D1602402

Quiet Diplomat

Quiet Diplomat

A Biography

of

Max M. Fisher

By

Peter Golden

A Herzl Press Publication

Cornwall Books
New York • London • Toronto

Cornwall Books
440 Forsgate Drive
Cranbury, NJ 08512

Cornwall Books
25 Sicilian Avenue
London WC1A 2QH, England

Cornwall Books
P.O. Box 39, Clarkson Pstl. Stn.
Mississauga, Ontario,
L5J 3X9 Canada

Herzl Press
110 East 59th Street
New York, NY 10022

LIBRARY OF CONGRESS CATALOGUE CARD NUMBER: LC 92-71441

ISBN 0-8453-4846-9

PRINTED IN THE UNITED STATES OF AMERICA

For my wife, Annis,
and my father, Lance,
and in memory of my mother, Evelyn

"Don't you see the significance of what I'm trying to do? [Judaism] is finally taking its place in this country, and think what it'll mean if I can get up to be a . . . big industrial magnate and run down and advise them in Washington . . . and at the same time be a Jew that's fully accepted in the inner circles of . . . society. . . . These things are coming."

Novelist Myron S. Kaufmann,
Remember Me to God, 1958

"The movement of Jews into the American political elite marks one of the most radical social transformations in Jewish history, and probably, for that matter, in history in general."

Historian David Biale
Power and Powerlessness in Jewish History, 1986

CONTENTS

AUTHOR'S NOTE

Q *UIET DIPLOMAT* is an authorized biography. It is based on more than 200 hundred hours of interviews with Max M. Fisher, and many more hours with his family, friends, and associates — supporters and detractors alike. I have had access to the 300,000 documents in the Fisher Archives in Detroit, Michigan, among them official and personal letters, memos, jottings on the back of airplane tickets, photocopies of canceled checks, speeches, photograph albums, balance sheets, ledgers, maps, newspaper and magazine articles, journals, diaries, notes on private and public meetings at the State Department and White House, and an oral history section that holds dozens of audio- and videotapes.

Having enjoyed the cooperation of the subject, however, raises several questions, the first two being how objective was the author's viewpoint and how free was his hand?

Everything of relevance that I culled from the Fisher Archives, interviews, articles and books found its way into this biography. I spent over three years working on the *Quiet Diplomat* and fully half of that time was devoted to research. Do I like Fisher? Yes. And because I like him I have been on guard not to bend these pages to the arc of my affection. Do I agree with everything he's ever done? Hardly. But this book contains Fisher's view of the world — not mine — and the perceptions that others hold of him. Events are witnessed through his eyes, while I have concerned myself with his motivation and attempted to gauge the outcome of his efforts. Does Fisher always find his portrait flattering? I hope not. That wasn't my intention. However, being a pragmatist, Fisher is fond of saying that the world has few unalloyed devils or saints and that he, like most of us, falls somewhere in the midst of the Great Moral Middle.

There is another bias common to studies of people immersed in politics — authorized or not. This bias, though rarely mentioned by authors and just whispered about by critics like some shameful disease, is often discernible within the opening pages of most political biographies. I am referring to the political stance of the writer, which on far too many occasions precludes anything approaching objectivity.

Fisher has been referred to as *the* Jewish Republican. I match up with him on one of these — I am a Jew. I do not count myself a Democrat or Republican. Our area of strongest compatibility is that we believe it is in the interest of the United States to be vigorously involved in world affairs, supporting democracies wherever they bloom and helping to counter aggression against them. Fisher feels — and again, I agree — that the costly lessons of history support this position. As the distinguished foreign correspondent, C.L Sulzberger, observed in his study of the Second World War: "As soon as the sound of aggression from across the seas . . . began to be disturbing, we [Americans] insulated ourselves with neutrality laws that forbade trade with either side in the conflict. It made no difference that our neutrality always seemed to harm the victim more than the aggressor. We were safe — so we thought — and that was what mattered."

American isolationism has proved cataclysmic for the world, and provided one of the worst moments in 4,000 years of Jewish history — the murder of the 6 million. Thus the subject and author of this biography maintain that U.S. support of Israel — and other proven democratic allies — is vital to our national security.

Fisher has dedicated a good portion of his life to this view. And while I do not always approve of the particulars of his political exertions, I do, in the broadest sense, applaud what he has tried to accomplish. This is my prejudice.

There is one last question, perhaps the most crucial. Why should the reader be interested in this biography? The nineteenth-century historian Thomas Carlyle's oft-quoted pronouncement that history is nothing "but the biography of great men" is only partially correct. Belonging to more romantic days, Carlyle was overly enamored of heroes and less impressed with the subtle tides of history, which draw their power from all people — great, small and in between. Closer to the point is that historical movements are clearer when examined within the microcosm of a single life. Naturally, the more involved the individual is in his times, the more history that is revealed.

The two seminal events of twentieth-century Jewish history are the Holocaust and the birth of Israel. For better or for worse, both consciously and unconsciously, these two occurrences have shaped the present politics of Jews in the United States. The psychological ramifications are equally profound. Upon confronting either event, American Jewry can't help but demonstrate its complex feelings about being American and Jewish.

Because Fisher's life has touched every decade of this century and because he was intimately involved in Jewish communal work and national politics, the backdrop of his activities illuminates modern American Jewish history. Furthermore, the most historically noteworthy of his endeavors took place behind the scenes. So his career offers a glimpse into the lesser-known workings of government and diplomacy.

In the end, though, the drama of any life boils down to what was accomplished? How long were the odds? How high was the price?

Fisher's accomplishments are notable. As a young man, he joined the first rank of industrialists, then became a force in Jewish and nonsectarian philanthropy. In his early fifties, pursuing his lifelong interest in the political process, he entered Republican Party politics, eventually becoming a valued adviser to an assortment of governors, congressmen, senators, secretaries of state and four presidents. The odds against him were steep. He was the son of Jewish immigrants and, financially, started with little. Personally, Fisher is the opposite of gregarious, which is no help to those who plunge into the frenetic social whirl of philanthropic fund-raising and politics; probably no man who is as temperamentally unsuited for public speaking as Fisher has faced so many audiences from a podium. Finally, what about the price? Listen to him, and the voices of his wife and children, and judge for yourself.

Introduction

EISENHOWER AND THE REVELATIONS OF SINAI

O N A GLIMMERING October afternoon in 1965, Max
Martin Fisher was driving through the autumn-gold
Pennsylvania hills to the Gettysburg farm of former
President Dwight D. Eisenhower. Fisher had an appointment
to see Eisenhower in connection with his position as general
chairman of the United Jewish Appeal, a national organization that, in coordination with local federations, raises funds
for immigration to Israel and for Jews in distress around the
world. The year, 1965, was the twentieth anniversary of the
liberation of the Nazi concentration camps. To honor the
anniversary, Fisher and the executive vice president of the
UJA, Rabbi Herbert A. Friedman, conceived of a medal that
would be awarded to three military leaders — one from
France, Britain and the United States — who played a pivotal
part in rescuing the remnants of Europe's Jews. Fisher was
driving to the farm to invite Eisenhower to accept the medal.

At fifty-seven, Fisher was still physically impressive. He
was six-foot-two; his weight fluctuated between 200 and 230
pounds, his burly chest and wide shoulders recalling his days
as a football lineman at Ohio State University in the late
1920s. In 1959, he had merged his Aurora Gasoline Company
with Ohio Oil (later to become the Marathon Oil Company),
earning himself and his partners $40 million. Since then, he
had been immersed in philanthropic fund-raising. By nature,
however, Fisher was not suited for the whirl of socializing and
speech making that accompanied his style of philanthropy.

He seemed friendly enough, with a broad open face and a firm handshake, yet he wrestled with an innate shyness. He tended to slouch and to swallow his sentences. Despite a boyish optimism about most everyone around him — a legacy of his small-town boyhood in Salem, Ohio — Fisher's inclination was to remain distant, enveloped by a gentle elusive sadness. Even when he smiled there was a melancholy remoteness in his eyes that his family, friends and colleagues noticed, but could not explain.

As of late, Fisher had carried his fund-raising expertise into Republican Party politics. In 1962, he helped George W. Romney become governor of Michigan; he helped Romney win again in 1964, and now the popular governor was being touted as a front-runner for the party's 1968 presidential nomination. By 1965, Fisher's first year as general chairman of the UJA, his speeches began to blend philanthropy and politics as the interests themselves coalesced in his mind. Fisher believed that Jewish philanthropic organizations, if politically unified, represented a constituency with the proven capability of gleaning millions of dollars, the key to a successful presidential campaign. Fisher, a consummate proponent of the practical, embraced — and repeatedly quoted — the observation of the nineteenth-century statesman, Otto von Bismarck, who professed that "politics is the art of the possible." Logically, it followed that Fisher had to uncover *what* was possible for an American Jew. There was the worn road of serving as a fund-raiser for a candidate and, if he won, collecting your quid pro quo by accepting a slot within the administration. This was, for instance, how Henry Morgenthau Sr. won his ambassadorship to Turkey from President Woodrow Wilson.

At gut level, Fisher found the notion of an official role in an administration unappealing. As far back as high school and college, when he was involved with prom committees and theater groups, Fisher preferred to work in the background, and typically, on the business side. Beyond the emotional unattractiveness, Fisher sensed — and in this he was significantly different from Morgenthau Sr. — that to take a titled post would curb his ability, especially in the event of a crisis, to make his voice heard at the White House. As a member of an administration he would owe his boss — the president or the secretary of state — his allegiance, and one who too often disagrees with his boss soon finds himself without a job, and thereby, no voice at all.

Eventually, Fisher opted to become, in the words of Malcolm Hoenlein, who in 1989 was serving as the executive director of the Conference of Presidents of Major American Jewish Organizations, "the dean of American Jewry." This deanship, however, was well in the future. Fisher's choices in 1965 were far from clear. All he had was an undefined vision of carving out a niche for himself as an insider-outsider amid the overlapping rings of power. He realized that he required an official platform in a *unified* Jewish community to have any chance of influencing an administration on behalf of that community. Fisher would have these platforms, several simultaneously, during his career. The UJA general chairmanship was a giant step. Abraham J. Karp, in *To Give Life*, his study of the UJA's shaping of the American Jewish community, writes: "It is significant . . . that [Fisher's] first position of national leadership was in the UJA. It was the one enterprise which could serve as both coalescing agent and the fountainhead of united Jewish communal enterprise."

When it came to national politics, the question remained: how large a role could he play unofficially in an administration? Surely, if you raised an impressive amount of money, you could get yourself invited to dinners at the White House. You could take a wide-eyed gaze at princes and prime ministers and have your photograph snapped with the president and maybe impress some in your social circle who didn't know how the game was played by having the photo autographed and framed and then hanging it conspicuously in your den. But what did that mean? Nothing. Presidential campaign chests were swelled by this ploy. You traded money for prestige, for a seat near the king, and were granted everything you ever wanted — except influence. Perhaps Morgenthau Sr.'s choice had been the only choice. When you stripped away the pomp of protocol, what possible chance did even "a dean of American Jewry" have of influencing a president?

For the moment, the answer appeared to be none.

*　　*　　*

By the time Fisher called on Eisenhower, the former president was nearing his seventy-fifth birthday and in frail health. After leaving the presidency, he claimed to be "bone tired," and chose to emulate George Washington at Mount Vernon by retiring to the bucolic joys of a 500-acre farm on the edge of the Civil War battlefield. The chief crop was hay, which was used as winter feed for the Angus cattle that roamed the fields. His colonial house was elegantly furnished, and Eisenhower passed the hours on the glass-enclosed sun porch, where he could read or paint or, on occasion, receive visitors.

Fisher, upon entering the house, was directed to the porch. Eisenhower stood and Fisher shook hands with him. In spite of his poor health, the former president maintained the erect posture of a military man. Since the mid-1950s, Fisher had thought that the popular perception of Eisenhower as an inactive president was woefully off the mark. He felt that Eisenhower exhibited a devout — yet prudent — willingness to confront the Russians and demonstrated strong leadership by ordering troops in to ensure the desegregation of the schools in Little Rock, Arkansas.

Fisher took a seat and presented his proposal. Eisenhower listened. Then he began to reminisce about his efforts to aid the Jewish displaced persons in Europe during 1945. He promised Fisher that he would make every effort to come to New York and accept the medal.

In retirement, the former president kept a keen eye on Republican Party politics, and his advice and endorsements were coveted by candidates and officeholders. He was aware of Fisher's burgeoning reputation as a fund-raiser for the GOP, and so it was only natural that their talk turned to how the party would heal itself in the aftermath of Senator Barry M.

Goldwater's resounding defeat in the 1964 presidential election.

Their discussion went on for a while and, Fisher remembers, gradually veered toward the Middle East, with Eisenhower recalling the 1956 Suez Crisis. The former president's reminiscences proved to be a major turning point in Fisher's life.

For American Jews and for many in Israel, the Suez Crisis, while somewhat of a forgotten conflict when compared to the euphoric Israeli victories in 1948 and 1967, and the somber reaction to the heavy casualties of the 1973 Yom Kippur War, had immense geopolitical ramifications for the United States and Israel. On July 26, 1956, Egyptian President Gamel Abdel Nasser declared that he was nationalizing the Suez Canal and its future revenues would be applied to the construction of the Aswan Dam. Nasser, writes historian Howard M. Sachar, "was hailed as a national hero. His domestic position had never been more secure, nor his reputation in the Arab world higher." The initial reaction to the nationalization in Western capitals was outrage. Yet by the fall of 1956, Eisenhower thought the dilemma was behind him, and Secretary of State John Foster Dulles agreed. The French, however, devised a covert plan to attack Egypt, convincing the British and Israelis to join them. Israel would land paratroopers near the Suez Canal. The French and British would demand that both sides withdraw. Nasser, his stature among the Arabs on the line, would refuse, thus providing France and Britain with a pretext to strike.

On Monday, October 29, Israel attacked. Eisenhower was livid; he had been tricked by his allies. He thought their strategy would invite the Soviet Union into the fray and the United States would be forced to bail everyone out. The British and French issued their ultimatum for withdrawal. When Nasser declined to heed it, the British and French bombed Egyptian airfields. Eisenhower contacted Britain's Prime Minister Anthony Eden via transatlantic telephone and vented his outrage in a spate of language more familiar to an enlisted men's barracks than to the stately rooms of 10 Downing

Street. On Wednesday, Eisenhower sent an ominous message to Israeli Prime Minister David Ben-Gurion: "Despite the present temporary interests that Israel has in common with France and Britain, you ought not to forget that the strength of Israel and her future are bound up with the United States."

The Israelis did not withdraw, and by November 5, they controlled the Sinai and the Gaza Strip. Two days later, Eisenhower's warnings to Jerusalem became more menacing. He said that there could be severe repercussions if Israel did not evacuate the Sinai and Gaza, a combination of U.N. condemnations, counterattacks by Soviet "volunteers," the termination of all U.S. governmental aid and philanthropic assistance — a move that included the threat of a Justice Department investigation into the tax-exempt status of the United Jewish Appeal and other charities that furnished funds vital to Israel's survival.

Eisenhower's arm-twisting was effective.

The following morning, Ben-Gurion announced that Israel would withdraw.

Richard M. Nixon, who as vice president under Eisenhower was close to the Suez Crisis, recalls his boss's thinking in 1956.

"Eisenhower," says Nixon, "never had any illusions about Nasser. First, there were Nasser's unpolitic statements at that time — to put it mildly. And there were so many interests to consider: we had French interests, British interests, Israeli interests. But what really happened in 1956 was that it came at a very bad time politically. It came right after the Hungarian revolution, after we had bashed [Soviet Premier Nikita] Khrushchev as the 'Butcher of Budapest' [for ordering Russian troops into Hungary]. So it was difficult to say, 'Well, we're going to support our own people when they are doing the same thing.' Although ours was justified — and the two were not the same — nevertheless, it was difficult. The second thing is that it came shortly before an election, which we were going to win anyway as it later turned out. But on the other hand it was an election in which we were running on the platform of 'peace and prosperity.' And so all of these factors led to Eisenhower's decision to force the Israelis out."

Eisenhower's forcing the Israelis' hand so close to the election brought the American Jewish community to the polls in record number. In his study, *Political Cohesion of American Jews in American Politics*, M.S. El Azhary records that over 90 percent of American Jews who were registered to vote came to the polls in the 1956 presidential election, 74 percent of them voting for Eisenhower's Democratic opponent, Adlai E. Stevenson.

This illustration of an expansive unified Jewish vote, with Israel as the central motivating component, would be a major factor in Fisher's future — as well as for Nixon and all ensuing presidents. Eisenhower, though, chose to ignore the concerns of American Jews.

In the 1956 race, Stevenson used Eisenhower's stance to swing voters, insisting that the Israelis ought to be given the arms required to guarantee their territorial integrity. His strategy did not pay off. On November 6, Eisenhower defeated him by more than 9 million popular votes.

Although Eisenhower did not require the American Jewish community's support at the polls, he did try to operate through "Jewish channels" to influence Ben-Gurion. But Eisenhower had not developed alliances within the power structure of the American Jewish community, which weakened his efforts. Eisenhower's dealings with America's Jews and the Israelis were most conspicuous for what was missing: a reliable conduit between the Oval Office and the community, someone who could have functioned as a diplomatic navigator between Washington and Jerusalem.

Beyond domestic politics lay the question of whether or not Eisenhower made the correct decision, because the geopolitical fallout from his actions was profound.

Nixon explains: "The French, of course, had their problems [with foreign policy]. But the British are very sophisticated in foreign affairs. They had been our close allies not only [in the Middle East], but all over the world. What happened at Suez split the British wide open. The people who disagreed about Suez in Britain still won't speak to each other.

But it was also the beginning of Britain withdrawing as a world power east of Suez. As of the present time [June 9, 1989], you have Britain with a very strong leader in Margaret Thatcher who plays a very significant role, but not nearly the role that could be played if Britain were still a major player. After Suez, the writing was on the wall."

The implications were equally great for the United States. Even though they were not apparent until eleven years later — on the heels of Israel's Six-Day War — they drastically altered the American role in the Middle East.

"As a result," says Nixon, "of our turning on the British and the French when they were trying to protect their interests in the Canal, it meant that they were finished in other parts of the world as well. That was a very unfortunate thing because it meant that the United States then virtually had to act alone."

Despite the geopolitical consequences of Eisenhower's pressure, history has recorded that Eisenhower had no second thoughts regarding his decision. According to Stephen E. Ambrose, author of an Eisenhower biography, editor of the Eisenhower papers and director of the Eisenhower Center at the University of New Orleans, the former president "never wavered on or regretted his decision to force the invading parties out of Egypt, no matter what."

Fisher, though, on that October afternoon in Gettysburg, would hear a different story. Evidently, the ensuing decade had provided an opportunity for Eisenhower to reflect. For as Fisher's conversation with him drew to a close, the former president wistfully commented: "You know, Max, looking back at Suez, I regret what I did. I never should have pressured Israel to evacuate the Sinai."

Fisher was astonished by the statement, but apparently he was not the only one to whom Eisenhower had divulged this information.

"Eisenhower," says Nixon, "many years later, in the 1960s, told me — and I'm sure he told others — that he thought that the action that was taken [at Suez] was one he regretted. He thought it was a mistake."

Fisher started to say goodbye to Eisenhower; it was then, almost as an afterthought, that Eisenhower revealed another startling facet of his reconsideration. Although the former president did not live long enough to witness the results — in doing so he clarified the course of Fisher's political career.

"Max," Eisenhower said, "if I'd had a Jewish adviser working for me, I doubt I would have handled the situation the same way. I would not have forced the Israelis back."

Eisenhower's statement struck Fisher with the impact of epiphany. If Fisher had been unsure of the extent of power that an unofficial adviser could wield with a president, he now had his answer, and from an unimpeachable source: the influence exerted could be decisive. It was exactly the role Fisher hoped to play. Fisher thanked Eisenhower for his time and the former president again promised to try to be there for the UJA dinner.

*   *   *

On December 11, 1965, the United Jewish Appeal gathered for its Annual Conference at the Hilton Hotel in New York City. It was there, in the Grand Ballroom, that the medal was presented. Fisher spoke of the three honorees: General Pierre Koening, leader of the French Resistance; Field Marshall Alexander of Great Britain, who evacuated British troops from Dunkirk and later fought the Nazis in North Africa; and Eisenhower. In a voice edged with emotion, Fisher repeated what General Eisenhower had said two decades ago while paying a Yom Kippur visit to the Jewish displaced persons camp in Feldafing, Germany:

"'I feel especially happy,'" Fisher quoted, "'to be in a Jewish camp on the holiest day of your year. You are only here temporarily, and you must be patient until . . . you will leave here and go to the places you wish to go. I know how much you have suffered and I believe a sunnier day will be coming soon.'"

Sadly, Eisenhower was not at the Hilton to receive his medal: General Lucius D. Clay, Eisenhower's erstwhile dep-

uty commander in Europe, was standing in for his friend, who
had suffered another heart attack and was in the hospital.

Fisher, saddened that Eisenhower was not there on that
evening, was grateful for the political gift that he had given
him. Let Nixon then, the first president to allow Fisher to
exercise his influence in Washington, define the position to
which Fisher aspired.

"There is no question about it," says Nixon. "A private
citizen who has no selfish interest, who, like Max, is not in
business for himself, who is a supporter of the administration,
can have a substantial influence on a close decision. He can't
create policy, but when it is a very close call, as it was at Suez,
someone like Max can change the president's mind."

Now, all Fisher had to do was choose the right man in
1968. Romney was emerging as a favorite in the polls. But two
other hopefuls were courting him — Nixon and Governor
Nelson A. Rockefeller of New York. Picking the winner,
Fisher soon learned, would prove a far harder task than it originally seemed.

Chapter 1

WHAT NORMAN ROCKWELL
NEVER DREAMED

HAD NORMAN ROCKWELL cast his eye on Salem, Ohio, in those rapturous days just after the century turned, he would have seen the sights he loved: high-school football captains slouching in the middle of Reilly Field waiting for the coin toss, the autumn blazing behind them; a scoutmaster and his troop camped in the summery, starlit woods beyond town; a winter dusk gathering over the storefronts and awnings along East and West State Street; and farther out, a brakeman standing beside the railroad tracks as a train thundered past, all of it bathed in Rockwell's small-town American light, cool and clear and furiously nostalgic.

Without question, Rockwell could have captured the boyhood of Max Fisher in dozens of his paintings, but Fisher, son of an immigrant and, more significantly, a Jew, would not have fully belonged there.

*　　*　　*

Velvil Fisch, Max Fisher's father, also grew up in a small town — Yakshitz, in White Russia, among the most poverty-stricken regions of the Russian empire. Velvil was born on April 15, 1888. By the age of seventeen he was tall and broad-shouldered, with dark eyes and thick, dark wavy hair. Velvil was eager to join the two million Russian Jews who fled their land between 1881 and 1920. Although his parents, Icheh and Soreh Fisch, had a daughter, Devora, and two other sons, Yosef and Beril, they had no intention of permitting Velvil to go; nor did they have the money to give him for his passage.

They prevailed upon Velvil to marry, arranging a match with Malka Brody, who came from a nearby town, Lyakhovich, and was a year older than Velvil.

At five-foot-four, Malka Brody was six inches shorter than Velvil. She was an attractive young woman, with dark oval eyes and flowing dark hair, who had been orphaned as a child and raised in poverty by an aunt who sold sewing notions. The match with Velvil did not appear to be her best prospect; the idea of marrying and moving into a house with a dirt floor was especially unappealing. But Velvil was stubborn; in spite of his parents' wishes he planned to emigrate and this plan tilted Malka's decision in his favor.

In April 1905, Malka and Velvil were married.

Velvil shortly discovered that his new bride possessed a small fortune: nearly $200. (Later in life, their children would tease them, saying their father married their mother for her money.) And Malka must have trusted Velvil, because despite the accounts drifting back of husbands who had gone off to the United States, never to be heard from again, she gave the money to him for his passage. She even wrote her cousins, the Darefskys, and told them to expect Velvil. (The Darefskys had left White Russia in 1903 and settled outside of Philadelphia, Pennsylvania.) So Velvil packed a few belongings in a cardboard valise, kissed Malka goodbye, and promised to send for her as soon as he saved enough money.

On June 2, 1906, Velvil Fisch, booked into the steerage section of the *S.S. Zeeland*, sailed from Antwerp, Belgium. Almost two weeks later, the ship docked in New York City. Upon landing, Velvil claimed his occupation was that of locksmith and declared ten dollars in assets. His first night in the *goldeneh medina*, the golden land, he slept on a park bench. The following morning, he traveled to the Darefskys, who advised him to try his luck farther west.

He set out for Pittsburgh, stopping to work odd jobs. By now, Velvil Fisch had changed his name to William Fisher. In Pittsburgh, William rented a flat at 87 Fulton Street and decided to become a peddler. He spent his last money on a horse and wagon and an assortment of cloth and sewing notions, picked a territory in eastern Ohio, and began the wandering life of a peddler — in those years, an immigrant's first rung on the ladder of success, what has aptly been described as "schooling for Americanization."

William was easily schooled. He was friendly and curious by nature. He easily picked up English and learned how to read it. The long hours of travel appealed to his restlessness. He did not enjoy staying in one spot for long; there was always something else a farmer or a farmer's wife required. In just over a year, he saved the money to send for his wife. Malka docked in Baltimore on August 24, 1907. Her name was changed to Mollie Fisher, and she came to the flat in Pittsburgh to live.

On July 15, 1908, a son, Max, was born.

For a peddler in the early 1900s, the next step of his imagined rise was to sell his horse and wagon and buy a store. William kept his eye out, and in 1909 he bought a clothing concern in Salem, Ohio, sixty-two miles west of Pittsburgh. Salem, with a population of approximately 14,000, had been founded in 1806 when the Quakers came across the Appalachians to settle.

William adapted readily to small-town life. His store, with living quarters on top, was located at 24 Lincoln Avenue, a block from the center of town. At the outset, he had to supplement his earnings by periodically peddling in the surrounding countryside. Within a year, though, he was making enough at the store to support his family and to put some money aside. In 1910, Mollie and William had a daughter, Augusta, whose name was later changed to Gail. That same year, William got word that his father had died, and he stepped up his efforts to bring the rest of his family to America.

Tragically, before he could arrange it, William's sister, Devora, died, leaving her children in her mother's care. Yosef, William's brother, was running the family farm, and it was not until 1913 that William managed to bring his brother Beril to Salem. In 1916, a typhoid epidemic struck the town, and William briefly took his family to Detroit, where another daughter, Anne, was born. The Fishers returned to Salem and William established The Fisher Company, selling men's clothing at 142 East Main Street. In 1920, the Fishers' final child, a daughter, Dorothy, was born, and they moved down the block to larger quarters at 63 Roosevelt Street, where the family had a garden and William had a garage for his new Stoddard-Dayton automobile.

William soon set up a larger store at 66 Main Street, Fisher's Underselling Store, stating in his *Salem City Directory* advertisement that "Men, when in need of quality merchandise such as suits, shoes and furnishings, and you don't have much to spend, you should visit the low price store of Salem."

By 1923, Beril, now Ben Fisher, had married a woman in Pittsburgh and returned to Salem, opening a junk business. William turned over his place on Roosevelt to them and relocated his family to a spacious gray stone house at 68 Jennings at the end of town. The porch had honeysuckle vines twisting over it, and there was a big yard with white roses, a chicken coop and a creek running past.

William's business prospered. The store, because William was so gregarious, became a social center. It was open six days a week, and William worked behind the counter, wearing his steel-frame glasses and wing collar, and invariably puffing an El Producto cigar. In the evenings, he would come home, have a bite of pickled herring along with a shot of schnapps and preside over the family dinner table.

His daughter, Anne Fisher Rose, recalls: "My mother was always cooking. *Kreplach*, stuffed cabbage, pot roast and her coffee cakes. She never knew how many people my father was going to bring home for dinner, but there was always enough."

While William became fluent in English early, Mollie did not. She spoke Yiddish to her husband, usually to prevent the children from eavesdropping, and read the Yiddish papers, the *Forvets* (*Forward*) and *Der Tog* (*The Day*), which she had delivered by mail. Mollie spent her time cooking, cleaning, canning the vegetables she grew in her garden and caring for her children. She was close to her daughters, often reading to them from the Yiddish papers, particularly the love-advice columns. But Max, according to his three sisters, was her "sonny boy," and she doted on him, sometimes to the detriment of his siblings.

For example, when Max and his sister Gail were taking piano lessons, they were both supposed to practice for one hour each day. Max, as restless and impatient as his father, had no interest in being glued to a piano bench. So he explained to his mother that boys learned at a far faster rate than girls: four times the rate to be exact. Therefore, while Gail required the hour, he could learn the same amount in fifteen minutes.

"And she believed him," Gail Fisher Rossen recalls today, laughing. "That's how it was with Mother and Max. He was her 'sonny boy' till the day she died."

"My mother," says Max Fisher, "was a real *Yiddishe Mameh*."

This statement is more than it seems, certainly more complex than Irving Howe's description, in *World of our Fathers*, of the immigrant Jewish mother: "It was from her place in the kitchen that the Jewish housewife became the looming figure who would inspire, haunt and devastate generations of Jewish sons."

Zena Smith Blau, in her essay, "In Defense of the Jewish Mother," offers an alternative view of the mother-son relationship, one that has particular relevance to Mollie's relationship to Max: "*Yiddishe Mamehs*," writes Blau, "were active, responsible, stable, expressive and verbal women for whom *naches fun die kinder* [satisfaction from the achievement of children] represented the highest form of self-fulfillment and achievement for a woman. . . . With no other human being did the Jewish child develop as close, as trusting, as free and fearless a relationship as with his mother, and therein lay the secret of her power to gain his compliance ultimately in those areas of behavior in which she chose to exert pressure during the entire period of maturation."

Considering the adult Max Fisher's active role in Jewish philanthropy, it is no surprise that his mother's greatest demands involved his participation in her specific form of

Jewishness. Perhaps Mollie saw how immersed her son was in the Gentile environment of his playmates and hoped to provide some tie to her past. And since for many years Mollie insisted on keeping kosher, riding the trolley to Youngstown, twenty-two miles north, to buy from the kosher butcher, she concluded that it was a job that should be passed on to Max. And so Max was directed to travel to Youngstown to buy live chickens and take them to the *shokhet* to be properly slaughtered. He accomplished his assignment with occasionally amusing results, like the time the chickens got away from him on the trolley car and flapped wildly among the passengers.

Charity was another responsibility Mollie handed down not only to Max, but to her daughters. Her favorite charity was the Jewish National Fund (JNF), which acquired land, planted trees and prepared the soil for the pioneers who were struggling to build a Jewish homeland in Palestine. Mollie dropped coins into her blue-and-white JNF box every Friday and encouraged her children to do the same.

As for Mollie's leniency with Max, according to Blau this would not damage a child's later capacity for discipline: "For all their warmth and indulgence *Yiddishe Mamehs* were demanding, determined women . . . [whose] standards and expectations were extremely high. . . . And, just because he needs his mother's approval, the young child will work harder to develop the skills *she* values and be more resistant to the influence of 'the other kids.' By the time he matures he will have internalized the motivation and goals that make . . . excellence possible."

*   *   *

If Max could depend on Mollie's good-natured tolerance, this was not the case when it came to his father. William was critical of Max. He felt that his son should help out more around the house and the store. This disagreement between father and son was exacerbated by a cultural gap. William, the immigrant, the man who had made his way alone, was providing a life for his native-born son that must have seemed abundantly comfortable, and Max, in William's estimation, was taking undue advantage of that comfort. Whereas from Max's perspective, this was no less than he had the right to expect.

Nevertheless, the conflict, although tense, was a quiet one. William periodically punished Max with a strapping, but there was little shouting. William, when angered, grew coldly silent, and Max did the same.

Even as a child, Max was reserved. The silence suited him, both his need to control his feelings and as a method to keep from stepping outside of his inherent shyness.

"I was very insecure when I was a kid," says Fisher. "I was driven to be a success. I wanted to make my mark."

His fantasies were fueled in Salem's Carnegie Library, one of the 2,500 libraries erected by industrialist Andrew Carnegie. There, curled up on a comfortable chair, Max read and reread biographies of Carnegie and John D. Rockefeller, and the novels of Horatio Alger, the Unitarian minister who authored over 130 books for boys, all based on the principle that fighting against poverty and temptation leads a boy to wealth and fame. It was this orderly world view, great reward for great effort, that Max would carry into adulthood.

Fisher's philosophy of wealth also seems to have been shaped by Alger, who wrote: "Money is said, by certain moralists, to be the root of all evil. The love of money, if carried too far, may indeed lead to evil, but it is a natural ambition. . . . The wealth of [fictional characters] Amos Lawrence and Peter Cooper was a source of blessing to mankind, yet each started as a poor boy and neither would have become rich if he had not strived hard to become so."

Max's other passion, as a youngster, was the Boy Scouts. Scouting was relatively new in the early 1920s; the Boy Scouts of America was incorporated in New York City in 1910, and registration, with annual dues of twenty-five cents, began in 1913. Max enjoyed the typical scouting activities: hiking and camping in the woods outside Salem, fishing and swimming in the streams, learning signaling and First Aid.

In his junior-high yearbook, the 1922 edition of *The Mirror*, Fisher paid homage to the Boy Scouts in an essay, leading off with what sounded like a rejoinder to William's criticism: "People sometimes think that Boy Scouts are only a bunch of boys out for a good time. But the Scouts have a larger job than this."

Scouting did have a lasting effect on Max's development, for it was there that he met his first mentor, a scoutmaster who was instrumental in furnishing Fisher with the confidence to shrug off his protective shell.

"His name was Lee Chamberlain," recalls Fisher. "Funny that I should remember his name."

Chamberlain, according to Charles Roessler, who has been active in the Salem Boy Scouts for seventy-seven years, was a strong, lanky man, a devout churchgoer and an employee of the Buckeye Engine Company.

"Lee was dedicated to scouting up until he died," Roessler says. "He was a perfect gentleman and absolutely dedicated to the boys. There wasn't a finer man in town."

Besides reviewing the Scout saws with his troop, instructing them on the advantages of being responsible and trustworthy, Chamberlain was also sensitive to boys like Fisher in need of a compassionate paternal hand.

"I remember going into a barn," Fisher says. "And one of the things we had to do was jump out of a hayloft. Everybody jumped, but I got scared and the other kids started razzing me. Lee Chamberlain sat down and counseled me and the next day I went there and I jumped off and I came back as one of the boys."

*   *   *

If William and Max had an uneasy truce when Max was a youngster, this did not hold true when Max entered high school in 1923. The cultural differences that divided father from son suddenly widened, and the similarities of their personalities — their drive and stubbornness — terminated the peace.

William's criticism sprang from his opinion that Max was neglecting his chores and wasting his time. This was not altogether true. Because Mollie suffered from eczema on her hands, she could not do the wash, so Max regularly carried the laundry to a neighbor. He also worked in his father's store on Saturdays, but he preferred finding his own jobs, mowing lawns, caddying at the golf course, delivering papers or splitting logs.

However, Max's grades, which in junior high school had been in the eighties and nineties, dipped once he was in high school. He excelled in math and history, but struggled with Latin and French and was an average English student. He was too shy to date, so girls did not fill his time, but he played on the football, basketball and track teams, handled the business side of the school plays, participated in numerous clubs, chaired the junior and senior proms, and began keeping a scrapbook of each of his accomplishments. He frequented the local poolroom, developing into a sharp pool player. But he was betting on games, and since he occasionally lost, he would sneak small sums of money from his father's register.

A note from Charles B. Coffee, a star of Salem's football team, sent to Fisher more than a half-century after they had last seen each other in the 1920s, captures the spirit of those years: "Do you ever think back to our high school days?" Coffee wrote, "when you and I ran around together? We sure had some good times then. Even when we practiced football in your basement and drank some of your dad's booze."

Today it sounds like the guileless mischief of high-spirited boys, yet one can imagine the disdain with which William Fisher viewed it.

The strongest conflict Max had with William was over Max's football career. At six-foot-two and 148 pounds, Max was one of the biggest boys in Salem. He played center, on defense and offense, and was considered one of the finest lineman in Columbiana County. But both William and Mollie, terrified that Max would get injured, refused to watch their son play. (Max's sister Anne, as athletic and feisty as her brother, with a habit of climbing and tumbling out of trees, never missed a game.) What William would have seen on the field was that Max showed the same sort of tenacity playing football that his father showed in business.

Fred C. Cope, a year older than Fisher, was a star track man at Salem. Cope recalls Max as a boy who, although lacking the natural athletic ability of a Charles Coffee, was intent on succeeding at football.

"The thing that I remember about Max more than anything else," says Cope, "is that at the end of practice he'd come up to Coach [Wilbur] Springer and say, 'What did I do wrong?' or 'How can I improve?' Then they'd practice some more. The other kids couldn't wait to get away from Coach after practice. Not Max. He was constantly trying to better himself."

Once, when Coach Springer was staying late with Max to tutor him in the finer points of blocking, Max, always aggressive and eager to learn, broke his coach's collarbone.

So Max continued to play football, parrying his mother's worries with hurried reassurances and his father's disapproving silence with a silence of his own, a studied distance that would one day make him a gifted negotiator, but also would interfere with his personal relationships. He was soft-spoken, and yet Fisher admits, sixty years after leaving Salem, that underneath the serene exterior he was "pugnacious as hell."

*   *   *

When the Fishers lived in Salem there were only five other Jewish families. The closest Jewish communities of any size were in Alliance and Youngstown, approximately twenty miles away. Alliance and Youngstown had synagogues, which Mollie and William attended sometimes on the High Holidays, without their children. Mollie, in an effort to prevent her young children from feeling left out at Christmas, allowed them to hang stockings in the house. Over the years, she became less observant and no longer shopped at the kosher butcher. Instead, she sent Anne to Votaw's Market to buy meat and then soaked and salted it before cooking as if it were kosher. She did maintain two sets of dishes and a separate set for Passover when William led a traditional seder. On Friday nights, William chanted the blessing over the wine and Mollie lit candles. Charity, with its obligatory status in Judaism, was observed. In addition to Mollie's and the children's JNF contributions, William dropped coins into the *pushkeh*, a tin box with the name of the charity on it, and when the collectors — the *meshulakhim* — came to collect the money, William invited them home for dinner and provided them with a place to sleep.

Other than these rituals, Max Fisher had no Jewish education. He did not have a bar mitzvah at the traditional age of thirteen and he did not go to Hebrew school. His friends were not Jewish, nor was his community. How then, did he become so identified with his Jewishness, growing up in Salem where American culture — Christian culture, the culture that Norman Rockwell enchantingly preserved in his art — was so pronounced?

The philosopher Horace M. Kallen provides a partial answer. Kallen wrote extensively on the concept of Jewish identity and understood the lessons that families like the Fishers were learning in America: that the Americanization of Jews did not mean Jews would become indistinguishable from Christians. But rather, by preserving their Jewish identity in a myriad of ad hoc ways, they would live not only as citizens of a nation, but also as Jewish citizens of a nation. Then, too, Jewish identity, for Kallen, would be fortified in America *because* of anti-Semitism, which would serve as a safeguard against assimilation. Jews could not disappear into a society that did not wish to hide them.

Kallen writes: "Of all them which say they are Jews, each may be the synagogue of Satan to [other Jews], but all, whether they speak with the old tongues of Sephardi and Hassid, or the new tongues of Zionist or American Council for Judaism, Inc., are equally the synagogue of Satan for the anti-Semite. The common enemy imposes on them a common identity and a common cause."

And the Ohio of Fisher's boyhood was filled with anti-Semitism. During the 1920s, the state had the country's largest enrollment in the Ku Klux Klan. Membership estimates exceeded 400,000. Politically, the Klan won an imposing array of victories. It supported mayors who were elected in Toledo,

Akron, Columbus, Hamilton, Marion, Elyria, Newark and at least five smaller cities. The mayor of Youngstown belonged to the Klan, as did his law director, Clyde W. Osborn, who became the state's first grand dragon.

In Salem, the Klan staged cross burnings just outside of town and marched through the streets in their white hoods and robes. Still, the Klan was not taken too seriously, and Salem's children, Max and his sister Anne among them, watched them parade by and taunted them.

As Dr. Henry K. Yaggi Jr., a classmate of Fisher's, remembers: "In those days, the Klan wasn't violent. They were all show and no blow."

Even though some of the Fishers' neighbors did belong to the Klan, Max can remember no earnest anti-Semitic feelings among the people in Salem. One of William's closest friends and best customers was a Mr. Shepard, who held a leadership post with the Salem Klan. Shepard, who owned a coal mine, was friendly enough with William to give Max a summer job splitting logs. As a teenager, Max's application for a membership at the YMCA was rejected because he was Jewish, and several private parties were closed to him, but these were the exception, not the rule.

Max Fisher's recollections of his hometown are of the realized American dream, a beautifully simmering melting pot. His sister Anne remembers Salem in a similar spirit. As a girl, Anne accompanied her Christian friends to church and Sunday school and was an ardent fan of the Episcopal Church's annual picnic.

More than fifty years after leaving Salem, Anne Fisher Rose says: "I never heard the expression 'dirty Jew' till I moved to the big city."

In the 1920s, although the Salem Klan disliked Jews and blacks (there was only a smattering of black families living in Salem then), they focused their resentment on immigrants, chiefly Catholics, who were referred to as "cat-lickers."

There are other indications that the anti-Semitism Fisher was exposed to in Salem went beyond — and deeper than — white-hooded parades and denied memberships, was more subtle and lasting. Some interviewers, when confronting Fisher's recollections of Salem, have implied that his observations have been sugarcoated by memory, as if they have been revised in accordance with the words etched into the stone hearth in the basement bar of Salem's Elks Club: "The faults of our brothers we write upon the sands, their virtues on the tablets of love and memory."

For instance, in a July 1980 magazine profile of Fisher in *Monthly Detroit*, senior editor Kirk Cheyfitz writes: "Fisher says he remembers no anti-Semitism [in Salem]. The Salem of his memory is an American Eden. . . . But it wasn't exactly that way. Laura Mae Whinery grew up across from Max's house on West State Street. . . . She remembers a quiet, polite Max Fisher. . . . And then, with no prompting, she offers: 'Of course, I suppose he had his moments with being Jewish.' But she cannot or will not name those moments."

These moments should not have been difficult to identify, beginning with Fisher's nickname, "Rabbi," which he carried with him through public school and which was inscribed under his picture in the 1926 edition of *The Quaker*, Salem High School's yearbook. Fisher, his family and his friends appeared to consider the sobriquet a warm-hearted joke. As late as 1988, when Fisher celebrated his eightieth birthday, his son, Phillip, presented him with a professionally produced audio cassette, complete with a play-by-play announcer and roaring crowd noises, which contained an affectionate parody of Fisher's high-school football career. The name most often used on the tape: "Rabbi."

Dr. Henry Yaggi Jr., who played next to Fisher at left guard on the Salem football team and whose father owned the hospital where the boys wound up — with sprains, bruises and the random break or concussion — following the games, explains the meaning of the nickname: "Most of the people [in Salem] weren't concerned with [a person's religion]," says Yaggi. "There was never any discrimination. Hell, Red Cosgrove was captain of the football team and he was Catholic. The only reason that you didn't like someone was because you didn't like him. Just like you wouldn't like somebody in your Sunday-school class. Max and I, we always hit it off. We called him 'Rabbi,' the same way you'd call a guy 'Butch' or 'Joe.' It was just the first Jewish name that everybody would recognize."

Why, one wonders, would they require a name that everyone would recognize as Jewish? Yaggi's logic does not address this point; it focuses on the issue of intent. "Rabbi," to his mind, was used by Fisher's friends with wit and affection, and thus should not be confused with anti-Semitism.

Yet paging through *The Quaker* published in 1923, when Fisher was a freshman, a more revealing, unequivocal nickname can be found. This one under the picture of a handsome, light-skinned black man. His real name, Donald Woods, was duly noted, as was his nickname: "Jigaboo."

Only an enormously generous opinion could mistake this sobriquet as an amiable substitute for "Butch" or "Joe."

In contrast to the manner in which Dr. Yaggi reflects on his teammate's nickname, Fred Cope remembers it as having a distinctive significance.

"Max and I were on the periphery of the student body," Cope recalls. "They used to kid me about wearing boots to school because I was a farm boy and [they said I should] get the smell of the farm off me. And Max was not treated like one of the regular students. He was called 'Rabbi,' stuff like that."

Cope continues, highlighting Fisher's identification with another student who was a victim of prejudice. "I remember a track man," he says. "A black fellow. He always liked Max. I was down in the dressing room and somebody had called the black a derogatory name, 'Steppin' Fetchit,' I think. Max was patting him on the back. I don't know what Max was saying because I was over across the room, but he was encouraging [the black man] not to pay any attention to these guys."

Additionally, there is reason to believe that the discrimination may have extended to the football fields of Ohio.

On December 1, 1925, when H.P. Braman selected the all-county high-school football team in *The Salem News*, a piece appeared in the paper that went so far as to wonder whether or not someone was harboring a particular animosity toward Fisher.

"A storm has been brewing around the selection of the center," the story began. "Fisher of Salem stands far and above any other center, not only in this county, but he was better than the Alliance, Niles, Akron West, Cleveland West and Struthers centers. Some persons close to athletics have held some grudge against Fisher or else do not know his ability. The only excuse one of these persons could give for keeping him off the [all-county] team was that he made three miscues all year, and this the year of the big mud. There isn't a college center that could claim that record. There are other good centers, with Larkins of East Liverpool, the only snapperback given a rank near Fisher, but he was not the bear on the defense that Fisher was, for the Salem boy made nearly half of his team's tackles."

What is noteworthy about this story is that the other players named to the all-county team were just given a brief mention. And interestingly enough, although this was the longest, and most laudatory, piece ever written about Fisher's football career, he did not clip it and paste it into his scrapbook.

The evidence suggests that most Salemites — like many other small-towners — managed to accept their Jewish neighbors by the psychological maneuver of "exemption." Peter I. Rose, in his study of small-town Jews and their neighbors, *Strangers in Their Midst*, explains: "Small-town 'natives,' most often having fixed images of what Jews are supposed to be . . . differentiate Jewish friends from these images. In most instances we found that exemption served as a device useful for the circumvention of prejudice."

This addresses why Fisher would remember his hometown as an "American Eden." The anti-Semitism, to some extent, was not personally aimed at him, but at an overly fantastic conception of what it meant to be a Jew. In addition, Fisher was reserved and, as in his adult years, kept his feelings to himself. In fact, Fisher was past his eightieth birthday when he admitted that being refused a membership at the

Salem YMCA because he was Jewish was "one of the most painful experiences in my life."

Although being surrounded by non-Jews and some expressions of anti-Semitism enhanced Fisher's sense of Jewishness, it also led to the development of a phenomenon Peter Rose refers to as "biculturalism": Rose writes: "While [the small-town Jew] identifies with fellow Jews — a reference group he can 'feel' rather than 'touch' — and in many ways expresses a feeling of kinship with his people, he adapts himself to the folkways of the small town in a variety of ways. He enjoys the advantages of sharing two 'cups of life' and, in a word, is bicultural."

This biculturalism is often noticeably absent in those who were raised in the teeming Jewish enclaves of America — the Lower East Side of author Harry Golden, for example, where everything Jewish was no farther away than the corner candy store and a bubbling glass of two-cents plain. Unlike Salem, in Irving Howe's *World of Our Fathers*, Jews effortlessly imported their Judaism from Europe, making the requisite adjustments, gilding their ghettos until they became suburbs, but remaining insular and what they deemed a prudent distance from the pitfalls of Gentile America.

Fisher's capacity to live in two worlds, one Jewish, one Christian, was among the distinctive talents that he took with him from Salem. It was the town's legacy to him and prepared him for the leaders of the oil industry, the basis of his fortune and the beginnings of his clout. And it also prepared him for the WASP power elite in Detroit and Washington, D.C.

Yet while Fisher propelled himself through the Protestant establishment — whether it was sailing off around the Greek islands with his friend Henry Ford II, or addressing the 1988 Republican National Convention in New Orleans — his identity prevailed. He spoke as Max Martin Fisher, wealthy oil man, investor, philanthropist, power broker, fund-raiser — and Jew.

*   *   *

By the winter of 1925, William Fisher had a decision to make. His wife was anxious to relocate to a big city. With three daughters to marry off — the eldest, Gail, was now fifteen — Mollie felt that her girls should have access to a Jewish social life. William agreed. But in addition to his concern for his daughters' dating opportunities was his own desire to achieve, his dissatisfaction with the present, his restlessness, all of which he would bequeath to his son. Immigrants by definition and by nature are voyagers. And for William, because his ship had landed at one port did not mean his journey was over. When he was peddling door-to-door, the store in Salem had represented his highest aspiration; now he had another rung to climb. The store had provided a decent living, but not much else. And America was, as William knew, the *goldeneh medina*, where opportunity was supposed to be as boundless as the nation's borders.

William and Mollie settled on Cleveland, sixty-two miles northwest of Salem, a city they were familiar with from their visits with one of Mollie's cousins. A new suburb was being built, Shaker Heights, and William saw his chance to make a start as a general contractor. He was not discouraged that he knew almost nothing about construction. Business was simple arithmetic, and as with his clothing store, William would learn by doing. He sold his property in Salem and rented a house in Cleveland, at 3673 East 146th Street. He packed his wife and daughters into his car and off William went to pursue his fortune.

Meantime, Max moved in with his Uncle Ben's family to finish his senior year of high school.

*   *   *

During his final six months of high school, Max continued his frenetic pace. His grades improved, rising above average, but this was partly due to the fact that he no longer had to take Latin. He was again a member of the Science Club, served on the business staff of the senior play, was sports editor of his yearbook and chairman of the senior prom. He was on the basketball and track teams, and made the all-county football team. If Fred Cope's assessment of Fisher's ability on the football field was correct — that what he lacked in talent he made up for with hustle — this quality was sufficient to impress the scouts from Ohio State University in Columbus, who offered Fisher a football scholarship, which he accepted. That June, Max was among the eighty-five students who graduated from Salem High School, and in the late summer of 1926, with $150 his father had given him toward his college education, he left for Columbus.

Forty-six years later, on June 10, 1972, Max Fisher returned to Salem for the 91st Annual Reunion of the Salem High School Alumni Association. (Organized in 1882, the association keeps track of Salem's graduates with remarkable success.) Fisher had come to the reunion to accept the association's award as the high school's outstanding alumnus of the year. Over 200 townspeople crowded into the Elks Club ballroom for the banquet. Following dinner, Fisher spoke. By then he had given hundreds of political and philanthropic speeches, yet he still was not a natural speaker; every pause and inflection was noted on his script.

After thanking everyone for the award, Fisher said: "Growing up in Salem provided me with some critically important guidelines. I'm not sure that I could have acquired them by growing up in a city. In cities people tend to break up into smaller groups that have the same interests. . . . [In Salem], I got to know something about people, [and] I can't think of a better place to learn about the American people, with all their virtues and shortcomings, than in a small town."

Fisher talked about discovering the importance of charity not just in his parents' home, but also by watching the Salvation Army in Salem. He digressed to how his love of automobiles, which began in Salem, influenced his decision to enter the oil industry, and how the sweeping technological changes of the 1920s affected his boyhood. Then he discussed the satisfactions of working with the Jewish Agency to help the Israelis, who are "making the desert bloom again."

Finally, he concluded: "It occurred to me one day as I

stood in the city of Jerusalem that I had only come from my boyhood Salem to the original city of Salem. Jerusalem: City of Peace. Salem: peace. I can only hope that some of the things I have been privileged to do since my high-school days have added a little to the cause of 'Salem,' of peace, of *shalom*. And I am delighted to be able to come back here to a place that in a sense I never left, where I learned that people are important, and say *shalom* again."

The crowd applauded. Fisher announced that he was giving a $5,000 annual gift, in perpetuity, to the alumni association scholarship fund. The audience rewarded him with a standing ovation. Fisher smiled, enjoying the pleasure of being his hometown hero. It was a fleeting pleasure, so keen it could not last, the pleasure of vindication. Fisher watched men and women approach him. He shook their hands, accepted their hearty thanks, meanwhile thinking of what he did *not* mention in his speech: that although he had grown up among the people of Salem, he never felt as if he were part of them; he always sensed that, as a Jew, he was an outsider. And because he was Jewish, he was amazed that they had invited him to return.

Chapter 2

THE ROAD NOT TAKEN

IN THE FALL of 1926, there were 10,000 students on the Ohio State University campus in Columbus, almost as many students as townspeople in Salem. Max Fisher arrived with one suitcase, a mackinaw and high boots, footwear favored by the boys in rural Ohio, but seen as strictly "farmer" by the college men, many of whom came from Cleveland and Cincinnati. Along with their up-to-date cosmopolitan dress, these young men had a breezy sophistication — popularized in the magazine *College Humor* — and their style was foreign to Fisher.

Forty-four years after matriculating at OSU, Fisher came back to be honored with the Ohio State Centennial Achievement Award. In his speech, Fisher praised the Land Grant colleges because by creating them the United States declared that higher education was no longer the exclusive domain of the wealthy few, but also the right of men and women of modest means. Fisher described OSU as a place with "wide, wide doors," and although this was true academically, Fisher quickly discovered in 1926 that this egalitarianism did not extend to OSU's social world.

His friend from Salem, Charles Coffee (who, like Fisher, had won a football scholarship) was also entering Ohio State. One day, Fisher ran into Coffee crossing the campus. They talked about their classes and the football season. Then Coffee, explaining to Fisher why he had been out of touch, said: "Max, I can't invite you to my fraternity for dinner."

"Why not?" Fisher asked.

"You're Jewish," Coffee replied.

So Fisher joined his own fraternity — the Alpha Epsilon

chapter of Phi Beta Delta, which by definition was nonsectarian, but whose members were primarily Jewish. Fisher moved into their solid three-story house at 1918 Indianola Avenue, a winding, tree-shaded road one short block from the campus.

Fisher had grown up as the only Jew among his peers. Now, he underwent his first exposure to Jews. But he was the only country boy among his urban fraternity brothers, and initially he was intimidated. "They were [second- and third-generation] Jews," says Fisher today. "They came from the cities, were more polished and more sophisticated — and more Jewish. They had a style I didn't have. They were more affluent and exposed to [education and traditions] I had never seen. And suddenly I was shoved into this mix. They were too fast for me. It was hard for me to get adjusted."

His fraternity brothers, says Fisher, found him difficult to understand. But his roommate, Lou Horowitz, who was from Cleveland, helped him get through this period. "Lou and I used to walk and talk for hours," Fisher says. "We used to try to explain to each other our feelings about things. And Lou would tell me: 'Max, you're going to be a great businessman.' The fellows at the fraternity didn't like me at the beginning because they didn't understand me, and Lou would tell them: 'You're making an awful mistake. This man's going to be a big success someday.'"

During the next four years, Fisher would deal with his uncertainties as he had dealt with them in Salem: by plunging into activities. He worked in the fraternity, cleaning up in the kitchen to pay for his meals. He was the "Richman Brothers' Man" on campus, taking orders for the clothier, and when football season was over, he worked in Richman Brothers' downtown Columbus store. He maintained a B average in his course work and played on the football team until his sophomore year, when he was clipped during practice and severely injured his knee. He managed the basketball team and was on the business staff of several social and fraternity committees.

Along with the Jewish social milieu that Fisher experienced in his fraternity, he was introduced to formalized Judaism. "I attended my first religious service at the Hillel House on campus," Fisher recalls. "And the Rabbi — Lee Levinger — had quite an impact on me. He and his wife used to invite me to their house for kosher meals and for Passover. I would play with their [young] son. I learned about being a Jew. I didn't become more observant, but I understood more and became more conscious of being Jewish."

Fisher also became more involved in Hillel. He served as its president and produced a play, *The Dybbuk*, under its auspices, taking it on the road to Cleveland, Dayton and Cincinnati. Fisher was responsible for financing the production, and he drummed up support in Cleveland from Rabbi Abba Hillel Silver, the noted Zionist and later the country's foremost Jewish Republican.

As in his adult life, Fisher preferred the business end, because despite the scope of his college activities, he retained his shyness. A woman who dated one of his fraternity brothers recalls: "I remember Max as very quiet. He was so tall and thin and I thought he was awkward. A very nice boy, but very shy."

Although Fisher was eventually popular enough to be elected president of his fraternity, Aron M. Mathieu, a fraternity brother, remembers him as someone who kept his own counsel. "He stayed out of political discussions," says Mathieu. "His best friend was Lou Horowitz — 'Duke,' we called him. Duke was a Communist back then, and we were always arguing with him, but Max didn't like to argue. You could tell Max was determined to succeed. We knew he wanted to make money. When he returned from football practice, his mouth was full of bloody cotton from practicing with those giants, and we teased him, really trying to comfort him, by lining up, bowing and chanting, with put-on Yiddish accents, 'Don'ta worry, Maahx, you'lla makea money, Maahx.'"

Money, the lack of it, was on Fisher's mind. The single voiced ambition that he can recall from college was "to walk into a clothing store and buy what I wanted without looking at the price." Once he had lost his football scholarship due to his injuries, his budget was tight; there were tuition, books, fraternity dues and a car loan to pay. So every Sunday evening, when the fraternity kitchen was closed, he walked over to Tim's, a restaurant across from the campus, and for fifteen cents got a bowl of chili and all the crackers he could eat. In this manner, Fisher managed not only to fill himself up and to save money, but to cultivate a lifelong dislike for chili.

Fisher augmented his work during the school year with summer work when he returned to his family in Cleveland.

"I delivered ice," says Fisher, "for City Ice and Fuel. It was the best paying job [a college student] could get. Thirty-four bucks a week. That was a of lot of money. I was the only Jewish boy who worked at the icehouse, which was on Superior and St. Clair. It [was] a tough neighborhood. This was during Prohibition. We served the speakeasies along with the butcher shops and grocery stores. Well, one morning, when I went to work, I didn't have my gloves on. The foreman saw my hands were blistered and said: 'What's the matter with your hands?' 'Nothing,' I told him. We were carrying 200-pound blocks of ice, and I earned a lot of respect because I kept up even with the blisters on my hands."

The icemen, Fisher learned, had a profitable scam going. They would load up, say, a butcher shop with 4,000 pounds of ice and charge the shop for a little more ice than they delivered. The extra money went into their pockets.

Late one afternoon, Fisher remembers, the foreman, who would go with the men once a month, was riding with him. They had just stocked a grocery store and were en route to the icehouse when the foreman turned to Fisher and asked: "How much money did we make?"

"What do you mean?" Fisher said. "'How much money did we make?'"

"How much did we knock down?" the foreman said. "I want my cut."

Fisher replied: "I don't know what you're talking about."

When they returned to the icehouse, the foreman, laughing and jerking his thumb back at Fisher, said to the other ice haulers: "This guy's not a very smart Jew boy. No sir, this Jew boy's not very smart."

In several ways, anti-Semitic remarks were easier for

Fisher to abide than the strange sophistication of his Jewish fraternity brothers.

"I had no problem relating to Christians," says Fisher. "I never carried a chip on my shoulder about that."

Clearly, Ohio State University afforded Fisher a glimpse of broader and brighter horizons and the opportunity to test himself on a more competitive field than Salem. It also hardened and gave new form to some of what he had learned at home. He no longer had his father around to criticize him. But Fisher must have internalized this process, because it was early in his college days that he began to construct self-improvement lists and to mete out his own punishments.

For example, if he spoke in class or to others without thinking, if he said something hurtful, if he didn't manage his time or money properly, he wrote it down, promised himself to try not to do it again, and skipped breakfast or subjected himself to what he considered some appropriate deprivation. Perhaps of greater relevance to Fisher's later careers — since it partially explains the source of his abundant drive — Fisher does not remember ever rewarding himself for his accomplishments. Whatever he achieved, it was not enough. The peaceful rewards of satisfaction were not in his plans.

*   *   *

While Max was earning his degree at Ohio State, the fortunes of his family wavered. William, upon arriving in Cleveland, established an office in the Guarantee Title Building. When general contracting did not pan out, he switched to carpentry contracting. After two years of steadily losing money, William contacted a childhood friend, Nathan R. Epstein, who was now living in Philadelphia. Epstein had made enough money as an electrical contractor to become a major investor in the Woodrow Wilson Building and Loan Association, a thrift institution. It was precisely the sort of success William had in mind for himself. He recounted his recent troubles to his friend, and Epstein suggested that William come to Philadelphia and learn the electrical business.

Again, William set off, packing up his wife and daughters,

and renting an attractive row house in the Roosevelt Boulevard section of Philadelphia. Six months later, the family was back in Cleveland. Electrical contracting had not proved profitable, and although William maintained his friendship with Epstein, the two men had not gotten along in business. William now made another stab at carpentry contracting and did fairly well.

Then, on October 29, 1929, the stock market crashed. The United States skidded off into the Depression, and William lost his business.

He got in touch with friends and relatives, and came up with a lead — Louis J. Chesnow. Five years younger than William, Chesnow was an architect. Because the Depression had ground the building trade to a halt, there was no demand for Chesnow's professional skills. So he was in the market for a good investment, and sifted through the city tax rolls hoping to find a failed business that might have some promise.

Finally, Chesnow spotted one: the Solaray Sales and Manufacturing Corporation, which had foundered due to a number of nearly worthless shares of stock being issued before the crash. But Solaray did have potential. The company produced lubricating oil reprocessed from used automobile crankcase oil, which they refined in their own plant. Since the current models of automobile engines required frequent oil changes, and since it seemed that the only profitable businesses during the Depression would be in the essential areas of either food or fuel, the $5,000 down payment for Solaray appeared to be a sound investment.

At least Chesnow thought so, and he lined up four other men to invest with him. William Fisher wanted in — this was the opportunity he had been waiting for. There was, however, the problem of capital, specifically William's share of the down payment. He quickly proceeded to raise the money. He went to see Nathan Epstein, his former partner in Philadelphia, whose business had suffered at the start of the Depression. Epstein was as excited about the possibilities of Solaray as William, and not only agreed to invest, but decided to move his family to Detroit.

In the winter of 1930, not long after the deal was finalized, William and Mollie Fisher relocated from Cleveland to Detroit. Their daughter Gail, now twenty years old, accompanied them, as did their youngest, Dorothy, who was ten. Anne stayed behind in Cleveland with friends to finish junior high.

William Fisher inspected the refining plant of which he was now a partial owner and was disappointed at the grim collection of steel jammed onto a lot at Beaufait near Gratiot, in the middle of a residential area. Yet William was brimming with optimism, even though none of the partners was familiar with the complex process of refining oil. This *was* the oil business! You could make a fortune — real money and all that it represented to an immigrant stuck in the trough of the Depression: a rapidly dwindling chance for security.

As William got things under way, it naturally never occurred to him that he was altering the course of his son's life.

*   *   *

Tuesday, June 10, 1930, was a beautiful day in Columbus. The sky was blue as turquoise, the sun warm and bright.

That morning, Max Fisher was in a hurry. Ohio State University's 53rd annual commencement exercises were slated to begin at 9:30, and Fisher had to pack. Richman Brothers, pleased with his work at its Columbus store, had offered him a job at its Cleveland headquarters, which he had accepted. He was supposed to depart immediately after graduation. Fisher, still uncertain what direction to head in, yet still dreaming of great success ("Maahx, you'lla makea money, Maahx"), wasn't certain he wanted to forge a career in the men's clothing business. But any job for a new college graduate in the Depression was a rare opportunity. So even though his parents had moved from Cleveland to Detroit, Fisher was determined to drive to Cleveland and get to work.

Fisher dressed, finished packing his suitcase, ate breakfast, grabbed his cap and gown, and dashed out of the fraternity house, crossing the campus and stopping outside the high stone walls of the stadium, where over 1,300 graduates and a host of faculty and honorees had gathered.

The Ohio State University concert band played Meyerbeer's "Coronation March," and the processional began. The robed graduates paraded past the stadium gates, unwinding toward the north curve of the grandstand like a shining black ribbon, while 8,500 relatives and friends watched them on both sides.

Fisher took his seat among the College of Commerce and Administration graduates and faced the canopied platform. Professor Manley Ottmer Hudson of the Harvard University Law School gave the annual address. His theme centered on how drastically and rapidly the world was changing. Technocracy, the domination of technology, was a widely discussed — and to some, a feared — phenomenon. Solo air flights to distant parts of the globe, in record time, were increasing, and picture telegraphy service began. The Depression continued, while the Smoot-Hawley Bill, which raised tariffs on foreign imports, elevated protectionism to an all-time high. France was busy constructing the Maginot Line. The Soviet Union was gearing up its industrial capacity. In Germany, Adolf Hitler was gaining ground and Heinrich Himmler was shaping up the SS — the Nazi Party's military arm. In the Middle East, Arabs were attacking Jews over Jewish use of the Western Wall, and in England Lord Passfield was issuing a twenty-three-page White Paper, repudiating Zionism and suggesting that Jewish immigration to Palestine be halted. Albert Einstein completed writing *About Zionism*, and the Jewish Agency, in which Fisher would play a vital role, became the representative body of all Zionist and non-Zionist Jews.

Professor Hudson exhorted the OSU graduates not to be afraid of the current sweeping changes. "These changes," Hudson said, "have been so upsetting that as citizens we are now confronted with social and political problems of which the first graduates of this university did not even dream. We must adjust ourselves to a world which seems wholly different from that of our grandfathers. The geographical frontiers of our society have ceased to correspond to the political boundaries of our . . . nations. Each new extension of our knowledge . . . enlarge[s] the area in which we live."

Hudson's words must have struck the audience as especially meaningful, because seated under the canopy on the platform, waiting to receive an honorary degree, was the aviator and inventor, Orville Wright, whose airplane would contribute mightily to the future's global village.

Gazing out across the graduates, Hudson concluded: "The thought that I would place before you is not a vague ideal of world citizenship. I am suggesting a world outlook for a citizen of America, because it seems to me to be necessitated . . . by our interests as Americans. If we would prefer to be ruled by the past . . . we shall neither prove to be useful nor shall we be sure of serving the interests of our own local communities."

Hudson completed his talk to polite applause, and if Max Fisher, sitting with the sun beating down on his mortar board, was listening, it is now impossible to discern. That recollection is lost. But the spirit of Hudson's address would be echoed by Fisher throughout his multiple careers in business, philanthropy and politics, and this turn-of-the-century progressivism indelibly marked Fisher, for better or for worse, as a child of his time.

*　　*　　*

As the Ohio State University graduation of 1930 drew to a close, bugles sounded the "Call to the Work of the World," and the recessional began. Fisher filed from the stadium and ambled through the golden afternoon. He took his time now, scanning the campus, the magnificent brick buildings and the blooming buckeye trees, and returned to the Phi Beta Delta house. He said goodbye to his fraternity brothers, then walked out to where his 1916 Model T Ford was parked. He tossed his suitcase into the back and gripped the car-door handle.

In 1983, more than a half-century after this shining spring afternoon, seventy-five-year-old Max Fisher — moneyed, powerful, credited with more accomplishments than a recent college graduate would dare to imagine — went to the Westin

Hotel at the Detroit Renaissance Center to receive the Business Statesman's Award, which was being presented to him by the city's Harvard Business School Club. Standing on the dais, Fisher spoke briefly after accepting the plaque, ruminating about his past. What, he wondered aloud, would have happened to him had he gone to Cleveland as originally planned?

This is a question to which there is obviously no definitive response. Yet as Fisher grew older and allowed the press greater access to his life, it was a question that he often discussed in interviews. To some degree, Fisher's interest in the concept of fate had been heightened in the mid-1960s by his wife, Marjorie, who, upon reading Edgar Cayce, developed an interest in mysticism. Fisher also admitted, in scores of interviews, that behind any notable success, including his own, you would find not only intelligence, hard work, foresight and all the qualities extolled by Horatio Alger, but also an equivalent portion of luck. Still, the question of what might have occurred had he wound up in Cleveland seemed to fascinate him for another more important and personal reason. As someone who has periodically kept self-improvement lists, the question provided a method for him to evaluate his life. So on the evening he was being feted by the Harvard Business Club, Fisher posed the question, not anticipating a reply. He was pleasantly surprised.

"A young man stood up," recalls Fisher. "And he said: 'Mr. Fisher, if you'd gone to Cleveland instead of Detroit you would be getting this award in Cleveland.'"

This response, though flattering, was not satisfying, as though something in Fisher resisted the solution because it would be the decisive settling of accounts, signaling the end of his relentless self-evaluations, which had been critical during his college years and his later financial and political successes. He would, in short, no longer have the drive to achieve.

But certainly on June 10, 1930, with the sunlight glimmering on the lush green leaves like a glaze, no such question existed. And as Fisher stood outside of his fraternity house, he took one last look around him. Children were playing on the neatly clipped lawn of the Indianola Avenue public school over on the corner of East 16th Street, and Ohio State students, newly graduated, many accompanied by their parents, were loading up their cars.

It had been a productive four years, Fisher thought. He had made some friends, Jewish friends, big-city friends. He had attended his first Jewish religious service and become active in Hillel. He still had his insatiable hunger to distinguish himself, but he had no specific goal in mind. On the credit side of the ledger, he did have five dollars in his pocket, his bachelor of science degree in business administration, a job waiting for him, and he would no longer have to eat the chili and crackers at Tim's.

Fisher climbed into his car. As he drove the Ford from Columbus it struck him that he might enjoy checking in on his family before getting situated in Cleveland. Whether it was homesickness — brought on by the sight of other students with their families — or a yearning for his mother's stuffed cabbage and noodle pudding; whether it was a distant memory of an old joke, "Cleveland is Detroit without the glitter," or pride and wanting to share the accomplishment of his degree with his parents and sisters, or simply a desire for a final stay with his family before venturing out alone into the world, Fisher headed for Detroit.

True, he was heading toward the type of extraordinary fortune that even as a youngster, sitting in Salem's Carnegie Library with the novels of Horatio Alger on his lap, he could not have conjured up in his most spectacular dreams. Yet, despite all of his success, it was a decision he would reflect on forever.

Chapter 3

IN PURSUIT OF HORATIO ALGER

I WAS PAST midnight on June 11, 1930, when Max Fisher
pulled into Detroit. William Fisher had rented a wood-
frame house with a tiny yard and an even tinier porch on
Collingwood, in the northwest section of the city (which was
predominately Jewish in the 1930s), and Max navigated the
dark, unfamiliar streets until he located the house. Inside, his
parents and sisters were sleeping. Max stretched out on a
couch. That morning, William woke him, saying that he
needed his help. He and his partners in Solaray had acquired
a four-and-a-half-acre brickyard in southwest Detroit, on
Greyfriar and Northampton, across the Rouge River from the
Ford Motor Company's Rouge complex, and they were physically relocating their oil-reclaiming plant from the Beaufait
site and rebuilding it on the new lot. Max accompanied his
father, and the dismantled plant was trucked to the brickyard.

As Max unloaded equipment, his career in men's fashion
ended. From childhood on, he liked tinkering with radios and
cars, and perhaps it was the sight of the plant's pipes and
engine components that changed his mind. Or perhaps it was
the concept of literally being in the oil business — even if it
was purifying used crankcase oil, a thick sludge, that was
pumped from the floor pits of gas stations. Within days, he
notified Richman Brothers that he would not be relocating to
Cleveland.

The relocation and construction of the reclaiming plant
went on for months. It was finished in the fall of 1930, and by
New Year's the Keystone Oil Refining Company was hawking
its lubricating oil. William hired Max as a salesman, paying
him fifteen dollars a week — when there was money. (At one

point, due to a paucity of funds, Max had to turn his car over to a finance company.) Keystone's difficulty was rooted in the oil market of the time. Beginning in 1928, virgin oil was selling at one dollar per barrel. According to Daniel Yergin, author of *The Prize*, "all over the world, there were too many producers and too much production," which made reprocessed oil less appealing. Max recalls working ten- and twelve-hour days and, despite his exhaustion, found that selling over the phone and soliciting potential customers in their offices had an unforeseen benefit: it kept him out of his parents' house. His four years at Ohio State gave him a taste of independence that now made living among his family feel confining. With his three sisters, he picked up where he left off: he constantly teased them, especially Gail, who invited her large circle of friends over every Sunday. Max would come downstairs, roll his eyes and proclaim: "Ah, my sister is holding court." Most troublesome, however, was that he was again at odds with his father.

The conflict between William and Max may have been based in the head-butting between an equally stubborn father and son, but once Max signed on with Keystone he and William had a divergence of opinion about the company. William became a partner in the plant because he viewed it as an investment. He did not believe that he was required to know the technology of the oil business. He would learn what he needed by doing it, as he had learned to speak English, to peddle and to run a clothing store. Max, on the other hand, was convinced that success in the oil business would be based in knowing as much technical detail as possible. He was obsessed with it. He read everything he could find on petroleum engineering, enrolled in night classes in petrochemistry at the University of Michigan, and engaged a tutor — a University of Michigan chemistry professor — to direct his studies. With the backseat of his car loaded with oil samples, he visited refineries throughout the Midwest, comparing their operations to Keystone's and suggesting improvements that William typically ignored. On those rare evenings he had a date, he drove out to the Keystone refinery and was dismayed when the young woman failed to share his pleasure in gazing up at the crisscross of steel pipes.

"In [the oil] business," Fisher recalled in a 1972 speech, "I was caught up almost immediately in the process of change that was affecting American industry. I don't want you to think that forty years ago I suddenly had a full-blown vision of all the incredible things that were going to happen. What I did get was one small inkling that change was becoming a basic factor in the way Americans live. . . . You could see how the car was bringing an end to the isolation of our small towns."

Fisher would become noted for his ability to envision change; it would be considered among his greatest assets as a businessman, and he would bring it with him into the civic, philanthropic and political arenas. He would tell groups that one has "to be a visionary if he wants to accomplish any-thing," and that "a person who goes through life on a day-to-day basis — he just lives." He would tirelessly reiterate this theme — sometimes to the chagrin of his colleagues. In 1932, William Fisher was the first to hear it and, coming from his twenty-four-year-old son, whose résumé was limited to work-ing in a kitchen and lugging blocks of ice, it understandably annoyed him.

Max's efforts began to pay modest dividends. Service sta-tions and department stores were stocking Keystone prod-ucts, and Max initiated a marketing program, writing a his-tory of oil refining that Keystone used as a sales manual and bestowing brand names on their rerefined oil — Korlube, Penny and, his favorite, Maximile, for which he composed a bit of advertising copy: "Max Sez/more miles/more smiles/ with Maximile."

Financially, though, Keystone was hampered by the Depression-ravaged economy. And Detroit was hit hard. In 1931, total U.S. car sales dropped below two million for the first time in a decade, and that summer Henry Ford I closed his production lines. Nearly one out of every seven persons was on relief and, according to Robert Conot, author of *American Odyssey*, a comprehensive history of Detroit, "children scavenged through the streets like animals for scraps of food. . . . Among high-school students in the inner city the incidence of tuberculosis tripled. Each day 4,000 children stood in bread lines. With their sunken, lifeless eyes, sallow cheeks, and distended bellies, some resembled the starving children in Europe during the war."

A half-century after the 1929 stock-market crash, Fisher told an interviewer: "[The Depression] gave [me] a point of view. It helped [me] build a little character. . . . Whenever I hear about people who are washed out or lost their homes . . . I feel tremendous sympathy, because I [think] back to those days and remember. . . . It was very rough. People were selling lubricating oil out of barrels on the street corner along with apples. You learned to do almost anything to get by. I'll never forget paying my dentist with five-gallon cans of lubricating oil. It's funny, you couldn't give oil away then."

Other than the occasional date, Max's chief form of entertainment was strolling along West Grand Boulevard, in the soaring shadow of the Fisher Building, the twenty-eight-story masterwork of architect Albert Kahn. Kahn had been commissioned to build it in 1928 by the seven Fisher brothers (no relation to Max), who earned their fortune providing bodies for the automobile industry. The brothers picked a parcel of land a few miles from the heart of the city, in the New Center, their vision of a secondary business district that would relieve the congestion downtown. The building itself, arguably the most prestigious edifice in Detroit, was magnificent, Gothic in design, with a tapering majestic tower and pinkish-gray granite and white marble facing.

Attracted by the name of the building, Max enjoyed pausing in front of the ornate display windows of its expensive street-level shops and watching the executives and lawyers and bankers file in for lunch. They would walk down the grand, arch-ceilinged, marble-walled arcade, past the plush Fisher Theatre, and ride the elevators up to the exclusive, members-only Recess Club, renowned for its deft waiters in tuxedos, starched table linen, muted oak paneling and opulently prepared food.

In the early 1930s, Max was stuck on the outside looking in, a quarter-inch of shining plate glass standing between him and his dreams. It seemed as though everything that had ever made him feel like an outsider — his growing up Jewish in Salem, his poverty at Ohio State, his father's criticism — was still conspiring to make him feel that way. He was a Jew in Detroit, a city not only closed to Jews, but hostile toward them. Henry Ford I had turned anti-Semitism into a local pastime, and a new right-wing group, the Black Legion, casually murdered WPA workers, trade unionists and the treasurer of the Auto Workers Union. Meanwhile, Father Charles Coughlin, stationed nearby in Royal Oak, Michigan, became among the most popular radio personalities in the country, broadcasting anti-Semitic invective from his Shrine of the Little Flower.

In addition, Max's fiscal situation was hardly improved. Although he was earning fifteen dollars a week, more than most men who had families to support, Keystone rarely made enough money to pay him. Decades later, Max recalled "walking through the lobby of the Fisher Building and staring up at the beautiful architecture. This was . . . when they had vaudeville there, and I didn't have the money to go in and see the shows." Most trying of all for him was that he was chafing under his father's thumb at Keystone. In these years, his yearning to be among the privileged and powerful who lunched inside the Fisher Building was almost palpable.

By 1932, Keystone was selling one million gallons of reprocessed lubricating oil per year. The volume was heavy enough that William Fisher hired another salesman, Maurice S. Schiller.

"I had graduated from the University of Michigan the year before," says Schiller. "My parents were a hair away from losing their house and I wanted to help them. I needed a job. My father played pinochle with Bill Fisher, so I went to see him."

"You'll get fifteen dollars a week when we have the money," William said. Schiller wasn't thrilled with that prospect. Then William said: "And I'll give you a car and gas. Hell, you'll be able to go out on dates."

That clinched it. Schiller accepted.

Schiller remembers that Max would go to extreme lengths to nail down a deal. One afternoon, Schiller recalls, he and Max had driven to Ohio to see a distributor. He was out hunting geese when the two men arrived at his office. Max got directions and, dressed in overcoats, suits and oxfords, he and Schiller hiked through the woods with mud up to their knees and an icy wind snapping at them until they located the distributor, who was walking through a meadow of brown grass with his shotgun. While they waited for the geese to appear, Max closed the sale.

Despite the increased volume, there was not much profit in reprocessed oil. The Keystone plant was inefficient, and the owners lacked the technical expertise to correct it. (Leon B. Komisaruk — later Leon B. Kay — who had been hired as an electrical contractor to help reassemble the plant, was made a partner because he had a degree in chemical engineering, the only one with the vaguest notion of how the plant should operate.) Even though the used oil was obtained by Keystone at no cost, they had to pay truckers to drive to the service stations to collect it, and that expense, along with their other operating expenses, kept Keystone in the red.

Max's entry into the oil industry coincided with the discovery of crude oil in eastern Michigan, where, during the next decade, over a dozen oil fields were uncovered. As Max traveled around the state he learned of the strikes and saw that the most profitable end of the petroleum business was in crude-oil exploration and refining. He finally persuaded his father to dedicate a small section of Keystone's refinery to crude, and Max shortly had the operation under way, arranging to have the oil trucked in from the Michigan fields and personally supervising the technical modifications to the plant.

"It was only 200 barrels a day," Fisher says. "But, at a dollar a barrel, we were making $200, which was fantastic money then."

In the fall of 1932, Fisher cast his first vote in a presidential election. "I voted for Franklin D. Roosevelt," remembers Fisher. "Being a good Republican now, I don't talk about it too much. I remember [his 'We have] nothing to fear but fear itself' [speech]. I heard [it] on the radio in the lobby of the Detroit Leland Hotel. It gave you quite an uplift. . . . Those next couple of years were very tough, and that speech helped."

Actually, with Keystone now refining 200 barrels of crude per day, Max was feeling sanguine enough about his financial future to take a vacation. Max had a friend, Joseph Falk, a hardware salesman who occasionally drove around Michigan with Max in order to share traveling expenses. Max and Joe had each been saving a dollar a week in a Christmas club, and by late December of 1932 they saved enough to visit Cuba.

"It was quite an experience," says Fisher. "It was my first trip on an airplane, a Pan Am Clipper, fifteen dollars round-trip. In Havana, we stayed at the Isle of Cuba Hotel for three dollars a day, including food. While I was down there we found this tailor who made me a wonderful suit — a three-piece gray gabardine — and was willing to accept an American check. Well, on my return from that trip, I heard that the banks had closed. And, gee, I was worried about that because I thought the tailor had trusted me and now my check wouldn't clear. But he must've deposited it just in time because the check cleared and cleaned out my account."

What Max also learned when he returned from Cuba was that, due to faulty equipment, the Keystone plant had burned down.

"It took a long time to get the insurance settlement, and those were the darkest days for me," says Fisher. "I figured I was one of the lucky ones — at least I had the new suit from Havana."

Keystone received a $90,000 insurance settlement, and with the money, William bought out most of his partners, leaving himself as president, Nathan Epstein as vice president and Leon Kay, secretary. Max felt this was the opportune moment to build a crude-oil refinery and drew up technical and financial plans, which he presented to his father. Max pointed out to William that a refinery with a 1,000-barrel-a-day capacity would cost $40,000, and would yield $10,000 a month.

William was not impressed. "We're only rebuilding a reprocessing plant," he said. "Our trouble started with your refining crude. The factory burned because of it."

Over the next several weeks, Max pressed and William sank into an angry silence. It was as though Max were a teenager again and William was disgusted with him for wasting his time playing football. One afternoon at the office, their argument boiled over and William turned to Max and said furiously, "You're so smart, college boy. Go do it on your own."

It was then that Max went to Henry E. Wenger.

*   *   *

Two mentors significantly influenced Max Fisher, both of whom he met by the age of twenty-five. The first was his scoutmaster in Salem, Lee Chamberlain; the second was Henry Wenger. These two men had little in common except that Fisher was able to seek them out when he was battling with his father. Chamberlain gave Fisher the confidence to pursue the pleasures of his American boyhood despite William's criticism that hiking and camping were frivolous. Wenger was, in a sense, an extension of Chamberlain. He helped Fisher surmount William's provincialism in business, enabling him to achieve his conception of what it meant to be an oil man — that is, a modern industrialist.

Henry Wenger was a year older than William Fisher, and like William, he was an immigrant. Wenger was born in Basel, Switzerland, in 1887, and came to the United States in 1912, after having lived in England and France. He was a gentle, urbane man who loved opera and golf and bore a striking resemblance to the actor Adolphe Menjou. In Chicago, after World War I, he married Consuelo P. Slaughter, and they moved to Detroit in 1929. Three years later, Wenger, along with his brother-in-law, William E. Slaughter Jr., founded the Aurora Gasoline Company, which sold gas to service stations in tank-car lots, at markups as low as a quarter-cent per gallon. Wenger was in charge of the selling, and Slaughter, who was nineteen years younger than his brother-in-law, handled the books. They ran Aurora out of the basement of Wenger's brick Tudor house on La Salle Boulevard in northwest Detroit.

Max, who had dabbled in the gasoline-brokerage business on the side, knew of Wenger, and drove over to his house and presented his financial projections. The success of the venture, Fisher said, rested on the fact that the few refineries around Detroit were committed to buying crude oil from Texas and Oklahoma and were forced to pay enormous shipping charges. But this new refinery would rely exclusively on Michigan crude, thus saving a significant sum in shipping and making it possible to undersell local competitors and to compete with the major oil companies. He added that he had a good location for the refinery, on the Keystone lot; he had experience in crude-oil refining; and the refinery would be a joint venture with Keystone, thereby minimizing the risk.

Wenger said he would consider it. Discussions continued for two months, and Wenger agreed to invest all of his cash, $38,000, if the first profits were used to pay off his investment.

In his later years, when interviewers asked Fisher how he convinced Wenger to invest with him, Fisher jokingly replied that he "must have hoodwinked him." Fifty years after the fact, Fisher is at a loss to answer why Wenger bankrolled the venture. He simply states that "Wenger was sold on refining and my strategy for getting into it." William Slaughter, who also listened to Fisher's pitch in 1933, says that "Henry looked at the figures and they made sense." Neither of these statements seems adequate to explain why a forty-six-year-old man with a wife, young son and daughter to support would hand over $38,000 in the depths of the Depression to a twenty-five-year-old who had been in the oil reclaiming business for three years.

Wenger's son, Henry Penn Wenger, who became a successful oil man, supplies a more complete explanation: "My father was a dreamer," says Penny Wenger. "And so was Max.

Dad wanted to earn his fortune and he sized up Max and thought that he had a lot of promise. Max was among the first Jews to be involved in oil refining and the Texas Anglo-Saxon oil industry wasn't waiting for a smart young Jewish boy from Ohio State. That didn't matter to my father. He was a maverick and I think he saw the same thing in Max. They were kindred spirits."

As Wenger mulled over the proposal, Max approached his father with his new proposition. Although William was in the midst of rebuilding his reclaiming plant, he consented to participate in Max's plan since his son assured him that it would only require Keystone to put up land, not money. Max then negotiated a half-interest in Keystone's 50-percent share of the venture for himself as compensation for putting the deal together. Certain that the refinery would never show a profit, William gave Max his share without a fight.

Hearing that The Ohio Oil Company was scrapping three of its Oklahoma refineries, Max went out west and purchased their old equipment. He hired an engineer, E.G. Guy, to design the refinery. Max supervised its construction and oversaw every aspect of the refining. (Until 1945, Aurora had no engineering staff beyond him.) The projected cost of the refinery, $40,000, was too low by $28,000, but Max's prediction of the refinery's financial success was on target. He had projected a $10,000-a-month profit; the first month they cleared $10,125. Although Max had predicted it, the swiftness of their success startled him. He discussed it with Henry Wenger, and the older man gave him a piece of advice that Fisher was still quoting sixty years later.

"Max," said Wenger, "don't be afraid of big numbers. A hundred or a million — it's only a matter of zeros."

Within months, Aurora moved out of Wenger's basement, setting up offices in a converted bank — a wedged-shaped, sandstone building — on the corner of Wyoming and Puritan. It was around this time that Max met Irving L. "Bucky" Goldman, a Brooklyn native who had relocated to Detroit to be near his wife's family, and the two men, so different in appearance and temperament, became fast friends. Goldman, who had worked in New York and California as a salesman, was a small, compact man, an extrovert comfortable in groups of people, a nonstop talker and amusing storyteller. Fisher brought him to meet Wenger, and Aurora hired him as a salesman for fifty dollars a week and the use of a Ford. From the beginning, Goldman felt that Wenger was "one of the smartest guys I ever met," and he saw a side of Wenger that surprised him. Wenger was a member of the Detroit Golf Club and the Detroit Athletic Club, both of which excluded Jews from membership. Yet, Goldman says, Wenger was without prejudice, even when it cost Aurora a substantial amount of money.

"I went to see a man whose company sold gas nationally," says Goldman. "I made my pitch and he told me he would have to think about it. [After I left], he called Henry at the office and he said he'd like to do business with Aurora, but he wouldn't deal with a fellow named Goldman. Henry replied, 'There's nothing we'd like more than to do business with you. But Mr. Goldman will be handling your account.' The distributor said no thanks, and we didn't do business with him."

In the fall of 1934, with Aurora piling one profitable month on top of the other, Max decided to get married. Bucky Goldman's wife, Frances, had introduced Max to her friend, Sylvia Krell. Two years younger than Max, Sylvia was a pretty, dark-haired, dark-eyed woman, with high cheekbones and fine features. She had grown up in Detroit and lived on Poe Avenue, just off West Grand Boulevard, an area that, when her parents, Max and Edith Krell, moved there, was more like the country than the city, with gardens bordering the wide streets. Sylvia, a talented pianist, had a large circle of friends. She attended Northwestern High School and, upon graduating, worked at Pack-Wolin, a tony women's shop downtown.

On their initial date, Max drove Sylvia to the refinery, his bottles of oil samples rattling in the backseat, and proudly guided her on a tour. Although it was not Sylvia's ideal of romance, over the next several months Max treated her to more traditional romantic fare, and on October 4, 1934, they were married at Sylvia's parents' house. The Fishers, Krells, Wengers and assorted friends crowded into the living room. The rabbi kept calling upstairs for Max to come down. The delay was not due to nervousness. Max and his best man, Bucky Goldman, were in a bedroom huddled around a radio listening to the Detroit Tigers playing the St. Louis Cardinals in the second game of the World Series. The Tigers were batting in the bottom of the 12th, the scored tied 2-2, with Charlie Gehringer on base and Hank Greenberg, the slugging first baseman (and eventual Hall-of-Famer) at bat. Fisher and Goldman were devoted fans of the Tigers, who had not won a pennant in a quarter-century, but their devotion was more than home-team fealty. Hank Greenberg was a rare, great Jewish big-leaguer, a folk hero to Jews of the era who were struggling to swim into the American mainstream, and Fisher and Goldman would not consider budging from the radio. Greenberg walked, and after Goose Goslin knocked in Gehringer with the winning run, Fisher and Goldman joined the wedding party. Following the ceremony and a supper, Sylvia and Max left on their honeymoon, boarding a United Fruit Company ship for a cruise through the Panama Canal.

*   *   *

When the Fishers returned they rented a series of flats and then settled at the Wilshire Hotel-Apartments. At Aurora, Max was responsible for the procurement of crude, refining and sales, and he was gradually buying into the company. In 1936, for instance, he assigned Aurora his contract for one-half of the Keystone profits and chose to forgo his salary of $21,000 in lieu of stock. (He eventually owned 38 percent of Aurora; Wenger had 40 percent; and the rest was divided among Slaughter, Goldman and several other executives of the company.) His original notion of relying on Michigan crude oil had earned substantial sums for Aurora, but now an obstacle arose. Aurora was refining 3,000 barrels a day and Michigan crude was high in sulphur and did not yield a good quality gasoline. Fisher utilized the local oil and produced cheaper gasoline by installing a blending plant. When the plant supervisor complained that the high-sulphur oil was corroding the refinery's overhead condensers, Fisher, instead of switching to a different crude, scribbled some figures on a pad, factored in the costs of rebuilding the condensers every month and continued producing premium gas from the cheaper crude.

"Everybody wanted to operate on 'sweet crude' in those days," Fisher recalled for *Forbes* in 1981. "I would take any grade of oil because it would be cheaper [than sweet crude]. Then I'd build a process to operate on it. . . . If you are an independent competing against the large companies, you have to do something different. . . . To compete against Standard Oil we had to turn out a better product more cheaply. Those were the only things we could do. We sold only one grade of gasoline — premium — but we sold it for the price of regular."

With Aurora's rapidly rising volume, Fisher was obliged to tap other sources of crude. He made the rounds of the Michigan fields and traveled to Texas and Oklahoma. His constant traveling, his seventy- and eighty-hour work weeks, were interfering with his personal life. Sylvia was unhappy and he attempted to reduce his schedule, but by the beginning of 1938 Aurora was expanding beyond his expectations. One February evening, Bucky Goldman remembers, Fisher came to his apartment. When Goldman opened the door he was alarmed. Fisher was shaking as though suffering from malaria. Goldman asked him if he wanted a drink. Fisher shook his head and blurted out, "Sylvia's pregnant."

Goldman understood why his friend was frightened. Doctors warned Sylvia against pregnancy. A teenage bout with rheumatic fever had caused mitral stenosis, a narrowing of the valve between the upper and lower chambers of the heart, which disturbs blood flow. She was also developing a serious fibrillation, the heart twitching instead of contracting smoothly, a condition that frequently leads to congestive heart failure. Sylvia was often tired, her legs swollen, and on occasion she had to gasp for breath. Becoming pregnant, the doctors told her, particularly if it was a difficult pregnancy, would tax her heart, causing further — and potentially fatal —

damage. Though aware of the risks, Sylvia would not allow her illness to rob her of having a child.

"Sylvia was a brave woman," says Goldman. "She was terribly sick. She just lived to try to live."

Her pregnancy was without complication, and Max was soon immersed in a deal with The Ohio Oil Company that would springboard Aurora into the front ranks of independent petroleum companies. (In 1962, The Ohio adopted the better-known name of a subsidiary, Marathon.) The deal that Fisher struck is renowned in the petroleum industry and has been extensively examined, from *The Wall Street Journal* to Hartzell Spence's definitive history of Marathon, *Portrait in Oil*. However, what has not been discussed is why he sought the deal, which, Fisher says, was the result of a humdrum incident familiar to the oil business in the late 1930s.

Because of a gross overproduction of crude, independent refiners could buy all the oil they wanted at a considerable discount from the posted price. Now, several weeks prior to approaching The Ohio, Fisher ordered a shipment of crude from a Michigan supplier. In between the time he placed the order and the day of delivery, the price of oil jumped slightly. Pressed for cash, the supplier did not ship the oil to Aurora, but peddled it to another refiner who was willing to pay the higher price. Furious, Fisher promised himself that Aurora would never again have to worry about a steady supply of crude, and so he drove to the town of Findlay, Ohio, to meet with The Ohio Oil Company's vice president, James Donnell II.

Donnell was glad to see him. By 1938, The Ohio was heading toward trouble. With its prolific production in Illinois and Wyoming and heavy yields from wells in eight mid-continental states, the company had amassed critically high levels of unsold crude. The Ohio had recently tried to capture a share of Aurora's 3,000-barrel-a-day business, but without success.

Donnell was a tall, impeccably mannered man, two years younger than Fisher. His grandfather, James, had headed the company, as his father, Otto, was now doing, and though James Donnell II was a product of a privileged boyhood and a

Princeton education, he shared a number of personality traits with Fisher. A hard-working, imaginative perfectionist with an abiding respect for technology, he had a phenomenal memory and a precision of mind that effortlessly grasped the crux of a dilemma and its prompt solution. He disdained small talk and was impatient with factual errors and muddy thinking. Most important, in light of the deal Fisher had come to make, Donnell possessed what historian Hartzell Spence describes as "an inviolate honesty and fairness."

Fisher sat in Donnell's office and got right to the point. "I want to buy some crude," he said. "And I'm willing to pay the posted price."

Donnell leaned forward, shocked at what he thought Fisher had said. Paying the publicly announced field prices for crude in 1938 was unimaginable — an oil man's shortcut to a career change. "Did I hear you correctly?" Donnell asked.

"Yes," Fisher replied, "you did."

"Excuse me a moment," Donnell said, and summoned two colleagues, Hal Stewart, the company counsel, and Charles Bunje, head of the pipeline division, to listen to Fisher's proposal.

When Stewart and Bunje were seated, Fisher outlined his deal. True enough, he said, right now he could purchase all the crude Aurora could handle below the posted price, but he was looking toward the day when crude would be in short supply.

"I'll pay full price now," Fisher told the men, "provided that when the shoe is on the other foot, you'll protect me and deliver all the crude I need."

It did not take Donnell long to decide. "Done," he said, and shook hands with Fisher.

Their agreement was never drawn up in writing. With a handshake, The Ohio gained its largest single crude oil customer when it desperately needed the new outlet. Over the next three years, Aurora forfeited some profit by paying the posted price, yet it continued its expansion. Aurora built storage tanks on a seven-and-a-half-acre tract adjoining the Keystone lot and erected a thermal cracking unit, which made it possible to manufacture a range of higher-type petroleum products, particularly high-test gasolines. By the end of November 1941, Fisher, Wenger and Slaughter divided a cash dividend of $100,000, and the deal with The Ohio would become even more lucrative weeks later, after the Japanese bombed Pearl Harbor and the United States entered the war.

*　　*　　*

On September 9, 1938, Sylvia gave birth to a girl, Jane Ellen, at Harper Hospital in Detroit. Sadly, soon after her daughter was born, Sylvia who was contending with a painful recuperation, suffered a series of setbacks.

"She became depressed," says her younger sister, Shirley Krell Schlafer, "a postpartum depression. And then my mother became ill. She had a congenital heart problem. She was at home in an oxygen tent with nurses [attending] her. It was so sad because [neither Max nor I] could bring Sylvia to visit. We didn't want my mother to see her in that condition."

Sylvia recovered, but six months after Jane was born, her mother, Edith Krell, died. There was more bad news. Dr. Laurence F. Segar, along with a number of the Detroit physicians who treated Sylvia, told her and Max that because of her rheumatic heart disease, "her life could be jeopardized by repeated colds and their complications." A warm climate was suggested. Sylvia chose Tucson, Arizona. For the next fourteen years, Sylvia spent part of the year in Detroit, the other part in Tucson. Max joined her for weeks at a clip. Business always brought Max back to Detroit and then sent him around the country in pursuit of more deals and sources of oil. Initially, Jane went to Tucson with Sylvia, but even before she began grammar school Sylvia decided she should be in Detroit, near her aunts and uncles, cousins and grandparents.

Bucky Goldman recalls the effect of the separation on Max. "Most men," says Goldman, "work until six or seven, or, if they stay late at the office, until eight. Once Sylvia was away, Max had no family to go home to, nothing to organize his life around. He lived on and off with my wife and me. Max had always worked hard. Now, instead of just working hard, he worked all the time. Day and night."

Since college, Fisher had been plagued now and then by an inability to sleep, but by 1940 he was a full-fledged insomniac. He rarely managed to sleep for more than a few hours and often not until four o'clock in the morning. So at night he drove out to the refinery by the Rouge River, or to Aurora's newly acquired refinery in Elsie, Michigan, and talked with the men working the graveyard shift. He studied petroleum journals and geology reports or sat in his office — with his shoes off and his feet up on the desk — scanning financial statements or phoning business contacts in Texas, Oklahoma, Chicago and New York.

Fisher also filled his time traveling through the Southwest in search of oil. He had been attracted to the industry by technology. But as he became acquainted with a wider circle of oil men, he started to enjoy their legendary flamboyance. By nature shy and reserved, he secretly savored — even envied — their outlandish antics. He relished the faith of the wildcatters who believed they could smell oil and pinpointed wells through nasal wisdom; the "poor boys," who drilled with any equipment available in order to get in the game; the promoters who put together big-money deals over poker hands or shots of bourbon — men who bet it all on black-gold dreams and acted as though it were nothing more than a wager at the two-dollar window.

One such man was Max Pray, an oil promoter who operated out of Chicago. Maurice Schiller remembers Pray as "a hail-fellow-well-met." Pray also enjoyed a drink and he knew instinctively who would dig a dry hole and who would tap a gusher.

Now, one Saturday, Fisher and Schiller were in Dallas, Texas, on business. According to Harry Hurt III, author of *Texas Rich*, "Dallas was then the queen city of Texas ... [boasting] the 46,000-seat Cotton Bowl stadium and the sophisticated fashions of Neiman-Marcus ... and transcontinental airline service from Love Field." Oil men were drawn to the downtown hotels, which overflowed with promoters, investors, pipeline operators, oil-well scouts, lease hounds and drilling contractors. Fisher and Schiller were staying at the Adolphus (built by the Busch brewing family of St. Louis), with its beautiful German baroque facade and lobby of rich loamy carpeting and deep leather chairs. Fisher and Schiller were planning to drive to South Oak, Oklahoma, on Sunday, to look in on the drilling of a new well in which Aurora owned a quarter-interest. That Saturday, they got a call from the site; the well had just come in and, Schiller says, "it was a monster." To celebrate, Schiller made reservations at the Cipango Club, an exclusive dining establishment frequented by oil men. Fisher phoned Max Pray, who also had an interest in the well and had participated in several deals with Aurora. Shortly before Fisher called him, Pray had received a payment of $300,000 for one of their joint ventures and he had yet to forward Aurora their half of the money. Fisher told Pray the good news. Pray, who was in Chicago, said: "Hold on, I'll be right there."

Neither Fisher nor Schiller thought much of it, though Fisher did hope to see Aurora's $150,000. It was late in the evening as the two men ate at the Cipango Club when an inebriated Max Pray burst in, explaining that he had chartered a plane and flown down to celebrate.

"Did you check into the Adolphus?" Fisher asked Pray.

"Nah," Pray said, shaking hands and taking a seat. "I sent my bag up to Maury's room on the twelfth floor."

"I'm on the eleventh floor," said Schiller.

"Aah, so what," Pray replied, signaling the waiter for a drink. "I didn't bring much luggage. I only got a suitcase with a pair of underwear and the hundred and fifty grand I owe you."

Pray drained his drink and requested a menu, while Fisher and Schiller stood, paid the check, grabbed Pray and hurried to the Adolphus. Fortunately, Schiller was known in the hotel and the suitcase was in the correct room. Pray must have been talking about the money because a house detective was in the room guarding it. The money was wrapped in a map. Pray removed the package from the bag, tore off the cover and started jumping up and down on the bed flinging $100 bills in the air and shouting: "You guys thought I was bullshitting you, didn't you? You didn't think I brought the dough, did you?"

The house detective was not amused. He said: "The bell-hop knows that money is here and you can bet that in five minutes so will every thief in Dallas. I want that money counted and put in one of our safety-deposit boxes."

Fisher and Schiller complied. By Sunday evening, Pray had flown back to Chicago, and Fisher and Schiller were preparing for their drive to South Oak. They checked out of the Adolphus and the clerk handed them a manila folder stuffed with $150,000.

"We don't want that," said Fisher. "Keep it here in the safe. We'll come back for it."

"Sorry," said the clerk, "we can only extend that courtesy to guests of the hotel. You have checked out."

Schiller said: "Then we'll check in again."

"I'm sorry," said the clerk, "you can't check in without a reservation."

"So we'll make a reservation:" Fisher said.

"You can't," replied the clerk. "We have no reservations. We're full."

Fisher and Schiller quickly departed with the money, and in the middle of the night, on a dirt road somewhere between Dallas and South Oak, Oklahoma, one of their tires blew. They had no flashlight or matches, and it was pitch dark, so while one changed the tire the other kept a lookout for stickup men. At five o'clock in the morning they pulled into South Oak and parked outside the bank.

"I won't say that we were scared," Schiller says. "But we were awfully relieved when the bank opened and we could deposit the money."

*　　*　　*

With the United States enmeshed in World War II, the nation's oil supplies were taxed to the limit. Emergency fuel rationing could have provided The Ohio Oil Company with a convenient excuse to slip out of its old unwritten bargain with Aurora. Fisher was aware that they could have pleaded that government regulations or the inordinate appetite of the war machine made their deal unacceptable. But Fisher was pleasantly surprised. Donnell kept his word, and the deal Fisher struck with The Ohio paid off. Aurora had all the oil it needed. Aurora had added another refinery in Muskengon, on the eastern shore of Lake Michigan, and its capacity reached 65,500 barrels per day. Detroit, as "the arsenal of democracy," had an enormous industrial market for oil, and Aurora captured much of it.

"We were able to plug into the public-service pipelines," says William Slaughter. "And we built a pipeline right from our Detroit refinery to Ford in Dearborn. Once you're a public carrier, it's like a railroad. We could buy here, there and everywhere. [Crude oil suppliers] put crude in the pipeline and then we would refine it."

Additionally, Aurora was slowly diversifying. "During the war," Fisher says, "we got further into the chemical-engineering phase of the industry. For example, when the war began, there was a shortage of rubber, and as a result there was a crying need for isobutylene — which was used to manufacture synthetic rubber. Washington wanted it and so we installed a plant to produce it. It wasn't that successful, but later on we revamped this plant and turned out codimer — a high-powered ingredient of aviation gasoline. That was very profitable."

When the war ended, Aurora was among the largest independent petroleum companies in the Midwest, employing 1,150 workers; and the pipeline they had installed made Detroit's heavy industrial firms (automobile manufacturers, steel producers, forge plants and chemical companies) particularly dependent on Aurora to maintain their winter production schedules. Since Michigan is surrounded on three sides by water, a greater burden falls on railroads and trucking companies when the lakes are not navigable. While other petroleum suppliers were hampered by shipping delays, Aurora was the only refinery of its type in the city that was capable of transporting its product by a pipeline that ran underground to Trenton, Michigan, where it connected to a supply that drew crude from the midcontinent, Southwest and Illinois Basin. Perhaps most attractive to industry was Aurora's ability to convert crude into finished products and ship to its customers within hours after receiving the raw materials.

Aurora's productive capacity and its stature as a supplier was underscored by the figures released in a 1949 report of the Bureau of Mines. That year, Aurora produced almost one-fifth of the industrial fuel oil refined in Michigan — 90 million gallons of a total statewide production of 475 million. Of 625 million gallons of domestic fuel oil, Aurora supplied 83 million gallons — more than one-eighth of the state's gallonage. These numbers consistently climbed after World War II until Aurora was annually producing over 500 million gallons of petroleum products.

Along with its increased volume, Aurora was about to win a reputation for technological sophistication.

"With the peacetime economy," explains Fisher, "Detroit was churning out cars, which generated demand for even higher-octane gasoline. Aurora had to get in a favorable position to meet the rising octane specifications. To keep the costs down we wanted to use as much of our existing equipment as possible, and we did it by installing the first postwar fluid catcracking unit. It gave us the flexibility to produce everything from maximum quantities of high-octane gas to distillates for whatever way the market changed. The technology had been invented during the war. It had never been used commercially. If we wanted to stay competitive, we had to do it. So we took the chance."

The unit, dubbed the "Aurora type," was widely adopted by smaller refiners throughout the world.

Business steadily improved, in no small measure due to the deal Fisher cut with The Ohio Oil Company in 1938. Even with the postwar fuel shortages and the escalating requirements for gas and oil because the country was back on the highways, Aurora never lacked for crude. The Ohio made no effort to strike another bargain with Aurora or to press for a written contract. The basic commitment, sealed with a handshake, was sustained by mutual trust. And the profits from oil refining financed Aurora's continuing expansion.

Says William Slaughter: "If there was a way to make money from oil, Max found it. He didn't miss a trick."

Aurora was now manufacturing asphalt and kerosene, and Fisher, through his connections to different types of industry, was able to purchase vast quantities of scrap steel. Right after the war, oil drillers were scrambling for pipe and fittings. Since there was a shortage of steel, Aurora was able to meet the demand and even bought into oil wells with pipe, because just at that moment, it was more precious than cash. The investment in steel was also the beginning of Fisher's relationship with John S. Bugas, Fisher's first friend among the city's Gentile elite. Since the mid-1940s, Bugas, once head of Detroit's FBI bureau, was a powerful executive at the Ford Motor Company and a confidant of Henry Ford II. One day, Bugas heard from an acquaintance that there was an oil deal brewing in Wyoming, but there was no pipe. Bugas worked his contacts, but everyone told him the same thing: You need pipe, call Max Fisher. "I didn't know [Max] from a load of lumber," Bugas told *Monthly Detroit* in 1980. But before too long they were investing in Wyoming oil wells together, along with Ernest R. Breech, the Ford president who had been hired to teach Henry Ford II how to direct an automobile company. Fisher and Bugas soon became close friends.

Southern Michigan was proving to be a bonanza for oil companies, and Aurora discovered both oil and natural gas there. What was unique about this discovery was that Aurora relied on the advice of a fortune-teller.

Fisher explains: "Aurora owned land in Southern Michigan, but we had drilled twenty-four dry holes. Back then, it cost about $15,000 to drill a hole, so we had a lot of capital tied up. One day, a man by the name of Clifford Perry came to our office and spoke to Maurice Schiller, who was in charge of Aurora's production and handled requests for dry-hole contributions — meaning, we would stake drillers, and if they came up dry then they wouldn't have to absorb the whole loss. Perry was retired and drilled in his spare time. He wanted to drill on Hosneck Farm. We owned much of that land and our geologist swore that there was nothing underneath it except dirt. But we gave Cliff Perry $1,500 to drill and forgot about it. Eleven months later, Schiller walked into my office and said Cliff had hit natural gas. Gas is often on top of oil and so I gave Cliff more money to drill deeper. The typical time to drill a hole is thirty days, but it took Cliff almost a year because he worked on it with his son part-time. He knew where to drill because a gypsy fortune-teller, traveling through the area, had informed Mrs. Hosneck that there was oil under her house. So Mrs. Hosneck gave Perry $3,500, told him where to drill, and he made her rich because it turned out that there was oil under the gas. This was the beginning of the Albion-Scipio field, which subsequently became one of the largest fields east of the Mississippi River."

Huge gas and oil strikes, of course, were welcome, but Fisher had always hoped to transform Aurora into an integrated oil company, where it would own or control or have easy access to every link in the supply-and-demand chain. Already, Aurora had refineries, oil wells, a supply of natural gas, steel and the ability to manufacture a multitude of petroleum products. In 1947, the company became fully integrated when it bought its best customer, the Speedway 79 gas stations. Fisher had his eye on Speedway for some time. Aurora had been its principal supplier for years, and the gas-station chain was owned by relatives of Sylvia Fisher — C. William and Harry Sucher. An extremely prosperous operation, Speedway was coveted by several oil companies, but Fisher devised a sure-fire method for making his pitch to the Suchers. He invited them for a discussion and locked them in his office.

"I've got tickets to the Army-Navy football game," Fisher told them. "So we've got to get this done."

"Max!" Bill Sucher protested.

"I'm leaving in two hours," Fisher replied. "Let's go."

Perhaps impressed by Fisher's resolve and undoubtedly amenable to his terms, the Suchers agreed to sell Aurora a

50-percent interest in Speedway for $2.5 million. A decade later, Aurora acquired the other half of the corporation in a stock swap, and went on to operate and supply 680 service stations.

*   *   *

In 1947, the Fishers, after nine years of living in apartments, hotels and rented houses, finally bought a home in Detroit, a brick colonial on Parkside Road, in the Sherwood Forest section — an island of greenery that seemed far from the city, with broad lawns and old shade trees and kids playing baseball in the streets. Every October, Sylvia would depart for Tucson, and during Jane's Christmas vacation from school, Jane and her father traveled by train to Arizona, and along with Sylvia stayed in one of the adobe houses at the Double-U Ranch.

"My father taught me to horseback ride when I was four years old," says Jane Fisher Sherman. "We would ride out through the foothills to Sabina Canyon for picnics."

During the winters in Detroit, with Sylvia in Tucson, Jane was her father's main companion. He taught her how to play gin rummy and took her to Briggs Stadium for Lion football games and to Olympia Stadium to watch the Detroit Red Wings play hockey. Each night they listened to the news on the radio, and Jane must have picked up her father's interest in politics because she attacked his Republican sympathies by chanting, "Phooey on Dewey!" (Max cast his first Republican vote for presidential candidate Wendell L. Willkie in 1940, saying that he did not think any president, even FDR, should serve more than two terms.) On Thursday evenings, they dined at Beauchamps, a pleasant family restaurant on Six Mile Road, where Fisher, a constant dieter, introduced his daughter to a ritual that he would one day share with his other children. He instructed Jane to order a chocolate parfait for dessert, and when it was set in front of her he swooped in with his spoon and ate it. Jane, like her father's future children, gazed at him quizzically.

"The calories don't count if they come from *your* plate," he explained.

But the central factor in the Fishers' family life was Sylvia's illness. She was now periodically confined to a wheelchair, and the enforced separations during the interminable Michigan winters were a strain on both her and Max. Their daughter, Jane Fisher Sherman, recalls brief stretches when her mother was well, but says that "basically she was always ill." Fisher was at his best when confronted with practical puzzles he could solve. This was beyond his comprehension. Though he was characteristically reserved, his anguish about Sylvia's suffering and his helplessness in the face of her physical deterioration overwhelmed him. His insomnia grew virulent; he now needed a prescription for phenobarbital to get his four hours of sleep each night. And he fought a triweekly battle with migraine headaches, the pain so severe that he required intramuscular injections of Gynergen, a vasal constrictor, to relieve them.

Nathan Appleman, a Jewish oil man raised in Tulsa, Oklahoma, was a boy wonder who earned a fortune in oil and then relocated to New York and earned another fortune in stocks and bonds. Along the way, he met Fisher and they invested in oil and gas wells in the West. They also became close friends. Appleman remembers that when Fisher was in New York on business he would come to his apartment at the Hotel Pierre and talk about his distress over Sylvia's failing health for hours. Appleman also remembers Fisher's migraines.

"Max's headaches were occasionally so intense," says Appleman, "that he couldn't hold the syringe, and I had to give him his injections."

Sylvia's health steadily declined. Cardiac surgery was in its infancy, and Max sought advice from cardiologists around the country. On June 1, 1951, Max wired birthday flowers and greetings to Sylvia, saying how "wonderful [and] courageous" she had been while undergoing the necessary tests and hospitalizations. A month later, though, Dr. Benson Bloom wrote Max from Tucson that a surgical solution to Sylvia's repeated bouts with congestive heart failure was too risky, "since the operative mortality in her type of case seems to be 75 percent and more."

By the beginning of 1952, Fisher, trying to cope with Sylvia's situation, did what he had not done since he was a student at Ohio State: he attempted to examine his feelings in writing. He bought a green leather-bound diary for the purpose and religiously made his entries. His examination met with mixed success. It becomes clear early in the diary that his overriding feeling with respect to Sylvia was guilt that he could not help her. At the same time, his insomnia and migraines besieged him, and so the diary became a record of a husband's horror at witnessing the painful physical deterioration of his wife.

By June 1, 1952, Sylvia's forty-second birthday, she was bedridden in Detroit, her breathing badly labored, her heart not beating strongly enough to prevent fluid from collecting in her lungs. Jane Fisher Sherman, at the time just thirteen years old, remembers walking into the house one afternoon — it was June 22 — and seeing her father sitting on the sun porch. It was odd for him to be relaxing at that hour. She went to him. His face was calm. He told her that her mother had died that morning. The next day, after services at the Ira Kaufman Chapel in Detroit, the funeral procession drove down Woodward Avenue and stopped outside the city, in Birmingham, where Sylvia was buried beneath a circle of oaks in the Clover Hill Park Cemetery.

*   *   *

By the conclusion of the Second World War, William Fisher and his partners at Keystone were rich men. Although Keystone had expanded since 1930 — testing and grading reprocessed oil in its own laboratory and canning it in its own plant — the reprocessing operation remained marginally profitable. However, Keystone's quarter-interest in the joint venture with Aurora was a bonanza for the partners. William Fisher, never enthralled by the oil business, was now free to indulge his passion: speculating in real estate. He invested in Detroit and, after 1934, when he and Mollie took their first annual winter vacation in Miami Beach, in Florida. William and Mollie loved the balmy weather and dependable sunshine. William was adamant about not missing his vacation, and it was this adamancy, coupled with his penchant for real-estate speculation, that propelled him into the hotel business. During World War II, the Army and Navy ran short of barracks and requisitioned nearly every hotel in the Miami area. Ever resourceful, William guaranteed himself a room by buying a hotel, the Winterhaven. After the war, the Florida tourist industry erupted, with hotel and apartment construction booming in Miami and Miami Beach, particularly along what would become known as "the Gold Coast." By the early 1950s, William and various partners had bought and sold the Atlantic Tower Hotel, the Palm Beach pier, and an apartment house on Biscayne Bay. In 1952, he sold the Winterhaven, and with some Detroit investors purchased the Martinique in Miami Beach, the first luxury hotel built in south Florida after World War II. Three years later, Aurora bought Keystone, giving William several million dollars more to invest. He and Mollie moved into the Martinique in 1957, and William soon bought the hotel next door, the Delmonico.

Mollie shortly became a dance fanatic, taking daily lessons from the hotel instructor. Her favorite step was the rumba. She also had two of her grandchildren, Stephen and Sharon Ross, to dote on. (Gail and David Ross had moved to Miami from Detroit.) William, when he was not digging up a new deal or checking in on his hotels, could be found at his cabana playing pinochle. His only other distraction was fishing, which he pursued with his accountant, Norris Friedlander.

Friedlander was twenty-eight years old when he met William Fisher. With Max, William had encountered someone who was stubborn and determined to go his own way. Friedlander was more malleable, and his father had died when he was three, so he was grateful when William took a paternal interest in him. They met regularly. William had a French chef at the Martinique who specialized in oxtail soup, William's favorite, and he insisted that Friedlander have lunch with him whenever the soup was served. William helped Friedlander establish his own accounting firm, loaning him and his partner the capital to open their office and sending them clients. William urged Friedlander to hold his son's bar mitzvah party at the Martinique, and when Friedlander replied that it was beyond his means, William told him not to worry, that he would pick up much of the tab.

At the Martinique, William established a life to which he was perfectly suited. He popped in and out of offices, greeted guests, contemplated deals and played pinochle. But there was one problem. He loved investing, not the day-to-day grind of overseeing a business, and so within three years of moving permanently to Florida, William Fisher, without mentioning a word to anyone, was on the brink of bankruptcy.

*　　*　　*

The past year, 1952, had been confusing for Marjorie Switow Frehling, but as Thanksgiving approached there was one thing she was sure about: She did not want to go to Carolyn Alexander's party in Detroit. Marjorie's divorce from George Frehling had recently been finalized and she was living with her children — four-year-old Mary and two-year-old Phillip — in her parents' house in Louisville, Kentucky. Marjorie was relieved to be among her family. Her mother, Florence, was a genteel southern lady, a housewife who had assiduously looked after Marjorie and her younger sister, Joyce, and was treating Mary and Phillip to the same care. Her father, Harry, owned and operated a string of movie theaters in Indiana, Kentucky and Ohio. He was a generous, gregarious man who loved to sing and accompany himself on the piano, and by all accounts, he worked as hard as he played. As a bonus, Marjorie's sister, Joyce, was now married to Stanley T. Burkoff and residing across the street.

Marjorie's ex-husband, George, had been her high-school sweetheart, a relationship that endured through her fine-arts studies at Marjorie Webster Junior College in Washington, D.C. Now, though, after eight years, their marriage was over, and Marjorie was feeling content and unwilling to dive into

another relationship. Which was why she didn't want to fly
up to Carolyn Alexander's party in Detroit. Carolyn, Marjorie's distant cousin and erstwhile college roommate, was
insisting that Marjorie attend. She had lined up a platoon of
potential suitors who kept questioning her about her cousin,
the pretty southern belle.

"Marjorie," says her sister, Joyce Switow Burkoff, "was
definitely the beautiful one. When we'd go horseback riding
— you had to ride if you lived in Kentucky — and Marjorie fell
off her horse, everyone would run over to see if she had been
hurt and she'd stand up and ask, 'How's my hair?'"

Since her separation, however, Marjorie often refused
dates, or went out and then returned disappointed. Carolyn
was on the phone to her every day, and Florence Switow urged
her daughter to fly to Detroit, and so Marjorie relented and
packed her bags.

*　　*　　*

Five months after Sylvia's death, Max was getting a
stream of phone calls from self-appointed matchmakers
among Detroit's Jewish community. Reticent, he rejected
most dates, and submerged himself in work. He did purchase
a Cadillac in case he had a change of heart. However, he preferred his old Plymouth, and the Cadillac was chiefly driven
by one of his employees, Randall Martin. He had promised
Carolyn Alexander to drop by her party — but just for a few
minutes, because he was taking Jane to the theater to see *The
Four Posters*. Fisher was standing inside the door of Carolyn's
house when a young woman appeared at the top of the stair-
way. She was wearing a magnificent red satin dress. Another
guest at the party remembers that while the men were
impressed, they affected a suave nonchalance. Fisher did not.
He was transfixed as Marjorie gracefully descended the stairs.
Her thick dark hair framed her face, which was lovely as a
cameo. She was small and beautifully built, a collection of
curves meandering into other curves. Carolyn introduced her
to Max.

Recovering his equilibrium, he quipped: "Hello, Scarlett."

"Hi, Rhett," she replied.

"How about a date next Monday night?" Fisher asked.

"Fine," Marjorie answered, and disappeared into the party.

When Fisher met Jane at the theater, he told his daughter: "I just met the cutest little girl and she's only" — he raised his hand five feet from the floor — "this big."

Fisher flew down to Louisville to take Marjorie to dinner. He had always been somewhat withdrawn and serious, but as they saw each other over the ensuing weeks his demeanor changed. Right out of college, he had responded to the Depression by burying himself in the oil business. He had earned enough money to feel safe about starting a family, but then his marriage was tragically marred by Sylvia's illness. Now, he was past forty and there was something about this winsome twenty-nine-year-old woman from Kentucky that coaxed him from his shell. At Carolyn Alexander's party, he had been bowled over by her beauty. Yet there was also her sudden laugh and swift repartee — there was something so lighthearted about Marjorie — and he courted her as enthusiastically as a high-school sophomore with a crush. He inundated her with flowers, telegrams and phone calls. He picked her up in Louisville in a private plane, flew her to Detroit for dinner and then returned to her parents' house late in the evening. Marjorie loved his courtly manner.

"After my divorce," says Marjorie, "the men I dated were in such a rush to paw me. Since I was divorced, maybe they thought that was appropriate. Max was different. He was such a gentleman. And I appreciated that."

Fisher responded to Marjorie's gaiety by becoming more outgoing and, on occasion, what for him would have to qualify as outrageous. For example, in the spring of 1953, he went to a seder at the Switows' house. When the gefilte fish was put on the table, Max stared at it and said: "Your fish is black."

Southerners, he was informed, preferred spicy food. Pepper was regarded as "Kentucky sugar" and lavished on many dishes. Max ate several platefuls, perspiring and complaining that gefilte fish should not have pepper on it. Then the chicken soup and *kreplach* were served.

"The *kreplach* are too white," Fisher said. "There's no chicken fat on them."

As everyone watched, Fisher stalked into the kitchen, donned an apron and demonstrated the proper method — that is, Mollie Fisher's method — for fixing *kreplach*. He rubbed chicken fat on the doughy pockets, then broiled them. The Switows were laughing hysterically, and they must have been impressed by the recipe. According to Marjorie's brother-in-law, Stanley Burkoff, from that Passover on, the *kreplach* were prepared with chicken fat.

Fisher realized he was in love with Marjorie, but he was hesitant to propose marriage and thought a trip would help him decide. He visited Mollie and William in Miami. Bucky and Francis Goldman were also in Florida. Bucky recalls that there was an attractive red-headed judge who was pursuing Fisher. Uncomfortable, Fisher suggested that the Goldmans accompany him on an overnight jaunt to Cuba. The judge invited herself along. At the hotel in Havana, Fisher and the judge registered in separate rooms. That evening, while Fisher was chatting with the Goldmans in their suite, the phone rang. The judge was phoning from down the hall saying that she had a headache and asking if Max would please bring her two aspirin.

"Don't go," Bucky warned.

Ignoring his friend's warning, Fisher took the aspirin to the judge and was back with the Goldmans in five minutes. The next thing Bucky knew, Fisher was asking the hotel operator to ring Louisville. When Marjorie got on, Fisher proposed. She accepted.

Max and Marjorie were married in New York City on July 1, 1953. Nathan Appleman and his wife, Janet, arranged for them to be married in a rabbi's study, and they gave a lunch for them after the ceremony. The Fishers spent their honeymoon in Hawaii, and then Marjorie gathered up Mary and Phillip in Louisville, and they moved into Max's house on Parkside.

* * *

Mollie Fisher had encouraged her son to donate money to charities in general and Jewish ones in particular. Even in 1932, when Fisher's fifteen-dollar salary was a hit-or-miss proposition, he pledged five dollars to Detroit's Allied Jewish Campaign. Each year, as his finances improved, so did his pledges. Now, with his wealth in the millions, Fisher promised himself to do more. Yet getting involved in high-level fund-raising meant turning himself outward, not an easy task for a man so innately shy. He was supremely confident in his facility for speaking at business meetings or for talking oil with the boys at the refinery, but the notion of addressing a crowd was unthinkable, and he lacked the talent for sprightly chitchat, as de rigueur at formal, big-dollar fund-raising dinners as tuxedos and gowns.

Fisher was fortunate in his selection of a wife. Marjorie believed deeply in charity and glided through social situations, putting her relaxed charm and easy humor and the gentle southern cadence of her voice on display. And Marjorie felt that her husband was selling himself short.

"I told him," Marjorie Fisher says, "'Max, you're wonderful. People like you. You just don't have any confidence. Anything you want to do you can do.'"

In October 1954, Max made his initial visit to Israel with the first United Jewish Appeal study mission. (Marjorie, five months pregnant with their first child, a daughter, Julie Ann, stayed home.) The purpose of study missions is to witness the results of campaign funds and to demonstrate the importance of giving. Historically, the missions have helped to increase pledges.

Although thrilled by the improbable reality of a Jewish state, Max was horrified by how poorly many Israelis were forced to live. Across the arid, rocky hills, he saw 200,000 Jewish immigrants huddled under makeshift tents, reminding Fisher of the shanty towns during the Depression. Jobs and medical care were scarce; so were food and water. The Arabs were an ever-present danger. As rapidly as the UJA provided money, the Israelis spent it; progress was slow. Fisher must have impressed the others on the mission, for they elected him to represent their group at a talk with Israeli leaders. And so Fisher, the creative, prosperous American businessman, met Finance Minister Levi Eshkol. Fisher was anxious to help, and voiced what he conceived of as a logical stopgap solution to some of the fledgling country's economic woes.

"Because you're short on money," Fisher asked, "wouldn't it make sense for Israel to shut down immigration for a while?"

Eshkol's reply was instantaneous. "Every Jew in Israel remembers how six million fellow Jews died under Hitler because they had no place to go," the finance minister said. "Even if you don't give us another dime, no Jew is ever going to add to that six million. Israel may go under, but one thing we'll never do: we will never close the gates. There has to be an Israel so there can be one place in the whole world where Jews may come in — any Jew, in any condition — as a matter of right." Then Eshkol added: "Israel exists so Jews may exist."

In retrospect, Fisher says that Eshkol, who would later serve as prime minister, taught him "the greatest lesson I would ever learn about Zionism." He returned from Israel with an even stronger commitment to Jewish philanthropy and discovered that he was a more effective fund-raiser than he initially thought. According to Carl Bakal, who wrote *Charity U.S.A.*, "One reason Jewish philanthropy is so spectacularly successful is because of its . . . techniques, some of them unique to Jewish fund-raising." Bakal cites how Jews pioneered solicitations of a single donation on behalf of multiple charities and how they personalized Benjamin Franklin's concept of the matching gift. "However," Bakal writes, "sui generis as a means of raising money is the arm-twisting techniques of 'card calling' or . . . public pledging, invented in the 1930s, and still a uniquely Jewish phenomenon. . . . Upon hearing his name . . . the person publicly announces his new pledge. Naturally, it behooves him to pledge an amount that makes him stand tall in the eyes of his . . . friends [and] neighbors."

While Jewish fund-raisers concede that this style of raising money can be harsh, they point out that it is effective, delivering over 60 percent of the funds raised, with an incalculable influence on the other 40 percent.

"Obviously," writes James Yaffe, author of *The American Jews*, "the effect of card calling depends on who calls the cards," and Fisher seemed to have a knack for it. Fisher's friend, John Bugas, who described card calling to an interviewer as "putting the slug on people," claimed that Fisher "developed a hide as thick as an alligator's as he perfected his art."

James Yaffe recounts a story that illustrates Fisher's technique: In 1957, Fisher "had just been appointed chairman of [the Jewish Welfare Federation of Detroit], and a Gentile friend of his, who was the new campaign chairman for the nonsectarian [United Foundation], came to him for advice. 'How do you Jews manage to raise so much money?' asked the friend. Fisher invited him to sit in on the first meeting of the board for the new Jewish campaign. A dozen men attended this meeting, all of them wealthy and prominent. Fisher opened the proceedings by telling them that they themselves, in the past, had always made inadequate contributions to the campaign. How could they expect other Jews to be generous if they didn't lead the way? 'I'm naming no names,' he said, 'but I'm going to start the ball rolling with a pledge of $30,000.' He then asked the man on his right for his pledge. In a tentative voice this man pledged $3,000. The man said, 'Isn't that enough, Max?' Fisher shook his head wearily. The man said, 'How much do you think I should give?' Fisher said, 'In view of your circumstances, Sam, I think you could afford $35,000.' Sam gulped a little, but he came across with his pledge. When Fisher continued around the room to the other board members, none of them wasted his time with inadequate pledges. By the end of the meeting the board itself had pledged half of the campaign goal.

"Afterward, Fisher went up to his Gentile friend and said quietly, 'That's how we do it.'"

Fisher raised $5,841,000 for the 1957 campaign, the most in the Detroit federation's history. His success attracted the attention of the board at the United Foundation's Torch Drive. The drive was started by Henry Ford II in 1948. The board was exclusively drawn from the Christian power elite of the city's auto executives and bankers. It was, traditionally, a closed shop, particularly to Jews. One day, a United Foundation board member ran into Fisher and he asked him why the Jewish community raised money so out of proportion to their numbers and yet did not participate in the Torch Drive.

"That's easy," replied Fisher. "You don't have enough Jews on your board."

With a phone call, Benson Ford, Henry II's brother, changed all that, and Fisher became the first Jew to head the United Foundation's annual Torch Drive and to be chairman of the UF board.

*   *   *

At the beginning of 1957, the Fishers left the city of Detroit for the suburb of Franklin, moving from the Parkside house into a white-brick Georgian with a sprawling garden that bordered the eighth fairway of the Franklin Hills Country Club. On December 30, 1957, they had another daughter, Marjorie Martin, called "Little Margie" by the family. (In 1960, Max legally adopted Mary and Phillip.) Now, along with his charity work, Fisher was expanding his friendships by reaching out to the younger members of Detroit's Jewish community.

One of those young men was A. Alfred Taubman. Born in 1924, the son of immigrants, Al Taubman grew up outside Detroit, in Pontiac and then Sylvan Lakes. His father was a custom-home builder and, after studying fine art in college, Taubman dropped out to enter the building business. His interest was not in following the spread of suburbia, but in creating it, and he did so by erecting commercial malls across the country. He built his initial shopping center, North Flint

Plaza, in 1952, and ultimately became one of the premier developers in the United States, being among the first to build malls with two and three levels connected by ramps, elevators and escalators, which assured equal traffic — and equal rents — on every level. He then parlayed his real estate earnings into a variety of immensely profitable ventures.

There is a wonderful, oft-told story in Detroit of how Taubman became lifelong friends with Fisher and how both men wound up wheeling and dealing together and rising on the *Forbes* 400 list. Taubman, so the story goes, was a young, financially strapped builder when, in the mid-1950s, Fisher requested that he redesign the islands of Aurora's Speedway gas stations. Taubman redesigned the islands, a break that boosted his career and established his multifaceted empire, his wealth rocketing into the billions.

It is a charming story. And it is also not true. Fisher did ask Taubman to redesign Speedway's islands and Taubman assisted him, but he says he did it out of friendship, and that it would be at least ten years before he reached the front ranks of developers. Three decades after that first phone call, Taubman was eating dinner with the Fishers in Palm Beach. He had recently read the story again and mentioned it to Max.

"I don't know why the journalists keep writing it," Fisher said.

Taubman laughed. "Because they repeat it when they interview you and you smile and you never tell them it's not true."

Smiling slyly at his friend, Fisher placed his hand over his heart and said with all sincerity, "Al, would you deny me the pleasure of that story?"

No, Taubman would not. Fisher was seventeen years his senior and, according to associates of both men, their relationship was that of a loving father and son. They spoke on the phone several times a day, regardless of what they were doing or where they were. But in the 1950s, the first call that Fisher made to Taubman had nothing to do with business.

"Max contacted me at work," says Taubman, "and said that he wanted to see me in his office. It wasn't the sort of invitation that someone starting out in Detroit turned down. Young businessmen measured their dreams by what Max had accomplished. It was flattering to be invited."

Fisher says, "There was something about Al. I knew when I met him that he was going to be incredibly successful. He just had this way, and he was so intelligent."

What Fisher wanted was for Taubman to join the Franklin Hills Country Club. Their membership was aging and they needed young blood.

"I told him," says Taubman, "'Max, the dues have to be $5,000 a year. I can't afford that.'"

"Don't worry about the money," said Fisher. "The important thing is that you have to join before the other members get to know you."

Taubman says that he wasn't sure if Fisher was teasing or insulting him, and he didn't know him well enough to ask. Then Fisher explained that there were so many petty feuds in country clubs that membership committees invariably had a case against someone they knew. Those who did not belong to their social circle could not be condemned because they lacked information about their personalities. It made sense to Taubman — and even if it didn't, Fisher was requesting him to do it — and he agreed to apply for membership.

*　　*　　*

As the Fishers settled into their new house, Aurora was about to undergo an enormous change. Henry Wenger, the controlling partner, turned seventy-one in 1958. Because Aurora was a tightly held company, Wenger was concerned about what taxes would do to his estate. Also, says Wenger's son, Penny, "Aurora had gone through gas-price wars, had their oil and chemical workers on strike, and my father thought it was time step back from the daily operations of an independent oil company."

Gossip spread in the industry that Aurora was shopping for a tax-free stock swap with a public corporation. They attracted a dozen offers; Ashland Oil was especially interested, but The Ohio Oil Company did not bid. Fisher, however, favored a merger with them because he trusted James Donnell II, who was now president, and The Ohio was a well-managed, financially sound company whose stock would hold its value over the long term. Pocketing his best offer, Fisher flew to Findlay. Donnell was interested. The Ohio could only refine 40 percent of its crude and had to sell the balance; Aurora's three refineries would solve that predicament, and its 680 gasoline stations would give The Ohio a foothold in the tremendously profitable Detroit market. But Donnell had bad news for Fisher. The Ohio could not meet Aurora's top offer. Fisher, primarily concerned about what the merger would be worth in ten or twenty years, was willing to merge with them anyway. His partner, William Slaughter, was not.

"I wanted more money for it than we got. Max made a deal too short for me. I knew what our potential was."

But Wenger sided with Fisher, who argued that The Ohio "gave Aurora what we wanted — security."

The merger, which historian Hartzell Spence characterized as "one of The Ohio's largest forward thrusts," was finalized in the summer of 1959. The Ohio Oil Company gave Aurora 874,422 shares of its stock and assumed $2,800,000 in debt, and Aurora became a wholly owned subsidiary of The Ohio. The deal was worth nearly $40 million, Fisher's portion in excess of $15 million.

The July before the merger was Fisher's fiftieth birthday, and Marjorie gave a spectacular party, with a fireworks display lighting up the sky above the Franklin Hills golf course. Al Taubman was a guest at the celebration. The rumor that Aurora was seeking a merger had already spread. Taubman recalls standing off on the edge of the party and watching Fisher talking to his family and friends.

"I was thirty-three at the time," says Taubman, "and I stood there, watching Max and putting myself in his place, thinking about what I would do if I suddenly sold my business. I was terrified for him. I kept wondering: what would he do with the rest of his life?"

It was a question that was also on Fisher's mind.

*   *   *

In 1957, William Fisher suffered a coronary that was so serious neither his family nor his physicians thought he would survive. He fooled them. But the following year he had another, though less severe, attack. The stress of operating the Martinique and the Delmonico were not aiding his recovery, and although Mollie and their children were unaware of it, he was pouring his personal money in to keep his hotels afloat and he was frightened about the drain of his capital.

William's accountant, Norris Friedlander, saw what was happening. "The hotels in Florida were changing," says Friedlander. "They were becoming family hotels, with meal plans, and William did not want to change the way he did things at the Martinique. He wanted top-quality food, at top prices. Miami Beach wasn't like that anymore. Also, William did not like paying attention to details and that got him into trouble."

A rash of unseasonably cold weather kept tourists away and contributed to William's financial reverses. Gail discovered her father's plight and contacted her sisters and brother. Together, they prevailed upon William to sell his properties — to Max. Max paid his father every dollar he had invested, and then William and Mollie moved to a penthouse apartment at the Fontainebleau Hotel. In 1958, Jane Fisher married Larry Sherman, and they were willing to transfer to Miami and try the hotel business. After Larry decided that he didn't want to manage hotels as a career, the Shermans returned to Detroit and Max shed his holdings in Florida real estate.

*   *   *

Once the excitement of the Ohio Oil-Aurora merger passed, Fisher saw several options. He had been named president of the subsidiary, agreeing to remain in management until Aurora's operations were integrated with The Ohio's, which took until early 1963. (He also served on the board of directors.) He worked with his friend, oil man Leon Hess, for a year, and through his efforts in Jewish philanthropy, he met Vice President Richard Nixon, and began dipping into national politics. He also learned that philanthropy, Jewish and nonsectarian, could be a vocation. In 1959, in response to pressure from communities for his presence, he tentatively ventured out as a public speaker. Representing the United Jewish Appeal, he spoke at a UJA federation fund-raising meeting at the San Francisco home of Madeleine H. Russell, a nationally known philanthropist whom President Kennedy would appoint director of the State Department's reception center in San Francisco.

According to Irving Bernstein, who in 1959 was head of the UJA's West Coast region, Fisher was tense. He had his speech written on index cards and insisted on keeping them out of the audience's sight. So Russell seated him at a desk and he stashed the cards behind a gold-inlaid box, which Bernstein claims "was probably worth more money than I was making." Fisher was anxious and spoke haltingly, but his willingness to speak in public, despite his diffidence before groups and extreme nervousness, was a personal milestone. In 1961, he chaired the United Foundation's Torch Drive, raising a then-record $19.5 million. And once he was relieved of the daily obligations of directing a company, he was free to take a more aggressive stance as an investor. He began with a multimillion-dollar deal that possessed enough rags-to-riches irony to qualify as a twentieth-century addendum to the collected works of Horatio Alger.

In the late autumn of 1962, Fisher and two prominent Detroit real estate men, Louis Berry and George D. Seyburn, formed the Fisher-New Center Company (FNC). Then, on December 7, after nine months of negotiations with the four surviving Fisher brothers, FNC purchased the Fisher Building and adjacent properties — the eleven-story New Center Building and parking lots — for $10.3 million.

Following the purchase, Fisher told reporter John M. Carlisle of *The Detroit News*: "I have great admiration and respect for everything [the Fisher Building] stands for. When Lou [Berry] came to me to discuss this I felt as he did that this great building should always belong to Detroit and be owned by Detroiters. We both felt it was a symbol."

In broadest terms, what the Fisher Building stood for was the grand triumph of capitalism in Detroit. Fisher had portrayed it as a symbol, and, for him, the symbolism extended past his civic pride. For Fisher, owning the landmark was a proclamation that his face was no longer pressed against the glass of the exclusive shops downstairs, that he was no longer stuck on the outside looking in. Although he had been journeying through the highest echelons of the Detroit business community for some time, being among the landlords of the Fisher Building marked his spot beyond a reasonable doubt. Perhaps the doubts had only been in his own mind, but now he was undeniably part of "this great building," inseparable from its meaning and the city to which it belonged. And as Robert Lacey, biographer of the Henry Ford dynasty, wryly noted, when Fisher established his headquarters there in a twenty-second-floor, four-room suite, he even "saved himself the expense of putting a new nameplate on the door."

Chapter 4

BUILDING BRIDGES

O N SUNDAY MORNING, December 13, 1964, Max
Fisher was in the Grand Ballroom of the New York
City Hilton, seated among the delegates at the United
Jewish Appeal's annual meeting. Fisher had just been elected
general chairman of the UJA from 1965 to 1967. The position,
among the most prestigious in American Jewish philan-
thropic life, had been held by such moneyed and influential
men as Henry Morgenthau Jr., Edward Warburg, William
Rosenwald, Philip Klutznick (whose tenure was cut short
when President Kennedy appointed him ambassador to the
United Nations Economic and Social Council), and the man
Fisher was succeeding, Joseph Meyerhoff.

Fisher would characterize the importance of the chairmanship when he told a group: "When you say to me then,
that a man is 'an American Jewish leader,' I take it for granted
that you are also saying he is a leader in UJA. I see the two
things as synonymous. And I can't see how it can be any other
way."

The UJA was founded in 1939, but until Meyerhoff and
Fisher the general chairmanship had been almost the exclusive domain of German Jewish immigrants, those gilded representatives of Stephen Birmingham's *Our Crowd*. But in the
early 1960s, the baton of UJA leadership passed to the
descendants of Eastern European Jews, the children of immigrants like Malka and Velvil Fisch, the waves of "homeless,
tempest-tost," a phrase from the poet Emma Lazarus that
Fisher was fond of quoting in his speeches. These were the
Jews that Birmingham described in *The Rest of Us*, his soci-
ological sequel to *Our Crowd*.

"Fisher represented the Eastern European prince," says Irving Bernstein, who by 1964 had left Los Angeles and was working as the assistant executive vice chairman of the UJA in New York. "He was the counterpart to Warburg and Rosenwald. He had made it — in politics, in the oil business; he was friends with Henry Ford II, and he had roots in his local Jewish community."

A son of Polish immigrants, Bernstein grew up during the 1920s in Ellenville, New York, which he describes as "a transplanted *shtetl* in the Catskills." Bernstein felt that Fisher "made [the children of Eastern European] immigrants look good. He was our role model. He was a different kind of Jew. Very comfortable with himself and the Jewish world, very comfortable in the non-Jewish world. He was a totally different type of personality. That's one of the reasons for the impact he had."

However, the change in UJA leadership — in fact, the financial ascendancy of America's Eastern European Jews — had far more potent consequences than a shift in social structure. Certainly there was, as Birmingham meticulously documents, a class struggle between the two groups, a cultural gap and the discordant strains of Old Money versus New Money. But Birmingham, who admits that his "interest has always been in the romance of people," and is "more concerned with what people *are* than what they do," understandably passes over the net political outcome: the marriage of American Jewish philanthropy and Israel.

At the dawn of the twentieth century, the German Jewish elite who guided the UJA focused the organization's resources on the Jews residing in Eastern Europe as opposed to those who returned to Palestine. (Morgenthau's father, Henry Sr., had been a doctrinaire anti-Zionist; Julius Rosenwald was a practical anti-Zionist; Felix Warburg and Jacob H. Schiff were non-Zionists.) Their argument was that Eastern Europe was in the midst of the Enlightenment and was another latent America for Jews, a land brimming with tolerance and opportunity. That is where the funds should be spent, developing a sister community to the one already flourishing in the United

States. Why squander it on those dreamers — a fair amount of whom were socialists — who were knee-deep in the dangerously disputed sands of Palestine?

The cause of the reluctance, it would seem, was not fiscal, but psychological.

For Jews in the United States, Zionism frequently presented the predicament of "dual allegiance." Simply stated the predicament is: To whom do I belong? Am I a Jew who has been longing for a home in Israel? Or am I an American? In back of this identity crisis was the specter of anti-Semitism. Jews, having struggled to enter a Christian society, did not want to furnish ammunition for the anti-Semitic allegation that, because of their allegiance to Palestine (and later on, Israel), Jews were incapable of being faithful Americans.

Barbara W. Tuchman, in her essay "The Assimilationist Dilemma," writes movingly of this concern, one that plagued her renowned grandfather, Henry Morgenthau Sr. He was among the largest contributors to President Woodrow Wilson's campaign, but, Tuchman writes, "the reward was not, as [Morgenthau Sr.] had hoped, a Cabinet post . . . but a minor ambassadorship . . . to Turkey, the more disappointing because it was a post set aside for Jews. Given Morgenthau's passionate desire to prove that a Jew could . . . be accepted in America on equal grounds . . . the offer was peculiarly painful. It was . . . the fear of being thought to have another loyalty, that made him and others like him resist . . . a movement for a . . . Jewish state. . . . Jews like my grandfather . . . felt that . . . Zionism would supply an added cause for discrimination."

However, there were other distinguished American Jews who were not haunted by the charge of dual allegiance — Louis D. Brandeis, for one, the first Jew to sit on the Supreme Court. Brandeis, raised in Louisville, Kentucky, and a graduate of Harvard, was an assimilated Jew. His approach to Zionism, he stated, "was through Americanism. . . . Jews [are] by reason of their traditions and their character peculiarly fitted for the attainment of American ideals. . . . To be good Americans we must be better Jews, and to be better Jews we must become Zionists. Jewish life cannot be preserved and developed . . . unless there be established . . . a center from which the Jewish spirit may radiate and give to the Jews scattered throughout the world that inspiration which springs from the memories of a great past and the hope of a great future."

Fisher, like Brandeis, was bicultural, at ease among Jews and Gentiles. Yet where Brandeis's view of the compatibility between Zionism and American ideals sprang from his philosophical bent, Fisher, the utilitarian, the businessman, grounded his belief in the realpolitik. For by the time Fisher became general chairman of the United Jewish Appeal, he was convinced that the policies of Israel were not only in harmony with U.S. foreign policy, but complemented it.

"Jews would come," recalls Fisher, "and argue with me. They used to say: 'If the United States attacked Israel, what would you do?' That's silly. The United States is not going to attack Israel. There's no hang-up there. I can be a good citizen of the United States and be a supporter of Israel. Israel is something that I love. It's something that the Jewish people have dreamt about: they wanted a homeland. Where's the dual allegiance?"

And on that Sunday in the last weeks of 1964, Fisher stood on the dais at the Hilton Hotel and addressed the UJA delegates. He thanked them for honoring him with the chairmanship and spoke about "Israel — proud and progressing — a dream of generations, realized." Fisher mentioned the $109.4 million in pledges he hoped they would raise. The amount was staggering. Even Fisher, renowned for his fundraising skills, knew that his objective would be an exacting one to reach. But he had a more strenuous goal on his agenda. He wanted to lessen the historical competition over procedures and fiscal allocations that existed between "the alphabet soup" of Jewish groups, particularly between the UJA and the CJF — the Council of Jewish Federations. Fisher's purpose was twofold. He felt that cooperation among the groups would translate into more dollars raised, and if he could bring the organizations closer together he would have the makings of a coalition, a cohesive block of voters, a precious commodity to those in Washington. And so he concluded his address by reminding the UJA delegates of an old Chinese saying: "'A journey of 1,000 miles begins with a single step.'"

* * *

Only in a broad sense is the United Jewish Appeal a fund-raising agency. It organizes campaigns, but collects funds only in the smaller communities that do not have an established federation to conduct the campaigns. (The federations, although independent, are under the umbrella of the CJF, which is the coordinating body of all the organized Jewish communities in the United States and Canada.) A UJA in-house report of the Long Range Planning Committee, issued in March 1982, stated that the organization's role was: a) "to facilitate and enhance the fund-raising efforts of the American Jewish communities by actively providing services to federations and non-federated communities so that through joint efforts maximum funds may be raised for local, national and overseas needs," and b) "to be an advocate for overseas needs."

Operationally, the UJA resembles a variety of fund-raising bodies in that it is an amalgam of volunteers and professionals. This arrangement presents the possibility of operational tensions. Lay leaders, like Fisher, make policy, and professionals implement it. The lay leaders rotate every few years, while the professionals are involved over the extended course of their careers.

Over the years, Fisher quoted a homily that he used as a guide when directing organizations: "If you run a business like a charity, then you won't have a business. But if you run a charity like a business, then you won't have a charity."

This, combined with Fisher's first rule of leadership, "You're only a leader as long as you keep looking back to see if people are following you," were his guidelines for directing the UJA. His method was to set policy with the board of directors and turn the implementation of that policy over to the professionals.

"Max," says Irving Bernstein, "was probably the best

chairman that I've ever worked with in terms of division of labor. Once the policy was formulated, he didn't interfere. Most leaders have difficulty making the decision. Then, after it's made, they don't know where policy stops. Max wasn't like that. That's why he can do so well in so many areas. For example: you establish a budget for a staff and you hire your people. Another [chairman] would say: 'I want a breakdown of the salaries!' That wasn't how Max operated. He let professionals be creative. He's the only one I know of in my forty years of professional life who knew how to use professionals constructively."

While Fisher was general chairman of the UJA, he was also serving as president of the United Foundation of Detroit; was deeply involved in other Jewish and nonsectarian charities; was pursuing political financing in his role as vice chairman of Michigan's state Republican committee; was looking after his personal investments; and was sitting on more than a dozen corporate boards — Michigan Bell, Consolidated Gas, the Loyal American Life Insurance Company and Fruehauf Corporation among them.

"I've always been able to compartmentalize things," says Fisher, "and keep a lot of balls in the air."

This ability was bolstered by Fisher's drive, a feeling, he says, "that I never made it," and even his recurrent insomnia: late-night and early-morning phone calls to associates were commonplace. For despite his operational laissez-faire, he was not as removed as it might appear. Just as he regularly telephoned business partners, politicians, fund-raisers and the big givers — Fisher became a constant presence in the lives of the UJA professionals.

"Max calls people," says Irving Bernstein, "at least once a day, maybe twice or three times, to get a sense of what's happening. At first, you think you're the only one he's doing it to. Then you find out he's calling this one and that one, he's calling twenty people. He calls more than any other layman I've met. And you appreciate it, his always asking for your opinion. So [professionals] speak well of him. And he's a gentle man in most areas, so there's a good feeling about him."

Although Fisher was respectful of the separate realms of the lay leader and professional, he had little patience with those whom he felt stepped beyond the bounds of their responsibilities.

"There is a tendency in all professionals to do things without consulting the chairman," says a UJA professional. "It's part of life; things happen quickly, or you don't want to bother the guy, or you don't want to do it. I forget the specific incident that Max felt impinged on policy. But he told the [top professional] point-blank that policy was a matter for leadership, and administration was the responsibility of the professionals, and if that wasn't adhered to then it would be a problem for the board to deal with. Max looked him straight in the eye and said it; he didn't play games. With Max, you knew exactly where you stood."

*　　*　　*

Fisher, "the Eastern European prince," brought another dimension to the UJA, a social dimension that, according to a professional colleague, "softened the atmosphere surrounding any highly charged fund-raising group."

"That was [one of] his [goals]," adds Irving Bernstein. "[Fisher] created something that has never existed since [in the UJA] and may never exist again: a prestigious social venue. I think it was the first time we had a black-tie affair, the first time we had a meeting on a [yacht]. Because of this, Max brought in more men and women from around the country. He was not like [other leaders], who dealt with business and were gone. Instead, there seemed to be a sense of welcome."

What, perhaps, was most uncommon about Fisher's approach was that it transgressed the classic skyrocketing mobility of America's moneyed Jewish elite.

In his essay on the relationship between Jews and the Protestant establishment, E. Digby Baltzell writes that while most Americans "are moving up the class hierarchy within each of our larger religious communities . . . class tends to replace religion as the independent variable in social relationships at the highest levels of our society."

Fisher had developed friendships among the WASP upper crust, but by 1964 he was too involved in Jewish affairs to separate himself from his identity. His social egalitarianism was in some measure a result of his small-town beginnings. (As one Salemite recently observed: "In a small town, the richest man knows the poorest man, and may even have grown up next door to him.") But Fisher's approach had another, more politic purpose: it was the start of his relentless consensus building among the major Jewish fund-raising groups.

"The question for me," says Fisher, "was how could I get [people] to work together? I started by gathering them socially for a common purpose. You have to make people feel comfortable, and they have to be part of the process. The next question was: how could I start a cause? The answer — you have an idea and you sell some people on it and then you expand the cause from there."

In a further attempt to unite people, Fisher widened the UJA's Study Mission Program. The missions, which brought UJA members throughout the United States to Israel, were designed not only as educational expeditions, but occasions to socialize. Under Fisher, the meetings also took place in London, Paris, Rome and Geneva.

"It was Margie," says Irving Bernstein, "together with Max, who created the gracious social atmosphere."

Max may have provided the impetus, but the countless nuts and bolts of the social planning fell to Marjorie Fisher. "We hold [these parties] wherever we are," says Marjorie. "To pay back people. And not just that, but to spend time with people we like. I did it in Israel and Europe and Detroit and New York. I wanted the parties to be lovely, so Max would be proud of them."

Marjorie was responsible for pushing Max to turn his attention outward. Yet if she had intended back in 1953 when she married him to live a relaxed suburban life with their children, by the start of 1965 she found herself drawn into a frenetic lifestyle more familiar to the wives of politicians than those of prosperous businessmen. It may have been slight compensation, but at least the political wives had some vague notion of what would be asked of them during their marriage.

On the other hand, Marjorie Fisher recalls: "I had no idea what I was in for."

Marjorie, always the perfectionist, always hoping every party proceeded as planned and suffering when they did not, faced that pressure, along with the added burden of raising children, her husband's traveling and his focus on events outside the family.

"An interviewer once asked me," Marjorie says, "'[Max is so busy], where do you fit into his life? What comes first for him?' And I said: 'The Jews of the world, then the people of Detroit and after that the political arena. I'm fourth. But that doesn't bother me. He could have had three mistresses.'"

Despite the amusing quip, and the snapshots of her beaming in the Jewish press, and such other quotes in the Detroit papers as "Life is just a bowl of charities," Marjorie would grapple with her role. She would tease her husband by hiding his vitamin pills — "to conserve his boundless energy," she said, although later conceding that it had no noticeable effect. Marjorie Fisher's outgoing nature, her flair for doing the unexpected, her humor and well-known generosity, would only take her so far. There would be a price to pay, and decades would pass before Marjorie and Max could look back and determine that it had all been worth the cost.

*   *   *

The underlying causes of the friction between the UJA and the Jewish federations had its roots in two explosive issues: money and power. Although, when reduced to its simplest form, the UJA is a service agency for the federations, its primary interest is in supplying funds for overseas needs, chiefly Israel, but including Jews throughout the world who require financial backing to maintain their educational and religious institutions.

It had long been asserted by some leaders in the federations that it would be more efficient for the UJA to be incorporated into the machinery of the federations. This proposed incorporation, though, posed a problem. Since there was, by definition, a built-in tension between those who promoted domestic needs and those who championed overseas needs, if the UJA was removed, one side would suffer at the hands of the other.

Those, like Fisher, who opposed the incorporation, argued that the UJA, as an outside advocate for overseas needs, provided a safeguard against the local interests of the federations. Furthermore, as Jonathan S. Woocher points out in *Sacred Survival: The Civil Religion of American Jews*, Israel was the ballast on which much of America's Jews now rested their identity. For a rapidly growing percentage of America's assimilated Jews, Israel had replaced religious ritual as the exclusive tie to their Jewishness. It was a sentiment that Fisher reiterated in his speeches across the country in 1965.

"We face the obligation," he told audiences, "to help Israel show the world, as America once showed it, that 'from the wretched refuse of teeming shores' we Jews can build a new, modern successful society. We are a chosen generation. In our time we have seen the lowest point in Jewish history [and] we have also seen the greatest revival of the Jewish people on record. We must continue to make the revival possible."

Fueling much of the friction was the issue of power. The federations, their hands gripping the reins of the fund-raising network, were responsible for 80 percent of the collections, while Israel's unflagging promoter, the UJA, was revered for its formidable skills in organizing fund-raising campaigns. Thus, the politics of the Jewish community had become a circuitous and, occasionally, acrimonious debate over budget allocations.

Fisher, with his ability — and need — to cast conflict in its least divisive light, cornered representatives of the federations and the UJA and used a rebuttal to their positions that he had used when confronting the battling camps of self-proclaimed Zionists and non-Zionists.

"Don't you want to have a place to bring all the refugees?"

Fisher would ask. "Don't you have a responsibility to all of the Jewish people — in America and abroad? All of these Jews are troubled. Don't they have a right to a Jewish education? Do you agree with all of this? Yes? You don't want to live in Israel — O.K. You want to allocate funds for a Jewish day school in Cleveland — fine. You are still as much a Zionist as anyone. You have got to preserve unity. It's precious."

Unity became Fisher's abiding theme. "There is more that unites us than divides," he would say repeatedly, while he tried to lead warring factions to common ground. Fisher's critics would eventually claim, not without some justification, that he was not comfortable in the thin air of ideology, disdaining it to pursue certain goals and, in the process, shedding layers of principle. To some degree, Fisher's reaction to ideological debates came from his dislike of conflict, but as a rule he avoided them because he felt they were useless.

"Look at American politics," says Fisher. "Do you think you can convince the far-right conservative to change his view? Or the fellow on the far left? You can't. But if you can bring these parties into the mainstream than you'll have a coalition and you will get things done."

When it came to deciding on monies for Israel versus domestic needs, Fisher thought that in practical terms it was counterproductive to sever the two. Realistically speaking, barring any domestic disaster, it was Israel that supplied the drama for any Jewish fund-raising campaign. Upon visiting a new Jewish home for the elderly in Long Island, a giver might increase his contribution from $10,000 to $15,000. But Israel — and only Israel — was the basis for dramatic giving, because then it was no longer charity: it was nation-building. After a study mission, meeting with ministers of the Israeli government and touring *kibbutzim*, hospitals, military bases and schools, contributors have been known to jump from $5,000 to $25,000, from $25,000 to $100,000. The aftermath of Israel's wars has seen the most spectacular rise in UJA donations: following the Six-Day War, when Fisher was the chairman, contributions rose 230 percent; and in the wake of the Yom Kippur War, the increase was in excess of 150 percent.

Fisher, according to Abraham J. Karp, author of *To Give Life: The UJA and the Shaping of the American Jewish Community*, "recognized the symbiotic relationship between the UJA and federations." After all, most of the UJA's money came *not* from the backwater hamlets where UJA field operatives passed through like migrant workers, but from cities: Los Angeles, Chicago, Detroit, Cleveland, New York and Miami. Here, in these metropolitan centers teeming with the institutions of Jewish life, the federations were firmly planted in the community and superbly organized.

Fisher also knew that while it was viable for him to use his contacts and friendships among corporate heads and the rich to court a select conclave of sizable contributors — those willing to pledge $50,000 or more — the federations remained, in Fisher's words, "the salesmen for the UJA." Fisher understood that there was no percentage in alienating the people who carry your product — in this case, a philanthropic message — door-to-door.

Conceivably, Fisher's greatest asset in his attempts to bridge what one commentator euphemistically described as the "formal and cool relationship between [the federations and the UJA]" was that unlike other UJA heads, Fisher had not erupted onto the national philanthropic scene. He did not begin as a "prince." Rather, as with his start in the oil business, he began on the bottom rung of the ladder.

The ultimate importance of this facet of Fisher's philanthropic — and later on, political — career was identified by Abraham Karp in his history of Jews in America, *Haven and Home*. Karp writes: "[Fisher] came to national leadership through activity in the Detroit Jewish community as president of its Jewish Welfare Federation, one of the most powerful in the nation. He went on to become president of the Council of Jewish Federations and Welfare Funds, while at the same time serving as chairman of the United Israel Appeal. Later he became chairman of the Board of Governors of the reconstituted Jewish Agency, as well as chairman of the executive committee of the American Jewish Committee. He thus held leadership positions in all the power bases of the American Jewish community. In a sense, he represented the final consolidation of the Jewish community into a unified entity."

Karp's point became apparent immediately upon Fisher's election to the chairmanship. Boris Smolar of the Jewish Telegraph Agency headlined an article, "Fisher, '65 UJA Head, Is Grass Roots Man!" The resentment that the members of the CJF might have felt toward a UJA leader was absent in Fisher's case because to the federations his ascension at the UJA was a tale of local-boy-makes-good. As if to underscore this point, the same year Fisher was elected to the chairmanship of the UJA, he was also elected vice president of the CJF. Fisher united the groups by assuming leadership posts in both. It was an unprecedented paradigm of coalition building that Fisher would repeat in 1969, when, as president of the UJA, he was elected to the presidency of the CJF.

As for the competition over funds, that was lessened by long-range allocation agreements and, in the end, Fisher reached his goal. In 1981, Boris Smolar reported: "Elaborate preparations are now being made by the leadership of the United Jewish Appeal to honor Max Fisher in grand style as a unique leader of the American Jewish community." Smolar compared Fisher to other eminent Jewish personalities: Louis Marshall, Rabbi Stephen Wise, Felix Warburg and others, but indicated how Fisher had differed from his predecessors: "While each of these great Jewish men reflected the philosophy of just a certain segment of American Jewry — they were either outspoken Zionists or non-Zionists — Fisher represents all segments of the American Jewish community. His philosophy is based on the idea of achieving Jewish unity." Then Smolar called Fisher what he had always aspired to become. "Max Fisher," Smolar said, "is a builder of bridges."

Chapter 5

FISHER AND NIXON: LONELY MEN OF FAITH

NEITHER MAX FISHER nor Richard Nixon can place the exact year they met, but both men indicate that it was probably 1959. Fisher recalls that he went to Washington to talk with then-Vice President Nixon about a problem facing the United Jewish Appeal. After the 1956 Suez Crisis, Arab spokesmen argued that the U.S. government, in granting the UJA tax-exempt status, was underwriting Israel's "military aggression." Senator Allen J. Ellender, a Democrat from Louisiana, called for an investigation into the UJA's status. Since the right to deduct UJA gifts from their taxes was a substantial incentive to major contributors, American Jewish fund-raisers were concerned about the call for an investigation, and a battle ensued.

At their first meeting, Fisher told Nixon about the conflict. Nixon was sympathetic and promised to look into it. Eventually, the investigation was repulsed by Senator Jacob K. Javits, a Republican from New York, and other legislators. (In the long run, the issue was put to rest by a group led by the United Israel Appeal's Gottlieb Hammer and Maurice M. Boukstein, and by the designation of a separate nonprofit corporation that would oversee the funds funneled to Israel.) Fisher and Nixon arranged to meet more regularly, a routine they would maintain until Nixon entered the White House in 1969, when their visits had to be fit into the president's schedule.

"We saw the world pretty much the same way right from

the start," Nixon says. "We didn't drink booze. We never played golf. We never played poker. I never partied with Max or was on a boat for a weekend with him. We liked it better that way. We discussed politics. I might say, 'How about a bite of lunch?' and we'd talk. And it was never those martini lunches with us. Max was serious. We could discuss issues."

"We shared the same philosophy," adds Fisher. "In those early years, we had a lot of long philosophical discussions, especially about the Middle East. Dick is a great admirer of the Israelis. We also talked about the Russians and his attitude toward China. He had traveled so much; he had read so much. He was quite a student."

Fisher and Nixon soon found that they also shared an obsessive interest in their work — to the exclusion of nearly everything else. One of Nixon's classmates at Duke Law School, echoing the consensus on Nixon during those days, recalled that he was "the hardest-working man I ever met." On the campaign trail, it was said that Nixon worked "like a horse," and it was a trait that he respected in others. In 1968, Nixon told Garry Wills, author of *Nixon Agonistes*: "I have seen those who have nothing to do . . . the people just lying around at Palm Beach. Nothing could be more pitiful." Wills observed that when Nixon made this statement "his voice had contempt in it, not pity."

Fisher, by 1959, could have afforded to sun himself forever in Palm Beach; he did, along with his family, vacation at his apartment there in the winter. But free time jangled Fisher's nerves; he was incapable of relaxing. Instead, he sat, picking at a bowl of grapes or a platter of chocolate-chip cookies — the choice depending on whether or not he was dieting that week — and leafed through *The New York Times*, *The Wall Street Journal* and *The Jerusalem Post*, piling the sections of newsprint at his feet. Then he dialed the phone. There was always another detail to check or a deal to investigate and, as soon as he could schedule it, a meeting to attend. It was as though Fisher was still the insecure Salem Boy Scout and athlete trying to disprove his father's accusation that he was wasting his life.

Fisher's lawyer and friend Jason Honigman recalls that "Max was always working, always probing into something. Once, we were on business in New York and sleeping in the same [hotel suite]. I was awakened at six o'clock in the morning by this simmering noise. Then I caught on. Max was talking business on the telephone. There is another incident I remember, a Saturday-night party at the Standard Club [a private club in Detroit's Sheraton-Cadillac Hotel]. Max was there with Margie and another couple, George Patterson [president of Buckeye Pipeline] and his wife, who had been Max's secretary at Aurora. The four of them had just come from a cruise in the Caribbean. George's face was red as a beet, but Max was as pale as the morning he left. So I said to George: 'I assume Max isn't sunburned because he spent his vacation on the phone.' And [George] said, 'Of course.'"

The Fisher-Nixon rapport was not built solely on the attraction of kindred spirits. An ample portion rested on the conventional quid pro quo of politics. Since Fisher had achieved some newsworthy financial success with the Ohio Oil-Aurora merger, Nixon had to realize that in Fisher he had a potentially generous backer for his 1960 try at the White House. In November 1958 — months before the initial Nixon-Fisher meeting — Nixon had decided to run and had a campaign manager and finance chairman in place.

Fisher's motivations for supporting Nixon were less obvious. He respected him, particularly his hard-line stance against Soviet expansionism. Nixon was going to be the candidate, no question about it, and therefore represented an opportunity. Fisher suspected that his own entrée into national politics would come through a partnership with a president that merged sympathetic visions of the world, a compatible personal relationship and, the usual bill of fare, hefty financial support. Fisher also believed in the standard Republican torch song that the country required less government, not more, and that a healthy economy, strengthened through the unencumbered growth of private enterprise, was good for everyone, regardless of where they stood on the economic ladder.

But by the close of the 1950s, Fisher's feelings toward his Republicanism were changing. If, in the 1940 presidential election, he had switched his vote from FDR to his Republican opponent, Wendell Willkie, because he believed that no one should occupy the Oval Office beyond two terms, Fisher had now come to see his party affiliation in an increasingly practical light. His Republicanism was less reflective of his moderately-to-the-right political convictions than of his Jewishness, and the reasoning behind it was as elementary as the logic that induced investors to diversify their portfolios.

Fisher says: "I thought it was a mistake for the Jewish community to be locked in by the Democrats because they were taken for granted. Every election the Democrats knew they could count on 75 or 80 percent of the Jewish vote. They didn't even have to go out and listen to the concerns of [the Jewish community]. They didn't have to work for it. This was one of the big arguments I made [to Jews]."

However, it was not an argument he would make effectively until the 1968 election; he was in 1960 only beginning to enter the leadership of the national Jewish community and therefore lacked a constituency. As always, Fisher began his fund-raising efforts with his own check. He cannot recall the precise amount of his contribution — somewhere in the range of $10,000, a decent sum in a campaign that collected approximately $2 million. Then he got on the phone and drummed up support. It was not until the final days that the Nixon campaign people realized the range of Fisher's skill.

In 1960, Nixon pledged to campaign in every state, and he was, despite the protests of his staff, determined to keep his promise. And so on the Sunday before the election he flew to Anchorage, Alaska. Next, Nixon moved on to Madison, Wisconsin, and then on Monday, to Detroit, Michigan, where a telethon was scheduled.

In *Six Crises*, Nixon recalled that he "had wanted to have several telethons in the last days of the campaign but funds had not been available. Only three days before air-time were we able to obtain enough contributions to finance this one show."

David J. Mahoney, then-president of the Good Humor Company (and later the head of Norton-Simon), was helping with the Nixon campaign. Mahoney explains how Nixon managed to raise the money for the telethon. "I was in Washington, D.C.," says Mahoney, "when I got a call from [Nixon campaign manager Robert] Finch. Finch was in Alaska, overseeing Nixon's visit, and he said that we had a serious problem. Because the polls were predicting that the race was too close to call, the TV station in Detroit [WXYZ] wanted their payment in advance for the telethon. That made sense: losers sometimes don't pay their bills. The problem, Finch said, was that we didn't have enough money for the buy. Then he asked me to meet him at the Cadillac Hotel in Detroit to see what we could do about it."

Mahoney met Finch the following day. They got busy on the phones, but could not come up with the money. Finch, Mahoney says, phoned Nixon; Nixon said he had a friend in Detroit they should try — Max Fisher. "I can't recall the exact amount," Mahoney says today. "But it must have been close to $250,000 that we needed. And Max raised it right away. If there hadn't been a Fisher, there wouldn't have been a telethon."

The 1960 presidential election was the closest in American history. Nixon carried three more states than Kennedy, but lost in the Electoral College, 303 to 219. There were 68.8 million votes cast and, with the shift of one-tenth of 1 percent of the vote, Nixon would have been president.

Fisher, naturally, was disappointed, but he was about to discover an aspect of Nixon that increased his admiration for him and confirmed his belief that he would have been the right man for the job and perhaps still would be. Following the election, rumors of voting fraud began to circulate. The rumors focused on Texas, Vice President-elect Lyndon B. Johnson's home state, and Cook County, Illinois, where Mayor Richard J. Daley, chief of Chicago's monolithic Democratic machine, had delivered a dubious Kennedy vote. (Years later, Fisher heard the story of Edward Bennett Williams, the powerful Washington attorney — and, for a while, Nixon enemy — who decided to heal his rift with Nixon by inviting him to lunch at the exclusive Manhattan restaurant, Le Cirque. At lunch, Williams told Nixon that when Daley was dying Williams visited him, and Daley said: "God forgive me for stealing Illinois from Nixon in 1960.") Because the rumors appeared to have a hint of truth and because Kennedy's margin of victory had been so narrow, many of Nixon's friends and associates urged him to demand a recount.

Fisher attended a meeting in which several people tried to persuade Nixon to ask for a review. Nixon replied that a recount would create chaos, leading to bitterness across the country and a loss of confidence in the election process. Finally, it would serve as a sad example to all of those nations who were striving to establish democracies. Nixon concluded that not demanding a recount was his only responsible course of action.

Fisher left the meeting impressed by Nixon's response. Paradoxically, despite his deep disappointment over Nixon's defeat, it can be claimed that Nixon's loss brought him closer to Fisher — and provided Fisher with a greater opportunity — than if he had won.

*　　*　　*

In part, Fisher's chance to befriend Nixon came because Nixon did not have a smooth transition into private life. Upon leaving the vice presidency, he accepted a consulting job at the Los Angeles law firm of Adams, Duque and Hazeltine. His wife remained behind in Washington so their daughters could finish school, and Nixon moved out to California alone, renting a small apartment on Wilshire Boulevard, where he passed his evenings eating TV dinners and reading. It was not, Nixon confessed in his memoirs, *RN*, an easy time. One of the major difficulties was that since losing the election, Nixon had started to notice a sharp falling-off of friends. What hurt the worst, he remarked, was to see that those for whom he "had done the most were often the first to desert."

Fisher was not one of the friends who deserted. Shortly after Election Day, he wrote Nixon, and by early December, Nixon replied: "Pat and I want you to know how very much we appreciated the letter which you sent us after the election. A message of congratulations after winning an election is of course always appreciated although not unexpected. But nothing could have meant more to us than to receive such a warm and thoughtful message after losing. Your act of thoughtfulness will always remain close to our hearts."

Nixon wrote Fisher again on January 3, 1961, telling him how he and his office staff had been busy, "dig[ging] its way out from under the mass of mail that has come to us in the days since November 8. Nixon said he sensed in himself and his supporters "a renewed determination to continue to fight for [their] principles." He then assured Fisher that he "intend[ed] to do everything that I can in working for those principles in the years ahead."

For Fisher, the message was clear. Nixon, despite his loss, was still running.

And Fisher continued to treat Nixon as a candidate. The two men maintained their steady flow of correspondence and phone calls and, whenever possible, got together to discuss domestic politics and foreign affairs. In view of Nixon's painful discovery after the 1960 election — the flight of his fair-weather political friends — it becomes clearer why he valued Fisher's enduring interest in his career and why he would, in 1989, talk of his "unbounded admiration and affectionate friendship for Max."

"Max Fisher," says Nixon, "is a solid man, and there are very few solid people in anything, especially in the big-business community. I'm not against them, but they're very enthusiastic only if you're winning. They didn't get there by supporting losers. But if Max believed in an individual, he'd stand by him. Max had qualities of great personal loyalty."

Nixon was going to need those qualities, because he could not keep away from politics. By the spring of 1961, Nixon was increasingly interested in taking up the role of titular leader of the Republican Party. He agreed to write a book, which later became *Six Crises*, and he was writing political columns for the Times-Mirror syndicate. In May, Nixon began a speaking tour. He stated that he was making the tour as a private citizen, but his talks were blatantly political. On May 9, Nixon was in Detroit, addressing a capacity crowd of newsmen, broadcasters and businessmen at a Detroit Press Club luncheon.

Nixon, appearing far more rested than during his Detroit campaign stops in 1960, spoke for over an hour. He told the audience that the United States must maintain a nonbelligerent but firm attitude toward the Soviet Union. He exhorted the businessmen "to work for the Republican Party," and advised Michigan Republicans to beef up their organizations in urban areas. To win the Negro vote, he observed, the Republicans must continue a program "that talks with Negroes, not down to them." He added that his party leadership would be along the middle ground, "in the Eisenhower tradition."

Fisher was unable to attend Nixon's talk — he was out of town — but two days later they spoke on the telephone. Fisher told Nixon that he had been tremendously pleased with the press coverage and the reactions of people to his visit. Fisher said that Nixon had made a good start at solving some of the political problems in Michigan by bringing them into focus, adding that he "[felt] more of this should be done."

Due to his speeches, Nixon found himself in the national limelight as the leader of the "loyal opposition," and it was not long before the pressure on him to seek the governorship of California escalated. Polls indicated that he could defeat the incumbent, Governor Edmund "Pat" Brown, by a margin of 5 to 3. Nixon stewed over the decision during the summer. Eisenhower, Thomas E. Dewey and a number of Nixon supporters — including Fisher — felt that the governorship could be Nixon's springboard back onto the national scene.

In July, two weeks after his fifty-third birthday, Fisher wrote to Nixon: "I have been following with a great deal of interest your speeches and your columns, and [I] think they have been very constructive. However, I would like to add some comments which I have heard in my travels, [from] many people who are good friends of yours and [from] others who are looking into the future for leadership. These revolve around your re-entry into the political field in the near future.

To a naive observer, as I sit here, it appears to me that you could win the election for governor hands down, which would result in some very definite pluses [for your] long-range plans.

"First of all, one must consider that California will be the largest state in the Union in the future, and the man who speaks from the forum of the highest office of [that] state would certainly carry a great deal of prestige nationally and internationally. Secondly, it would be a great help to the Republican Party to have the state of California locked up. More important, the fact that you could command an election to this top post would be a tremendous demonstration to most people of your ability to command a following now and in the future. The impact of this to me would be tremendous and would go a long way toward welding some dissident factions in the Republican Party, as well as giving greatest impact to messages on the national and international level. I certainly hope that you are giving this matter some consideration. Meanwhile, these comments are worth about as much as you pay for them, but I really have a sincere desire for [you to succeed] in your future plans."

In terms of predicting a Nixon victory, what a *Wall Street Journal* reporter referred to as Fisher's "keen sense of timing" failed him. Nixon would later claim that "the importunings of many close friends" convinced him to try for the governorship, but on August 15, 1961, he was still ambivalent about becoming a candidate. He wrote Fisher: "I have been leaning strongly against the idea of running for what appear to me to be some compelling reasons. Before I make a final decision, I will be in touch with you again. I can't tell you how much I sincerely appreciate your taking the time and trouble to pass along your own recommendation. Our mutual friend, Cliff Folger, [also] takes your point of view."

Clifford Folger was a banker and former U.S. Ambassador to Belgium. He had also been, in the 1950s, the GOP's finance chairman and then, in 1960, he had served as Nixon's finance chairman during his presidential campaign. Now, on Tuesday evening, August 29, Fisher flew from Detroit to Washington, D.C., to attend a dinner at Folger's home. Nixon was there, and during the meal Fisher discussed the pros and cons of Nixon's being governor of California. The governorship may well have provided a prestigious platform and a pathway to the Oval Office, but Nixon was convinced that Kennedy would be unbeatable in 1964. Then, too, Nixon was not all that certain he wanted to be a governor. Fisher understood Nixon's hesitancy, but he was concerned that Nixon not lose his place in public life or be overshadowed: Nelson Rockefeller was running for governor in New York and William W. Scranton in Pennsylvania.

Despite his ambivalence — or perhaps because of it — Nixon welcomed the chance to hear the thinking of an inner circle of advisers. Over the Labor Day weekend, he wrote Fisher: "It was certainly most thoughtful and generous of you to take the time, particularly on such short notice, to come to [the Folgers']. This is a difficult decision but I feel most fortunate in having the benefit of your thinking as to what I should do."

On September 27, Nixon announced that he would seek the governorship of California in 1962. Governor Pat Brown publicly responded that Nixon "sees the governorship of this state only as a steppingstone for his own presidential ambitions." It was a charge that would be echoed throughout the campaign. Californians, pollsters soon discovered, came to accept it. One poll showed that 36 percent thought that Nixon was truly interested in serving as governor, while 64 percent believed that he was far more interested in running for president. Whatever the truth of the charge, the White House — at least his try for it in 1960 — was much on Nixon's mind. During the fall, Nixon wistfully told Fisher: "As I looked at my desk calendar this morning, it seemed hardly possible that a year had gone since our campaign of 1960 came to a close. I would not want this day to pass without . . . [telling] you again how deeply grateful I am for all that you did for our cause. No candidate for the presidency could have had a more dedicated and loyal group of supporters."

Fisher believed that Nixon still had his eye on the White House. On March 14, Nixon mailed Fisher an autographed advance copy of *Six Crises*. (Nixon sent dozens out to prominent Republicans.) Fisher's reply to the gift is revealing, for it illuminates what Fisher perceived as Nixon's mixed feelings about his race in California. After thanking Nixon for the book, Fisher said: "I am more convinced than ever that what I have felt always of your ability to fill the highest office is confirmed. Good luck to you in your forthcoming campaign. I will be in touch with Cliff Folger since I would like to be as helpful as possible."

Fisher was helpful: his best recollection is that he gave somewhere between $5,000 and $10,000 to Nixon's gubernatorial campaign. The dollars that Fisher contributed were small compared to what he would contribute to Nixon in 1968 and 1972, and almost negligible when compared to the millions he would raise for him in those election years. (Nixon's entire 1962 race cost $1.42 million.) But it would seem that the reality of Fisher's continued confidence was drawing Nixon closer to him. Fisher's willingness to be involved, to put his money up, was heightened because Nixon was having trouble raising funds. Large contributors who were willing to aid a potential president were reluctant to write checks when the stakes were a governorship.

In July, two days before Fisher turned fifty-four, he flew to Washington for another dinner with the Nixons at the Folgers' house. For a while, the dinner conversation centered on the California race. But then the discussion became more general, drifting toward the politician's difficult lot, and Nixon told the group that "constant and loyal friends in political life are rare indeed," and he felt particularly fortunate to be among those sort of friends now.

In a note thanking Fisher for taking the time to fly to Washington, Nixon expressed what may well have been his premonition that he would lose the governorship. For if he intended to move into the governor's residence in Sacramento, it seemed odd that he would conclude his note with "[Pat and I] hope it will not be too long before you will be out this way so that we can welcome you in our new home in Beverly Hills."

On Election Day, November 7, 1962, Nixon watched the

returns on his television in a suite at the Beverly Hills Hotel. That evening, Fisher phoned him from Detroit.

"It doesn't look like I'm going to quite make it," Nixon said. "I'm glad things are going better for Republicans in Michigan."

The next morning, after Governor Brown had defeated him, Nixon went to face reporters. By his own account, he "looked terrible and felt worse," and he angrily told the journalists: "You won't have Nixon to kick around anymore, because, gentlemen, this is my last press conference."

It was a statement that would trail Nixon like an unfortunate shadow, establishing him as a "sore loser," an image that, as he stated in *RN*, he would fight against in his 1968 bid for the presidency. But in 1962, the prevailing wisdom was that Nixon was walking out of history. The next day, in *The New York Times*, James Reston wrote that Nixon "will have to be left to the historians and the psychological novelists." Four days later, on ABC television, Howard K. Smith hosted a special, "The Political Obituary of Richard Nixon."

Fisher, of course, was distressed by the loss in California, partly because he had encouraged his friend to run and also because he realized that without a political base, Nixon's chances to become president were limited. Even though he saw Nixon's biting retirement statement on the news, Fisher felt that he was far from through with politics.

Soon after the gubernatorial race, he wrote to Nixon: "This is just to let you know we are thinking of you and hoping we can continue our very fine relationship. It is unfortunate that there have to be losers in political battles, but I remember your philosophy on this and it is my hope that this will not be the end of political activity for you. However, whatever you do I would like to hear from you."

Nixon's reply arrived in the form of gift. "In view of the frost damage to the citrus crop across the nation," said the enclosed letter, "I thought you might enjoy these navel oranges, grown in a frost-free area in the foothills of Southern California."

The letter did not mention politics. On the surface, Nixon's exit appeared complete.

*   *   *

In the winter of 1963, Nixon believed he was ruling himself out as an active political figure for the foreseeable future by relocating to New York City and joining a renowned Wall Street law firm, which shortly became Nixon, Mudge, Rose, Guthrie and Alexander.

Nixon, although he told *The Los Angeles Times* that Manhattan was very exciting — "the fast track" — was having difficulty adjusting. One of Nixon's new partners was Leonard Garment, a litigating partner at the firm. Eleven years Nixon's junior, Garment, a Jew born in Brooklyn, was a former saxophonist with the big bands of Woody Herman and Henry Jerome, a self-described "band manager and general utility musician." He would play a large role in Nixon's 1968 campaign and would serve in both Nixon administrations and under President Gerald R. Ford. Garment also would become a close friend and associate of Fisher. He was the one who had arranged the Edward Bennett Williams-Nixon lunch at Le Cirque and then told Fisher of Mayor Daley's dying regret of stealing the 1960 election from Nixon.

When Nixon began his stint on Wall Street, Garment noticed that the former vice president seemed to feel out of synch.

"I took it upon myself to help him become oriented to a New York law firm," Garment says. "I knew that he was uncomfortable with the jargon and all that. My motives were: one, my great personal curiosity about [Nixon] — he was a man out of history, suddenly my partner, and I was very interested in seeing what made him function; number two, I had a self-interest in him as an up-and-coming partner to fit him into the firm and help him establish credentials as a lawyer; and three, I was aware, from the time he joined the firm, that he was not finished with politics.

"But Wall Street," Garment continues, "was not Nixon's natural field of action. In politics, people are very direct — it's almost a physical encounter. However, on Wall Street, it's a very complicated, convoluted language. And then you have country clubs and golf and the private clubs in town. That was not Richard Nixon's cup of tea."

Fisher met often with Nixon in New York, but Fisher saw that the erstwhile candidate was unquestionably cut off from politics, that he was wandering — in the words of William Safire, who would become a speechwriter for President Nixon and then a columnist for *The New York Times* — in the "wilderness." Nixon had no power base and slim hope of establishing one, since New York's Republican Party was controlled by Governor Rockefeller, who also coveted the White House. Still, Fisher and Nixon continued to discuss politics and foreign affairs, and Nixon, now the outsider, began to sense a kinship with Fisher.

"Max," says Nixon, "was never part of the big-business Eastern Establishment, though he had a lot more stroke than most of them. And he had his lines into more than Marathon Oil. But just as I was never the candidate of Wall Street — I was the candidate of Main Street — Max was the [Bernard] Baruch of the heartland. Baruch was influential because people thought he was so wise and smart; that's because he was part of the Eastern Establishment. Max [would become] a key adviser to presidents, and a very influential one, more so than Baruch ever was. But the general public knew little about him."

Nixon was correct in assessing that Fisher perceived himself as an outsider because of his origins, but it was not because Fisher was a child of the heartland. Rather, it was because Fisher was Jewish, a fact that in Fisher's mind influenced how he conducted himself in every facet of business, philanthropy and politics.

"In order to be successful," says Fisher, "you have to be good at what you're doing. But because I was Jewish I always felt that I had to be twice as good."

Fisher's discussions with Nixon led him to conclude (as Garment had) that Nixon was not as removed from the arena as it appeared. In early 1964, Barry Goldwater had decided to contest President Lyndon Johnson in the upcoming presidential election. Politically, Goldwater and LBJ were seated on opposite sides of the Great Society ballroom. Johnson was on the left, an updated version of his hero, FDR, with an aggressive stance on social programs and civil rights. Goldwater, conversely, appealed to those who desired a simpler America, before the advent of government safety-net systems. Goldwater was also a hard-liner on the deployment of military force. He claimed that he would consider giving field commanders control over the use of tactical nuclear weapons, and he became a proponent of an escalated effort in Vietnam. He was popular with Southern segregationists and a smattering of formalized groups on the radical right — notably, the John Birch Society — and although Goldwater stated that he did not agree with many of the Birchers' views, he said that he "refused to engage in any wholesale condemnation of them."

It was not just the Democrats who attacked Goldwater. He managed to alienate moderate Republicans, Fisher and Nixon among them. And so in the first week of June 1964, when Nixon, en route to the National Governors' Conference in Cleveland, came to Detroit for a fund-raiser, he had a private breakfast meeting at the Book-Cadillac Hotel with Governor Romney of Michigan and Fisher.

Romney, a popular centrist Republican with a strong record on civil rights, had been critical of Goldwater's "extremism." Nixon and Fisher, like all liberal and mainstream Republicans, were concerned about the effect of Goldwater's rightist stance on party unity; losing the White House was one thing, but the fallout in statehouses and in Congress was potentially disastrous. So now, over breakfast, Nixon attempted to convince Romney to challenge Goldwater for the nomination. Romney was not sure he was ready to make that move. Fisher said that he felt it was far too early for the governor to seek national office; the party was hopelessly divided, the election machinery was not in place, and Romney's reputation was still circumscribed by Michigan's borders.

The breakfast broke up, and from this point, the story

grows muddled, the truth depending on whose version one accepts.

Romney and Nixon traveled separately to Cleveland; Fisher remained in Detroit. The governor and Nixon conferred again during the conference. Nixon spoke to reporters and flew on to Baltimore to board a plane for a business trip to London. Here, though, the tale shifts. The press started to spread the word of a Romney candidacy. According to Jules Witcover, in *The Resurrection of Richard Nixon* (published in 1970), when Nixon arrived in Baltimore, his aide John Whitaker told him: "It's on the radio that Romney's *not* going to run."

Nixon was stunned. He said: "What do you mean he's not going to run? He told me he was."

Romney claims that he never said he was going to enter the race. Fisher, who does not remember Romney ever agreeing to become a candidate, does recall that Nixon phoned him from Baltimore, saying that he had not told reporters Romney was going to challenge Goldwater. Nixon apologized for the mix-up and asked Fisher to pass the message along to the governor.

By the summer of 1964, the relationship between Fisher and Nixon began to shift, becoming more personal — particularly for two men whom associates often characterized as strictly businesslike and distant.

Leonard Garment, who observed the Fisher-Nixon friendship for more than two decades, felt that it was based on their similarities.

"They are both men of action," says Garment, "both dependent on being part of large events. They are very pragmatic people, distrustful of the big gesture and a lot of talk about clout. Now in Max's case, he made money and achieved status and then he wanted to reach the next stage — to be a player on the field of politics. [So they had] that in common. And Richard Nixon had real admiration for Max. He saw him as somebody who had come out of the Midwest, not wealthy, who worked hard and eventually [earned his fortune]. There are very similar elements to both lives: relentless work and deprivation and struggle and then getting up the ladder. So I think there was a real empathy between them. They were both very ambitious, hard-working men who had finally broken through to a kind of clear horizon."

The emotional foundation of their friendship, then, was a blend of constricted pasts and expansive futures, of memory and dreams, and by the summer of 1964 they were close enough for Nixon to let down his guard and show Fisher another side of his personality, a side not generally known to the public.

Nixon, despite his claims that he was "the candidate of Main Street, not Wall Street," had traditionally been seen as someone who cared little for the common man. It was a perception that Kennedy exploited in 1960.

Historian Stephen Ambrose writes: "Kennedy had never spent one day of his life at manual labor for pay, yet he managed to duplicate the FDR miracle of convincing millions that he was a real friend of the poor workingman. Nixon had worked at manual jobs every day of his life until he became a lawyer, but even his maudlin accounts of his youthful poverty failed to convince most people that he cared one fig for the common laborer."

The side of Nixon that did indeed care for the common man was what he revealed to Fisher in an exchange of letters beginning in July 1964. For all of the light it sheds on Nixon, it also indicates the turn his friendship with Fisher was taking.

"Dear Max," Nixon wrote. "As you know, I get my hair cut in the — barbershop. John, the barber, was originally from [Europe]. Alex, who shines shoes, handles the telephone appointments and acts as valet for the shop, also came from [Europe]. When [Alex] lived [overseas], he worked as a stone dresser, which I understand is a highly skilled type of masonry for which there is no demand in this country.

"When I was in the barbershop last week, Alex had just returned from Detroit where he had spent six weeks with his wife and children. This was the heartrending story he told me. His wife has had a very serious nervous breakdown and is now receiving shock treatment in one of the public institutions in Detroit. For four weeks, Alex went to the various employment offices and tried to get a job as a laborer, maintenance man or anything else that might be available. He was unable to get work there and had to return to New York in order to be able to send at least a small sum each week to his family.

"[Alex] was obviously desperate in his desire to find some kind of work in Detroit so that he could be with his wife and his children during this period. As he put it to me, 'I would willingly let somebody cut off my right hand if it would mean getting a job in Detroit.'

"I do not know why he and his wife have been separated in the first place. I do know that his desire to be with her and to provide for her and the children is genuine in every respect. He fears that if he is unable to return to Detroit, his wife may commit suicide because of her very disturbed mental condition.

"I hesitate to ask someone as busy as you are to look into a matter of this type, but I thought that possibly through some of your many contacts in the business and political world you might find some company or individual who could provide employment for Alex in the maintenance or common-laborer category.

"Perhaps the next time you are in [New York], you might like to check out Alex's story yourself. In any event, I felt compelled to pass it on to you."

A cursory glance at Nixon's childhood can partially explain why Nixon "felt compelled" to pass Alex's troubles on to Fisher. There were the financial hardships suffered by Nixon's family; the terminal illnesses of two brothers; and the painful three-year separation from his mother when she moved from Whittier, California, to Prescott, Arizona, to nurse his oldest brother, Harold, who was dying from tuberculosis. So when he became aware of Alex, an immigrant in search of his small slice of the American dream while beset by family and financial problems, Nixon's urge to assist him must have been overpowering.

Fisher, too, as a youngster, had endured the struggle of his father to provide for his family, and the ensuing separation from his parents and siblings when he was left behind with his uncle in Salem, so William could set up a business in Cleveland. He also found Alex's story compelling and soon after receiving Nixon's letter, Fisher replied to him: "I suppose somewhere in Detroit we probably could find a job for Alex. But before doing so, I would like to have a little background on what work he has done in the past and how much he is earning at the present time. If you will have him write me a letter directly as to what he has done in the last few years, I will try to find something for him."

Nixon did not wait for Alex to contact Fisher. Instead, he took it upon himself to discover the specifics of Alex's background and to send them to Fisher.

"This is in further reference to Alex," Nixon wrote. "He will be forty years old [this year], speaks good English with a slight accent, makes a good personal appearance, and is in good health. He has been at [the barbershop] since March 1963 as the valet, but also handles appointments for the barber by phone and serves as the cashier. From January 1962 to February 1963, he worked at — as an elevator operator; during 1960 and 1961 he worked at — as the porter/maintenance man; before that he had a similar job at — . All of these jobs were in New York City. He has never worked in a gasoline service station, but his English is certainly good enough to do so, and I know of no reason why he couldn't perform such a job well. Again, my appreciation for your willingness to take an interest in this matter."

Three days later, Fisher instructed his corporate attorney, Max Isberg, to get in touch with Alex and help place him in a job at one of Speedway 79's gas stations.

*   *   *

It is not surprising that Nixon approached Fisher with a request to use his influence. Besides the healthy amount of clout he had around town, by the early 1960s, Fisher was celebrated for his charitable instincts. He once told an interviewer that he "always felt a great obligation to the community because of the great success of Aurora. You can't take without giving something back."

As the interviewer observed, though, Fisher's gift-giving and fund-raising had become a vocation. And to some degree it had rewards beyond an altruistic glow. Fisher was, after all, publicly acclaimed for his charity work. A pavilion at Detroit's Sinai Hospital is named for him and his wife, as is a third-floor sunroom of the Detroit Jewish Home for the Aged and a gymnasium in West Bloomfield, Michigan. There is the community center in Ramla, Israel, and a park in Jerusalem (an honor he shares with Al Taubman). Then there are the scholarships that send students to study in Israel; and the Max Fisher Scholarships in Salem, Ohio. His office walls are crammed with honorary doctorates from colleges and universities — Ohio State, Eastern Michigan, Gratz, Yeshiva and others. There are also proclamations of Max M. Fisher Days, the Salvation Army's William Booth Award, plaques, citations and certificates of every size and hue, and an oceanic silver-gold-and-glass montage praising his generosity and fund-raising efforts.

Yet, far away from the public fanfare of conventional philanthropy, with its ribbon-cutting ceremonies, stately dinners and photographers capturing 1,000-watt smiles for society pages, stood Fisher the private benefactor, who gave in secret, who spotted someone in need and offered to help, his rewards more solitary, more personal. It was a feature of Fisher's philanthropic activity that he never alluded to in interviews, and he must have kept it quiet around Detroit because reporters, who habitually questioned him on the minutiae of his charity work, did not even bother to ask him about it.

It is difficult to say when it began; Fisher claims he cannot recall, but his brother-in-law, Stanley Burkoff, discovered it in 1963.

Burkoff had recently brought his family to Detroit from Toronto, and, unknowingly, started to frequent the same downtown barbershop as Fisher. Burkoff noticed that the barber and manicurist were unusually attentive to him.

"I didn't understand why I received such good service,"

says Burkoff. "Until one afternoon Max came up in the conversation and I learned that he had put the barber's son, and the manicurist's daughter, through college."

There were other examples of men and women whom Fisher helped. Some were relatives of friends or employees; others, strangers, simply sought him out, made their case and were helped with tuition bills, down payments for houses and medical expenses. One afternoon, a longtime associate of Fisher phoned him upon inheriting a real estate company that was hard-pressed for cash. He told Fisher that the company was about to go under and, by the end of the day, a signed, blank check was on its way, eventually to be filled in for $500,000. Joseph Nederlander, who, among other interests, operates the Fisher Theatre, recalls that producers whose shows were in trouble often came to Fisher to bail them out; some loans were repaid, some were not.

"But Max never put any pressure on anyone," says Nederlander. "He helped you and that was it. If you paid him back — fine. If you didn't — that was fine, too."

A more extreme illustration of Fisher's confidential philanthropy — since it involved not only his money but his time — was that of Joseph J. Wright.

Wright began working at the Fishers' Franklin home when he was a sixteen-year-old high-school student at Brother Rice, a Catholic school in Birmingham, Michigan. Wright raked leaves, polished floors and performed a variety of odd jobs, part-time during the school year, full-time in the summer. His relationship with Fisher was casual: they would just say hello or chat about local sports.

In the winter of Wright's senior year in high school, his father committed suicide. Wright phoned the Fishers' house manager, Richard Morse, and told him why he would be unable to come to work. Morse, in turn, called the Fishers, who were in Palm Beach, and told them what had happened.

Two days after the funeral, Fisher flew up from Florida, and Wright received a call that he wanted to see him. Wright drove over to the house. Fisher was waiting for him in the glass-walled garden room. The room, where Fisher conducts his business at home, is furnished with bright chintz-covered sofas and chairs centered around a low glass table and overlooks the Fishers' pool and the eighth fairway of the Franklin Hills Country Club.

Wright sat across from him, and Fisher quietly said: "Joe, this is a situation, like others are going to be in your life, that can either destroy you or make you a stronger person. You have a lot of responsibility now. You're the oldest in your family [Wright had three sisters and a brother]. The ball is in your court. But I'll do anything I can to help you."

Wright was unaware of it, but this was a standard Fisher reaction to a problem, particularly one laced with tragedy. Fisher would offer a series of clichés — what technicians of the English language refer to as "dead metaphors." But because Fisher himself believed so fiercely in what he was saying, the metaphors were transformed into a layman's homily on conquering adversity. Fisher would sit back, stretch out his long legs, and, in his soft voice, pass along a folksy wisdom that might have sounded more appropriate coming from a nineteenth-century country lawyer than a present-day industrialist and investor. The effect was heightened by the deep furrows in Fisher's forehead, the sad expression in his dark eyes, and by the fact, which was not lost on Wright, that Fisher's power and wealth created a number of opportunities.

"I was stunned," recalls Wright. "Here he was, Max Fisher. His associates are presidents and prime ministers, senators and CEOs, and he was taking the time out to help a kid who rakes leaves. I'm not Jewish and this wasn't the United Foundation. [The help Fisher was offering] was not about flag-waving or fanfare. It was just a guy who cares about people."

That afternoon in the garden room, Wright, although embarrassed, explained to Fisher that he had developed a problem with drugs and that his grades were terrible.

"You've got to put that all behind you now," Fisher replied. "It's time to take the bull by the horns."

Wright returned to work at the Fishers' on weekends, and he talked regularly with Max about his plans. As a result, Wright says, he decided to attend Oakland Community College and "busted my ass to get into a good four-year school."

Wright was accepted at Michigan State. He was nervous about going, doubted that he could handle the more competitive scholastic requirements. Fisher encouraged him to enroll, and the Fisher Foundation paid for Wright's room and board, tuition and books.

"Given my family circumstances," Wright says, "there was no other way I could have gone to school without the money from the foundation. And Mr. Fisher was strict. He wanted nothing less than a B average out of me and he got it. But it wasn't a complete freebie. [To earn spending money], I continued working part-time for him. We would sit down every six weeks or so and he would question me about school and review my grades."

Wright graduated from Michigan State and, at Fisher's urging, decided to attend graduate school. Wright applied to the Detroit College of Law, and while his grades were adequate, Wright was concerned that his law-board scores were not high enough. And so Wright went to Fisher's office and told him about his concern.

"What do you want me to do about it?" Fisher asked.

"He knew," Wright says, "but he wouldn't let him take the indirect route. So I asked him, flat out, 'Can you help me?'"

Smiling, Fisher quipped: "I hope I don't have to build them a library."

"I don't think I'll need that much help," Wright said.

Fisher asked Wright for a Detroit School of Law brochure, and Wright handed one to him. Fisher scanned the list of trustees, recognized a name and had his assistant call him. Fisher took the phone and said to the trustee: "I've got a young man here who works for me and wants to go to your law school. I'd like you to talk to him. No, no, next week's no good. How about today? He's here now. I'll send him over to see you."

Wright was accepted by the Detroit School of Law. The Fisher Foundation paid for his tuition and books and loaned him money to cover his living expenses. Fisher continued to meet with Wright to discuss his academic career.

"I had gotten a poor grade," says Wright, "and I went to Mr. Fisher's office to tell him about it. I remember that I was very nervous. I was perspiring."

"Hey," Fisher said when he saw Wright, "you're sweating. You don't have to be nervous around me. I'm your friend. What happened? Did you flunk a course?"

"Yes," Wright answered.

"So take it over again," said Fisher. "And let me know how you make out."

"I got a B the second time," says Wright. "My motivation was that I didn't want to disappoint him. When I graduated from law school, he gave me a check for $500."

Joseph Wright went on to become a product-liability attorney at a prestigious Detroit law firm. The job, he is proud to say, he got on his own.

Explains Wright: "I wanted one day to be able to go back to Mr. Fisher and say: 'Look what you helped me accomplish.' I feel so much love for him it's unbelievable."

*　　*　　*

In biographical detail, the parallels between the lives of Fisher and Nixon are marked. Born five years apart (1908 and 1913), and growing up in small Quaker towns (Salem and Whittier), their boyhoods spanned the cusp of the era before technology altered the face of their country forever. These were — as purveyors of nostalgia assure us — the halcyon days of America, days of clear rushing streams and boys marching through woods with fishing poles fashioned from mop handles and string, genteel days so radically at odds with the nuclear age, when both men ascended toward the pinnacle of their power. Nixon's mother, Hannah, was a diligent homemaker, and his father, Frank, an industrious shopkeeper, much in the mold of Mollie and William Fisher. More than a half-century later, when Nixon wrote about his parents in his memoirs, he could well have been describing Fisher's perceptions of Mollie and William.

"My father," Nixon remembered, "was a scrappy, belligerent fighter. . . . He left me a respect for learning and hard work, and the will to keep fighting no matter what the odds. My mother loved me completely and selflessly, and her special legacy was . . . the determination never to despair."

Nixon and Fisher grew up working in their fathers' stores. As teenagers, both were enthusiastic athletes who found inspiration in the discipline of their high-school football coaches, who were active in school clubs and fraternities (frequently heading them), and who, due to the limited financial resources of their families, required scholarships and jobs to finish their educations. Both met with early success: by the age of forty Fisher was well en route to amassing his fortune; Nixon was vice president. Although certain aspects of their lives may have varied (Fisher was more athletic, Nixon more intellectual), the themes Leonard Garment mentioned — deprivation, turmoil, hard work and their belief in their ability to shape their futures — were interchangeable.

One could flip through the pages of a considerable catalogue of American men born between 1908 and 1913 who could recount journeys akin to Fisher's and Nixon's, from modest, quaint-and-nameless-town childhoods to a middle age that flourished in the urban halls of answered prayers and privilege. Therefore, it is not merely the background that formed their bond, but it is the analogous temperaments that came along for the ride, temperaments that engaged the concealed territories of each man's mind. Here, in these darker places, Fisher and Nixon were men more guarded than most. Regardless of the public necessities of their chosen professions, they nursed a passion for privacy, a secret love of secrets, devout in their belief that emotionally one should never tip one's hand. Thus, neither man had much tolerance for personal conflict; they found it excruciating. When challenged by a lacework of potentially explosive political complexities, their impulse was to sidestep nimbly to the wings, to tug on the cable and curtain backstage, giving their penchant for secrecy full rein.

In foreign affairs and the politicking within the American

Jewish community, this proclivity would prove to be a propitious match. However, in another arena, where Nixon was concerned, it also would underlie his resignation from office.

Nixon biographer Fawn Brodie, commenting on *Six Crises*, said that in the book she detected a "kind of terror" in Nixon's "fear of loss of control." It was a fear that Fisher shared. He had one steadfast rule in dealing with conflict, personal and professional: "You stay calm," Fisher says. "You have to control your emotions."

As to be expected of men who strive for control, Fisher and Nixon were generally guarded. Initially, what is most striking about this ingredient of their personalities is that since they played their emotional cards close to their vests, despite two decades of meetings and lunches and letter writing and conversations over the phone, they knew little of each other's background. Whatever bonds abided between them abided in silence, remaining wholly intuitive. The similarities between their lives were too remarkable to ignore, and yet before each began reading about the other they were unaware of them. (In 1981, when Nixon was told by an interviewer that Fisher had grown up in a Quaker town in Ohio, much like the town Nixon himself had lived in, Nixon was astounded.) It was not until May 1978, when Nixon sent Fisher a copy of *RN*, that Fisher's knowledge of Nixon's past exceeded what the press had written about him. And the same was true with Nixon's knowledge of Fisher. In January 1982, Nixon, traveling to Florida, dashed off a note to Fisher that demonstrated just how uninformed he was about his friend's background.

"On a flight to Miami," Nixon wrote, "I picked up the airline magazine & saw the fine [profile of] you from *Forbes*. What a career you have had! My only reservation is whether the $100,000,000 [estimate of your net worth] might be on the low side in view of your Horatio Alger successes in your business career!"

Predictably, another aspect of each man's seeking emotional discipline was that Fisher and Nixon had a potent dislike of personal conflict, both having learned to dislike it as children while encountering their fathers' anger.

Nixon recalled: "It was [my father's] temper that impressed me most as a small child. . . . He was a strict and stern disciplinarian. . . . Perhaps my own aversion to personal confrontation dates back to these early recollections."

Fisher, too, as a youngster, preferred to dodge William's wrath — especially his criticism — as opposed to meeting it directly. As an adult, Fisher was known to go to great lengths to avoid open conflict. His reputation as a consensus builder within the American Jewish community was founded on his need to view events in their least divisive light. Better, he thought, to solve everything off in the wings. Better yet, to cast everything that appears to be a battle as nothing more than a misunderstanding or, at worst, a mild difference of opinion among friends. This was, in Fisher's case, the foundation of his pragmatism.

"I always see good in people," Fisher says. "You can look at a person and if you look at his faults, he's a devil; if you look at his virtues, he's a saint. [But] there's no such thing as a devil or a saint. I am an optimist and focus on the best side of the people. The result is — I get along. You know, people have fixed ideas about a person. 'Oh,' they'll say, 'that guy's screwy.' I take [people] on balance. *As long as I get along with them.*"

The portraits that emerge from this sketch of Fisher and Nixon are of two men who are controlled and reticent. Yet Nixon pursued the most visible office in the world; Fisher ventured out on a smaller — although highly visible — scale in the Jewish community. The politically pragmatic basis of the Fisher-Nixon alliance is contained within this paradox.

Nixon once remarked that the media portrayed the late President Herbert Hoover as "sour, stiff, and sullen," but the truth, Nixon claimed, was that Hoover "was an introvert in an extrovert's profession." Nixon's image in the press approximated Hoover's, and it may be that Nixon, in observing Hoover, was divulging something of himself. It has been said of Nixon that he was a president with the soul of a secretary of state, and this assertion is not limited to Nixon's love of foreign policy. Instead, it captures the aura of privacy, of distance, that Nixon maintained — if not in an ivory tower then in numerous private offices.

Because occupying a leadership platform in the American Jewish community is a far narrower stage than the Oval Office, Fisher's distance was more complete than Nixon's. He moved through Washington unobserved, with rare exception, by those outside the inner sanctums of government. Fisher was so secretive that even Marjorie could not track him down when calls came to their Michigan home. Maybe, she would tell the caller, Max was in Palm Beach; try him there. No, he wasn't in Florida. How about New York? No. Washington? No again. Well, he's not supposed to leave for Israel until next week.

Even associates who attended Fisher's confidential talks with leaders were uninformed about other avenues of influence that Fisher walked. Jacob Stein, for one, who as chairman of the Conference of Presidents of Major American Jewish Organizations participated in many private meetings with Fisher and Henry Kissinger on Israel and Soviet Jewry, had no idea that Fisher was also back-channeling on the same issues with Attorney General John N. Mitchell. The reason that Stein did not know: Fisher never told him. Seymour Milstein, an old and trusted friend who along with Fisher would guide United Brands, was aware that Fisher had contacts in politics, but never realized the level of his involvement until one morning, while sitting with Fisher in a New York hotel suite, there was a knock on the door. When Fisher opened it, Israeli Prime Minister Menachem Begin was in the doorway. He had come to talk.

Throughout each one of his years spent in secrecy, when the specialized fruits of his efforts were devoured by the more substantial appetites of history and credited to others, Fisher seriously contemplated pursuing public life. He was offered ambassadorships and Cabinet posts, and he regularly refused them. But to stand before the footlights was a constant temptation, a rainbow just out of reach.

"I thought about it a lot," says Fisher. "I could have had a public career. But I turned it down. I'm not sure why."

There are some readily identifiable components to his resistance. There is Fisher's innate shyness and his fear — mastered in his fifties — of addressing crowds. Then there are the random humiliations of public office, the rude invasion of privacy. Fisher had worked too hard to control his world; publicity, in the form of unwanted scrutiny and criticism by the press, would have forced him to relinquish his control, and this was not the sort of life he envisioned. Finally, and what may be the underpinning of his refusal, was that Fisher believed his obscurity, his reveling in secrets as the insider's insider, was the source of his enduring and singular power, what gave him the flexibility to move from president to president, from Washington to Jerusalem, from the issues of arms shipments to the fluctuations in Israeli-American relations. He was never too closely identified with one president or prime minister or secretary of state or senator because hardly anyone beyond a select circle could identify him at all. His diplomatic ghost ship was exclusive, with a passenger list of one.

And so it was that Nixon, a public man longing for privacy, and Fisher, a private man with his eye on center stage, became friends. Yet in the early 1960s, the world knew little of their friendship. Fisher was far more identified with another presidential hopeful. In fact, at his "last press conference," Nixon commented that the most significant results of the 1962 election were the Republican gubernatorial winners in four major states — Nelson Rockefeller in New York, William Scranton in Pennsylvania, James J. Rhodes in Ohio and George Romney in Michigan.

Fisher had helped pave the way to Lansing for Romney; he had, more accurately, been responsible for financing it. And in one of those quirks of history — one of those puzzling coincidences that seems entirely logical from the distance of two decades — Romney also would become a thread in the Fisher-Nixon story, a strand inextricably woven within the tale.

Chapter 6

FISHER AND ROMNEY
AND THE LEGACY
OF THE SIX-DAY WAR

MAX FISHER MET George Romney in 1962. Perhaps by then it was only a matter of time before Romney was approached to enter politics. As political writer Theodore W. White observed, Romney could have been a candidate ordered up out of "Hollywood's Central Casting," and in the aftermath of the 1960 Kennedy-Nixon debates, politicos were starting to understand the magic that television possessed to sway voters.

Romney was a natural for television. His all-American, square-jawed good looks were accentuated by his silvered shock of hair and laser-blue eyes. He had worked his way through Latter-Day Saints University in Salt Lake City, Utah, and served as a Mormon missionary in Europe. By 1938, at the age of thirty-one, Romney was lobbying for the Automobile Manufacturers Association. Impressed by Romney's record, George Mason, chairman of Nash-Kelvinator, hired him in 1948 as his special assistant. American Motors was formed through the Nash-Kelvinator-Hudson merger and when Mason died, Romney took over the corporation.

By 1959, American Motors, on the strength of its compact car, the Rambler, was showing profits of $60 million. Michigan was not doing as well. The state general fund was so depleted that 26,000 state employees could not cash their paychecks. The problem was an outmoded state constitution and a feud between Democratic Governor G. Mennen Williams and the Republican-controlled Legislature. Soapy Williams, so named because his maternal grandfather founded the Mennen Company, a soap and pharmaceutical firm, was elected governor for six consecutive terms between 1948 and 1960, a record unequaled in the United States. (In 1960, when Williams accepted a Kennedy appointment as assistant secretary of state for African affairs, he was replaced by his machine's choice, John B. Swainson.) Williams was noted for his trademark crew cut, green polka-dot bow ties and his avid backing of a state tax on personal income and corporate profits, which Republican legislators opposed, producing a stalemate.

To break the deadlock, Romney organized a statewide committee, Citizens for Michigan, whose purpose was to direct public action toward "a more responsible political climate." He gathered a coterie of powerful men, among them Robert S. McNamara, head of Ford Motor Company and later secretary of defense under Presidents Kennedy and Johnson. Through the efforts of Citizens for Michigan, voters approved a referendum in favor of a constitutional convention. "Con-Con" convened in Lansing in October of 1961, with Romney as a delegate, and when the rewriting was complete, Michigan had a constitution that was lauded as one of the outstanding charters in the nation.

For years, people had urged Romney to pursue politics. Richard Nixon was one; Robert McNamara was another. And when Romney finally determined his course, he did so in a way that was consistent with his Mormon faith. On February 8, 1962, he began praying and fasting for twenty-four hours. When he was done, he declared that he would seek the Republican gubernatorial nomination. A campaign manager was selected, Arthur G. Elliott Jr., the chairman of the Republican organization in Oakland County, home to many of Michigan's well-heeled Republicans, including Max Fisher. Signing up a high-powered fund-raiser was a priority. Richard VanDusen, a young attorney on the rise who was among Romney's inner circle, was given the assignment of recruiting one.

VanDusen and Romney agreed that Jason Honigman, a

Detroit lawyer and former Republican candidate for Michigan attorney general, would be the best choice for the job. And so it was, in the winter of 1962, that VanDusen and Romney met with Honigman and invited him to sign on as finance chairman.

Honigman had one problem: "I hate asking people for money," he told them.

But, Honigman added, he had a friend and client, Max Fisher, who would be terrific. Max had gumption, Honigman said, and was not apprehensive about asking people for money or handing them back their checks when he thought they were not being as munificent as possible. Romney replied that he had heard of Fisher through his wife, Lenore, who was familiar with Fisher's work at Detroit's United Foundation, and he would like to talk to him. Honigman promised that he would get in touch with Fisher.

Years before, Honigman and Fisher had struck up a friendship at the Franklin Hills Country Club. By 1962, Honigman was handling much of Fisher's legal work. Beyond business, the two men shared a casual attitude toward golf. Despite the snowbound Michigan winters, they conceded that in the interest of health they should exercise. So, on occasional weekends, while waiting for a football game to start on TV, they tramped behind Fisher's house to the course at Franklin Hills and proceeded to drive, chip and putt through the snow.

After talking with Honigman, Fisher says, "I was intrigued. Romney was a popular figure and he had a great reputation for integrity. He was controversial, but he was right about calling those big American cars 'gas-guzzling dinosaurs' and years ahead of his time. I thought he was top-notch."

Fisher was scheduled to fly to a board meeting at Marathon Oil in Findlay, Ohio, and he arranged to meet Romney at a hangar-office out at Pontiac Airport, a private airfield.

"We visited out there for an hour," says Romney. "Max wanted to know my basic philosophy and I told him. I was impressed by him and thought he would make an excellent finance chairman. But it wasn't a case of his selling me; I was selling him."

"We just hit it off," says Fisher of that meeting. As for Romney's qualifications, Fisher felt that he might do for Michigan what he had done at American Motors. And his moderate attitudes also appealed to Fisher. There was Romney's position on race — one that was diametrically opposed to the Mormon church, which claimed, according to Theodore White, "that blacks were eternally consigned to outer darkness in the Hall of God." Ignoring the political backlash, Romney called for the dismissal of Richard Durant, a key Republican leader in Michigan, because he had affiliated himself with the John Birch Society. Romney also directed his campaign staff to reach out to the black community. Albert B. Chennault, a black builder, would serve as his treasurer, and Charles M. Tucker Jr., a black business executive who had been active in the civil-rights movement, would oversee race relations.

The basis of Fisher's support for Romney was multifaceted, encompassing more than their communal nest under the moderate wing of the Republican Party. In May, already three months into the campaign, Fisher told one Romney contributor: "The way things have been going in Michigan, we are certainly due for some changes." In light of this remark it is probably safe to say that Fisher would have aided any middle-of-the-road Republican gubernatorial candidate. But Fisher recognized that Romney was not merely any candidate: he had a rugged, apple-pie charisma. His metamorphosis from blue-collar worker to head of American Motors, combined with the triumph of the Rambler, had the quality of a fairy tale. His picture had graced the cover of *Time* and he had been favorably profiled in numerous national magazines. Undeniably, he had potential for office outside of Michigan — perhaps the presidency. And as nebulous as Fisher's political ambitions were in 1962, it is unlikely that they were confined to his home state.

First, though, Fisher had to win the approval of Romney's closest advisers — Elliott and VanDusen — and another meeting was scheduled a few days after the Fisher-Romney chat at Pontiac. On a bitter cold evening, Fisher rode to Rom-

ney's house in Bloomfield Hills. Elliott and VanDusen were
there and the four men sat by the living-room fireplace.
Elliott, the single party regular in the group, was impressed by
Fisher's practical questions on the mechanics of Romney's
campaign structure and policy. Elliott might have been less
impressed if he knew that, according to Fisher, he was posing
the questions to see if signing on would be — borrowing an
expression from the oil business — "pouring money down a
dry hole."

Upon concluding that Romney would be a viable candidate, Fisher stood in front of the fireplace and quietly said: "I
believe in leadership giving," a phrase that was new to Romney and his men, but one that Fisher used regularly when
fund-raising. "I don't think I can effectively go out and ask
people for money if I haven't given, and if the candidate hasn't
given, and if the people close to the candidate haven't given.
So I want your check, George. And I want your check, Dick,
and I want your check, Art. Right now."

The three men complied. Then Fisher wrote a check of
his own — for $20,000. From then on, even before the official
announcement of his position, Fisher was accepted into Romney's inner circle, filling a role beyond his duties as finance
chairman.

Richard VanDusen explains: "At the outset, Max indicated that if he was going to be responsible for raising money he
felt that it was important for him to have some participation
in how it was spent. That gave him access to discussions on
campaign direction and strategy. Max was very wise in the
way he used that access. His suggestions were good and he
didn't come in and throw his weight around. He had a nice
sense of discretion as to when his comments were appropriate
and when he should listen."

On March 28, 1962, George Romney formally announced
that he was appointing Fisher as his finance chairman.

"Getting Max," says VanDusen, "was a real coup. I don't
know that we appreciated at the time how much of a coup it
was. He was a consummate pro."

Fisher's professionalism was essential — as was his need

to direct his area of responsibility alone — since Romney, other than appearing at functions, wished to remain aloof from raising money. "I didn't want to pay attention to [the fund-raising]," Romney says, "because that left me in a freer position politically. I had an understanding with Max that he would raise it properly with no involvement on my part. And he got it done." Fisher constructed a Republican fund-raising network from the ground up. Remer Tyson, a national political correspondent for Knight-Ridder newspapers who followed Fisher for over a decade while at the *Detroit Free Press*, recalled that at the time "the Republican Party in Michigan was Max Fisher and a telephone." Fisher circled the state, speaking on behalf of Romney and assembling his machine. He gathered small groups, building upon them, pyramiding support, and he discovered that political fund-raising was not dissimilar from chasing charitable contributions.

"You've got to be a giver yourself," says Fisher. "But the real secret is to get people to give without feeling fleeced. If people disappoint me, if they don't give as much as I think they should, it troubles me, but it doesn't destroy my faith in them. Their contributions may be small, but it's better than nothing. Sure, I'd like them to give me a big piece of pie. And some people will give you a big piece; some a little. It takes a combination to put the whole thing together."

A group that had the potential to cut out some larger slices for Romney was the leadership of the Big Three — Chrysler, Ford and General Motors. The problem was that when Romney was at American Motors, he attacked their control of the car market and they considered this an ungrateful response to their having encouraged him to produce the Rambler back when American Motors was floundering. (The notion of producing a compact was partially an outgrowth of conversations Romney held with Harlow H. Curtice, president of General Motors.) Consequently, in the beginning, with the exception of Henry Ford II, the Big Three leaders were not eager to contribute to Romney. Fisher knew of the difficulty, and had even heard a story from an acquaintance, Elton F. MacDonald, who charged that Romney's behavior toward General Motors surpassed ingratitude. In the 1950s, MacDonald said, Romney had "begged Harlow Curtice to stop General Motors from taking any of [American Motors'] dealers — which Curtice did."

But Fisher felt that Big Three support was indispensable to a Romney victory and so, he says, "I wooed them."

A GM executive, who asked not to be identified, told *The Detroit News*, "We know Romney's bent on dissolving the big motor companies, but most of us have contributed something to his [campaign] anyway. Max Fisher . . . [has] gotten to just about everybody."

Fisher says that he gave the Big Three leaders his standard, common-sense fund-raising pitch. "I went to see them face-to-face," says Fisher, "which is required when you're dealing with that level of leadership. And I told them: 'Look, the Democrats have been in control of Michigan for fourteen years. They have the unions behind them; they're very strong. But Republicans — Romney — will be better for industry, better for you. And he needs your help.' That's how I convinced them to donate to George['s campaign]."

Fisher may have been underestimating the value of his personal involvement. It was not false modesty, but rather his predilection for not digging at causes that were buried too far beneath the surface. According to Henry Ford II, Fisher's ability to raise funds for Romney was not solely based on his entreaty to the economic sensibilities of corporate leaders.

"Let me describe the influence of Max Fisher this way," says Ford. "There are some things you do only because it's Max Fisher asking you to do them."

Anteing up for Romney would appear to be one of them. Among those who contributed was General Motors executive Semon E. "Bunkie" Knudsen, who in the early 1960s transformed GM's stodgy Pontiac line into some of the hottest cars on the market. Knudsen, says Fisher, was suitably forthcoming: he handed over a check for $5,000. Fisher augmented his tête-à-têtes with a series of dinners, the bread-and-butter of major-league fund-raising. Among other places, he organized them at the Bloomfield Hills Country Club, the Knollwood

Country Club in West Bloomfield Hills, the Little Club in Grosse Point and at the country club where he belonged, Franklin Hills.

VanDusen, who attended many of the dinners, had never seen anything like it.

"I remember the dinner at Franklin Hills vividly," he says. "It was my first exposure to that high-powered method of fund-raising. I had heard about it, but never experienced it firsthand. Max got the group warmed up by telling them how important it was [to have Romney elected governor] and what a great opportunity we had to bring Michigan back, to get the economy on the right track again. Max obviously had everything primed. Because then Al Borman, who owned the [Farmer Jack] supermarket chain, stood up and gave his 'banana peddler' speech. Borman talked about what a marvelous country America is that it allows a humble banana peddler to rise to economic success. 'This country has been good to me,' Borman said. 'And this state has been good to me. And I will give X.' I don't remember the amount Borman pledged, but it was substantial. And then, one after the other, everybody rose to make their contributions. I found myself so moved that I wrote another check. I did not get up and say, 'Here I come down the sawdust trail.' But I really was so caught up in the occasion that even though I had already made a contribution I considered substantial, I made another one."

Elliott, too, was amazed. "I was at a fund-raising dinner Max had at the Knollwood Country Club in West Bloomfield Hills," says Elliott. "Max gets up and gives his very sincere, very nice hearts-and-flowers talk. Then Romney spoke. After that, Max worked the room. People stood — I'm sure Max had set some of this up beforehand — and said what they would give. I was stunned. You have to remember: this was 1962, when a $100 contribution to a politician was considered significant. And yet in about a half-hour, Max raised over $100,000. I had never seen this type of fund-raising or these kind of results. It was revolutionary."

Supplementing these appeals, Fisher contacted everyone

within his rapidly growing reach. His social and business life, his Jewish and nonsectarian fund-raising, had always dovetailed, and now he took advantage of the connections. Al Taubman, the Sucher family, builders George Seyburn and Louis Berry, oil man Harold McClure and hundreds more — all were solicited and came through for Fisher. And he did not stop there. Even when a friend made a contribution, Fisher nudged them a step further. Using their display of interest as a fulcrum, he enlisted them in his cause. Edward C. Levy Sr. is a good illustration of how this practice worked. Levy, who lived across the street from the Fishers on Fairway Hills Drive, contributed $1,000 to Romney's campaign. Upon thanking Levy for his donation, Fisher notified him that he should now consider himself "a committee of one whose goal it is to raise at least $1,000 from your friends and associates." In the event Levy required a little help, Fisher sent him a pack of pledge cards. Nor did Fisher limit his endeavors to Michigan. He went to his old friend Nathan Appleman in New York, and to California, soliciting Leonard Friedman of Beverly Hills, who ran a highly successful steel business. Fisher knew Friedman through their fund-raising efforts on behalf of Jewish causes. He told Friedman that he was so enthusiastic about Romney he had taken on the job of finance manager and "of course we will require a tremendous amount of money to combat the great reserves of the unions in financing politics." Next, Fisher shifted to Dallas, Texas. He contacted oil man Jake L. Hamon, who responded with a generous check, saying that the contribution should be made in Fisher's name because "a Texan in Michigan is a liability. I am for [Romney] but don't care for any credit in this matter."

It was the sort of discretion Fisher appreciated, a discretion for which he would become noted. He told Hamon that Romney wanted to thank him personally for his check, "but in deference to your remarks will wait until he meets you."

Throughout the campaign, the focus of Romney's attack on Governor Swainson was the alarming loss of jobs in Michigan. Between 1956 and 1962, said Romney, 300,000 workers had deserted the labor force. Swainson countered by having

President Kennedy and Vice President Johnson swing through Michigan to campaign for him, a strategy that backfired, for it provided Romney with an opening for some first-rate sniping. "We'd better get leadership," he commented, "that doesn't need . . . coattails to get re-elected."

Fisher had to keep at his task until November, and when he was finished he had raised just under a million dollars, a sum that, according to Arthur Elliott, Romney and his staff considered "amazing."

"With Max in charge," says Elliott, "we never ran out of money and we always paid our bills."

On Election Day, Romney squeaked past Swainson, capturing 1,419,046 votes to the incumbent's 1,340,549. Ballot-splitting by Democrats was cited as the basis for Romney's victory. The moderate Republican had bitten deeper into the vote of labor and the black community than any Republican had been able to do since 1948.

*　　*　　*

Romney's win gave Fisher what he had hoped for: a working relationship with a high-profile governor. Two years later, Romney won again, but the Republican Party, as Fisher, Nixon and Romney had feared, was reeling from Goldwater's decisive defeat in his 1964 race for the presidency against Johnson. (LBJ outdistanced Goldwater by more than 16 million popular votes, and in the Electoral College by a vote of 486 to 52.) The party itself was split into warring factions on the right and left, with no candidate to bring them together in the center.

"I know," Nixon wrote Fisher after the election, "there are some who believe that a public repudiation of Goldwater would be good for the 'image' of the party. The argument goes that the number of hard-core Goldwater voters is only four or five million and that 1964 proved that this group cannot elect a candidate. However, the converse of this proposition is that while the hard-core supporters cannot elect a candidate, they can certainly defeat one [in 1968] if they decide to sit it out."

There appeared to be no Republican who could seriously

challenge Johnson in the next presidential election. But then in 1966, Romney was resoundingly re-elected again, which thrust him into the national spotlight, and pundits — Fisher among them — were describing the governor as "presidential timber." In the '66 race, Romney defeated Zolton Ferency, the Democratic state chairman, by a 568,000-vote margin, astonishing observers by capturing 50 percent of the labor vote and 34 percent of the black vote, constituencies normally hostile to Republicans but warming to Romney's (and Nelson Rockefeller's and Jacob Javits's) liberal Republicanism. Since the national machine of both parties endeavors to elect not only a president, but also a confederation of candidates to advance that president's agenda, Romney attracted the attention of Republican kingmakers because he had long coattails: Michigan Republicans won the five congressional seats they were seeking and sent Robert P. Griffin to the U.S. Senate.

Nor did Romney's victory go unnoticed by the national press corps. The Michigan election was held on November 8, 1966. By December 11, even before Romney was sworn in for his third term, the *Detroit Free Press* was publishing the results of a nationwide survey, conducted by a team of eight Knight Newspaper reporters from around the country. The reporters had toured thirty states from Maine to California, talking to nearly 200 Republican governors, senators, party officials, county chairmen and political experts. And what the reporters discovered was very good news for Romney: "The dynamic governor of Michigan," wrote *Free Press* Washington staffer Robert S. Boyd, "has it within his power to capture the Republican presidential nomination in 1968." The survey also uncovered three major impediments to a successful Romney candidacy: the governor had to get out of Lansing and campaign; he had to boost his stature in the area of foreign policy; and he had to lay to rest the doubts about his personality — his tendency to appear holier-than-thou. Fisher felt this personality trait was an outgrowth of Romney's genuine commitment to his Mormon ideals, a deep faith that was sometimes mistaken for imperiousness. Others, though, did not consider this idealism sufficient when selecting a president. "Being a super Boy Scout," *The Washington Star* said of Romney, "is not enough."

There was a fourth requirement for a victorious candidate, though this one was not unique to Romney. Jim Farley, one of the masterminds behind FDR's 1932 presidential victory, identified the key to winning elections by remarking: "There are three requirements for a political campaign. The first is money; the second is money; and the third is money." And in this pivotal area, the Knight Newspaper survey judged that Romney was in excellent shape. The survey said: "Romney's chief money man, Detroit oil magnate Max M. Fisher, heads the United Jewish Appeal and is one of the most influential men in American Jewry. Romney, incidentally, addressed that organization in New York Thursday night [December 8]."

Fisher insisted that Romney speak to the UJA. During the past four years, he and Romney had reassembled the state's Republican machinery, establishing a dynasty of moderate Republicans that held the Statehouse into the 1980s. In the process, Fisher tucked himself into an influential niche within Michigan's Republican Party. From his job as Romney's finance chairman in 1962, he moved on to the job of Republican state finance chairman, a position he held until 1969. He served as a delegate to the 1964 Republican National Convention in San Francisco, and was soon to begin heading up the finance committee for Romney's campaign for the presidency.

The dinner at which Fisher presented Romney was no run-of-the-mill UJA reception. UJA executive vice president Rabbi Herbert Friedman said that invitations had been restricted to "a very thin layer of the apex of American Jewish life." (So many people wished to attend that the site had to be switched to the Grand Ballroom of the Waldorf-Astoria Hotel from a smaller room at the New York Hilton.). Over 600 guests sat at tables set with gold cloths and ivory candles, and danced to the music of the Lester Lanin orchestra. Despite the evening's frivolity, and its resemblance to an aristocrat's ball, the purpose was to raise money, large amounts of it, for the affair was what is known on the fund-raising circuit as a "call-dinner." After a meal of rock Cornish hen, the doors were

closed to the press, and guests were called by name from the
dais to announce their contributions. The minimum pledge
was $10,000, a sum *The New York Times* declared "a record."
The exact size of each donation was not revealed, but numerous individual gifts were said to exceed $333,000.

Romney was impressed. In his speech, he saluted the generosity of the guests: "American citizens, armed with this
sense of responsibility, and blessed with greater material prosperity than any nation in history must give leadership in
rebuilding and healing a torn and damaged world."

It was Romney's pet sermon, one he had been preaching
since he announced the formation of Citizens for Michigan
before he ran for governor. It was also an approach favored by
Jewish self-help organizations. And so Romney had to wonder: if this group can raise this much for a cause, then what
could they do for a moderate Republican presidential contender who agreed with them?

For Fisher, as a fund-raiser and chairman of the UJA, providing Romney with an expanded Jewish forum was a logical
move. Beginning in 1962, he had canvassed Detroit's Jewish
community biannually for Romney's gubernatorial races and
the community had delivered. Since Romney was now contemplating national office, it followed that Fisher would present him to a more formidable national body.

But December 8, 1966, marked a more significant
moment in Fisher's political quest. There was more at stake
here: the Oval Office, not the statehouse, and the likelihood
of a position of consequence for Fisher, an opportunity for
input beyond local issues. In Fisher's case, this meant problems dear to the heart of the American Jewish community; it
meant Israel. The circumstances were transparently political.
Fisher was arranging a betrothal. In short, bringing George
Romney to address "the apex of Jewish American life" was
Max Fisher's first overt attempt to politicize American Jewry
on behalf of the Republican Party. What made it such a monumental step for Fisher was his timing, because by December
1966, when he introduced Romney at the Waldorf-Astoria,
American Jews were on the brink of becoming more cohesive

— and therefore a more potent lobbying and voting bloc — than ever before in their history.

The opportunity was created by a serious threat to Israel's survival. During the following year, Egyptian President Gamel Abdel Nasser closed the Straits of Tiran to Israeli shipping, then ousted the United Nations Emergency Force from the Sinai, replacing them with the Egyptian Army. Israel petitioned President Johnson to uphold Eisenhower's promise, made in 1956, to keep the Straits open, and while LBJ did not deny U.S. commitments to the freedom of shipping, he advised the Israelis to wait for an international flotilla to break the blockade. Johnson had his own problems: opposition to the war in Vietnam was escalating daily, as though in proportion to the rising American body count, and his attention was centered on his own waning popularity and besieged foreign policy.

* * *

On May 26, Fisher was sailing in the Greek Isles with Marjorie, and Henry Ford II and his second wife, Cristina, when a call came from Herbert Friedman, executive vice president of the UJA. Things were approaching the boiling point, Friedman said, and he and Fisher were needed in Israel. Fisher immediately flew to Tel Aviv, landing at Lydda.

In a speech to the UJA, Fisher later recalled his arrival in Israel:

"The one moment I shall never forget," he said, "is the moment we stepped from the plane when the people at the airport and the people we met everywhere saw us and said, 'They are here! The American Jews are here! They have come!' In a critical hour — in your name — I was able to bring a message of complete support and I was able to assure them that American Jews would give full help. I was never more privileged and never more honored."

Fisher was taken to a meeting with Prime Minister Levi Eshkol and his Cabinet that lasted six hours. When they finished, Eshkol escorted him out of the office; it was then that the prime minister introduced Fisher to an Israeli with whom much of his later work between Washington and Jerusalem would be entwined: Yitzhak Rabin.

Rabin, who was serving as chief of staff of the defense forces at the time, recalls: "There was a tension period prior to the Six-Day War. It was during what we call the *hamtana* — the waiting period. Eshkol was talking with leaders of the Jewish communities, especially from the United States. The leaders came over to learn about the situation. It was after midnight that I arrived. Max came out of a talk with Eshkol and it was the first time I met him. We had a little talk in which I explained to Max the awful situation of the Arab countries mobilizing around Israel and the almost inevitable consequences of it. Political negotiations had not produced any results. I told Max that even though we had lost the strategic surprise element, at least the tactical surprise element must be retained by us. It was a relatively short conversation because I had to go to sleep."

Fisher listened to the assessments of how much money would be required during and after the fighting. "The estimates," he said later, were "beyond belief." Harold Berry, who was vice president of the Fisher-New Center Company, remembers encountering Fisher at a board meeting of the corporation after his visit to Israel. Fisher was obviously distressed. The exhaustion of his traveling was etched on his face, deepening the furrows of his forehead, the lines around his eyes and mouth. When the meeting was finished, Berry walked over to Fisher and asked him how he was feeling. Fisher shrugged.

"Max," Berry said, "what's going on in Israel?"

Fisher gazed at the younger man. Then he said: "There's going to be war."

On June 5, 1967, when the Six-Day War broke out, Fisher was in Detroit. He scheduled a fast fund-raising session at a friend's house. Then he flew to New York to oversee the national fund-raising from UJA headquarters, and he found himself in the midst of what will be remembered as one of the American Jewish community's finest hours. Although the majority of local communities had recently completed their annual UJA drives prior to the war (raising $65 million), emergency funds flowered and money poured in. Fisher, for all of his experience with fund drives, was astounded. He later described what transpired to *The Jerusalem Post*: "I just can't emphasize enough this unity of the leadership of all the communities. Everybody had to give up their particular plans to raise more for Israel. It was unprecedented. There is a much deeper feeling for Jewish causes among American Jews than some people realize." Synagogues froze their expansion funds; businessmen applied for personal loans and donated the proceeds to the UJA. In fifteen minutes, $15 million was raised at a New York luncheon. In Boston, fifty families contributed $2.5 million. Overnight, the Jews of St. Louis raised $1.2 million; those in Cleveland in excess of $3 million.

Fisher entered into a round of speech making and fundraising. He spoke at a UJA Big Gifts meeting at the Americana Hotel in New York and from a nationally televised hookup from UJA headquarters. The UJA had sent a delegation to Israel to witness the effects of the war, and across the United States, in city after city, Jews now listened to the report. Then Fisher came on again. "It is clear," he said, "we must continue as we began — with full vigor. This means that every community, every leader, every worker, every Jew must dedicate themselves to raising every last possible dollar."

The success of the Israel Emergency Fund exceeded any other previous campaign in the history of the American Jewish community. Within the initial month, $100 million rolled in; in September, the figure passed $180 million with an additional $100 million worth of Israel bonds purchased. In all, during 1967, between the regular and emergency campaigns, American Jews raised $240 million in donations and $190 million in bonds.

The stunning Israeli victory over the Arab armies resulted in more than a torrent of funds. A Zionist priority was immigration, *aliyah*. On the eve of the war, in a U.S. Supreme Court decision, *Efroyin* v. *Rusk*, the justices reversed precedent, holding that Congress did not possess the power to deprive Americans of their citizenship without their consent. (The issue arose because an American citizen had voted in an Israeli election.) Now, in light of this reversal, Americans could hold dual citizenship, Israeli and American, and Israel's government quickly revised its immigration laws to enable Americans to obtain Israeli citizenship without having to give up their American rights. In the wake of this decision and the war, the number of American immigrants to Israel jumped nearly 50 percent, while temporary residency doubled.

The Six-Day War had a long-term energizing effect on Jews throughout the United States. Norman Podhoretz, editor of *Commentary*, explains that up until 1967 "a certain degree of [American Jewish support for Israel] remained reluctant. . . . The old anti-Zionist doctrines might have been consigned to the trash can of history, but the sentiments that had accompanied them still fluttered in many a Jewish heart. Mostly they took the form of a disposition to blame Israel for the trouble it was in with the Arabs. . . . Some of us can still remember . . . the almost vindictive relish with which certain former non-Zionists joined the Eisenhower administration in pressuring Israel to retreat from the Sinai [in 1956]. We can also remember how eagerly many of these same people rushed to condemn the seizure of Eichmann by Israel as a violation of international law. But not even this kind of thing could manage to survive the Six-Day War. . . . Confronted with Nasser's explicit threat to drive [Israel's] Jewish inhabitants into the sea, and faced with a world prepared to watch him do it, the Jews of America went through a kind of mass conversion to Zionism. . . . Thus did Israel now truly become the 'religion' of American Jews."

Fisher was quick to recognize the change. Four months after the fighting ended, he was in Israel. He was awarded Bar-Ilan University's first honorary doctorate and then, later, at the Tel Aviv Hilton, he spoke at the Prime Minister's Dinner of the UJA's thirteenth study mission. In a speech entitled "From the Heights of June," Fisher said: "From June 5 through June 10, [Israeli] Defense Forces and Israel's people changed the Middle East. But, in the same month of June,

American Jews changed all ideas of their love for Israel — all estimates of what they are prepared to do for its brave people. To our great joy, it was our young men and women, so many of whom you see here, who made it crystal clear that the cause of Israel's people is their own great cause as well."

All of this — the renaissance of pride, the flourishing cohesiveness among Jews in the United States with the security of Israel at its core, Romney's front-running and Fisher's role in the governor's budding campaign, the open field for the Republican nomination for the presidency coupled with LBJ's plummeting popularity — coincided with Fisher's own rise as the symbolic head of the American Jewish community.

By now, Fisher was an established force in numerous major national Jewish organizations from — alphabetically — the American Jewish Joint Distribution Committee to the United Jewish Appeal. The perception of Fisher as the leader of this newly invigorated American Jewish polity, along with his seat in Romney's inner circle, increased his visibility and was beginning to draw attention. Roger Kahn (later famous as the author of *The Boys of Summer*, his tale of the Brooklyn Dodgers then and now) was, in between 1966 and 1967, working on *The Passionate People*, a study of what it means to be a Jew in America. Kahn was particularly interested in anti-Semitism and came to Detroit to interview Fisher. In his book, Kahn, after cataloguing Fisher's business triumphs and multifaceted contributions to Detroit, commented, "On the way to his fortune, Max Fisher became a devout Zionist." Kahn then quoted a conservative automobile executive. " 'To tell you the truth,'" said the executive, "'I respect [Fisher] for it. I respect almost everything about [him]. He's a straightforward guy. Nothing devious about him. You never have to wonder how he stands. . . . He's done a lot to open the eyes around here to what kind of people the nicer type of Jew can be.'"

Leaving aside that dubious homage, Kahn moved on to Denver, Colorado. And it was there, in a city that Kahn characterized as "completely and rigidly separatist" with respect to Christians and Jews, that the author unearthed the deeper meaning of Fisher's developing importance to the Jewish community. "A point about *our* town," a local stockbroker told Kahn, "is that we've never once had a major national Jewish leadership figure like Max Fisher here. Maybe that's why things are the way they are."

If Fisher's star was ascending over the national Jewish community, it had already climbed to exaggerated heights in Michigan. During the Six-Day War, Jews in Ann Arbor convened to raise emergency funds for Israel. Professor William Haber of the University of Michigan, who chaired the gathering, recalls: "We assembled on the second night of the war. The whole [Jewish] community was at Temple Beth Israel; the place was packed. A man who usually only gave $500 [as a yearly donation to the UJA] suddenly sprang up and said, 'Mr. Chairman, I rise to make an announcement: I am prepared to give $20,000 on the condition that you get Max Fisher to get a tanker and fill it with oil and break the blockade at the Straits of Tiran.'"

Haber says: "Here's a meeting in Ann Arbor and a guy who probably never met Max Fisher. But Max is *the* symbol. Sure, Max Fisher can get a tanker, and sure Max Fisher would know how to put oil in it, and he even had enough influence to break open the Straits of Tiran. What are we doing just sitting here and talking, the guy wanted to know. I'll give you the money for the oil; let Max get the tanker. That's the symbolism of Max Fisher throughout the Jewish world. Don't just get [some rich bigshot]. Get Max Fisher — a doer, a leader, recognized."

*　　*　　*

Fisher never doubted his ability to raise money. But what was required, he thought, was what Eisenhower had told him he could have used in 1956 — a voice at the White House that would bring the American Jewish community's fear for Israel to the attention of the president. So Fisher aimed his political energies beyond the borders of Detroit. And the media started to track him, as though the story of his ascendancy were an entertaining sidebar to the more substantial story of Romney's march toward Washington. Now, whenever Fisher was asked about his success, he more often than not gave the impression that he owed it all to the grace of smiling fortune. One interviewer asked him how his oil company survived the Depression. And Fisher, who, in the 1930s had an oil expert at University of Michigan tutoring him, who traveled the country hunting down deals and fresh sources of crude, who regularly made 2 a.m. jaunts to oil refineries to talk with the men working graveyard, replied: "[We survived the Depression because] we had one great advantage. I didn't know any better."

"I never felt like I had it made," Fisher was to say repeatedly, long after it was obvious that he had achieved far more than most.

There had always been something self-deprecating about Fisher, as if he could not assimilate this new image of himself into the old. This feeling was heightened by his own gnawing lack of satisfaction with his accomplishments. But that was a conflict that had plagued him since college and would continue to plague him into his eighties: after all, vast success rarely satisfies the vast hunger that creates it. Fisher's view of himself, on the other hand, was not wholly inaccurate. Much of what he accomplished depended on events well out of his control. Just as World War II and its aftermath of shortages created opportunities in the oil industry, so did the Six-Day War, by bringing Israel to the forefront of American Jewish consciousness, sharpen the political appetite of that constituency. And Fisher was ready to combine his communal work with his political beliefs.

Romney began organizing his push for the nomination. Along with Fisher he went to a suite at the Waldorf-Astoria and was joined by J. Willard Marriott, a Mormon and Romney supporter who headed the national motor-hotel chain; Clifford Folger, Nixon's finance chairman in 1960; Leonard Hall, former chairman of the Republican National Committee; and several Romney aides. The parley attracted the attention of *The New York Times*. Upon learning of the meeting, a reporter approached Romney, who again repudiated the claim that he was a candidate. Later, Fisher was asked by the same reporter if it was not unusual for the session to be convened in New York as most of those attending were from Michigan. He replied that it just happened to be convenient for everyone and that he had been in town pursuing his duties at the UJA.

Although Fisher had been tight-lipped in New York, once he returned to Franklin he momentarily dropped his guard and spoke about Romney's aspirations with Patricia B. Smith, who was profiling Fisher for the Sunday magazine section of the *Detroit Free Press*. Her feature, headlined "Detroit's Gentle, Massive Max Fisher," encased Fisher in the cotton-candy aura his hometown press habitually reserved for him. The lead-in full-page photograph caught Fisher, pensive as a Talmudic sage, sitting on a low wall beneath a leafy tree outside his house in Franklin, with the family toy poodle, Tiger, nestling against him. Smith touched on the "happy mosaic" of Fisher's boyhood, his "Horatio Alger" career and, apparently impressed by his height and broad shoulders, deduced that Fisher was "quite unshakable."

Toward the conclusion of the article, she asked him about Romney and he replied: "Romney is a man of integrity . . . who can set an example. . . . He has been a success as a man of business, a family man, a governor. He would be a great symbol."

Fisher revealed nothing of his own hopes, and Smith did not press him. She wrote: "If Romney should become president one wonders what might be in mind for his great backer. Max Fisher says he has no plans for himself."

The interview was vintage Fisher. He succeeded in projecting what Kahn had called his "benevolent presence," acting as though there were no reward in it for him if Romney were to win the White House. Smith also quoted Romney in her story. The governor said of Fisher: "He has a rare gift of empathy and great organizing ability. He is a leader who inspires others by doing. . . . He avoids offense and has a warm, friendly personality."

Romney had sufficient cause to be flattering. Looking back at the nascent days of his campaign, he says: "Max was an exceptional fund-raiser. [But] he was more than that for me; he was an adviser. Max would come over [to my house in Bloomfield Hills] every week and we would discuss politics — state, national and so on. He had a wide acquaintance with many people of significance. And he had this ability to give good advice."

It was Fisher's acquaintance with people of significance and Romney's increasing respect for his advice that led him to advise the governor in 1966 on a potential vice presidential running mate. From Fisher's perspective, it would have been a dream ticket, combining the governor of his home state with a man who was arguably the most powerful Jewish holder of national office in the country, Senator Jacob Javits of New York. (The only other Jewish presence of equal stature on the national scene was Senator Abraham A. Ribicoff of Connecticut. However, Connecticut lacked New York's punch in the Electoral College, and alas, Ribicoff was a Democrat.) Elected to the Senate in 1956, Javits was an old-time liberal Republican and a tireless defender of Israel. He was four years older than Fisher and had been acquainted with him since the 1950s, when Javits had gone to Detroit to speak at a fund-raiser. They had been friends ever since. Both men were unique as Jewish Republicans, Javits aligned along the left wing of the party, Fisher nearer the center. The two constant concerns they had in common were the direction of Republican politics — especially in the wake of Goldwater and the rise of the party's right wing — and the relationship of the United States and Israel. Fisher and Javits often met in Washington and New York, but for the most part kept in close touch through frequent phone calls. Javits's widow, Marian, remembers that Fisher was in the habit of calling her husband early on Sunday mornings, waking her. Sleepily, Marian would answer the phone, mumbling that "Jack would call him back." According to Marian, Jack, as a rule, invariably reached over and took the phone.

In his autobiography, Javits writes that it was "through Max that I was invited to a rather ceremonial lunch at Governor Romney's summer mansion on Mackinac Island in Lake

Michigan." Javits went to the mansion with his wife, Max and Marjorie, cruising on the Fishers' boat from Detroit. After the social pleasantries, the talk got down to politics. Romney, Javits and Fisher discussed their fears that the Republican Party would never recover from Goldwater unless it took a new, more liberal direction. Then they discussed Romney's emergence as a presidential candidate. Fisher cannot recall who initially brought up Javits as a running mate, although he had broached the idea to the governor several times before. In addition to the ideological affinity between Romney and Javits, the three men saw numerous advantages to the proposed ticket. It would be well balanced in geographic and ethnic backgrounds, and by the differing governmental experience of the governor and senator. Javits's considerable experience in foreign affairs and national legislation would complement Romney's excellent domestic record in business and state administration.

Soon after the luncheon, Romney told reporters that if he were nominated, then Javits would be his choice as vice president. Since Romney was so far ahead of the pack of Republican contenders, his announcement stirred up enormous political speculation.

Javits remembered: "The press was suddenly beating on my door . . . and I certainly did nothing to quiet the talk. . . . *U.S. News and World Report* weighed in with the story declaring that Rockefeller had not only urged the Republican Party to nominate Romney and Javits but was pledging the ticket all kinds of support. A couple of weeks later I was on the cover of *Time*, the subject of a favorable story that commented on the idea of my becoming vice president: 'Audacious, perhaps. But preposterous? Not really.'"

With mounting satisfaction, Fisher watched his matchmaking take hold. Well into 1967, Romney remained the favorite to be tagged as the Republican presidential candidate, but his nomination was by no means assured. Rockefeller, because of his personal fortune and his state's commanding presence in the country and the Electoral College, was always a possibility. And Richard Nixon was still a candidate, though due to his losses to Kennedy and to Governor Brown, he was saddled with a loser's image, an impression that he could not carry an election without Ike as a running mate. A leading Colorado Republican confirmed this opinion to the political experts from the Knight Newspapers survey when he said: "Isn't it too bad we can't elect Nixon? But we can't, and so I think we'll go with Romney."

Fisher, although pleased with his candidate's progress, felt that the experts were still underestimating Nixon.

"The party was in rough shape after Goldwater," Fisher says, "and in 1966 Dick did a great job of trying to heal it. He went around the country, speaking about Vietnam, about the Soviet Union, and doing favors for [local Republican machinery], campaigning for candidates. We talked about it. He built up a lot of chits in 1966. None of the other potential presidential candidates realized that Nixon still had a lot of juice. Nobody really knew the power of his connections, all of the county organizations who supported him, all of the favors he was owed. And he had raised plenty of money. In 1966, Nixon's power was his best-kept secret. Romney was still on the rise, and, of course, in Rockefeller's case, the Republican Party didn't quite trust his liberalism."

While campaigning, Nixon predicted that 1966 would be a banner year for Republicans, erasing their humiliating defeats in 1964. His prediction was, as he observed in his memoirs, "vindicated with a vengeance." In 1966, Republicans won a net of 47 House seats, 3 Senate seats, 8 governorships and 700 state legislature seats.

This impressive Republican victory was, Nixon later conceded, "a prerequisite for my own comeback." And he and Fisher did far more than talk about it. Says Nixon: "Max contributed financially [to my travels]. He footed the bill — and I don't mean just in Michigan. This was nationally."

One of the reasons Fisher did not reveal his hopes to Patricia Smith was that he was unsure who would win the Republican nomination and he did not want to be tied to a single hopeful. ("He avoids offense," Romney had said.) Fisher understood that the price of admission into the political arena was loyalty. Yet it was clear to him that loyalty would not help if a Republican did not win. Furthermore, his objective was to represent the American Jewish community. He was loyal to his party; that was enough. His support did not have to be for a specific candidate. But that candidate did have to be a Republican, and that Republican had to be president. At bottom, he reasoned, the best person for the job would be the one who could unseat Johnson.

Two decades after the 1968 election, Fisher says: "Even though Romney was winning, I maintained relationships with Nixon and Rockefeller. Both of them lived on Fifth Avenue, and when I was in New York I'd go from one apartment to the other. Whatever was going to happen in 1968, I wanted to play a part."

It was an attitude that rankled Romney. In 1980, when asked about the social vision Fisher had been pursuing for the previous twenty years, Romney laughed and said: "I never saw much of what you'd call a vision. He tends to move where the power is."

In response, Fisher said, "History alone will have to decide." Then, dropping the guise of historical speculation, he gave an answer that was more consistent with his bedrock pragmatism: "Look," he said. "You can't please everybody."

Fisher, as Romney noted, indisputably gravitated toward power. But that explanation is only half correct, and thus an incomplete accounting. For what Fisher was surprised to discover, as the 1968 election drew closer, was that power was also gravitating toward him.

William and Mollie Fisher with Gail and Max (standing), Salem, Ohio, 1912.

Fisher's Underselling Store, Salem, Ohio, 1919. Because William was so gregarious, his clothing store became a social center. It was open six days a week, and William worked behind the counter, wearing his steel-frame glasses and wing collar, and invariably puffing an El Producto cigar.

Max Fisher at Reilly Field, 1923. The strongest conflict *M* had with his father was over his football career. At six-foo two and 148 pounds, Max was one of the biggest boys Salem. He played center, on defense and offense, and w considered one of the finest lineman in Columbiana Count But both William and Mollie, terrified that Max would g injured, refused to watch their son play.

Max Fisher outside his fraternity house on Indianola Avenue in Columbus, Ohio, 1929. Barred from a number of fraternities at Ohio State University because he was Jewish, Fisher joined the Alpha Epsilon chapter of Phi Beta Delta, which by definition was nonsectarian, but whose members were primarily Jewish. It was his first exposure to Jews. But he was the only country boy among his urban fraternity brothers. "They had a style I didn't have," says Fisher. "It was hard for me to get adjusted."

Sloppy Joe's in Havana, Cuba, New Years Eve, 1932. Left to right: Joseph Falk, Kurt Saloma, Max Fisher. Upon returning to Detroit, Fisher learned that, due to faulty equipment, the Keystone plant had burned down. Fisher recalls: "It took a long time to get the insurance settlement, and those were the darkest days for me."

Left to right: Max Fisher, Henry E. Wenger and William E. Slaughter Jr., mid-1950s. Beginning in 1929, Wenger and Slaughter ran the Aurora Gasoline Company from the basement of Wenger's house in Detroit. In 1933, Fisher persuaded Wenger to put up $38,000 to build a refinery. Years later, when interviewers asked Fisher how a twenty-five-year-old convinced a middle-aged man with a wife and two children to invest all of his cash in the depths of the Depression, Fisher jokingly replied that he "must have hoodwinked him." However, Wenger's son, Henry Penn Wenger, says: "My father was a dreamer. And so was Max. They were kindred spirits."

Sylvia Krell Fisher. On their initial date, Max drove her to the refinery, his bottles of oil samples rattling in the backseat. Although it was not Sylvia's ideal of romance, over the next several months Max treated her to more traditional romantic fare, and on October 4, 1934, they were married. A teenage bout with rheumatic fever had damaged Sylvia's heart. In 1952, she died of congestive heart failure. She was forty-two years old.

Max Fisher, 1941. Because of Sylvia's fragile health, she spent the winters in Arizona. During their daughter's Christmas vacation from school, Jane and her father traveled by train to Arizona, and along with Sylvia stayed in one of the adobe houses at the Double-U Ranch. "My father taught me to horseback ride when I was four years old," says Jane Fisher Sherman. "We would ride out through the foothills to Sabina Canyon for picnics."

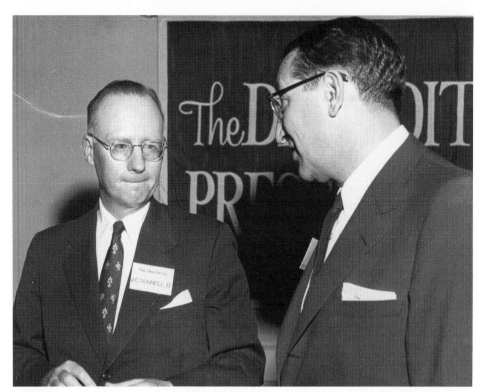

James Donnell II and Max Fisher, mid-1950s. In 1938, Fisher approached The Ohio Oil Company, offering to pay the posted price for crude. Donnell was shocked. Paying the publicly announced field prices for crude during the Depression was unimaginable—an oil man's shortcut to a career change. All Fisher wanted in return was a guarantee that Donnell would ship Aurora oil when supplies were short. Their agreement was never drawn up in writing. With a handshake, The Ohio gained its largest single crude oil customer when it desperately needed the new outlet. During the Second World War, when oil was scarce, Donnell kept his word.

Left to right: William Avrunin, Max Zivian, Israeli guide, Herbert Abeles, unidentified woman, Max Fisher. In October 1954, Fisher made his initial visit to Israel with the first United Jewish Appeal study mission. Behind him, the sign warns: "Danger. Frontier Ahead. No Passage."

Max Fisher and George W. Romney, New York City, 1964. In 1962, Fisher helped Romney become governor of Michigan. He helped him win again in 1964. Two years later, the popular governor was a front-runner for the Republicans' 1968 presidential nomination.

Groundbreaking for a Howard Johnson Motor Lodge, September 17, 1964. The Fisher Building is in the background. Left to right: Eugene Charles and Arthur Kroog, Howard Johnson Company; Willis McFarlane, 300 Blvd. Co.; James McDonnell Jr., Blvd. Restaurant Co.; Jack Cassidy, 300 Blvd. Co.; Max Fisher, chairman, Fisher-New Center Co.; Louis Berry, president, FNC; Ben Berry, director, FNC; William Pegley; David Miro, secretary, FNC; Tom Moore; Harold Berry, vice president, FNC; Jack Caminker, general manager, Fisher Building; Barney Smith; William Springer, editor and publisher, New Center News; and H. L. Volkes contractors Sanford and Stanley Simon.

Max Fisher presenting former Israeli Prime Minister David Ben-Gurion with an ancient glass vessel as a gift for his eightieth birthday, at the Sheraton Hotel, Tel Aviv, Israel, October 1966. In his remarks, Fisher said: "That this glass has remained intact for 2,000 years represents a small miracle. It symbolizes the even greater miracle that the Jewish people have remained intact over an even greater span of time." In reply, Ben-Gurion whispered to Fisher: "You should come live here."

Left to right: Max and Marjorie Fisher, Israeli Prime Minister Levi Eshkol and his wife, Miriam, 1966. Fisher had remarried in July 1953, and Marjorie encouraged him to broaden his philanthropic horizons. Fisher was particularly bound to Prime Minister Eshkol. He credits him with teaching him "the greatest lesson I would ever learn about Zionism." Fisher's first official act on behalf of President Richard Nixon was to attend Eshkol's funeral in 1969.

Former President Dwight D. Eisenhower and Max Fisher, 1965. During their discussion, Eisenhower reflected on the 1956 Suez Crisis and clarified the course of Fisher's political career.

Max Fisher and Governor Nelson A. Rockefeller of New York at a Romney fund-raiser in Detroit's Pontchartrain Hotel, February 24, 1968. At a press conference following the luncheon, reporters peppered Rockefeller with questions until he said that, if drafted, he would accept the Republican nomination for president. Romney believes Rockefeller's statement submarined his candidacy. Nixon's campaign manager John N. Mitchell later told Marjorie Fisher that he had fed some reporters the question with instructions to repeat it until Rockefeller answered it.

Vice President Hubert Humphrey and Max Fisher, 1965. During the 1968 campaign, Fisher's fund-raising for Nixon dried up traditionally Democratic sources. Humphrey contacted Fisher, reminding him that over the years he had been a good friend to Israel. Fisher agreed. Then Humphrey asked if Fisher would raise money for him. Fisher declined, explaining: "Hubert, I'm a Republican."

Shortly after the 1968 election, Fisher spoke privately with Richard Nixon. The newly elected president thanked Fisher for his assistance in the campaign and said that Fisher was welcome to an appointment as an ambassador. The offer, Nixon explains, was pro forma, because he never expected Fisher to accept anything. "And he never did," says Nixon.

Mollie and William Fisher with their four children, mid-1960s. Left to right: Max Fisher, Anne Rose, Mollie, William, Gail Rossen, Dorothy Tessler.

Left to right: Albert Arent, Yehuda Hellman, Charles Zimmerman, Phillip Hoffman, Jacob Stein, Secretary of State William Rogers, Charlotte Jacobson, Max Fisher, and Rabbi Israel Miller at the State Department, Washington, D.C., March 26, 1971. The meeting was requested by Jewish leaders to seek clarification on a Nixon administration Middle East proposal—the Rogers Plan—which Fisher vehemently opposed. Fisher thought that the meeting was a failure. Rogers had been unable to persuade anyone that American policy toward Israel had not veered off course.

Israeli Prime Minister Golda Meir and Max Fisher, 1971. Fisher's opinion of her was summed up when a reporter asked him to describe her via a word-association game. When the reporter said, "Golda Meir," Fisher quickly replied, "Oak tree. No, two oak trees."

Louis Pincus and Max Fisher, shortly after initialing the Agreement for the Reconstitution of the Jewish Agency, August 1970. For both men, the ideological distinctions between Zionist and non-Zionist held little weight.

Phillip Fisher. In January 1971, Phillip Fisher, at the age of twenty, had his first extended period alone with his father when he accompanied him to Israel. Upon arriving, they learned that William Fisher had died.

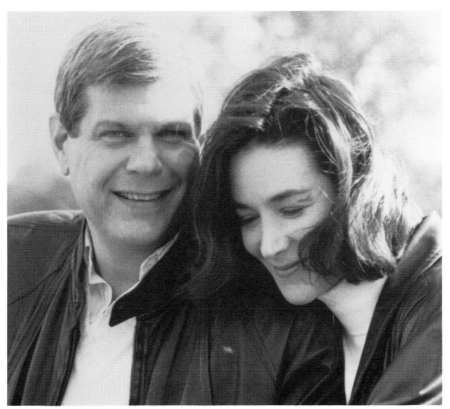

David Aronow and Marjorie Fisher Aronow. As part of Max's promise to himself to spend more time with his children, his youngest daughter accompanied him to his boyhood home of Salem in 1972.

Signing of a contract between the United Israel Appeal and the State Department, which provided $31 million for Soviet Jews emigrating to Israel, in the Thomas Jefferson Room, State Department, April 1973. Left to right (seated) Gottlieb Hammer, executive vice chairman of the United Israel Appeal; Melvin Dubinsky, president and board chairman of the UIA; Frank Kellog, special assistant to the secretary of state; (standing) left to right: Simcha Dinitz, Israeli ambassador to the United States; Leonard Garment, special consultant to President Nixon; Walter Stoessel Jr., assistant secretary for European Affairs; Joseph Sisco, assistant secretary for Near Eastern and South Asian Affairs; Marshall Wright, assistant secretary for congressional relations; Max Fisher, chairman of the Jewish Agency Board of Governors. The mood at the signing was upbeat, with plenty of handshaking, backslapping, and even a memorable quip by Senator Edmund Muskie of Maine. When Fisher leaned over to sign for the $31 million, Muskie said: "That's the smallest check Max has signed this year."

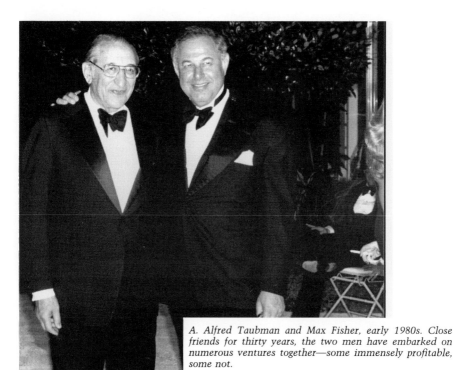

A. Alfred Taubman and Max Fisher, early 1980s. Close friends for thirty years, the two men have embarked on numerous ventures together—some immensely profitable, some not.

Left to right: Robert Surdam, Henry Ford II, Max Fisher and Robert McCabe in front of Detroit's Renaissance Center, late 1970s. Fisher urged Henry to undertake the project. Henry agreed, saying: "It won't be a Ford Motor Company deal. Everyone has to contribute. You too." Fisher promised that he would do his share.

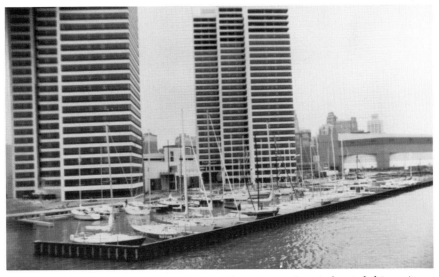

Riverfront. Along with Taubman, Fisher pursued his vision with a single-minded intensity unmatched in his professional life, and en route he authored what urban experts at Michigan State University have declared "a kind of textbook case in the application of power to realize an urban development project."

Max Fisher, Mayor Coleman Young of Detroit, and Governor William Milliken of Michigan at a press conference to discuss Riverfront, September 12, 1980. In Michigan, helping Detroit was always a bipartisan effort.

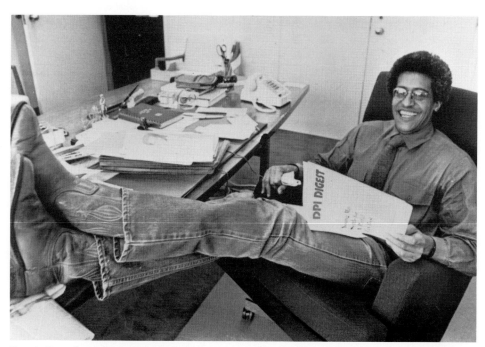

Detroit Councilman Kenneth Cockrel, who opposed city tax breaks for Riverfront. Cockrel distributed T-shirts stenciled with the refrain: "Tax Max and his Pal, Al!" Photo courtesy of the Detroit Free Press.

Chapter 7

IN THE HEAT OF THE SUMMER

IN JANUARY 1967, Richard Nixon met with seven men at the Waldorf Towers in New York. The purpose of the meeting, Nixon said, was to start preparing "to win the nomination [for president]." When Nixon's coterie encouraged him to sprint out front, Nixon replied that Romney should take the lead. Speculation arose that Nixon and his supporters welcomed Romney's candidacy because they doubted he could hit big-league pitching — the national press would cut him down to size, and at the nominating convention in Miami, Nixon's come-from-behind victory over Romney would appear more dramatic. Not every member of the campaign team shared Nixon's confidence. One of his law partners, John Mitchell, who would become Nixon's personal chief of staff, was wary.

"We felt Romney would stumble," Mitchell says, "but we were worried about him to this extent: he had Max Fisher and all that meant. It made Romney formidable early on. Rockefeller wanted [Fisher's backing], and reportedly tried to buy it. We wanted it, too. And we went after it. Max Fisher's support meant a hell of a lot in '68."

Franklin Roosevelt's man, Jim Farley, identified the importance of money in political campaigns in the days before television. Since then, TV had become an expensive and critical coast-to-coast stump. Nixon says that although he "knew [television] was going to cost a great deal of money, I didn't dream it was going to cost as much as it did."

So Nixon concurred with Mitchell that they should talk to Fisher. And they both did, asking him to sign on. Fisher told them, "Just because I'm for George doesn't mean I'm against you."

He was not making any enemies. He was, however, committed to Romney and he would have to wait until the governor had run his race before supporting another candidate.

It was a hectic spring for Fisher. What time he could spare from the emergency fund-raising campaign for Israel, he allotted to Romney. Then, in July, as the storm in the Middle East subsided, Fisher turned on his television one Sunday at his house in Franklin and saw that war of a different kind was raging closer to home, only sixteen miles down the John C. Lodge Freeway, in Detroit, where police rushed to barricade the streets, while fire-engine sirens screamed and pillars of smoke corkscrewed into the sky.

*   *   *

Throughout the 1960s, "civil unrest" became a synonym for long hot summers of rioting in the predominately black inner cities. Watts, Tampa, Cincinnati, Atlanta and Newark had suffered through it. Now, at 3:30 a.m., on Sunday, July 23, it was Detroit's turn. At Twelfth Street and Clairmount, a warren of bars and tenements and locked stores, four vice-squad policemen raided a "blind pig" — an after-hours drinking and gambling joint. When the police herded the eighty-two arrestees out, the sidewalks were still teeming with miniskirted hookers, junkies, winos, good folks praying for a breeze and rows of young men leaning against cars. It took over an hour and four paddy wagons to ferry the suspects to jail. Two-hundred spectators were kidding the cops and the folks getting busted. Inevitably, as suspects were herded into the wagons, bystanders were jostled by police. A college student kept shouting at the officers to "leave my people alone!" Word was that the cops had beat up a woman. As the last patrol car left at 5 a.m., a bottle was hurled against its rear window. Suddenly, rocks were thrown. The police returned. A lieutenant was struck by a brick. Around 6:30 a.m., burglar alarms, set off by broken store windows, were ringing down Twelfth Street. Shops were being looted and burned. By midafternoon, Mayor Jerome P. Cavanagh was requesting the assistance of the State Police.

When Fisher heard the news of the riot he phoned his assistant, Richard Van Tiem, and asked him to come to his house. Van Tiem arrived and Fisher said, "Let's go."

"Go where?" Van Tiem asked.

"Down Twelfth Street," Fisher replied. "I want to see what's going on."

Van Tiem's reaction was that his boss was being a bit rash. Van Tiem said, "Max, there's a riot going on. We can't go for a ride down there."

Fisher evidently thought that they could, because he said, "Drive, Dick," and strode out the door. Van Tiem followed.

Twenty-two years later, Van Tiem recalls, "Max was in a rush to find out what was happening to his city. I, on the other hand, went under duress."

Traffic was light on the Lodge. The radio reported the spreading arson, shooting, rock throwing and looting. Van Tiem was not comforted by the news. He exited and drove along Twelfth. Smoke was rising from the blackened shells of buildings, and looters, wading through the shattered glass, were wheeling televisions and stereos and frozen hams in shopping carts. Fisher was quiet. It was possible that the radio was wrong, that the havoc had not spread. He wanted to see for himself and told Van Tiem to drive to the office. The rioting had not yet filtered over to West Grand Boulevard. The streets around the Fisher Building were deserted. Fisher wondered aloud if that was a positive sign. Van Tiem wanted to go home. The two men rode the elevator to the twenty-second floor. Fisher opened his office, hurrying to the sweep of windows, with their panoramic view of downtown. He saw a patchwork quilt of flame blanketing the city and burning toward the Canadian border. Neighborhoods were dotted with fires as though the cityscape were a campground during a Boy Scout jamboree, the sky now so black with plumes of smoke it was as if night were falling. Fisher stood silently at the windows, looking down.

The writer Tom Shachtman has named the years from

1963 to 1974, from the assassination of JFK to Nixon's resignation over Watergate, "the decade of shocks." And indeed, it was as though a malignant genie were loose in the land: students dynamiting university buildings; children going to the corner store for milk and being shot by snipers from rooftops; political leaders from the neo-Nazi George Lincoln Rockwell to the pacifist Martin Luther King dying as violently as American soldiers in a jungle firefight.

Meanwhile, Vietnam played on the nightly news, the prime-time show America was not ready for, a grisly miniseries without end.

For Fisher, though, the riots in Detroit touched a chord of sadness in him, stirring him in a way he cannot describe. Ask him about it and he shakes his head. Press him for an answer, he shrugs. Some two weeks before the riot began Fisher celebrated his fifty-ninth birthday, but nothing in his past had prepared him to watch people, in the city he had so willfully claimed as his home, burning their houses.

As Fisher stood at his office windows, the surge of helplessness he felt with the city in flames was overpowering, and helplessness is an uncomfortable and confusing sensation for a pragmatist, particularly one who has spent much of his life accumulating influence of one kind or another. His response to any problem was to solve it. He liked to fix things — radios, cars, oil equipment, the problems of his family and friends — and the riot, for the moment, was something he could neither fix nor fathom, and it left him without a card to play.

"I didn't know what to do," Fisher says. "I stood at the windows. Then I called the governor."

The governor did not know what to do either. By the evening of July 23, Romney had been badly shaken by a helicopter tour over the city. It gave him a view similar to the one Fisher had from his office. He saw "entire blocks in flames" and had the impression that Detroit "had been bombed." At 3 a.m., on Monday, July 24, Romney phoned Washington, requesting that 5,000 federal troops be dispatched.

President Lyndon Johnson was reluctant to grant Romney's request. Johnson, who often consulted a hand-drawn

graph that compared his latest Gallup Poll strength against
Romney, had no intention of aiding a contender for the presidency. What defined Johnson's reluctance as political was
that he had not displayed the same hesitancy with Democratic governors. Governor Pat Brown of California had been
offered "all the assistance in the world" during the Watts riot,
as was Governor Richard Hughes of New Jersey when rioting
erupted in Newark.

And so it was not until 2:30 a.m. on Tuesday, July 25,
nearly eighteen hours after Romney had made his request,
that paratroopers from the 101st and 82nd Airborne waded
into the riot.

Gus Cardinali, a Detroit police sergeant who later went
to work as a personal assistant to Fisher, was patrolling the
streets during the riot. Cardinali recalls that the police and
firemen were furious with the politicians. "We needed all the
help we could get," says Cardinali, "because the fire fighters
required escorts. Snipers were shooting at them and kids were
throwing rocks and bottles and the firemen couldn't get the
trucks in. That's why the fires spread. [The politicians] let the
whole thing get out of hand. The rioting should have been
suppressed immediately. Or at least contained. But Detroit
was a victim of the times. The politicians quibbled while the
city burned."

This political theater of the absurd paled beside the cost,
in human and financial terms, of the rioting. There were
7,200 arrests, 43 deaths and a minimum of 1,000 injuries.
Conservative estimates of the damage put the figure at $42.5
million, with 2,500 stores either looted or burned. In the
sobering wake of the destruction, the first urban coalition in
the United States was founded. Christened the New Detroit
Committee, its goal was to channel private resources into
rebuilding the city. Committee membership embraced a
cross-section of block-club bosses, militant blacks, industrialists such as Henry Ford and Max Fisher, and numerous corporate heads. Joseph L. Hudson Jr., the thirty-six-year-old president of Hudson's, which would become the world's largest
privately owned department store, was elected chairman.

Hudson explains the beginnings of New Detroit: "I was invited [to head the committee] because I was young and fresh. I phoned Max and he immediately agreed to serve — even though the structure of the coalition hadn't been invented yet. Max saw the whole community and system as unresponsive [to the inner city] — the public sector even more than the private. We obviously had to get some money and people together. I couldn't do both. Max had been the big fund-raiser in town. So he poured himself in, and he did another very significant thing: he called to my attention that I was running around trying to put out fires instead of saying and doing things that attracted people to join in. Max became my adviser and in the process he got more involved. And when a year had gone by and I had pretty much burned myself out, he became the next chairman. He was highly respected by Detroiters as a businessman, as a person who was independent, committed and concerned about his community. Max was able to command immediate attention, in person or on the telephone. He brokered ideas and people and groups. When a lot of people were vegetating, Max had this fervent vision of something better."

Fisher had been enraged by Johnson's stalling, but, not having access to the circle of power within the Democratic administration, his choices were limited. (Choices he promised himself to broaden after the 1968 election.) If he had not known what to do when he first saw the city ablaze, when Hudson called him he had a clearer idea. New Detroit got off to a fast start, and Fisher threw himself behind it. Within two years he was addressing groups of prominent business people around the nation, trumpeting the inroads the coalition had made against poverty: the jobs found for 35,000 previously hard-core unemployed; the Michigan Consolidated Gas Company sponsoring the construction of low- and moderate-income housing; General Motors providing an interest-free loan of $1.1 million to a nonprofit housing corporation of blacks and Hispanics; New Detroit's anteing up $4.5 million to investigate alternative low-cost housing; and an offshoot of New Detroit, the Economic Development Corporation, earmarking $2 million to help blacks establish businesses.

"There is no force more powerful," Fisher said at the time, "no force which has shown itself more creative, more talented and responsive to change, no force which can provide greater leverage for meeting urban social problems than business and businessmen. In the final analysis, as business helps in meeting social problems it truly helps itself." Fisher's devotion to this doctrine matched the devotion he brought to the cause of Israel. Arthur Hertzberg, in his 1989 *The Jews in America*, ascribes Fisher's dedication to the residents of urban ghettos to the social conscience taught by Judaism. In 1968, Hertzberg says, Fisher, despite his status as "the leading Jewish Republican," was telling the organized Jewish community, "If Jews truly believe that advancing social justice is a Jewish obligation, there can be no . . . doubts that helping people in the inner city . . . represents a genuine Jewish commitment."

Hertzberg's assessment was partially correct. Fisher's commitment to the poor was fashioned at the feet of William and Mollie, who, when they lived in Salem, donated what meager sums they could spare to the Jewish National Fund or fed and housed the traveling representatives of Jewish charities who passed through town. But Fisher was also a product of Salem's belief in the benevolence of the good Christian. The father of his boyhood friend, Henry Yaggi, was the town doctor, a prosperous man who set up charge accounts at the grocery store for the less fortunate and paid their bills. One of Fisher's enduring memories of Salem is of the Salvation Army soliciting donations, and one of the honors he took special pride in as an adult was the Salvation Army's William Booth Award, which he won in 1977.

The legacy of the riots to Max Fisher was a longing to see Detroit restored into the model of orderly industriousness he remembered from the 1930s, when he would gaze up at the imposing granite and marble of the Fisher Building and dream his great American dreams. Fisher's work with New Detroit evolved into his work with the Detroit Renaissance Corporation and, in the end, cost him (and Al Taubman) in excess of $30 million. Maybe, by the late 1960s, Fisher was chasing an America that had been vanquished by the cunning of time. In 1969, when he spoke before the American Chamber of Commerce executives, he wistfully recalled: "With all their terrible shortcomings, the city ghettos of other years served as a sort of natural Americanization machine: the immigrant came in at one end — a stranger to American ways and American mobility. After a passage of years, he and his children emerged at the other end — a part of American society and capable of taking care of themselves. That in a crude way is how our inner cities once worked. It isn't the way they are working today."

Trying to answer that question became a consuming passion for Fisher. It occupied him in the face of Detroit's bleak islands of abandoned buildings, the needle tracks along the heroin mainline and the anguish of disintegrating families. It continued to occupy him, a decade later, through a new pestilence of gang gun battles and burning crack pipes, and it occupies him still, twenty-three years after the day of the "blind pig."

*　　*　　*

At the beginning of August 1967, with the rioting under control, talk of a Romney candidacy picked up again, and Fisher was increasingly wearing two hats — as a fund-raiser and adviser. Among the most critical areas in which he advised Romney was on how to approach the media. Ever cautious and methodical, Fisher, the ex-stage manager, was leery of the limelight — too much is revealed, too many mistakes are possible. An abundance of exposure, whatever its personal satisfactions, tended to form legions poised for counterattack. Fisher had been discussing the finer points of media relations with Romney for some time. In 1964, when Nixon had come to Detroit to persuade Romney to challenge Goldwater for the nomination, Fisher not only told Romney that allowing himself to be used as a figurehead to split the Republican Party would have dire consequences for his political career, but that it was too soon to take that step, that exposure to a presidential election-year circus of reporters would hurt him.

"George," says Fisher, "was a great believer in input from

other people, and I respected him for it. I used to try to explain to him how to handle the press. They're human beings, too; sometimes they recognize people for what they are and sometimes they've got their own hang-ups. George was a very above-board, decent politician. But his trouble was that he said too much. So [the press] started in on him. I remember there was a woman who wrote for one of the Washington papers, and she told me the press was going to goad him — they were out to get him. And I told George: 'They are gunning for you. Be careful.'"

Fisher had his own distinctive association with the press, and it is instructive to examine it since the examination not only highlights the role of the media in the political process, but also shows why Fisher's assistance would one day be sought by leaders in the United States and Israel.

Fisher, as to be expected of any reasonably informed person, was well aware of the power the press had to undercut a program or a candidate, and he was skeptical of its motives. Yet he rarely refused any persistent requests for interviews and, even more paradoxically, often appeared to grant his interviewers free access to information.

Steven Flax, a journalist who grew up in Detroit and who would favorably profile Fisher in the September 14, 1981, issue of *Forbes*, explains Fisher's style. "[During the interview], Max comes on like your grandfather," says Flax. "He's very kind, very solicitous, as if he not only wants to give you all the information you need, but wants you to impress everyone [at your magazine or newspaper] with all of the inside details you were able to incorporate into the profile. But don't be fooled: Max is tough, he's smart and nothing gets by him. He's no media innocent. He tells you what *he* wants you to know."

Al Taubman has watched Fisher deal with the press for over thirty years. Taubman is a shopping mall developer and operator, real estate investor, majority shareholder of Sotheby's, owner of A & W Restaurants and of the department stores Woodward & Lothrop and Wanamaker's — with an estimated wealth of $3.7 billion. A focus of media curiosity,

Taubman does not share his friend's affable relationship with
the press or his interest in dealing with them. (In print,
Taubman has been accused of everything from banning carry-
around food at his malls because he slipped on an ice-cream
cone, to dousing Mike Wallace of "60 Minutes" with a drink
when Wallace peeked inside Taubman's Lear Jet while doing
a story on corporate executives who had flown to New Orleans for Super Bowl XII.) Taubman considers many reporters
"on a par with inside traders." He feels they are only after the
story they want, regardless of facts. It is not surprising then
that in March 1981, when *The Detroit News* ran a two-part,
two-day feature on Taubman, he declined to talk to them,
agreeing to respond to written questions. Predictably enough,
when the reporter, Steve Konicki, interviewed Fisher on
Taubman, "Fisher lamented that he had tried but couldn't
convince Taubman to talk for himself."

Taubman, according to Fisher, had nothing to fear from
the media; if he made himself more accessible, he might find
the press less harsh. But Taubman disagrees and says that
Fisher has his own special relationship with reporters, that he
handles them with an adroitness based on a subtle combination of his personality, skill and reputation.

"Max," says Taubman, "is basically a listener. I have
been at dinner parties with him and afterward spoken to the
people he was seated with. They go on about what a charming
man Max is to sit next to. People will tell him things they
wouldn't tell their husbands or wives. And I've watched the
whole time [they were eating]. Max hardly said a word. He let
them talk and listened and they came away feeling that they
had participated in a brilliant conversation. They may have —
but it was definitely one-sided. In a way, the same principle
applies [when Max talks to reporters]. Max is a patrician, in
the best sense of the word. He is so courtly that reporters are
charmed by his taking the time to talk and seeming — when
he does say something — to talk frankly with them. Yet I
wonder if they ever analyze what he tells them, how little he
reveals. You won't get any secrets from Max. He's too
guarded. Also, as far as the Detroit media is concerned, Max

is a sacred cow. He's good for Detroit, he's a symbol of all that is progressive about the city and the media responds to this. He is above reproach."

Romney's evaluation of Fisher's ability to deal with the press is more succinct. "Max," Romney says, "has good judgment."

Whatever judgment Fisher possessed did not alter the outcome of Romney's bid for the presidential nomination. The hammer blow that permanently knocked Romney's campaign off course came at the end of August 1967. (Romney disagrees; he says it was in February 1968.) August began promisingly enough. A Gallup Poll claimed that Romney was leading Johnson 49 percent to 41 percent with 10 percent undecided. Fisher, meantime, was busy with the fund-raising. His offhand estimate, according to what he told Will Muller of *The Detroit News*, was that it would take $2 million to pay for the Romney foray until the GOP convened to choose a candidate in Miami next summer. He revealed to Muller that he was in the process of drawing up a budget and that "ten top people [have] volunteered for the finance committee and we expect to build that to fifty."

What Fisher did not mention was that he already had commitments for contributions in excess of $2 million. Nelson Rockefeller, whose urge to be president had momentarily slackened, threw his support behind Romney with a pledge of $250,000. Five others promised Fisher an equal amount, bringing the opening bankroll to $1.5 million. Fisher then raised another $1 million from friends who were each willing to give $25,000 and up, like Ford Motor Company executive John Bugas and General Motors executive Bunkie Knudsen. The money that Rockefeller mailed Fisher came in the form of fifty checks from $4,000 to $6,000, each made out to a different committee. Under 1968 election laws, there was a limit to the maximum gift allowed to a committee, but no limit on committees. So committees were created as fast as Rockefeller and the others could sign checks: Romney Boosters Committee, Friends of George Romney, Romney for Good Government, Romney '68,

Citizens for Urban Progress, Citizens for Progress. The list was long, not overly poetic, but effective.

On Thursday, August 31, Romney taped a television show with Lou Gordon, a Detroit broadcaster with dreams of becoming a sort of Eliott Ness-Walter Cronkite combo. Fisher says that Gordon was a friend of his and of Romney, and the commentator had been favorably disposed toward the governor since 1963. Fisher occasionally mailed transcripts of Gordon's WXYZ radio program to Romney in Lansing. Even when Gordon disagreed with a Romney initiative, he more often than not gave the governor "an 'E' for effort."

"Lou liked George," says Fisher, "but I was worried about George going on with him. I never spoke to George about it. I wish I had. To this day, I wish I had been there with him."

Romney got ready on the set; there were no aides off-camera; he had not been briefed, unaware of what his competitor, Richard Nixon, had grasped long ago: "No television performance takes as much preparation as an off-the-cuff talk."

Romney's stance on Vietnam, like the stance of many politicians of that era, had vacillated. Once a hawk, he was reincarnated as a dove. So, had he been briefed prior to the show, he may have anticipated Gordon's question, which was, "Isn't your position [on Vietnam] inconsistent with what it was, and what do you propose we do now?"

Romney replied: "Well, you know when I came back from [my trip to] Vietnam, I just had the greatest brainwashing that anybody can get when you go over to Vietnam. Not only by the generals, but also by the diplomatic corps over there, and they do a very thorough job. And since returning from Vietnam, I've gone into the history of Vietnam, all the way back into World War II and before. And, as a result . . . I no longer believe that it was necessary for us to be involved in South Vietnam to stop Communist aggression."

The show aired on Labor Day, September 4. The following morning, *The New York Times* announced: "Romney asserts he underwent 'brainwashing' on Vietnam trip." That evening, a thirty-second clip of Romney's quote — edited until it was stripped of its context — played on the national news programs. The Democrats accused Romney of impugning the integrity of General William Westmoreland and Ambassador Henry Cabot Lodge. By Sunday, a *Detroit News* editorial was stating that Romney should drop out of the race because of his incompetence.

"It was poor choice of words," Fisher says. "Except George was correct. In the beginning, everybody got brainwashed on Vietnam. But his statement blew us out of the water."

Romney officially declared his candidacy for the nomination on November 21, saying he would enter the New Hampshire primary in March. Although Romney was spiraling downward, Fisher pumped close to $4 million into his campaign coffers. In January 1968, Romney was stumping through New Hampshire, where he made a slight recovery. Fisher went to New Orleans to speak at a banquet of the Jewish Welfare Fund. A reporter from the *Times-Picayune* asked him about Romney. Fisher assured the reporter that Romney would get the GOP nod, citing his gains in New Hampshire.

Nelson Rockefeller, at Fisher's request, agreed to speak at a Romney fund-raiser on Saturday, February 24. (Romney was campaigning in Oregon.) The luncheon was slated for the Versailles Room of Detroit's Pontchartrain Hotel. As Fisher wrote the governor of New York, the event was for "prominent business people who need a little persuasion." Over 200 guests were invited. The list read like a Who's Who of Michigan: Senator Robert Griffin, Al Taubman, Harold McClure, Joseph Nederlander, John Bugas, Harold Berry, Jason Honigman, Bunkie Knudsen — enough wealth and clout to ease a man down the road to Washington.

Rockefeller, accompanied by his wife, Happy, arrived on his private jet Friday night, landing at Metropolitan Airport. The Fishers hosted a small black-tie dinner for them at their home. The luncheon began at noon and ran until approximately 2 p.m. Then, riding the elevator upstairs to Suite 1912, Rockefeller, with Fisher beside him, went to meet the press. It was here that Romney believes Rockefeller submarined any possibility he had to win the nomination.

Everyone in the suite knew that Romney's candidacy was dying, and so it was no surprise when one reporter asked Rockefeller if he would enter the race if Romney lost in New Hampshire.

Rockefeller said: "I'm not a candidate. I'm not going to be a candidate. I'm supporting Governor Romney and I think he's the best man."

Then someone asked him if he would accept a draft. He answered: "Although I don't believe there is such a thing as a draft, I said if there were a draft even though I don't believe it, if it came, I would face it at the time."

When another questioner asked if facing it meant accepting it, Rockefeller said: "I don't see how you can face it without accepting it."

A reporter persisted, but before he could finish repeating the question, Rockefeller cut him off, saying: "Apparently, he didn't hear my answer."

The reporters would not let it go. At the conclusion of the press conference, a TV newsman asked the governor: "Did I understand you to say you would accept a draft from the Republican National Convention?"

An exasperated Rockefeller responded: "I said exactly that, but I don't think that's going to happen."

Standing off to the side with Happy Rockefeller, Marjorie Fisher was enjoying the circus-tent atmosphere of her first live press conference. She thought the faceless chorus of reporters was rude with their cross-examination of Nelson, pushing him to admit that he was a candidate. But she dismissed this insight, writing it off to her inexperience. Later, she would hear a different explanation from Nixon's campaign manager, John Mitchell.

Across the country, on Sunday morning, newspapers ran photos of a beaming Rockefeller shaking hands with Fisher. The headlines were variations on the same theme: Rocky will run if drafted. By then, Rockefeller was in New York, and Max and Marjorie were en route to Acapulco, Mexico, for a brief vacation at the villa of their friends, Lisa and John Anderson. Max was only staying until the following week. He had another Romney fund-raising affair scheduled in Michigan, this one featuring Governor John H. Chaffee of Rhode Island.

For the next several days the Fishers relaxed — swimming, touring the countryside and cruising the calm blue waters in the Andersons' boat. On Wednesday, February 28, Max and John went deep-sea fishing. By lunchtime, Max had radioed shore, proudly informing Marjorie that the fish were biting. Late that afternoon, the telephone in the villa rang. Marjorie answered it.

"Is Mr. Fisher there?" someone asked.

"May I ask who's calling?" Marjorie said.

"The New York Times."

"My husband," said Marjorie, "is not here. He's fishing."

The reporter told Marjorie that he wanted a quote from Max on the Romney announcement. When Marjorie asked what announcement, the reporter said that Romney had announced that he was dropping out of the race before the New Hampshire primary because his candidacy had not won wide enough acceptance among Republicans.

"I'll tell my husband," Marjorie said.

Marjorie contacted the boat and filled Max in. There was a short silence, a flash of loss, disappointment. He was surprised that Romney had not waited until after the New Hampshire primary and equally surprised that he had not phoned him.

"Well, Max," Marjorie said. "At least today hasn't been a total disaster. You did catch two fish."

Max and Marjorie finished out the week in Acapulco. During that time, Romney never called.

*   *   *

Twenty years after the fact, George Romney is convinced that Nelson Rockefeller gave his time and money to his campaign for two reasons: to use Romney as a stalking horse for his own moderate Republican candidacy and to woo Fisher into his camp. It was not his plunge in the polls, Romney says, that persuaded him to get out, but Rockefeller's press conference on February 24.

"I saw Max [when he came home from Mexico]," says Romney. "And he expressed disappointment that he hadn't had a chance to persuade me not to get out of the race. As long as I was active politically, Max was loyal. But I knew I couldn't win the nomination if Rockefeller was also in, because we would split the vote that wasn't going to Nixon. So the one thing I made certain of before I declared my candidacy was that Rockefeller was committed [to me]. As a result of a lack of understanding of my Vietnam position, I began to slip in the polls; [Rockefeller] began to rise. Then Rockefeller came for that fund-raising luncheon — ostensibly for me. I say 'ostensibly,' because previously [when reporters asked him if he would consider the nomination] he always said no; at that press conference [on February 24] he said he would accept a draft. That made him a candidate. The minute he did that I knew the jig was up. That was the reason I withdrew. In 1968, I was caught between two men who were determined to become president regardless of what it took. One was Nixon and the other was Rockefeller. Their methods were different, but both of them were taking care of me."

Fisher saw it differently. "George," he says, "always felt that Rockefeller was using him as a stalking horse. He started saying that, but it wasn't true. I had spent hours talking with Nelson. George knew it. Nelson just couldn't make up his mind. As for Nixon, everyone was underestimating him."

The particulars are now relegated to the fine-tunings of history. For the moment, in the late winter of 1968, Fisher was in demand. Rockefeller and Nixon called on him again, and so it was that the last chess moves of the '68 campaign were played.

Chapter 8

THE FINAL CURTAIN

UPON RETURNING FROM Mexico, Fisher did something that is highly unusual in American presidential politics: he went back over the Romney campaign books and refunded the surplus money. On March 4, 1968, he sent the following letter to Romney contributors: "We were all greatly surprised by the sudden withdrawal of our friend, Governor Romney, from the presidential race. This leaves me with a problem concerning the contribution you made to the governor's campaign, which today would be very useful as far as paying off some of the campaign debts. However, since this money was requested for the primaries in New Hampshire and Wisconsin, it is my feeling that in all conscience, this money should be returned."

The motives for the refund were manifold. Fisher had always been meticulous about money, a habit from business that carried over into fund-raising. Every penny he raised had to be accounted for. During Romney's second race for governor, Fisher went so far as to write a twelve-year-old a thank-you note for the fourteen cents he had contributed. Fisher felt that "the responsibility for money doesn't end when it's raised. Whoever raises the money must retain some supervision over it."

While the overt sentiment in this approach appears to be fiscal accountability, it is also true that Fisher preferred keeping his hands on the financial reins and utilized his grip to enter the decision-making process of Romney's inner circle. In addition, since Fisher intended to stand in the wings of power as long as possible, he knew that to be welcomed backstage by a president his reputation for honesty must be unblemished. Fisher even had one of his folksy sayings for the occasion: "It takes a man's whole life to build up a reputation for integrity. And only one day to lose it." The cruel truth of his observation was discovered by those indicted during Watergate. Fisher, from his beginnings in politics, had no intention of trusting his reputation to others and risking such a loss.

Finally, there was a practical impetus for Fisher's refunding the balance of Romney's war chest. Quite simply, Fisher wanted to be an adviser to a president and recognized that this would come through his ability to raise funds. With Romney out of the race, Fisher had to align himself with a contender and he would need the money again. From his years as a fundraiser and ample giver, he was aware that contributors, even wealthy ones, have a specific sum they earmark for contributions. If they exceed their budget, they are disinclined to hand over additional money.

Many of the contributors were surprised by the refunds. John B. Martin of the Republican National Committee wrote Fisher that he appreciated the return of his check, though he "had not really expected to see this again." But the shrewder contributors expected the letter or phone call that came months later: Fisher was now raising money for another presidential candidate and would they be so kind as to donate again.

Now, though, in mid-March, Fisher was being romanced by other Republican hopefuls. Governor Nelson Rockefeller was the first to call. He phoned Fisher in Palm Beach, saying he was probably going to run and would announce next Thursday.

Rockefeller said, "Come to New York and we'll have a lot of fun with this thing."

Fisher replied that he would consider it, but right now he was staying uncommitted.

Rockefeller went to Washington to confer with Republican leaders. They were not as optimistic as he had hoped. On Thursday, March 21, Fisher was in Findlay, Ohio, attending a board meeting at Marathon Oil Company. In the middle of the meeting, Fisher told everyone that he would have to stop and find a television set. Everyone hurried out and crowded into an office with a TV. Rockefeller was onscreen, telling reporters: "I have decided today to reiterate unequivocally that I am not a candidate campaigning directly or indirectly for the presidency of the United States."

Fisher was astounded. "That was Rockefeller," he recalls. "He was indecisive. He was running, then he wasn't running and then he ran. God, but he spent a lot of money."

The 1968 campaign was full of surprises, as if those vying for political leadership could do no better than mirror the psychic disarray of their society. On March 31, President Johnson told the nation that he would not seek or accept the nomination for another term as president. The Democratic candidacy was now up for grabs. Vice President Hubert H. Humphrey was a prospect. So was Senator Eugene J. McCarthy of Minnesota, who was pledging to end the war. McCarthy's competitor along the Democratic left wing was Senator Robert F. Kennedy of New York, who proved promising in the polls. Then there was the segregationist, former Governor George C. Wallace of Alabama, who by the summer of 1968 was showing a poll strength of 30 percent, enough to threaten that no candidate would receive a decisive majority in the Electoral College and the selection of a president would fall on the House of Representatives, which itself was acrimoniously divided on Vietnam and civil rights.

On April 4, Martin Luther King was assassinated in Memphis, Tennessee. Arson, vandalism and shooting broke out in New York, Washington, Boston, Detroit, Chicago and other cities across the country.

Nixon canceled all political activity for two weeks after King's death. On April 24, at 6 p.m., he landed at Pontiac Airport in Michigan to attend a private dinner with Romney and Fisher at Romney's house in Bloomfield Hills. Michigan delegates to the Republican National Convention in Miami were scheduled to be slated that weekend. Nixon wanted Romney's support and he wanted Fisher to raise money for him. Nixon was also in the market for a running mate. During the three-hour dinner, Romney discussed what was happening in the inner cities and told Nixon that he thought the answer to many of the problems could be found in volunteerism, involving local big business in the ghettos. When the three men finished discussing the urban crisis, Romney briefly spoke about his view of a vice president's responsibilities. Fisher later characterized Romney's perception of the job as "a super-vice president." Nixon, although appearing to listen intently, was most likely not impressed. Romney must have seemed even less impressive when he told Nixon that he would not come out publicly for him before the nominating convention. He said that he was going to stay neutral and would encourage the Michigan delegation to do likewise. This position disappointed Nixon on two fronts: he would not have the Michigan votes locked up prior to the Miami convention and Fisher would not go to work for him.

"I wanted to keep our options open," Romney says today. "It was not clear who was going to get the nomination and I thought by remaining uncommitted we would have some influence in Miami."

"Out of a sense of loyalty to George," Fisher says, "I [also] had to remain neutral. I had to keep our [Michigan] delegates pledged to him and he was pledged to remain neutral until after someone was nominated in Miami. It was Romney's idea. I'm not sure it was the best one he ever had, but he was a friend and we had been together through a lot and I just felt I owed it to him to remain neutral."

At a patio press conference, Nixon and Romney denied that their talk had been political. Nixon said that he had come to swap ideas on the Republican platform and that he and Romney had "agreed on many things." The reporters were not buying it. They asked about Fisher's presence. Romney answered that Fisher was invited because "he's a close mutual friend of both of us," adding that Fisher had participated in the discussion of issues. The reporters nodded politely at the formula responses, then focused on what everyone was wondering: Was Romney a candidate for vice president?

Nixon hedged, saying: "[Governor Romney will] play a

vital role in future politics. [He] ran a vigorous race and his decision to withdraw didn't take him out of politics. He's going to play a great role at the convention and he's going to play a role in any future administration that he may want to play."

Although Romney is convinced that "I was never on Nixon's short list to be vice president," his desire to remain neutral might have cost him the second spot on Nixon's ticket. In order to sign Fisher up, it seems that the Nixon team may well have been willing to cut that deal. According to John Mitchell, "Once Romney nose-dived, Dick and I talked a great deal with Max about the possibility of George Romney as a running mate. We wanted Max Fisher on board. He had great contacts in the Jewish communities and in the business world. I visited Max at his home [in Franklin] and discussed it very seriously. Max brought with him a whole network of contacts around the country, practically his own committee-to-elect. It meant a lot getting him. We discussed Romney's vice presidency very seriously as a result. But, well, Romney being Romney, it just wasn't in the cards."

Primarily, it was not in the cards because Romney formed a pact with Governor James Rhodes of Ohio and Governor Spiro T. Agnew of Maryland, all three pledging to withhold their support from any candidate until after Miami. Mitchell and Nixon got wind of Romney's pact, from which Agnew ultimately distanced himself to put Nixon's name in nomination at the convention. Romney's move was seen as disloyalty. And in politics, where memories are long — and Nixon's memory among the longest — Romney lost any chance he may have had to be on the Republican ticket.

Fisher continued to campaign with the Nixon people on behalf of Romney, particularly with John Mitchell, who, along with his wife, Martha, visited the Fishers in Detroit. "I did try to get George the vice presidency," says Fisher. "But he had gotten himself into a messy situation. And his conception of a 'super-vice president' — that just didn't fly."

One benefit of the Mitchells' visit to Detroit accrued to Marjorie, who had been perplexed at the behavior of the journalists during Rockefeller's February 24 press conference at the Pontchartrain Hotel. She had not understood the reporters cornering Rockefeller until he said he would accept a draft. Now, John Mitchell was about to solve the mystery.

Marjorie Fisher explains: "The four of us were going out to a fund-raising dinner and I had a hairdresser come to the house for Martha. She was off having her hair styled and Max was upstairs getting dressed. I had a drink with John downstairs. We talked about the campaign and I told him that I had never been to a political press conference before, and that I found it interesting when the reporters kept asking Nelson the same question. John said that he had never been worried about Romney [as a candidate]."

"I was worried about Rockefeller," Mitchell said. Then he told Marjorie that before Rockefeller went to talk to the press he had fed some reporters the question about whether or not he would accept a draft, with instructions to repeat it until Rockefeller answered it. He had been pleased with the resulting confusion. Marjorie, admittedly a stranger to the grittier tactics of campaigns, asked Mitchell how he could do such a thing.

"Weren't you the attorney representing both of them?" she said.

"Yes," Mitchell replied. "But we're all in politics. And I wanted Nixon."

*   *   *

If Marjorie Fisher was distressed by her husband's perpetual motion, she did manage to find a foolproof way of slowing him down: she kidnapped him. It was, she explained later, "the only way to get him to relax." What she did not mention was that it was also the only way, particularly in the heat of the 1968 campaign, to redirect his attention toward their family.

On Thursday afternoon, July 11, as Max was drumming up financial support for Nixon, he got a call at his office from Sol Eisenberg. Eisenberg, owner of Ken-Wal Products, a highly successful steel firm, was eight years younger than Max and had met him at a UJA of Detroit meeting in 1945. They rapidly established a rapport. From that time on, whenever Max was in town, Eisenberg spoke to him at least once a day, often twice. Eisenberg was a natural to be in on Marjorie's kidnapping plot because he also felt that Max needed to slow down. He knew the toll his interests took on him: the insomnia and exhaustion. And like Nathan Appleman, Eisenberg was one of the few men to whom Max would reveal his fears and frustrations, the growing criticism of him in the Jewish community as "Nixon's man," which would, after November, be transformed into "Nixon's court Jew." Whenever Eisenberg phoned Fisher's office he jokingly said to Fisher's assistant: "Tell the boss his psychiatrist wants to talk to him."

Now, on July 11, Eisenberg said to his friend: "Max, I'm going to make this deal. A man has a product playing and he's out at [Metropolitan] airport. He wants to have lunch on his plane. Will you come out and help me?"

Fisher agreed and drove to the airport with Eisenberg. They went to a private jet on the tarmac. Eisenberg boarded first, then Fisher. Marjorie and the forty family members and friends who were waiting for him cried out in unison, "Happy birthday!"

"Where are we going?" Max said, a little stunned. His birthday was not until the following Monday. "What are you doing with me? How long are we going to stay?"

"Good afternoon, Mr. Fisher," a stewardess said. "Welcome aboard. We're on our way to Las Vegas."

Max yelled: "I hate Las Vegas! And I don't have any clothes."

Marjorie replied: "You're all packed: your golf clubs, your swimsuits, everything."

"I have to see [Detroit] Mayor [Roman S.] Gribbs tomorrow," he said.

Marjorie said: "Everything's been canceled for the next four days."

In Las Vegas, the party checked into the Riviera Hotel. During the day they sat by the pool; at night they enjoyed dinner and a show, then went to gamble in the casino. Max pursued his political fund-raising by phone, but Marjorie made sure he spent most of his time by the pool. She felt that she was rewarded for her efforts. On the last morning of the trip, Marjorie, a self-described "five-dollar bettor," went to a dice table; though she knew nothing about the game, she won several thousand dollars.

*   *   *

In early August, Fisher went off to the Republican National Convention in Miami as a delegate-at-large from Michigan. Fisher was good to his word. He stood next to Romney on the convention floor and waited until Nixon defeated Rockefeller and Governor Ronald Reagan of California before declaring his support. When Nixon announced that Agnew would be his running mate, Republican liberals revolted. Mayor John V. Lindsay of New York entered Romney's name for the nomination, but Romney lost by a vote of 1,128 to 186.

When Fisher arrived back in Detroit, he wrote to Nixon, congratulating him on winning the nomination and complimenting him and his organization on their superb planning.

"I enjoyed meeting with your associate, John Mitchell," he said, "and as I have told you and John, I will try to be helpful in any way I possibly can. It is very important we have a discussion on the phone or in person at some time in the near future, and work out some personal problems I see developing with key persons. Today, it seems to me we should be rebuilding relationships so that we are united in a single purpose."

Nixon phoned him. "Max," he said, "I really want you on board [my campaign]. Help me out and there'll be a prominent position in it for you."

"Thank you," Fisher answered, "But I want a prominent position for George."

Nixon said that was a possibility and again asked Fisher what he wanted — for himself. Fisher's response was immediate; he had been thinking about it for three years, ever since that October afternoon in Gettysburg with Eisenhower. "All I want," he told Nixon, "is to be able to talk to you about issues that are of interest to me: the Middle East, energy, the economy."

Nixon replied that he would honor Fisher's request.

*   *   *

Fisher started his work for Nixon by making a contribution to his campaign of $150,000. Then he scoured the country by phone, tapping familiar sources: Benjamin Fixman in Missouri gave $25,000; Joseph Meyerhoff in Baltimore, $3,000; Bernard H. Barnett in Louisville, $25,000; Nathan Lipson in Atlanta, $5,000; Nathan Appleman in New York, $10,000. The list was culled from Fisher's phone book and ran for over 100 pages. Fisher saw his responsibilities as twofold, each one reinforcing the other: to raise money and to reach Jewish voters.

In *Before the Fall*, his memoir of his years working for Nixon, William Safire identifies the importance of the Jewish community in presidential elections: "The 'Jewish vote' should be insignificant. This 4 percent of the population could hardly affect the popular-vote totals. But this complicated American electoral system . . . has a way of preventing a tyranny of the majority. Jews make a difference in New York, Illinois, California, Florida, Ohio, and New Jersey . . . the 'battleground states.' Moreover, as Nixon pointed out to several of us in 1968, Jews are in the habit of voting, increasing their significance in the critical states by nearly half again. On top of that, every new Jewish vote Nixon could get was really two votes, since it usually meant the reduction of a vote against him. Traditionally, the Jewish vote for the presidency ran about four-to-one Democratic, but candidates for state races like Rockefeller and Javits would get as high as 35 percent, indicating that there was room for a 10 percent turnaround, enough to swing a key state in a tight election."

Fisher knew that Nixon's image in the Jewish community was poor. In 1960, gossip of Nixon's alleged anti-Semitism was so rampant in Jewish communities that the Anti-Defamation League felt compelled to release an official communiqué, stating that Nixon had always been a friend of the Jews. However, Fisher felt that Nixon's problem was that he had dismissed the Jewish community as a political liability and had not endeavored to win them over. When, in conversation with Fisher, Nixon disagreed with that analysis, Fisher said, "Dick, they don't dislike you, but you haven't made yourself known to them. Talk to them. They'll listen."

To facilitate his outreach program, Fisher convinced John Mitchell to establish a "Jewish Desk" within the campaign committee, a first in the history of either party. Martin R. Pollner, a senior associate at Nixon's law firm, was given the job. His qualifications, Pollner says, "were that I was Jewish and I was cute. Max underwrote the whole thing. I worked with the speechwriters, called around the country and set up meetings."

It was an expensive proposition. "A hundred thousand dollars didn't go very far, even back in '68," one Nixon campaign worker recalls. "There were ads to buy in the Jewish press, and the telephone bill alone to keep up with the amazing national structure Fisher was building was staggering."

Fisher kept encouraging Nixon to take his message straight to the Jewish community, and on the evening of September 8, Nixon did, speaking at B'nai B'rith's triennial convention at the Shoreham Hotel in Washington. Fisher volunteered to introduce him, one of the numerous signs of approval he was sending to the community. In addition, he discussed the content of Nixon's speech with him. Fisher said that because the Johnson administration had reneged on its shipment of Phantom jets to Israel, Nixon should focus on his belief that Israel should have military superiority over its Arab neighbors. He also warned the candidate against sounding unduly evenhanded, a message that the Jewish community believed was politicians' code for favoring the Arabs.

The Shoreham Hotel ballroom was packed when Fisher introduced Nixon. His speech, "The Cradle of Civilization Must Not Be its Grave," ranged over an assortment of topics. But within the opening two minutes, Nixon swung into the section that the B'nai B'rith audience would find sweeter than the lilting musical cantata that was performed to mark the organization's triennial. He said: "Israel must possess sufficient military power to deter an attack. . . . Sufficient power means the balance must be tipped in Israel's favor. . . . If maintaining that margin of superiority should require that the United States should supply Israel with supersonic Phantom F-4 jets, we should supply those jets."

Nixon was given a standing ovation by B'nai B'rith and the text of his address was published in its monthly newsletter. Fisher had the speech printed as a brochure and instructed Martin Pollner to send it to Jewish leaders around the country. Fisher mailed Pollner the names of thousands of suggested recipients; Pollner sent them off as fast as Fisher supplied them.

Following his address, Nixon flew to New York with Fisher. The candidate was pleased with his warm reception and grateful to Fisher for handling the introduction. Fisher thought they were sending the proper signs to the Jewish community. And Nixon had another one for them. On September 26, he appointed Fisher his special adviser on urban and community affairs. On the surface, the appointment appeared to be apolitical; Nixon was a fan of Fisher's philanthropic bent and enamored of his latest work with New Detroit, which he characterized as "a remarkable effort that is setting the pace for the country in solving some of our most urgent inner-city problems." But to the Jewish community, with rare exception excluded from the cherished clique of America's power, it was a signal that Nixon, if elected, was going to alter that precedent, and Fisher, among the best known of Jewish leaders, was going to be his man. The story of Fisher's appointment was deemed newsworthy enough to Jews that in Israel *The Jerusalem Post* ran a feature story on it.

"As a longtime friend and admirer of Richard Nixon," Fisher was quoted as saying, "I have joined the effort to elect him president because I firmly believe that he offers this country the qualities of leadership needed to meet the great problems that face us. Richard Nixon has a long and distinguished record in civil rights, a deep understanding of the problems of our cities and a profound knowledge of the situation in the Middle East and other critical areas."

After Israel's frustrating dealings with Johnson over delivery of the promised Phantoms, one can only guess at the joy with which this news was greeted in Jerusalem.

*　　*　　*

With Bobby Kennedy dead and Eugene McCarthy slipping, Vice President Hubert Humphrey won the Democratic nomination in Chicago, choosing Senator Edmund S. Muskie of Maine as his running mate. The Democratic Party was marred by dissension, a status that was not improved by television coverage of young protesters rioting during the convention nor the tear gas and free-swinging billy-club response of Mayor Daley's police. By September 30, Humphrey was trailing Nixon by fifteen points in the Gallup Poll. But in a nationally televised address from Salt Lake City, Humphrey altered his stance on Vietnam and stepped out from President Johnson's unpopular shadow. Previously, the Democrats asserted that any bombing halt would have to be accompanied by a reciprocal sign of peace from North Vietnam. Now, Humphrey said, "As president, I would stop the bombing of the North as an acceptable risk for peace because . . . it could lead to success in the negotiations and thereby shorten the war."

Within forty-eight hours, 5,000 letters of support flooded the Democratic National Committee. More important, for the DNC was drastically short of funds, the letters contained checks that totaled over $200,000. The favorable reaction to his speech and the money was a shot in the arm for Humphrey, and three weeks later, Nixon's lead dipped to five points. Humphrey, by then, with the bottom of his campaign chest showing, was as concerned with collecting six-figure contributions as he was with getting votes. Eager to cash in on his surge in the polls, he brought his campaign to New York City, the tried-and-true trough for presidential hopefuls. But, as one journalist observed: "When Hubert got there, the cupboard was bare."

Humphrey immediately ran into trouble at a private conference in the Waldorf-Astoria. Arthur J. Goldberg, former justice of the Supreme Court and United Nations ambassador, told the candidate that little money was available. His opinion was seconded by Humphrey's New York finance chairman, industrialist Marvin Rosenberg.

Reporter Robert Hoving of Michigan's *Grand Rapids Press* related what lay behind the scarcity of funds: "Max Fisher put a funnel under that source long before Humphrey [arrived]. Fisher now is collecting his political debts in cash from the wealthy Jewish community after having been a workhorse in raising money for [the UJA]. Fisher has been having success here in pointing out that Nixon supports increased military aid to Israel and believes that the Middle East military balance must be weighed in [Israel's] favor. This has been Humphrey's pitch, too. But here in New York, it seems to be a case of too late and too little."

As with his refund of the Romney contributions, Fisher was operating on his experience as a fund-raiser and benefactor, knowing that in a presidential election year, patrons would swiftly exceed their contribution limit. So, soon after Miami, Fisher harvested New York's bumper crop. Humphrey, however, should not have been surprised that Fisher beat him to it. The vice president had, six weeks before, asked Fisher to raise money for him. Just after Labor Day, Fisher was sitting in his Detroit office when the phone rang and his secretary told him that Humphrey was on the line. Fisher picked up and had a friendly chat with the vice president, discussing the trials and tribulations of a campaign, the disturbances in Chicago, the latest on Vietnam and the Middle East. Because, Fisher says, the true purpose of any business or political conversation is not disclosed until the final moments, he was not taken aback when, as the talk concluded, Humphrey said, "Max, you ought to raise money for me. I've been a good friend to Israel."

"You have been a good friend," Fisher replied. "But Hubert, I'm a Republican."

"Yes, Max," the vice president said, "you are."

The two men laughed and said goodbye.

Now, in October, Humphrey contacted Fisher again. He sent a note, saying, in effect, "Max, you are drying up funds that have been ours for years."

John Mitchell later remarked, "I think that Hubert probably thought that somewhere along the line Max would at least split the money with him fifty-fifty."

Humphrey, one suspects, thought that he was providing Fisher with the chance to don both jerseys, and regardless of who became president, he would have won the favor of the administration. Fisher was a pragmatist, but that cynical sort of pragmatism was distasteful to him. And since he felt that loyalty was the primary component of lasting political careers, he rejected Humphrey's offer and the vice president did not get his split.

Long after the election was over, Humphrey was haunted by his lack of funds. "We could have won, and we should have won," he was to say, and pointed to his poor financing. "It's not the amount of money you get," he said, "it's when you get it," for without a steady stream of financing there can be no coherent plan for producing radio and TV spots and buying airtime.

At least one member of the Nixon campaign team agrees with this assessment. He says: "At the end Dick was running out of gas and Humphrey was absolutely on top of his game. The last few weeks the only thing we could do was outbuy them on airtime. We spent and spent heavy. Some of us thought the campaign war chest was the margin of difference. [If] Humphrey could have matched the kind of money Max and [Maurice H. Stans] brought in, well, then it might have been a different story."

*   *   *

Fisher's capacity for finding money for Nixon in 1968 was based not only on his singular standing in the organized Jewish community, but also in the community itself. Maurice Stans, who directed Nixon's fund-raising efforts, is convinced that "the Jewish people are much more relaxed as contributors to any good cause because they are public-spirited. Those that have the means expect to contribute. Max knew best how to tap that particular faculty. His effectiveness was due to the force of his personality, his reputation, his ability to talk to important people one-to-one and his credibility. He knows his prospects going in and he doesn't waste any effort. They know him and his own reputation for giving. We'd send him out to someone who usually only gave $1,000 and Max would come back with $50,000 or $100,000. He was magnificent."

Rabbi Herschel Schacter, who has had a protracted and distinguished career in Jewish communal life, feels that Fisher "was able to corral enormous support in the upper echelons of Jews around America because all of them felt flattered to have Max Fisher call personally on them. Therefore, they contributed heavily. Fisher raised a lot of money from American Jews who respected his role in the leadership of the Jewish community."

Nixon saw Fisher's skill as a mixture of ingredients, not the least of which was his aptitude for identifying with the cause he was backing. Nixon says: "If I had something I wanted to raise money for — for cancer, a candidate — I would pick Max. There's no baloney with him. He'll put up his own money, make a big commitment himself. Then he'll get on the telephone with that network of his. But that's not all. Max becomes an alter ego to the candidate."

Fisher did bring a multitude of talents to this task. But it would be misleading to grant him full credit, for he was aided immeasurably by the tenor of the hour. A sudden shift in the political winds within the American Jewish community blew open a window of opportunity for him; he was perceptive enough to spot it and agile enough to climb through it. As with his accomplishments in business, his achievements during the campaign were founded on his uncanny timing, what Fisher would later describe as "luck."

In 1968, the American Jewish community, identified with the liberal wing of the Democratic Party since the 1920s, appeared to be drifting to the right of political center. Although dozens of highly visible Jewish leaders and celebrities were outspoken critics of U.S. involvement in Vietnam —

qualifying them for their left-wing colors — their fears for Israel's survival impelled them to reconsider any candidate who was a hard-liner in the face of indirect Soviet aggression, namely the supplying of weapons and advisers to the Arabs. On this score, Nixon was definitely the one. As syndicated columnists Evans and Novak pointed out: "Nixon took an unequivocal pro-Israel position, advocating, early and often, U.S. jets for Israel. Humphrey's tardy echo of the proposal was weakened further by President Johnson's move in the opposite direction."

Another cause of the apparent Jewish drift was the vocal anti-Semitism of black militants, which alienated and bewildered Jews, since the community was a champion of the civil-rights movement. There is some indication, though, that anti-Semitism had been rife — if concealed — among blacks for decades. In 1948, James Baldwin wrote: "I remember no Negro in the years of my growing up who did not . . . exhibit for [Jews] the blackest contempt. . . . When the Negro hates the Jew *as a Jew* he does so partly because the nation does and in much the same painful fashion that he hates himself. It is an aspect of humiliation whittled down to a manageable size and then transferred."

But by the late 1960s, these feelings were overtly expressed. Folksinger and activist Theodore Bikel and Rabbi Arthur J. Lelyveld, president of the American Jewish Congress, resigned from the Student Non-Violent Coordinating Committee when SNCC started vociferously condemning Israel, a motif that ran through the philosophy of other groups, such as the Nation of Islam and the Black Panthers. Even more distressing was that black anti-Semitism was also expressing itself in displays of violence. Rabbis, whose synagogues had not relocated from inner cities to suburbs, discovered swastikas painted on their buildings and had their stained-glass windows pelted with stones. Furthermore, the majority of white merchants burned out during the last few summers of urban rioting were Jewish.

Civil unrest was responsible for the introduction of the law-and-order theme into the campaign and it was stressed so ardently that Mayor Joseph Alioto of San Francisco quipped: "None of the candidates is running for president. They're all running for sheriff." Nixon appeared particularly tough on law and order, which now appealed to Jews, a majority of whom, like blacks, resided in cities. This disquieting new element in the relationship between the two minorities was characterized by Evans and Novak as "an unexpected dividend to Nixon."

The perceived shift in attitudes of the Jewish community received wide play in the press. Joseph Cummins, the influential publisher of California's *B'nai B'rith Messenger*, which had the largest circulation of any Jewish newspaper on the West Coast, told *The National Observer*: "When Dick Nixon ran for governor against Pat Brown in 1962, there was one nearsighted Jew in Boyle Heights who voted for Nixon because he didn't have his glasses on. That's the only one I know of."

Cummins, of course, was exaggerating, but he added that while he had been voting Democratic for a half-century, in 1968 he was voting for Nixon, and he believed a large bloc of Jewish Democrats would do the same.

A Gallup Poll predicted that in 1968 droves of Jewish Democrats would take a leave of absence from their traditional voting pattern. Gallup suggested that Humphrey could expect only a 20-percent plurality among Jewish voters, giving him, roughly, a 60-40 split, with George Wallace getting a minuscule vote. That would mean a dramatic shift from the 80 to 90 percent that Jewish voters had consistently given Democratic presidential candidates since the days of Calvin Coolidge.

The reasons mentioned in *The Observer* article for the switch were Israel, the urban crisis and that the Nixon organization had established a committee of prominent Jewish leaders, chief among them, "Max M. Fisher of Detroit, who is also special assistant to Mr. Nixon for urban and community affairs and national chairman of the [United] Jewish Appeal."

At Fisher's urging, Nixon capitalized on his freshly minted reputation in the Jewish community. He not only reached out on Israel, Soviet Jewry and interracial animosity, he paid attention to a matter of lesser urgency, a matter that, in the minds of many Jews, counted as a clear signal of how sensitive the candidate was to their community.

Back on June 21, Chief Justice Earl Warren submitted his resignation to President Johnson. Warren and Nixon disliked each other. The conventional wisdom was that Warren had resigned because he thought Nixon might win the election and have a chance to appoint a new chief justice and Warren wanted Johnson to make the appointment. Five days later, Johnson did just that, nominating his old crony, Associate Justice Abe Fortas, who happened to be Jewish. Senate Republicans were outraged and vowed to fight, threatening a filibuster to prevent Johnson from influencing the Supreme Court in the waning hours of his presidency.

In June, Nixon appeared to side with the Republican senators. He said: "I felt that it would have been wise for the president to have delayed his appointment until the new president had been elected."

Privately, Fisher told Nixon that his acquiescence in a Senate filibuster to block Fortas's confirmation would be held against him by Jews. The Jewish community had a special feeling for the Supreme Court, a conviction that they should be represented there since historically they had been excluded from the more visible posts in the White House and Cabinet. Then in September, according to Fortas's biographer, Bruce A. Murphy, Fisher "called a meeting between Nixon and twelve Jewish Republicans. . . . Once again Nixon tried his waffling routine, explaining that while he 'liked Fortas, some senators were . . . jealous of their prerogatives, especially Southern senators.' But for the first time he faced directly the charge that his policy of silence was fueling anti-Semitism. So, like a good politician, Nixon agreed to change his policy. He told the Jewish leaders that if the nomination became entangled in a Senate debate he would personally 'let it be known that he does not favor filibuster on the nomination.'"

*   *   *

Fisher believed that simply raising money for a presidential candidate was too shortsighted an assignment, too narrow a corridor of influence. Then the president would only require the assistance of the Jewish community every few years. Naturally, there was, Fisher realized, a synergy between support at every socioeconomic level of Jewish America and his facility for soliciting large givers; after all, everyone, rich or poor, was sensitive to the opinions of his neighbor. But, if Nixon were to win the election and Fisher and the Jewish community hoped to be heard at the White House, the community would have to become a factor in the ongoing mechanisms of day-to-day government, not merely the hugging-and-handshaking hoopla that accompanied a presidential campaign. To be included, the community would need to function as a cohesive bloc on an assortment of *issues*, never a strong suit when Israel was not directly involved. Thus, seeking grass-roots support for the programs Nixon would initiate as president, Fisher traveled the country, speaking to groups from New York to Los Angeles.

"I never used my titles [in Jewish organizations] when I campaigned for Nixon," Fisher says. "Of course, I couldn't help that every time I got up to speak, they used all my titles to introduce me." The national Anglo-Jewish and secular press included his titles in the coverage of his speeches and the list was impressive: president of the United Jewish Appeal, chairman of the United Israel Appeal (the major beneficiary of the UJA), chairman of the Executive Board of the American Jewish Committee and vice president of the Council of Jewish Federations and Welfare Funds.

As Rabbi Schacter says, "The message was clear. This wasn't just some wealthy Jew speaking. This was a recognized leader of the community. *Your* leader."

"It meant something to Jews all over the country," adds Irving Bernstein, "that a man of Max's caliber and integrity trusted Nixon. It also made political activity more kosher. And it gave people more hope that you could achieve something. [Yet] Max was never a parochial militant in politics. He has always taken the position that it is important for Americans — particularly Jewish Americans — to be involved in the process, whether you are a Democrat or Republican. His view would be, 'I wish you were a Republican, but if you're a Democrat, that's fine.' Max has always been a political animal."

"This type of politicking wouldn't happen again," Fisher says. "The Jewish organizations are a lot more careful about leaders taking political stands now. But then, in '68, what were they going to say to me? Resign from the UJA? Resign from the UIA and CJF? Nobody tells you to resign when you're doing the job."

On October 18, with Humphrey gaining on Nixon, Fisher was at the New York Hilton Hotel, addressing the publishers of Anglo-Jewish newspapers from across the country. He referred to the Gallup Poll showing Jewish support for Nixon and promised that 1968 would be "a precedent-shattering election." After citing Nixon's pledge to tip the balance of power in the Middle East toward Israel and reviewing the reasons for Jewish dissatisfaction with the Johnson administration's performance at home and abroad, Fisher threw a roundhouse right at Humphrey's campaign team. He said: "The fact that George W. Ball has become Vice President Humphrey's chief political adviser has not reassured American Jews with regard to Mr. Humphrey's Middle East position. Mr. Ball, as United States ambassador to the United Nations, joined with the United Nations Security Council in censoring Israel. And now that he is out of government, he offers pious words about trying to bring about arms control in the Middle East, while the Soviet Union continues to provide massive arms, including jets, to the Arab states."

Yet what may well stand as Fisher's greatest single coup during the 1968 campaign harked back to what he had told Nixon in August: that the candidate had to make himself known to American Jews. Fisher had helped fill in this void, bringing Nixon before B'nai B'rith and then crisscrossing the country to proselytize for him. Now, he wanted Nixon to face a more intimate and influential circle of the community, the segment that held sway over the breadth of Jewish communal operations. So Fisher courted the Conference of Presidents of

Major American Jewish Organizations. The Presidents Conference, as it has come to be known, was founded in 1955 by the World Zionist Organization's Dr. Nahum Goldmann and comprised the leadership of nearly every significant Jewish communal group, twenty-four in all. (Like most Jewish communal assemblies, the Presidents Conference had a professional leader, Yehuda Hellman, who served as its executive director until his death in 1986, and a rotating volunteer chairman, drawn from the heads of its member organizations.) The concerns of the Presidents Conference extended beyond internal organizational issues. It had evolved into the recognized voice of organized American Jewry in international affairs. Fisher felt that if Nixon could persuade these leaders of his commitment to Israel, they in turn would carry his message to their constituencies.

For almost two months, Fisher tried to arrange a meeting between Nixon and the Presidents Conference. Fisher was not well acquainted with Hellman, but knew the chairman, Rabbi Herschel Schacter. However, by design, the Presidents Conference was a nonpartisan assembly. The members were resistant to being politicized in the name of any party. They had, in fact, never met with a presidential candidate. But the Six-Day War sensitized American Jews as never before to the stake Israel had in who sat in the Oval Office, and with Fisher, among others, influencing him, Nixon was speaking the language the community longed to hear.

Obviously, the Presidents Conference was listening, because soon after Nixon's speech to B'nai B'rith, Fisher received a letter from Rabbi Schacter. "We have noted with satisfaction the recent statements by Mr. Nixon on the serious threats to Israel's security," Schacter wrote. "We would therefore appreciate an opportunity to meet with Mr. Nixon for an off-the-record discussion of the various vital issues currently of paramount concern to us. We feel that such a meeting, where Mr. Nixon could hear and exchange views with the authentic leaders of the American Jewish community, would be of inestimable value to him and to us."

The meeting took place on October 21 in the Presidents

Conference headquarters at 515 Park Avenue in New York City.

Yehuda Hellman recalls: "It was my first exposure to Max Fisher. I had heard of him. I knew he was a wealthy Jew, a respected leader. But what struck me so strongly that day was that here was this powerful figure and yet no detail was too small for his personal attention. Where should the chairs be? Where should the pencils be? Who should sit here? Who should sit there? How should questions be addressed? Who would introduce? He literally arranged the chairs himself. He was nervous. But who wouldn't be? This was a historic meeting in terms of the Jewish community, and he had set it up. Who knew how it would go?"

Fisher admits he was nervous. "I was worried that they might be cruel to Nixon. There was a lot of opposition to him in parts of the [Jewish] community. It was emotional. I caught some of it when I was out speaking for him. The Alger Hiss hearings; the Checkers speech; the way he lost his cool with the press after he lost in '62 for governor of California."

At the meeting, Fisher introduced Nixon and the candidate went to work. It was a perfect match: Nixon, the anti-Soviet hard-liner, and Jewish leaders who were frightened of how Russian support would encourage the Arab states to renew their attacks on Israel.

Nixon told the Presidents Conference that it was necessary for the Soviets to understand that the United States will not tolerate any Russian takeover of the Middle East or the destruction of Israel. "That," he said, "was 'preventative diplomacy.' The Soviet Union must not believe that we will remain idle if one of the Soviet client states in the Middle East made a move toward Israel." He reiterated his belief that it was in the vital interest of the United States and the cause of world peace that Israel possess military superiority to deter Arab aggression. "The Arabs," he said, "are seeking vengeance against the Israelis, while Israel is only seeking to defend its own independence."

Nixon was asked about the religious-cultural repression of Jews in the Soviet Union. He replied that the concern of

Americans for the freedom of Soviet Jews must be adequately communicated on many levels to Russian leaders. When questioned about the urban crisis, Nixon voiced appreciation for the role of Jewish voluntary associations in advancing human rights and in the war on poverty. He said the time had come to involve private citizens, as well as the government, in the problems of the cities, and said he hoped to establish machinery for Jewish voluntary organizations — as well as those of other faiths, and civic bodies — to play a more direct part in solving the problem.

Nixon had been saying these things throughout his campaign; Jewish leaders could have read them in the newspaper over coffee at their breakfast tables. What made Nixon's talk with the Presidents Conference so triumphant was the intimacy of it, a give-and-take intimacy in which grand pronouncements that had echoed along the campaign trail were reduced to the trustworthy size of personal vows. It was also a sign of access; if the candidate would meet with Jewish leaders, wouldn't that suggest that he would do the same as president? Word spread in the Jewish community; the meeting was regarded so favorably that Humphrey's campaign strategists promptly requested one for their candidate and got it. But Nixon had been there first and it was his triumph that was reported in the national and Jewish press, under banner headlines proclaiming, "Nixon Says Soviets Must Understand USA Will Not Permit Takeover in Mideast."

In spite of Fisher's efforts in the Jewish community, the choice of a president appeared to be turning on the war in Vietnam. On October 31, with the election five days away, President Johnson announced a bombing halt and maintained that North Vietnam had assented to expanded peace talks and to desist from attacking South Vietnamese cities. Polls taken the next day showed that Americans favored this course of action by a 2-to-1 margin. On November 2, the Louis Harris Survey had Humphrey surging past Nixon, 43 percent to 40 percent, with Wallace at 13 percent, and 4 percent undecided. That same day, however, President Thieu of South Vietnam weakened Johnson's claim when he said that his government would not sit down with their enemies. Now, peace seemed improbable and the election was shaping up as a dead heat.

* * *

Election Day fell on November 5, which happened to be Marjorie Fisher's forty-fifth birthday. That evening, her friends Bea and Sidney Solomon hosted a lavish black-tie dinner in her honor at their house. During the party Max made brief appearances to eat and to socialize. But he spent most of the evening closeted in the Solomons' library staring nervously at the television set. The presidential race was too close to call. The returns rocked back and forth and, Max thought, appeared to be repeating the pattern of 1960 — not a good sign. He had the same uncomfortable feeling he had experienced eight years ago, the same edginess, a vague sense of foreboding. At nine o'clock, Nixon had 41 percent of the vote; Humphrey had 38 percent. By ten, the two were running even, and at midnight, as the guests said their goodbyes outside in the wintry Michigan wind, Humphrey had shouldered ahead by 600,000 votes.

The Fishers returned to their house. Max tossed and turned and then quit trying to sleep. He got out of bed, put on his robe and slippers, and went downstairs. He sat in the library watching the early news programs until it was announced that Nixon had won by less than 1 percent of the vote, outpolling Humphrey 31,770,237 to 31,270,533. Fisher stared at the TV for an instant, then went upstairs to shower and dress. By 11:30 a.m., when Humphrey phoned Nixon to concede the election, Fisher had boarded a plane and was en route to Nixon headquarters in New York.

* * *

In assessing the scope of Fisher's contribution to the 1968 campaign, one could point to the money he gave — $150,000 — which qualified him for what Maurice Stans called Nixon's honorary "Century Club," twenty-six people who donated $100,000 and over. (Fisher spent close to another $60,000 in expenses that he incurred for his own traveling and to fund activity in the Jewish community.) You could also point to the money Fisher raised: $3.5 million out of the $36.5 Nixon spent for his nomination and election. The Jewish vote, however, the focus of such optimistic speculation by Fisher and others, tallied a disappointing 16 percent for Nixon. Humphrey had remained attractive to Jews. Compassionate, liberal, strongly on the side of Israel, any vote Nixon won from him would have to be counted as a victory. Fisher's investment in turning the Jewish community away from the Democrats would not pay dividends until 1972. The most evident result of Fisher's work was the forging of his own national identity as *the* Jewish Republican leader. As if to confirm this perception, Nixon would affectionately call Fisher the "Republican Bernard Baruch — without the park bench."

Nixon's intention was to flatter. Baruch was a Wall Street investor and philanthropist who was a power in the Democratic Party. He served, often unofficially, nine presidents, from Wilson to Johnson, as an adviser and troubleshooter. Yet there was a glaring distinction between the way Baruch and Fisher operated. And it is here, in this distinction, that one ascertains the range of Fisher's achievement. It is perhaps his tightest claim on history, and lay the foundation for much that he accomplished in Washington, in Jerusalem, and between the leaders of both capitals.

Yehuda Hellman states: "Fisher's philosophy is diametrically opposed to Baruch's. Baruch saw himself as a great individual. He wanted to shape events and insisted that the [American Jewish] community be behind him. Baruch never wanted to take anyone with him. Fisher insists on it. Historically, American Jews have had a series of strong personalities, but they acted as individuals. Fisher has a community consciousness. He is a master of the art of inclusiveness."

The net result, according to Hellman, was that "starting in 1968, Max Fisher politicized Jewish America as it had never been done. He defined the new parameters of the Jewish community's relation to the presidency and politics."

Chapter 9

LEARNING HIS PART:
1969-1970
THE NIXON WHITE HOUSE,
PART I

SHORTLY AFTER THE election, Fisher spoke privately with Nixon. The newly elected president thanked Fisher for his assistance in the campaign and said that Fisher was welcome to an appointment as an ambassador. The offer, Nixon explains, was pro forma, because he never expected Fisher to accept anything.

"And he never did," says Nixon. "Max is a very successful, self-made man. He likes associations with important people, but he didn't need status, and some major business people do need it. That's all an ambassador has — status. Maybe if you're ambassador to China when there's trouble, then you might play a part. But usually a person doesn't make that much difference as an ambassador — as long as he doesn't make an ass of himself. I should add that Max's wife, Marjorie, didn't need it either. Sometimes, the wives push these people. They think it's a big deal to get an honored place at every state dinner and be referred to as 'Madame Ambassador.'"

Fisher told Nixon that he was flattered by his offer, but he declined it on the grounds that an ambassadorship was incompatible with his interests. The president inquired if Fisher might be interested in a Cabinet post. No, Fisher said, but he had hoped that there would be room in Nixon's Cabinet for

George Romney. There was, Nixon said. Romney was going to resign as governor of Michigan to head the Department of Housing and Urban Development (HUD).

Fisher characterizes his unwillingness to accept a spot in the administration as "keeping his eye on the ball," meaning that he wanted to remain fixed on his goal — becoming the sort of adviser that former President Eisenhower had mentioned in 1965. Since Fisher shared Nixon's opinion that an ambassador's function was chiefly ceremonial, an ambassadorship would be of no use to him. Nor would a position in the Cabinet, even though it was closer to the seat of power than a foreign embassy. But Fisher believed that to sign on with an administration in *any* official capacity was to be indebted to the president who bestowed the distinction on him, and you paid off that debt by relinquishing your influence. Now influence is the currency of politics, hoarded in the treasuries of government. Therefore, to owe a favor is the antithesis of influence, an unacceptable state to Fisher, who planned to spend the rest of his life perfecting his own personal fulcrum and studying the responsible uses of its leverage.

What then, Nixon asked, did Fisher want?

Fisher repeated what he had told Nixon during the campaign; he just wanted to have access to him.

Nixon agreed, and they shook hands. And with that handshake Fisher's influence at the White House began, an influence that was both celebrated and attacked and, as a rule, mistaken for a power that he did not possess.

Power and influence are frequently used as synonyms. Yet though these two terms are political siblings, they are not identical twins. Power is defined as the control or authority over situations or people; influence is the ability to affect or alter by indirect or intangible means. To confuse the words in casual conversation is a petty error, say, on the order of eating your steak with your salad fork — not altogether proper, but entirely functional.

However, to confuse the difference between power and influence when trying to understand Max Fisher's association with the Nixon (and Ford and Reagan and Bush) White House is to miss his genuine function. Because Fisher was outside the government, he had no sanctioned power; he was not a prime mover. The events in which he was invited to participate were not of his own making, nor were the policies that gave rise to the events. Of course, Fisher's influence — his *restricted* and *indirect* capability to alter the *outcome* of events — was based on his positioning as a supporter of Nixon. But the most pivotal factor in creating Fisher's diplomatic chance evolved from Nixon's method of conducting foreign policy and his consequent relations with his State Department.

In *RN*, Nixon admits that well before his inauguration on January 20, 1969, he "planned to direct foreign policy from the White House." This plan led him to appoint his old friend, William P. Rogers, as secretary of state. Rogers, according to Nixon, was "a strong administrator," with demonstrated ability, as attorney general under Eisenhower, to "get along with Congress." During the Nixon administration, Rogers's primary purpose would be "managing the recalcitrant bureaucracy of the State Department." Nixon naturally does not write of Rogers's experience in foreign affairs, since Rogers did not have any.

Nixon appointed a Harvard University professor, Dr. Henry A. Kissinger, his assistant for national security affairs. Kissinger's global view of the U.S.-Soviet conflict matched Nixon's; he and his staff operated out of the White House; and his appointment furthered Nixon's aim of directing foreign affairs from the Oval Office. Finally, once Nixon had the machinery in place to circumvent the bureaucracy, he realized that he required lines of diplomatic communication outside of official channels.

Nixon explains: "It is important for a president to have input beyond what he gets from State and Defense and the National Security Council, because while they are all very good, they are also very parochial. The communications you get from them tend to be terribly formalized. The same is true of leaders of other countries. They do not speak candidly; they talk to their constituencies and to history. So a president occasionally finds it useful to reach out to someone who can give you an understanding of the players, of what they really feel. You can throw out ideas that foreign leaders would have to deny publicly, but that they can consider privately. You could run foreign policy without these people, but you wouldn't run it as well.

"You read *The Washington Post* and *The New York Times*, and you'll see all these experts burbling about the need to do things through official channels. Let me tell you: if we had done things through channels, we wouldn't have had the opening to China; we wouldn't have had SALT I; we wouldn't have had negotiations to end the war in Vietnam. Generally, you should try to get it through channels so that you have an orderly procedure. But when you have controversial and complex issues, like the Middle East, it is necessary to use private communication."

As the Nixon administration got under way, the president did arrive at a quasi-official designation for Fisher: he named him his liaison to the American Jewish community. His duties, however, were unclear — even to White House staffers. One assistant, John R. Brown III, sent Chief of Staff H.R. Haldeman a memorandum asking: "Since the president has charged Max Fisher with responsibility for liaison for the Jewish community on a nationwide basis, does this mean that presidential correspondence concerning the affairs of the Jewish community should be forwarded to him for response?"

Haldeman's reply did little to clarify Fisher's assignment. After initialing the no-line on the memo, Haldeman wrote: "But he should be informed on general activities relating to the Jewish community."

The first of these activities was ceremonial. On February 26, 1969, Israeli Prime Minister Levi Eshkol died suddenly of a heart attack. Nixon asked Fisher to be part of a four-man delegation representing the United States at the funeral. The delegation was headed by Secretary of Health, Education and Welfare Robert N. Finch, and included U.S. Ambassador to Israel Walworth Barbour, and Assistant Secretary of State for

Near Eastern and South Asian Affairs Joseph J. Sisco. Eshkol
had been the first Israeli leader that Fisher had met, back in
1954, and the leader that Fisher credited with teaching him
the raison d'être of Israel. Yet, as Fisher stood before Eshkol's
grave on Mount Herzl, his sadness was compounded by the
sense that his potential for aiding Israel at the White House
was at the moment as dim as the chilly gray light obscuring
the hills of Jerusalem.

*   *   *

However undefined his role between Washington and
Jerusalem, Fisher was clearer on his domestic goals. As a special presidential consultant on voluntary participation, Fisher
had an office in the Executive Office Building and at HUD,
where since January he had been spending three days a week
working with Secretary Romney to found a national center
that would coordinate volunteer urban-renewal and social-
welfare programs across the country. During the campaign,
Nixon had pledged to provide "a new measure of reliance on
voluntary efforts." Fisher and Romney were anxious to set
private industry to work on the inner cities. They hoped that
their program would partially mirror what Fisher was doing at
New Detroit, Inc.

In part, Fisher was pushing for a national center on volunteerism because of his experience at NDI. But while he felt
that the lessons of philanthropic organizations could be
applied to the U.S. social agenda, he was even more troubled
by the expanding polarization between blacks and whites, and
he believed that uniting leaders from both communities could
ameliorate this trend. His belief hardened into conviction in
late March, when violence erupted at the New Bethel Baptist
Church in Detroit, and the city was again seized by tragedy
and racial rhetoric.

Historian Sydney Fine, author of *Violence in the Model
City*, characterizes the Bethel incident as "the most serious of
the postriot confrontations between the police and the black
community." It occurred on the evening of March 29, 1969,
when approximately 250 members of a black militant separat-

ist group, the Republic of New Africa, were meeting inside the New Bethel Church on Linwood and Philadelphia, an area that had been hard hit by the 1967 riot. At around midnight, two patrolmen, Michael Czapski and Richard Worobec, were cruising past the church when they saw about a dozen RNA members on a street corner, some of them carrying firearms. The patrolmen left their cruiser, and as they approached the men, shots were fired at them. Czapski was killed; Worobec, hit in the thigh, dragged himself to the patrol car and radioed for assistance.

Fifty police officers were soon storming the church. The police later claimed that riflemen in the church shot at them, which led the police to return fire. However, a church janitor said that the police were lying and that the women and children in the church were "screaming and completely hysterical trying to get away from the [policemen's] shots." The police arrested the 142 people inside the church, confiscating nine rifles, three pistols and some ammunition.

The prisoners were taken to the First Precinct downtown, and by 6 a.m., Recorder's Court Judge George W. Crockett Jr. (who was black) was holding hearings in the police station. He heard the cases of thirty-nine prisoners, releasing sixteen of them on personal bonds of $100 with instructions to reappear at noon in court, discharging one with the consent of the assistant prosecutor and remanding the other twenty-two to police custody until the noon hearing. When Prosecutor William Calahan (who was white) arrived, he protested Crockett's actions, contending that the police lacked sufficient time to process their prisoners and that Crockett had released some prime suspects. Crockett retorted that the police had already had several hours to process their prisoners — most of whom had no benefit of counsel, a violation of their constitutional rights. Crockett warned Calahan not to interfere with the prisoners' release, but Calahan ignored the warning. Crockett charged that Calahan's behavior was "not only a personal affront, but it also had racial overtones."

The violence was shortly overshadowed by the racial malice loose in the city. The media portrayed Crockett as the villain, but their portrayal paled beside the criticism from the Detroit Police Officers Association, who called for Crockett's dismissal in a full-page ad in *The Detroit News*.

In defending himself, Crockett stoked the fires of racial resentment. Stating that "a black judge's views in Detroit will be obeyed as long as he has the power to act," Crockett posed a rhetorical — and loaded — question at a press conference: "Can any of you imagine," he asked, "the Detroit Police invading an all-white church and rounding up everyone in sight to be bussed to a wholesale lockup in a police garage?"

Crockett's actions had almost universal support in the black community. More than 500 blacks of every political stripe formed the Black United Front and picketed the Recorder's Court until halted by an injunction. The attitude of young black militants was succinct: "If Crockett goes, Detroit goes."

Fisher and New Detroit, Inc. had long been concerned about the relationship of the police to the black community, regarding it as the most critical barrier to progress in race relations in the city. Because of their concern, eighteen days before the New Bethel incident, Fisher disclosed that NDI was initiating a police-community relations study and a police-management study. Then came New Bethel, and whatever Fisher and NDI might have learned from the studies would have to wait. By April 2, when New Detroit held its monthly board meeting, Fisher felt that the city was about to erupt. At the board meeting, during a discussion of Judge Crockett's decision, Novell Harrington, a twenty-year-old black board member, stalked angrily out of the closed session. Harrington told reporters he walked out because he wanted NDI to convene a committee to meet on police-community relations and Harrington wanted to be on it.

"We have to have [that committee] today," Harrington heatedly told reporters. "If not, you don't know what kind of hell I can raise." When Harrington was asked if that could include a riot, he answered, "It could."

Minutes after Harrington spoke to the press, Fisher took Harrington aside for a private conversation. According to reporters, Harrington seemed "partly mollified." Fisher had promised to look into the relations between the police and the community and to get in touch with him within a day.

Then Fisher addressed a news conference, asking Detroit's black and white citizens to examine events since the slaying of patrolman Michael Czapski "on the basis of facts, not rumors or nitpicking. We as a community are at a crucial time. Let us examine what is happening in a calm atmosphere. We cannot afford to go back to 1967. There has been a tendency to polarize, which I consider unfortunate. [We should not] choose up sides."

Breaking with his usual procedure as the chairman of New Detroit and hoping to use his personal credibility to stem the white backlash, Fisher said that he was going to comment as a private citizen. He told reporters that he believed that Judge Crockett used "honest judgment" when he ordered the release of a number of blacks who had been arrested after the incident. "Judge Crockett," said Fisher, "is an honest man who is trying to do what is right."

The white backlash persisted. Upon hearing Fisher's comments, a high-ranking police officer remarked that "the big guys are on the niggers' side."

Fisher was struggling to keep his own anger in check. He had been incensed by the roundup in the church because the police had grabbed dozens of children and kept them in jail overnight. But he confronted the imbroglio with his standard combination of pragmatism and consensus building. NDI solicited funds to repair the New Bethel Church and offered a $7,500 reward for information leading to the arrest of Czapski's killer. (No one was ever convicted of the shootings.) Then Fisher met with the media, and with black and white civic leaders, enlisting them in his vision of harmony. It was a modest vision and a portable one, for Fisher carted it with him into each of his endeavors. In the case of New Bethel, he gathered representatives of opposed viewpoints and asked them to solve the same dilemma, thereby reducing their volatile disputes to friendly differences of opinion on solutions to practical problems. To Fisher, this was the craftsmanship of the possible. He knew it would not heal the racial scars in Detroit, but it would ease the city past the crisis.

At a press conference on May 2, Fisher announced that New Detroit's Law Committee had completed a thirty-six-page document, *The New Bethel Report: The Law on Trial.* Fisher stated that the report vindicated Crockett, showing this his actions were just. When Carl Parsell, president of the Detroit Police Officers Association, read the report, he said that members of New Detroit would be "cowards or fools" if they approved it. Fisher replied: "Mr. Parsell is entitled to his opinion," and the report was adopted unanimously by NDI following what *The Detroit News* described as "an unusually short meeting."

The Bethel incident may have been behind the city, but Fisher was well aware that the germ of the conflict was present. He felt that the police would never get cooperation from the community if the people believed that they could not expect fair treatment from the police. By November 21, 1969, Fisher was demanding that he be given a copy of the study made of the Detroit Police Department management by the International Association of Chiefs of Police. It was the first section of the two-part study that NDI had put into motion less than three weeks before Czapski and Worobec were shot.

"[NDI was] asked to pay for it," Fisher told reporters, "but we haven't seen it. I don't know if the report is critical or not critical of the department. I won't know until I see it."

Fisher had personally requested a copy and been rebuffed. The study cost somewhere between $3,000 and $5,000, and Fisher said that NDI wasn't "going to pay for the study if we don't get a copy of it."

Both studies were eventually released, and according to Sydney Fine: "Of seventy-three administrative changes recommended by the Police-Community Relations Committee, the Police Department had implemented sixty-eight within two years. . . . It had recruited more blacks, who made up 14 percent of the department . . . and the department had resolved ambiguities regarding the use of deadly force. . . . Although New Detroit judged what had occurred to be only 'a qualified success,' police-community relations were in a far less troubled state as of July 1972 than they had been during the final seventeen months of the Cavanagh administration that followed the July 1967 riot."

Fisher's experience with NDI was one of the compelling reasons he pressed executives to enlist in his volunteer program in Washington. On April 15, Fisher, Romney and a dozen executives from life insurance companies around the nation came to the White House to meet with Nixon. The companies, urged on by Fisher and Romney, had committed $1 billion to core city areas in housing, health care and jobs.

Four days later, Fisher and Romney spent an hour with Nixon and his domestic adviser, John D. Ehrlichman. Romney said that their program, a nonprofit, nonpartisan group, would be known as the National Center for Voluntary Action (NCVA), and it was almost ready to go. The center, headquartered in Washington, would be a depository of information on successful volunteer programs throughout the United States, and would dispatch task forces to help communities tailor volunteer projects to local needs. Nixon asked Fisher to be the chairman. Fisher accepted and suggested that Clem Stone, a Chicago insurance executive and a Nixon friend, serve as the center's finance-committee chairman. It was, Fisher said, important to involve as many leaders of big business as possible; therefore, a board of directors would be established with the eighty or ninety members drawn from industry, volunteer organizations and civic groups. Fisher and Romney were in the process of selecting a nominating committee for the board.

In closing, Romney said that he thought they could have the center operational by Thanksgiving.

* * *

In 1969, Fisher was elected president of the Council of Jewish Federations and Welfare Funds, an association of 200 local federations throughout 800 communities in the United States and Canada. At the General Assembly in Boston where Fisher was elected, he was immediately confronted by hun-

dreds of college students protesting at the entrance of the
hotel, in the halls and conference rooms. The students felt
that the CJF wasted time, energy and resources by just
meeting mundane local needs — for example, building community centers or supporting day camps — and not promoting
the loftier ideals of Jewish culture through increased funding
to Hillel Foundations on campuses or sponsoring intellectual
journals. The students planned to disrupt the plenary session
— chain themselves to microphones and picket in the aisles.
Though one can scarcely categorize the student protest as a
grave crisis, Fisher's reaction to it is one of the most lucid
illustrations of his technique for handling conflict.

Philip Bernstein, who served as chief executive officer of
the CJF from 1955 until 1979, recalls: "Max invited about
twenty of those young people to his suite. He sat around on
the floor with them and said, 'All right, tell us what you
want.' And they did. Max replied: 'We're not going to just
hand out money. We have to be responsible. We're trustees of
funds. But in terms of suggesting programs and helping to
implement them, you have an open door. I promise: you will
be involved in our committees and our ongoing work.' And
that's what he did. He put them on committees. Fifteen years
later, some of those kids were deeply involved in the Jewish
community. Hillel Levin — he was the students' spokesman
— became head of Judaic studies at Yale."

In 1971, the CJF General Assembly was again targeted by
college-age protesters. They represented Rabbi Meir Kahane's
Jewish Defense League (JDL) and wanted the CJF to adopt a
more militant stance toward the Soviet Union's treatment of
its Jewish citizens. The JDL members locked arms and snake-
danced through the audience, singing Hebrew songs loud
enough to drown out the business that Fisher was trying to
conduct from the podium. Fisher considered the JDL destruc-
tive, and since they had been threatening to disrupt the CJF
Assembly for weeks, he was prepared.

Philip Bernstein remembers: "Max arranged to finish the
important business at the beginning of the meeting to make
sure that we got through as much as we could before the JDL

showed up. When they arrived, Max kept his cool. He would not call the police, nor would he have them thrown out. He just let them sing and dance while he ran through his agenda. The JDL protesters wanted to be arrested; they wanted publicity. The next day the newspapers carried maybe one line about them. Max acted as if they weren't even there. He was just that smart."

*   *   *

Despite the progress at New Detroit, the CJF and with Romney, Fisher was at a loss for where he fit in between Washington and Jerusalem. Ironically, Nixon already had a spot in mind for him — a historical paradigm that the president adjusted to match his concept of how to proceed with the pragmatic chores of foreign affairs.

"The most famous example in American history of a private citizen becoming involved in diplomacy is that of Colonel Edward M. House," says Nixon. "House was a close friend of President Woodrow Wilson and was a quasi-government official by the time they started to negotiate the Versailles Treaty. Prior to that time, House was an intermediary whom Wilson often used because Wilson trusted him. Wilson was not that close to his secretaries of state. He didn't like William Jennings Bryan. Nor did Wilson get along with his other secretary of state, Robert Lansing. So House became the president's closest adviser. Now that's an extreme position. And it wasn't Max's position with me."

In his book, *Leaders*, Nixon writes that Woodrow Wilson was the "ideal" man to be president, and judges him "a great creative thinker" and "a decisive man of action." So an affiliation modeled on the one Wilson enjoyed with House appealed to him. And like Wilson — albeit for different reasons — Nixon was bypassing his secretary of state. While Fisher's friendship with Nixon did not duplicate the inordinate Wilson-House closeness, it did provide the president with other advantages. Fisher, unlike House, returned a political dividend to Nixon — besides the money he contributed and raised — namely access within the organized American Jewish community and the use of his friendships with Israeli officials.

"Max," says Nixon, "had excellent credentials with the Israelis. He had excellent credentials with me. I trusted him as someone who would honestly report to me what he thought and who had unusually good political judgment. Max also suggested ideas that would not come from the bureaucracy. I knew that if we relied solely on the bureaucracy we would just continue along the same lines. We needed to be bold. And boldness is not something that bureaucrats get involved in: bureaucrats protect their butts. It's true in the business world as well. Max knew that. Your average CEO isn't just going to rely on his bureaucrats — he's going to go out and break a little china."

With regard to domestic politics, Nixon knew that by granting Fisher access to him, he was strengthening Fisher's hand in the American Jewish community, while Fisher, by having the access, was increasing the value of Nixon's stock in that community.

"I was happy to do it," says Nixon. "After all, I am a politician, and I hope, at times, a statesman. But by building up Max, I was building up a responsible person. A president has to realize that there are some irresponsibly partisan people in the Jewish community. Max believed in a balanced approach. He was not what I would consider — and this is not said in derogation — a professional Jew. There are professional Jews. There are professional Quakers: I happen to be one. There are professional Irish; some of the worst, in my opinion. And the Greek lobby is the toughest. [They] take an attitude toward the Turks that would get rid of NATO's southern hinge if you didn't support them on Cyprus.

"Now, what we call 'the Lobby for the Cause of Israel,' " Nixon continues, "has a deeper connotation for reasons that [a number of] people do not understand. [Because of] what happened to the Jewish community during World War II, and then [their establishing a new nation], there [exists] a support for Israel in the United States that goes far beyond any written piece of paper. It is often said that Israel is our best ally in the

Middle East. [Yet] we have no alliance on paper with Israel. But we have something much stronger: we have interests — maybe emotional interests, but also strategic interests.

"Which brings us to Max Fisher. Max is very proud of his American heritage and he is also passionately for Israel. He makes no bones about it. If you talk to Max you always have the feeling that he's trying to weigh Israel's interests with American interests. But his loyalty is not divided. [Besides], there is nothing wrong with being for Israel. Max believes that Israel's interests and American interests [coincide]. And usually, they do. That's the fortunate thing about it."

In the spring of 1969, however, the dovetailing of U.S and Israeli interests was not immediately apparent. Seventy-year-old Golda Meir had left retirement to replace Eshkol as Israel's prime minister. Meir was deeply distressed about the War of Attrition that Egyptian President Nasser had launched against Israel along the Suez Canal. Russian ships would bring SA-3 surface-to-air missiles (SAMs) to Egypt, along with an imposing array of other military equipment. Israel would retaliate by bombarding Egyptian positions, but the fighting would drag on for eighteen months — at a terrible cost in lives and an alarming quantity of downed Israeli aircraft. Meir wanted America to resupply Israel with Phantom fighter jets and Skyhawk bombers to offset Israeli losses and the arms that the Soviet Union was shipping to Egypt.

The reluctance of the United States to furnish Israel with aircraft had recently become a serious bone of contention between the two nations. In October 1968, in what numerous observers deemed a pre-election gambit, President Johnson finally promised to sell fifty Phantoms to Israel, but the deal was not signed until three months later, just days before Johnson left office, and the planes would be slow to arrive. Nixon appeared no more eager to sell Israel planes than Johnson had been. At the outset of the Nixon administration, Secretary of State Rogers, and his capable assistant secretary, Joseph Sisco, were overseeing policy in the Middle East. Nixon, believing that there was a slim probability for success in the region, distanced the White House from it. The president had restricted

Kissinger from becoming involved because he felt that the national security adviser would be busy enough with Vietnam, the Soviet Union, Europe and Japan, and that Kissinger's Jewishness would be a liability when approaching Arab leaders.

The framework for an Arab-Israeli peace agreement had been formalized by the United Nations in the aftermath of the Six-Day War. On November 22, 1967, the U.N. Security Council unanimously approved Resolution 242. As political scientist Steven L. Spiegel points out, the resolution "affirmed positions valued by each side." Attractive to the Arabs was that the resolution called for Israeli withdrawals "from territories occupied in the recent conflict," and for a "just solution to the refugee problem." Of interest to the Israelis was that the resolution insisted on freedom of navigation through international waterways, for an end to the state of belligerency and the right of every state in the region to "live in peace within secure and recognized boundaries."

Secretary of State Rogers (and U.N. special representative Gunnar V. Jarring, who was trying to bring peace to the area) saw Resolution 242 as a straight swap. Rogers was inclined to force the Israelis back to their pre-June 5, 1967, borders in exchange for a pledge of peace from her Arab neighbors. In retrospect, Rogers's perception of 242 was a formula for deadlock, since Israeli Prime Minister Golda Meir's response to his view was that Rogers (and by extension, Ambassador Jarring) did not appreciate that "the verbal reliability of the Arab leaders was not, in any way, similar to his own."

Frustrated with Washington (and the United Nations), Meir contacted Fisher. In June, Fisher visited her in Israel.

Fisher had become acquainted with Meir through his work at the United Jewish Appeal. His opinion of her was summed up in 1983 when a reporter asked Fisher to describe her via a word-association game. When the reporter said, "Golda Meir," Fisher quickly replied, "Oak tree. No, two oak trees."

Says Fisher: "Golda's resolve was unbelievable, and her commitment to her vision of Israel's safety was unshakable.

When we talked in June 1969, she was clearly upset about Nasser's intentions along the Suez Canal. She also wanted the Phantoms that had been promised during the Johnson administration. We spoke for three or four hours. I told her that she could trust Nixon. The Russians were obviously behind the Egyptians, and the president would stand up to the Soviets. She was worried about Rogers, and I agreed that his opinions on the Mideast were wide of the mark. I suggested that a private meeting with Nixon would be worthwhile. She said that she had been considering it, but given the charged political atmosphere, would it be possible? I told her that I would pass her wish along to the White House."

Upon his return, Fisher phoned Leonard Garment, who was now working in the White House as a consultant to the president, and told him that Meir thought that an official visit to Washington would be beneficial. Garment passed along the message. Meir, at a White House dinner in 1973, credited Fisher with prevailing on her to go see Nixon. She was, by all accounts, extremely fond of Fisher, but it is likely that she would have gone to meet with Nixon on her own. Yet in terms of the role that Fisher would come to play between Washington and Jerusalem, his June 1969 meeting with Meir marked his initial foray as an intermediary between the two governments and taught him his first small lessons on the use of private diplomacy.

"Max and I," says Nixon. "set up our communications so that messages could go back and forth without putting anything on the record. Max knew that I would hold everything he passed along from Israel in confidence, and I knew that everything I told him would be treated the same way. And Max never spoke to the press. A president has many good friends who love to come in and talk, and then they go blurt out the details to reporters. That destroys their usefulness. Part of the justification for personal diplomacy is that a president can get a foreign leader to say things to his representative that he wouldn't say to the ambassador or to the secretary of state. If the emissary talks to the press, the president and the foreign leader [lose their options]. That wasn't how Max did business. He was discreet."

As time would prove, Fisher's variety of back-channeling was an effective method for keeping negotiations private. It was particularly effective because Fisher was so closed-mouthed with the media — reporters were rarely even cognizant of the fact that he was involved. In general, the media is frustrated by back-channel diplomacy, and, according to one distinguished journalist, actually assists the government in carrying it out.

"Rather than examining the process of government, reporters are hung up reporting the government's official line," says Bill Kovach, who covered the Nixon and Ford administrations for *The New York Times* and presently serves as the curator of Harvard University's Nieman Foundation, a midcareer fellowship program for journalists. "Reporters become quasi-government officials, laying down the smoke screen behind which the maneuvering occurs. This is not by choice. It's because the conventions of journalism that we've adopted — the notion of objective reporting — has led us to become dependent on official statements. Most of the good news stories, if you read deeply enough into them, have a sense of the process — of what's really going on. But it's two-thirds of the way down and there is not enough [space and time] to develop it. The headline and the thrust of the story, and what winds up on television and radio, are just the official position."

It was this narrow strip of territory between the outer and inner workings of government that Fisher traveled. The meeting with Meir had been fruitful, but one question nagged at him: How much ground would the White House permit him to cover? The answer, Fisher would soon ascertain, would depend as much on his own initiative as on the needs of the administration.

*   *   *

On Friday, August 8, Mollie Fisher, who had been ill on and off since the 1950s, died at St. Francis Hospital in Miami

Beach. She was eighty-two years old. Funeral services were held on Sunday in Southfield, Michigan.

Despite the arc of Mollie Fisher's life from *shtetl* to Fontainebleau penthouse — she had clung to the values she brought with her from Russia in 1907. She cooked, cleaned, raised her children, doted on her six grandchildren and eleven great-grandchildren, and accepted the dips and swells of her fate as a matter of course. Her life, she had surmised, was unfolding as designed, and it was this calm certainty about things working out for the best that she bequeathed to her son. Max's doggedness in pursuing his objectives may have come from William, but his faith that his pursuit would be successful came from Mollie. His apparent willingness to accept things as they were — which others commonly misinterpreted as equanimity or pragmatism — was actually Max's unwavering inner conviction that regardless of obstacles his efforts would be rewarded.

Max was sixty-one when Mollie died, and he had remained her "sonny boy," right up until then, but he says that his mother never really comprehended the scale of his success at Aurora or his work with Romney and Nixon or what it meant that he had become a national leader in Jewish philanthropic organizations. Charity, however, was something Mollie understood. She belonged to Hadassah, the National Council of Jewish Women, the Order of the Eastern Star, the Jewish Old Folks' Home Association, the Women's European Welfare Organization; and she was active in the Mt. Sinai Hospital Association, which, together with other organizations, founded a Jewish hospital in Detroit. If Mollie had been certain that she would find good fortune in America, then once she found it she believed that she owed something in return. This belief was also something that she bequeathed to her son.

When the service for Mollie was over, the funeral procession wended through the Sunday afternoon traffic and turned past the gates of the Clover Hill Park Cemetery. As Max read the Mourner's Prayer, the *Kaddish*, over his mother's grave, tears rolled down his cheeks. It was the first time that his wife and children had seen him cry.

*   *   *

Almost immediately, Fisher's connection to the White House, coupled with his prominence in Jewish communal life and the instability in the Middle East, had an unsettling effect on his business interests.

In September 1969, a military coup deposed the pro-American monarchy of Libya's King Idris I. Shortly thereafter, twenty-seven-year-old Colonel Muamar el-Qaddafi assumed power. His regime was Islamic and pan-Arab. Qaddafi challenged Western oil interests in Libya, singling out the Marathon Oil Company on Libyan television because of Fisher's seat on the company's board of directors.

Fisher loved the oil business. Throughout his life, decades after merging Aurora with The Ohio (Marathon since 1962) and relinquishing the daily tasks of running an oil company, Fisher still thought of himself as an oil man and spoke wistfully of the years spent studying the technology of the industry and putting together oil deals around the country. But when Qaddafi threatened Marathon with nationalizing their holdings, Fisher believed that he had to choose. No one on the board demanded his resignation, but Fisher says, "Being so active in Jewish affairs and with Israel, I didn't want it on my conscience that I was hurting Marathon's stockholders."

He passed one long night discussing the situation with John Bugas, and in the morning he flew to Marathon headquarters in Findlay, Ohio, and addressed the board of directors.

Fisher said: "I am identified on Libyan TV as an enemy of the people. They say that I take millions of dollars out of their country and donate it to Israel. They're right. I am their enemy. And so, I formally tender my resignation to this board."

Expressing their regret, the board accepted his resignation.

Though Fisher lamented his decision to resign from Marathon, his deepening involvement between Washington and Jerusalem was ample compensation. At the end of September, Golda Meir made a triumphant visit to the United States. In private talks with Nixon, her rapport with the president was instantaneous and extraordinary. At a state dinner in her honor, which Fisher and numerous leaders from the American Jewish community attended, the president and prime minister exchanged munificent toasts. Meir departed in a wash of warm feeling and confident that Israel would receive more shipments of Phantoms and Skyhawks.

On October 9, Fisher sent Nixon a memo telling him that his openness toward the prime minister and his empathy for Israel's circumstances "had a tremendous impact on the Jewish community." More important, said Fisher, was that "in visits of the prime minister with [Jewish] leadership throughout the country, she referred to the warmth of your reception and said, 'I am much happier now than before my visit.' In my own private conversations with her, she indicated reactions to the visit which were very favorable. I believe we can build upon this reservoir of good will for the future."

The optimism of Meir and the Jewish community was short-lived. On December 9, Secretary of State Rogers unveiled his plan for Middle East peace. Known as the Rogers Plan, the proposal recommended that Israel withdraw to the pre-June 1967 borders with Jordan; hinted at a united Jerusalem with Jordanian participation in the city's civic, economic and religious life; called for a settlement of the refugee problem and a cease-fire between Israel and Egypt.

The next day, the Israeli Cabinet rejected the plan, claiming that the major powers could not impose a peace on the region. Meir, though, was shaken by Rogers's proposal, and, as she recalled in *My Life*, by the fact that "the number of Soviet military personnel in Egypt was increasing by leaps and bounds, including combat pilots and crews of the ground-to-air missiles." On December 29, Meir wrote Fisher: "I am writing to you as one of Israel's proven friends. I am sure you understand that we are passing through difficult days, attempting to carry on in face of the enmity which surrounds us. If it were possible for you to come to Jerusalem, I would be delighted to receive you in person and tell you in detail the problems facing our people. Since that might not be feasible and time is urgent, I am sending to you, within the next few weeks, my personal emissaries to explain in depth, with new confidential material, some of these problems. I want you to listen to them as though you were listening to me."

The confidential information that Fisher saw offered evidence of the Kremlin's generosity in supplying the Egyptians with arms. Meir hoped that Fisher would share the information with the White House, and that Nixon, as a hard-liner against Soviet designs throughout the world, would speed up the delivery of combat aircraft to Israel.

Fisher passed on the information, but at the beginning of 1970, he was immersed in his own controversy. The leaders of the American Jewish community had been outraged by the Rogers Plan, feeling that the administration, which had extolled its firm backing of Israel during the campaign, was now reneging on its promise. Fisher, as the Jewish Republican most closely identified with Nixon, was in the uncomfortable position of having to explain why the administration had allowed Rogers to announce his plan — a plan to which Fisher vehemently objected.

Fisher phoned Assistant Secretary of State Joseph Sisco. He had met Sisco during their trip to Eshkol's funeral, and once they returned he frequently called him to discuss the Middle East. Fisher was impressed by Sisco's intellectual grasp of the region's complexities; his shrewd perceptions of all the players; and his steady, measured temperament — the sign of a first-rate negotiator. Sisco says that he and Fisher became "fast and close friends," aided by the fact that Sisco's wife, Jean, had lived in Louisville and knew Marjorie Fisher.

"Max's forte," says Sisco, "was a pragmatism not unduly constrained by emotional ideology. He saw that Israel had a fundamental interest in the United States being the global leader, and he continually tried to see whether Israeli and American interests could be pointed in the same direction. Yet Max understood that while the interests of both countries

were parallel, they were not one in the same. That made leading the Jewish community difficult. Contrary to popular
belief, it is not a monolith, but very individualistic. Max managed to lead the community because he was a consummate
diplomat. He was also a sensitive indicator, to me, of difficulties that could arise from certain policy decisions. He was an
excellent lightning rod."

When Fisher contacted Sisco about the Rogers Plan, the
assistant secretary told him that the administration had no
intention of pressuring Israel to accept the secretary of state's
proposals. (Nixon passed the same message to Fisher through
Leonard Garment.) Sisco added that he was personally in
favor of providing Israel, at the earliest possible date, with
increased economic and military aid, an idea that Nixon
seemed to endorse.

In a series of meetings in New York City, Fisher reiterated
the administration's assurances to American Jewish leaders,
but they were irate, and several members of the Presidents
Conference began to refer snidely to Fisher as the Republican's "court Jew," a charge that would be leveled at Fisher,
on occasion, for the next twenty-three years.

The term "court Jew" dates to sixteenth-century Europe,
when rulers permitted favored members of the Jewish minority to participate in the life of the state. As a rule, court Jews
were wealthy and assimilated. Their responsibilities varied,
but in the main they functioned as mediators between the rulers and the ruled, elevating their own social station by
assisting the monarchies in conserving their exploitative
position in society.

Fisher was frustrated by the appellation — the community was being unrealistic. The White House had a broader
agenda than the Middle East. Nixon had entered the Oval
Office committed to the principle of détente, which held that
since the interests of the United States and the Soviet Union
were hopelessly entwined, then a relaxing of tensions
between the superpowers would lead to a lessening of tensions throughout the world. The United States was already
fighting Soviet-backed clients in Vietnam. Although the Rog-

ers Plan may have been unrealistic — as Nixon later admitted in *RN* — the administration had to leave the door open to Arab states who, because of America's unstinting support of Israel, were being driven into the Soviet camp.

Attempting to stave off a collision between the Jewish community and the Nixon administration, Fisher arranged for Jewish leaders, Republican and Democrat alike, to meet with Secretary of State Rogers in Washington to voice their objections. On January 8, forty-three leaders met with Rogers for two hours of questions and answers. Many of those who attended were later quoted in the national Jewish press as saying that they were satisfied with Rogers's contention that his recommendations signaled no change in the administration's policy toward Israel and that his plan was merely an effort to kindle cease-fire negotiations between the Arabs and Israelis. Even playwright Dore Schary, a prominent liberal Democrat who was acting chairman of the Anti-Defamation League of B'nai B'rith, appeared pleased with the results. Schary told a reporter that the group had come out of the meeting "reassured that there is no basic change in U.S. policy on the sovereignty of Israel. Secretary of State Rogers was warm, candid and forthright."

Fisher was thankful that no one had blasted Rogers in the press, but he knew that the meeting was a failure. Rogers had been unable to persuade anyone that American policy toward Israel had not veered off course. As for the secretary of state, Fisher felt that Rogers was an honorable man who suffered from his lack of knowledge and diplomatic experience, and who, in the final analysis, did not belong in foreign affairs.

The announcement of the Rogers Plan had also weakened Fisher's credibility within the American Jewish community, and Fisher was upset about it for two reasons. One, the administration was going to need the support of the Jewish community to get any type of Middle East settlement through Congress, and the Rogers Plan engendered nothing but acrimony. Secondly, Fisher had worked assiduously to shore up Nixon's image among Jews, and now the administration was undermining his labors by not sticking to the Middle East

approach that had been promised in the 1968 campaign —
that of keeping the military balance tipped in favor of Israel.

Worst of all, Fisher thought, with a bit more attention to
detail the fallout could have been avoided — or at least contained. Fisher decided to inform the president about it. On
January 12, he wrote Nixon: "It was unfortunate that I did not
have the opportunity to be briefed on the [content of the Rogers Plan]. I have been overwhelmed with mail and telephone
calls [protesting his proposals]. I have tried to reassure the
community that there is no basic change in U.S. policy
toward Israel. [At our January 8 meeting], Secretary Rogers
was most gracious and displayed great patience by going into
the position of the State Department. However, I would be
less than candid if I did not say that there are great concerns
still being expressed throughout the Jewish community.

"I'm afraid this concern will now be increased tremendously by the French sale of arms to Libya, which most people
feel will finally be delivered to Egypt. I am disturbed that
there will be quite a storm of protest over the visit of [French]
President [Georges] Pompidou to the United States, over what
looks like his very pro-Arab policy. He could have hardly
timed his sale of Mirage [fighter jets] at a more disadvantageous period. The fact that he holds back delivery of arms to
Israel at the same time he makes a sale to Libya, creates a
problem, [since France hopes to be involved in Middle East
peace talks]. The feeling now will certainly develop that such
peace talks are based on the mainly pro-Arab positions [of
France, Britain and the Soviet Union], while leaving the
United States isolated.

"I believe some review of the situation may be necessary.
I have some suggestions that might be helpful in solving these
problems — as to keeping the Jewish community cool and on
how some political benefits may be derived."

The president was not unaware of the corner into which
he had backed Fisher. Nixon says that "Max took risks supporting me. He took a lot of heat from his friends and family.
And I knew that many of the people in the Jewish organizations were attacking him — they called him 'court Jew.' It was

hard on him having to be balanced — not always taking the Israeli line without regard for American interests. But that's why I trusted Max — because of his balance."

Fisher advised Nixon to reaffirm his support for Israel to Jewish leaders. He told the president that it could be accomplished without publicly contradicting the secretary of state. Nixon consented, but wondered how it should be done. Fisher already had an approach and a forum in mind.

Two weeks later, on January 26, the Conference of Presidents of Major American Jewish Organizations convened an emergency session of 1,000 Jewish community and organization leaders at the Statler-Hilton Hotel in Washington to express their disapproval of the Rogers Plan. (Protestant, Roman Catholic and black leaders also attended the session and spoke in support of Israel.) Nixon had a letter delivered to the session. It was addressed to Dr. William A. Wexler, chairman of the Presidents Conference, and Fisher read it aloud to the audience.

The letter professed that the United States believed peace in the Middle East could come only after a negotiated agreement between Israel and the Arab states. The president stated that he knew that American Jews feared "that Israel might become increasingly isolated," but added that this was "not true as far as the United States is concerned." Responding to the community's consternation that the sale of French jets to Libya would tilt the balance of power in the region, Nixon said that while he would prefer "restraint" in the shipment of arms to the area, the United States was "maintaining careful watch on the relative strength of the forces there, and we will not hesitate to provide arms to friendly states as the need arises." In a statement of blanket reassurance, the president wrote: "The United States stands by its friends," and "Israel is one of its friends."

After the session, Dr. William Wexler, speaking for the conference, told *The New York Times* that the letter "shows that the president understands and shares our concerns. It indicates that he wants no further erosion in American policy."

For the moment, then, the protest within the organized American Jewish community abated. And Israel started turning the tide in the War of Attrition by embarking on air strikes deep inside Egyptian territory. Nixon had not filled Golda Meir's request for a new shipment of planes, claiming that he was still weighing it. But there were the fighter jets that the United States had agreed to sell Israel during the Johnson administration — most of which were bogged down in a political and bureaucratic swamp. With the increased raids into Egypt, Israel sorely needed them. Fisher believed that even if the administration chose to hold off on new Phantom shipments in order not to induce the Soviets to expand their military aid to Egypt, then the administration could speed up the delivery of the remainder of the fifty Phantom jets by claiming that the United States was simply honoring a previous commitment. So Fisher approached Nixon's national security adviser, Henry Kissinger, and in the process, uncovered another facet of his role between Washington and Jerusalem.

*   *   *

Fisher had met Henry Kissinger on a few occasions, but all he knew about him was what he had read in the newspapers. Kissinger was a Jewish refugee from Nazi Germany with impeccable intellectual credentials — a Harvard professor who, in 1957, had published the influential *Nuclear Weapons and Foreign Policy*, and who had also served as a foreign-affairs adviser to Nelson Rockefeller. Fisher, however, was about to discover that Kissinger possessed other skills crucial to diplomacy — a sapient understanding of bureaucracies and a genius for surmounting them.

In his conversation with Fisher, Kissinger came right to the point. While he was sympathetic to Israel's predicament, Nixon had directed him to leave the Middle East to Secretary of State Rogers. But the Phantoms had been approved in 1968, said Fisher, and Israel needed the rest of them. Who could make this case to the president?

"Go see John Mitchell," said Kissinger.

Fisher was astounded. The attorney general could shake the Phantoms loose?

As Kissinger later revealed in *White House Years* (and Nixon confirmed in his memoirs), the president had included Mitchell in discussions of foreign policy as early as the summer of 1969, because "Nixon valued his political judgment."

So Kissinger told Fisher that Mitchell could help. And with that suggestion, the security adviser taught Fisher a type of lesson that Kissinger himself would humorously describe as the "dimensions of political science not taught at universities." The lesson was important to Fisher, but years later, during the Ford administration, it turned out not to be nearly as important as the fact that Kissinger had been the one to teach it to him.

* * *

For Fisher, it was a source of great sadness that John Mitchell, who died of a heart attack on November 9, 1988, would invariably be identified with the Watergate scandal and remembered as the big, gruff, pipe-smoking ex-attorney general who glared at prosecutors and never revealed a thing. Fully 75 percent of Mitchell's lengthy obituary in *The New York Times* was devoted to Watergate, the impact it had on his family and the nineteen months that Mitchell spent in prison.

"What's tragic," says Fisher, "is that John never wanted to come to Washington. He was Nixon's campaign manager in '68, did a great job and helped him win, and thought that afterward he'd go back to being what he'd been — a terrific bond lawyer. He never wanted to be attorney general. But Nixon asked him to join the Cabinet, and John said he'd do it."

The most enduring memory Fisher has of Mitchell is the afternoon in 1971 when they traveled to Philadelphia to watch a group of Russian Jews file off a plane, free for the first time in their lives. The immigrants had undergone colossal hardships to leave the Soviet Union; they had lost their jobs, been harassed by their government and charged an exorbitant exit tax. Mitchell had made their journey possible by clearing several obstacles through the Justice Department. Fisher watched as the Russian Jews walked toward the terminal, and a lump rose in his throat. He glanced at Mitchell. The attorney general was crying openly, not bothering to wipe the tears from his face.

And so Fisher spoke with Mitchell about the slowness of the Phantom delivery and Nixon's delay in agreeing to additional shipments.

Recalls Mitchell: "Max wasn't in the position of making the decisions. Rather, he was inducing other people to make them. Under those conditions, he was a cool operator. He didn't come into my office and shoot from the hip. He was well prepared and knew what was going on. He was extremely low-key, very warm, very congenial. But Max was persistent. Persistency was one of his prime virtues and it enabled him to carry the day."

Mitchell was inclined to aid Israel. He admired the Israelis, relished the success of their bombing raids against the Russian-backed Egyptians, and thought that supporting them was a wise political move for Nixon.

"We had a situation," says Mitchell, "where Henry Kissinger, who was Jewish, was on the National Security Council, and the secretary of state, Bill Rogers, was a little mixed up in his perception of the Middle East. And so we handled things like the Phantoms outside of the State Department and the NSC. I saw to it that the Phantom deal received proper consideration. I worked on it with [General Alexander M. Haig Jr.], who was on Kissinger's staff. We met with Israel's ambassador to Washington, Yitzhak Rabin. Of course, Max followed the progress of it, assuring the Israelis and [the American Jewish community] that it would be taken care of."

Fisher departed from Mitchell's office believing that the attorney general would see to it that Israel got her Phantoms. In fact, not long after the Fisher-Mitchell meeting, Israeli Ambassador Yitzhak Rabin noticed an abrupt shift in the attorney general and the administration. In *The Rabin Memoirs*, Rabin recalled that in late January 1970 "the American public's sympathy for Israel was growing stronger every day. I now observed a similar trend within the administration itself, especially on the part of . . . John Mitchell."

Mitchell spoke to Nixon, but six weeks later the administration collided again with the American Jewish community. Fisher's prediction to Nixon back on January 12 about the demonstrations during the visit of Georges Pompidou to the United States proved accurate. In early March, Jewish War Veterans in Chicago, protesting the French arms sale to Libya, harassed Pompidou. Madame Pompidou was so upset that she threatened to go home. In New York City, Governor Rockefeller and Mayor Lindsay snubbed the French leader. Nixon was enraged and one-upped the governor and mayor by going to Manhattan to substitute for Vice President Agnew at a dinner honoring Pompidou. Leonard Garment phoned Fisher to see if he could assist in modulating the reaction to Pompidou, but the damage had been done. In *Before the Fall*, William Safire records that Nixon, in a show of pique, put "a hold on all routine messages to Jewish dinners, yearbooks and bar mitzvahs." However, when John Mitchell heard of the embargo, he "picked up the phone to the White House and started the flow of congratulatory messages moving again."

What appeared to be of greater consequence to the Israelis was that Nixon announced he was postponing delivery of the Phantoms to Israel. In his memoirs, Nixon explains that he made this decision because he was attempting to "slow down the arms race without tipping the fragile military balance in the region. I also believed that American influence in the Middle East increasingly depended on our renewing relationships with Egypt and Syria, and this decision would help promote that goal."

Nixon's explanation, though, is misleading. Obviously, Mitchell (and Kissinger, whose fight over foreign policy with Rogers was escalating from skirmish to war) had helped to persuade the president to send more Phantoms. According to Yitzhak Rabin, less than two weeks after Nixon's announcement, he was summoned to the White House for a secret meeting with the president. Nixon informed him that while he would supply Israel with arms, he would no longer expose this commitment to public debate. The president told Rabin: "The moment Israel needs arms, approach me, by way of Kissinger, and I'll find a way of overcoming bureaucracy."

"And that's how Israel got her Phantoms," Mitchell adds. "[The Israelis] never sent me the Order of the Court. But I understand they appreciated it."

Israeli Defense Minister Moshe Dayan certainly appreciated it. When Fisher was in Israel, the defense minister saw him admiring a beer jug that dated back to 1200 B.C. Dayan presented the jug to Fisher as a thank-you gift for his assistance in securing the Phantoms.

"The jets had already been promised," says Fisher. "It was only a matter of getting them through the bureaucracy. I just helped move things along faster. That's it."

For the moment, Fisher thought, it was enough.

*   *   *

In late March 1970, Fisher resigned as chairman of the National Center for Volunteer Action. Speculation arose in the press that Fisher's resignation was due to Nixon's postponing the delivery of the Phantoms to Israel. Of course, since John Mitchell was keeping Fisher apprised of the delivery's progress, Fisher was aware that the Phantoms had not been truly postponed, but rerouted through the Oval Office. Still, newspapers cited reports that Fisher was unhappy with the administration's policy in the Middle East. Fisher tried to dispel the confusion by telling Jerald F. terHorst, Washington bureau chief of *The Detroit News*, that he was leaving the NCVA chairmanship because "the job ought to be given to somebody else every year." Fisher also told terHorst that "the president is 100 percent right on Israel." The speculation, however, was especially pointed in Israel, where *Haaretz* reported that Fisher had resigned from the NCVA to protest Nixon's Mideast policy. *The Jerusalem Post* ran a similar report, but they did phone Detroit to check the story with Fisher, who said that his resignation "meant no such thing," and that Nixon was "a real friend of Israel."

Given the political balancing act the White House was

performing with the Phantoms, the administration was anxious about the political repercussions of Fisher's resignation in the American Jewish community. Murray M. Chotiner, special counsel to the president, wrote a memorandum to Peter M. Flanigan, one of John Ehrlichman's assistants, saying that although Fisher had resigned because he felt the chairmanship should be a twelve-month position, "the timing turned out to be bad. Many people in favor of the jet transaction with Israel construed Max's resignation as a protest against the president's decision. It was *not* that. As a possible effort to show Max is still working with the president it is suggested that he be named chairman of some committee, or what have you, of substance."

Fisher already had something else on the back burner, but first he wanted to find someone to replace him at the NCVA. His choice was Henry Ford II, who was not only eminently qualified to be chairman, but was someone whom Fisher had been trying to recruit to work for Nixon since the beginning of the 1968 campaign. According to Peter Collier and David Horowitz, authors of *The Fords: An American Epic*, Henry II was "an LBJ man down the line." When Johnson withdrew from the '68 race, Ford's support for Nixon was, at best, half-hearted. Fisher told Ford that he was wrong about Nixon, and thought that getting Henry involved at the NCVA would change his thinking. Once Ford accepted the chairmanship, Fisher was free to tackle another unofficial role — this time as a consultant on the economy.

Nixon approved of the idea. "When Max and I talked," says Nixon, "we didn't just talk about Israel. Max is a fine businessman — his understanding of the business cycle is better than most economists. I listened to his advice on everything from wage-and-price controls to taxes and energy. Max and I discussed the whole field."

Fisher contacted Dr. Paul W. McCracken, a conservative economist from the University of Michigan, who was serving as chairman of the Council of Economic Advisers. He asked McCracken if he could be of assistance. McCracken replied that he would be glad to have his input, and from then on the two men spoke regularly about the economy — a practice that continued through McCracken's three-year tenure as chairman.

"All through Nixon's first term," says McCracken, "Max was very helpful to me. Being prominent in business, he had a feeling for the pulse of that world. We have to remember that the president lives in a cocoon. He needs to hear from business leaders. Max could get ideas in front of the president. He had access, and Nixon trusted him."

On May 27, at a White House dinner honoring businessmen, Fisher and Nixon conferred about the economy, which appeared to be heading toward recession. Inflation and unemployment were up, and both would have to be addressed soon. The president was contemplating asking business and labor to support his conception of moderated demands for price-and-wage increases, an unheard of move for Nixon, a long-standing economic conservative with an abiding faith in the free market. Fisher told the president that while he understood the political imperatives, he felt that economic controls would eventually exacerbate the downslide. Nixon answered that "his mind was still open on the matter of guidelines." Fisher thought it unwise to rush — perhaps the recession was not going to be as severe as anticipated by economists.

Their discussion was interrupted by the evening's ceremonies, but on June 13 Fisher sent the president a long letter telling him that he was growing "increasingly concerned about the negative attitudes of business leaders toward the economic policies of the administration." The thrust of the letter was that the administration was relying on economists to the exclusion of industry decision makers. Both were vital, Fisher said, but it was "essential that business leaders have the feeling of being involved. By having their involvement, the programs that you will adopt to control inflation will ultimately be much more successful."

Fisher was reluctant for the government to tinker with the free market, but his suggestions centered around his trust in the efficacy of consensus building. According to Paul McCracken, Fisher had been talking to the administration about instituting a forum for industry leaders and government since the fall of 1969. Fisher spoke to John Mitchell about it, who, along with McCracken, agreed that it would be prudent to give Fisher's recommendation a try.

On June 17, in a nationwide telecast, Nixon addressed the declining economic situation, asking business and labor "to raise their sights by lowering their [price and wage] demands," and thereby "helping to hold down everybody's cost of living," and reducing inflation. The president also announced that he was establishing a National Commission of Productivity, which would include business leaders, and instructed the Council of Economic Advisers "to prepare a periodic Inflation Alert."

Nixon wrote to Fisher the next day, saying how pleased he was that their thinking on the economy was "so close." McCracken, however, was eager to meet with business leaders before the productivity commission was up and running. Fisher arranged it for him.

"Max brought in five or six CEOs from around the country," says McCracken, "and we talked. The economy was in a dip, and, in order to gauge how aggressive the administration's reaction should be, I wanted to know if they thought that it looked like we were entering a monumental downturn. They said no, it wouldn't be too severe, and that's exactly the way it happened."

*　　*　　*

Despite Fisher's delving into other subjects on the national agenda, his most intensive involvement was between the American Jewish community and the administration, and between Washington and Jerusalem. Fisher's high visibility in Israel stretched back to December 1964, when he was elected chairman of the United Jewish Appeal. After all, the UJA had raised billions of dollars for Israel, and as head of the organization, Fisher received a fair amount of attention from the Israeli government and the press. Thus, in 1968, as Fisher emerged on the American political scene, it was only natural that when he landed in Tel Aviv, Israeli leaders and reporters shifted their emphasis from questions about philanthropy and sought his opinion on election-year politics, Congress, the propensities of the president and secretary of state.

However, what neither the government ministers nor the press noticed was that while Fisher was gaining political access in the United States, he was also on the verge of expanding the role he and other fund-raisers would play *within* Israel, a role that extended well beyond that of a man whose UJA chairmanship symbolized the beneficence of American Jews.

In September 1968, Fisher succeeded Dewey D. Stone as the chairman of the United Israel Appeal. Stone, a businessman from Brockton, Massachusetts, had chaired the UIA for nearly two decades and was ready to step down. (He was elected honorary chairman.) On the surface, Fisher's replacing Stone was not extraordinary. By the fall of 1968, Fisher was the president of the UJA, vice president of the Council of Jewish Federations and Welfare Funds, chairman of the board of governors of the American Jewish Committee and on the board of the Joint Distribution Committee. Apparently, in ascending to the top of the UIA, Fisher had predictably won himself another honor.

Yet titanic changes between the American Jewish fundraising community and Israel would transpire during Fisher's tenure at the UIA, changes so profound that, in varying degrees, those involved would be embroiled in them twenty years later. Examined from an historical perspective, these changes are entirely logical — perhaps unavoidable is the more precise word — when reflecting on the mandate of the UIA, and Fisher's relationship to money and power.

In his study, *The Smoke Screen: Israel, Philanthropy and American Jews*, Israeli journalist Charles Hoffman refers to the UIA as "the gilded funnel." It is, he writes, "the least known part of the American Jewish fund-raising establishment," but the one with potentially the most clout vis-à-vis Israel. The UIA is the organization through which the money raised by American Jews is transferred to the Jewish Agency for Israel (JAFI). The Jewish Agency, originally the brainchild of the World Zionist Organization's Chaim Weizmann, was founded in 1929 with the goal of uniting world Jewry to assist in the founding of a Jewish national homeland in Palestine. Once Israel was born, Agency leaders migrated to the official government, but the scaffolding of Weizmann's dream remained. Although its definition grew blurred, the Agency carried on, providing services or grants in Israel for rural settlement, immigration and absorption, youth education and training, urban rehabilitation, housing and other activities.

By the late 1960s, the Jewish Agency was in disarray. Political scientist Daniel J. Elazar states that it had "become little more than another branch of the government of Israel." And Zelig Chinitz, in his history of the reconstituted Agency, *A Common Agenda*, writes that after 1948 "the Agency was criticized for its inability to attract settlers from the West, for its dependence on the Israeli government for the funding of Zionist activities, and for becoming a 'second line' institution for the placement of party officials for whom there were no positions in the government. . . . These conditions generated a rising tide of criticism in Israel and elsewhere, to the point of questioning the raison d'être of the Jewish Agency."

These conditions coincided with Fisher's rise to the chairmanship of the UIA. Suddenly, Fisher was standing in the path of a financial stream. And as Romney's campaign team learned, Fisher never liked relinquishing control over funds that he was responsible for without having some say on the allocation of those funds. Fisher had few peers as a fundraiser, but the price for having him in your camp was that he would not permit money to pour through his hands without influencing its course. Still, in 1968, the notion of fashioning a power base for American philanthropists within Israel — within the Jewish Agency — seemed farfetched to representatives from both countries.

By the spring of 1971, all of that would change.

Chapter 10

THE STRONGEST SINGLE LINK: RECONSTITUTING THE JEWISH AGENCY FOR ISRAEL

WHEN IT CAME to the Jewish Agency, Fisher thought, history was the key. History and culture. Both had been on a collision course from the start.

In 1897, journalist and playwright Theodor Herzl convened the first Zionist Congress in Switzerland and formally transformed the religious vision of Jews returning to live in the Holy Land into the practical movement of Zionism. Herzl thought that his World Zionist Organization would provide the political framework for establishing a Jewish homeland. Funding would come from institutions sustained by world Jewry. However, WZO membership was largely drawn from Eastern Europe, where Jews were subjected to the harsher vicissitudes of anti-Semitism. Jews in Western Europe and the United States did not suffer the same fate. Moreover, they identified themselves as citizens of the countries in which they lived, and Zionism raised the specter of dual allegiance. Therefore, for most of world Jewry, joining the WZO was unthinkable.

Herzl died in 1904. Thirteen years later, Britain's Foreign Secretary Lord Arthur James Balfour issued a proclamation declaring that his government favored "the establishment in Palestine of a national home for the Jewish people." In 1922, the League of Nations went further, stating that a "Jewish agency shall be recognized as a public body for the purpose of advising . . . the Administration of Palestine in . . . matters [that] may affect the establishment of the Jewish National Home."

Chaim Weizmann, leader of the Zionists, recognized that because the WZO was the symbol of world Jewish nationalism, it alienated large numbers of Jews whose backing would be integral to the founding of a Jewish homeland. In the United States, Weizmann met Louis Marshall, president of the American Jewish Committee, which was the citadel of non-Zionism. Marshall, like many in the AJC, championed a Jewish national home, but did not endorse the establishment of an independent political state. In August 1929, Weizmann and Marshall set up the Jewish Agency, which would represent world Jewry in its efforts not to found a state in Palestine, but to build a homeland.

Tragedy intruded. Soon after the inaugural meeting of the Agency, Marshall died. Practically all of the formalized support from non-Zionists died with him. A decade later, the Agency and WZO became virtually synonymous in the eyes of Britain, the mandatory power. In 1945, with hundreds of thousands of concentration-camp survivors trapped behind the barbed wire of displaced persons' compounds, the call for a Jewish state intensified.

After Israel was founded in 1948, the WZO-Jewish Agency stayed tied to the nation's political parties. The Agency's chairman was parallel to Israel's prime minister and its Executive (comprised of the chairman and the department heads) was analogous to the Israeli Cabinet. As defined by the Knesset, the Agency's role was to ingather the "exiles" and to absorb them into Israel. WZO-Agency leaders in Israel also clung to the tenets of classical Zionism, which holds that Jewish Diaspora life is unhealthy, untenable and incomplete. But the WZO-Jewish Agency, unable to encourage *aliyah* from the West, had become an institution in search of a purpose. Still, writes Zelig Chinitz in *A Common Agenda*, "the [earlier] efforts of Weizmann and Marshall provided the inspiration for the second attempt at enlarging the Agency which was initiated on behalf of the Zionists by Louis A. Pincus

[and] Max Fisher, the recognized leader of the 'latter day non-Zionists.'"

*　　*　　*

At first sight, Fisher and Pincus appeared to be an odd pair. Fisher was tall, broad-shouldered, informal in conversation, with a muffled voice that sometimes trailed off before a sentence was complete. He was a private man who, because of his interests and circumstances, discovered himself in the center of a public arena. Like Marshall, Fisher was passionately concerned about the quality of life in what was now Israel, and he always regarded himself as an American Jew at home in the United States. Nor did Fisher have any interest in participating in the political inner workings of the Jewish state, which was part and parcel of becoming a leader of the WZO.

Pincus was four years younger than Fisher and nearly a foot shorter. A South African by birth and a lawyer by training, he was an eloquent advocate of classical Zionism. At the age of thirty-six, Pincus walked away from a lucrative legal career and emigrated to Palestine just months before the state was born. From 1949 until 1956, he headed El Al Airlines, steering the company from its modest beginnings to its position as a respected international carrier. At heart a politician, Pincus remained active in Israel's Labor Party and the WZO-Jewish Agency. At the 1961 WZO Congress, he was elected to the Executive. Seven years later, he became its chairman.

Fisher and Pincus grew close in the mid-1960s. Fisher would later credit Pincus with having "had a great impact on my life. It was from Louis that I began to understand what Zionism means. I looked up to him." Despite their divergences in background and temperament, the connection between the two men was clear. They shared a true believer's certitude in the importance of Israel to world Jewry, and in the inflexible demands of the bottom line. They were unapologetic pragmatists whose practicality was leavened with vision and faith.

By the late 1960s, Pincus saw that the "non-Zionist" philanthropists — the people who raised the bulk of the WZO-Jewish Agency budget — would have to be given a role in running the Agency. A number of Israel's leaders and some American Zionists objected to granting Diaspora Jews a significant say in an Israeli institution. Pincus argued that if the philanthropists were not included, then they might prefer dispersing their donations to Israel through an American-controlled group such as the Joint Distribution Committee. Then the Jewish Agency, and indirectly the WZO, would lose their primary source of income. Pincus's fiscal logic was irrefutable, but the resentment of some Zionists over being compelled to open their doors to non-Zionists would linger for more than two decades.

Fisher sensed that the American Jewish fund-raising bodies were interested in retaining more control of the money they raised for Israel. Melvin Dubinsky, Fisher's friend who would succeed him as chairman of the United Israel Appeal in 1971, elucidates: "Max had been the chairman of the UJA, CJF and UIA. He knew that there was a consensus in Jewish fund-raising circles that although we were happy that the state of Israel had been brought into being, if we were going to spend our resources to further the good of the Jewish people in Israel, then at least we should have the right to have some say about what was done with the money."

Fisher had been watching the WZO-Jewish Agency since the mid-1960s. He saw its decline and discussed it with Pincus, telling him "not to be discouraged by what was happening at the moment," and assuring him that "there were wellsprings of support for Israel that have yet to be discovered in the Jewish communities of the free world."

The vanguard of this support, Fisher believed, was in the American Jewish community, which, by and large, was rapidly growing secularized. The result was that for most American Jews, Israel was now the cornerstone of Jewish identity. Fisher was a prime model of the secular Jew whose sturdiest bond to Judaism is Israel. In practice, he was nonobservant. He belonged to two synagogues in suburban Detroit: the Conservative Shaarey Zedek, and the Reform Temple Beth El. He attended each one once a year — on the High Holy Days of Rosh Hashana and Yom Kippur.

One afternoon, following the Yom Kippur memorial service, Rabbi Morris Adler of Shaarey Zedek walked over to Fisher and said: "I missed you at services last week on Rosh Hashana. Where were you?"

"I was at Beth El," answered Fisher. "I have to divide my business up."

"Well," said Adler, "I had lunch with Rabbi [Richard C.] Hertz at Beth El the other day and we decided that — in this case — you don't have enough stock to split it."

Fisher laughed, but he still only attended services twice a year.

Yet Fisher was convinced that living in the wake of the Holocaust foisted a singular responsibility on world Jewry — that of assuring the existence of Israel. In 1965, when he was elected chairman of the UJA, his speeches were laced with this conviction. By the summer of 1967, after the Six-Day War, American Jewry seemed to concur with this conclusion. Charitable giving to — and political support for — Israel reached record proportions.

Fisher hoped that Israel would not have to depend on the exigencies of war for assistance from the Diaspora. Most American Jewish organizations, though, were not rooted enough *in* Israel to guarantee long-term interest. And philanthropists would want to avoid the labyrinth of Zionist politics.

"Most philanthropists," says Fisher, "are successful business people. They aren't interested in sitting around and talking about philosophy. You've got to give them something to do."

He required a formalized instrument — an organization — that could represent the partnership between Jews in Israel and the Diaspora. In talks with Pincus, Israeli government officials, representatives of the Agency, and American philanthropists, Fisher saw that the time was ripe to institute such a forum. Nevertheless, he knew that leaders from North America would refuse to join the WZO, since its ideological goal was to bring all of world Jewry to live in Israel. Yet, to create another instrument would take too long, engender mistrust in the WZO and add another layer of bureaucracy. So Fisher and Pincus concurred that the existing WZO-Jewish Agency would have to be reshaped. Fisher told Pincus that their main intention had to be to make this reconstituted Jewish Agency "the strongest single link between Israel and the Diaspora."

The Zionists and the non-Zionists differed on numerous details, but their pre-eminent differences were over governance and structure.

The Zionist Congress, which is convened every four or five years, fixes policy for the WZO. There are approximately 650 delegates to the congress: 29 percent come from the United States; 33 percent come from all other countries in the Diaspora; and 38 percent are from Israel. The Israeli delegates are chosen in proportion to their party's representation in the Knesset. From the day Israel was founded, handing out jobs at the Agency was considered a perk of the patronage system.

In contrast, the lay and professional leadership of American-Jewish philanthropic organizations, while not being free from infighting, are selected on the basis of ability and involvement as demonstrated over a considerable period of time. Fisher and Pincus ascertained that the only way to bring together in one body two disparate systems and operational styles was through a separation of powers and functions between the WZO and the "reconstituted" Jewish Agency.

Heightening the tensions over these elements was the ideological gulf between the Zionist and the non-Zionist.

Jacques Torczyner, a WZO member, felt that the fundraisers had no right to be involved in the Agency. "They are not real Zionists like us," says Torczyner. "We are Jews first, and they are Americans first and Jews second."

For Fisher and Pincus, these ideological distinctions held little weight. Pincus had serious misgivings about the non-Zionist tag that was attached to the fund-raisers. In the summer of 1970, Pincus told a reporter from *The National Jewish Post*: "I doubt very much whether I can regard Max as a non-

Zionist. I am confident, however, that the day will come when I can say with certainty that he is a Zionist."

Fisher's response to Pincus was not only based on the realities of the War of Attrition that Israel was fighting against Egypt in 1969 and 1970, but also on the fact that Libyan leader Muamar Qaddafi had threatened to nationalize Marathon's oil fields in Libya because Fisher, the Jewish philanthropist, sat on the Marathon board.

Fisher told Pincus: "It is really quite unnecessary for you to exercise yourself over this question: all of the Arab propagandists have already determined that I am indeed a Zionist."

Understandably, the WZO was reluctant to relinquish their control over the Agency departments and to allow the philanthropists to invade their kingdom. Harry Rosen, a former secretary-general, the key professional position between the Agency and the Diaspora philanthropists, believes that Fisher's refusal to get bogged down in the historical debate about Zionism and over operational details was crucial to the eventual agreement.

"Better than anyone," says Rosen, "Max understood the organizational and cultural differences between Israel and the Diaspora. Therefore, he became the ideal bridge. He understood the parliamentary nature of the Israeli political system; that the head is not a boss of bosses. Decisions are made by consensus. It is something that many Americans in the Agency have trouble understanding. Max made it possible to develop an ideological framework for this partnership. He didn't get lost in theoretical considerations. His attitude was, 'If there's a problem, let's solve it.' For Max, function is equivalent to ideology."

Moshe Rivlin, who served as the Agency's director-general, the chief operating officer of the WZO and the Jewish Agency, states that without Fisher the reconstitution of the Jewish Agency would not have been possible. Says Rivlin: "Max has a unique standing — with Republican administrations in Washington and with the prime minister in Israel. And he was the unchallenged leader of the fund-raisers. Yet with all this power in his hands, he was a mobilizer of people.

His art was finding the common denominator among groups and creating an atmosphere of consensus. He never dictated what had to be done. You could be sure that if four people were scheduled to be at a 9 a.m. meeting, Max spoke to one of them at seven. He ate breakfast with another at eight. He phoned the other one at 8:30, and if he didn't speak to the fourth person, then that was only because he wasn't in. This is how Max operates."

Fisher's sedulous consensus building sprang from his perspective on the responsible uses of power. He says: "When you start thinking about power, that's when you don't have it. When I chair a meeting, I don't just shut people down. I allow everyone to express their views or vent their frustration. But I always have an agenda. I know what I'm shooting for. At the end of the meeting, when everything is summed up, I make sure that it's not a summation of everything they wanted accomplished, it's a summation of what I wanted to accomplish. I find people are more agreeable if they have already expressed themselves. Then they often go along."

Some in the WZO and in the American Jewish community objected to Fisher's manner. Nonetheless, declares Morton L. Mandel, an ex-president of the Council of Jewish Federations who would be elected to the Agency Board of Governors, Fisher's tactics were startlingly efficacious. "Sometimes," says Mandel, "Max moves more slowly toward objectives than some people would like. When he captures ground, though, he holds it. In other cases, people make lightninglike moves and two years later they're five yards behind where they were. Max is a consensus builder — the single most able consensus builder I have ever seen in any form of activity. He's a genius at it. He has the fewest number of enemies of anybody I've ever met. He manages to retain credibility with people whom he does not support on a given cause at a given moment. That's a rare quality. It's what virtually separates him from the world."

Every inch of Fisher's consensus-building talent was indispensable to him as negotiations dragged on through 1969 and 1970. Finally, it was determined that the reconstituted Jewish

Agency for Israel would be divided into an Assembly, Board of Governors and an Executive. Fifty percent of the Assembly would be from the WZO; the other half from among the fund-raising leadership in the Diaspora. The Assembly would elect a Board of Governors — the policy arm — whose members would be 50 percent from the WZO and 50 percent from the Diaspora community leaders; its chairman would be from the Diaspora. In turn, the BOG would elect the Agency Executive — the implementation group. The chairman of the Executive would be from the WZO and most of its members would be Israeli, since these people were responsible for the operations of the departments — Immigration and Absorption, Youth Care and Training, and Agricultural Settlement.

The Agency would retain its political shadings. The chairman of the WZO Executive would also be the chairman of the Agency Executive. Furthermore, candidates to head the departments would emerge from the World Zionist Congress. But there was a new twist — although the nominees to lead departments were intertwined in Israeli politics, each one would be subject to the principle of "advise and consent." This rule stated that the non-Zionists on the Board of Governors must be consulted about the selection of department heads and that the BOG retained a veto over the candidates.

Numerous American philanthropists objected to this compromise, but Fisher told them "that the main thing was to create the instrument. Once we start working together, people will realize that aims and objectives are more important than structure and organization."

The "Agreement for the Reconstitution of the Jewish Agency for Israel" was signed in August 1970. Less than one year later, in June 1971, the four-day Founding Assembly was held in Jerusalem with David Ben-Gurion and Prime Minister Golda Meir on the podium. Pincus was elected chairman of the Executive; Fisher was elected to chair the Board of Governors.

In his closing address at the Binyanai Haooma — the Jewish People's Convention Center — Fisher told the members of the reconstituted Jewish Agency for Israel that they had come "to correct history," meaning that the charge of upbuilding the Jewish state was now going to be a responsibility of every Jew — regardless of where he resided. "The test for admittance to this Assembly was simple enough," said Fisher. "Does one carry the welfare of Israel in his heart? And there is no one here who does not bear this badge of admission." He spoke of the traditional responsibilities of the Agency — the social welfare programs and immigration, which Fisher referred to as "the sacred work of *aliyah*." But again he emphasized that "these must be done by us — *by the world Jewish community* — through the Agency."

Reinforcing this point — that the Jewish Agency was now the institution that represented the partnership between Jews in the Diaspora and in Israel — was a task that, in great measure, Fisher labored at for the next twelve years as chairman of the Board of Governors.

*　　*　　*

Among the foremost critics of the reconstituted Agency is Professor Eliezer D. Jaffe, an American-born sociologist who has lived in Israel since 1960 and teaches at The Hebrew University's school of social work. Having written widely on the subject, Jaffe concludes that the presence of Israeli politics in the Agency has led to "sloppy, wasteful philanthropy," and that "more time is spent at [a Zionist Congress] haggling over the spoils of office and setting up political coalitions than in debating and evaluating Zionist programs and welfare projects."

Jaffe says that "Fisher should have demanded a bigger say for the philanthropists. It was their money. They give over $400 million dollars a year. He could have depoliticized the Agency when it was reconstituted and made it purely a philanthropic organization. He chose not to. He made a lousy deal."

Fisher felt that attempting to extend the reach of the philanthropists would have scuttled the reconstitution. Gradualism, after all, is the guiding principle of a pragmatist. As Fisher explained to another energetic critic of the reconstituted Agency, Israeli journalist Charles Hoffman: "Our first big problem was to bring people together from two different cultures. We had to learn what the Jewish Agency had been doing, and to create rapport with our partners. As we got involved we discovered a lot of inefficiency and 'bureaucracy.' You know, the Israelis saw our role at first as an infringement of their turf. People don't like to give up power and turf. It took a lot of time to change their basic philosophy. People asked why we didn't move faster. I told them that change had to be evolutionary and it had to be by consensus, not by hitting people over the head. If we had acted differently, this would have destroyed the partnership."

Internal and external critics of the Agency found this hard to accept, which was indicative of their impatience with the overlapping implementation systems. For instance, the man who replaced Fisher in 1983 as chairman of the BOG was Jerold C. Hoffberger of Maryland, erstwhile owner of the Baltimore Orioles and Baltimore Colts. Hoffberger was impatient with the Agency bureaucracy. Yet Hoffberger believes that in 1971, Fisher had no choice but to live with the imperfections.

"Max's most valuable service," says Hoffberger, "has been as the bridge between the various communities in the Jewish Agency. The problem has not been an easy one, bringing together the ideologues of the Zionist organization and the practical people in the Diaspora who provide most of the funds. He balanced all of the different factions. Had he not done it, [the reconstitution of the] Jewish Agency would have not been possible."

Just as the Agency was getting off the ground, tragedy intervened as it had during the days of Weizmann and Marshall. In 1973, Louis Pincus died suddenly. Fisher was heartbroken. Pincus had not only been an effective advocate in the WZO for establishing a partnership with Jews in the Diaspora, Fisher had considered him a dear friend.

He was followed in June 1974 by Pinhas Sapir. A former finance minister, Sapir was a chief architect of the Israeli economy and a power broker without peer in the Labor Party. The prime ministership had been his for the asking. Sapir, however, felt comfortable in financial matters and doubted that he had the emotional stamina to send young soldiers into battle. He chose to head the Executive of the Agency. Fisher was delighted. Sapir possessed a pervasive influence among Israeli politicos — he could get things done — and his image rivaled that of the prime minister. In addition, Sapir deeply appreciated fund-raisers like Fisher, about whom he said: "I see in these people the most precious group that I ever met in my entire life." Sadly, Sapir died in August 1975.

His successor was Yosef Almogi, the mayor of Haifa and a Labor Party leader. Primarily, he was a political appointment by Prime Minister Yitzhak Rabin, who was warring with Shimon Peres within the Labor Party. In 1977, the Likud election victory deposed Labor. In February 1978, Leon Dulzin was elected chairman of the Executive at the World Zionist Congress.

After seven years, the reconstituted Jewish Agency still had its severe critics. In an article in the *London Jewish Chronicle*, David Elias was confidently predicting that the Agency's days were numbered. Other critics persisted in lectures and in print to expound on why the Agency should be abolished. Much of the criticism still revolved around the inundation of Israeli politics in the Agency.

Fisher appreciated the objections. But it was not until 1977, when Menachem Begin and his Likud Party rose to power, that Fisher felt the Agency was stable enough to withstand a confrontation with the Israeli political machine over who had the final say in selecting the officers of the Agency and the heads of departments. Personally, Fisher liked Begin. He was struck by the contrast of Begin's history as the leader of the *Irgun* — the militant underground — prior to 1948 and his gentle demeanor and soft voice. Unhappily for Fisher, Begin, like all politicians, jealously guarded the privilege of being able to dispense jobs to his supporters.

One morning, Fisher had an appointment to see Begin. When he entered the prime minister's office, Begin was standing with a man whom Fisher did not recognize. Fisher greeted Begin and the prime minister replied: "Max, I want you to meet the next treasurer of the Agency, Yoram Aridor." Fisher said to Begin that, with all due respect for Mr. Aridor, this was not how the system functioned. According to the principle of "advise and consent" in the 1971 partnership agreement, the Board of Governors must be consulted about the candidates. Begin demonstrated that he was not always soft-spoken. He became, says Fisher, "quite upset," and insisted that appointments to the Agency were the prerogative of the ruling party in Israel and in the WZO.

Fisher answered: "That's not how we're going to do things anymore."

Aridor was rejected by the philanthropists, who also rejected Begin's second choice for the post, Raphael Kotlowitz, whose sole qualification was his loyalty to Begin and the Likud. In a gesture of conciliation, Fisher and the other philanthropists accepted Kotlowitz as head of the Immigration and Absorption Department. Five-and-a-half years later, though, Fisher was in Begin's office telling him that Kotlowitz had overly politicized his department — in disregard of BOG policies. Begin protested, and Fisher replied that Kotlowitz would not be reappointed.

Fisher then sent a letter to Dulzin, the chairman of the Executive, reminding him that the fund-raisers held a veto over Jewish Agency appointments. Fisher's successor as chairman of the Board of Governors, Jerold Hoffberger, was in place when Kotlowitz was ousted. This was the first time the Board of Governors had been able to discharge a senior department head for lack of competency. And the decision of the philanthropists stood, despite Kotlowitz's petitioning the new prime minister, Yitzhak Shamir, to intercede, and even challenging the BOG's ruling in an unsuccessful civil court case.

On the heels of this victory, the philanthropists forged ahead to persuade their Israeli partners that department directors should be selected by merit, not political connections. Although Fisher was proud of these gains, he saw that the politicization of the Agency would endure to some degree, a byproduct of its entanglement with the government of Israel. Partisan politics infiltrated social and fiscal policies, and appointments at the lower administrative levels. But merit had been elevated to a qualification, and this, Fisher felt, was a vast improvement from 1971.

*   *   *

The politicization of the Agency was not the greatest challenge that Fisher faced during his tenure; nor did he see it as the gravest danger to the survival of the Agency. Rather, it was the division between the members of the World Zionist Organization and the fund-raisers on the question of who was actually a Zionist. Fisher's response to the debate, oft-repeated while he was BOG chairman, was that "there are no non-Zionists at the Jewish Agency. History has made Zionists of us all." In other words, the non-Zionist label had lost its meaning, because everyone working with the Agency was hoping to strengthen Israel. Fisher termed these men and women "new Zionists," and an ideological commitment to live in Israel was not a prerequisite to qualify. Generally, it was recognized that the WZO *and* the Diaspora were crucial to Israel's survival, and the philanthropists' money and efforts were critical to the functioning of the Agency.

To heal the rift between the two factions, Fisher and Dulzin instituted the Caesarea Process, which began in February 1981, when the Board of Governors convened a special meeting at the seaside resort of Caesarea. Speaking to the conference, Fisher said: "The key issue today is not how many of us belong to Zionist parties. The key issue is how do we strengthen the Agency? How do we make the Agency the strongest single link between Israel and the Diaspora?"

Dulzin spoke next, telling the audience that the conference offered an opportunity to understand each other. "In this connection," he said, "I want to tell you a story about Max Fisher. A year or two after we reconstituted the Jewish Agency, Max and I appeared before a press conference in Tel Aviv, and he was asked what is his belief as a non-Zionist. He said: 'We are one people, we have a mutual responsibility to each other, Israel is the center of Jewish life, and we have to do everything possible to bring a maximum of Jews to Israel; also, we have to be concerned for the future of our Jewish children and give them a

Jewish education.' When Max finished, I was asked what I think. I said I believe more or less the same thing — the only difference is that I proclaim myself a Zionist."

From the start, Fisher had maintained that the true discord between the WZO and the philanthropists was "functional, not ideological." Thus, the intention of the Caesarea Process was to examine the decade-long partnership between the WZO and Diaspora fund-raising bodies in Agency operations. Six commissions emerged, dealing with goals and objectives, governance, immigration, Jewish education, finances, and fiscal policy and management. Fisher's hope was that as the Agency became more efficient, the WZO would see the value of the increased efficiency and not resent the greater voice of the philanthropists in the allocation of funds.

His efforts were rewarded. As Charlotte Jacobson, one of the best-known Zionist leaders in the United States, observed: "It was worth the trip to Israel just to participate in this exchange." Another longtime Zionist remarked: "Thanks to Fisher, we discovered that we are one family with one heart."

Philosophically, though, there were Zionists like Uri Gordon, head of the Agency's Youth *Aliyah* Department, who refused to relinquish the concept that every Jew belonged in Israel. In his essay, "My Zionism," Gordon writes: "I was brought up to believe that going to kibbutz was the most important thing one could do. Kibbutz, they told me, is the highest rung on life's ladder. What kind of ladder does today's Zionist movement offer? Today the movement is afraid to reject the Diaspora. Yes, I want strong Jewish communities, but I have a Zionist world view which says, 'Israel's the target.'"

The hard-core Zionists, Fisher felt, would never be swayed, but he had other serious concerns — these ones regarding the philanthropists. Since 1971, he had been worried that the fund-raisers would grow indifferent to the Agency because they had no say in its operation. Out of this concern, Fisher became a prime supporter of Project Renewal, a program that formalized links between the Diaspora and communities within Israel. Project Renewal twinned neighborhoods. The Jewish Federation in Detroit, for example, became responsible for the revitalization of Ramla, while the New York community took on the Tel Aviv neighborhood of Hatikvah. Project Renewal also nurtured Fisher's overall objective. As Zelig Chinitz points out in *A Common Agenda*: "Project Renewal succeeded in creating a direct bond between Israel and Diaspora Jews, whereby each has had a personal stake in the process. . . . [It] transcended the conventional philanthropic relationship — that is to say, the benefactor became the beneficiary as well."

The enterprise that most emotionally engaged Fisher was Jewish education. Interestingly enough, it was the World Zionist Organization that pushed for it, and Fisher found himself on the opposite side of the table from the American philanthropists, who were initially reluctant to earmark funds for education, since they believed that their responsibility was limited to rescuing Jews in distress. But beginning at the Caesarea Conference, Fisher started talking about the need "to save Jewish souls." He was referring to education in the Diaspora and told the Board of Governors that teaching youngsters about Judaism and Israel should be added to the traditional goals of the Agency.

Leon Dulzin remembers: "When Pincus died, I spoke to Max and said: 'Let's form a Pincus Fund for Education.' At first, everyone was against it. Except Max Fisher. I'll never forget: Max said to me: 'I never had a Jewish education. I miss not having one. I lived in a very dramatic time of the Jewish people — the Holocaust and the founding of Israel. So these things brought me here. Who knows what will happen with my children?' Max persuaded everyone on the Board of Governors. He did it by telling them about himself. It had tremendous impact."

Two entities were created for Jewish Diaspora education: the Pincus Fund, which Fisher chaired and which, from 1975 until 1988, furnished $13.7 million in grants. And then there was the Joint Program. This was headed by Mort Mandel and spent $18.2 million.

*   ⋆   ⋆

Of all the undertakings in which Fisher immersed himself, the Jewish Agency for Israel was the one that was molded most closely in his image. It was the institutional embodiment of realpolitik, a pragmatist's dream — evolving, filled with philosophical and procedural tensions. It was noble at times, petty at others; it was flawed — but it worked. After twenty years what will stand as Fisher's greatest achievement at the Jewish Agency is the singular fact of its reconstituted existence.

Israeli political scientist Dr. Daniel Elazar explains: "The Jewish Agency is important in two ways. First, it is the vehicle through which the Jewish people as a whole — in the Diaspora and in Israel — have been able to participate in a systematic way in building Israel. Secondly, the Agency has become the nexus of what I call the 'world Jewish polity,' which is the organized governance of world Jewry. After 1948, Jews had to rebuild their relations to each other around the fact that we now had a politically sovereign state. At the same time, we also had a Diaspora, which somehow had to be linked to this state if we were going to keep the Jewish people connected. The Jewish Agency, through the reconstitution, provided this link. In my book, *The Jewish Polity*, I discuss three types of Jewish political leaders: constitutional founders, constitutional interpreters and statesmen. I include Max as a statesman, because he's the only Diaspora leader I know of who saw the necessity of having this link. Whether he used the term or not, Max was a polity builder. He was not seeking a more streamlined method for giving money to Israel. He had this vision of a polity, in the larger sense, and he stuck with it. That was his accomplishment."

Chapter 11

PERSONAL BUSINESS

ONCE MAX FISHER added his work at the Jewish Agency to his other commitments, his life became an unending series of telephone calls and meetings from Detroit to Jerusalem, from Washington to New York.

"For a long while there," says Marjorie Fisher, "Max just came home, changed clothes and left."

Marjorie, beginning in the 1960s, began to drink more heavily. Max, she thought, was unaware of it. Initially, she did not see the problem and only noticed that she had less patience, felt on edge. Her most overwhelming feeling was of loneliness.

She recalls: "Several nights a week, after dinner, I would take all four of the children on the bed with me. Everyone would get in their nightgowns and pajamas. They'd ask me questions; we'd talk about anything they wanted to discuss. Little Margie would fall asleep and they'd carry her back to [her room]. That's what we would do when Max was away."

For Marjorie, the answer seemed to be to accompany Max on his trips.

"We had to go here," says Marjorie, "and we had to go to there. I was torn. I went with him, but I had children at home. Julie needed me to go with her for shoes. Mary needed to go to the dentist. I felt guilty about leaving them. But after we got to where we were going, I hardly saw Max. He would be in meetings from seven o'clock in the morning until midnight. I'd sit in the hotel room with a stack of books. Traveling with him was fine if I wanted a long rest."

Marjorie may have felt forced to lead an event-filled life more familiar to the wives of politicians, but she did not feel the typical constraints of a political wife. "Their husbands are always running for office," she says. "Mine wasn't." Therefore, she considered herself free to use her sense of humor to lessen the demanding aspects of her and Max's social obligations. And her behavior sometimes produced unusual quasi-geopolitical results.

One afternoon, Marjorie's friend, Lisa Anderson, phoned her in Franklin and told her that she and her husband John had asked the Princess of Morocco to visit. Lisa was calling to invite the Fishers to join them for dinner.

"Do you speak French?" Lisa asked Marjorie.

"High-school French," Marjorie answered.

"I'm having fourteen for dinner and I'm trying to find people who speak French. You have to come."

"Max doesn't speak French."

"Don't worry about Max. Morocco's ambassador to the United Nations [Ahmed Taibi Benhima] wants to meet Max. You come and talk to the princess."

After Lisa hung up the phone, Marjorie sat, holding the receiver and thinking about the invitation. Then she quickly dialed the Andersons' number.

"Lisa," she said, "do you know who you invited? You invited a Jew with the Arabs?"

"I know. They want to meet you."

"Fine. But the day after your party, you come aboard the *Marmara,* and I'll have lunch for your guests."

Marjorie and Max went to the Andersons' for dinner. Afterward, with Max deep in conversation with Ambassador Benhima, Marjorie sat on the couch with the princess, and by her own account, "was getting along pretty well with her high-school French." She asked the princess what she did during the day in Morocco.

"I play Gin Rummy," the princess replied. "I love it more than anything."

Marjorie recalls: "I thought that the princess might be a bit bored with my French because I can't carry on much of a conversation. So I asked her if she wanted to play cards."

Lisa Anderson supplied a new deck. Marjorie unwrapped

the cellophane, took the cards out of the box and shuffled them.

"What shall we play for?" Marjorie asked.

"Whatever you like," the princess said.

"Well, let's make it exciting. Let's play for Israel and Morocco. Two hands out of three."

"Splendid."

Marjorie dealt and won the first hand. Then she won the second.

"The princess," recalls Marjorie, "was so upset. But I told her not to be depressed, that tomorrow I would give her a chance to win back Morocco. So we had them for lunch on our boat and the princess couldn't wait to play again. As soon as lunch was finished, she said: 'Where are the cards?' I won two straight hands and so Israel owned Morocco. The princess was literally depressed that she had lost her country, but the afternoon ended nicely and then I forgot about it."

Several months later, Marjorie and Max were attending a dinner at Israel's Embassy in Washington. While chatting with another couple, Marjorie turned and saw that Israeli Prime Minister Golda Meir had just entered the room.

"I adored Golda," says Marjorie, "She was straightforward. With Golda, it was 'These are the facts. Let's make up our minds.' But she was also terribly sensitive. I remember when she traveled all over Israel to pay condolence calls to the families of boys who were killed. Every Israeli soul was precious to her."

Marjorie walked over to Golda, kissed her and said: "You look wonderful."

"You listen to me," Golda snapped, pointing her finger and yet barely containing a smile. "Don't you ever, ever play Israel for Morocco in a card game again. You could have lost."

"Why are you screaming at me? All you have to do is go pick up Morocco. You own it."

"Next time, you play for the United States against Morocco. You could have lost."

"No, I couldn't have," Marjorie retorted. "And why are you yelling at me? I got you Morocco. With no bloodshed."

Golda, now openly smiling, said: "Don't you ever do that again."

Then she kissed Marjorie on the cheek.

* * *

Like many men of wealth, Fisher had regularly received crackpot mail and phone calls — strangers requesting small fortunes or asking to use his box seats at Tigers games or hurling anti-Semitic slurs at him. However, once his connection to the Nixon White House and Israeli leaders became known, the letters and phone calls took a terrifying turn: his life and the lives of his family were threatened. A security detail was hired to guard the house in Franklin. Soon after, assassination plots against Fisher surfaced — plots originating with Libyan leader Muamar Qaddafi and the PLO. The White House ordered protection for Fisher from the FBI, but the threat of assassination continued, becoming familiar to international experts on terrorist and anti-terrorist activities. For instance, Amos Aricha, former chief superintendent of the Israeli police force who became a novelist, published a political thriller, *Hour of the Clown*, in which the Mossad and the CIA uncover a plan to assassinate a group of men who are "known for their unqualified support of the Jewish state," among them, Senator Daniel Moynihan, Senator Jacob Javits and "Max Fischer [sic], adviser to the [president] on Jewish affairs."

The plots and the around-the-clock security men made an already complex home life even more complicated. Julie Fisher Cummings recalls: "It was a very difficult time for our family to begin with. The FBI came and spoke to the children. We were not allowed to go to school alone; we were told to memorize the locations of the police stations between our house and school, and if we ever believed we were being followed, to head straight there. I'll never forget coming down to the kitchen in the mornings and seeing shotguns on the table. It was just sort of hard living like that."

Max was unnerved by the thought of an assassination attempt, but his attitude toward it was grounded in his pragmatism. He knew that if the 1960s proved nothing else, it was

236 : Quiet Diplomat

that anyone could kill anyone — John Kennedy, Medgar Evers, Martin Luther King, Robert Kennedy — the list was as long as it was tragic. Max had no intention of being scared off, and besides, there was little he could do about it. He told Marjorie that he wouldn't even be able to hate the person who pulled the trigger. All he could do was hire extra guards and heed the advice of the FBI man in charge of his case, Special Agent Jack Jackson.

Fortunately, Special Agent Jackson appreciated the pressure that Max was under, because Max, along with Marjorie's brother-in-law, Stanley Burkoff, were inclined to test his patience.

One evening, Stanley, his wife, Joyce, and Marjorie drove to Max's office to pick him up. They were going to dinner at the London Chop House and then to a show at the Fisher Theatre.

"I drove into the garage of the Fisher Building," says Stanley Burkoff, "since the FBI wouldn't let Max stand outside. Jack Jackson was there behind the wheel of a nondescript dark green Ford. He waited for Max to come down on the elevator and get in my car. Then he told us: 'You drive to the Chop House. I'll be right behind you. When you go into the restaurant, somebody will already be there. I'll be with you through dinner and before you go to the show.'"

"At the Chop House," continues Joyce Burkoff, "Marjorie and I tried to figure out who the other FBI fellow was. We were convinced it was a guy at the bar who was watching our table in the mirror. It was the most obvious thing you ever saw. When we were finished eating, I said to Jack Jackson: 'That tail you planted was awful.' He said: 'Why? Who do you think it is?' I said: 'That fellow at the bar.' He said: 'You're wrong. It was the guy sitting behind your table.'"

"After the show," says Stanley Burkoff, "Jack Jackson tells me to take my normal route home, down the Lodge Expressway, and he'll be in his car behind us. I start driving. Joyce is in the front with me and Marjorie's in back with Max. Kidding around, I said to Max: 'Do you think that I could lose this guy?'"

Without hesitation, Max replied: "Good idea. Try it."

"I step on the gas pedal," says Stanley, "and I'm going ninety miles an hour, and weaving in and out of traffic. I keep checking the mirrors and everyone else is looking around, out the windows, and no one can spot the FBI car. I'm sure I'd lost the tail. Max is really hysterical. He can't stop laughing."

As Stanley pulled into the Fishers' driveway, he glanced in his rearview mirror. Jackson's dark green Ford was right behind him.

"How did he do that?" Stanley said to Max once they were out of the car.

"It's my business," Jackson answered.

Max was still laughing when Burkoff asked the FBI agent: "Was I any good?"

Jackson looked at Stanley and Max, and sadly shook his head. "You were fair," he said. "But both you guys better forget about a life of crime."

*   *   *

For Max's younger children — Mary, Phillip, Julie and Margie — the central fact of their childhood and teenage years was that their father was rarely present. (By the late 1960s, Jane Fisher was no longer living with Max and Marjorie. She and her husband Larry Sherman had three children of their own — David, Sylvia and Scott.)

Says Mary Fisher: "Up until 1968, Dad had always been busy. But his work had mainly been in Michigan — for Romney, the local federation, the Torch Drive and his business interests. After Nixon's first election, though, he was working nationally, and in Israel, and he was gone all the time. I remember wanting to tell him: 'Look, Dad, these people are not as important as we are.' I understood what his priorities were, but that didn't mean I liked them or that I didn't try to change them every chance I got."

But changing his priorities was impossible for Max. He brought the same blind energy to politics and the Jewish Agency that he had brought to the oil business. Engulfed by these commitments, he was unable to scale back. Even on those evenings when he was in Franklin and promised himself to focus his attention on his wife and children, he was constantly being called to the telephone, which was, as an interviewer once remarked, his "favorite instrument." A photograph, often referred to by the Fisher family, shows Max sleeping on a couch, his right hand still pressing a "telephone" to his ear — long after he had dozed off and the phone had been pried from his fingers.

However, there were times when everything appeared to be in place with his wife and children — fishing jaunts to the Bahamas, parents' day at summer camps and school graduations. Max fretted that his absence would rob his children of the necessary discipline, and so he attempted to rein them in by spanking them when they misbehaved. Margie Fisher Aronow recalls that her father "would have difficulty with it. He'd say: 'This is going to hurt me more than it's going to hurt you,' but his heart wasn't into punishing us, and he'd start laughing. We used to put books in our pajama bottoms, which made him laugh harder."

On occasion, it would strike Max with excruciating clarity that he was abandoning one of life's grander pleasures by not being around to watch his son and daughters grow up, and he would turn to Marjorie and say: "I miss the children. There's never enough time."

"And the children," says Marjorie, "never knew it. Max is so quiet about the way he feels. But he told me over and over again: 'I've missed so much.' "

Max decided that one way he could rectify the situation was to bring his children with him to meetings or on his travels. After graduating high school, Mary went with him to Israel and California; Julie used to sit on his lap at business conferences; Margie traveled with him to Salem, Ohio, when his high school named him alumnus of the year. And in January 1971, Phillip, at the age of twenty, had his first extended period alone with Max when he accompanied him to Israel.

They almost didn't make the trip. William Fisher had suffered another heart attack and was admitted to the intensive care unit at St. Francis Hospital in Miami Beach. Unhappy about being confined, he tried to escape from his room. As someone who had unremittingly followed the news, William was also unhappy about being deprived of his radio. But Max had just received a series of death threats and several news services reported them. Max's sister Gail, worried that their father would hear them, removed the radio from beside his bed. The doctors assured Max that William was in no imminent danger. He could go to Israel with Phillip.

*   *   *

The late 1960s and early 1970s were fertile ground for father-son dissonance. The cultural antagonism was cast around what was then described as "the Generation Gap." Logically enough, each side had a uniform. Fathers were neatly barbered and wore pinstripe suits. Sporting beards and hair past their shoulders, sons dressed in work shirts and bleached denims.

"I went off to the University of Hartford in 1969," says Phillip Fisher. "I thought going to Connecticut — actually, getting away from Detroit — would be the best thing for me. I was really striving to form an image of myself, to get out from under my father's shadow. I had been pretty sheltered in high school and I moved into my dorm room and met my first hippie. By Christmas break, my hair was long; I had a motorcycle — the whole nine yards. Dad was Establishment, and he wasn't very happy about these developments. He gave me a hard time, particularly about my hair."

Although fathers and sons were often at loggerheads over cultural styles, for many the greatest rift occurred over America's involvement in Vietnam. Max and Phillip disagreed mightily about the war, and their debate intensified in the spring of 1970, when President Nixon announced that he had ordered U.S. troops into Cambodia. Nixon's announcement ignited antiwar protests on college campuses across the country. At Kent State University in Ohio, National Guardsman fired on protesters, killing four students. The next day, 450 colleges and universities went on strike. Antiwar rallies escalated into riots. A national day of student protest was scheduled for May 9 in Washington, D.C.

Max supported Nixon's decision, believing that the United States had to confront the Soviet Union wherever the Kremlin chose to fight — whether in Southeast Asia or the Middle East. On May 2, Max wrote the president: "My congratulations to you. It takes great courage to make the decision you did on Cambodia, when you knew there would be an outcry against it from people who do not have the facts and who do not appreciate what long-range effects it might have on this country and the world."

Phillip, at the University of Hartford, was considering leaving school and joining the protesters. He phoned his father.

"Dad," he asked, "what's Nixon doing?"

Max explained the geopolitical reasoning behind the U.S. push into Cambodia. Phillip said that the whole war was wrong — how could this latest installment of it be right?

Max thought for a moment. He recalled how unyielding his father had been about what he should do and what he shouldn't. Was that the way he wanted to deal with his son? No, he decided, it wasn't.

"Look," Max said, "you asked for my side of the story and I gave it to you. But it's your decision — you make up your mind."

Phillip left school to join the protest marches.

Though Max was a believer in conducting important business via the phone, he did not feel that parenting fell into that category. So the trip to Israel in 1971 was going to be, in part, an opportunity for father and son to become reacquainted.

On the morning of January 23, Phillip and Max flew from Detroit to Washington, D.C. While his father attended a two-hour meeting at the State Department to discuss William Rogers's conception of land for peace in the Middle East, Phillip toured the capital. Their next stop was New York City, where Max, with leaders from the United Jewish Appeal and Council of Jewish Federations, attended meetings on the upcoming reconstitution of the Jewish Agency. Phillip took another tour. Late that afternoon, they left for Tel Aviv. On the flight, they talked about Phillip's schooling, what he enjoyed about college and what he found difficult, and his plans for the future. When they stepped off the plane at Lod Airport, an Israeli man who worked for the Jewish Agency approached them and said: "Mr. Fisher, I am very sorry to have to tell you that your father has died."

Recalls Phillip: "My father stopped; he froze. I'm used to him making split-second decisions, but not now. He stopped for a full minute. It was as if he were praying. I said: 'Dad, I'm so sorry.' But he was oblivious to me or to anyone else."

Finally, Max, in control again, told Phillip: "I've got to see Golda and Dayan, and President [Zalman] Shazar. When I've finished, you'll stay in Israel and I'll go to Detroit and arrange everything. Then I'll come back next week and pick you up and we'll go home."

Phillip said that he would prefer to return to the United States with his father; he didn't want him to be alone. Max looked at him and nodded. Then they went to visit Golda Meir. The prime minister hugged Max and offered her condolences. Defense Minister Dayan walked in. Golda served coffee and cookies, and Phillip sat in as they discussed Secretary of State Rogers's proposals. The discussion lasted for an hour and a half. Afterward, Max and Phillip rode to President Shazar's house. Max spoke to the president for an hour regarding plans for the June reconstitution of the Agency. Late that afternoon, Max and Phillip returned to New York and then caught a flight to Detroit.

* * *

Funeral services for William Fisher, eighty-two, were held on January 27, in Southfield, Michigan. In a private room at the Ira Kaufman Chapel, before the crush of family and friends gathered, Max stood over his father's open casket. Even in death, William's face retained its determination. Max stroked his father's hair and turned to his niece, Sharon Ross Medsker, saying: "Dad always liked that."

The squabbles between Max and William in Salem and

during their salad days at the Keystone plant were long forgotten. Until the end, though, their relationship was unusually formal. At one point, after Mollie died in the summer of 1969, Max invited his father to attend a White House dinner with him. William refused without explanation. At the dinner, Max was seated with President Nixon. The president offered to sign Max's place card as a memento. Max asked him to inscribe it to his father, which Nixon did. Max later presented the card to William, who pocketed it and said nothing.

Norris Friedlander, William's accountant in Florida who did double duty as a surrogate son, says that "William was very proud of Max and loved to hear someone compliment him, but he would never tell a stranger: 'My son's such a success in business and is a friend of the president and Israel's prime minister.' Bill Fisher had an East European Russian mentality. He couldn't let himself go. I know something about that because my family came from the same place that Bill came from. They were reticent people. It was how they lived. So Bill's ways did not surprise me — not a bit."

Nor should William's ways have surprised Max, since they essentially mirrored his own. And it was not only a penchant for reticence that they had in common. In his eulogy for William, Rabbi Irwin Groner remarked on traits that those familiar with both men claim were interchangeable facets of their personalities. "There was," said Groner "a certain dominant quality about Bill Fisher that one sensed in every encounter with him. He lived by fundamental and fixed principles to which he offered his steadfast loyalty and his unswerving dedication. He was a man for whom the standards of integrity conveyed great meaning. His word was his bond."

William and Max may have been much more alike than otherwise, but there remained an unmistakable — and somewhat mysterious — distance between them. In commenting on the scope of William's life, Rabbi Groner unwittingly located the barricade that divided the father from the son. Said Groner: "Bill belonged to a generation of pioneers who came to an unknown land and who coped with strange and difficult circumstances. They were sustained on this odyssey by a vision of freedom and of peace, and by the hope of giving their children an opportunity for a better life."

William's resoluteness provided Max with opportunities that were unavailable to a Jew in a Russian *shtetl*. Yet it was William's fate to rear an equally resolute son who, in his own manner and on his own terms, was also a pioneer. Of necessity, Max's perceptions of freedom and peace were more Americanized than William's. They were a product of a small, turn-of-the-century town and an efflorescing nation in love with progress and poised on the threshold of a technological gold rush. Thus, Max's goals contained ideals of economic and social potential for American Jews that projected his father's immigrant aspirations beyond William's bravest dreams. If, in moments, William felt left behind, then perhaps that is simply the bittersweet lot of fathers who are courageous and industrious enough to hand their sons a better world.

William understood the breadth of Max's accomplishments — how far the son had traveled from the gloomy steerage of the ship that had brought the father to Ellis Island in 1906.

Not long after William was buried next to Mollie at Clover Hill, Max was sifting through his father's personal effects. Tucked safely in the top drawer of a bureau, Max found the place card that President Nixon had signed.

*   *   *

Of all the friends that Fisher made in business, philanthropy and politics, two men can be judged to have grown closest to him: Al Taubman and Henry Ford II. Taubman's friendship with him began in earnest in the early 1960s. Fisher's friendship with Ford dates to a few years before, in the late 1950s, when Ford's first wife, Anne, was raising money for the Detroit opera. But Fisher and Ford became particularly close during Romney's 1962 campaign for governor.

Their backgrounds could not have been more different. Fisher was the son of Jewish immigrants; Ford was the WASP heir to one of the world's premier industrial dynasties whose grandfather, Henry I, was an ardent backer of anti-Semitic publications that were treasured in Hitler's Third Reich. But Henry II's antipathy for his grandfather was well known. Henry Ford I, an imperious man, had cruelly mistreated Henry II's father, Edsel, who died before the age of fifty. Explaining his father's death to a friend, Henry II commented: "Grandad killed my father."

Henry Ford II was eager to distance himself from his grandfather's reputation. For example, after Chaim Weizmann became the first president of Israel, Henry presented him with a new Lincoln limousine. There were only two of its kind in existence. Henry gave the other one to President Harry S. Truman. Twenty years later, Ford sponsored Fisher and Alan E. Schwartz for membership to the Detroit Club, which had a policy of excluding Jews.

Today, according to Tim Kiska, author of *Detroit's Powers & Personalities*, Schwartz is a "legal patriarch [with] the best Rol-o-dex in town," who "helped build the Honigman, Miller, Schwartz & Cohn law firm, the most prestigious Detroit legal shop begun in the last forty years." But in 1952, when Schwartz returned to Detroit from Harvard Law School, he was struggling to win a spot for himself, and Fisher, as he had done with Taubman, took him under his wing.

Explaining the problem at the Detroit Club, Schwartz says that "Henry just thought it was time that they had some Jewish members. Max and I agreed. So Henry and Joe Hudson sponsored us. On our first try, the board turned us down."

When Schwartz learned that he and Fisher had been rejected by the Detroit Club, he phoned Fisher and said: "Well, Max, how do we deal with this? What do you think we should say about it?"

Fisher answered: "Alan, you don't understand it. This isn't our problem. It's the Detroit Club's problem. They now have to wrestle with the question of whether they were really prepared to open up to Jews or not. Just let it sit. Don't let it concern you."

A year later, Fisher and Schwartz were approached again by Ford to join the club and were accepted. More Jewish members followed.

Schwartz had the chance to observe the Fisher-Ford friendship and says, at bottom, the two men just "trusted each other. Henry had a lot of confidence in Max because he was a self-made man who had been so successful in every sense — financially, socially and politically. Henry felt very comfortable with him as the person whom he could confide in and who wasn't seeking anything from Henry. They were pals."

Henry's son, Edsel B. Ford II, who in April 1991 was named president and CEO of Ford Motor Credit, believes that his father and Fisher grew so close because "there were few people in the world who were at the same power level as my father. Max was one of them." In addition, says Edsel, "Max was the angel on my father's shoulder. He talked everything over with him. Max is the great calmer, and my father was impulsive. Max was willing to listen to him. He is the kind of man who can talk to the president about a global issue one minute and then the next minute he's discussing a mundane personal problem with someone else."

Fisher's ability to listen and calmly offer suggestions was something that Edsel valued after he graduated from college and entered the family business. They were trying years for the great-grandson of the company's founder; the Ford mantle, he says, is not easy to wear, and Edsel had his troubles with his father.

"When I couldn't get through to my father," says Edsel, "I used to use Max. I could say things to him that I couldn't say to my father and then Max would talk to Dad. More than anyone, Max has been a mentor for me. Generally, I had a wonderful relationship with my father, but he was Henry Ford first and foremost and that's very difficult. It was very hard for him, and hard for me being his son. Max helped me when I was frustrated. I would say: 'Max, Dad's not listening.'"

In Henry Ford, Fisher saw someone who "honestly does things from his heart. [But] he finds it very hard, quite often, to express his emotions. I'd say 'Come on, Henry, why don't you let it go?' But really, he finds that side of things pretty difficult."

Regarding his relationship with Fisher, Ford told an interviewer: "I've always felt that I could count on Max when I was in trouble."

And Ford was well acquainted with trouble. Fisher helped him through upheaval at Ford Motor Company, the dissolution of his second marriage to Cristina, and saw him through the scandal that erupted when Ford was arrested for drunk driving in California with his girlfriend, Kathleen King DuRoss, beside him. Along with Marjorie, Max encouraged the romance between Ford and DuRoss. She later became Ford's third and final wife.

In February 1972, when the Fords and Fishers visited Israel together, Henry was still married to Cristina. The two couples flew from England with Irving Bernstein, executive vice president of the United Jewish Appeal, and Walter Hayes, an English friend of Henry who served as a public-relations officer at Ford. Henry had decided to visit Israel to determine whether Ford Motor Company might supply automobile components to an Israeli businessman, Joe Boxenbaum, who had recently opened an assembly plant in Nazareth.

The deal was not without economic risks. According to Walter Hayes "the Arab boycott offices in the Middle East were alert and alive to companies setting up in Israel, and . . . the prospect of Ford being placed on the boycott list could probably be taken for granted. . . . Other companies, some of them household names, had closed subsidiaries in Israel to protect their bigger and more profitable Arab markets."

Discussing the boycott with Fisher, Ford told him: "Nobody's gonna tell me what to do."

The first day in Israel, Teddy Kollek, the burly indefatigable mayor of Jerusalem, guided the group on a tour of the Old City. Kollek, who had known Fisher for nearly two decades, held him in the highest esteem, because, he says, "many men like Max would've stayed home and pampered themselves. But he feels a responsibility for Israel. And when he's here he doesn't throw his weight around. He's very sensitive to the complicated nuances of life in Israel."

One of these complexities was the ailing Israeli economy.

During the week, Fisher introduced Ford to Israeli leaders: Golda Meir, Shimon Peres, Abba Eban and David Ben-Gurion. The politics surrounding Arab oil were frequently the focus of conversation.

Fisher was impressed with how thoroughly Henry had prepared for these meetings. Yet when he questioned Ford about them, Henry smiled modestly and replied: "It was over my head. I didn't understand half of what they were saying." Fisher answered with a phrase that he invariably used when Ford was being self-deprecating or sidestepping his obvious emotional reaction: "Henry," Fisher said. "You're full of shit."

Ford expressed interest in seeing the Suez Canal, so early one morning, Max, Henry, Walter Hayes, Irving Bernstein and his nineteen-year-old son, Robert, who was spending the year living on a kibbutz, hopped on a twenty-eight-seat French Frélon helicopter in Jerusalem and headed for the Sinai.

In *Henry*, his affectionate biography of Henry Ford II, Walter Hayes writes: "We were over the Sinai Desert . . . when the helicopter shuddered as though it had met bad weather and then began to gyrate as if wounded. Henry fastened his seat belt; I was torn between the desire to do the same and get my camera out. I managed to do both before we hit the sand with an almighty thud. . . . We piled out of the Frélon onto the Sinai, which was covered with shells of some snaillike creature and stretched forever."

A rotor blade had snapped, and while the pilot radioed for another helicopter, Fisher set off on a stroll.

Irving Bernstein called: "Max, where are you going?"

Ford quipped: "Don't bother him. He's looking for oil."

Actually, Fisher was looking for oil. The shells littering the sand were, Fisher believed, signs that an ancient sea had once covered the area. And that could signal oil below.

However, Fisher's exploration was cut short. Within twenty minutes, the relief helicopter landed and the pilot stepped out. Before anyone could climb in, Ford asked the two pilots to stand next to each other and remove their aviator headgear. The two young men appeared dumbfounded by the request, but they complied. Underneath his headgear, the first pilot wore a *yarmulke* — the skull cap worn by observant Jewish men. But the second pilot was not wearing one.

Nodding to himself as if he had finally solved a knotty problem, Ford said: "I want the religious guy flying the new helicopter."

"What?" Fisher asked, incredulous.

"It can't hurt," Ford replied. "He got us through the crash. No use taking any chances."

The pilots explained that it was against regulations for them to swap helicopters.

Ford said: "Max, can't we do something about this?"

Irving Bernstein had an idea. He radioed Bir Gafgafa, headquarters of the Israeli Defense Forces in the Sinai, and was patched through to Hakirya — Israel's version of the Pentagon — in Tel Aviv. Bernstein reached Ezer Weizman, who was then chief of the air force, and explained Ford's reluctance to fly with a nonobservant Jew at the controls. Weizman started laughing so hard that Bernstein began to break up as well. At last, Weizman gave the pilots permission to switch helicopters. As they boarded for the flight to the Canal, Ford was obviously relieved.

Two days later, Ford visited Joe Boxenbaum's assembly plant in Nazareth. Says Walter Hayes: "[Though] Henry was not convinced the agreement would make economic sense for Israel or Ford . . . he was not prepared to have anybody stop him from carrying on the nonpolitical everyday business of the Ford Motor Company."

As a result, the Ford Motor Company was placed on the Arab boycott list, where it remained for fifteen years.

"It was just a pragmatic business procedure," Henry said years later. "I don't mind saying I was influenced in part by the fact that the company still suffers from a resentment against the anti-Semitism of the distant past. We want to overcome that. But the main thing is that here we had a dealer who wanted to open up a agency to sell our products — hell, let him do it."

Fisher felt that more lay behind the decision than business. Despite the countless tabloid pages Henry filled in his lifetime, he had an insatiable need to do what was right when it came to issues of fairness. And he'd be damned if he'd let any pressure group push him around — regardless of consequences.

This quality drew Fisher to Ford. By nature a cautious man who excelled at patiently constructing a consensus behind the scenes, Fisher admired his friend's sudden, ham-fisted method for reaching a decision and barreling into action. Impetuousness had its place, but each man would need the other's talents by the mid-1970s, when they, along with Al Taubman, endeavored to restore the deteriorating face of Detroit.

*   *   *

By the end of 1972, Fisher was exhausted. Nixon's re-election campaign was behind him, but the reconstituted Jewish Agency, still in its infancy, required constant care. So the last week of the year, he paused for a vacation in his Palm Beach apartment.

Following their marriage in 1953, Marjorie had insisted that Max take an annual winter break in Florida because she said that the sun rejuvenated him; he could stretch out in the oceanside light, visit with friends and see his children. Best of all, Marjorie thought, was that her husband was away from his office, and although he was never far from a telephone, he was able to relax. And so in the years before they purchased their house on the shores of Lake Worth, the Fishers rented a penthouse apartment at the Sun and Surf, on Sunrise Avenue, in Palm Beach.

Now, it was 6:30 a.m., on New Year's Day, 1973. After tossing and turning from midnight on, Max woke with a start. He was still scared. A bad dream? Hardly. It was real. Last night, the doctor had come. The scene hung on the dim edge of memory. Then Max rolled over. Marjorie was sleeping. Careful not to wake her, he slipped out of bed, put on his robe and walked into the living room. Through the wall of windows, he saw the pink streaks of dawn coming up over the ocean. Usually, gazing out at the blue-green water calmed him, so he went to the book-lined den just off the living room, sat in his chair and watched the sun rising above the water.

Last night, Max had been terribly frightened. While dressing for a New Year's Eve party, he suddenly grew dizzy, then short of breath. Marjorie says that "his skin turned gray." She phoned the doctor, helped Max onto the bed and loosened his tie. The doctor arrived and examined Max. He said that Max had suffered from an arrhythmia, a variation of the normal heartbeat. There was medication to treat it. But Max would have to reduce his work load, watch his diet and generally lead a less stressful life; after all, he was only six months shy of his sixty-fifth birthday.

Recently, Max had experienced a round of health problems, reminders that — as the saying goes — always is not the same as forever. (Also, eighteen months after William's death, Henry Wenger, Fisher's mentor, had died.) A bout with cataracts was Max's most immediately distressing ailment, making it nearly impossible to read.

Yet the underlying predicament was his time commitments. Philanthropy, politics and serving on boards of directors had its rewards, but he was stretched too thin. And his cluttered schedule kept him from his family, aggravating problems that required his attention.

Mary and Phillip were in their twenties and on their own. His daughters, Julie and Marjorie, were living at home, and Max was, at the moment, at odds with Julie. She had been steadily dating a young man since she was sixteen. Her boyfriend was nine years her senior, which concerned Max. He felt eighteen-year-old Julie was too young to be so seriously involved with someone who was twenty-seven. During Christmas vacation, Julie had asked her father if she could get married. Max said no and would not discuss it further. Julie threatened to elope. Max became furious. Julie asked what he would do about it, get the FBI after her? In his frustration, Max replied yes, that's exactly what he'd do.

The standard adolescent gyrations of his children, although exasperating, were not unexpected. He felt that within a few years the worst of the conflict with his children would die a natural death. There was, though, a grave dilemma that would not vanish, that had actually grown in intensity, namely, his wife's drinking, which frightened Max as much as his own declining health.

Even among professionals who treat alcoholics, the border between excessive drinking and alcoholism is subject to debate. To Max, by the early 1970s, Marjorie appeared to have crossed it. Marjorie believed that Max was unaware that late each afternoon she started pouring herself vodka and drank for two hours. Some of the Fisher children also believed that their father did not notice their mother's startling alcohol consumption or, like in a host of other families with an alcoholic in their midst, chose to overlook it, thinking, unrealistically, that the malady would correct itself. But Max confided to one of his oldest friends that he was "beside himself with Marjorie's drinking," and, other than being with her more frequently, did not have a clue about how to handle it.

Marjorie Fisher says: "I was very lonely, but I would never blame [my drinking] on Max."

She didn't have to. Max blamed himself, his interminable traveling.

There are three identifiable crisis points in Max Fisher's life. The first transpired shortly after he departed Salem for Ohio State; the second was during the final year of Sylvia's life; and the third was at approximately 7 a.m. on New Year's Day, 1973. What makes them identifiable is the manner in which Fisher chose to deal with them. At the three junctures, he attacked his turmoil by examining it in writing, cataloging his distress and proposing solutions to himself — a pragmatist's makeshift guide to subduing adversity. In college, he compiled self-improvement lists and deprived himself of meals when he missed his mark; in 1952, he kept a running commentary of his despair in the face of Sylvia's heart disease; and in his Palm Beach penthouse, in 1973, he removed a yellow legal pad and pen from a side table, and sketched out his troubles and his plans for countering them.

"Have been trying to put into perspective a new life style,"

Fisher wrote. "There is no question continuation of the past would create many problems — physically, mentally and emotionally. Most important, [my] relationships to my family have been adversely affected when some changes were delayed. [My wife, Marjorie], in this regard has shown great patience. There is no question that the lack of balance in [my] family relationships has robbed me of a great deal of happiness.

"Looking into the future, I would like to consider certain changes.

"Let us start with physical — No question I cannot continue what I have been doing — certain obvious physical problems are developing. The abuse I have been giving my body is beginning to show — [my] weight is [my] number one problem. I have put on over twenty pounds which have hurt me physically.

"The question is — realizing this — what will I do about it? A crash diet will bring about a reduction — but this does not solve the problem. Do I have the will power to adjust my style of eating for my own good over a period of time? I believe I must and will.

"At the same time I must learn to exercise again. My refusal to even move coupled with [my extra] weight is a serious physical problem. I can walk — swim, ride, bicycle and play golf — but I must also be consistent about it.

"The problem with my eyes is serious. There again I must get other advice — but I will be positive — eyes are so important to me because of my love of reading — yet [up until] now I have not been willing to sacrifice. Will I? [I] must do something.

"I know also that my heart rhythm is out of balance because of the above reasons. I believe I must have the best medical advice on this and I must adjust myself to what needs to be done.

"Business and outside activities — There is no question I must make serious adjustments. A great deal of [the] things I now am doing are not necessary and I must withdraw. I have reached the top of all the [Jewish] charities and I must confine myself to [the Jewish] Agency and [in] the rest [of the Jewish charities] become a senior statesman.

"I have plenty of things to do in Detroit and some activities in Washington.

"On Washington scene — I should be willing to take on special assignments to maintain my relationships and responsibilities — but there again [I] must be phased out to a reasonable degree.

"Now comes the most important [part] — relationship to my family. There will [be] little time to capture what I have lost — but to whatever extent I can I should spend [time] with my children and my wife.

"I have lost a great deal — no one can really appreciate what I have lost except myself. This is something I will suffer from more than anything else. I can gain so much from all of my family if I would allow it.

"Marjorie has been so patient [with] — and tolerant of — me. But this cannot continue. I must give of myself because she has so much to give. This of all things I have mentioned is the most important.

"I have locked all my thoughts and ambitions within me. Can I open myself up? I feel I must. The love of a woman like Marjorie is something to treasure and not to fight. I am so fortunate and I badly need her help and patience. We can have much to look forward to if I can allow myself to give. It is too much to ask but I hope she appreciates my problems and will be patient with me.

"All of this is a tall order — Can I make all these adjustments?

"All it will take is will power and an understanding of what really matters.

"I remember when I was eighteen — I kept a diary [and] I had the will power to bring about changes.

"Can I do it now?

"I promise to give it a good try. I am going to grade myself as I did when I was eighteen on these requirements — health; weight; exercise; eyes; diet; business and charitable activities/ balance; MF family relationships."

*　　*　　*

When Fisher completed writing the document, he signed and dated it as if it were a contract, then slid the sheets into a folder and consequently had them filed in his office, inspecting them on occasion to gauge his progress. For the next eighteen years, with differing degrees of success, he wrestled with his goals. He underwent the routine physical ailments of aging. In the main, he was scrupulous about doctor appointments, weighed himself each day, cut back on chocolate ice cream and the brownies, chocolate chip cookies and coffee cake that Manya Kern, the Fishers' longtime Detroit housekeeper, baked with inimitable skill, and adhered to a regimen of swimming, calisthenics and a modified weight-lifting program.

Striking a balance between business, philanthropy, politics and the requirements of family would prove more challenging. Fisher would be engaged in this process for the next twelve years. By then, Marjorie was conquering her addiction to alcohol, and Max was discovering that his involvement in causes had cost his family far more than he had ever imagined.

Chapter 12

PLAYING HIS ROLE: 1971-1974
THE NIXON WHITE HOUSE,
PART II

THE LACK OF progress toward peace in the Middle East frustrated Fisher and most American Jews. No matter how turbulently the political sands shifted, the landscape remained the same.

For example, in August 1970, the "stop-shooting, start-talking" initiative of Secretary of State Rogers paid off. Egypt and Israel agreed to an unofficial cease-fire. Within days, the Egyptians violated the truce. Russian technicians manned Soviet-supplied SAM batteries in the Canal Zone, while Soviet pilots flew missions against the Israeli Air Force. Egyptian President Nasser died in September 1970. Although his successor, Anwar el-Sadat, grew disenchanted with the Kremlin, he balked at a formal treaty.

Also in September 1970, the Palestine Liberation Organization tried to overthrow King Hussein of Jordan. Syria hurried to shore up the PLO attack with tanks. Nixon viewed the Syrian invasion as a Soviet-inspired, global chess move against the United States. He put U.S. forces on alert and requested that Israel intervene for Jordan. The Israelis mobilized; Syria withdrew. In the aftermath of the crisis, Kissinger won a battle with Rogers. The White House shelved the notion of imposing a Mideast peace and leaned toward rearming Israel to restrict Soviet inroads in the region.

Kissinger's methodology had vigorous backing in the Sen-

ate. Senator Henry M. "Scoop" Jackson of Washington, a powerful Democrat, pushed through an amendment to the
Defense Procurement Act that — according to Jackson's biographer Peter J. Ognibene — "made an essentially open-ended
commitment to fulfill Israel's need for military weapons."

Nixon and Kissinger continued to extricate the United
States from Indochina and to implement their policy of
détente with the Russians. Reducing tensions between the
superpowers appeared to be a strategy that the American Jewish community would embrace. Israeli security could only be
strengthened by the Soviet restraint of its Arab clients. Therefore, as historian Melvin I. Urofsky observes in *We Are One!:
American Jewry and Israel*, it stunned the administration
when "the monkey wrench thrown into the gears of détente
[originated] . . . from a totally unexpected area: American Jews
suddenly wanted their government to pressure the Soviets
into allowing Russian Jews to emigrate."

Between 1945 and 1966, conventional wisdom held that
the once-flourishing Jewish population of Russia had been
devastated by the Second World War and then crushed by the
Communists' resolve to abolish religion. In 1966, though,
novelist and Holocaust survivor Elie Wiesel published *The
Jews of Silence*, an account of his recent trip through the
Soviet Union. Wiesel documented that three million Jews had
survived the Kremlin's assault on Judaism. In the wake of the
1967 Six-Day War, thousands of Soviet Jews applied for exit
visas to Israel. Russian authorities punished the applicants by
stripping them of their jobs, expelling them from schools and
harassing their families. As Urofsky writes, it was not long
before "Jewish agencies saw the Russian emigration problem
as second in importance only to Israel."

*　　*　　*

Fisher first approached the administration about Soviet
Jewry during his tenure as president of the Council of Jewish
Federations and Welfare Funds. On December 30, 1970, a Jew-
ish leadership conference had gathered in Washington to ask

the government for assistance in seeking clemency for the Leningrad 11.

The case had begun on June 15, 1970. At 8:30 a.m., Russian authorities arrested the Leningrad 11 at Smolny Airport as they boarded a single-engine Aeroflot plane that was scheduled to fly from Leningrad to Petrozavodosk, a city on the Finnish border. Nine of those apprehended were Jews who hoped to leave for Israel. Russian authorities alleged that the group, armed with knives and pistols, intended to hijack the plane. Six months later, on December 24, a Leningrad court convicted all eleven under Article 64-A. The article declared it treasonous to flee abroad and equated a planned crime with one that had been committed. Nine of the defendants were ordered to serve prison-camp terms ranging from four to fifteen years. The other two defendants — both of whom had applied for exit visas to Israel — were sentenced to die before a firing squad.

According to Soviet law, the Leningrad 11 had seven days to file their appeals with the Russian Federation's Supreme Court.

By December 30, only twenty-four hours remained for the condemned. Through the morning, Fisher attended meetings with congressional leaders. He had also scheduled an afternoon visit with Secretary of State Rogers at Foggy Bottom. Dr. William Wexler, head of the Presidents Conference, and Rabbi Herschel Schacter, chairman of the National Conference on Soviet Jewry, accompanied Fisher to the State Department. They implored Rogers to intercede or to ask Nixon to speak with the Soviets. Rogers was sympathetic, but he replied that his options were limited.

"What about the president?" Schacter asked. "This is an apolitical cause — purely humanitarian."

"The president's busy," said Rogers, "but I'll call him."

Rogers left the room, returning five minutes later. "Let's go," he said. The four men took the back elevator to the garage, entered the secretary's limousine, and rode to the White House.

At 4:20 p.m., they walked into the Oval Office. Nixon sat

behind his desk. Chief of Staff H.R. Haldeman and George P. Shultz, director of the Office of Management and Budget, were talking to the president. (Fisher had been friendly with Shultz since 1969, when, as secretary of the treasury, Shultz investigated how industry could provide training and jobs for inner-city residents and discussed the subject at length with Fisher.)

Before entering the Oval Office, Rogers had cautioned the three Jewish leaders that Nixon's schedule was tight and not to engage him in an extended dialogue. So they hastily repeated their request — could he intercede for the Leningrad 11?

The president did not rush them, nor did he immediately answer their question. He reminisced about his 1959 kitchen debate in Moscow with Soviet Premier Nikita Khrushchev. Nixon recalled telling Khrushchev that "a real test of a society is the manner in which a government treats its Jewish citizens." The president then remarked on his admiration for Israel and said that had the Leningrad 11 been Israeli pilots, they would have escaped with the plane.

After a half-hour, Nixon said: "I'd be happy to help the Leningrad 11, but you know I'm Public Enemy Number One in the Kremlin. The minute I try, they'll probably shove these guys up against a wall and shoot them." He paused. "There's a way, though. Listen, last time Golda was here I said to her, 'Trust me.' Which is what I'll say to you: 'Trust me.'"

That evening, Fisher received a call from a presidential assistant. The death sentences of the two Russian Jews were being commuted to fifteen-year prison terms. Fisher never learned how Nixon managed it. He guessed that the president spoke to Kissinger, who contacted the Soviet Embassy in Washington. The Russians would soon be seeking several concessions from the United States — i.e., an arms limitations agreement and most-favored-nation trade status. The Kremlin probably surmised that granting Nixon's request was an investment in the future.

*   *   *

With such a promising start between the administration and the American Jewish community on the fate of Soviet

Jewry, Fisher anticipated that the cooperation would continue. Early in 1971, he saw that he had miscalculated. Nixon believed that a superpower such as the Soviet Union could not let the United States dictate its internal policies — after all, would the United States allow Russia to set its national agenda? Hence, Nixon believed that the way to obtain freedom for Soviet Jews was to apply pressure to the Russian government without humiliating them. Fisher subscribed to Nixon's method. Regrettably, a considerable portion of the American Jewish community did not. Protests against the Soviet Union burgeoned. Since Nixon would not openly nudge the Kremlin, the organized Jewish community felt that Soviet Jewry was not a priority at the White House. Consequently, the protests intensified. A radical element, Rabbi Meir Kahane's Jewish Defense League, planted a bomb outside the Soviet cultural center in Washington, D.C., while in New York, JDL gangs stalked Soviet diplomats and cursed them in Russian.

Nixon publicly deplored the anti-Soviet violence. Fisher and seventy-three American Jewish leaders sent him a telegram stating that they were "united in our abhorrence of these acts," but added that "they believed that Soviet Jews should be permitted cultural and religious freedom and should have the right to emigrate from Russia if they wish."

Because Fisher was pressed for time, he was grateful that the quarrel over Soviet Jewry did not reach its zenith until after the 1972 election. Caught between the White House and the Jewish community, he had the sinking, helpless sensation of watching the battle lines being drawn and knowing that there was, just then, nothing he could do to prevent the impending showdown. For the first six months of 1971, Fisher was traveling back and forth to Israel in preparation for the Founding Assembly of the reconstituted Jewish Agency. On his visits, when he had a break between Agency meetings, he buttonholed American Jewish leaders and encouraged them to give the Nixon administration the benefit of the doubt. He also spoke frequently with the Israeli press, repeatedly telling them that "the president understands the Soviet Jews' situation and takes much more action on it than he is given credit for."

But Fisher's election to the chairmanship of the Board of Governors in June further crowded his schedule, and then he had to focus his attention on the upcoming presidential campaign. The Nixon organization for 1972, the Committee to Re-elect the President (CRP), was in place by the spring of 1971, with Fisher one of its eight original members. At this point, CRP's primary goal, according to its chairman, Francis L. Dale, publisher of the Cincinnati *Enquirer*, was "to study the manner in which the campaign should be waged." Fisher was again anxious to take a stab at the Jewish vote. Nixon had garnered 16 percent of it in 1968; Fisher thought that the president had a shot at doubling that percentage.

For two months, Fisher worked the phone, calling his contacts around the country and in Israel, talking to Jewish leaders and professionals, fund-raisers, journalists — anyone who could give him an up-to-the-minute reading on the swaying political sensibilities of the Jewish electorate. In August, Fisher sent a six-page précis to John Mitchell, who in March 1972 would resign as attorney general to direct the Nixon campaign. In his abstract, Fisher outlined his ground plan for enlarging Nixon's percentage of the Jewish vote.

"It is my feeling," Fisher wrote, "that a swing could be made in the voting pattern of the Jewish community — if we understand the basic issues and we start organizing now on a low-key basis."

For Fisher, the basic issues were — Israel: "The one thing the Jewish community is united on." Economic policies: "I find a strong tendency [among leaders] toward some sort of controls, plus a stimulation of the economy through investment tax credits [and] an adequate money supply." Law and order: "There is a strong feeling on this issue among Orthodox and Conservatives who live in cities and have not been able to move because of low-income status and age limitations. They have suffered considerably from crime." Fisher said that the next issue, Soviet Jewry, was important for two reasons: the "great emotional response" it engendered, and because college students were attracted to it. (The 1972 election was the first in which eighteen-year-olds were eligible to vote.) He

did tell Mitchell that "the president has a very deep understanding of this problem," and that he had "discussed it with
him on previous occasions."

Noticeably absent from Fisher's evaluation was the
expanding dispute between the White House and the organized Jewish community. Fisher thought that it would be
sapient to get past the election before the controversy
careened out of control. To circumvent future hostilities and
to assist Soviet Jews in their emigration, Fisher lobbied
Mitchell in his précis to speak to the president about doing
more for Soviet Jewry. Fisher wrote: "The matter of Yiddish
broadcasting in Russia by Radio Free Europe is a very important issue. In addition, [how] about a statement by the Department of Justice and the State Department allowing [Soviet
Jews] entry into the United States? I believe this was done in
the case of Cuba."

Considering these priorities, Fisher said, CRP should
have a full-time man in Washington, who understands "the
pluralistic nature of the Jewish community [and] its high
degree of organizational life." He recommended Lawrence Y.
Goldberg, a young, active Republican from Providence, Rhode
Island. Fisher's next point to Mitchell was notable because it
was perhaps the most straightforward statement Fisher ever
made on the political challenges of dealing with Jewish communal groups.

"The community," Fisher wrote, "is over-organized. [But]
one must not be taken in by the claims of the organizations
as to the control of their constituency. For example, B'nai
B'rith may say they have a million members they control.
They may have a million members, but they hardly control
the votes. [However], having their help can be very constructive, especially among their leadership."

Fisher stressed that the campaign had to inform "the rank
and file of what the president has done for Israel. Though a
broad section of the leadership knows of his involvement, this
has not filtered down. One of the great opportunities we will
have is publicizing the assistance Israel receives in credits,
grants and arms."

Fisher proposed that they approach the Anglo-Jewish press, making certain "that the proper information is carried through the news or editorial section." He volunteered to write letters "to opinion makers and leaders from the various [Jewish] communities." Fisher believed that a letter-writing campaign would underscore the political slant he brought to his work as a leader in Jewish America.

As he told Mitchell: "One of the things I have tried to do very carefully in my relations with organizations and the leadership of the communities (I make almost forty or fifty appearances a year before some of these organizations) is to be as factual as possible without being political. The fact that I have been able to do this is evidenced by a great deal of newspaper coverage that I have received from the Jewish press, which makes me believe that we have built a base from which we can become actively *political*."

Fisher promised to organize the general fund-raising activity, but only if it was "part of the regular structure and not on an ethnic basis." In conclusion, Fisher stated that he was prepared to begin and would wait for Mitchell's comments.

*　　*　　*

Over the next several months, Fisher and Mitchell discussed campaign tactics. By February 1972 (while Nixon was making his historic visit to the People's Republic of China), the operation was under way — an operation that was characterized in *The New York Times* as the "most broad-based vote-getting effort [that] any Republican presidential candidate has ever directed at the American Jewish community." Fisher had Lawrence Goldberg running the nuts-and-bolts of the effort: locating regional campaign chairmen around the country, setting up fund-raising events, and overseeing the 375,000 direct-mail pieces that were sent to influential Jewish groups.

According to Maurice Stans, who chaired the Finance Committee to Re-elect the President (FCRP), Fisher and Taft B. Schreiber, chairman of MCA in California, were the two people that had the responsibility for bringing the Jewish community into the Nixon camp. "This was not just for funds," says Stans, "but for votes. Taft worked in California and Max did the rest of the country. Max doesn't have a fund-raising machine in the sense that he had 1,000 people scattered around he could call and say: 'Get to work.' It was that black telephone book of his, of people he knew who revered him and who would contribute because he thought they should. Max is so highly respected that his direction influences the direction of a lot of other people."

In keeping with his long-standing practice, Fisher began his fund-raising activities with his own pledge — $250,000. Then he culled his list of "campaign workers" from his contacts in the business world and Jewish communal life. He even persuaded Henry Ford II to support Nixon. Perhaps chairing the National Center for Voluntary Action had changed Ford's mind. He donated $100,000 to the campaign.

In New York, Fisher enlisted the aid of, among others, Gustav Levy, head of the investment banking firm Goldman Sachs; George Klein, president of Barton's Candies; and financier Bernard J. Lasker. So spectacular were the fund-raising efforts of Fisher and Lasker that William Safire, in *Before the Fall*, writes that he and Leonard Garment "tried to play it down," because the emphasis in the press was on "Jewish money" from Fisher and Lasker and "that kind of thing was not, to use an old expression, 'good for the Jews' or for Nixon."

Fisher's organization spread itself across the country. Some of its members included: in Florida, investor Robert Russell; in Georgia, Dr. William Wexler, former head of B'nai B'rith and the Presidents Conference; in Illinois, Samuel Rothberg, chairman of Israel Bonds; in Maryland, Joseph Meyerhoff, one of the biggest builders in America and a former chairman of the UJA and Israel Bonds, and his daughter-in-law, Lynn Meyerhoff; in Missouri, Mel Dubinsky from the UIA; in Ohio, Edward Ginsburg, a former chairman of the UJA and current chairman of the Joint Distribution

Committee; and in Wisconsin, Albert Adelman, a former vice chairman of the UJA.

As Fisher had urged, the administration reached out to executives from the national Jewish press. On March 13, one hundred of these executives attended a kosher lunch provided by the CRP and received briefings from Herbert Stein (who had replaced Paul McCracken as chairman of the Council of Economic Advisers), Leonard Garment, William Safire and Joseph Sisco. Following the briefings, Fisher hosted a cocktail party for the executives.

Between April and October 1972, Fisher spoke to sixty groups in thirty states. He also personally recruited potential big givers — sometimes in conjunction with Maurice Stans. In early June, after Fisher spoke to 100 members of Philadelphia's Jewish community at the Bellevue Stratford Hotel, he and Stans encountered one of the more unpleasant circumstances of soliciting big gifts.

Maurice Stans recalls: "Max brought a man in who wanted to make a substantial contribution. The man sat down; we shook hands, and he said: 'Mr. Stans, how much for Luxembourg?' I replied: 'Pardon me.' The man said: 'Well, I don't know how these things are done. But I want to be an ambassador to Luxembourg. How much do I have to give?'

"I told him: 'We are not in the business of selling ambassadorships. There is no way that I can commit to anything like that. I can tell the White House that you are interested. I'll do it whether you contribute or not, but your contribution should be based on what you want to do to help re-elect the president.'

"Max was astonished. He had no idea that the guy was going to talk that way. I would say that during the next year Max was still so embarrassed about it that he apologized to me six times for having brought the guy in without having a better measure of what he was going to say. That wasn't a typical case. Max would usually size an individual up before bringing him in."

Two weeks later, Fisher left the campaign fund-raising

circuit to pursue his responsibilities as president of the Council of Jewish Federations.

Hurricane Agnes had struck the Northeast, which had already been saturated by a week of incessant rains. The storm left over 100 people dead. According to the Associated Press, "the impact was especially severe along the Susquehanna River in [Wilkes-Barre], Pennsylvania. . . . Three hospitals had to be evacuated and several radio stations were forced to go off the air."

Fisher traveled to Wilkes-Barre to assess the damage and to confer with community leaders. It was a harrowing trip. Roads, railways and airports were flooded. Fisher and several members of the CJF executive staff discovered that because of breaks in the flood control dike, nearly 90 percent of the town's 1,600 Jewish families had to be evacuated from their homes; 800 of its 900 Jewish businesses were destroyed; synagogues, a religious school and a recreation center had collapsed in the mud.

During a telephone conference with the CJF's national executive committee, Fisher described the tragedy and estimated that $2 million would be required to rescue the families and the community. The executive committee unanimously approved Fisher's request that every federation contribute to the emergency fund. Fisher brought in caseworkers to counsel the families and help get them back on their feet. Youth volunteers were organized to clean up. Within two months, the waters receded, building foundations were shoveled from beneath banks of mud, and the CJF's aid to Wilkes-Barre topped $2.27 million.

* * *

One of Fisher's major thrusts in the 1972 campaign was to identify distinguished Jewish Democrats who would be willing to endorse Nixon. He knew it was a long shot because the pattern he was endeavoring to change was well rooted in American Jewish history.

In a 1988 article published in *Judaism* magazine, "The Republican Party and the Jews," Professor Herbert L. Solomon points out that during the seventeen presidential elections between 1860 and 1924, Jews primarily voted Republican — the party of Abraham Lincoln. (One exception was when Jews backed the erudite Woodrow Wilson in 1912 and 1916.) But in 1928, the Democrats nominated Alfred E. Smith, a Roman Catholic. Jews, hurt by the overt anti-Semitism of the day, felt a kinship with Smith, since Catholics were then victims of discrimination; a Catholic president might herald a declension of prejudice. Thus, a cohesive Jewish Democratic vote materialized.

This trend resumed in 1932 with Franklin Roosevelt. In his next four elections, FDR averaged 58 percent of all votes. Yet in light of his Jewish appointees to the Cabinet and Supreme Court, his Jewish advisers and his apparent sympathy for the oppression of European Jewry by Nazism, Roosevelt captured an average of 86 percent of the Jewish vote. Furthermore, Roosevelt was the father of modern liberalism and seen as the protector of the disenfranchised, while Republicans were now perceived as the party of the rich. As bellwethers in trade unionism and civil rights, Jews carried the banner hoisted by Roosevelt until 1972. By then, another issue had become central to Jewish American life — the survival of Israel.

Although Fisher had bored in on several issues dear to Jewish hearts, the statistic he quoted again and again to the groups he addressed was that "the Nixon administration has given $1.1 billion of military and economic aid to Israel — as much as the United States expended in the previous nineteen years."

It was a compelling argument. And when Fisher picked up his campaigning again after July 15 — his sixty-fourth birthday — the argument was even more compelling, because at the Democratic National Convention, Senator George S. McGovern of South Dakota had been nominated to oppose Nixon.

Professor Herbert Solomon explains: "Regarding Israel, the former Jewish distrust of conservative sincerity . . . shifted to doubts of liberal trustworthiness. The first signs of these doubts were evident in 1972. The Democratic nominee, George McGovern, was the most liberal major party candidate for president in modern times. Because of his third world sympathies, however, he was considered by the Jews as unreliable vis-à-vis Israel. . . . To many Jews, so attuned to every nuance relating to Israel's needs, the liberals (thus the Democratic Party) [became] at best unreliable, and, at worst, a potential threat to Israel's safety."

Fisher recruited Democratic proselytes to the Nixon cause all across the country, and they, in turn, were enlisted to convert other Democrats. For instance, one of the most prominent converts was Louis Boyar, a Los Angeles real estate investor, who for years had contributed heavily to Democratic candidates. In 1972, though, based on the administration's massive assistance to Israel, Boyar was endorsing Nixon. Boyar invited forty of his wealthy Democratic friends to his Beverly Hills home for a private meeting to ask them to side with the president. According to Fisher, when the gathering was over "all but a handful" had pledged contributions to the Nixon campaign.

Besides raising funds, Fisher was eager to reach a broader base of American Jewry. To do this, Fisher says, it was critical "to send signs" to Jewish America that their communal leaders were behind Nixon. Fisher saw to it that one of these salient signs was beamed over network news cameras on August 21, at the start of the Republican National Convention in Miami Beach. He arranged for Rabbi Herschel Schacter to deliver the RNC's opening prayer.

Schacter remembers: "Max really pushed for me to deliver the prayer at the first session of the convention. I was reluctant to do that, because I was not a Republican. I am still not a Republican. I did commit myself to support Nixon as vice chairman of Democrats for Nixon. But not this. Max said to me, 'You have to do it. The president thinks highly of you. The people around the president think highly of you.' So I went out and delivered the prayer."

For Jewish America, the sign was unequivocal. Would an individual like Schacter, a former chairman of the National

Conference on Soviet Jewry, support a nominee who was not sensitive to the plight of Russian Jews? Would Schacter — the presiding head of the Religious Zionists of America — back a candidate who did not believe in a militarily robust Israel?

Nixon easily won his party's renomination, and by early September Fisher was certain that the president would capture one-third of the Jewish vote. He predicted this remarkable shift in Jewish voting patterns to John Mitchell over Labor Day weekend, betting him "the best dinner either of us ever had" that his prediction would prove true. Fisher's confidence was based on two categories of evidence — one statistical, the other anecdotal.

To Fisher, his mathematical proof was unassailable. He was in the process of raising $8 million for Nixon. While financial resources were vital for conducting campaign activities, Fisher felt that the funds also provided a reliable poll. He knew that in presidential campaigns money did not readily flow toward losers. McGovern was finding the financial well in the Jewish community far drier than Humphrey had found it in 1968. (For example, Fisher spoke to one Jewish Democrat in Baltimore, known for generous contributions to the Democratic Party. He told Fisher that when McGovern contacted him, he said that while he would not donate to or work for Nixon, he was "sitting this election out.") Although only a minuscule percentage of Jews could afford to make large donations to the CRP, the number of contributors and the size of their contributions indicated that support for Nixon among Jews was unprecedented for a Republican presidential candidate. Fisher had raised $3.5 million for Nixon's '68 race, and the president had won 16 percent of the Jewish vote. Now that Fisher was more than doubling his fund-raising total, he believed that the percentage would rise accordingly at the voting booths.

Fisher regarded his anecdotal evidence with skepticism, but it gave him a greater sense of personal satisfaction than the money he raised.

One August morning, Fisher walked out of the Regency Hotel in New York City on his way to a meeting with John

Mitchell. The doorman hailed him a cab and Fisher got into the back. The driver pulled into traffic. He was a bulky young man, in a white shirt and wearing a yarmulke, his long *payos* spilling past his shoulders. As he drove down Fifth Avenue, Fisher asked him where he was from.

"Brooklyn," said the driver, adding that he was studying at a yeshiva and driving a cab until he completed his education.

Figuring he could conduct a little informal polling, Fisher asked the driver who he was voting for in the presidential election.

"Nixon," the driver announced proudly.

"Why's that?" Fisher inquired.

"Because," the driver explained, "Nixon has an ambassador to the Jews. A man who takes care of us in Washington."

"What's his name?" Fisher asked.

"His name is Fisher," the driver answered. "Max Fisher. He's from Detroit."

"I'm from Detroit," Fisher said, barely containing a grin.

"Do you know Max Fisher?" asked the driver.

"I am Max Fisher."

At best, Fisher thought that the driver would smile or his eyes would widen or he would make some cordial gesture of surprise. Instead, in the midst of morning rush-hour on Fifth Avenue, with cars, cabs, buses and trucks swirling past, the driver slammed on his brakes. Traffic swerved around the rear of the taxi, horns blaring. The driver turned, gaping at his passenger.

"You're Fisher?" he asked.

Fisher nodded. Ignoring the horns and the shouts to get moving, the driver uttered a prayer, beseeching God to grant Fisher good health and long life. Then he drove on.

When Fisher reached Mitchell's office at 20 Broad Street, the driver refused to take any money from him. Fisher pressed, but the driver was adamant. Fisher thanked him and climbed out of the cab. As he walked toward the building, the driver called from his open window, "It was an honor to meet you, Max Fisher. I want you to know: I'm going to take the rest of the day off to pray."

Fisher watched as the driver pulled out and the cab blended back into traffic.

*   *   *

Despite his optimism about the election, Fisher knew that following Election Day the Nixon administration and the Jewish community were going to clash over how to deal with the Russians on the right of Soviet Jews to emigrate. So Fisher scheduled a meeting between the president and Jewish leaders for late Tuesday afternoon, September 26, at the Waldorf-Astoria. It was part campaign swing, part conflict management.

At 4:30 p.m., Fisher met with Nixon and Mitchell in the president's suite. Fisher told the two men that Jewish support for the president would range from 30 to 35 percent. It was unlikely, Fisher said, that the president would garner more than that because the community was wrestling with its deep-seated habit of voting for Democrats. Nixon replied that he understood the problems Fisher faced.

"I know you've worked your butt off, Max," Nixon said. "No one could have done any more."

Fisher said that *there* was more that could be done. The Jewish community could be made to feel comfortable at the White House. If the community were given more opportunities to fill jobs in the administration, then it would also tie them in to the Republican Party over the long term. Nixon acknowledged that Fisher had a point; he would try to do more.

Their conversation moved to Soviet Jewry. Nixon said that he "would do his utmost." Yet he was still adamantly against embarrassing the Soviets with demonstrations and public-relations campaigns — neither approach would work, he insisted. Fisher agreed, but said it was an emotionally loaded topic for world Jewry. The Jews in Nazi Germany had pleaded for help, and few had answered them. The Jewish community was not going to allow that to happen to the Jews in Russia. A labor camp or a concentration camp — it didn't matter, they were the same thing.

At least, Fisher said, the community and the administration are in agreement on Israel. Nixon said that there was absolutely no question about his stance — there would be no imposed peace settlement and the Israelis would get as much military assistance as they required.

At a quarter to five, Nixon and Fisher walked to a hospitality suite where Jewish leaders from around the country were waiting. William Wexler was there, as were Herschel Schacter, Albert Spiegel, Gustav Levy — thirty-one in all. Nixon began by expressing his appreciation for the leaders' work in the campaign. He said that in his second administration the Jewish community would still have access to him. Max, he said, has been to the White House on many occasions and he will have an open door.

The president spoke about the Middle East. He said that while he greatly admired the Israelis, the U.S. policy in the region of keeping Israel strong was in "our own national interest." Nixon delved into the particulars of the policy for twenty minutes, the gist of which was that an independent Israel kept the Soviets out of the area and promoted stability. Next, Nixon went on to Soviet Jewry. He said that if he were to make a big speech predicating U.S. foreign policy toward the Soviet Union on the Soviet's willingness to grant exit visas to Jews, the results would be the opposite of what American Jews desired. No one would get out.

The audience questioned the president on the Mideast, and on the issue of hiring quotas, which much of the Jewish community (and Nixon) opposed, believing — as William Safire has noted — that for Jews "a quota is a sign on a closed door that says, 'Stay in your place.'" The most pointed questions, though, focused on Soviet Jewry. The Russians had unexpectedly started to levy a stiff "exit tax" on Jewish emigration, claiming that the tax reimbursed the state for the emigrants' education. In all likelihood, the tax was a Soviet bid at reconciliation with Egyptian President Sadat, who had ordered Soviet military personnel out of Egypt. The tax was the Russians' promise to the Arabs that they would severely restrict emigration to Israel. Repeatedly, the audience asked the president what he intended to do about these ransoms.

"I'm concerned about Soviet Jewry," Nixon said. "But a superpower like Russia can't allow another country to dictate its internal policies. I've had much experience dealing with the Soviets. This sort of thing must be dealt with quietly. And that's what I am doing — Kissinger constantly mentions it to them. We're getting results. Between 1968 and 1971, only 15,000 Soviet Jews were allowed to emigrate. This year over 35,000 will leave. I ask you to trust me."

The president's assurances were attacked the next day in the press by two leaders who did not attend the Waldorf-Astoria meeting and who were not supporting Nixon's re-election — Rabbi Arthur J. Hertzberg, president of the American Jewish Congress, and Harold Ostroff, president of the Workmen's Circle.

Rabbi Hertzberg said: "The abhorrence our government feels over the persecution of Soviet Jewry is consoling but ineffective as long as it finds no expression in practical action. We do not see it as confrontation for the president to make clear both to the American people and to the Soviet leadership that the United States will not grant major economic benefits to the Soviet Union while that country continues to blackmail Russian Jews seeking to emigrate."

Ostroff stated that he was "shocked" at the view that pressures on the Soviet Union to eliminate exit fees on Jewish citizens constitute unwarranted harsh confrontation and that the issue is not worthy of public debate. Voicing additional "shock" at the administration's opposition to withholding favored-nation treatment until the ransom demands are withdrawn, Ostroff claimed that "gains for Soviet Jews have surely been abetted by vigorous public activities on their behalf."

Concerned that the debate would get out of hand prior to the election, Fisher moved to answer the critics. He phoned Louis Pincus, chairman of the Jewish Agency Executive, in Israel. Several days later, the national Anglo-Jewish press in the United States was carrying a story that quoted Pincus as saying that Jews should "bless President Nixon for the manner in which he deals with the issue of Soviet Jewry."

Forty-eight hours after the Waldorf-Astoria meeting, Fisher threw himself back into the campaign. He spoke at the Radisson South Hotel in Minneapolis. On October 1, he repeated his pitch at a Jewish community center in Norfolk. On October 6, he hosted a cocktail party at the Stouffer's Inn in Cincinnati. On October 10, he spoke at a rally in Silver Springs, Maryland, and nine days later, he addressed a private dinner in Dayton.

As Fisher plugged away, the president was cutting a deal with Senator Scoop Jackson that would become the flash point between the administration and the Jewish community during Nixon's second term.

On October 3, in the White House, Nixon and Soviet Foreign Minister Andrei A. Gromyko signed documents implementing two pacts limiting the use of nuclear arms. (The agreements had been hammered out during Nixon's May Summit in the Soviet Union.) After the signing, Nixon strolled through the Rose Garden for forty-five minutes with Senator Jackson. As an anti-Soviet hard-liner, Jackson had objected to the pacts, calling the interim agreement a "bum deal" because it permitted the Soviets heavier throw weights in missiles. Now, in the Rose Garden, Nixon and Jackson discussed trade agreements with the Soviet Union.

Back in May, Nixon had delayed signing such agreements with Soviet General Secretary Leonid I. Brezhnev. The public explanation for the delay was that Congress maintained that before any economic considerations were extended to the Soviets, they had to repay a portion of their lend-lease debt from the Second World War. Privately and perhaps more important, Henry Kissinger insisted that trade with Moscow be linked to Soviet help in ending the war in Vietnam. Gromyko agreed to both points, and Nixon was prepared to bestow most-favored-nation status on the Soviet Union.

Jackson thought that the United States was being too generous with the Russians. The senator wanted to link MFN status to the issue of the Soviet exit tax on Jewish emigrants.

Jackson told Nixon that he was planning to introduce an amendment that would deny MFN status to any Communist country that restricted emigration. Jackson then offered Nixon a deal. The senator said that he would neither turn his amendment into a campaign issue, nor press the 92nd Congress to vote on it, if Nixon would release the Republican senators who refused to co-sponsor the amendment without Nixon's approval. Nixon cut the deal.

On October 4, Jackson brought his amendment before the Senate. It had seventy-two co-sponsors. (Six days later, Representative Charles A. Vanik, a Democrat from Ohio, introduced a similar amendment in the House.) Initially, Brezhnev responded by hardening his stance. Kissinger continued to talk privately with the Soviet Ambassador to the United States, Anatoly F. Dobrynin, about the matter. Within weeks, the Soviets granted hundreds of exemptions to the exit tax, and allowed 4,500 Jews — the most yet — to emigrate in October.

Nixon rewarded the Soviets by signing a comprehensive trade agreement and pledging to seek congressional approval for their MFN status. When the Kremlin promised to pay $722 million of the lend-lease debt, Nixon authorized Export-Import Bank credits for the Soviet Union, and the Russians used the loans to purchase American grain.

*   *   *

Richard Nixon won his 1972 election against George McGovern by 18 million popular votes — the widest margin in American history. (Nixon beat McGovern by 513 votes in the Electoral College, second only to FDR's triumph in 1936 over Alfred M. Landon, who lost in the Electoral College by 515 votes.) Fisher was pleased about the Jewish turnout for the president — which some said reached 42 percent — because, as he told John Mitchell, he felt "for the first time that the Jewish community voted on issues rather than tradition." Repeating what he had said at the Waldorf-Astoria in September, Fisher told Mitchell that it was "tremendously important that we build on this [support] and not let it disappear. This means that [the administration] must be able to relate to this constituency and let them know they are welcome at the White House."

Nixon was impressed by his level of support in the community, and surprised. "We really soared among Jewish voters in '72," Nixon says. "And my support would not have been as strong had Max not been involved. Max is a good politician. But it isn't just Max, see, he's a got a network. He's got a guy in Ohio; he's got guys in California and New York and Illinois. I call it 'the Fisher Mafia, the gang.'"

A week after Nixon's second inauguration, the Vietnam peace accords were signed in Paris. However, the situation in the Middle East was deteriorating, momentarily quieting the debate over Soviet Jewry. Beginning in late February 1973, the administration tried to broker a deal between Egypt and Israel. Hafez Ismail, a chief adviser to Egyptian President Sadat, visited Washington, followed by Golda Meir. The Egyptians were still demanding that Israel withdraw from the conquered territories in exchange for a cessation of hostilities, a concession that Meir and her Cabinet had repeatedly rejected. The Nixon administration's strategy was to arm Israel in order to win its trust for a future peace process. So the Israeli prime minister was promised more weapons.

On March 1, a dinner was held in Meir's honor at the White House. With the relationship between Washington and Jerusalem on an even keel, it was a happy occasion. Fisher later told the president that "the Jewish leadership was thrilled at being invited," and that the "honor was one of the highlights of their lives." During dinner, Fisher sat talking with Nixon and Meir. As he had after the 1968 election, the president offered Fisher an ambassadorship or a spot in his administration. Fisher said thank you and declined. He explained that he was assisting John Ehrlichman on some energy matters. (By summer, an acute energy shortage would have American motorists lining up at the gas pumps, and in the fall, an Arab oil embargo would compound the shortage.) Fisher added that he would be willing to lend a hand on any

other projects that Nixon thought worthwhile, but he preferred working in an unofficial capacity.

Nixon turned to Meir and said: "You know, Golda, I've
offered Max any job he wants, but he won't take one."

Meir looked at Fisher. She understood that trading his
influence outside the administration for a minor role inside it
was not a good deal — a fact that would be underscored for
Meir six months later when the Yom Kippur War broke out.
Now, over dinner, she laughed and said to Nixon: "That's
Max's problem. He's lazy."

The warm feelings between the White House and the
organized Jewish community lasted until the end of the
month. On March 30, Fisher represented the Jewish Agency at
a State Department ceremony. Although Fisher disagreed
with much of American Jewry over publicly attacking the
Kremlin, he did agree that the Soviet Jews who escaped to
Israel would need help. And so in 1972, Fisher had gone to his
old friend, Jacob Javits, and discussed how the Jews emigra-
ting from Russia to Israel might receive a financial boost from
the United States. Javits, along with Senator Muskie of Maine
and Democratic Congressman Jonathan B. Bingham of New
York, sponsored the eventual legislation, which provided $50
million of resettlement aid. The money was to be given
through a contract between the State Department and the
United Israel Appeal, who would then pass the funds to the
Jewish Agency. The money would go toward the maintenance
of Soviet Jews in transit, the operation of Israeli absorption
centers, and for housing, language training, and vocational
and professional education.

The bill passed, and on March 30, the first $31 million
installment was formally turned over in the Thomas Jefferson
Room at the State Department. Frank Kellogg, special assistant to the secretary of state, signed for the United States; Mel
Dubinsky and Gottlieb Hammer for the UIA; and Fisher for
the Jewish Agency. Because the agreement was free of any of
the political acrimony that accompanied the fracas over
Soviet Jewry, the mood at the signing was upbeat, with plenty
of handshaking, back-clapping, and even a memorable quip by

Senator Muskie: When Fisher bent to sign for the $31 million, Muskie, obviously aware of Fisher's business success, said: "That's the smallest check Max has signed this year."

Not quite true, but Fisher smiled at the sentiment.

*   *   *

By spring, the conflict over Soviet Jewry escalated into a full-scale political war. Nixon recalled in *RN* that he got caught between "the liberals and the American Zionists [who] had decided that now was the time to challenge the Soviet Union's highly restrictive emigration policies . . . [and] the conservatives, who had traditionally opposed détente because it challenged their ideological opposition to contacts with Communist countries. My request in April 1973 for congressional authority to grant most-favored-nation trade status to the Soviet Union became the rallying point for both groups."

Blocking the path to Soviet MFN status was the Jackson-Vanik amendment, which a majority of American Jewish leaders supported. Fisher invited Senator Jackson to his apartment in Palm Beach and tried to dissuade him from pushing his amendment through Congress. They argued back and forth. Fisher concluded that nothing would deter the senator. Among other grievances Jackson had against the Soviets, he cited their assistance to the North Vietnamese as one of the primary reasons for the fighting in Southeast Asia.

In a last-ditch attempt to learn if Jackson could be convinced to back off, Fisher asked: "How many Jews a year do the Soviets have to let go before you'd vote for granting them MFN status?"

Without a trace of irony, Jackson replied: "About 100,000."

His reply effectively ended their discussion, and the clamor to adopt Jackson-Vanik heightened, much to the discomfiture of Nixon and Soviet authorities, who hoped that if they issued 2,500 exit visas per month, Congress would relinquish its objection to the trade bill.

"Jackson-Vanik was a mistake," says Nixon. "At the

time, if someone wanted to do the Russians in, I was all for it. But Jackson-Vanik was not going to do the job. The year I entered office [1969], less than 600 Jews were allowed to emigrate from the Soviet Union. In 1973, that amount had gone over 34,000, which was not exceeded until [1979 and not again until 1989]. We were able to do that by leaning on the Soviets — in private. I would say to the Russians: 'I know your argument against my talking about freedom for Soviet Jews; you say it's an internal matter. But I need support in Congress for the arms-control agreement, for trade agreements. I'm not going to tell you what to do, but it would be useful if you could be more liberal in your emigration policy.' This is called linkage. I let the Soviets know that if they wanted agreements in other areas, then they had to loosen up their policy. But you can't link publicly. Basically, Jackson-Vanik said to the Russians: 'Change your internal policy or we're not going to trade with you.' You can't do it that way.

"Max understood it," says Nixon. "I met with him and he brought in the Presidents Conference and other leaders from the American Jewish community. I explained it to them, and some said, 'Maybe you're right — we shouldn't go on and on about Soviet Jewry.' Max told them, too, and it showed Max at his best. It was a bloody scene at times, though."

One of these many scenes occurred on April 19, when Fisher and fourteen other Jewish leaders met for over an hour in the Cabinet Room at the White House with the president and Kissinger. Nixon reiterated his sympathy for Soviet Jewry, but he emphasized the difficulties that would arise in his quest to reduce East-West tensions if the Jackson-Vanik proposal passed. He then asked Kissinger to recount some of his private communications from the Kremlin to the group. The communications reassured the president that Soviet Jews would be free to emigrate.

Fisher prodded the leaders to carry this message to their constituencies, but American Jews were in a bind. Why should they be less combative in pursuit of freedom for Soviet Jews than a Gentile senator and congressman? When several of the leaders in the Cabinet Room expressed their displeasure with Nixon's quiet diplomacy, the president became visibly angry and said: "You gentlemen have more faith in your senators than you do in me. And that is a mistake. You'll save more Jews my way. Protest all you want. The Kremlin won't listen."

After the meeting, Jacob Stein of the Presidents Conference, Charlotte Jacobson of the Conference on Soviet Jewry, and Fisher issued a statement to the press, reaffirming their determination to aid Russian Jews and expressing their appreciation to Nixon for his help. However, at Fisher's insistence, the statement was vague regarding whether or not American Jewry would advocate the adoption of the Jackson-Vanik legislation. Fisher thought that the vagueness would stanch the public debate and permit the rising emigration statistics to demonstrate that Nixon's methods were effective.

In theory, Fisher's maneuver was reasonable. The jump in exit visas for Soviet Jews should have mitigated the dissension between the White House and the American Jewish community. Yet the emotion energizing the community was a combustible fusion of sorrow and guilt over their failure to rescue millions of Jews from Nazi brutality. "Never again" was the shibboleth of the Jewish Defense League, and though most of American Jewry scorned the JDL's militant tactics, this intense emotional commitment to deterring any semblance of a Holocaust was common in the community.

The atmosphere became even less favorable for settling the dispute when, several days after the meeting, 100 Soviet Jewish dissidents forwarded an open letter to American Jewish leaders pleading for their assistance. "Remember," their letter concluded, "the history of our people has known many terrible mistakes. Remember — your smallest hesitation may cause irreparable tragic results. Our fate depends on you. Can you retreat at such a moment?"

In the spring of 1973, the administration was facing a far greater political challenge than the argument over Soviet Jewry. Right after the meeting on April 19, Fisher dashed off a note to Nixon, saying, "Mr. President: With all your problems, let me say that anything I can do to [be] helpful to you,

I am available to the fullest extent of my time and ability."

Fisher was referring to the Watergate scandal. In June 1972, five men were arrested breaking into the Washington, D.C., headquarters of the Democratic National Committee at the posh Watergate complex of apartments, offices and boutiques overlooking the Potomac River. Ten months later, as revelation piled on top of revelation, the Nixon White House was besieged with allegations that sapped the president of his political strength.

Nixon phoned to thank Fisher for his note, and on May 14, three days before the Senate Watergate hearings started, Fisher wrote to him again: "Dear Mr. President: In the last couple of days I have found signs at my various board meetings that people are beginning to question the extreme position of the media in trying to make a judgment on Watergate by innuendo and hearsay, and that there is great feeling that the office of the President is being attacked unnecessarily. And I believe there is definite indication that the support will increase. What is particularly encouraging to me is the many calls I have had from leaders of the Jewish community. There is a very warm feeling toward you, and very strong support for you during these troubled times. For me, personally, some of the attacks on you have been unnecessary and biased. If there is anything I can do, please do not hesitate to call on me."

Undoubtedly, his letter was designed to cheer Nixon and to let him know that Fisher and many others were in his corner. But Fisher sensed something ominous about the temper surrounding Watergate — the ire that flashed across editorial pages each morning, the indignant comments he heard from his colleagues and friends. Yet, to Fisher, it did not seem plausible that the scandal could drive a president from office. Two months later, he would change his mind.

*   *   *

Nixon's second summit with Soviet Secretary Leonid Brezhnev was about to begin. Brezhnev was coming to the United States to explore expanding the SALT agreements and to

seek most-favored-nation status. Despite the importance of
Summit II, the gathering momentum of Watergate eclipsed it in
the news. By June 4, when Nixon replied to Fisher's letter, the
president had admitted to the 1969 buggings and 1970 surveillance plan along with the creation of the "plumbers," stating
that these acts were necessary in the interest of national
security.

"Dear Max," Nixon wrote. "It was so thoughtful of you
to write to let me know of your continuing support. I am
deeply grateful for your words of encouragement and for the
concern which prompted you to offer your assistance.
Although developments in recent months have posed a very
great test of our administration, your message of confidence
and understanding renews my faith that, working together,
we can achieve the great goals of peace and progress all Americans seek."

Outwardly, Fisher thought, Nixon was keeping his attention riveted on the summit. For some reason Fisher could not
pinpoint, this tack worried him, as though the president had
misjudged the national anger about the alleged cover-up. If
Nixon had misjudged, that would shortly change. White
House counsel John Dean was scheduled to testify before the
Watergate Committee in the last week of June.

Brezhnev landed in Washington on Saturday, June 16. On
Monday evening, a state dinner was held in his honor at the
White House. Along with the usual government officials, the
guest list included numerous celebrities and business leaders:
June Allyson, Van Cliburn, Cornelius and Marylou Whitney,
Teamster head Frank E. Fitzsimmons, Marjorie and Max
Fisher, and Jean and Jack Stein.

Many leaders in the American Jewish community were
opposed to Fisher and Stein attending the dinner.

Says Stein: "Max and I heard a lot of 'How can you go
have dinner with a guy who is persecuting Jews?' They were
very vocal about it. But that kind of protest is not my style.
I'm a businessman. So is Max. We prefer to meet things head
on. Something productive could come from being at the dinner. As it turned out, something did."

Furthermore, Fisher adds, in the symbol-laden universe of diplomacy, it was significant that Nixon invited two prominent members of the Jewish community. It let the Russians know that Soviet Jewry was a priority item on the president's agenda and could not be ignored by Brezhnev if he banked on departing the summit with the possibility of winning most-favored-nation status for the Soviet Union.

Nixon was taking no chances that Brezhnev would miss the signal. As the guests passed through the receiving line in the Blue Room, Nixon introduced the Fishers and Steins, emphasizing that the two men were Jewish leaders. Brezhnev got the message. Stein remembers that when the interpreter translated Nixon's introduction, he used the Russian for Hebrew, *Yevrey*. Brezhnev nodded.

During the cocktail hour, Fisher and Stein cornered Soviet Foreign Affairs Minister Andrei Gromyko. They began to talk, warily at first, and then Stein started peppering Gromyko with questions: "Why are you doing this to the Jews? Why can't we sit and talk this thing out? Why do you need people in your country that you don't want? Why are you jeopardizing your MFN status?"

Gromyko listened. Finally, he said, "Everything will be all right. The road will be wider."

The foreign minister spotted Soviet Ambassador Anatoly Dobrynin nearby, and requested that he join the conversation. Then he recapped what had been said and asked Dobrynin,"Why don't you talk this out with Mr. Fisher and Mr. Stein?"

Dobrynin answered that he would do so in the near future. Dinner was announced and the four men went to their tables.

On Friday, June 22, after Nixon and Brezhnev signed the Agreement for the Prevention of Nuclear War, the two leaders flew to the president's house in San Clemente, California, to continue their talks.

That afternoon, Fisher phoned Jack Stein in his office. There was a demonstration planned in California, Fisher said, to protest the treatment of Soviet Jews. Was it really in everyone's best interest to heap some more public embarrassment on the Russians? Brezhnev's talks with Nixon were crucial, a matter of world peace. And we know that Nixon is behind us and has been talking to him about getting the Jews out to Israel.

"Jack," Fisher asked, "can't you do something about this rally? It's not good for the president and it's not good for us."

Stein later recalled: "I hung up with Max and got back on the phone. But I was in a tough position. People felt strongly about Soviet Jewry. I was able to relocate the protest, to moderate it. But again, we were dealing with an emotional issue, and it had spread to the college campuses. This was the age of demonstrations: against Vietnam, for civil rights. Soviet Jewry was mixed in with these issues."

As support for the Jackson-Vanik legislation swelled, the Soviets grew alarmed about the threat to their MFN status, and they sought to head off the bill's support. Among their gambits was to try to convince American Jewry that they were sincere about free emigration for Russian Jewry. To that end, in early July, as Soviet Foreign Minister Gromyko had suggested at the White House dinner, Ambassador Dobrynin invited Fisher and Stein, and their wives, to lunch at the Russian Embassy in Washington.

When Fisher discussed the invitation with Stein he said that Marjorie wasn't eager to go. Stein replied that Jean also would prefer not to attend. Stein phoned Dobrynin to see if he and Fisher could come alone, but the ambassador was disinclined to remove the social facade from the luncheon.

"I would very much like your wives to come," Dobrynin told Stein. Although he did not add that the two men could not attend without their wives, his meaning was clear. The ambassador would never let it appear as if he were courting American Jews on substantive concerns.

The lunch was scheduled for Wednesday, July 25. Before riding over to the Russian Embassy, Fisher and Stein met with Kissinger at his NSC office in the White House. When Kissinger was asked if certain issues should be avoided during their lunch, he replied, "You can say things the administration can't say. You can raise issues we can't raise. Go ahead and raise them."

"Kissinger," says Stein, "was all along very supportive of trying to get the Soviet Jews released. We met with him a number of times. But all of us kept it quiet."

From Kissinger's instructions to Fisher and Stein, it would appear that he was using the pressure generated by the American Jewish community to help force concessions from the Soviets, who desperately wanted MFN status. For, if the Soviets pressed him or the president on that subject, they could point to the opposition back home as the major impediment.

"Brezhnev," says Fisher, "may not have liked democracy, but he certainly understood how the game was played."

The social front for the lunch with Dobrynin was maintained after a compromise was reached. Marjorie Fisher stayed home; Jean Stein attended. The ambassador and his wife greeted Fisher and the Steins when they arrived at the embassy, ushering them in to an anteroom, where they were received with great pomp and, in Jack Stein's words, "sat around exchanging polite nonsense."

The party shifted to the dining room. The table was set with elegant china, cut crystal, polished silver and a sterling candelabra. The ambassador sat at one end of the long table; his wife at the other. As soon as the guests were seated, Jack Stein took out his reference notes and unloaded on Dobrynin; Fisher, for the moment, hung back. Stein says that he gave the ambassador an earful of "the whole Soviet Jewry line — straight out — names, dates, facts and figures."

Dobrynin listened to Stein. Then he said: "I do not know why right now the Jewish community is pushing for Jackson-Vanik. I do not understand it. The levels of immigration are going up. I, myself, have a lot of Jewish friends in the Soviet Union; I play chess with them when I go home."

Dobrynin's wife, obviously angry with the way Stein had gone after her husband, said to the ambassador, "Why don't we put all of our Jews on a TWA plane and send them to the United States?"

"Could you do that?" Fisher asked. "We would be happy to pay their way."

He did not receive an answer, nor did he expect to, but he figured that it was worth a try. The tenseness was broken when a chef in a white hat and flowing apron entered the dining room, carrying a large silver tray.

"Ah," Dobrynin announced, "I have a very great delicacy for you to try. These are tiny birds from the Ukraine."

Lunch was served, to the delight of the Dobrynins; Fisher and the Steins were less enthralled. The discussion began again — on a softer note. Ambassador Dobrynin said that the matter of the Russian Jews had to be seen in the context of the Soviet Union's overall relations with the United States, adding that it could be worked out if it were done "without confrontation." Fisher said that the drop in exit visas to Israel during May and June had many concerned Americans skeptical of the Kremlin's willingness to let the Jews go. The ambassador replied that this was deliberate because the Soviets did not want Brezhnev's visit keyed to a rise in immigration.

But, Dobrynin said, the annual immigration figures would be 40,000. Fisher and Stein said that it would be helpful if that level could be maintained for the remainder of the year. It also would be helpful, Fisher said, if Dr. Kissinger could get confirmation on the Soviet's emigration statistics. For example, Fisher said, of the 800 names submitted to Kissinger, only 50 or 60 could be confirmed. If the ambassador could provide the names of the other 750, then perhaps Americans might have more confidence in the Kremlin's sincerity with respect to emigration.

"That is a fair request," Dobrynin said. "I will see what I can do."

Fisher broached the subject of harassment of the Jews who applied for visas, but as Fisher later told Len Garment at the White House, he was "not confident that much will happen in this regard." Dobrynin said that the activists who were in jail would eventually be released, but "not now, because doing so would create an internal problem." Dobrynin said that no activists were allowed to roam the streets of the Soviet Union — Jewish or otherwise. It was a question of national policy and would not be altered in the foreseeable future.

The final issue Fisher raised was that Brezhnev had stated that 90 percent of the Jews who applied for exit visas would receive them. Yet, Fisher said, reports from the Conference on Soviet Jewry and other groups indicated that roughly 100,000 people hoped to secure visas. Was there any way to reconcile these reports with — and confirm — Brezhnev's statement?

"No," Dobrynin replied, and shortly thereafter, the luncheon was over.

In a letter that Fisher wrote to the White House about his "frank and friendly visit" with the Soviet ambassador, he said that Dobrynin seemed willing to assist in solving some aspects of some problems. Fisher recommended that if the president was going to defeat Jackson-Vanik, it was essential that the administration find the names of the people who were on the list of 800 and verify that they had left Russia; nail down the Kremlin's promise of allowing 40,000 Jews to emigrate each year; and confirm that the people who have applied for visas get them, as per Brezhnev's statement.

"If these things did take place," Fisher concluded, "we could then provide this information to the community, which would be *very, very* helpful."

Two days later, Fisher wrote to Nixon on another matter — the rapidly accelerating Watergate scandal. Weeks ago, John Dean had testified before the Senate Watergate Committee that Nixon was involved in a cover-up of the break-in. Then Alexander P. Butterfield, the administrator of the Federal Aviation Administration and an erstwhile White House aide, disclosed to the committee that listening devices and taps had been installed in all the president's offices and phones for the purpose of preserving Nixon's conversations for posterity. Now, the committee wanted to hear the tapes and Nixon refused. He was threatened with a subpoena.

"Dear Mr. President," Fisher wrote. "In view of the Watergate hearings, I would like to give you my own comments and those of a great many people across the country with whom I have talked — both Republican and Democrat. The underlying theme I find is that everybody wants you to continue with the great programs you have started. My feeling is that it would be very helpful if you could make your own statement of position to the nation. This would have the effect of uniting all the elements who want to support you and help offset the destructiveness of the Watergate hearings, both in this country and abroad. I feel that your presentation should be of a conciliatory nature to counteract the abrasiveness of the confrontation which has taken place. After all, the good citizens of this country do not support the aggressive, pugnacious type of encounter we have seen on television, plus the political overtones present in the hearings. To conclude, Mr. President, I feel a low-key conciliatory statement to the people would be very helpful. Please be assured of my cooperation and support during these difficult times."

Nixon responded with a short note, telling Fisher that "I have always valued your friendship, as well as your counsel and advice, and I want you to know how much I appreciate your interest in passing along your suggestions and comments on the current political picture. It is good to know that I can continue to count on you!"

Watergate gradually bled Nixon of his domestic support, which appeared to hinder his ability overseas. But then, as the president had predicted to Kissinger, war suddenly blazed across the Middle East and set the stage for what Nixon would recall — in his 1990 memoir, *In the Arena* — as "his last major foreign-policy decision."

The war also would demonstrate how far Fisher's role had evolved since that autumn afternoon in Gettysburg less than a decade before, when Eisenhower, relaxing on his sun-splashed porch, had articulated a vision to Fisher and, unknowingly, helped to define his future.

*   *   *

October 6, 1973, was the Jewish High Holy Day of Yom Kippur, the Day of Atonement. At 2 p.m., the Egyptian army launched an assault to cross the Suez Canal, while Syrian forces stormed the Golan Heights. That evening, leaders from the Conference of Presidents of Major American Jewish Organizations, the United Jewish Appeal, and Council of Jewish

Federations and Welfare Funds met in New York City. Everyone was troubled by the fighting, but given the decisive Israeli victory in the 1967 Six-Day War, the leaders were confident that Israel would repel the attack. Fund-raising programs were mapped out, and a national leadership convocation was scheduled at the Shoreham Hotel in Washington, D.C., for Tuesday, October 9.

However, by Tuesday, as 1,000 people gathered at the Shoreham, the situation had radically shifted. The Egyptians had barreled into the Sinai, planting their flags on Israeli bunkers, and the Syrians had captured the high ground on Mount Hermon in the Golan. Israel's losses were unprecedented. Egypt's Soviet-supplied surface-to-air missiles were devastatingly effective against the Israeli Air Force, an alarming new twist for Israel, since it had invariably relied on air superiority to offset the larger Arab ground forces. (During the Yom Kippur War, Israel lost 114 planes — nearly 20 percent of its fighter-bombers — and more than double the number lost in June 1967.) Equally frightening was that the Soviet Union was determined that its Arab clients would prevail. On October 9, a massive Soviet airlift began, bringing tanks, guns and fighter jets to Syria and Egypt. Three days later, eighteen Soviet planes were landing every hour.

In light of the Israeli losses and the Soviet airlift, the top priority for Israel and American Jewish leaders was to persuade the U.S. government to resupply Israel with military equipment. In her memoir, *My Life*, Israeli Prime Minister Golda Meir recalls phoning Simcha Dinitz, Israel's ambassador to Washington, "at all hours of the day and the night" to prod him into action. Dinitz was a magician at mobilizing the American Jewish community. Among those he contacted was Fisher. "My relationship to Max," says Dinitz, "was such that we would talk to each other four or five times a week and in periods of crisis, like the Yom Kippur War, every day. For me, Max was a person whose commitment to Jewish survival was so strong; his contacts in the U.S. government were so intimate that he could be for them, and for me, another channel of transmitting information and feelings that existed in Israel."

Now, Dinitz told Fisher how desperately Israel needed to be resupplied. Fisher was in Washington for the convocation at the Shoreham, and he began phoning his contacts. Leonard Garment, who at the time was a special adviser to President Nixon, recalls that "during those early, terrifying days of the war Max was a one-man campaign all over Washington, pressing every button, calling every card."

Late Tuesday morning, Fisher was in Jack Stein's room at the Shoreham with several leaders from the Presidents Conference. Fisher had set up an appointment to see Nixon. The leaders were discussing the best way for Fisher to present their case.

"I had a portable typewriter," says Stein, "and we drafted a letter for Max to take to the president urging him to resupply Israel. Then we went downstairs to the rally."

On the afternoon of October 9, Fisher went to the Oval Office. Nixon was glad to see him, but the president seemed fatigued. Besides the crisis in the Middle East, the president was in the midst of locking horns with U.S. District Court Judge John J. Sirica over whether or not White House tapes should be turned over to the Grand Jury. In addition, Nixon's vice president, Spiro Agnew, was being investigated on suspicion of accepting kickbacks while serving as governor of Maryland. (Agnew would resign the vice presidency the next day; Congressman Gerald Ford of Michigan would later replace him.) Fisher handed Nixon the letter from the Presidents Conference, and sat across from him as he read it. Nixon finished reading, folded the letter and placed it on his desk.

Fisher looked at him and said: "I've worked hard for you and I've never asked anything for myself. But I'm asking you now. Please send the Israelis what they need. You can't let them be destroyed."

Nixon assured him that the United States would see to it that Israel got everything it needed. When Fisher left the Oval Office he was certain that Nixon would resupply the Israelis.

On Wednesday, Fisher flew to New York City with Stein.

"We were delighted," says Stein. "The rally had been a

290 : QUIET DIPLOMAT

success; congressional support for Israel was strong; and Max told us that Nixon had committed to the resupply. On Thursday — this was October 11, the sixth day of the war — we had meetings at the Presidents Conference headquarters at 515 Park Avenue. We were mustering support from non-Jewish groups. But we kept getting calls from Israel saying that the Israeli military was in trouble and asking us why the American airlift hadn't started. Some members of the Presidents Conference thought that Max had been had by the president, that Nixon was not going to help. Max got on the phone and called Kissinger."

Kissinger, who had supplanted Rogers as secretary of state in late August, told Fisher that the United States was committed to the airlift, but there were logistical problems. Fisher informed Kissinger that all his sources in Israel were telling him that the Israelis' situation was deteriorating.

Still, the delay dragged on.

The cause of the delay in resupplying Israel has become a lingering historical debate, and the blame has often erroneously been dropped on Kissinger's doorstep.

In *Decade of Decisions*, his inquiry into American policy toward Arab-Israeli conflicts between 1967 and 1976, Middle East expert and former NSC staffer William B. Quandt writes: "When Dinitz complained about the slow American response, Kissinger blamed it on the Defense Department, a ploy he repeatedly used with the Israeli ambassador over the next several days."

Richard C. Thorton, a professor of international affairs and a consultant to the State Department, also blames Kissinger. In his study of the reshaping of American foreign policy, *The Nixon-Kissinger Years*, Thorton writes: "Kissinger, in describing his relationship with Israeli ambassador [Simcha Dinitz], all but says the delay in resupply was deliberate: 'Like all experienced diplomats, we took great pains to keep our disagreements from becoming personal. One device is to blame — usually transparently — someone else for painful decisions. . . . When I had bad news for Dinitz, I was not above ascribing it to bureaucratic stalemates or unfortunate decisions by superiors.'"

In response to the assertion that he was stalling in the face of American objectives in the Mideast and with the American-Soviet relationship in mind, Kissinger says: "Who are the people who could claim this? There has to be a limit to ingratitude. The war started Saturday morning [October 6], and we were delivering weapons to them — over violent bureaucratic opposition in our government — by Saturday night [October 13]. The Israelis had told us that they were going to win the war by Thursday. They grossly overestimated their own capabilities. So initially our priority was not to resupply them during the war, but after a cease-fire. The first time we knew the extent of their needs was on Tuesday morning [October 9]. By Friday night [October 12], they had the all-American military airlift operating. Sure, we explored the possibility of civilian airlifts. That took all of thirty-six hours. Before you put your whole military-airlift capability at the disposal of a foreign country, you do look at alternatives."

Former President Richard Nixon also cites a bureaucratic wrestling match as the cause of the delay: "There was great opposition in the Defense Department and among some in the foreign-service bureaucracy to coming down on the side of Israel in this conflict," says Nixon. "Their opposition was due, in part, to the energy problem — the threat of an oil shortage. There was also concern that if the United States came down solidly on the side of Israel against those Arab nations who had launched the attack, then we would permanently damage our relations with the [Arab] oil-producing states.

"Consequently," continues Nixon, "when we got the request [for the resupply] from Golda Meir, there was a Soviet airlift to Syria operating. I said to Kissinger: 'Let's see what we can do about this.' So [the National Security Council] came up with all these cockamamie schemes — we'll paint over the Star of David on the Israeli airplanes; we'll charter planes from private companies; we'll do this, that and the other thing. It was all nonsense. Finally, we agreed upon a position. Kissinger said we should send three C-5A military transport planes. I said: 'How many do we have?' Kissinger said: 'Twenty-six.' I said: 'Send them all.' Kissinger repeated the bureaucratic objections. 'Just send them all,' I said. My point was that if you send three, then we were going to get blamed by the Arabs just as much as if we had sent twenty-six. It's important to do enough. Always do enough."

General Alexander Haig, who was serving as Nixon's chief of staff and fielding calls from State and Defense during the Yom Kippur War, explains what he believes was behind the delay: "Defense Secretary [James R.] Schlesinger was not inclined to help the Israelis," says Haig. "Kissinger, on the other hand, was sensitive to the need for prompt assistance to Israel. The Pentagon was hiding behind a number of trumped-up legalities about airlift allocations. The delay was due to several days of bureaucratic infighting between State and Defense. The fight was over substance and between personalities. The hatred between James Schlesinger and Henry Kissinger was severe. Schlesinger, for some reason, saw himself in a power struggle with Kissinger. Jim's a good friend of mine, but it was a mismatch. Kissinger gave Nixon his recommendations, and the president dramatically increased them. Then Nixon drove it down Schlesinger's throat. Nixon's decision demonstrates what presidential leadership can do when it's properly exercised. And I think Nixon deserves the credit for it."

Between October 14 and November 14, the United States sent 566 resupply flights to Israel, delivering 22,000 tons of equipment.

Prime Minister Golda Meir recalled: "The airlift was invaluable. It not only lifted our spirits, it also served to make the American position clear to the Soviet Union and it undoubtedly served to make our victory possible. When I heard that the planes had touched down in Lydda, I cried."

*　　*　　*

In assessing Fisher's part in loosening the bureaucratic logjam blocking the airlift, it is crucial not to ascribe to him an overly dramatic role, to view him as an Eddie Jacobson reborn. Since 1948, the American Jewish community has been enamored of the Jacobson paradigm — the heroic individual who intercedes on behalf of his people and miraculously alters the path of Jewish history. Jacobson was President Harry Truman's ex-partner in a Missouri haberdashery. In 1948, Chaim Weizmann, soon to be Israel's first president, was seeking President Truman's backing for the founding of the Jewish homeland — backing that Truman's State Department opposed. Weizmann, however, was unable to get an appointment with the president. Eddie Jacobson went to the White House and convinced his old friend to meet with Weizmann. Truman ultimately recognized Israel, and Eddie Jacobson was inscribed in the Zionist book of heroes.

Historically, though, Jacobson's role — and Truman's love for Israel — have been exaggerated. For instance, since Truman was guiding his own war-weary nation, it is unlikely that he would have supported the founding of a Jewish state if the Zionists had required a guarantee of American troops. Nothing Jacobson or later, Weizmann, could have said, would have changed Truman's mind. In the end, his decision was based on the interests of the United States.

Truman recalled in his memoirs: "I was not committed to any particular formula of statehood in Palestine or to any particular time schedule for its accomplishment. . . . The simple fact is that our policy was an American policy rather than an Arab or Jewish policy."

The same rule applies to Nixon. He did not order the airlift out of empathy for the Israelis, but because he thought it was the proper U.S. foreign-policy move.

"After Israel won the war," says Nixon, "all of the players tried to justify their position [about the airlift]. Mine was very clear-cut. Under no circumstances were we going to allow a Soviet airlift to Israel's enemies lead to an Israeli defeat. Part of the reason we assisted Israel was personal. I felt very sympathetic to Golda Meir, to Yitzhak Rabin and to others. I didn't want them to be defeated. Yet it was by no means entirely personal. Strategic considerations were crucial. For example, let's suppose that the United States was not concerned about Israel. From a geopolitical standpoint, given our relationship to the Soviet Union in 1973, we could not be in a position of having the Soviets prove to be a loyal ally to its clients, while the United States let its ally go down the tubes. The airlift was important as a measure of U.S. reliability."

Thus, in October 1973, Fisher's asking Nixon to begin the airlift may well have been a moot point. Yet what stands as historically significant is that Fisher was able to talk directly to the president at such a moment and the manner in which he presented his case. Both indicate Fisher's unique contribution to the political life of Jewish America.

Fisher did not come as a friend from long ago or as a privileged Jew at court. Neither he nor the Jewish community was going to be dependent on the grace of some Persian king or Córdoban Caliph. Nor was Fisher a lobbyist — that was the bailiwick of the American Israel Public Affairs Committee. But AIPAC worked Capitol Hill, not 1600 Pennsylvania Avenue. As I.M. Destler points out in *Presidents, Bureaucrats and Foreign Policy*: "The legislative branch can hardly be a force for foreign affairs leadership . . . [since] the Constitution . . . [gives] foreign affairs primacy to the president." That October afternoon, Fisher, with the Presidents Conference letter in hand, stood before Nixon as the formal embodiment of the organized Jewish community's ability to enter the Oval Office as a political constituency to ask the president for help.

According to Dr. Israel Miller, senior vice president of Yeshiva University who served as chairman of the Presidents Conference from 1974-1976, this capacity represented a considerable evolution in the Jewish community's relationship to political power.

"Max gave prestige to the Presidents Conference," Miller says. "He built it — and the organized Jewish community — up in the eyes of the political world. I, for example, would never seek a meeting with the president without talking to Max and discussing who would go or what would be on the agenda. Max set up the appointments. But afterward it was the Presidents Conference that spoke to the press, that represented the Jewish community. In hindsight, always involving Max was one of the most important things that the Presidents

Conference did. Max had access without us. He had his White House pass and could walk right in. But Max's strength was not in his being just a Republican and a Jew, but being an active member of the organized Jewish community. Bringing the community in with him was part of his vision and his greatness. No other 'Jewish friends' of the administration had ever done it before. Each of them went into the Oval Office, or to the State Department, as individuals. That all changed after 1968. And Max was the person who changed it."

*   *   *

As Secretary of State Kissinger attempted to arrange a disengagement among Syrian, Egyptian and Israeli forces, the American Jewish community resumed pressing for the adoption of the Jackson-Vanik legislation. Following the Yom Kippur War, Fisher and Jack Stein met several times with Jackson to try to curtail the punitive slant of his amendment, but to no avail. There were, says Stein, "some harsh words between Scoop and us." The senator said that Nixon's methods would not get the Soviet Jews out and he, personally, would make that known to the Jewish community and go over the heads of the Presidents Conference, Fisher, or anyone else who got in his way.

Says Stein: "The consensus of the bodies I represented was ardently pro-Jackson-Vanik. Even though Max found it hard to swallow, he wound up signing statements of support that he really did not believe in, statements commending Congress for their efforts, et cetera. He recognized that you can't be a leader if you don't have followers. But all along he thought the legislation was a mistake."

On December 11, 1973, the House of Representatives passed a trade bill that denied the Soviet Union most-favored-nation status because of its restrictive emigration policies. The congressional action was a calamity for Soviet Jews. Within twenty-four months, emigration dwindled from 34,733 a year to below 13,221. Fisher recognized that there were limits to his influence in the Jewish community, but that did not lessen the despondency he felt as the Kremlin shut the doors. His frustration chafed at him for fifteen years until a confluence of events provided Soviet Jews with another opportunity for freedom.

*   *   *

On January 30, 1974, Nixon announced that despite Watergate, he had "no intention whatsoever of resigning." Less than a month later he opined that he did "not expect to be impeached." Yet it was evident to Fisher that the scandal was devouring Nixon's presidency. Politically, Fisher regarded the break-in and cover-up as foolish. The outcome of the 1972 presidential race was never in doubt. Once the burglary was reported the predicament presented Nixon with a tidy surgical solution — fire everyone involved. But the president had not been paying attention and had followed some flawed advice. Now, the media was having a field day, and the Democrats were milking every rumor for all it was worth.

In May 1974, a story in *The New York Times* claimed that deleted portions of the White House tapes revealed that Nixon referred to members of the Securities and Exchange Commission and some attorneys attached to the Watergate prosecutor's staff as "those Jew boys." *The Times* contacted Fisher for a comment. Fisher stated that he did not think there was anything terribly wrong with the president using slang. "We all do the same thing once in a while," Fisher said. "I'd hate to have my business meetings recorded." Privately, Fisher thought that while Nixon may have exhibited bad taste, charging him with anti-Semitism was ludicrous. When the chips were down during the Yom Kippur War, Nixon had saved Israel. And domestically he had brought more Jews into the front ranks of government than any other president in American history.

Watergate held some personal ramifications for Fisher. His integrity was attacked, not directly, but by having his name linked in the press with men who were under indictment, several of whom would soon become acquainted with the more disagreeable aspects of the federal penal system. Fisher had regularly shied away from publicity. His strength on the national level was his anonymity. And the kind of publicity he was about to garner could rob him not only of his meticulously constructed veil, but his unblemished integrity as well. Fisher was a discriminating investor with his fortune, but he was even more circumspect with the air of professionalism and honesty that had surrounded him since his start in the oil business. He could, if a financial venture soured, cut his losses and reinvest. But Fisher knew that once someone was pigeonholed as corrupt, he was marked for life. An active political career, even if conducted in the shadows, was unthinkable. Fisher was hardly prepared to retire from politics.

He was called before a grand jury by the United States District Attorney in New York. The U.S. Attorney's office in New York had indicted John Mitchell and Maurice Stans on ten counts each of conspiracy, obstruction of justice and perjury, relating to the acceptance of a $200,000 campaign contribution — in $100 bills — from fugitive financier Robert L. Vesco, allegedly in return for promised assistance to Vesco in connection with an investigation by the SEC.

Mitchell and Stans were acquitted, but the damage was done. In his memoir, *The Terrors of Justice*, Stans described the ordeal as the violation of "the personal reputations of so many ... [and] the agony and heartbreak which the innocents in the line of fire and on the sidelines were made to bear." (In another case, Stans pleaded guilty to three counts of violation of the reporting sections of the Federal Election Campaign Act of 1971 and two counts of accepting illegal campaign contributions; he was fined $5,000. Mitchell also had other problems. He was indicted again and went on trial in Washington, D.C.)

Maurice Stans recalls that throughout his ordeal "Max was compassionate. He knew the attitude of the prosecutors and their hunger to pin something on the Nixon campaign group. I remember Max saying to me one time: 'Maury, don't take it so much to heart. You are respected and loved by the people who know you, and you ought to be content.' I spoke to Max when he was called to testify. He said: 'They told me I should bring a lawyer, but I told them I didn't need one. I'm not ashamed of anything I know or did.' Max testified and gave them statements in writing, but as far as I know, he never used a lawyer."

Although not a target of an investigation, Fisher had been asked to testify at a federal grand jury hearing in New York because two memos had surfaced that appeared to indicate he had been involved in the buying and selling of political jobs. One memo from Gordon C. Strachan, an aide to Chief of Staff H.R. Haldeman, stated: "Ford is in for 100; Fisher may be in for 250, but you weren't sure you could pay his price." The other, a Political Matters Memorandum dated September 18, 1971, said that Fisher was in for 250 and "the close by [Nixon personal attorney Herbert W.] Kalmbach will come later." It ended with: "Larry Goldberg will begin working with the Jewish community pursuant to Max Fisher's memo to John Mitchell."

At the time, these were not necessarily the names with whom a Republican insider like Fisher would want to be associated. Strachan was indicted on three counts by the Watergate special prosecutor for alleged complicity in the cover-up (his case was dismissed because he agreed to cooperate). Kalmbach pleaded guilty to promising federal employment as a reward for political activity and support for Nixon; he was sentenced to six to eighteen months in prison and fined $10,000. Haldeman and Mitchell were convicted of conspiracy, obstruction of justice and three counts of perjury. Both of them were sentenced to two-and-a-half-to-eight years in prison.

Fisher was nervous when he entered the courtroom, with its high, ornate ceiling and gleaming wood rails, tables and benches. He had done nothing wrong and yet he knew how this game worked. He did not have to be formally accused of anything. Just a hint that he had acted improperly would be sufficient to cut his career short.

Fisher faced the grand jury as an assistant U.S. attorney questioned him about the memos. What precisely did Strachan mean by Fisher's price? What was his price?

Fisher had made his contributions to Nixon in two phases: before April 7, 1972, he had given $125,000, and then another $125,000 in February 1973. He explained that he obliged himself to the full quarter of a million, but half of it was going to be in Marathon stock and he had waited for the stock to go up.

Yes, but what was his price?

Outwardly Fisher held himself in check, but he was furious. He had no idea what his price was so why was it in a memo? Henry Ford was going to give $100,000. Fisher had no price — he had never had a price — except for access to the president, which had been his since February 1969.

Were you seeking an ambassadorship?

This question rankled Fisher. An ambassadorship? He had been offered ambassadorships and Cabinet posts — all he had to do was name it. He wanted nothing, but to fill his narrowly defined role. How could he be buying influence he already had? That would have been bad business.

The close? Why would the close from Kalmbach come later?

"Close," Fisher wondered, no one had to "close" him. He told Stans he was going to give the $250,000 and that was it. He didn't need closing. He raised $8 million in 1972 for Nixon and somebody was going to put the close on him?

Fisher told his side of the story to the prosecutor. Yes, Larry Goldberg, on Fisher's recommendation, was in charge of Nixon's outreach to Jewish voters. And yes, he had dealt quite a bit with John Mitchell. He was Nixon's campaign manager.

The prosecutor asked Fisher if he was aware that his name appeared on Mitchell's calendar more frequently than any other?

No, Fisher said, he was not aware of that, but he was not surprised. Mitchell handled many things for the president. Fisher had gone to see him often — not just on political issues, but on matters that concerned Israel and Soviet Jewry, which he hoped Mitchell would bring to the president's attention.

The prosecutor was satisfied. Still furious at being called, Fisher stood and walked out of the courtroom.

Chapter 13

OLD FRIENDS

O N AUGUST 9, 1974, Max Fisher flew to Washington, at the invitation of Vice President Gerald Ford, for a meeting to discuss the economy. At the vice president's office, he was told that Nixon was resigning and Ford was being sworn in. Fisher was asked to join the audience in the East Room of the White House, where, at noon, Ford took the oath as the thirty-eighth President of the United States.

"History overtakes men," Fisher told an interviewer after the ceremony. "Many times President Ford said his ambition was to be Speaker of the House. The events of our time have changed his life. . . . Ford was the right man at the right time and place."

Fisher may well have been portraying his own position. For if it is true, as David Biale asserts in *Power and Powerlessness in Jewish History*, that "the movement of Jews into the American political elite marks one of the most radical social transformations in Jewish history, and probably, for that matter, in history in general," then Fisher's relationship with Ford elevated that transformation to its highest plain.

"Among all the yardsticks that Washington has for measuring power," writes Hedrick Smith in *The Power Game*, "access is primary . . . a privilege to be treasured." And according to President Ford: "Max had access whenever [he] asked for it. I trusted him and he had as good access as anybody, if not better."

Over the next two-and-a-half-years of the Ford administration, Fisher would officially visit the Oval Office twenty-five times and speak with the president, on his private line, nearly as often.

It is likely that Fisher would have continued his active role if, for example, John B. Connally, Nixon's first choice to replace Vice President Agnew, had been selected in October 1973. Probably, Fisher's status would have remained relatively unchanged under any Republican administration, for his services to the GOP were too valuable. He was a leader of Michigan's Republican Party, revered for his uncanny ability to raise funds and, unlike some of the other more prodigious Nixon fund-raisers, was emerging from Watergate with his integrity intact. Additionally, he now had his diplomatic work for Nixon to his credit, and respect for his political savvy, because of the jump in Jewish voter turnout for Nixon in 1972, was running high. Then, too, Fisher was able to get along with a line of Republican presidents, many with widely different personalities. This ability is to some extent a function of his pragmatism: regardless of which person Fisher may have wanted in the White House, a president represents, for his term of office, an immutable presence. As Fisher was fond of reminding those who complained about officials who thwarted their agendas: "The president [or secretary of state or secretary of defense, etc.] is not a movable object."

Leonard Garment, who, after serving as Nixon's counsel, went on to serve as an aide to Ford in the early days of his presidency, continued his friendship with Fisher throughout the transition. After seven years of working with Fisher, Garment began to observe what he felt fueled much of Fisher's political involvement and his facility for forming lasting affiliations with presidents.

"The greatest motivators," says Garment, "the powerful engines of our lives, are boredom and envy. Max doesn't have a lot of envy, but he's deathly afraid of boredom. And he attacks it by serving causes. That's where his energy comes from. And whether it is done consciously or whether it is part of the embroidery in his soul, Max has a sense of how to use his energy. Within limits, I don't think he cares that much what people are like. A man becomes president [and Max figures that] in order to do all the things that he likes doing — he learns how to deal with the president. Equally important is that Max doesn't need to be dragged in on anyone's coattails. He is a man who is above self-interest in the more narrow sense. Ford knew it and Nixon knew it. Max was trusted. He was seen as a very solid guy who thought his way through problems, who would never get anybody in trouble [by talking to the press] and who had great influence, not to mention a network of organizations and individuals that he built and tended to like a permanent prime minister. And I know this: from the Nixon administration into the Bush administration, you had all of those people who were pretenders to Max's role. He was very philosophical about it and said, 'You wait and see.' Then boom — [the White House and State Department] began to call him because they knew that he knew how to do it: he had the kind of sagacity that comes with doing it for a long time."

However perceptive Garment's view of Fisher, there was a uniqueness to the Fisher-Ford relationship that surpassed the shared ground of political allies. Ford's first recollection of Fisher dates to the early 1960s, when Fisher was helping Romney. He was impressed by what Fisher was doing for Michigan Republicans, not only the millions of dollars he raised, but his method for raising it, which involved putting his own capital and reputation behind a project.

"There is no question," Ford says today, "that when Max puts his personal reputation on the line, he can raise tremendous sums of money for causes in which he believes. Max was always a doer, but he doesn't project himself as a public person. I, for one, enjoy working with people like that because of their reliability. Any time Max says he's going to do something, he'll get it done."

Fisher, from the beginning, sensed something special about Ford, his clear and moderate views, his solid judgment — in short, his potential. Maurice Schiller, who worked for Fisher in the oil business, always felt that his erstwhile boss had a talent for discerning who would go far, for recognizing where and with whom to cast his lot. And Fisher recognized Ford's potential as far back as July 1964. That July, Republicans descended on San Francisco to choose a candidate to oppose President Johnson in November. It was an exacting period of upheaval for Republicans. They had divided into warring factions: liberals siding with Governor Nelson Rockefeller, conservatives with Senator Barry Goldwater. Marjorie Fisher recalls that one morning, during the convention, she and Max left their hotel and walked outside to hail a taxi to the Cow Palace. As the Fishers moved to the curb, Marjorie looked up and saw Gerald Ford. They exchanged greetings and chatted about the convention. Then, surprisingly, Max said: "Jerry, have you ever thought about the vice presidency?"

"I love being a congressman," replied Ford. "Betty and I have a house, and the three children, and we love our life. I don't want to be vice president."

"You'd make a fine vice president," Fisher said.

"Thanks, Max," said Ford. "But I'd like to be the Speaker of the House."

Over the next decade, Fisher and Ford crossed paths on numerous political occasions. Ford, as minority leader of the House, asked Fisher to help Robert Griffin in his race for the Senate, and Fisher was happy to lend a hand. Fisher invited Ford to appear at the Economic Club of Detroit, and Ford came and spoke about "Legislating for a Better America." When the Zionist Organization of America (ZOA) selected Fisher for their Rabbi Abba Hillel Silver Award, which Ford had received the previous year, Ford wrote Fisher that the ZOA "could not have chosen a finer American for this great tribute." Of course, after Ford was nominated for the vice presidency, Fisher sent his hearty congratulations and Ford replied with his "warmest personal regards and deep appreciation for [Fisher's] support."

Undoubtedly, Ford and Fisher had a deep respect for each other, but there is little here to illuminate the reasons underlying the uniqueness of their friendship. And Ford's memoirs shed no further light. In *A Time to Heal*, Ford refers to Fisher as "a close friend," and "my old friend."

As the years passed, Fisher developed an amusing anecdote about Ford, which he used whenever he introduced him at dinners and fund-raisers. "Jerry Ford and I have a lot in common," Fisher would begin. "We went to college on partial scholarships. We washed dishes to earn spending money. We played center on our football teams: he for the University of Michigan, me for Ohio State. He became president. And I became rich" — Fisher smiled — "betting with him on Ohio State-Michigan football games."

Their annual bet was five dollars and, in this good-natured ribbing, there is a hint of what bound the two men. It was the sort of joking that Fisher had participated in with his boyhood friends. It had the same spirit of friendly competition and good will.

"I'm not by nature suspicious of people or their motives," Ford recalls, and neither, as a rule, is Fisher. It was a nature bequeathed to them by their small-town heritage — a heritage owing more to the nineteenth century than to the twentieth — and it was responsible, in large measure, for their optimism and their willingness to trust. Fisher had different qualities in common with Nixon: an impulse toward obsessive work, of never being satisfied with any accomplishment, of always pushing, of discreet and agile politics. With Ford, on the other hand, Fisher recaptured the more relaxed rhythms of Salem.

It is no surprise then that Ford's hometown of Grand Rapids, Michigan, mirrored much of what Fisher experienced in Ohio.

"In the mid-1920s," Ford remembers, "Grand Rapids was known as a strait-laced, highly conservative town. The large number of Dutch immigrants and their descendants were hard-working and deeply religious. Almost everyone attended church and a strict moral code was scrupulously observed."

Like Fisher's Salem (and Nixon's Yorba Linda and Whittier), Grand Rapids was imbued with Christian culture.

"The local high school where I went, South High, had a very limited number of Jewish students," Ford says. "But they were always among the very smartest. This was a very cosmopolitan high school. We had a lot of poor people; we had a fair amount of rich kids; it was a good mixture. But even in high school I noticed that some of my non-Jewish schoolmates resented the ability, the hard-working characteristics, the success of the few Jewish students."

This animosity somehow missed the future president.

"I've always admired success," says Ford. "And in our high school [although] there were very few Jewish students, they were always in the top echelon academically and I had great respect for them. I wanted to do as well as they, and never did, but instead of being critical or feeling resentful, I [tried] to be as successful as they. And that attitude toward these Jewish students continued all my life in relationships with Jewish citizens generally. I've always felt that Jews as a whole work harder, aim higher, and probably have a higher I.Q. than any comparable group in our society. I admire them. And Max is a good example."

Beyond his admiration for Fisher was a similarity of style.

"Max," says Ford, "gives you a soft sell. He doesn't seek personal aggrandizement. He feels very strongly about certain fundamental issues and approaches you with a rational, fair point of view. That approach appeals to me. To my knowledge Max never sought, at least from me, any personal benefit or gain. He was truly dedicated to whatever viewpoint he was proposing and that generated trust and response."

From the outset of his tenure, Ford encouraged his official and unofficial advisers to be frank with him. Fisher's trust in Ford was predicated on this genuine openness combined with Ford's high tolerance for honesty, a rare attribute in powerful people in general and politicians in particular.

"Max would tell me what he thought," recalls Ford, "but he would do it subtly, in his quiet, unassuming way."

"I could talk to Ford about any problem," says Fisher. "I always tried to tell him the way it was. He was marvelous. What made him so good was that he understood the way the system worked. He would listen to all sides of a story before he made a decision. And he was a man of great sensibility, much smarter than people thought he was. And he had a deep sense of loyalty to the American people."

*   *   *

Loyalty was on Fisher's mind in the late summer of 1974. On Monday morning, August 26, as he was preparing to leave for Washington for his first visit with Ford in the Oval Office, Fisher sent a letter off to Nixon at his home in San Clemente, California.

"Mr. President," Fisher wrote, "as I look back on our relationship during the past [fifteen] years I think of all the events leading up to the present time and I can only reflect by saying that history will record the great contribution you have made to the world. In this emotional period, it is so difficult to sort out the real facts, but I want you to know you have many friends who fully understand what you have really done. I can only express my own feeling of personal satisfaction for having worked with you and to know the kind of man you are. Please be assured of my continued friendship."

Nixon, wounded by the circumstances surrounding his resignation, uncharacteristically did not immediately reply. Fisher did receive a phone call from Julie Nixon Eisenhower. There were tears in her voice when she said: "Mr. Fisher, we were at dinner the other evening, the whole family, and we were talking about how so few of my father's friends have continued to stand by him. I wanted you to know how grateful we are to you."

Fisher told her that he had always admired her father and he would do anything he could to help. There was, however, nothing to be done. Richard Nixon was again in the wilderness.

Four months after writing Nixon, Fisher received a reply.

"Dear Max," Nixon said. "As 1974 comes to an end, I want you to know how deeply grateful I have been for your loyal friendship from the time we first met each other, and particularly during these past difficult months. In the world of politics, this kind of friendship is very rare and therefore deeply cherished."

Indeed it was. As Nixon observed: "When you win in politics, you hear from everyone. When you lose, you hear from your friends."

The first conversation Fisher and Nixon had following the resignation was just before the New Year. Nixon phoned him and their chat, Fisher later said, was "awkward." They discussed Nixon's bout with phlebitis, his legal troubles and the Middle East. Fisher, as he had after Nixon's loss in 1960, continued to keep in touch with the former president, but his attention was now focused on the new administration.

*   *   *

On Monday afternoon, at 3:30, August 26, 1974, Fisher walked into the Oval Office for his first visit with President Ford. William J. Baroody Jr., who served as director of the White House Office of Public Liaison, was also there.

"Mr. President," Fisher said, shaking Ford's hand.

"Mr. President?" Ford replied. "Max, you've known me for twenty years and it's always been Jerry."

"And you'll be Jerry again," said Fisher, "when you've finished sitting in that chair."

Fisher had come to discuss the Middle East. He was scheduled to fly to Israel over Labor Day for a budget meeting at the Jewish Agency. The Middle East was undergoing a painful and potentially dangerous readjustment in the wake of the Yom Kippur War, and Ford was counting on Fisher to help smooth the transition between the new administration and Israeli leaders.

First, Ford said, Fisher would now deal directly with the president, not through a bureaucratic pipeline. Second, the president thought Fisher could provide some input on the energy problem. He also requested that Fisher handle the administration's relationship with the American Jewish community and to continue his liaison work with Israel.

Fisher gave the president his reading on the situation within the Jewish community. They were concerned, he said, about the United States keeping its financial and military commitments to Israel, especially since the oil crunch provided a convenient excuse to court the favor of Arab countries. Ford replied that his support for Israel was as strong as ever and that he was confident in the Israelis' judgment about how to proceed toward a lasting peace. Their discussion was lively and informative and went on for an hour. When Fisher stood to leave, Ford said, "Max, please tell [Prime Minister Yitzhak] Rabin that an early meeting between us is crucial."

That weekend, at the Beit Agron, a club where the press gathers in Jerusalem, Fisher trumpeted the backing of the administration, telling reporters that Israel had "no reason to fear a cooling of President Ford's longtime support." Fisher said that he had been asked to deliver the president's greetings to Prime Minister Rabin and Golda Meir, and that Ford promised to meet with American Jewish leaders in the near future.

On September 27, Fisher was in Washington, at Ford's request, to take part in the Conference on Inflation. Five weeks later, at the White House, Ford spent a half-hour with Fisher, Rogers C.B. Morton, secretary of the interior, and Michael Raoul-Duval, the associate director for natural resources of the Domestic Council. Fisher had submitted to Ford a seven-year energy program that was designed to reduce the growth rate of U.S. energy consumption and to increase domestic supplies. The administration had already implemented some of Fisher's suggestions: reducing the speed limit, recycling waste, converting industry from oil to coal, and promoting industrial and private conservation. But Ford was "intrigued" with Fisher's proposition that the president establish a Council on Energy and merge it with the Council on Environmental Quality.

"You know," Fisher said to Ford as he was leaving the Oval Office. "These are good suggestions. And," — he added, referring to his vast holdings in oil — "they are going to cost me a fortune."

Ford smiled. Yes, he knew, and what he did not have to say was that Fisher's willingness to make suggestions that ran contrary to his own interests was a major reason his trust in him was so complete.

The Wednesday before Thanksgiving, Fisher spent an hour and a half with Ford in the Oval Office discussing the finer points of Fisher's access to the president. Ford told him that he should feel free to contact him in the family quarters and that he would have immediate access to Donald H. Rumsfeld, Ford's chief of staff, and Richard B. Cheney, who was Rumsfeld's chief deputy. Ford asked Fisher to arrange a meeting with American Jewish leaders. Fisher promised to take care of it. Then he told Ford that he thought Leonard Garment would do a first-rate job at the United Nations and hoped Ford would look into it. Fisher left the meeting in good spirits and five dollars richer, because on the previous Saturday, Ohio State running back Archie Griffin, en route to the first of his two Heisman Trophies, had helped Ohio State defeat Michigan 12 to 10. When Ford handed Fisher the five-dollar bill, Fisher said to him, "I want you to sign it."

"Max," Ford grinned, "that's defacing government property. It's against the law."

"Mr. President," Fisher replied. "I don't want to spend it. I want to frame it."

"All right," said Ford, signing the bill. "And I know you'll do the same for me."

"Of course," Fisher said, and he did, several weeks later, when the University of Southern California defeated Ohio State in the Rose Bowl.

*   *   *

Late Sunday afternoon, December 8, Fisher was again in Washington talking with Ford, Richard Cheney and Dr. Paul McCracken. The three men spent forty-five minutes boring in on the economic picture. McCracken was convinced that the overheated demand phase of the present inflation was over and that renewed expansion of the economy would stabilize the price-cost level. He encouraged Ford to pursue a vigorous policy of expansion without fear of reactivating the inflation. Fisher suggested that an increased money supply was necessary to stimulate the housing market. He also recommended that Ford name his economic team as soon as possible and that the team should focus their energies on the recession.

The final order of business between Ford and Fisher in 1974 was the president's talk with Jewish leadership. As he had during the Nixon years, Fisher made certain that the president met with a representative body of leaders, not a partisan clique. His arrangements had a dual purpose: one, the administration would be able to view an ample and unified constit-

uency, which would give the desires of that constituency —
namely, a benevolent policy toward Israel — electoral weight;
two, the Jewish leaders would see Fisher as an effective advocate for the community.

It was, for Fisher, an exquisite transaction, each component nourishing the other.

So at noon on Friday, December 20, Ford welcomed nine-
teen men and women from all walks of Jewish American life,
Republicans and Democrats alike: Fisher and Jack Stein;
Rabbi Israel Miller from the Presidents Conference; David
Blumberg of B'nai B'rith; Charlotte Jacobson, head of the
World Zionist Organization's American Section; Mel
Dubinsky, chairman of the United Israel Appeal; Frank
Lautenberg, chairman of the United Jewish Appeal; and a
dozen more, all sitting around the gleaming wood table in the
Cabinet Room of the White House. Ford's briefing paper had
been prepared under the auspices of Secretary of State
Kissinger. The president began by assuring the leaders that he
was committed to maintaining the geographic integrity of
Israel.

"The Israelis," said Ford, "can count on our economic
and military aid. Israel is vitally important to overall American foreign policy in the Middle East."

Ford turned to current events: Kissinger's shuttle diplomacy and U.S. efforts to bring peace to the region. "Most
other countries," Ford said, "including those in NATO, disagree with our policy, and want Israel to return to her 1967 borders. If we go to a Geneva peace conference, the PLO would
have to attend, and Israel will not negotiate with the PLO.
Negotiations between Israel and the Arabs should be a quid
pro quo. If Israel gives something up, she should get something in return."

The crux of Ford's program was precisely what American
Jewish leadership wished to hear: the president would be a
champion of Israel. As the gathering adjourned in a wave of
warm feelings, Fisher wrote himself a note that reflected the
confidence of the leaders: "As long as Ford is president, there
will never be another Munich."

And Fisher was quick to praise Ford for his stance at the meeting. "You impressed the group immensely with your grasp of the issues and your directness," he told the president. "Even the most 'Democratic' members of the group came away with a strengthened sense of trust in your leadership. As you know, nothing is more important to this community than trust. My best wishes for the New Year to you and Betty."

For the moment, everything was as congenial as a honeymoon. And as 1974 drifted into 1975, this balmy air of congeniality obscured the diplomatic hurricane hovering offshore. The storm had its origins in the geopolitics created by the Yom Kippur War, and three months hence, it would lash across Washington and Jerusalem, testing not just the relationship between allies, but the bonds of friendship between the president and his "old friend, Max Fisher."

Chapter 14

THE REASSESSMENT

I N 1975, AS the United States grappled with the demons of
Watergate, Vietnam and the oil embargo, Israel wrestled
with her own grueling angels: the aftermath of the Yom
Kippur War and an internal debate on how to pursue peace
with her Arab neighbors.

The government of Golda Meir was a political casualty of
the war. She was replaced by General Yitzhak Rabin, a military hero and the first native-born Israeli, the first *sabra*, to be
elected prime minister. (Shimon Peres was named defense
minister and Yigal Allon was handed the foreign ministry.)
Once Egypt and Israel disentangled their forces in the Sinai,
Secretary of State Henry Kissinger sought to bring about
another interim agreement, "the second Egyptian-Israeli Disengagement." After a U.S.-Soviet supported peace conference
in Geneva fell apart in a blast of ill will, Rabin told Kissinger
that he was prepared to seek peace in stages. However, said,
Rabin, if Israel were to give up a "piece of land" without
acquiring a "piece of peace," then they would have relin-
quished everything and received nothing.

What Israel wanted from Egyptian President Sadat was a
public pledge of nonbelligerency. Sadat, Kissinger told Israeli
leaders, could not go public with such a commitment. Egypt's
president wanted Israel to give up the Abu Rodeis oil fields
and the Mitla and Gidi passes. Israel balked at that proposal,
but Foreign Minister Allon said that Israeli demands were
flexible and Kissinger should pass that along to Sadat.

Israeli leaders invited Kissinger to continue his shuttle
diplomacy. In March 1975, he spent ten days shuttling between
Israel and Egypt, but discrepancies over Israeli withdrawal and

Egyptian advance were not solved, and Egypt would not consent to a formalized renunciation of belligerency. On a flight from Egypt to Israel, Kissinger, in his standard guise of "senior official," told reporters that he was bringing "new Egyptian proposals to Rabin" that could dissolve the deadlock. Instantly, these revelations made international headlines. In Israel, Rabin asked Kissinger to spell out Sadat's new proposals. Kissinger replied that he hadn't said he brought anything new. But the journalists did, answered Rabin. Kissinger said he wasn't responsible for what they reported. Yes, Rabin replied, in most cases you are. Kissinger asked the prime minister if he truly desired peace. Rabin said yes, but not at any price.

On Friday, March 21, President Ford, presumably at Kissinger's request, forwarded an urgent letter to Rabin. "Kissinger has notified me," the letter said, "of the forthcoming suspension of his mission. I wish to express my profound disappointment over Israel's attitude. . . . Kissinger's mission, encouraged by your government, expresses vital United States interests in the region. Failure of the negotiations will have a far-reaching impact on the region and on our relations. I have given instructions for a reassessment of . . . our relations with Israel. . . . You will be notified of our decision."

If Ford and Kissinger banked on this tough talk to force Israel's hand, they were misguided and ran headlong into what Israeli scholar Shlomo Aronson calls Israel's "old, Holocaust-inspired, siege syndrome." Every indication is that the letter hardened the Israeli stance.

On Saturday, March 22, Sadat again refused to make a formal declaration of nonbelligerency, and the talks broke down.

Fifteen years later, Kissinger still feels that Israel should have accepted the plan at this point and maintains that he never would have resumed the shuttle if he did not believe he had a deal.

"It was an honest misunderstanding," Kissinger says. "Operationally, we were deceived. I'm not saying that it was the Israelis' fault. But the differences between Israel and us were a matter of a few kilometers at the Mitla and Gidi

passes, which the Egyptians were going to get anyway. Whatever the assessment of Egyptian [military] capabilities, we
were talking about ten to fifteen kilometers at the western
end of the Sinai, for God's sake. They weren't going to be any
nearer to defeating Israel."

In 1989, Rabin, now a defense minister immersed in the
dilemmas of the *intifada*, looked back at the breakdown of
the 1975 talks and commented: "We didn't want [the Egyp-
tians] to have total control of the eastern parts of the passes
because then they would be in better shape [during the next
phase of] negotiations. I realized it was not the end of negotiations, because the interim agreement, *by its name*, was [for
the] interim. Why lose cards? Why create a worse military situation knowing that I'd need the cards for the next phase of
negotiations?"

The "misunderstanding" was a result of conflicting agendas. Kissinger and Ford were correct: the distance within the
passes being debated over was not significant as a military
measurement. But as a card to be held for later it was, to
Rabin, invaluable. "It did not make any difference," Rabin
said in 1989, "*if* giving back the passes would have been the
final step in the peace process. But it wasn't."

On Sunday, March 23, Kissinger gave his farewell statement at Ben-Gurion Airport, his eyes glistening with tears.
During the next few weeks, Kissinger would be quoted as
blaming the Israelis for "humiliating" the United States, and
he would allegedly accuse Rabin of misleading him. The
"reassessment," which according to Wolf Blitzer, then-Wash-
ington bureau chief of *The Jerusalem Post*, "marked one of
the most acrimonious periods in American-Israel relations
[since] 1948," had begun.

*   *   *

On the morning after Kissinger's return, President Ford
intimated that America's political and financial support for
Israel might be curbed. Ford, recalling how he came to his
decision to reassess, states: "We had worked very hard to try
to get the Sinai agreement, which involved very detailed

negotiations with the Israelis and with Sadat. And we had gotten to a point where the Israelis were nitpicking over where a line ought to be drawn. It seemed to me that they were losing sight of the big picture. As much as I admired and supported the Israelis, I thought they were being shortsighted. And it finally was my judgment — and Kissinger agreed — that we had to somehow shake the Israeli government into doing what we thought was right."

Coercion was elevated to a less-than-subtle art form as the reassessment rolled on. Added to the public statements of Ford and Kissinger was an array of U.S. chokeholds. Negotiations were suspended on Israel's request for F-15 fighter planes and a shipment of Lance ground-to-ground missiles was delayed even while an Israeli Army team waited in the United States to learn how to operate them. Diplomatic hammerlocks were also used. A scheduled visit to Washington by Israeli Finance Minister Yehoshua Rabinowitz was put off. Israeli Defense Minister Shimon Peres, who was slated to come for a round of talks on a new military-aid package, was instructed to stay in Tel Aviv until the reassessment was finished.

Perhaps to remind Rabin and his Cabinet that other, more inimical viewpoints existed in the American government, Kissinger summoned home four U.S. ambassadors — three of them career Arabists — to participate in the reassessment. He encouraged other governments to assist with the pressure, telling them that the collapse of the talks was Israel's fault and that he would not resume his shuttle diplomacy without significant concessions from the Israelis.

The reaction of the American Jewish community was instantaneous. Seven-hundred American Jewish leaders descended on New York City to kick off a nationwide support drive for Israel. On university campuses, members of Hillel Foundations met with Protestant and Catholic student groups. The Jewish Labor Committee contacted trade unions. Leaders of the Jewish War Veterans addressed gatherings of the American Legion. These tactics were effective. A Harris Survey, conducted just before the negotiations collapsed, showed that American backing of Israel was hovering at an all-time high: 52 percent in the Israeli camp, only 7 percent sympathizing with the Arabs.

Kissinger felt the effects of the outcry. "I really felt the pressure," he says. "I talked to several [American] Jewish leaders [about the reassessment], and I think many of them understood it. But the [American Jewish community] doesn't give Jewish secretaries of state the same benefit of the doubt that they give non-Jewish ones."

Kissinger thought that the president felt far more let down by the Israelis than he did. "Ford is a very straight guy," says Kissinger. "One of the things that burned him up was that [Israeli Ambassador Simcha] Dinitz made it back [to the United States] before I did. And he called a meeting of [American Jewish leaders], and they came out with a position before I even landed."

Ford believed that the groundswell of protest from the American Jewish community was due to their "terribly misunderstood and misinformed point of view."

"They didn't understand that I was as dedicated to Israel's future as they," Ford says. "You had to move forward. The only way to do it was to appear tough. Max Fisher understood it. He was very smart, very wise."

In his autobiography, Ford wrote: "Predictably, our 'reassessment' jolted the American Jewish community, and Israel's many friends in Congress. The Israeli lobby, made up of patriotic Americans, is strong, vocal and wealthy, but many of its members have a single focus. I knew that I would come under intense pressure soon to change our policy, but I was determined to hold firm. On March 27, I met in the Oval Office with Max Fisher . . . [and said] that my comments about reassessing our policies there weren't just rhetoric. . . . I didn't have to ask Max to get the message back to the Israelis. Word would spread very quickly that I meant what I said."

Ford's recounting of the March 27 meeting with Fisher is, to some degree, deceptive, because it skirts a substantial part of their discussion. Fisher did fly to Washington on March 27 and at 3:15 p.m. was ushered into the Oval Office. Although it is not mentioned in Ford's written account, the president was not alone on that Thursday afternoon: Kissinger was with him. Ford was, by his own admission, "mad as hell." He was angry both at the Israelis, for what he saw as their intransigence, and at the American Jewish community, for what he considered their unfair attacks against him.

But Ford was aiming his sights higher than indulging himself in a verbal tantrum. He needed the talks to progress for other reasons, primarily because his administration's foreign policy had been steadily losing credibility with Congress in the backwash of the oil embargo and the suspension of arms deliveries to the Turks. Also, two days prior to the meeting, King Faisal of Saudi Arabia had been assassinated by his nephew. The Saudi monarch, who had ruled over the world's largest proven oil reserves, had been regarded in Western capitals as a moderate who tried to tone down the oil policies of such extremist nations as Libya and Algeria. Faisal believed that the United States was a natural ally of Saudi Arabia, for the Saudi royal family lived in deadly fear of communism. Faisal's death left a problematic question mark. The continued fighting in Southeast Asia was also a problem for the United States — and for Israel, since it demonstrated what could happen to an ally of the United States who was forced to live with an American-inspired (and -imposed) peace agreement. In January 1973, Kissinger and North Vietnam's Le Duc Tho concluded the cease-fire agreement between North and South Vietnam. Yet, by March 15, the Communists were driving closer to Saigon. It was only a matter of weeks before the North Vietnamese Army entered the capital and the country fell.

It was with these difficulties erupting around the world that Fisher entered the Oval Office and shook hands with the president and secretary of state.

Fisher was disturbed about the reassessment, but outwardly he was composed, his distress mitigated by his trust in Ford and Kissinger.

Joe Sisco noticed Fisher's calm. Sisco, undersecretary of state for political affairs, the highest career policy-making position in the State Department, was an old hand in the Middle

East and had coined the phrase "shuttle diplomacy" as he was flying between Egypt and Israel in January 1974 with Kissinger. Sisco saw much of Fisher during the reassessment and says that "Max has the orientation of a problem solver. And when you are a problem solver you are less concerned with the whole conceptual structure than you are with how one alleviates the problem in a practical way. And he does not panic; he is calm. I would be surprised if there was any evidence in Max's lifetime, in critical business decisions or in his role as a [Jewish leader], where he would be anything other than a calm operator. I don't mean he doesn't get emotional like anyone else."

True enough, as Sisco observed, Fisher's basic response to conflict was to rein himself in and to focus his energy on anything that might solve, with a minimum of hostility, the problem. Fisher's measured productive calm was deceptive, though, for by his own design, it revealed little about his stubbornness and anger. It was a response rooted in his profound aversion to public outbursts of hostility. His oft-repeated phrase "You're only living for today" was not merely advice to those who disagreed to step out of the entanglements of the moment into the promise of the future; it was Fisher's way for rising above — and thus circumventing — conflict, his method for not participating in it, for chasing it away.

So as Fisher sat before Ford and Kissinger, he did what he thought was best to defuse the emotionally charged question of reassessment: he listened.

Ford started by telling Fisher that he was upset about the breakdown of the talks, that he held the Israelis responsible, and was considering a televised speech to make his feelings known. "Max," he said, "it is the most distressing thing that has happened to me since I became president. Rabin and Allon misled us into thinking they would make the deal. I never would've sent [Kissinger] if I didn't think we had an agreement. The Israelis took advantage of us."

"Israel," Kissinger said, "made a terrible mistake." He added that going to Geneva would be a disaster; the world would line up against Israel and the United States, and a peace conference that brought together the Russians and Arabs could very well mean a potent pressure on Israel to retreat to its 1967 borders.

Many people, Ford continued, including the Congress, were upset about the stalling of the talks, and the whole Cabinet was in an uproar. Israel was endangering American activities; there was now a chance of another oil embargo, another war, or even a confrontation with the Soviet Union. Ford felt that Israel did not consider America, while America did consider Israel; if Israel has no respect for our interests, he told Fisher, then we must act alone. Israel has damaged America's position with her clients and, by doing so, increased Soviet influence around the world.

Fisher gently broke in, asking Kissinger why he thought the talks failed. The secretary replied that maybe events in Southeast Asia caused Israel to lose confidence in America as an ally.

Ford emphasized that if Israel accepted American assurances on peace, the United States would be locked in — in spite of what was presently happening in Vietnam. He repeated that he had full confidence in Kissinger. The president then mentioned the attacks on him and the secretary of state. He said that he was not anti-Israel; he had been their friend for twenty-five years. The reassessment did not mean the end of military aid and political support. However, that aid and support would be measured in terms of self-interest. It was one thing for support in war and quite another in the context of peace.

The three men rehashed the issues surrounding the dispute. Fisher, realizing that his old friend had been acutely hurt, pointed out to Ford that the breakdown of the talks was not the end of the world. Everyone must keep cool; all the countries involved knew that only the United States could assist the parties in reaching an agreement. He said that he didn't think there had been any deceit intended by Israel, and dropping the blame on them for the disintegration of the talks served no purpose, except to alienate the Israelis and make the Egyptians more demanding. With respect to the attacks on Ford and Kissinger, Fisher said that in his judgment there was still a substantial reservoir of good will in Israel and the

American Jewish community for the president and secretary of state.

Fisher's final note on the forty-minute meeting, which he wrote later, said: "I settled the president down."

When the discussion was over, it was decided that Fisher would go to Israel and learn what, from the Israelis' point of view, had happened to derail the negotiations; what ultimately could be done to heal the rift between the two allies, and to discover if it was feasible to get the peace talks back on track.

Whatever bending would be done, Ford and Kissinger knew, would be done in private. The negotiations had broken down under a cloud of bitterness; personal reputations were on the line: the president's, the secretary's, and the prime minister's. The Israeli press was reporting that "Kissinger was picking on Rabin," and highlighted the tensions in the American Jewish community and the downward spiral of its relationship with the Ford administration. According to *The Jerusalem Post*, Israel's government had "acted to constrain American Jewish leadership from launching an all-out counterattack against Dr. Kissinger — though some of the American Jewish organizations are visibly [champing] at the bit." This back-door diplomacy required someone who would tread lightly and who was not enamored of seeing his picture splashed across a newspaper or television screen.

"I wanted Max to get us the background information on what the unofficial thinking of the Israeli government was," President Ford says. "[The situation was so sensitive the Israelis didn't] like it going through official channels. It had to be kept quiet. That's the way the world has operated for centuries. You have purely official channels where the record has to be made by both parties, but there's a way of information being transmitted that tells you what is do-able. [And this is done] without putting it on the record for future historians to follow. That's what Max did. He was involved in many historic events, [but] the great thing about Max was that he never called a press conference."

Ford's assertion that future historians would have trouble

tracking Fisher's contributions proved correct. Even a scholar as thorough as Steven Spiegel, in *The Other Arab-Israeli Conflict*, his incisive study of American Middle East policy from Truman to Reagan, missed it. Spiegel writes that Kissinger's "opinions and prejudices were paramount; contrary ideas rarely received a hearing. Even when outside consultants were approached, as during the 1975 reassessment, they served as instruments for pressuring Israel rather than as genuine contributors to the diplomatic process."

Secrecy then was a key element if the process were to succeed. And so was trust. Ford did not suspect Fisher, regardless of his sympathies for Israel, of having a hidden agenda.

"Max," says Ford, "never tried to fool you with something."

Kissinger states that while believing Fisher, as a Jewish leader, "had a bias toward the Israeli position," he trusted him "to do an honorable job," relaying the American viewpoint and returning with Israel's answer.

"[President Ford and I] also considered ourselves friends of Israel," says Kissinger. "And I had a lot of confidence in Max. I [used him] to convey our thinking to the Israeli government. And where he agreed with [us] to add his weight to it. I would say, 'Look Max, you know President Ford, you know me. We don't lie to you; this is the way we look at things. [The Israelis] have to understand that this is our thinking, not a negotiating position. This is our analysis and what we think their options are.'"

During the spring of 1975, Fisher had the perfect cover for a trip to Israel. In early April, leaders of the Jewish Agency were convening to prepare for the Fourth World Assembly in June. Upon leaving the White House, Fisher returned home from Washington. On the flight, he put his head back, closed his eyes and replayed his discussion with the president and secretary of state. Both had been angry and disappointed. It would be no small task to communicate this anger and disappointment to Rabin without angering the prime minister, hardening the Israeli position, and permanently undermining this opportunity for peace.

"The reassessment," Fisher says today, "got all out of proportion. I don't think Ford and Kissinger realized, at the time, the extent to which the controversy was mushrooming out of control."

Fisher rummaged under his seat, removed a legal pad from his black leather briefcase, and noted, point by point, what the president and secretary had said, adding his own impressions until he had filled four pages. He leaned back and closed his eyes.

If Fisher managed to elude American journalists, he was not as lucky with the Israeli press. On March 31, *Haaretz* announced on page one: "Three days ago, the Jewish leader with the main contact to the White House, Max Fisher, met with [President] Ford. Mr. Fisher heard criticism of Israel, but his impression was that Ford had hoped for an arrangement between Israel and Egypt and was convinced that this was assured. In [Ford's] opinion Israel should have been flexible for America, which is facing [foreign policy] difficulties. It is possible that part of the president's ire is directed toward the State Department. . . . According to Jewish leaders, Fisher's report indicates that the situation is not encouraging."

Fisher was not interviewed for the story. It was likely that sources in the American Jewish community passed the information along to inflame the protest against Ford and Kissinger's claim that Israeli intransigence had scuttled the peace initiative.

On Thursday, April 3, Fisher arrived in Tel Aviv. As always, when on Jewish Agency business, he was picked up at Ben-Gurion Airport by his driver, Shlomo Osherov, and checked into his usual suite at the King David Hotel in Jerusalem.

"I knew," Fisher says, "that the Americans and Israelis had faith in me. Both sides could speak honestly and trust that the things they wanted kept in confidence I would keep in confidence. I didn't consider myself a messenger boy. I tried to interpret what the messages meant. When I thought either the Americans or Israelis were wrong, I told them. My fundamental responsibility was as an American. Then as an American Jewish leader. And finally, I had my love for Israel."

Throughout April 3, 4, and 5, Fisher attended a nonstop circuit of meetings. He talked with Foreign Minister Yigal Allon and Defense Minister Shimon Peres. He stopped at former Prime Minister Golda Meir's house in a tree-lined Tel Aviv suburb and spoke with her. She told him that although she had a high regard for Kissinger, in this case he was wrong: Israel had not misled him, and he himself had created the rift with his leaks to the press. Fisher then left to exchange ideas with members of the conservative Likud bloc, whose right-wing politics were opposed to those of Rabin's Labor Party, and whose support would be pivotal if an accord with Egypt were to be signed.

On three separate occasions, Fisher spoke with Prime Minister Rabin. They met *ledabare arbah anaiyim*, a Hebrew expression meaning literally "to speak in four eyes," privately, frankly. It was the mode of communication favored by Fisher, and Rabin, who felt that "the importance of [political dialogues] is usually in inverse proportion to the number of participants."

By 1975, the relationship between Rabin and Fisher was on solid ground, but it had not always been that way. In 1968, as Israel's ambassador to Washington, Rabin felt that American Jews misguidedly exercised their influence by means of a *shtadlan*, a court Jew. Rabin was convinced that the Israeli Embassy should speak for Israel at the political level, while America's Jews should muster support for Israel among all the American people.

However, Fisher, who was the intermediary in Republican administrations, felt that Rabin was under the impression that he should act as if he were "a private in the Israeli Army." This was not, Fisher says, how he viewed his role. "If a friend," says Fisher, "asks you a question and you don't give him an honest answer — even if he'd rather hear something else — you're not being much of a friend by lying to him."

Early on in his relationship with Fisher, Rabin referred to him as "a cold Jew." Irving Bernstein, who as executive vice chairman of the UJA ultimately helped bring Rabin and Fisher together after the 1972 presidential election, explains what Rabin meant: "Max," says Bernstein, "is not a great guy for small talk. For a lot of people Max is difficult to communicate with. He mumbles and is a typical American in his approach: he leaves many things unsaid. Rabin, the Israeli general, likes everything on the table. And Max was a Republican, where most Jews were Democrats, and Rabin felt that Max's first priority was his relationship with the administration, not the welfare of the Israelis. He was not a 'true' Zionist. There was, perhaps on Rabin's part, a lack of trust which was made worse by Rabin's assistant, Shlomo Argov, a very emotional man who did not understand Max's reserve."

Bernstein arranged a meeting between Fisher and Rabin, because, he says, Rabin's negative impression of Fisher "was bad for Israel and an injustice to Max." Bernstein wanted Rabin to feel comfortable, so he brought along Edward Ginsburg, a previous chairman and president of the UJA, who was apolitical and trusted implicitly by Rabin. The meeting was held on the mezzanine of the Madison Hotel, where Fisher stayed when he was in Washington. (Rabin would also feel comfortable there. The hotel was owned by one of his friends, Marshall Coyne.) Rabin arrived with his assistant, Argov, who proceeded to outline why he felt Fisher was too reflective of Washington's official perspective. Bernstein and Ginsburg spoke on Fisher's behalf. Fisher said nothing. The discussion turned into a tennis match of mild allegations and polite responses. Finally, Fisher broke in. In lieu of parrying Argov's criticism, he looked at Rabin and quietly told his life story, how he was raised far from things Jewish, his financial struggles, the depth of his horror in the face of the Holocaust, how he would do everything in his power to prevent it from happening again and that meant seeing to it that Israel was secure.

Argov interrupted Fisher, but before he could complete a sentence, Rabin said: "No. Enough. Max is committed."

The meeting was over.

"Max cares about everything that happens to the Jewish people," Rabin commented in 1989, "and [therefore] to Israel. But he has found a way to remain a Jewish leader and never betray the United States. He has mediated when there was a sharp difference of opinion about policies or approaches between the United States and Israel. He understands the problems of Israel, but he does not pretend to be an Israeli. He has the point of view of an American, and is ready, as an American, to try to convince the president to do what must be done."

"One has to understand," says Fisher, and it was a point that he made repeatedly to the Israelis in the spring of 1975, "that the United States functions globally and has interests in the Middle East besides Israel."

Fisher, in dealing with Rabin, felt that as the prime minister, the former general could not match the political charisma and finesse — crucial in foreign diplomacy and for holding the road against the turbulent turns of Israel's domestic politics — of a Golda Meir. Yet, Fisher says, "for sheer brainpower, Rabin is the best. He's a brilliant strategist, with the long global view."

And so Rabin remembers that Max came in April 1975 and "we talked. I explained, point by point, the problem: what brought it about, what needed to be changed, what were the major issues that caused the break from my point of view."

Rabin assured Fisher that he had tremendous regard for the friendship of the United States and the president. He emphasized that he understood American interests and respected them. But he was worried about the impression that Israel had intentionally misled Kissinger. Rabin said the Israelis desired peace and were willing to take risks for it, but they would not barter away their security. He was, along with the other ministers, realistic about the obstacles confronting Israel because of the breakdown of the talks. Even though they were now dealing with Egypt, they realized that they would have to deal with Syria next, and soon. They had already met with Jordan's King Hussein four times in recent months, and the discussions between Jordan and Syria were another complicating factor.

One particular worry of the Israelis, Fisher learned, was the vagueness of Sadat's proposals and whether or not the Egyptian president would keep his pledge to end hostilities. Previously, Sadat had promised Hussein to support him on Jordan's right to negotiate the future of the West Bank. Then, under pressure from other Arab leaders, Sadat suddenly reversed fields at an Arab summit, voting with the crowd and crowning the Palestine Liberation Organization as the only legitimate representative of the Palestinians. If Sadat would break his pledge to fellow Arabs, how binding would he view an agreement with Israel? This distrust also applied to the "private" Geneva accord. The agreement was far too vague, and while Israel was willing to accept less than they thought reasonable, they were troubled about securing the renewal of the United Nations' supervisory force after one year with the Russians holding veto power. In conclusion, the Israelis had no responsible alternative but to accept Sadat's promises with caution.

During his discussions with Rabin, Fisher tried to discover areas where concessions might be made by both sides. He listened, gauging what he had to bring back to Ford and Kissinger. He enumerated the American position and reassured the prime minister that the president and secretary could be relied on to work with Israel toward a realistic peace.

On Saturday, Rabin concluded their final meeting by saying: "Max, tell Kissinger and Ford not to worry — the process will continue. The talks will be resumed. But there is no need to rush."

Later, in the Hebrew edition of his memoirs, Rabin wrote: "It was always true that [U.S.] administrations had a proven method of incurring favor with any Arab leader who showed signs of cooperating with America. Namely, reduction of arms to Israel. On the other hand, it is also true that Israel is not alone, provided it knows how to harness the support of its friends, Jewish and non-Jewish, in a discreet and judicious manner. From Max Fisher I always received great support; the door of the White House is always open to him and in time of need, Max moves its hinges."

Now, more than ever, with the Passover festival finished and the hills around Tel Aviv green in the warm seaside sunlight, Rabin would need Fisher to open the White House door, and keep it open, until the crisis was over.

Chapter 15

BEHIND THE WHITE HOUSE DOOR

FISHER'S WEEKEND TRIP to Israel fueled speculation about his activities and the status of the reassessment in the American and Israeli press.

On April 5, *The New York Post* headlined a story, "U.S. pushes Israel on Sinai pact," and stated that Israel's national radio had announced that the U.S. government had enlisted Fisher "to coax Israelis into taking new steps that would bring Secretary of State Kissinger back into a leading mediating role. These new initiatives would have the effect, the radio said, of pushing back the reconvening of the Geneva conference." In Israel, *Haaretz* jumped into the fray by saying that "Dr. Henry Kissinger claimed, in a talk with Jewish Agency Board of Governors chairman Max Fisher, that Israel had 'misled him.' Sources close to Mr. Fisher further reported that though a slight shift has occurred in Kissinger-Israeli relations, the stand of [President Ford] is more moderate and [the president] has remained a true friend of Israel."

Fisher kept his customary distance from the press. When he was questioned by *The Detroit News* about a report in *Newsweek* magazine that said he was asked to be a special emissary for President Ford to Israel regarding the stalemate in the Middle East, Fisher termed the report, "absolutely false."

Meantime, Kissinger was pursuing some stateside diplomacy. Perhaps he hoped to deflect the criticism leveled at him by the American Jewish community and to garner support for his rendition of the breakdown, thereby heaping further pressure on Israel. At the very least, it was an attempt to demonstrate that the secretary was not deaf to the community of which he was a part. Kissinger requested and held a one-hour meeting at the State Department with political science professor Hans Morgenthau, writer Elie Wiesel and Max Kampelman, a leading Washington attorney and former adviser to Vice President Humphrey. According to an unnamed source who attended the meeting, Kissinger was "very sad" during the hour, and "very critical" of Rabin's insistence that Egypt make a formal declaration of nonbelligerency in exchange for the Sinai passes and the Abu Rhodeis oil fields. Israel, he allegedly said, would have received much more from the Arabs by sustaining the U.S.-initiated step-by-step diplomacy. Wiesel, a survivor of Auschwitz, had recently written in *The New York Times* that he feared another Holocaust, and reportedly told Kissinger that he had trouble sleeping at night because of it and asked him if he experienced such difficulties. The secretary replied that he too did not sleep at night, but did not elaborate.

The failure of Kissinger's impromptu caucus was due to his guest list: although the participants were among the luminaries of the Jewish community, none of them was a guiding star or, more important, had the ear of the president. Kissinger was undoubtedly aware of that. But given the lack of sympathy for him by American Jews, his hunting expedition was understandable.

Fisher thought that Kissinger's pressure campaign against the Israelis was not in anybody's best interest, except possibly Sadat's. By eleven o'clock on Tuesday morning, April 8, Fisher was boarding a flight for Washington at Metropolitan Airport in Detroit. He had an appointment with Ford the next day. The president was scheduled to deliver a nationally televised speech, his "State-of-the-World" address, to a joint session of Congress on Thursday, and so Fisher was anxious to convince the president to soften his public position on Israel. A hardening of his stance, on the other hand, would be a catastrophe. The news was not optimistic. That morning, flying to Washington, Fisher read a piece in *The New York Times* asserting that the secretary of state was reluctant to attempt a new mediation role in the Middle East unless the outcome was certain and that Kissinger "had detected no sign that Israel is willing to go beyond what she was willing to do on March 22." The story concluded: "The State Department today denied a report Max Fisher had been sent to Israel on a special mission. . . . [Fisher] has told State Department officials that he neither proposed or received any new ideas."

Northwest Flight 334 touched down at National Airport at one o'clock, and Fisher was off to a round of meetings. At the White House, he talked with Ford's chief of staff, Donald Rumsfeld, who, predictably, was backing up his boss. Rumsfeld was critical of Israel's posture, saying that if the talks were to begin again, the United States must not move too fast. Fisher then met with the secretary of state. He informed Kissinger about his discussions in Israel. The secretary was still "emotional," according to the notes Fisher jotted down afterward. His anger at Rabin for "misleading him" had not cooled. There was, Fisher saw, a desperate need to relieve tensions. That would have to wait until tomorrow's meeting.

Fisher registered at the Madison Hotel. At nine-thirty that evening, he rode over to have dinner with Jacob Javits at the Sans Souci, a French restaurant that was enjoying the distinction of being the in place for Washington's in crowd of White House staff, businessmen, politicians and lobbyists.

From the Romney years on, Javits and Fisher maintained their friendship. When Romney dropped out of the 1968 race, Javits lost his shot at the vice presidency, but since 1969 he had been a member of the powerful Senate Foreign Relations Committee. A committed supporter of Israel, Javits recalled in his memoirs that during the Nixon and Ford administrations Fisher "had a greater influence regarding Israel than any other American not in public office." Javits considered Fisher's work not only vital for Israel, but for the United States as well. "[Fisher's] intercessions," he said, "have always been made with an eye to the highest national interest of the United States, which he [and I feel] is parallel to the interest of Israel."

330 : Q_{UIET} D_{IPLOMAT}

Now, as Fisher and Javits conferred about the crisis, the senator felt that Fisher's intercession could be used to avert a disaster. Javits was also concerned about the administration's shift in attitude toward Israel and the talk in Congress of selling planes and missiles to the Arabs. Javits had just come from Israel. En route from Teheran, after visiting the Shah of Iran, Javits had stopped off and spoken to Rabin. Javits had urged Rabin to steer the dialogue with America away from recriminations over the breakdown toward molding a fresh consensus in advance of the Geneva conference.

The dinner lasted for over two hours. Fisher told Javits his ideas about healing the rift between Ford and Rabin, and the senator encouraged him. It had to be done, Javits said, and before Ford addressed Congress. Fisher said goodbye to the senator outside the restaurant; it was midnight when he walked through the doors of the Madison Hotel. The lobby, with its crystal chandeliers, antiques and glimmering marble floor, was deserted. Fisher had one last meeting to go, the most critical of the day. He stepped into the elevator.

Upstairs, Fisher opened the door of his suite. The lights of Washington were glittering through the wide sweep of windows. Fisher walked in and greeted Leonard Garment, who had been waiting for him. Garment was now living in New York City. Since resigning as an assistant to President Ford, he had returned to New York to practice law; when that proved unrewarding, he accepted a position as the U.S. representative to the Human Rights Commission at the United Nations. Garment's relationship to Fisher had become as personal as it was professional. Garment would one day write to Fisher of the profound love he felt for him and thank him for having "given the same time and attention to my personal problems that you have given to the problems of presidents and prime ministers. You have taken me through the toughest times of my life."

Garment would suffer a tragedy that, he later said, plunged him into a depression. Soon after his meeting with Fisher, his first wife, Grace, committed suicide. Garment left work to care for their teenage children. It was during this period that Garment relied on Fisher's advice, talking to him on the phone or walking along the ocean with him in Palm Beach. Through these talks, even though they centered on career and personal difficulties, Garment came to see why Fisher grew to become so useful to leaders in the United States and Israel.

"Max," Garments states, "doesn't process information like the average person. He doesn't go from A to B to C to D. He goes from A to Z. [And when we would discuss my problems], he would get right to it. I'd go through a long thing with him and then he'd say: 'Don't do it.' And I'd say: 'But why, Max?' And he'd say: 'Don't do it.' He just *knew* the answer. Max has assimilated so much information about the whole rich variety of things — the good and bad things, the decent and stupid things, treachery — name it, Max has seen it. That's why he is so valuable. The most valuable process in life is the distillation of experience into judgment. At a certain level, we call that wisdom. Max was an adviser to leaders on the most difficult problems because they wanted the benefit of his wisdom."

So on the evening of April 8, 1975, Garment traveled to Washington at Fisher's request to help him prepare a written document that Fisher planned to read to Ford and Kissinger the following morning. Fisher wanted Garment to serve as a sounding board and to help him construct the thrust of the document. Garment believed that it was method well suited to the talents of both men.

"A lot of Max's processing of information is internal," says Garment. "Through a kind of free-associative self-kibitzing, he constructs a private narrative that shapes itself into a point of view, rather than a coherent argument."

Garment, the former Wall Street litigator, would, in part, supply the coherent argument. Garment has a reputation for eloquence and persuasion. He is considered, according to a 1987 *Regardie's* magazine article, a master of "the arcane Washington art of persuading the press to see the world his way. His . . . education in the art of rehabilitating reputations began in the 1968 presidential campaign, when he directed

media relations for 'the new Nixon.' Joe McGinniss's landmark study, *The Selling of the President, 1968*, is . . . an illustration of Garment's genius."

Actually, it had been Garment's idea for Fisher to read a
written declaration to Ford and Kissinger. The formality of it,
so uncharacteristic of Fisher's typical relations with Ford,
would underscore the significance of what Fisher was saying.

Another strategic thrust behind Garment's recommendation was directed at Kissinger.

"I suggested that Max read a paper of State," Garment
explains, "because I was sure Henry would interrupt him if he
didn't. Henry was still very angry with Rabin, and Henry can
throw a whole basketball team off balance once he starts talking. If Henry launched into one of his tirades, Max's argument
would never have been presented."

Fisher approved of Garment's technique because it coincided with his general approach to business and political
transactions. "I study a person's character," Fisher says, "and
try to discern where they might be touchy. You also have to
be sensitive to their egos, because if you're not, you won't
know how to work with them. During these negotiations,
Kissinger's responsibility was to the United States. He's a
dynamic man and was one of our great secretaries of state. But
he wasn't always tolerant of what someone else might have to
say to him."

Offsetting this disadvantage was Fisher's unique friendship with the president.

"I knew that Max and Ford had a very good relationship,"
Garment says. "Ford had genuine respect for Max's acumen,
not just in business, but for his shrewdness in matters of this
kind. Ford would listen to him and, because of their relationship, trust Max not to give him a bum steer. Henry was
always outwardly respectful toward Max, and I think Henry
respected him, but Henry wouldn't yield to anyone in foreign
policy."

That night, at the Madison, Fisher and Garment were
banking on the president's trust, believing that Ford would
give Fisher a fair hearing and be persuaded to suspend the

reassessment. Fisher summarized his conversations with Israel's leaders for Garment, outlining ways America and Israel could reach common ground. Then they began to draft the document on legal pads.

"Max," says Garment, "is a 'back-door adviser.' There have been others in American politics. Presidents don't write about them in their memoirs because they don't want to admit that this is the way the country is run. But that's how business is done. Those are the important people. Forget the guy at the State Department and dinners in tuxedos. The meeting on April 9 was [going to be] one of the most important meetings in the history of American-Israeli relations. If I didn't believe that going in, I never would've been sitting around a hotel room at midnight."

It was 3 a.m. before Fisher and Garment were satisfied with the statement.

On the morning of Wednesday, April 9, as President Ford was meeting with Kissinger and Lt. General Brent Scowcroft, deputy assistant for national security affairs, Fisher was finishing his breakfast at the Madison. Earlier, Garment had gone to the White House and had his former secretary, Eleanor Connors, type a clean copy of the presentation; it came to nine typed pages. Now, Fisher carefully reviewed the text, practicing his delivery, deleting some phrases, writing in others. Then he climbed into a cab and rode to the White House, showing the guard his pass and entering through the northwest entrance.

A *New York Times* reporter spotted him going in and asked him where things stood with the reassessment.

"No comment," Fisher replied.

By 10:55 a.m., with the spring sunlight filtering in through the Oval Office windows, Fisher was seated in front of the president's desk, with Kissinger sitting on a chair to Ford's left.

Fisher began by listing the various people he had spoken with during his trip to Israel, making it apparent that he had spent a good deal of time with the prime minister. Then, reading from his statement, he said: "On no occasion did I tell

[Rabin] what to do, but I undertook to give an assessment of the situation in accordance with my conversation with the president and on the basis of my general impression of attitudes of representative leaders and groups in America."

Fisher spoke slowly, keeping his voice steady, and loud enough for Ford and Kissinger to hear. "The prime minister," he said, "was extremely concerned about the president's reported negative reaction to the termination of the talks. He has a warm feeling for the president and great confidence in him, so my report was not a very happy one. Rabin spent considerable time discussing the issue of whether the United States was misled in the Rabin-Allon visits. He was very frank in stating that Israel might have been 'too confident' in expressing a willingness 'to be flexible.' They had said they would be forthcoming and, in fact, they thought they were in taking the very positive position of yielding up the passes and oil fields.

"According to Rabin, they failed to appreciate that going public as early on in the negotiations as they did would put them in a very disadvantageous position. On the other hand, Rabin felt that declaring their willingness to give up these vital areas at an early point would help Sadat in the negotiations. This, Rabin said, turned out to be a tactical mistake."

Fisher added parenthetically that an Israeli public-opinion poll that he had received before his trip showed that opposition to giving up parts of the occupied territory and getting nothing in return was almost 78 percent.

"One cannot," Fisher continued, "overemphasize the Israelis' preoccupation with the question of physical security. This subject came up again and again in my discussions. Another repeated theme, particularly on the part of the prime minister, concerned the importance of maintaining or restoring the president's confidence in the credibility of the Israeli government. Rabin said that as Israelis and Jews, they pride themselves on keeping their word. They consider this a fundamental ethical issue and vital to their relationship with the United States."

Fisher glanced straight at Ford and, lowering his eyes,

commented: "I do not believe there was any intention on the part of the Israelis to mislead you, Mr. President, or the secretary. My impression is that they were too optimistic in stating their ability to be flexible and failed to appreciate the connotation that would be placed on certain terminology such as their intention to be 'forthcoming,' all of which contributed to a serious misunderstanding. But, I repeat, I am personally convinced there was no intention to mislead." After that reassurance, Fisher said: "The prime minister was also very much disturbed about the president's reported concern that the Israeli government did not take into consideration broader issues of American foreign policy. This appeared to disturb him as much as anything else. They are crucially dependent on U.S. friendship and help. They feel they owe a tremendous debt to America, and, according to Rabin, these considerations weighed heavily on them during the negotiations. However, they feel that balancing Soviet influence in the Middle East is as important to the United States as it is to Israel, and they have played and will continue to play a central role in this area for the foreseeable future."

Fisher paused, allowing the president and secretary of state to reflect on this assertion. It was a subtle point, but a significant one, for it italicized the reality that the relationship between America and Israel was not a one-sided deal. The United States, as characterized by former Israeli Prime Minister Golda Meir, is indeed "the only real friend [Israel has], and a very powerful one." But doesn't Israel pay a nation's heaviest price — with the lives of its citizens — for U.S. support?

A moment later, Fisher was reading from his statement, telling the president and secretary that Rabin had asked him to convey his deep feeling of gratitude to the United States, along with his and his country's regard for the president. "Rabin," said Fisher, "also made clear that the Israelis desperately want peace either on an interim basis, step-by-step, or, if necessary, in the setting of Geneva."

Fisher, Ford, Kissinger and Rabin knew that Geneva was not a viable option for America or Israel. Since Ford and

Kissinger had used the prospect of a reconvened Geneva conference as leverage to pry Israel from her position on the passes, the prime minister evidently sent this message to indicate that the Israelis would not be intimidated about a decision to resume talks in Geneva, and would never retreat to their 1967 borders. In his memoirs, Rabin, remembering the events of 1975, said: "[Everyone knew that] the Geneva conference would lead to hopeless stalemate. . . . I could not believe that the United States was truly interested in convening a format that would literally invite the Soviet Union to resume a position of primary influence in Middle Eastern affairs. . . . The Arabs demand a total withdrawal to the June 4, 1967 lines, and those lines were the cause of the war. [Israel has] defensible borders, and those are not the same as the June 4 lines."

So now, Ford and Kissinger had the Israelis' response to that U.S. negotiating lever. Yet Fisher and Garment had prepared the statement meticulously, offsetting Israel's toughness with a more pliable tone. "Rabin and his government definitely do not favor the Geneva approach," Fisher went on. "Rabin understands the vital interests of America and respects them. He feels, however, that what is needed now is to overcome the crisis in confidence which has arisen. He suggested certain steps and timing for the future."

The tone of the text abruptly switched.

"First," said Fisher, "[Rabin feels] that no further negotiations [should] take place until the U.S. reassessment is completed; and that the reassessment be completed as soon as possible since Israel cannot negotiate with this uncertainty hanging over her head."

Candidly, Rabin was saying that Israel refused to be shoved into a settlement by threats of delayed American arms shipments or a reduction in any type of aid. If an accord were to be attained with Egypt, Ford and Kissinger must plane down the rougher edges of their rhetoric and desist from censuring Israel for the diplomatic imbroglio.

"Second," said Fisher, switching to the Israelis' more malleable posture, "they are prepared to make more concrete proposals for peace on any of the levels outlined above — that is, they are prepared to: revive the present negotiations; make more extensive territorial concessions for a declaration of nonbelligerency [from Sadat]; or develop a comprehensive set of proposals for Geneva. But they know that they must work closely with [the president] and the secretary and must have [American] support and understanding in connection with any of these approaches."

Fisher turned the page. In what was surely meant to assure Ford and Kissinger that the administration would not be embarrassed again by an unexpected twist in the talks, he said: "Rabin feels that negotiations should start on a lower level — or levels — and that the involvement of the secretary should be the last phase. Rabin pointed out that negotiations of such gravity must take time, citing Vietnam."

Then Fisher offered what, from the Israeli perspective, was "do-able."

"Rabin," Fisher explained, "said his government realized the delicacy of America's political policy vis-à-vis Israel and the Arab nations; accordingly, even after Sadat made it clear that he would not offer more than vague promises, Israel was still willing to give up the oil fields and half the passes on the basis of even vague assurances. This is a key point and was predicated entirely on the American relationship. As I mentioned before, Israeli public opinion would not tolerate yielding strategic territory for nothing of substance in return, but nevertheless the government made this move and, surprisingly, was supported. As a result, in future negotiations Israel will be represented by a government which is substantially strengthened and now capable of even greater movement."

Fisher, having let Ford and Kissinger know that Rabin would have more domestic room to operate politically, offered his personal assessment of the situation.

"This is a significant and positive development," he said. "And one which is directly traceable to the recently suspended negotiations. Even the party of the hawks did not oppose giving up $350 million in annual income from the oil fields and half the passes.

"Another basic point Rabin made," continued Fisher, "was that they were upset by the secretary's effort — which they acknowledge was made in complete good faith — to substitute his judgment for theirs in the matter of security."

Fisher had been reading for twenty minutes, barely moving his eyes from the pages, as Ford and Kissinger listened without interruption. Each sentence had been carefully crafted by Garment and Fisher. It was an honest document, and a cautious one. Until this juncture, Fisher had not uttered one extemporaneous word. But now, upon revealing what had infuriated the Israelis about Kissinger's approach and, in Fisher's mind, contributed much to the deterioration of the talks, Fisher looked up from his pages, shifting his body toward Kissinger.

"Henry," he said softly, staring at the secretary, "I know how badly you felt about the talks collapsing, but you can't play God with the Israelis. They have to make up their own minds about their security. They may not be right, but it's their decision."

Kissinger was silent. Fisher resumed reading.

"I emphasize, however," he said, "that there is a tremendous reservoir of good will, affection and admiration for the secretary in Israel. The problem is that, given the state of Israeli sensitivity, private criticism and official pressure tend to produce negative reactions and, to put it bluntly, are extremely counterproductive. The cutoff of the visit of their ministers to the United States was viewed as a break in communications and increased the sense of suspicion and anxiety — particularly on the part of the public — out of all proportion to what was presumably intended."

Fisher was being diplomatic by saying that the cutting off of communications produced anxiety beyond what was "presumably intended." In fact, it was precisely what was intended, and now, for better or for worse, the Israeli rejoinder to that tactic was on the table for Ford and Kissinger to see. Chastising Israel in the press, behind closed doors at Cabinet meetings or in the halls of Congress would not lead to an agreement — it would widen the gulf already separating the parties.

"During my visit," said Fisher, "several congressional leaders were also visiting the Middle East. They talked to the Israelis about Sadat's expectation that the United States will pressure Israel to do what Sadat wants. Sadat was also telling the congressional people that the United States should stop supplying arms to Israel, although at the same time Egypt was receiving more arms from the Russians. The dominant Israeli view is that Sadat is playing both sides — the Soviets and the United States — against Israel, particularly with a view to driving a wedge between the United States and Israel."

Fisher had issued a warning. Perhaps in their disappointment, and the resulting rush to assign blame, the president and secretary were being manipulated by the Egyptians. It was certainly something to reflect on, and might temper their judgment against Israel.

"After three days of discussion," Fisher read on, "I came to these conclusions: the talks apparently moved too fast and were suspended too soon. There is a substantially strengthened government in Israel and Israeli public opinion has moved considerably along the road in support of government initiatives for peace. There is still division in their negotiating team but there is greater unity than before. There is a very sober feeling that they must do something. They do not take the friendship of America lightly and suffer through any decision that threatens the strength of that friendship. There was a bad reaction to the pressure exerted on them toward the end of the negotiations. They are now working to develop and propose further concrete steps. They do not like Geneva, and, for the most part, would prefer to resume the three-party step-by-step process.

"I have given careful consideration to these matters since my return and have had useful discussions about them with many responsible and friendly persons. This included a lengthy and informative visit with the secretary yesterday afternoon.

"Mr. President, I would like to close this report by emphasizing three points:

"First, the private negotiating process that you and the secretary set in motion can and should be resumed. Second, there should be a cooling-off period while new plans are developed and discussed, and the emphasis shifts to the constructive possibilities of the coming year and away from the misunderstandings and disappointments of recent weeks.

"I repeat: new strengths and new opportunities exist now that did not exist before, and these are the direct result of the recent negotiations that you and the secretary set in motion. Finally, and most important, in order to clear the air, create confidence and to minimize suspicion and resistance, the most urgent need is to narrow the scope of your planned reassessment of Middle East policy. This should be done in your address to the Congress tomorrow. It is essential to make clear that reassessment does not suggest any change in the traditional U.S. interest in the maintenance of the security and national integrity of Israel, nor does it mean that Israel will be pressured or coerced into adopting negotiating positions which she does not believe are compatible with her long-term security needs."

Fisher, always the conciliator, troubled about the tarnishing of Israel's image — its divisive effect on the American Jewish community, and the corresponding political fallout, which, in light of the coming presidential campaign, would weaken Republican support — said to Ford: "A feeling of separation between the United States and Israel is growing in the American Jewish community and this could have profoundly harmful domestic as well as foreign-policy consequences. On the other hand," Fisher said, letting Ford and Kissinger know that the Israelis understood their half of the bargain, "it must be made absolutely clear to Israel that paralysis and turbulence in the Middle East threatens vital worldwide interests of the United States, and Israel therefore bears a heavy responsibility and must stretch itself to the utmost to contribute to a peaceful solution. It would also be helpful if you could state that both sides — Israel and Egypt — negotiated in good faith, and the suspension of the talks was the result of extremely complex political and strategic problems, but you are optimistic that progress is being achieved toward a just peace for all parties in the Middle East."

Fisher had been reading for thirty-five minutes. When he finished, Ford came from behind his desk. Fisher and Kissinger rose and then the president stood between them, with his arms over their shoulders, saying: "Max, I want to thank you. I feel a lot better about things now. We'll work together and try to make this thing possible."

The president asked Fisher for a copy of his statement and invited him to join the Ford family in the audience on Thursday, while he addressed Congress.

Garment's strategy had paid off. Ford had listened; Kissinger had not interrupted.

The next day UPI reported: "President Ford met Wednesday with Detroiter Max Fisher. The White House said Fisher went to Israel for 'a private and personal visit' and that he gave the president a report on his activities there. [Press secretary Ron] Nessen said Fisher 'did not go as an emissary for the president.'"

Despite the denial, word was spreading. And Ford had another signal for Israel and American Jewish leaders. On Friday morning, April 11, *The Washington Post* covered Ford's "State-of-the-World" address to Congress, running a page-one photograph of First Family members standing and clapping in the House gallery. The caption read: "As President Ford entered the House chamber for his speech, daughter Susan, son Jack, and Mrs. Ford joined in the applause." *The Post* did not identify the tall man with the glasses who was beside Susan Ford; it was Max Fisher.

In the event that Fisher's seat assignment was too indirect a gesture of reconciliation, the president was blatant in his message.

"The interests of America as well as our allies are vitally affected by what happens in the Middle East," he told Congress, and the television audience. "Unfortunately, the latest efforts to reach a further interim agreement between Israel and Egypt have been suspended. The issues dividing the parties are vital to them and not amenable to easy and to quick solutions. . . . The United States will move ahead toward an overall settlement or interim agreements, should the parties themselves desire them."

"Reassessment," the term that historians would designate as a symbol of the most embittered impasse in American-Israeli relations, was nowhere in the speech. Ford had said negotiations would proceed, but he had softened. His statement that "the issues dividing [Israel and Egypt] are vital to them and not amenable to easy and to quick solutions" implied that the disagreements between the two nations were complex. Pitfalls on the path to peace should be expected, and therefore his administration could not drop the burden of blame on Israel's shoulders.

Leonard Garment, exhibiting a talent for understatement, later remarked that "the suggestion that Max have his thoughts in writing and insist on reading them turned out to be correct."

"I just played a part," adds Fisher. "The real players were Ford and Kissinger."

Once again, because Fisher operated away from the media's broad, bright eye, history would pass over his role.

"The 'Jewish portfolio' was handled in a unique way in the Ford White House," writes political scientist Steven Spiegel. "Max Fisher . . . [was] crucial as a 'close' and 'old friend' of the president. However, this system left him much weaker than Niles or Feldman, the various figures under Johnson, or the combination of Garment, Safire and Kissinger under Nixon. . . . Fisher could not deal with details in the daily routine because he was outside the administration. In any case, as the Dulles era demonstrated, it is extremely difficult for someone in the White House to deal with Israeli affairs when a czar [like Kissinger] reigns over the foreign-policy apparatus. When there is only one foreign-policy channel to the president, the influence of an extra-bureaucratic adviser is likely to be negligible."

But Fisher had his own safe channel to the president; he

was on Ford's select list of three dozen individuals who could phone the president on a private number. Additionally, as Fisher's activities on Friday morning demonstrated, he carried more than the "Jewish portfolio."

That morning, at ten thirty-five, Fisher was in the Oval Office chatting with Ford. He congratulated him on his speech, its calming effect, the sense of unity that it encouraged. Then, along with the president's closest advisers, they got down to business. The subject: politics — the beginnings of Ford's 1976 election campaign.

Around dinnertime, an exhausted Max Fisher boarded Northwest Flight 367 and flew to Detroit. As he walked into his house, the phone rang. Henry Kissinger was calling.

*   *   *

Because Kissinger would stamp his personality on the diplomacy of the period, his personal relationship with the major and minor players became not just entertaining speculation for columnists, but a notable piece of history. In sunnier moments, from the Nixon administration on, Kissinger and Fisher were attentive friends. Kissinger, often at Fisher's request, briefed various Jewish leadership groups. The two men met when Fisher was in Washington, keeping each other apprised of developments in government and the American Jewish community. Beyond politics, especially after Kissinger was no longer secretary of state, their friendship deepened. Get-well wishes during the illnesses of both men were sent; affectionate notes, brimming with news and ending with regards to each other's wives, were fairly common.

As the years passed, Fisher and Kissinger appeared to establish a mutual-admiration society. In 1982, *The New York Post*'s "Page Six" reported: "Former Secretary of State Henry Kissinger rarely opens his mouth these days for under five figures, but he happily forgoes his usual lecture fees when it comes to friendship. [On] Thursday, November 18, [Kissinger will] be the keynote speaker at the Grand Hyatt when the American Jewish Congress hands out this year's prestigious Stephen Wise [award] . . . to Max Fisher. Henry's doing it for love [since he] has long been an admirer . . . of Fisher."

Less than a year later, Fisher attended Kissinger's sixtieth birthday celebration at the Hotel Pierre in New York City. Afterward, Fisher wrote him: "To have so many people all over the world honor you is certainly an expression of the gratitude people feel for what you have done. I particularly, Henry, have always had great respect for [your] work. To me you are the greatest. By the way, it was a distinct honor and pleasure to be seated next to your mother, who is not your severest critic."

Kissinger repaid the tribute when Fisher turned eighty, calling him "a lodestar of the American Jewish community," and with that compliment possibly revealed the shadow that dimmed a small corner of his relationship with Fisher.

For Kissinger it could not have been personal, nor even remotely reminiscent of his duel with Secretary of State Rogers over foreign policy during the Nixon administration. Fisher, located *outside* the daily gnashings of government and not involved in the formation of policy, did not pose a bureaucratic threat. And as Leonard Garment suggested, Kissinger was far too respectful of Fisher for that kind of infighting. And Fisher was too fond of — and too sensitive to — Kissinger for a war in the press; furthermore, it was not his style. Nor was there any reason to engage the secretary in a competition for the president's attention: Fisher's access to Ford was secure.

Yet, with the consuming conflicts of the reassessment, the darker edges of the secretary's ambivalent relationship with America's Jewish community — and their mixed response to him — began to sound a discordant note within the orchestrations of diplomacy. So it was only natural that Fisher, Kissinger's "lodestar," as the embodiment of that community, would inadvertently find himself in the path of the secretary's anger.

But on Friday evening, April 10, 1975, when Fisher picked up the phone at his home in Michigan, Kissinger was relaxed.

"Max," the secretary said, "I want to thank you for helping me turn the president around on the reassessment. I think the peace process can now continue. We're going to follow your suggestion and resume the talks at a lower level."

Fisher replied that he was glad to be of assistance. Kissinger, of course, had been behind the reassessment from the start, but the purpose of his thanks was clear: it was a bid for reconciliation between the administration — more specifically Henry Kissinger — and America's Jewish communal leaders. The administration would require their domestic support for the process to advance.

The phone call ended amicably. And Fisher would pass the word in the community and to Israel. Such is the duty of any pragmatist striving to be an artist of the possible. But Fisher's role was not done. The president's speech, and Kissinger's call, had only been a respite from the tremors of the reassessment. The noise from Israeli sympathizers in Washington in the spring and summer of 1975 swelled to a record pitch. Less than three weeks after his conversation with Kissinger, Fisher was in the Oval Office talking with Ford and Chief of Staff Rumsfeld. The president began by complaining about the perception of the American Jewish community that he was "cold" toward Israel.

"It's not true," said Ford.

Fisher agreed with the president, but indicated that the reassessment hardly bolstered the community's confidence in the administration. Also, Fisher said, Kissinger's emotional response to the breakdown of the talks — and the manner in which the controversy played out in the press — inflamed the disagreement between Washington and Jerusalem.

Ford replied that he hoped the worst of it was behind them now, and mentioned that he was optimistic about his upcoming June talks with Sadat and Rabin.

The final order of business was the 1976 presidential campaign. Ford asked Fisher to begin involving himself at the top level. Fisher said that he would get started.

Ford may have been sanguine about his chances for hammering out a second disengagement between Israel and Egypt, but he was underestimating the effect of the reassessment on the Israelis, the American Jewish community and Congress.

On May 9, *The London Jewish Times* ran a story on Ford's

early-April discussion with Fisher and Kissinger, declaring that the secretary of state had "clashed sharply and angrily with [Fisher] over the responsibility for the failure of Dr. Kissinger's last mission in the Middle East." After recapping Kissinger's claim that the Israeli government had misled him, the story said that Fisher was sent on a fact-finding mission to Israel. Upon his return, he informed the president, through a long memorandum, that Kissinger had not been misled, but had been "too optimistic." Ford, said the story, sided with Fisher, and "Kissinger's position was for a time in doubt. But the president was not prepared to see Kissinger resign at this particular traumatic period of American diplomatic failures, and the dispute was smoothed over."

"It never happened," Kissinger says today, "that Ford and I, in the end, disagreed."

But by May 1975, the administration was rapidly losing political ground in the Jewish community and Congress.

Advertisements in *The New York Times* and *The New York Post*, sponsored by the local chapter of the United Jewish Appeal, warned Jews about the reassessment, saying that "the price of silence was the Warsaw ghetto. Bergen-Belsen. Auschwitz. Dachau. Speak now, so that we never again pay the price of silence." On May 12, *Time* magazine reported on the formation of American Jews against Ford, a committee that was spearheading a national drive to defeat the president's bid for re-election. AJAF opposed Ford because "his policy runs counter to the survival of Israel," and was "a disaster for the United States and the free world." AJAF was noteworthy as an indication of the anger at Ford in the Jewish community because it backed no specific candidate and pledged to support any hopeful who could beat Ford in the primaries.

The biggest blow to the Ford administration's policy of reassessment landed on the president's desk on May 21. Seventy-six senators, from both ends of the political spectrum, sent Ford a letter stating that peace in the Middle East requires Israel to "obtain a level of military and economic support adequate to deter a renewal of war by Israel's neighbors. Withholding military equipment from Israel would be dangerous, discouraging accommodation by Israel's neighbors and encouraging a resort to force. . . . Within the next several weeks, the Congress expects to receive your foreign aid requirements for fiscal year 1976. We trust that your recommendations will be responsive to Israel's urgent military and economic needs."

In *A Time to Heal*, Ford wrote that the letter "really bugged me, and there was no doubt in my mind that it was inspired by Israel." He thought the Israelis were "overplaying their hand," and commented that, for him, this "kind of pressure was counterproductive. I was not going to capitulate to it."

Fisher saw that the power struggle unfolding threatened both Middle East peace and Ford's nascent 1976 campaign. Attempting to defuse the situation, he spoke to leaders in the American Jewish community, in Israel and to Simcha Dinitz, the Israeli Ambassador to Washington. Meanwhile, Ford and Kissinger had been encouraging Israel to develop fresh ideas for a settlement. Late Sunday afternoon on May 26, Fisher went to the Oval Office and spent forty-five minutes relaying the new Israeli formulations for peace to Ford and Rumsfeld.

Again, Ford expressed his displeasure with the pressure, and Fisher commiserated with him. But, Fisher said, despite the protests, he believed that the president had an opportunity to resolve the dispute.

Reading from two typewritten pages of notes, Fisher said: "I have always refrained from making detailed recommendations to you or to Dr. Kissinger on Middle East policy. It's not a useful or proper role for me to play. What I have tried to do is to make sure that the United States and Israel understand the thinking and feeling on each side; to help maintain a climate of trust; and to convey my perception of any changes in the position of the Israeli government and my assessment of the significance of those changes.

"Since we last met," Fisher continued, "I, along with others in this country and in Israel, have made it known to the Israeli leadership the belief that the Israelis must take the initiative. The failure to act is itself a decision and involves risks that may be as great, or greater, than those resulting from an affirmative proposal. There are many — particularly in Israel — who disagree with this view."

Glancing up from his notes, Fisher told Ford that he had asked Ambassador Dinitz to make it clear to Prime Minister Rabin and Foreign Minister Allon that movement on their part was crucial. Dinitz, said Fisher, raised the issue of the administration cutting off American aid. Fisher told Dinitz that this was irrelevant: aid had not been cut off, nor would it be. Remember, Fisher told Dinitz, Israel must move to keep the negotiations alive.

Ford said: "What's holding the Israelis back, Max?"

"They think Henry will take advantage of them," replied Fisher. "But that's too subjective a view — a result of all the deep emotions around the reassessment. Henry wouldn't do that."

Ford asked: "Do you think they'll show some flexibility?"

"Yes," said Fisher. "Dinitz called me back. He explained that Rabin and Allon were willing to move on an interim agreement. But only if there was some indication that Sadat was not being rigid with his demands. If Rabin and Allon had some proof that Egypt was being flexible, they feel they could get approval from the Cabinet. If they went ahead now with a Cabinet vote, they'd lose politically."

Dinitz, said Fisher, informed him that Israel might well evacuate the Mitla and Gidi passes in the Sinai if they could secure a lengthy agreement with Egypt; a commitment from Sadat not to use force to settle their differences; a buffer zone; and manned, early-warning surveillance stations.

"There is a lot of face-saving going on here," Fisher told Ford. "It is clear to me that these comments — although carefully thought through and authorized — are only a sign of the developing attitude [in Israel] and should not be taken as an intention on their part to act, at this time, on an isolated set of proposals. My feeling is that they would go to great lengths to get an agreement with Egypt on the non-use of force."

The last topic on Fisher's agenda was the proposed

Geneva peace conference. Fisher relayed the prime minister's message to Ford, saying that if the United States felt that Geneva was in the best interests of peace, then Israel was willing to sit at the table with America as a partner. In sum, Rabin's rejoinder was geopolitical eyewash — he knew that the United States would never invite the Soviet Union to assume a more influential posture in the Middle East. That Ford kept publicly and privately alluding to the conference — and would raise the possibility again with Rabin in June — was more demonstrative of the president's exasperation with the stalled peace process, and its personal political ramifications, than with any earnest U.S. game plan.

Fisher departed the Oval Office confident that there was enough room in the two positions for the president to jump-start negotiations.

*　　*　　*

At the beginning of June, Ford spoke with Sadat in Salzburg, Austria. Ford recalled that Sadat said Egypt was "willing to go as far as [the United States thinks] we should go [to achieve peace]." A buffer zone in the Sinai was discussed. Ten days later, Ford spoke to Rabin in Washington. According to the president, Rabin "seemed intrigued" about the notion of a buffer zone. The prime minister also agreed to a deeper Israeli withdrawal in the Sinai, but it was not deep enough to suit Sadat, who wanted Israel out of the passes.

On June 13, when Fisher conferred with Kissinger and Ford in the Oval Office, the president told him: "The Israelis could do more for peace. They have to leave the passes. Otherwise, we'll have to develop a comprehensive plan for Geneva. I'm disappointed with the withdrawal lines Rabin proposed."

Kissinger said: "Time is running out. If they would move on this, then there would be no problem of economic and military aid." The secretary of state added that Rabin's refusal to move out of the passes was based on political necessities — not military realities.

Fisher didn't even bother to address the prospect of

Geneva. He told the president and secretary that he would speak to Prime Minister Rabin and Foreign Minister Allon.

In Israel, Fisher spoke with Rabin and Allon. They were, Fisher says, "troubled by the president's reaction." Fisher gave them his assessment of their options: they could lose this opportunity for peace and deplete their good will at the White House; they could go to Geneva, which would lead nowhere and engender more bad feeling; or they could leave the passes and, with a sizable military-assistance package from the United States, Israel would have the weaponry to ensure that Sadat kept his promises.

The prime minister said that he needed time. Fisher thought that the secretary of state had been right; Rabin's problem was political. Upon his return from Israel, Fisher flew to Washington for a meeting with Kissinger at the State Department.

"Henry," Fisher said, "just give them a little while to formulate another position. They'll come around."

"I hope so," Kissinger replied. "We have one more shot at negotiations."

On a July trip to West Germany, Kissinger huddled secretly with Rabin. They consented to the Sinai intelligence-gathering stations. Soon after, Sadat relented to three annual renewals of the mandate for the U.N. peacekeeping force. However, the depth of the Israeli withdrawal from the passes remained an issue.

On August 18, shortly before Kissinger resumed his shuttle diplomacy in the Middle East, Fisher led a delegation of American Jewish leaders to Washington to talk with the secretary of state.

Fisher began the meeting by telling the leaders that the unrest in the Jewish community and the community's lack of understanding of what Ford and Kissinger were trying to accomplish was interfering with the diplomatic process. Fisher then turned the meeting over for questions.

Rabbi Israel Miller, chairman of the Presidents Conference, asked Kissinger why so much pressure was being put on Israel, saying that some pressure should be applied to the

Egyptians. Kissinger skirted the question by responding that in the negotiations Israel had been presented with several alternatives. Admittedly, said Kissinger, there were grave risks if Israel opted for an interim settlement, but on balance it would be better for them to have one. During further questioning, Kissinger affirmed that even if no interim agreement was signed, the United States was committed to furnishing Israel with military aid to maintain the regional balance of power. Yet, he said, it would be far better for everyone if an agreement could be reached.

Members of the delegation repeatedly raised the subject of pressure. Many in the group felt that the administration did not fully appreciate the internal political squabbling faced by Rabin — inherent in every democracy, particularly when the security of a nation was at stake. Kissinger said that he understood Rabin's problem, but that he thought the prime minister could overcome it. What, Kissinger was asked, would happen if the Egyptians broke this agreement? The secretary of state replied that Israel would have the full backing of the United States if such circumstances arose.

The point, though, that Kissinger wanted to accentuate was that an American presence in the Sinai — so crucial to closing the deal between Egypt and Israel — would require congressional approval. The administration hoped that the leaders of the American Jewish community would see fit to advocate for this action.

In his notes on the meeting, Fisher wrote: "I felt that almost everybody came out feeling reassured. We wished [the secretary] well on his trip."

Nine days later, when Fisher returned to Washington to talk with Ford, most of the details of Sinai II had been thrashed out by Kissinger with the Egyptians and Israelis. Israel would withdraw from the Abu Rhodeis oil fields and the Gidi and Mitla passes. Buffer zones, U.N. forces and a U.S. civilian presence to supervise the intelligence-gathering stations were also included. Egypt and Israel agreed not to use force to work out their differences, and the Egyptians publicly stated that the Israelis would be permitted to ship and to receive non-military cargo through the Suez Canal.

The Ford administration committed to a $2-billion aid package for Israel and agreed to consider Israeli requests for F-16 jets and missiles with conventional warheads. Furthermore, the administration pledged to confer regularly with the Israelis on their future economic and military needs and to ask Congress for annual aid. Moreover, the administration promised to remunerate Israel for the oil lost by relinquishing Abu Rhodeis, and to alleviate any shortfalls in the country's normal consumption.

At his August 27 meeting with Ford, Fisher later wrote that he "and the president went into the matter of the Mideast settlement very thoroughly." Fisher told Ford that he thought that the administration should meet with Jewish community leaders immediately upon initialing the accord, so that the White House could have their full support. After all, reaction to the disengagement in the United States and Israel would be laced with the anger and distrust that had infiltrated the relationship between Washington and Jerusalem as the reassessment wore on. Ford agreed that a meeting with Jewish leaders would be beneficial. Then Ford said that the American presence in the Sinai must be wholeheartedly endorsed by Congress so as to avoid a replay of the muddled consensus that led to U.S. involvement in Southeast Asia. Ford commented that Fisher could be helpful on this point by speaking to Republican leaders.

Their conversation shifted to politics. Fisher said that he was discouraged with the Republican financial campaign: they had only raised $600,000. He observed that the program appeared to be out of synch and something should be done to align it. Fisher suggested that a more formal approach be implemented. The president said that he would look into it.

Finally, they spoke about the economy. Fisher said that the tight-money policy of Arthur Burns, chairman of the Federal Reserve Board, was having a deleterious effect on the stock market, and a poor psychological impact on the business world and the public. Ford said that he would be talking to Dr. Burns, admitting that he knew if economic conditions didn't improve well before November 1976, "no Republican would be elected president."

Although Fisher later noted that his meeting with Ford had been "thoroughly satisfactory," he left the Oval Office feeling dispirited. He didn't have the heart to tell his friend that it would take far more than a revived economy for him to win the White House. Nearly a year ago, on September 8, 1974, Ford had granted Nixon an unconditional pardon for any federal crimes he may have committed as president. Fisher thought that Ford had done the proper thing — the only thing — to get the country past its obsession with Watergate. Now, though, as Fisher prepared for the 1976 campaign, he recognized that the electorate had not forgiven the Republicans for the scandal, and because of the pardon, Ford was, at best, a long shot.

*　　*　　*

The signing of the second Egyptian-Israeli disengagement was announced on September 1. Israeli right-wing critics declared the accord a failure since it did not produce direct negotiations or force Egypt to promise a policy of nonbelligerency toward Israel. Sinai II also had its critics in the United States. In the American Jewish community, much of the criticism was due to a lingering resentment of the administration for undertaking the reassessment. Then, too, with Vietnam still playing on the nightly news, Congress was leery of ordering American observers to the Middle East, and so the Sinai agreement began to undergo congressional scrutiny and debate.

On September 1, Fisher was in Chicago on business, but he found time to trumpet the administration's successful handling of the negotiations. He told the *Chicago Daily News* "that the American Jewish community will be overwhelmingly behind the agreement and the same sentiment will be found in the non-Jewish community." When asked about the controversy over stationing 200 U.S. observers in the Sinai, Fisher replied that this "should not be compared with the slide-into-Vietnam argument. In Vietnam, we sent in U.S. observers on the side of the South Vietnamese to help them fight a war. Here we are sending in observers for both sides to help them keep the peace. This shows a desire on the part of Egypt [for] peace. [Both countries] want the Americans there."

Fisher phoned Rabin in Tel Aviv to congratulate him. Then he called Ford at Camp David. The president thanked Fisher for his help. They toasted the agreement.

Fisher said: "The only one I haven't spoken to is Sadat."

The president laughed, and they arranged to meet the following week.

A week later, in a move to boost support for the disengagement, Fisher brought a delegation of thirty-three American Jewish leaders to talk with Ford and Kissinger in the Cabinet Room of the White House. During the talk, Ford said that "a large supporting majority in Congress" for placing technicians in the advance-warning stations between the new Israeli and Egyptian lines in the Sinai "would help the atmosphere for peace." Rabbi Israel Miller said that Ford and Kissinger convinced the group to support the agreement.

Following one month of debate, Congress approved the agreements. Yet criticism continued. In fact, the breadth of Sinai II's achievement can be discerned in the voice of its most vocal critic, President Hafez el-Assad of Syria. Assad protested that the accords amounted to a separate peace between Egypt and Israel.

Chapter 16

LESSONS LEARNED

THE ADMINISTRATION'S TRIUMPH in the Middle East did not translate into broad-based political support for Ford. Polls indicated that 40 percent of Republicans and 27 percent of independents preferred former Governor Ronald Reagan. The Harris Survey predicted that even if Ford won the nomination, he would lose the election to Hubert Humphrey by a margin of 52 to 41.

Fisher, however, had more parochial concerns. He was worried about the President Ford Committee's inability to raise money; the PFC had raised less than 10 percent of its projected $10-million goal. In Ford and Fisher's home state of Michigan, things were so bad that the local GOP feared that the economically depressed state might go Democratic in 1976. So on September 20, the state GOP held a weekend leadership conference on Mackinac Island. According to the *Detroit Free Press*, Fisher "made a rare public appearance before the Republican State Committee to promote the sale of tickets for an October 10 fund-raiser in Detroit to be attended by President Ford." The goal, said Fisher, was $500,000. Although the proceeds were earmarked for Governor William G. Milliken's re-election campaign, Fisher thought that a strong showing would stimulate support for the president.

At the October dinner in Detroit's Cobo Hall, Ford spoke to an enthusiastic audience of 4,000, each paying $50 a ticket. But Fisher discovered that raising funds for the 1976 campaign was harder than in earlier years, and it was not only because of the president's lagging popularity or the disorganization at the PFC. A new election law now restricted contributors to giving $1,000 to a presidential candidate. Political

Action Committees (PACs) were not allowed to donate more than $5,000.

Five days after Ford appeared in Detroit, Fisher went to Washington and appealed to the president to straighten out his campaign. As a result, the president appointed Robert A. Mosbacher Sr., a forty-eight-year-old Texas oil man, as head fund-raiser for the PFC. Fisher was delighted. He had been friendly with the Mosbacher family since the 1940s. Mosbacher, who, in the spring of 1990 was serving as secretary of commerce in the Bush administration, says that he marveled at Fisher's network of people who were willing to raise money.

"We wouldn't have done as well without Max," says Mosbacher. "He had so much experience at this sort of thing, and he knew everyone."

As the campaign got on track, problems flared again between Washington and Jerusalem. In October 1975, Sadat had become the first Egyptian leader to visit the United States, making an eloquent speech before Congress. The administration was leaning toward cutting an arms deal with Egypt, which concerned many in Congress and, of course, the Israelis. Then, too, the United States was about to shift the start of its fiscal year from July to October. Israel hoped to receive $500 million of transitional aid, which Kissinger had promised. However, with Ford's assent, the Office of Management and Budget removed these funds from the $4.5 billion aid request.

In mid-December, Fisher, upon returning from a trip to Israel, spoke to Scowcroft and Ford in the Oval Office for an hour and fifteen minutes. Fisher says that he gave the national security adviser and the president "my best assessment of the situation," which was essentially that Israel was starting to demonstrate an inclination to be more accommodating in the interest of peace. Fisher said that he thought he had "a calming effect" on Rabin. But he did tell the prime minister that continuing to build settlements on the West Bank would become troublesome in the not-too-distant future.

Next, the three men discussed the aid request. Fisher said that Rabin badly needed the military credits for payments on hardware. Fisher recommended that the president try to reach some compromise — maybe $250 million or $275 million. First, Fisher said, the aid would bolster Rabin's political posture, which would make him feel more secure and therefore more willing to climb out on a limb for peace. Secondly, to deny the aid put Kissinger in "an untenable position," since he had promised it to Rabin.

Lastly, there was the president's political status to consider. Fisher said that the perception of Ford in the American Jewish community — albeit incorrect — was that the president was anti-Israel. This was, said Fisher, a potentially damaging situation; Ford would need the community in his corner to win in November. Fisher said that if Scoop Jackson ran against Ford, then the senator would do well with Jewish voters. But if James E. Carter Jr. became the candidate, then Ford would have a tremendous opportunity because the Jewish community was not drawn to him. Fisher suggested that Ford address some Jewish organizations — the American Jewish Committee, for example, which was holding its annual dinner in Washington on May 13. An appearance before such a crowd, Fisher said, would provide the president with a chance to clarify his position on Israel and give him a robust start on his campaign.

Meanwhile, Ford was winning in the primaries. In February, he beat Reagan in New Hampshire and Florida. Then he won in Massachusetts and Vermont. In March, he captured 59 percent of the Republican vote in Illinois (where Reagan was born). At this juncture, the president had 166 delegates of the 1,130 needed to secure the nomination; Reagan had 54. Ford recalled in his memoirs that "both camps expected [Reagan] to quit."

Although optimistic about being nominated at the August convention in Kansas City, Ford abruptly found himself under fire from Congress and the American Jewish community for agreeing to sell Egypt six C-130 Hercules transport jets. Senator Henry Jackson, considered a leading contender for the Democratic presidential nomination, made the transport sale a focal point of his campaign, calling it "cynical and dangerous," and saying that it could "only increase the chance of war in the Middle East." The administration estimated that if the C-130s went to an up-and-down roll-call vote in Congress at the moment, the sale might easily be defeated.

On March 9, the president, hoping to skirt a blowup on the order of the reassessment, met with Fisher, Scowcroft and Richard Cheney, whom Ford had selected as his chief of staff when he sent Rumsfeld to replace James Schlesinger as secretary of defense.

Fisher started by saying that it appeared to the Jewish community — and perhaps more than half of Congress — as though Ford were forging a new relationship with the Arab world at the expense of Israel. Arming Egypt was a dangerous game.

"All we have in mind," Ford replied, "is trying to keep Sadat in power — to avoid making him the victim of a revolution — by showing his people that he is getting help from America. We also want to prevent the Russians from becoming his ally again."

"The best method," Fisher said, "for controlling the situation in the Jewish community, would be to bring some Jewish leaders to the White House to meet with you as soon as possible."

The president consented. Fisher said that he would talk to the Israeli ambassador, Simcha Dinitz, to see if Dinitz could help the administration muster some support. Ford made it clear to Fisher that he was adamant about selling Sadat the C-130s, and he would not be deterred by political repercussions.

Fisher nodded, later jotting down a note that said "if [the sale] doesn't go through, Israel will lose a very good friend."

The question of transitional aid was raised. The Democratic-controlled Congress seemed inclined to grant the request. However, Fisher said, he had heard that Congressman Otto E. Passman, a Democrat from Louisiana, who was chair-

man of the House Appropriations Subcommittee on Foreign
Operations, was passing a message around the Capitol that he
had received a nod from Ford not to do much about the
increased funds.

"Passman," said Ford, "is a foxy old guy, and he's probably using this strategy to keep within his budget."

Scowcroft said that $500 million was too much to add to
the budget. Fisher replied that Israel was going to receive the
money from Congress anyway, and the administration would
wind up "with egg all over its face" and get no political credit
for the approval of the package.

Ford scheduled a meeting with Jewish leaders for March
17. During the week prior to the conference, the wrangling
over the sale increased. Prime Minister Rabin was quoted as
telling the Knesset that Israel was locked in a "bitter argument" with the United States. Rabin explained that he was
less concerned over the particular items to be sold to Egypt
than over the creation of an "arms supply precedent."

Fisher thought that Rabin was misreading the president.
More important, America had its own interests to pursue,
namely making a friend of Sadat. The Egyptian leader was in
the process of severing his relationship with the Soviets,
demanding that they withdraw their ships and aircraft from
his country. The Kremlin responded by canceling deliveries of
spare parts to Egypt, refusing to reschedule debts and collab-
orating with Libya and Syria to undermine Sadat's power.
Ford was eager to remove Egypt from the Soviet sphere of
influence and felt that Sadat was in dire need of a show of
approbation from the United States.

Fisher phoned Scowcroft to discuss the situation. The
NSC adviser mentioned that he had been up front with the
Israeli ambassador, informing Dinitz that the president would
be quite displeased if Israel tried to mobilize opposition to the
sale of jets to Egypt. Then Fisher called Dinitz. He told the
ambassador that Ford was going to sell Egypt the C-130s —
nothing would stop him. Thus Israel would be well advised to
go along with it, and would the ambassador please pass this
message along to Rabin? Dinitz said that he would talk to the

prime minister, saying that he did not really feel that the sale of the transports was "an important enough issue to make a fuss about."

On March 17, thirteen Jewish leaders filed into the Cabinet Room. Ford sat at the head of the table, flanked by Kissinger and Scowcroft. The president opened by stating that he was pledged to the security and integrity of Israel. Yet forcing the Soviets out of Egypt was in the best interests of the entire free world. Kissinger said that Egypt could not be rearmed by America because it would take five to ten years, and the United States was simply extending symbolic aid to the Egyptians, not inaugurating a long-term commitment to sell them arms.

Ford listened as questions were fired at him. In his answers, he accentuated that his administration would do nothing to upset Israel's military advantage. Fisher, attempting to show that Ford was becoming more sympathetic toward approving transitional aid for Israel, asked the president if he were still set on vetoing the appropriation. Ford said the matter was now an open subject. He would have to wait and see. According to Fisher's notes, "the meeting lasted an hour and a half — far too long — and the kind of rough questioning [of the president] was unnecessary. [But] all in all, the president came off well — as a man who was in command of the situation and who would not mislead you."

As the debate over the C-130 sale cooled, the president sustained another blow. On March 23, Reagan, defying the pollsters, defeated Ford in the North Carolina primary, winning 52 percent of the vote and twenty-eight of the state's fifty-four delegates. Ford was shocked. It was, as he recorded in *A Time to Heal*, "only the third time in U.S. history that a challenger had defeated an incumbent president in a primary."

While Ford turned his attention to the upcoming New York and Wisconsin primaries, the relationship between Israel and America underwent another jolt. Delivering a speech before the United Nations Security Council, America's newly appointed U.N. ambassador, William Scranton, criticized Israel's policies in East Jerusalem and the West

Bank. Scranton stated that "unilateral measures" taken by Israel would not "prejudge the final and permanent status of Jerusalem" which would be "determined only through the instruments and process of negotiation, agreement and accommodation." Declaring that the "substantial resettlement of the Israeli civilian population in occupied territories, including East Jerusalem, was 'illegal,' " Scranton announced that "the presence of these settlements is seen by my government as an obstacle to the success of the negotiations for a just and final peace between Israel and its neighbors."

Fisher received dozens of calls from Jewish leaders, asking him why the administration would allow Scranton to say such things. Was Ford planning to cut a deal with Yasser Arafat and the PLO? Fisher had been among those who recommended Scranton for his post at the United Nations, believing that he had "a warm attitude to the Jewish community and to Israel." He phoned Scranton in New York and inquired about the wording of the statement. The ambassador told Fisher that he shouldn't worry; no one was going to let Israel down. Scranton explained that he was new to his job, and just learning that one could hardly utter a few words without them being misinterpreted. He never meant that the United States should negotiate with the PLO.

Fisher told Jewish community leaders that Scranton was a good man who had made a mistake. Still, the controversy about Scranton's remarks persisted. Arriving in Israel for meetings with the Jewish Agency Board of Governors, Fisher was confronted by reporters — notably from *The Jerusalem Post* and *Davar* — who grilled him on the rocky relationship between Israel and the Ford administration.

Fisher responded with an uncharacteristic display of pique. The pressures of an election year, the series of battles between the White House and the Jewish community, his circling from Detroit to New York to Washington and to Jerusalem, had taken their toll. When asked why the administration was reneging on its promise to approve transitional aid for Israel, Fisher retorted: "If a man wants to give you $4 billion instead of $4.5 billion is he an enemy or an ally?" Fisher then rebuked Israel and American Jewry for "overreacting" to the aid issue, to the Scranton speech, to the sale of six planes to Egypt, and in general to the "strains," which the Israeli press reports "without foundation" almost every other week.

"Is four billion dollars in aid over two years a sign of 'strain'?" Fisher asked reporters. "People here seem to forget about the $4 billion and talk only about the other half-a-billion. You have to understand [the president's] problems. He has vetoed thirty-nine bills for federal spending at home. He's stopped aid to the cities. People ask him 'Why send funds overseas when there are these problems at home?'"

In reference to the Scranton speech, Fisher was pressed for his view of the dispute over the West Bank, always a controversial subject in Israel. For someone in Fisher's position, answering such a question in Israeli newspapers was guaranteed to win him as many friends as enemies. Fisher didn't hedge. He said: "I see the Palestinian problem as the gut issue of the [Arab-Israeli] conflict." He acknowledged that his stance was frowned upon by government leaders, but said that "he does not feel restricted by [their opinions]." Fisher said that he had noticed "a definite shift in the attitude of Israeli intellectuals toward the Palestinian problem," but he "had not seen this reflected in government circles."

Fisher was then asked for his opinion of Henry Kissinger. In the course of negotiating the disengagements, the secretary of state had been vilified by Israel's right wing, particularly by the *Gush Emunim* (Guardians of the Faith), a movement of religious ultranationalists, who referred to Kissinger as "Jew-boy," and "the husband of a Gentile woman." In the spring of 1975, Kissinger came under renewed attack in Israel with the publication of Matti Golan's book, *The Secret Conversations of Henry Kissinger*. Golan, a diplomatic correspondent and columnist for the Israeli newspaper *Haaretz*, maintained that during the Yom Kippur War, Kissinger had blocked the resupply shipments to Israeli out of "strict political calculation." For Kissinger, wrote Golan, the airlift ran the risk of damaging America's "still hoped-for cooperation with Moscow and future relations with the Arab countries."

Fisher responded to reporters by stating that Kissinger was the only secretary of state who had generated momentum toward peace — the others had failed. "If he weren't Jewish," said Fisher, "he wouldn't be getting that kind of coarse criticism from Jewish leaders. The Jews had no impact at all on [Secretaries of State John Foster] Dulles or [Dean] Rusk. The [Jewish community] couldn't even get in to see them."

Dismissing the allegations that Kissinger deliberately delayed the airlift to Israel during the Yom Kippur War, Fisher said: "I was as involved in that episode as anyone — certainly more so than [Matti Golan]. One day I'll publish my version. You have to look at actions, results. Nixon and Kissinger delivered the goods, in time."

The reporter from *The Jerusalem Post* had a parting shot for Fisher. Are the Republicans, Fisher was asked, good for Israel? Perhaps the Democrats would be more friendly.

"Look at the record," Fisher snapped, "and consider who was more supportive of Israel — Kennedy and Johnson, or Nixon and Ford."

Five days later, when Fisher landed in Detroit, he discovered that his interviews had been picked up by papers across the country. He also discovered that many American Jewish leaders disagreed with him. On April 12, *The Boston Globe* reported that "Jewish leaders, who worked for Richard Nixon's re-election in 1972, believe President Ford, if nominated, will not attract more than a small percentage of Jewish votes" in the election. Their belief was based on "the growing apprehension among Jews about the Ford-Kissinger policy toward Israel." The article quoted, among others, Rita Hauser, a New York attorney and member of the Committee for the Re-Election of the President in 1972. Hauser said: "Mr. Ford will have a difficult time getting the Jewish vote this year." Bertram H. Gold, executive director of the American Jewish Committee, added that "at this rate, any Democratic candidate will get 85 percent of the Jewish vote." And former Nixon supporter Norman Podhoretz, editor of *Commentary* magazine, declared that the Republicans "certainly seem to have turned their backs on the Jewish vote."

The problem, says Fisher, was not limited to the administration's relationship to Israel. The new laws restricting campaign contributions made it impossible to fund the ethnic outreach programs that were so productive for Nixon in 1972.

Fisher broached several political uncertainties with Ford on the afternoon of April 20 when they spoke in the Oval Office.

They also discussed Fisher's trip to Israel. Ford told him that he thought a portion of the transitional aid could be arranged. Fisher replied that such a package would certainly help quiet the critics in Israel, Congress and the American Jewish community. Ford asked about the turmoil on the West Bank, and whether or not Israel would ever consent to trading more land for more peace. Fisher said that he didn't know, but the civil war in Lebanon did little to buttress Israel's feeling of security. Right before their talk ended, Ford said that he was going to step up his campaign efforts in the Jewish community; he was taking Fisher's suggestion and was scheduled to address the annual meeting of the American Jewish Committee at the Washington Hilton.

The president did speak to the AJC on May 13, pledging that the United States would "remain the ultimate guarantor of Israel's freedom." But by then, Ford was fighting for his life in the primaries.

Back in April, after Reagan defeated him in North Carolina, Ford fleetingly regained his political equilibrium when Reagan conceded the 199 delegates in New York and Wisconsin in order to concentrate on preparing a thirty-minute, nationally televised fund-raising appeal. Accordingly, on April 6, Ford led in delegates by a 3-to-1 margin. Reagan's speech, though, was stunningly successful. He raised $1.5 million, and lambasted the administration for, among other things, its feeble foreign policy. On April 27, Reagan won in Texas. Next, he swept through Alabama, Georgia, Indiana and Nebraska. Ford was victorious in West Virginia, Maryland and his home state of Michigan. Yet, on May 18, Reagan had 528 delegates to Ford's 479. The president stepped up his campaigning. By mid-June, he had recaptured the lead — 992 delegates to Reagan's 886.

Fisher, trying to persuade leaders of the American Jewish community to campaign for Ford, brought a thirty-member delegation to talk with the president on June 24. Two-thirds of those who attended were Democrats and erstwhile supporters of Senator Henry Jackson's unsuccessful bid for the Democratic presidential nomination. At 5 p.m., the group gathered in the Roosevelt Room. The president spoke generally about the economy and foreign affairs. Questions focused on Israel and Soviet Jewry. Ford was especially emphatic on the Middle East, stating that the security of Israel was both a moral commitment and a "linchpin of American foreign policy." Regarding the Russian Jews, Ford said that he would do everything possible to encourage the Kremlin to permit free emigration.

Although the president had previously covered similar ground with Jewish leaders, Fisher thought that Ford was unusually persuasive because the animosity of the reassessment had dissipated and he felt free to express the true range of his sympathy for Israel. The session lasted for nearly two hours instead of the scheduled forty-five minutes. The delegation, Fisher thought, left the Roosevelt Room solidly behind the president; Ford's performance, Fisher thought, had been "extraordinary." Two days later, Fisher received some more good news. The White House and Congress had reached a compromise on transitional aid for Israel — $275 million.

On July 2, Fisher was back in Washington talking with the president and secretary of state. With the reassessment finished, the atmosphere surrounding their conversation was calmer. Kissinger was kidding Fisher, asking him why he never called anymore. But the main topic of their talk was anything but lighthearted.

On June 27, Air France Flight 139 had departed from Tel Aviv with over 250 passengers. En route to Paris, two members of the Popular Front for the Liberation of Palestine (PFLP) and two West German "urban guerrillas" commandeered the airbus, forcing the pilot to land in Entebbe, Uganda, a country ruled by a sworn enemy of Israel, Idi Amin. The hijackers released all passengers, except for the Israelis and Jews. Then they demanded that the government of Israel free 40 convicted terrorists in exchange for the more than 100 remaining hostages.

Ford told Fisher that "the United States was doing everything to save the people who were hijacked," but he wanted him to impress upon Prime Minister Rabin that the Israelis should not retaliate against the Palestine Liberation Organization for the hijacking. (The PFLP was formed by Marxist physician George Habash, a Christian Palestinian, who is a rival of Arafat within the PLO.) The president said that he did not want Israeli retribution to unite the Arabs. Kissinger took a different tack. He said that if Israel backed down it wouldn't help their cause. But, the secretary added, this was not for him to decide. Kissinger also said that the civil war in Lebanon was dividing the Arab world and sapping the PLO's strength, which in the long run might bring about a measure of peace. Ford asked that Fisher raise one final point with Rabin — that he felt "quite touchy" about the settlements on the West Bank, because, Ford said, in the future they could undermine the Israeli position and create several complications. Fisher replied that a large portion of the leadership in the American Jewish community also had reservations about the settlements and that they were endeavoring to get this message across to Rabin and his Cabinet.

Following his talk with the president and secretary of state, Fisher met with Dick Cheney to mull over the campaign reorganization. Fisher said that he hoped the PFC would "get somebody in there who made sense." Cheney replied that they were interviewing two or three candidates. (James A. Baker III would eventually be chosen to direct Ford's campaign.) Fisher suggested that Ford should establish an independent political structure, of which Fisher would be a member, so that he could bring in leaders from the American Jewish community, not as a Jewish group, but as part of Citizens for President Ford. Cheney said that Fisher should get it organized.

On July 3, the hostages were rescued by Israeli commandos in a night raid on Uganda. On July 15 — his sixty-eighth birthday, Fisher was vacationing in Greece, and by the time he returned to Detroit toward the end of July, the Democrats had nominated Jimmy Carter for the presidency and Senator Walter F. Mondale of Minnesota for vice president.

In mid-August, Fisher attended the Republican National Convention as a delegate from Michigan. As he had done in 1972, Fisher saw to it that one evening a distinguished American Jewish leader (this time it was Rabbi Israel Miller) offered a benediction at the convention.

The closeness of the race between Ford and Reagan notwithstanding, Fisher told a reporter from *The Jerusalem Post* that the president would win the nomination on the first ballot. The initial vote was neck and neck, and Ford defeated Reagan — 1,187 to 1,070. Senator Robert Dole of Kansas was chosen for the vice- presidential spot on the ticket. Fisher was pleased that the convention hadn't been torn apart by internecine bickering.

Ford's first-ballot win, however, was a moot point as the campaign got under way. The president was trailing Carter in the polls by a huge margin. Gallup judged Carter's lead to be 56 to 33; Harris estimated it at 61 to 32. Ford's own pollster was projecting that the president could lose the election by 9,490,000 votes. There were seventy-three days until November 2, and, as Ford wrote in *A Time to Heal*, all he had to do to win "was convert 130,000 Carter supporters every day."

Unlike 1968 and 1972, raising money for the general election was not Fisher's chief concern. The bulk of the financing would come from public funds; Ford and Carter each received $21.8 million. Yet, since the polls were predicting the lowest voter turnout in a half-century, the Jewish vote was a prime target of the candidates, especially in the Northeast with its large representation in the Electoral College. Fisher set his sights on persuading Jewish leadership to back Ford. He arranged for a strategy session at the Statler-Hilton Hotel in Washington for 150 influential Jewish supporters of the president. The meeting took place on September 20, with presentations by Chief of Staff Cheney and Ford's campaign chairman, James Baker III.

After the session, a select leadership group went to the White House to meet with the president. Beforehand, Fisher met with Ford in the Oval Office to discuss the president's planned remarks. Then they walked to the East Room. For twenty minutes, the president mingled with the guests. Finally, everyone was seated. Fisher introduced Ford, and the president launched into his speech. He concentrated on the U.S.-Israeli relationship, saying that America "must maintain our own freedom and that of our friends. I can tell you that when we number our friends, nowhere do we find a nation where our relations are closer or more cordial than with Israel. I intend to keep them that way."

Ford, says Fisher, "is an honest, straightforward man," and the best moments in the East Room were when he simply stated how he would deal with the anxieties of the community. The president said there will be no imposed peace agreements on the Middle East and no one-sided concessions. There would be substantial military and economic assistance to Israel, and strong action in support of the Israelis should the United Nations make any more "absurd attempts" to defame Israel's people or to deprive the country of its rights. In addition, Ford said, the United States was committed to combat international terrorism and to freedom for Soviet Jews.

Fisher told *The Jerusalem Post* that he thought Ford's speech would "turn the tide in convincing many of the still undecided Jewish leaders in coming out publicly on the president's behalf."

To zero in on the wider Jewish community, Fisher set up a press conference at the White House with Ford taking questions from journalists of the American Jewish Press Association. The AJPA represented sixty-five Jewish community newspapers, with a combined circulation of 800,000 in the United States and Canada. Afterward, Robert A. Cohn, president of the organization, wrote Fisher: "As I have indicated to you in the past, your assistance in arranging this news conference reflects your continued awareness of the importance of direct communication to the American Jewish community through its ethnic and religious media."

It also reflected Fisher's understanding that Jews in the United States, excluded from the WASP power structure for so long, needed to feel that a candidate was not blind to their needs in order to vote for him. The AJPA's readership, consisting of hundreds of thousands of Jews *outside* the organized Jewish community, was the perfect forum for the president to reach out to this constituency.

Ford trailed Carter throughout the campaign. Because of the Nixon pardon, the president had been operating under a handicap, but in the fall he suffered two other significant setbacks. The president was clinging to a three-percentage-point lead over Carter in California, and desperately wanted Reagan to campaign for him there as well as in the conservative Deep South. In early October, he made a campaign swing through California. In *A Time to Heal*, Ford recalled that Reagan's speech to a GOP dinner "was disappointing," and his comments about the president "were noticeably lukewarm." Worst of all, wrote Ford, "during the rest of the campaign he refused to work directly for my election."

Secondly, the president made a serious slip in one of his televised debates with Carter, stating: "There is no Soviet domination of Eastern Europe." Carter was quick to capitalize, remarking: "I would like to see Mr. Ford convince the Polish-Americans and the Czech-Americans and the Hungarian-Americans in this country that those countries don't live under the domination and supervision of the Soviet Union."

But Ford was an experienced campaigner. He kept at it, arguing that he did, unlike Carter, have a record to judge, and Americans should cast their ballot based on his record. He spoke of his curb on federal spending, which appeared to touch voters around the country. On November 1, the day prior to the election, the Gallup Poll showed the president pulling ahead of Carter 47 to 46.

Along with Bob Mosbacher and other members of the Ford campaign team, Fisher waited for the election results in a Washington hotel. (Neither he nor Mosbacher can recollect which one.) Everything had been arranged for a victory party. The early returns showed Carter, as anticipated, sweeping the Deep South. But the race was tight. Fisher believed that he had helped to make some inroads for Ford in the Jewish community. He felt that the president's share of the Jewish vote would range between 35 and 40 percent, and that percentage would pay off later in the evening. For a while, Fisher's belief seemed accurate. By midnight, Ford clung to a narrow lead in New York. But at one-twenty, after the votes from New York City rolled in, the networks were declaring Carter the winner in New York. The president was also losing in Pennsylvania and Texas. Although Ford did not phone Carter to concede the election until late Wednesday morning, at approximately 2 a.m. Fisher said to Mosbacher: "It's over."

Fisher describes the realization that Ford had lost "as the most disappointing moment in my life." It would be small consolation that Lou Harris would estimate that Ford had won 45 percent of the Jewish vote. (CBS claimed it was 32 percent; Fisher says it was probably closer to 40.) Nor did it matter that shortly after the election, Ronald I. Rubin, writing in *New York* magazine, observed that the 1976 election proved that for Jews "it's no longer *trayf* [unkosher] to vote Republican." Of one thing Fisher was certain: from January 1977 until January 1981, he would not be participating in any Oval Office conversations with the president.

*   *   *

One afternoon, in the late winter of 1975, Marjorie Fisher walked into David Webb jewelers in Palm Beach and purchased a pair of diamond earrings. The saleswoman, teasing Marjorie, asked: "Does Mr. Fisher have a new mistress?"

"No," Marjorie replied. "Mr. Fisher has a new stock."

The new stock was United Brands Co. For many years, Fisher had owned 73,000 shares of the United Fruit Company, the venerable Boston banana firm. But in 1970, Eli M. Black, a brilliant forty-eight-year-old conglomerateur, merged his AMK Incorporated with the United Fruit Company and renamed it United Brands Co. Aside from producing and marketing bananas under the Chiquita, Fyffes and Amigo names, the $2 billion multinational United Brands operated John Morrell & Co., the fourth largest meat packer in the United States; A&W International, a fast-food restaurant chain; Inter-Harvest, a producer of fresh vegetables; and J. Hungerford Smith, a supplier of ice-cream toppings and flavoring.

According to *The Wall Street Journal*, Black, an ordained rabbi and active philanthropist, had "tried to combine his business with [his] social conscience." Black negotiated personally on behalf of the company's lettuce subsidiary with Cesar Chavez's United Farm Workers Union, becoming the first and only major lettuce grower to sign with the union. He was also dedicated to eradicating the historical perception of United Fruit as a Yankee exploiter. In Central America, the corporation provided free housing and electricity to its employees, and its agricultural workers earned approximately six times the wages that other companies paid. In 1972, *The Boston Globe* opined that United Brands "may well be the most socially conscious American company in the hemisphere."

In 1974, United Brands sustained several blows. In August, the governments of Panama, Costa Rica and Honduras instituted banana taxes to offset the higher fuel costs caused by the Arab oil embargo. During September, Hurricane Fifi ripped through Central America, causing $20 million in damage to United Brands' crops and facilities. Reeling from this loss and high cattle-feed costs in its John Morrell division, United Brands' losses in 1974 surpassed $43 million.

At eight o'clock in the morning on February 3, 1975, Eli Black was picked up at his New York City apartment by his chauffeur and driven to United Brands' corporate headquarters in the Pan Am Building. After entering his office on the forty-fourth floor, Black, using his briefcase, smashed a hole in a window and jumped to his death. The stress of corporate life was cited as the reason for his suicide.

With Black's death and the financial reverses, the United Brands board of directors split into warring factions. Fisher, as one of the largest stockholders in the company and with the reputation of a conciliator, was asked to join the board. On April 2, he accepted. Within a week, it became partially clearer why Eli Black, who had prided himself on his capacity to succeed in business without forfeiting his moral principles, had been so depressed. On April 8, United Brands admitted that in 1974 it had paid a $1.25-million bribe to General Oswaldo Lopez, the former president of Honduras, to lower the country's banana tax. The company also admitted that over the past five years it had paid bribes totaling $750,000 to officials of a European country (rumored to be Italy). Following the disclosure of these payoffs, United Brands faced stockholder suits, and investigations by the Securities and Exchange Commission, the U.S. attorney's office and a Senate subcommittee.

On May 12, the understandably troubled United Brands' board of directors convened in Boston. As Fisher recalled for *The Wall Street Journal*: "My long suit is bringing people together. If you have that ability and can help a bad situation, you can't turn your back. . . . [At the board meeting], I opened my mouth and both sides asked me to be acting chairman."

The national business and investment community was surprised that Fisher, who was two months away from his sixty-seventh birthday, agreed to tackle such a hopeless task. United Brands had dropped to five dollars a share, and the pending legal actions against the conglomerate promised to be an ordeal.

Looking back, Fisher explains his reasoning: "I took the chairmanship because of ego. I wanted to see if I could still run a big corporation."

Additionally, Fisher was in the process of upping his original 73,000-share stake in United Brands to over 600,000 shares, more than 5 percent of the company.

Upon filling the chairman's post, the board elected Wallace W. Booth president and chief executive officer. An experienced executive, Booth had been a senior vice president at Rockwell International Corp. for the previous two-and-a-half years.

United Brands' reputation was so tarnished that just the election of Fisher and Booth to their posts improved the value of the stock by 13 percent. In August, Fisher was officially designated chairman of the board. Soon after, Fisher, along with seventeen officers of United Brands and three partners of its accounting firm, Price Waterhouse & Co., were subpoenaed by the Securities and Exchange Commission to give sworn statements regarding the $1.25-million bribe paid to General Lopez. The SEC's suit against United Brands charged that the company had violated securities laws by failing to disclose the bribe. The commission was seeking a court order forbidding management from making false statements to its shareholders in the future.

Initially, due to the investigation, Fisher was unable to address United Brands' immediate business concerns. Instead, he sifted through paperwork and headed an investigating committee that was delving into the foreign payments. He testified before the SEC, and by January 27, 1976, the suit was settled. In New York City, U.S. District Judge Thomas Flannery signed a consent order barring the company from violating the antifraud provisions of federal securities law.

The Wall Street Journal judged the United Brands order "unusual." The decree was the first to prohibit a company from future antifraud violations in connection with foreign payoffs. It required United Brands to disclose any "unlawful payment" of corporate funds to foreign governments — a measure one SEC lawyer described as the "belt and suspenders approach," since the injunction barred such payments. Finally, the order granted the SEC permanent access to United Brands' books and records. SEC officials indicated to the press that the injunction was also designed to deter other companies from bribing foreign officials.

With the SEC ruling behind him (and Ford's campaign for the presidency finished), Fisher spent the winter of 1976-1977 checking on the far-flung operations of United Brands. He asked his friends, Seymour and Paul Milstein, to give him a hand. The Milstein brothers, partners in Manhattan-based construction and building-management firms, owned 958,000 shares of United Brands — 8.8 percent of the common stock. Seymour Milstein had joined the board of directors in April

1975 right after Fisher, and in August, he had been named its vice chairman.

For Fisher, touring the corporation's facilities reminded him of his beginnings at Aurora, stopping to talk with the rank and file, asking questions and listening to their suggestions. He and Paul Milstein flew to Sioux Falls, South Dakota, to look in at John Morrell Co. Fisher was talking to one of the managers, sampling uncooked hot dogs and attempting to convince Milstein to try one. When Milstein refused, Fisher said: "You don't have to live in a meat plant. But you are in charge of the food division." Gingerly, Milstein ate a piece of a hot dog.

Fisher devoted most of his energies to the corporate hierarchy. As was his practice at Aurora, and in his philanthropic and political endeavors, he phoned executives at all times of the day and questioned them about details of their reports. In the process, Fisher earned his share of critics — one of them telling *The Wall Street Journal*: "It's easy to tell the coach how to manage the team from the sidelines and save $100,000 on a minor issue, but [Fisher] doesn't comprehend how a professional manager manages a multinational" with company-wide systematic controls.

However, Fisher felt that "you have to pay attention to details in a business . . . where profit hinges on the weather and rapid changes in commodity prices. Sure I [called] my executives, and I [didn't] talk to them about their golf games."

By mid-January 1977, Fisher continued to be dissatisfied with the corporate environment at United Brands. He invited Seymour Milstein to Palm Beach and asked him to bring his wife, Vivian. When the Milsteins arrived, they socialized by the pool with the Fishers, talking and looking out at Lake Worth from the deck. After lunch, Fisher said to Seymour: "You and Paul have got a bigger stake in United Brands than I do. I think you ought to go back to work."

Milstein had toured the operations across the United States and in Central America, reporting his findings to Wallace Booth. So he did not quite comprehend what Fisher meant about him getting back to work. He said: "Max, what do you mean? I am working."

Fisher answered: "No, not just traveling around. You've got a big stake here. We're near the bottom, and things could get worse before they get better. This company's not being managed. Most of the people are discouraged in Boston. They get to the office late and they're gone by four or four-thirty. I think in our and the shareholders' interest — as well as the management that stayed on after Eli's suicide — you have to get more involved in the daily operations. You should replace Booth and spend your time up at headquarters in Boston."

Now, Milstein understood why Fisher had asked him to bring Vivian to Palm Beach. If Milstein accepted the proposal, then he would be spending the majority of his week in Boston. Fisher wanted Vivian to be aware of the time commitment her husband was making.

Fisher expanded on why he thought Milstein should run United Brands. He mentioned that Booth seemed more enamored of numbers than operations. This, said Fisher, not only had an adverse effect on earnings, it could be disastrous in light of the SEC ruling — if new bribes were paid out, then somebody was going to go to jail.

Though reluctant to take the job of president and CEO, Milstein says: "Max persuaded me because, when all was said and done, his logic was better than mine."

Once Milstein accepted (and Vivian agreed with her husband's decision), Fisher phoned the other directors of United Brands and told them what he had in mind. They quickly agreed. Explains Milstein: "Remember, this is 1977, and by then Max was held in very high esteem by the directors. He did a great job of organizing. He had brought harmony to the board. He had gotten rid of the directors who were looking for trouble for trouble's sake."

When he finished speaking with the other board members, Fisher said to Milstein: "Come on, let's go talk to Wally Booth."

The two men flew to Boston. Milstein remembers: "Max said to Booth, 'Wally, you're a fine gentleman. But I don't

think we're getting along. You're not happy with me being
involved. And I'm not happy with how you run things. The
Milsteins and I have got too much money at stake. Let's work
out a deal. Arrange it so economically you'll be well taken
care of.'"

On January 31, 1977, *The Wall Street Journal* announced
that Booth was resigning from United Brands, and Seymour
Milstein was replacing him. In a telephone interview, Booth
told the newspaper that he had a "friendly difference of opinion" over management style with Fisher, which convinced
him that it was "the better part of valor for me to step aside
and let Seymour take over."

For most of 1977, Milstein lived in a room at Boston's
Ritz-Carlton Hotel for five days a week. United Brands, he
saw, was still disorganized.

"There was a lot of uncertainty," says Milstein, "and people were depressed. All the heads of the divisions were battling with each other and pursuing their own agendas. I discussed it with Max and determined that if United Brands
remained in Boston, then things wouldn't noticeably improve
— the company would never overcome its ingrained habits.
Leaving the office early, for example. Not being available to
our West Coast operations. The marketing and sales people
were always in Manhattan because a lot of our overseas customers wouldn't even go to Boston. Many of them hadn't been
up to Boston in five years. As a result, United Brands was losing market share. We had a study done by consultants. They
concluded that if we wanted to change the psyche of the company, we should relocate to New York. So the board voted for
United Brands to move."

Numerous executives complained about the move, saying that the only reason United Brands was going to New York
City was "because senior management wants to live there."

Fisher expected the complaints. He answered his critics
by telling them that he lived in Detroit, and had every intention of staying there. In truth, Fisher was not sorry to lose
many of the executives who refused to relocate — in his opinion, they had been a big part the company's problems.

By the spring of 1978, Fisher had enough corporate adventure. Operations were running more smoothly, and the stock price had climbed. In 1974, the year before he accepted the chairmanship, the corporation suffered a net loss of $4.25 a share. In 1975, United Brands gained 80 cents a share; in 1976, $1.28 a share; in 1977, 50 cents a share, and in the first quarter of 1978, 36 cents a share.

On May 17, 1978, at the annual meeting of United Brands' stockholders in Cincinnati, Fisher announced that he would be retiring as chairman of the board of directors. Seymour Milstein succeeded him, and Paul Milstein, who had been vice chairman, took over as president and chief operating officer. Fisher remained on the board, with the title of honorary chairman.

Fisher had always known that his stint at United Brands was a momentary interlude, an irresistible last chance for him to relive his years running Aurora. He had proved to himself that he could still lead a corporation. Yet his heart was elsewhere. Business, he learned, had become an avocation; only philanthropy and politics fully engaged him. He had suspected as much in the early 1970s. After heading United Brands, he was sure of it. Since the 1967 summer riots, he had imagined various ways to help restore Detroit, and so it was that he focused his attention on matters closer to home.

Chapter 17

RENAISSANCE MAN

ARJORIE FISHER REMEMBERS that in the late 1960s, Max and Henry Ford II occasionally played a game they called, "What can we do for Detroit?" It was a fantasy game, an urban-renewal Monopoly, based on the shimmering memories each man had of the city decades before, a city charged with money and power and plenty of overtime at the auto plants. Back then, lights were forever glittering downtown, bright as a necklace of harvest moons; the swanky Book-Cadillac Hotel was jammed; and Hudson's department store was mobbed with shoppers. Lines formed outside Les Gruber's London Chop House, while inside, framed caricatures of the great and near-great who came to dine covered the walls. At night, after a Tigers game or a show at the Fisher Theatre, the hip ermine-and-pearl clubs like the Flame Show Bar and the Chesterfield swelled with the jazz of Dinah Washington and Sarah Vaughan. And then there were those sultry summer Sundays, the church bells silent by afternoon and city folks escaping to Belle Isle, crowding along the banks of the Detroit River or perched in canoes to enjoy the cool river breeze and the music floating up from the bandstand that rose above the Grand Canal.

In terms of Detroit, whether Max Fisher received as much as he invested — both financially and emotionally — would remain a hotly contested question in the city for decades. But two things were certain: Detroit's quandary would occupy — some say obsess — Fisher into the 1990s. And because of his obsession, the city skyline, and perhaps the city itself, would never be the same.

*   *   *

The story of the Detroit Renaissance begins in the spring of 1970. Dwight Havens, president of the Greater Detroit Chamber of Commerce, was trying to assemble a collection of business leaders to stem Detroit's spreading social and economic woes. Although a variety of corporate fathers told Havens that they liked his idea, securing commitments from them was another matter. Fisher had served on the board of the chamber, but he had gone to Washington to head Nixon's program on volunteerism and to help George Romney staff HUD.

Then, Havens says, "we got some good news. Max resigned from his post in Washington [in April] and I called him immediately and asked if I could come talk with him." They met at Fisher's house in a series of Saturday morning meetings. Havens remembers: "We talked about what Detroit needed. We had no notion what the program would include. We agreed on the membership and then Max finally said that he would be the chairman if Henry Ford and Bob [Robert M.] Surdam [president of the National Bank of Detroit] would be his co-chairmen."

Fisher had already headed New Detroit. (On January 12, 1970, after serving for seventeen months as chairman of NDI, Fisher stepped down and was replaced by William M. Day, CEO of Michigan Bell Telephone Company.) New Detroit was a broad coalition from every segment of the community. Despite its $10-million fund, which was raised by Fisher, and according to him, was "to help resolve some of [metropolitan Detroit's] social problems," NDI was more of a forum for expressing ideas and, Fisher believes, for venting anger — on the part of blacks and whites — after the cataclysm of the riots. New Detroit had its niche, Fisher thought, but this new group, which would shortly be named Detroit Renaissance, appealed directly to his emotional need to attack complex problems by doing something concrete, by making the wheels turn, galvanizing his power-laced network of politicians and businessmen.

Havens was able to recruit Robert Surdam for one

co-chairmanship, but though he knew Henry Ford agreed in principle with the projected aims of Detroit Renaissance, Havens could not pin him down on accepting the other co-chair slot.

One Friday in July, Havens got a call from Fisher. "Dwight," Fisher said, "why not let me talk to Henry about the co-chairmanship?"

Havens was glad to have the help. On Saturday evening, while the Fishers attended a party at the Fords, Max spoke to Henry, who agreed to co-chair the effort.

The final planning meeting was scheduled for 10 a.m., on November 20, 1970, at the headquarters of the Greater Detroit Chamber of Commerce. Fisher had hoped all of the automotive companies would be represented, but James M. Roche, chairman of General Motors, was unable to attend. Fisher, however, had obtained Roche's commitment at approximately 8:30 that same day, when he and Havens went over to visit him at his office.

"Max," Havens says, "came right to the point with Roche. He said: 'We want you involved, Jim, and we want General Motors involved. We want a commitment from you — your time and your talent. And we want a commitment from General Motors, that the company will give us the resources we need, people, money, whatever. We're going to put this thing together to stimulate some economic growth in Detroit. And you need to be aboard.' Roche replied that he would go along with it if everybody else went along."

Later that morning, twenty-three executives filed into the chamber of commerce conference room, among them officials from the auto companies, banks and utilities, and retailers like Joseph Hudson Jr., along with Mayor Roman Gribbs of Detroit and Governor William Milliken of Michigan. Detroit Renaissance, Inc., a nonprofit corporation funded by the leaders and leading companies of Detroit's business community, was founded.

Havens provided everyone in the conference room with background information and explained the mechanics of how

Detroit Renaissance would function. When he finished, Fisher stood to address the group.

"Max was beautiful," recalls Havens. "I wish I had it on tape. He said: 'I want to hear that you will commit yourself and your company to what we are going to do. I owe Detroit something because Detroit has been good to me and I want to put something back. And Detroit has been good to you and your companies and you have an obligation to put something back. So let's bring this together now and form an organization that will have the strength to do what Detroit needs.'"

Detroit Renaissance had a more formal coming-out the following spring, on March 29, 1971, when Fisher addressed the Economic Club of Detroit. Fisher began by chastising the national media for declaring that "Detroit is dying." He admitted that Detroit did have "the same bitter difficulties that face almost every major American city: unemployment, crime, poverty, drugs," and that it had lost a sizable portion of its population to the suburbs. "But this is a community," he said, "that still has great leaders [who] call Detroit their home — and mean it. And our United Foundation, supported by people who have gone to the suburbs, still remains the greatest community chest in the country."

Fisher proceeded to define the goals of Detroit Renaissance as "an attempt to put all of Detroit's great economic assets together," saying that it represented "the idea that Detroit can revitalize itself economically." The speech was Fisher's customary inspirational fare. The thrust did not come until the conclusion, when he introduced the directors of Detroit Renaissance in the audience, a list that would have been impressive as a national body, but was astonishing as a civic organization. A partial roll call included (after Fisher, Ford and Surdam), Virgil E. Boyd, vice chairman of Chrysler; Roy D. Chapin Jr., chairman of American Motors; Walker L. Cisler, chairman of Detroit Edison; Harry B. Cunningham, chairman of the S.S. Kresge Company; Ray W. Macdonald, president of Burroughs Corporation; Roland A. Mewhort, chairman of Manufacturers National Bank; Raymond T. Perring, chairman of Detroit Bank and Trust Company; Alan

Schwartz, a partner in the law firm of Honigman, Miller, Schwartz & Cohn; Al Taubman, chairman of the Taubman Company; and Kenneth J. Whalen, president of Michigan Bell.

On that March afternoon at the Economic Club, Fisher was unsure what course Detroit Renaissance should follow. Yet, for the moment, he was satisfied. The true strength of the coalition, Fisher realized, was its medley of power brokers, their influence circulating through every capillary of city commerce. There was nothing they could not accomplish in Detroit — if they would stick with it. Fisher pledged to stay on as long as the directors felt his services were required. It turned out to be longer than he anticipated. Fisher was chairman of Detroit Renaissance from November 1970 until November 1981, when he moved aside to let Henry Ford replace him. In an effort to buy some time to develop young leadership, Fisher would again be asked to take the chairmanship; his second tenure ran from December 1983 until December 1986, when he stepped down and was awarded the lifelong post of Founding Chairman.

Detroit Renaissance would make some headway during these decades — an inspection of downtown, particularly the riverfront, is all the proof one needs. However, the group's ability to cut significantly into the social despair it sought to excise is a debatable question and, Fisher claims, a continuing process. "You have to think about the year 2000," he often told dissenting citizens, cynical city fathers, cranky public servants, querulous tycoons, skeptical mavens of the media and anyone who cared to listen about the war to save Detroit.

If the early 1970s presented an urban mire almost beyond comprehension to a small-town boy born in 1908, then the obstacles that arose in the 1980s stretched reason and patience and compassion until they nearly snapped. Crack addiction, skyrocketing teenage pregnancy, nine-year-old drug runners, high-school gangs draped in gold and armed with Uzis, prisons without a cell to spare, and a new, disquieting twist, Devil's Night — an annual pre-Halloween rash of arson that in a three-day period in 1984, for instance, erupted in over 800 fires — seemed to have finally shattered the fragile veneer of the civilized that enveloped not just Detroit, but the crumbling schools, cracked pavement and depleted services of inner cities from New York to California.

In the face of this social decay, Fisher pursued his plans to help rebuild Detroit. What motivated him is a consideration that will have to wait. His motives were not publicly maligned until 1979, when he and Al Taubman sought to make their personal contributions to Detroit's revitalization (which is best understood in the context of that time.) Ask Fisher why he dug in his heels at Detroit Renaissance and for your trouble you will be treated to a homespun sermon on an individual's obligations to his community — Horatio Alger by way of Norman Vincent Peale, with an ample measure of Rabbi Hillel thrown in ("If I am not for myself, who will be? But if I am only for myself, what am I?"). Beyond that response, Fisher proffers a single explanation.

"You have to think about the year 2000," he says.

*　　*　　*

In the winter of 1971, once Fisher saw that the corporate clout was committed to Detroit Renaissance, his next step was to hire a professional to oversee the program. Ford Motor Company headhunters mentioned the name Robert E. McCabe, and Fisher flew to New York City to recruit him.

McCabe, a tall, elegant man, later dubbed "Champagne Bob" by the Detroit media for his grand and sophisticated style, was born in Mt. Pleasant, Michigan, in 1923. A graduate of Central Michigan University and the University of Chicago, by 1970 McCabe had spent much of his career on the public side of urban development. Between 1967 and 1969, he was deputy assistant director at HUD in Washington, D.C., leaving the post as Nixon assumed office (and Romney and Fisher arrived), and taking a position as general manager of New York State's Urban Development Corporation.

Fisher invited McCabe to have breakfast with him in his suite at the Waldorf. While they ate, Fisher talked about what his group hoped to accomplish in Detroit. McCabe told Fisher that the cities that were successful at redevelopment had established an intimate working relationship between government and business. One reservation that McCabe expressed was that perhaps Fisher's group was a little late in starting their redevelopment, but he emphasized that he thought it was a good idea.

Fisher said to him: "Bob, I'm glad you think it's such a good idea because we'd like to have you come out and run it."

McCabe said that he was happy with his job in New York, but that was not the answer that Fisher had flown to Manhattan to hear.

"Well," McCabe recalls, "then Max quickly said, 'Look, maybe if you just come out and talk to the guys you can give us some ideas.' I said I'd be glad to do that. He got me out [to Detroit] and then he [sicked Henry Ford and Robert Surdam] on me. And, lo and behold, I became president of Detroit Renaissance."

*   *   *

The economic hardships suffered by Detroit can be boiled down to one sad fact: in 1945, when Henry Ford II took over the company his grandfather had founded, the United States produced 80 percent of all the passenger cars in the world. By 1980, that figure had been reduced to 28 percent. The aftershocks reverberated through every segment of Detroit's economy.

Secondly, during this financial decline, the 1967 riot transpired, after which, Fisher says, Detroit, *unlike* every other riot-torn urban community, became "a rudderless city."

Coleman A. Young, who would be elected mayor in 1973 and would work closely with Fisher, feels that the problems in Detroit developed differently than in other cities.

"Detroit is almost an anachronism," says Young. "During World War II, it was the arsenal of democracy. We produced every damn thing from bombers to tanks. Right after World War II, when we entered the atomic age, a real paranoia of the Russians intruded [on Detroit's industrial economy]. It was said that the [Soviet Union] had an atomic bomb and decentralization [of our industry] became the official policy of the United States government. That meant that the government actually subsidized the breakup of the concentration of heavy industry around Detroit. I remember this distinctly because I was associated with the labor movement. It must've been a little earlier than 1950, [when] one of the Chrysler plants moved out to Ohio [because] of this decentralization. That was the beginning.

"Then there were the expressways," Young continues. "With government subsidies we began a system of expressways *out* of the city, a system that was unparalleled in the United States. The rest of the country learned a lot from us. [But] in the process of building our [roads], they truncated [neighborhoods] and a big percentage of Detroit's tax base was destroyed. The communities were just choked off. I know from experience. I had a dry-cleaning plant on Livernois. It was a good business. That particular block was one of the busiest outside of downtown Detroit. My partner and I, Jack Ashton, what did we know? Jack had been busy with the civil-rights movement. And I'd been busy with the labor movement. The guy who sold us [the dry-cleaning plant] knew there were plans to move the expressway within two doors. We did very well for a year until they dug that ditch. Then that whole block died. It's a ghost block [now, and] it once was prosperous. That happened to all kinds of [Detroit] neighborhoods."

Young believes that the existence of the expressways also expedited the eventual white flight from Detroit. (Between the late 1950s and the late 1980s, Detroit's population dropped from 1.8 million to 1 million.) Young blames both racism and greed for the flight.

"After the '67 riots," says Young, "it was a bonanza for the real-estate guys. Here you got white people caught in a frenzy — the blacks are coming! The blacks got to be very powerful when you consider that on a block of forty people, three blacks moved in and thirty-seven whites ran. And the real estate agents [took advantage of the situation.] They were block-busting. They could overcharge the frightened whites; they're desperate and could be charged twice what [a suburban house] was worth. Then the agents could overcharge the blacks to move into the homes that the whites deserted.

There ain't never been a golden era like that for the real-estate guys. It was a double-con."

Race has long been singled out as a major factor in Detroit's decay. Nineteen years after the founding of Detroit Renaissance, hostility between blacks and whites is still being cited as the origin of the city's troubles. On July 29, 1990, *The New York Times Magazine* published an article, "The Tragedy of Detroit," by Ze'ev Chafets, a native of Pontiac, Michigan, who moved to Israel in 1967. In his article, Chafets states that living two decades in the Middle East has given him a good eye for tribal animosity and in Detroit he recognized it. One white voice in the article depicts Detroit as "the place where the wheels came off the wagon of Western civilization." A black voice responds that whites from the suburbs "rape the city, and then they come and say, 'Look what these niggers did to the city.'"

Fisher believed that there were less histrionic explanations for Detroit's difficulties. The economic distress of the auto industry was indisputable; it would take, Fisher thought, thirty or forty years before the local economy would be able to plug the financial gaps. Like anyone familiar with the metro sections of numerous American newspapers, Fisher knew that muggings, rapes, robberies and murders were not endemic to Detroit. If the "wheels of civilization" had come off in Detroit, then the same could be said of New York City. Around the time that the Chafets piece appeared, a young woman jogger was battered and gang-raped in Central Park by teenagers; a twenty-two-year-old tourist from Utah was stabbed to death on a subway platform when he went to aid his parents, who were being robbed and beaten; a black high-school student en route to inspect a used car was murdered by a white mob in Bensonhurst; and in a span of six weeks, twelve children were hit by the stray bullets of drug dealers (five of them died).

In Detroit, though, some social critics suggested that white resentment toward blacks centered around the judgment by whites that blacks had stolen their city. Critics claimed that whites like Fisher and Ford, who pooled their money and talents to aid Detroit, were caught in a web of nostalgic illusions — a longing for what Detroit once was urging them on, futilely, to restore the metropolis to its previous greatness.

Undeniably, at some level, Fisher's passion to help rebuild Detroit was ignited by his remembrance of things past. But however magnanimous and caring Fisher is said to be, he is rarely described as sentimental, and it is implausible that when his own political skills, money and credibility were on the block, as they were at Detroit Renaissance, that his actions would be steered by sentiment.

Fisher never envisioned restoring the city to its heyday. Facing out-of-town journalists at a question-and-answer session, Fisher said: "[Cities] may not be the same in the future as they were in the past. We think of cities as naturally being the thriving retail development and entertainment centers. They may not have to be on that scale anymore. Too many people relate Detroit to the past. We have to think in terms of what is the city of the future."

Fisher and Detroit Renaissance had become focused on the riverfront as a spot to secure a foothold for the city's revitalization. Fisher, among others, concluded that what Detroit required was a venture of such enormous scope that it would dramatically alter the image of downtown, producing a suitable alternative to suburbia and providing a catalyst for further projects. So in 1971 Fisher, Ford and Taubman privately commissioned a study of the future of development along the riverfront.

It is ironic that the three men were so instrumental in the organized effort to reverse the trend of Detroiters relocating to the suburbs, since this trio had been indirectly and directly involved in developing these bedroom communities. Of course, Henry Ford I, with his mass production of automobiles, had furnished the opportunity for average Americans to reside outside the cities where they worked, and his grandson, Henry II, continued rolling cars off the assembly line. Fisher, the oil man and owner of Speedway gasoline stations, made his fortune fueling the engines. And Taubman, as one of largest shopping mall developers in the nation, constructed and managed the spaces where suburbanites shopped. Fisher had also invested in the suburbs that ringed Detroit — in the Somerset Apartments and Somerset Mall, a posh mecca for suburban shoppers. Meanwhile, Taubman and Ford teamed up to create the upscale Fairlaine shopping center in Dearborn, among the largest shopping centers in the country.

The irony was not lost on Detroiters who hoped to see the city revived. One black activist told Henry Ford that if he was serious about urban renewal, then he should cut back on his investment in the suburbs and put some of his money where he said his heart was — into redeveloping downtown. In commissioning the study of the riverfront, Fisher, Ford and Taubman hoped to determine the feasibility of creating a strip of parks, stores, office buildings, shops, and high- and low-rise housing that would stretch from Belle Isle to the Ambassador Bridge, which links Detroit to Windsor, Canada.

In the late spring of 1971, Bob McCabe went to Henry Ford to talk to him about building a shopping-mall and office-building combination on the site of the old Packard warehouse beside the Detroit River. Ford told McCabe that his staff at Ford Land Development Corporation insisted that there was no market for such a project.

"I know," replied McCabe. "It's for us to force the market."

That summer, Ford and Fisher were sitting beside Fisher's pool after taking a swim. They were drinking red wine, the bouquet of greater interest to Ford than to Fisher.

"You could do so much, Henry," Fisher said, referring to the proposed development project along the river. "The name 'Ford' is part of Detroit. You're the only one who can do it. And you ought to do it, Henry. You should."

Ford listened, sipping his wine, staring past the border of evergreens out to the neatly trimmed fairways of the Franklin Hills golf course. Fisher waited. After fifteen years of friendship he was used to Ford's tactical retreats into silence and knew that pushing Henry was never productive, that the only way Hank the Deuce ever made up his mind was on his own, and he did it while listening to his own private song, in his own sweet time. Now, it was taking him awhile. The sunlight was fading. Shadows fell across the grass.

Despite his silence, Henry Ford was certain that if Fisher felt so strongly about something, chances were that it was the right move to make. Ford trusted Fisher, and trust was not readily extended by the scion of the First Family of American industry. Shortly before his death in 1987, Ford would say of his friend: "Max is the one person I can turn to for straightforward advice. See, everybody is always trying to tell me what they think I want to hear. Not Max. He tells me what he believes is true."

At last, with the sun drifting beyond the greens of the golf course, Henry Ford stood to go inside the house to dress. He said: "Max, I'll do it. But not alone and it won't be a Ford Motor Company deal. Everyone has to contribute. You too."

Fisher promised that he would do his share.

That fall, after Ford Land Development acquired fifty acres along the riverfront from the bankrupt Penn Central Railway, Henry Ford announced his intention to undertake the largest single building venture in Detroit's history. The project was the Renaissance Center, known locally as "RenCen." Ground was broken in May 1973. Ford hired John Portman to design RenCen. Portman, renowned for his design of Atlanta's Peachtree Center and the Embarcadero Center in San Francisco, was striving, in RenCen, to design "an urban village," clustering as many of Detroit's services under one roof as possible.

Today, RenCen stands at the base of the city's main business district, extending along the river and spanning more than thirty acres. Like some imposing spaceship, RenCen emerges from an enormous landscaped podium. It has five gleaming glass towers — a 73-story cylindrical hotel with 1,400 rooms encircled by four, 39-story octagon-shaped office buildings with 2.2 million square feet of rentable floor space. There is parking for 6,000 automobiles, a shopping mall with more than 100 specialty shops, 13 restaurants and lounges. It includes what in the mid-1970s was the world's biggest rooftop restaurant, which revolves one full turn every hour and on clear days offers a panoramic view of Lake St. Clair, the Detroit River and the Canadian shoreline.

When the Renaissance Center finally opened its doors in April 1977, Max Fisher was interviewed in *The Milwaukee Journal* under the headline, "The Man Who Gave Ford the Better Idea."

* * *

As a means to restoring Detroit, the success of RenCen was both notable and, given the civic controversy surrounding it, interminably debatable. Among other criticisms, RenCen has been called a "fortress for whites to work in while the rest of the city goes to hell around them," and a "Noah's Ark for the middle class." The response to these characterizations underscored Detroit's most noted affliction — violence. People, it was said, would not frequent RenCen unless they were barricaded inside, a claim that was backed up not only by the fortresslike walls, but by the fact that the RenCen security staff outnumbered half of the nation's police forces.

One point that was not debated, however, was that for Henry Ford and his partners, RenCen was a financial disaster. Ford assembled a fifty-one-member Renaissance Center partnership (banks, insurance companies, manufacturers), but the largest financial commitment came from Ford Motor Credit Company. Once it was apparent that RenCen was not attracting tenants, Ford became a ferocious rental agent, ordering 1,700 of his employees to transfer from Dearborn to Detroit. Shortly, Ford Motor Company became RenCen's biggest tenant, leasing an entire office tower — thirty-four floors of space. When the relocated employees complained about the crime rate, the inconvenient commute and Detroit's income tax, the company promised a pay raise to defray expenses and took the employees on a tour of the impeccable security operations.

It cost $357 million to complete the Renaissance Center. The investment was eroded by wave upon wave of red ink. Between 1977 and 1982, RenCen's operating losses totaled $130 million. On January 1, 1983, the RenCen partnership defaulted on its second mortgage. By midmonth, the partners were offered $275 million for RenCen, $15 million less than the total debt. In the end, a new partnership, the Renaissance

Center Venture, bought a majority interest in the project. The depressed downtown real estate market, coupled with a declining local economy and a business district that emptied at the dinner hour, were blamed for the economic failure.

"Max and Hank the Deuce recognized from the beginning that RenCen wasn't a pure investment [or even] a good investment," says Mayor Young. "It was regarded as a potential catalyst for development up and down the riverfront and for the economic stability and the redevelopment of Detroit. I think it proved to be both of those. The investment that [Fisher] and [Taubman] eventually made in the Riverfront Apartments was really supportive of the Renaissance Center. It was made *possible* by the presence of the Renaissance Center."

Bob McCabe seconds the mayor's opinion. He states: "The project is an example of what [Max and Henry] asked people to do from the start — put their money and reputations on the line. They lost money. But the week after Renaissance Center opened, a number of buildings nearby in the old warehouse district were taken over and became restaurants and bars. The police force noticed a 30 percent increase in pedestrian traffic in the area. RenCen was built on the site of the old Packard warehouse, an abandoned railroad yard and a grain silo. No one would have been walking around there without the Renaissance Center."

"We were never in it for the money," Fisher says.

There were some in Detroit who did not accept this statement, accusing Fisher of being a carpetbagger from the suburbs, out to enhance his fortune at the expense of the city. By 1983, when RenCen passed to a second group of investors, Fisher had been through a civic controversy unmatched in his career. It required the use of his fortune and political power in Detroit, Lansing and Washington, D.C., the restraint of his anger, the strength of his personal friendships and tested his skills as a bridge builder to the limit. Still, even after it was clear that Fisher and Taubman had lost more than $30 million in pursuit of their vision, Fisher's critics and his supporters wanted to know: Why was he there?

Fisher replied that he was thinking about the year 2000.

Chapter 18

DOWN BY THE RIVER

AT A PRESS conference on January 3, 1974, Max Fisher and Louis Berry, respectively chairman and president of the Fisher-New Center Co., announced that they were selling the Fisher Building, the New Center Building and ten acres of adjacent land to Tristar Development, Inc. of New York. Over the years, investors approached Fisher and Berry to buy the building, but the offers were rejected. Fisher, says Berry, was originally disinclined to sell to Tristar, maintaining that it was not the proper time. Berry assured him that the timing was exactly right. Fisher relented, but it was not until years later that he told Berry it had been the right thing to do.

In 1974, though, Fisher was troubled about letting go of the building. Early one evening, a few weeks prior to the press conference, after the deal was nailed down, Fisher and several of his employees went to celebrate at Al Green's, a restaurant in the Fisher Building arcade. Fisher ordered a drink — scotch and soda — which he rarely did. As his employees chatted excitedly about the sale, Fisher sipped his scotch and stared glumly at the people entering the restaurant. One of Fisher's employees, noticing that her boss did not appear to be celebrating, asked him, "Would you feel so blue if you had just sold the Smith or Jones Building?"

"No," Fisher admitted. "Probably not."

His profit from the sale, after taxes, was $11.1 million, and it was some solace that Eli Master, vice president of Tristar, pledged that his company had no intention of renaming the building. But Fisher had to concede that a momentous phase of his life was over.

Five months before the sale, Fisher turned sixty-five, the

age at which men are traditionally supposed to slow down. Fisher had no intention of honoring that tradition. He was immersed in politics, the reconstituted Jewish Agency had just gotten off the ground, and there were his investments to nurture, but he knew that he was at a crossroads. Something was finished. Fisher could not put his finger on it, an elusive feeling of having left things undone, of debts not paid. There was no use kidding himself. If, on many occasions, he could be emotionally evasive with his family and closest friends, he could, paradoxically, be brutally frank with himself.

For him, the Fisher Building was a symbol of every business accomplishment he aspired to and, by 1974, achieved. His young Depression dream of being among the elite who lunched in the Recess Room was no longer deferred. Yet something was wrong. He had everything he ever longed for and now he was selling the Fisher Building, the gold-threaded emblem of that longing and its fulfillment. Oscar Wilde remarked that there were only two tragedies in life — one is not getting what you want, the other is getting it — but Fisher did not think that was the issue. For him, it was a matter of direction, of making certain that in whatever time he had coming to him that he settled his accounts, closed every circle. He had raised so much money for such a multitude of causes, but meantime the city he called home, the city he felt had given him his glorious opportunity, was struggling.

In January 1974, the conventional wisdom around Detroit was that Fisher's decision to sell to Tristar was based on his promise to make a sizable investment in the city. Henry Ford was doing his part; Fisher had vowed to follow suit. Fisher bolstered this perception at the press conference on January 3. According to *The Detroit News*, Fisher explained that "the sale of the prime property in the New Center area should not be construed to mean he is abandoning Detroit as a place to do business. He pointed out that [as] chairman of Detroit Renaissance . . . [he] could not get into the sticky position of quitting the city." Fisher concluded by informing reporters that he was going to utilize his profits from the sale to fund a "dramatic" downtown endeavor, but he would not disclose his intentions.

Despite these statements, much of what was driving Fisher had its inception one year before the press conference, on New Year's Day, 1973. That was the morning after Fisher had suffered an arrhythmia, and he sat in his Palm Beach apartment examining his life in writing. Although most of the document dealt with his familial relationships and his health, he did write two rather curious sentences about his finances: "I must learn to liquidate certain holdings and get out of debt. There is no excuse to be in the position that I am in."

What is remarkable about these comments is that Fisher's financial position, at the time, was enviable. Conservative estimates appraised his assets at over $100 million. He was not excessively leveraged, nor involved in any overly speculative ventures. In the fall of 1990, Fisher claims that the debts he referred to in 1973 consisted of some miscellaneous notes, but nothing that was financially pressing. Emotionally pressing was another matter. And the springboard for Fisher's plunge into the Riverfront development is highlighted in the 1973 document by the dual dimension that "debt" held for him — its fiscal *and* emotional encumbrances.

Fisher loathed financial debt. For instance, in 1984, his son, Phillip, started to assist him in managing the family assets. One afternoon, at a meeting with Max, Phillip suggested that his father mortgage his houses in Franklin and Palm Beach so as to benefit from the tax-deductible interest on residential mortgages.

"He really has so little opportunity to take meaningful deductions," Phillip Fisher says. "But when I presented my recommendation, [my father] just looked at me and said, 'Max Fisher doesn't do mortgages.' That was it. Next case. It's not as if he won't leverage a business deal. And he knows almost every home owner in the United States has a mortgage. He doesn't think there's something wrong with that. But he won't do it. It bothers him. He just refuses to borrow money against his homes."

Between 1973 and 1984, Fisher's net worth multiplied by

Max Fisher, Israeli Ambassador Yitzhak Rabin and President Richard Nixon, Oval Office, 1970. As ambassador, Rabin had his differences with Fisher, believing that he was a court Jew. However, after serving as prime minister, Rabin wrote in the Hebrew edition of his memoirs: "Israel is not alone, provided it knows how to harness the support of its friends, Jewish and non-Jewish, in a discreet and judicious manner. From Max Fisher I always received great support; the door of the White House is always open to him and in time of need, Max moves its hinges."

Max Fisher and Israeli Defense Minister Moshe Dayan, Jerusalem, Israel, 1970. On a visit to Dayan's house, the defense minister saw Fisher admiring a beer jug that dated back to 1200 B.C. Dayan presented the jug to Fisher as a thank-you gift for his assistance in securing the Phantoms. "The jets had already been promised," says Fisher. "It was only a matter of getting them through the bureaucracy. I just helped move things along faster."

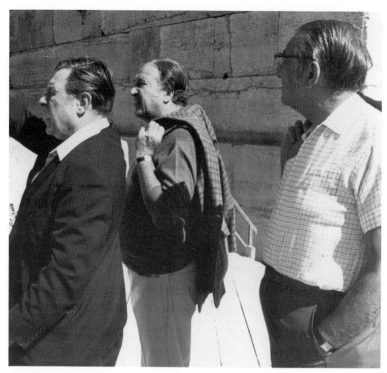

Mayor Teddy Kollek, Henry Ford II, Max Fisher, Jerusalem, Israel, February 1972.

Max Fisher, President Gerald Ford, and Secretary of State Henry Kissinger in the Oval Office, 1975. "The reassessment," Fisher says today, "got all out of proportion. I don't think Ford and Kissinger realized, at the time, the extent to which the controversy was mushrooming out of control."

Mary Fisher, working as an advance person in the Ford White House, May 1975.

Leon Dulzin, chairman of the Executive of the Jewish Agency, Israeli Prime Minister Menachem Begin, and Max Fisher, just after signing a covenant between the government of Israel and the Agency in the Knesset, Jerusalem, Israel, June 28, 1979.

Max Fisher, Egyptian President Anwar el-Sadat, and Israeli Prime Minister Menachem Begin at the White House dinner celebrating the signing of the Camp David accords, March 26, 1979.

Max Fisher and President Jimmy Carter, March 26, 1979. Prime Minister Begin introduced Fisher to Carter, saying, "Mr. President, I want you to meet the most important member of your country's Jewish community." As Fisher and Carter shook hands, the president replied: "Yes, I've heard of him."

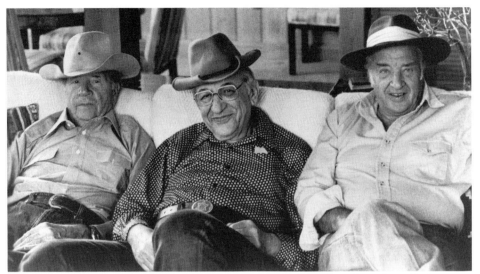

Left to Right: John Bugas, Max Fisher, Henry Ford II, at Bugas's Wyoming ranch. In the 1940s, Bugas was Fisher's first friend among Detroit's Gentile elite.

Max Fisher and Ronald Reagan's campaign manager William Casey, 1980. During the campaign, Casey asked Fisher to help make peace between former President Ford and Reagan.

Before entering the White House, Ronald Reagan did not know Fisher well, but he says that Fisher's stature was such that Republican presidents "inherited him."

Since President Reagan opted to leave the finer points of foreign policy to his advisers, Fisher found that his access to policy-makers ran through the stylishly appointed, oak-paneled office of Secretary of State Alexander Haig. Haig was eager to use Fisher's contacts with the leaders in Israel, believing that "it is always helpful to have an extra channel that influences more formal dialogue."

Secretary of State George Shultz, late 1980s. Although Shultz says that "it's better for the government to use official diplomatic channels" for communicating its positions, he found talking with Fisher helpful. Says Shultz: "I felt that Max was the person who knew the straight story and whose opinion carried real [weight in Israel and in the American Jewish community]. So I instinctively turned to him. You could speak confidentially to him and trust him. He told you what he believed and what he was going to do."

In 1984, when the Labor Party's Shimon Peres became prime minister of Israel, a compromise with the Palestinians seemed plausible. But violence scuttled the initiative. Of Fisher, Peres states: "I compare Max to a ship that has both engines and sails. When Max has the wind with him, he uses his sails. When he needs to propel himself further, he uses his engines. Max is a very good sailor."

On June 25, 1984, Fisher was bar mitzvahed at the Western Wall in Jerusalem. The bar mitzvah is a ceremony in which a thirteen-year-old boy is commanded to accept his share of Jewish responsibility. Fisher, growing up in the Christian community of Salem, Ohio, was sixty-three years late. After reciting the transliterated Hebrew prayers from an index card, Fisher said: "This is the most fortunate day of my life."

Max Fisher and George Bush in the Oval Office, 1990. The inscription reads: "To Max—Trusted Friend, Valued Adviser with Thanks and Best Wishes.

For Israeli Prime Minister Yitzhak Shamir, Fisher "represents the synthesis between the policies and aspirations of the United States and the goals and ideals of the Jewish people."

Secretary of Commerce Robert Mosbacher, 1989. Fisher became friendly with Mosbacher during Gerald Ford's campaign for the presidency.

Larry Sherman, Jane Fisher Sherman, and Shimon Peres, May 1988. The same year her father stepped down as chairman of the Jewish Agency Board of Governors, Jane Sherman was elected to the BOG.

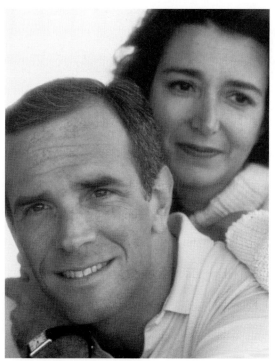

Julie Fisher Cummings and Peter Cummings. Recalling her father's constant traveling to pursue his philanthropic and political work, Julie Cummings says: "I gave my father to the world."

A working lunch, 1991. Left to right: Max Fisher, Chief of Staff John Sununu, Secretary of State James Baker, President George Bush.

Marjorie Switow Fisher. In the winter of 1984, Marjorie promised herself that she would never drink again.

Max Fisher, 1990, performing on what an interviewer described as his "favorite instrument."

a factor of three. So though the tax savings on mortgage interest would have been a negligible fraction of his fortune, Phillip's suggestion was fiscally sound. Fisher's objection to it was visceral, its origins in the second meaning of debt, to owe a favor or to be obligated to someone or something — debt as an emotional encumbrance. This category of personal indebtedness was as unpalatable to Fisher as residential mortgages. He was the one who did the favors and invariably stood ready to help. Hundreds of official and unofficial testimonies to Fisher's generosity exist — plaques and proclamations alongside impassioned handwritten letters of gratitude and the memories of phone calls brimming with appreciation. It is, however, a far smaller group who can claim that Fisher allowed them to do a favor for him. He was a believer in chits, notes one signs promising to pay later. He never missed an opportunity to lend a hand, to collect a chit and augment his store of favors owed. Nor did he ever redeem one without a compelling reason.

Phillip Fisher recalls that as a youngster his father instructed him in the intricacies of the chit system. "I was graduating from a private high school," he says. "Now, during my life, people have [often] been nice to me for some ulterior motive. And so one of the men running the school came to me and said, 'Phillip, we need somebody to give the keynote address at your graduation and we're trying to think of people.' Well, these type of guys always have a list where my dad is about three-quarters of the way down. Like they're disguising it or something. Their motive is that they want him to give the speech so that he'll make a contribution. So this fellow asks me if I'd ask my father to speak. I said that I didn't like to ask him favors. You see, when I was eleven or twelve my father told me that you earn chits in life and you don't want to use them unless something is really important. He did speak at my school and did a great job. When I got older I saw that he understood how to use his chits better than anyone else. But that's understandable. He's been doing it longer than most people."

And so on New Year's morning, 1973, Fisher promised

himself to wipe his debt clean. *There's no excuse for the position I'm in.* He planned to repay Detroit for what it had given him. He had been thinking about it for a while. Several months prior to that morning, Fisher accepted the Albert Einstein School of Medicine's Commemorative Award for Philanthropy. In his acceptance speech, Fisher articulated what he felt was the personal weight of his social obligation. He said: "I have long been interested not in philanthropy, but in what I call 'social responsibility,' in meeting the obligations that each one of us owes. Each of us can do something to help rebuild our cities. This is our obligation."

Mayor Coleman Young, who, in his effort to revive Detroit, worked his side of the political street while Fisher worked his, also sees in Fisher's impulse to give back an exigent need on Fisher's part to balance his emotional bottom line.

Says Young: "I think most of us who are involved in encouraging political and social change are moved by our memories of things as they were, or want [to pay back] the help [we received] from another quarter. Max came to Detroit as a relatively poor person and he made it in Detroit. And he never lost sight of [the discrimination he faced] because he was Jewish. That has been a strong, binding factor between those of us in the struggle for black civil rights and those who struggled for the same things in [the Jewish community]."

In his 1973 document, Fisher told himself that he would have to learn to liquidate certain holdings. He might have said that he would have to learn to put certain dreams attained behind him. He learned it soon enough.

"I always felt," Fisher says, "that because of the success of Aurora I owed, and owed a lot."

By the end of 1973, the Fisher Building was sold. By the beginning of 1974, Fisher began to pay.

*   *   *

As a wintry dusk settled on the banks of the Detroit River, Fisher turned up his coat collar and looked out over the leaden water to the lights of Windsor, Canada. Because he had just flown in from Palm Beach, the icy gusts felt particularly cold. He walked to keep warm, moving farther along the bank, careful not to slip on the rime. It was January 1974. Fisher was standing in the middle of an abandoned railroad yard with a crumbling storage shed under a grid of unused freeway overpasses. But the longer Fisher stood with the wind whipping around him the more he was able to imagine: the ultramodern towers of an apartment complex; a marina lined with boats; a bustling shopping center.

Before he returned to his car, a vision of Riverfront had taken shape in his mind. That was all anyone needed, Fisher thought, a vision fused to a blueprint. He had a draft of the blueprint by spring and announced that his Riverfront development would open its doors in 1976. He was off by seven years. During those years, as one frustration tumbled on top of another, Fisher pursued his vision with a single-minded intensity unmatched in his professional life, and en route he authored what urban experts at Michigan State University have declared "a kind of textbook case in the application of power to realize an urban development project."

*   *   *

Two years before Fisher's walk along the river, Al Taubman went to New York to bid on thirty-six acres of the Detroit riverfront owned by the bankrupt Penn Central Railroad.

"We wanted Detroit Renaissance to buy and control the land," Taubman says, "to put together packages to build residentials on those lands along the river. We did a study as to values and determined it would cost $5 million to build a sea wall and extended foundations. We figured the land was worth [between] $2.5 and $3 million. I made an offer of $2.5 million. The guy representing Penn Central promptly turned it down, saying they had an offer from [Southfield, Michigan, builder Adolph] Komer that would realize them $10 million."

But Fisher wasn't ready to relinquish his plans without a fight. So in 1974, he entered into a partnership with Komer and Penn Central, neither of whom believed in his vision. He was willing to wait and form the necessary partnerships in order to get his way.

Taubman says that ultimately Riverfront was more Fisher than him. "If not for Max, I probably wouldn't have been in Riverfront. It's his vision. In a sense, it's not a good deal. A good deal is one where everyone's in it for greed. Then it's simple: you make money and everyone walks away happy. The reasons [for building Riverfront] are too complicated. The test is: Could Riverfront be built in any other city? The answer is — no."

Adds Coleman Young: "I think Max had a real influence on Henry Ford and Al Taubman as a statesman. Max had a particularly powerful influence on Taubman. That relationship was almost a father-son relationship. They always argue with each other. Al complains [good-naturedly] that Max keeps him in trouble [and] causes him to lose money [with Riverfront]. But Al always comes through. When Hank the Deuce was alive, I regarded [Fisher, Taubman, and Ford] as a trio when it came to the economic development of Detroit and [other] supportive efforts for the city."

Hoping to pump some economic blood into Detroit, Young promptly forged an alliance between City Hall and developers who resided in the suburbs.

"Max," says Young, "is the person [who], as much as anyone, [is] responsible for adhering to the philosophy that the main mission of Detroit Renaissance should be the economic development of the city. And the theory upon which that is built is that the economic stability of the whole area depends on the economic stability of Detroit. I describe this as the 'doughnut theory.' Some would say that there is a new center and it ain't Detroit. And that the whole area surrounding Detroit could prosper while Detroit is nothing [but a] hole in the middle. The sweet meat is in the doughnut and Detroit is the sinkhole. Well, that is impossible. That ain't even physics. If it's a doughnut, it's a piece of cake, a solid piece of cake. And it can't taste good if the center is rotten. Max knows that. He always has."

The coalition between Young and business leaders partially explains Taubman's assertion that Riverfront could not have been built in other cities. What made the union unique was that while no one would ever accuse the electoral competition between Michigan Democrats and Republicans of being gentle, when it came to aiding Detroit the effort was fully bipartisan. Whoever had the contacts used them — in Detroit, Lansing and Washington.

An example, unrelated to Riverfront, illustrates how this coalition mobilized behind the city's banner.

On July 28, 1976, Richard Gilliland, a Republican administrator for the Department of Labor, ruled that Detroit could not use funds from the Federal Comprehensive Employment and Training Act (CETA) to rehire 289 police officers and emergency medical technicians that had been let go. Gilliland had some other bad news. He determined that as of September 1, Detroit would have to begin laying off another 1,200 workers who were paid through CETA. Mayor Young, by then a major liberal Democratic player on the national stage, was irate, describing Gilliland's ruling as "punitive and vindictive."

Young phoned Fisher, the quintessential Republican, who during that summer was in the midst of raising money for President Ford's campaign against the liberal Democratic governor of Georgia, Jimmy Carter. Young explained the situation. Fisher told him not to worry, that he would speak to the White House. On July 29, one day after Gilliland's pronouncement, President Ford reversed his own official's ruling, saying that not only could Detroit rehire the laid-off workers with money from CETA, but that the Labor Department would have to postpone any phasing out of the 1,200 CETA-paid city workers.

This bipartisan *modus operandi* was applied repeatedly to surmount the obstacles to getting Riverfront built — starting with the financing. Since the development had an estimated price tag of $78 million, Fisher recognized that in the inflationary economy of the mid-1970s the expenditures required for construction would propel rents above an acceptable limit (beginning at roughly between $350 and $450 per month).

Then, too, Fisher wanted the state and the city to have a stake in his project, to have their own commitment to making it work. And so he went to Lansing, where he lobbied for special state legislation that became known as "the Max Fisher bill." Representative William A. Ryan, a Democrat from Detroit, was the prime sponsor of the bill, which gave the Detroit City Council the power to grant twelve-year property tax-exemptions to new housing construction downtown. Fisher hoped the savings would be passed to him and then on to his future tenants.

The bill coasted through the Legislature. On January 13, 1977, Governor Milliken, a descendant of the moderate Republican dynasty founded by Romney and Fisher in 1962 and a grateful beneficiary of Fisher's fund-raising expertise, signed the legislation into law. By then, Fisher had lost his access to the White House, Carter having unseated Ford. This was unfortunate for Fisher, since he was now pursuing federal loans, grants and guarantees — $18.6 million, almost 25 percent of the estimated cost. Young, though, had been an "early rider aboard the Carter train." During the 1976 presidential race, Fisher told the mayor: "Well, regardless of who becomes president, at least Detroit will still have a friend in the White House."

That friendship was crucial because in the fall of 1977 Fisher's project collided with Elmer C. Binford, the head of the Detroit office of the Department of Housing and Urban Development. Binford had taken over Detroit's HUD in 1974, an office that the *Detroit Free Press* maintained had "a nationwide reputation for corruption and incompetence." From 1966 to 1974, FHA mortgage insurance programs administered by the HUD office lost close to $300 million. More than 200 persons, among them HUD employees, real-estate dealers and contractors, were convicted of fraud. Binford, according to the *Free Press*, successfully "fought with venal and inept HUD employees, with [Mayor] Young, all nine city councilmen, several superiors in HUD and a small army of shady real-estate operators, mortgage brokers and contractors."

Shortly before Labor Day in 1977, Binford made an inauspicious career move. Convinced that Fisher's proposed apartment complex would be a financial disaster, Binford sent evaluation reports to HUD headquarters in Washington that recommended the agency not participate in the financing, stating that HUD had enough problems in Detroit without getting stuck with another "multimillion-dollar white elephant."

Disturbed by Binford's evaluation, Fisher phoned Young as the mayor had phoned him the previous year to straighten out the CETA funding for city workers. Young was not only owed favors in the Carter White House, but had, according to *Fortune* magazine "installed a Detroit-made mini-machine within the federal bureaucracy to look out for the city's interests. . . . Young [had] also made and kept plenty of old friends around Washington."

Among Young's friends was HUD Secretary Patricia Harris Roberts. One phone call to her, and on September 4, 1977, Elmer Binford discovered that he had a new job — in Chicago.

In the spring of 1978, Fisher purchased the riverfront acreage from Komer and the railroad, then formed Riverfront Associates with Al Taubman, each man coming up with $100,000 in seed money. (While Fisher and Taubman owned 93 percent of the venture, they did take in eight minor partners: Robert C. Larson and Richard P. Kughn, officers of the Taubman Company; Gilbert B. Silverman and Irwin T. Holtzman, owners of the Holtzman and Silverman real estate company; developer David R. Nelson; and Miles Jaffe, one of Fisher's attorneys and a senior partner in the law firm of Honigman, Miller, Schwartz and Cohn.)

From the 1970s forward, Fisher and Taubman had participated in an assortment of philanthropic and business partnerships. They were equal contributors to the park they donated in their parents' names to the city of Jerusalem. In 1975, Taubman — with Fisher, Ford, Herbert Allen, Milton Petrie and Donald Bren backing him — opposed Mobil Oil in a bidding war for the rights to the Irvine Ranch in southern California. Taubman and company won, paying $337 million for the Orange County property. Taubman's acquisition — what the magazine *M Inc.* describes as "a nonpareil collection of office and industrial buildings, apartment complexes, luxury home parcels and 64,000 acres of mostly undeveloped land" — became the largest private real-estate holding in a major U. S. metropolitan area.

"Compared to Riverfront," says Taubman, "the Irvine deal was easy. All we had to do was line up the partners and the banks [to provide financing.] We dealt with private individuals, not public agencies."

Fisher agrees. He says: "I never ran into these kinds of roadblocks before. For three years, it was just one fight after another."

By then, the architectural plans for Riverfront had been finalized. The initial phase, situated on 10 acres, was a twin-towered, 29-story apartment complex with 604 units, all with a view of the Detroit River. Other amenities included tennis courts on top of the parking garage, a glass-enclosed swimming pool, a seventy-seven-boat marina, a health club, a gatehouse with private access, around-the-clock security, a gourmet shop, twenty-four-hour banking and a downtown People Mover that stopped not far from the front door. Opposition to the project came in three distinct flavors — environmentalists, government financiers and, most surprising and disheartening to Fisher, from a vocal activist segment of Detroit's black community.

The strongest of the environmental groups was the Michigan United Conservation Clubs, which represented 200,000 sportsmen. The Conservation Clubs threatened to block the project in a court fight because construction would restrict public access to the riverfront. Fisher settled that dispute by granting unlimited access along a 265-foot strip of the shoreline, while keeping 1,600 feet private. Other groups picked up the environmental flag, one charging that the development would interfere with the flow of the Detroit River's fish; another group said that the riverfront rat population would be disturbed.

Fisher solved the objections with the levelheaded forbearance for which he was revered. But, off the record, Fisher angrily asked a Detroit journalist: "Can't those damn fish swim *around* the shoreline?" He would not even discuss the dislocated rats.

The backdrop to Riverfront was an economy that, starting in 1976, deteriorated day by day. The money market tightened, while Fisher and his partners required more capital. And each new national headline about Detroit's economic woes decreased the odds of outside money coming into the city. *The New York Times* ran several articles on Detroit's distress. Columnist William Safire inveighed against the trend of Detroit leaders to sacrifice neighborhoods to corporations in order to save thousands of jobs. In a move that was uncharacteristic for a man who operated best backstage, Fisher rebutted Detroit's critics on the op-ed page of *The Times*. His reply was motivated not solely by team spirit, but also by the realization that stories in the national media would attract the attention of officials in Washington and bankers in New York, the very people he was going to ask to help finance Riverfront.

Financially, Fisher saw that the project was doomed without government support. That meant politics and at the federal level a series of alphabet headaches: HUD, UDAG (Urban Action Development Grant), UMTA (Urban Mass Transit Administration), GNMA (Government National Mortgage Association) and the FHA (Federal Housing Administration). Fisher bulled ahead, calling every one of his contacts on behalf of the city. For instance, in 1981, when it looked like Riverfront might fall apart because the Reagan administration was holding back on a $5.5-million UMTA grant, Fisher visited Secretary of Transportation Andrew L. Lewis Jr., whom Fisher knew from the Reagan campaign, and the grant was forthcoming.

Miles Jaffe, Fisher's lawyer and a partner in Riverfront, dealt with an unending string of legal and financial matters that arose during the development process. Jaffe says the process was like trying to fit a giant jigsaw puzzle together, except the pieces were animated and would not stay still.

"Forget for the time being getting the pieces to fit," Jaffe says. "Just on the financial side, between [the threat of] not getting the $5.5-million UMTA that we had anticipated and some serious problems we had in financing the construction bonds, the puzzle had changed enough that where before you at least had an objective picture on the puzzle box, you now had a Jackson Pollock. In 1981, a reasonable man would have bet that Riverfront would not get off the ground.

"In late September of 1981," continues Jaffe, "we picked up momentum. We got our initial FHA [mortgage guarantees]; we paid our fee to GNMA, not on the theory that we were at all close to putting the Riverfront package together — but because the terms of the financing were so good. In other words, it was a bad poker hand, but you couldn't let 7.5 percent interest rate on forty-year money go down the tubes if there was a shot."

When Jaffe spoke to Fisher about the dubious wisdom of paying out money that would be lost if the project didn't fly, Fisher's curt response was "Miles, if this can be done without breaking me, I want it built."

It was then that Jaffe understood how passionately Fisher felt about completing Riverfront. And the problems continued.

"Almost immediately after we put that package together," Jaffe says, "a problem came up on the bond side, which really seemed to be unsolvable. The underwriters told us we needed a certain kind of commitment from a rated bank. There aren't that many rated banks and most didn't want to provide this service as far as we could see. Finally, in the course of looking for someone to provide this rating, we came to Chemical Bank in New York. And Chemical said: 'We won't provide the rating, but instead of selling the bonds publicly, why not sell them privately to us, and we won't require this rating?'"

Chemical's offer, says Jaffe, was not standard practice. Explaining why Fisher was able to force it through, Jaffe observes: "Political clout helps, but the largest part is that people say, 'This guy Fisher is for real.' The thing that allows

Fisher to work with someone like Drew Lewis is that his past performance requires that he be taken seriously. So that when you go to Chemical Bank and you're representing Max Fisher and Al Taubman, you 'ain't screwin' around.' They are men who accomplish things. This isn't some flaky, off-the-wall operation. 'Build a 600-unit apartment building in Dee-troit?' They don't say that if you're representing Max and Al. They try and help you solve the complications."

The financing required the assistance of two banks, two federal agencies and one city, but after seven years, Fisher got the $77.49 million he needed to build Riverfront. Developers' equity accounted for $18 million, along with a pledge to cover cost overruns. HUD and the DOT kicked in $19.69 million — $17.2 million of which was to be repaid over forty years. A construction loan of $39.8 million was administered by Manufacturers National Bank of Detroit as trustee and funded by a Detroit Downtown Authority bond issue that was bought by Chemical Bank. On completion of construction, the note and mortgage would be purchased by GNMA — a guarantee that funds would be available to redeem the bonds. The note and mortgage would then be repaid over a forty-year term at a 7.5 percent interest rate, except for a small portion, which would be repaid over twelve years with monies from a city tax abatement.

This tax abatement was estimated to save Riverfront Associates — and cost Detroit — $700,000 per year, a fragment of Riverfront's budget. Yet when a fight broke out over the abatement, Fisher was tormented by it, because as the brawl was played out in the local media, Fisher's motives for undertaking Riverfront were assailed, raising again the ugly anxieties of black-versus-white in Detroit, an anxiety that since the 1967 riot Fisher had worked so vigorously to assuage.

*   *   *

In 1977, when Governor Milliken signed the "Max Fisher bill" into law, giving Detroit's City Council the power to grant twelve-year property tax-exemptions to new, downtown

housing construction, it seemed as though Fisher and his partners would only have to wait for the city council to rubber-
stamp the abatement. But after the council met on April 1,
1979, it was obvious that the approval would be slowed by
dissension and belligerence.

At the meeting, Jack Pryor, coordinator of Detroit's Community and Economic Development Department, informed
the council that due to escalating construction costs, the
apartments in Fisher's proposed high-rises would rent from
$500 to $600 a month, with some going for as much as $1,000.

Vexed at those projections, council president Erma
Henderson set the tone for the meeting by snapping: "I understand rich folks gotta have apartments, too."

Ignoring her implications, Pryor told the council that
Fisher was preparing to request a twelve-year tax abatement
from the city, explaining that Fisher "has to make the rents
affordable."

"Fascinating," said Councilman Kenneth V. Cockrel, his
voice lined with sarcasm. Then, referring to Fisher, he said: "I
never met the brother. Let him come before [the] council.
We'll have a look, see what kind of man he is."

Ken Cockrel would become the spokesman for the portion of Detroit's black community who opposed Riverfront.
He attacked Fisher regularly, along with Taubman and other
businessmen whom Cockrel considered white suburban elit-
ists profiteering on the backs of Detroit's poor blacks.

With the passing of time, Cockrel would mellow. When
he died suddenly at the age of fifty on April 25, 1989, civic
leaders had been predicting that he would supplant Coleman
Young as mayor. He was awash in the upper-middle-class
mainstream — a lawyer who was seen on billboards advertising Foster Grant sunglasses, a popular figure waving to friends
and admirers as he tooled down Woodward Avenue in his
black Porsche 944. But in 1979, Cockrel was on the opposite
end of the social and political spectrum from Fisher, the two
men having reached their respective positions by vastly divergent routes.

In the early 1960s, Ken Cockrel was living with his first

wife and son in the Jeffries public-housing project, working nights as a "jumper" on *Detroit News* delivery trucks — dropping newspapers at delivery points — and attending classes at Wayne State University during the day. Wearing an Afro hairdo, denim jeans and boots, and toting an olive-drab Army knapsack, Cockrel rose to prominence as a leader among the student radicals on the WSU campus, winning an impromptu debate with black Muslim leader Malcolm X, the start of Cockrel's lifelong reputation as a pugnacious oratorical opponent.

In 1968, following graduation from law school, Cockrel signed on with what *Time* magazine dubbed "the hippest and swingingest radical law firm in the country." The firm represented the League of Revolutionary Black Workers, welfare mothers, rent strikers, White Panthers and Black Panthers — underdogs of every leftist stripe and hue. Cockrel was soon in the headlines, successfully defending several black clients who had shot white police officers in self-defense. As an attorney, Cockrel was noted for continually putting the white Establishment on trial. In one case he labeled a white Recorder's Court judge a "lawless, racist, rogue, bandit, thief, pirate, honky dog fool." In 1977, Cockrel won a seat on the city council by calling for a "progressive, socialist agenda." Once seated at the council table, Cockrel exercised the same abrasive oratory and scathing wit that had been his trademark in the courtroom.

On October 7, 1979, six months after the council first heard of Fisher's plan to request a tax abatement, Cockrel appeared on the front page of *The Detroit News* decrying the tax breaks as "tools to enhance profit-making potential for millionaires."

Cockrel said: "I'm not going to charge Mayor Young with being a neo-colonialist puppet. Young did not invent Max Fisher. . . . The [architect] of these economic strategies [is] . . . the Detroit Renaissance, the elites. Coleman works for them."

Asked if the people and industry of Detroit wouldn't be

worse off if such tax breaks were rejected, Cockrel framed his response in racially antagonistic tones.

"I guess you could make the argument," said Cockrel. "At the time the niggers first resisted slavery, I suspect you could have argued that it didn't make much sense to resist. . . . [People] couldn't see the day slavery would be abolished in the United States of America. I'm saying the line has to be drawn somewhere."

Cockrel was drawing the line along Fisher's Riverfront. On Saturday, the day before his statements appeared in *The Detroit News*, Cockrel announced that he was sponsoring a petition drive along with the Detroit Alliance for a Rational Economy (DARE) — the political organization that helped him get elected to the council — to block the Riverfront tax break.

Beneath the slogan "Tax Max and his pal, Al!" Cockrel's petition read: "We, the undersigned citizens of Detroit, urge the Detroit City Council to Vote No! on the proposed 100%, twelve-year tax break for the Riverfront development. Max Fisher, Al Taubman and the other wealthy developers of Riverfront do not need a 100% tax break for twelve years. . . . [These public monies] will benefit the developers and the wealthy executives and professionals who will rent these luxury apartments. But if they get the tax break, Detroit will get very little from Riverfront. Only fifteen permanent jobs will be created! As homeowners or renters, we pay our property taxes. It is unfair to ask us to subsidize the well-off."

In public, as in his petition, Cockrel did not spare the us-versus-them rhetoric. In Detroit — as it would in many cities — this tactic swiftly divided people into two quarrelsome camps — one black, one white. Over the next two years, Cockrel claimed to have secured 15,000 signatures on his petition, and hundreds of black T-shirts, emblazoned with the phrase, "Tax Max and his pal, Al!" began appearing around the city.

By 1981, Fisher was impatient with the bureaucratic delays in Washington, but the rhetoric of Cockrel and his supporters hurt him. After all, he had poured a fortune into Riverfront — he was on the hook for $10 million and he knew that amount wouldn't cover it. He probably would lose his entire profit from the sale of the Fisher Building and then some. Had Riverfront been a straight business deal it never would have limped this far. He would have cut his losses and run. And Cockrel and his supporters were acting as if he were out to fleece the city. Damn it! He was trying to get out of debt. No one could see it; at times, not even Fisher. He owed — God, how he felt he owed Detroit for all of his good fortune, the respect in the business world, the friendship of presidents and prime ministers — and now they would not let him pay his bill.

Worse was the racial hostility. Fisher had gone out on a limb supporting civil rights within certain segments of the Republican Party, and later, when black militants were accused of anti-Semitism, he had championed them when speaking to the organized Jewish community. As far back as 1969, when liberal whites who had supported the efforts of Dr. Martin Luther King began to shy away from the rising black power movement, Fisher told *The Detroit News Sunday Magazine*: "The rise in Negro militancy and anti-Semitism does not give Jews any excuse to withdraw from the battle for equal rights and Negro justice. We are in this struggle to stay because it is the struggle of every American. . . . [We] must be ready to respond, to allow the Negro to achieve his self-set goals; and the militancy, the turmoil is good, because it shows that the Negro is himself concerned and involved. The growth of the black power concept is healthy. . . . I think that through my Jewishness I have a feeling of what [the Negro] wants."

But, from 1979 until 1981, the sniping about the tax abatement wore on and Fisher resented it. One afternoon, having heard enough, Fisher phoned Mayor Young.

"Look," he said to Young, "if the council thinks this is such a damn good deal for me, if they think I'm going to make so much money, then I'm going to go the hell down there and tell them they're welcome to buy it for what I've invested and the city can make all the profit."

"Max," replied Young. "There's no need to come down. They just want to throw darts at you. Don't you worry about the council. You leave them to me."

Miles Jaffe, who by the spring of 1981 was enmeshed in the jigsaw puzzle of Riverfront financing, believes that the combination of Fisher on the private side, and Young on the public side, was a good match.

"Young may be much more flamboyant than Max," says Jaffe. "But they are patient men who believe if you don't get it this year, you'll get it the next. And neither one of them is distracted by the crowd. They keep their eyes on the ball."

As pragmatists, Fisher and Young felt that it was an indulgence to argue about race, to point a finger and declare a villain. The issue, says Young, was plain and simple: Detroit needed investment. Fisher agrees.

"You make your deal," says Fisher. "You get the job done."

Says Young: "There was no room for pie-in-the-sky [debates], because that ain't where the pie is."

One of the most adroit mayors who ever steered a political machine, Young rushed into the Riverfront fray, fought Cockrel in the press and cooled the rhetoric in the city. When he was through there was no doubt that the council would approve the tax abatement. As one council staffer opined a month before the vote: "We all know the council is going to roll over. The question is: How much are they going to wiggle along the way?"

Young directed his people to work the wards, spreading the word that Detroit — and the mayor — had to have Riverfront. Surmounting the opposition was not that difficult a chore. Young was not even convinced that Cockrel's rhetoric was genuine. Asked about it in the summer of 1990, Young said: "[Ken's rhetoric] was a political ploy to prove how radical he was. I don't think it had anything to do with a personal animosity toward Max Fisher. And I don't think [Cockrel] was completely convinced that [Riverfront] was bad [for Detroit]."

Bob McCabe, president of Detroit Renaissance, seconds Young's opinion. "It was politics," explains McCabe. "You have got to remember that Cockrel was an old socialist — some would say he was a Marxist. He was a city councilman and Max and Al were good targets. And yet he had no animosity toward them. I'd meet Kenny on the streets and we'd kid about it. Besides, because of the things Max has done for Detroit, he is one of the most admired white people in the city's black community."

This is precisely the point that Coleman Young makes when discussing the fight over Riverfront. If Cockrel's objections were a political ploy, says Young, then he made a tactical mistake by attempting to focus black resentment on Fisher. Simply put, Cockrel chose the wrong target.

"Max," says Young, "is not swayed by differences between city and suburb, between black and white. I think his ability to view matters objectively and to express his concern for the poor [and] for the future of the city is responsible for his being regarded in the black community and in Detroit as a friend."

Fisher was taken aback by Cockrel's attempt to depict him as a racist come to steal the tax monies of black Detroit. The man who shied away from conflict discovered that he was now the focus of one. However, his greatest concern just then was that his project was in jeopardy. In the spring of 1981, a new administration in Washington threatened to cancel the funding unless the development got under way. Riverfront Associates needed the approval in a hurry. Disregarding the grass-roots support and racial enmity that Cockrel engendered, Fisher decided to go before the council to state his case.

What the press was billing as a showdown between Fisher and Cockrel took place on June 4.

The nine members of the council convened in the Committee-of-the-Whole room on the 13th floor of the City-County Building. It is a small, low-ceilinged, brown-carpeted room with rings of tables for the members, guests, the press, and a gallery. Through the windows to the west on this sunny spring day the Detroit River was a burnished ribbon of silver with the pristine skyline of Windsor beyond. The room was packed, the press and council staffers crowding the outer tables. Accompanying Fisher to the session were other representatives of Riverfront Associates — Larson and Kughn from the Taubman Company, the lawyer Miles Jaffe and developer Dave Nelson — but the attention soon focused on Fisher and Cockrel. They greeted each other warmly and shook hands — "almost like two old pals," *The Detroit News* reported. But both men were dressed in their respective uniforms: Cockrel in a "No Tax Break for Riverfront: Tax Max and his Pal, Al!" T-shirt; and Fisher in a blue silk suit highlighted by a burgundy silk handkerchief in the breast pocket.

Facing the council, Fisher started by stressing that Riverfront's future hinged on rapid approval of the tax-abatement plan by the city council.

"We're under a real time constraint because of changes in Washington," Fisher said. "If we don't meet the deadline dates, with the change of administration and the cutting-out of so many projects we're dead." He paused. Then he said: "It's almost seven years since we started, and we still have some problems. The cooperation and understanding of the city council is needed to bring this to reality. The city deserves everything we can do for a real renaissance. If we could make the whole riverfront a teeming city with people living on the riverfront, we could have a city in the year 2000 that everyone would be proud of. I've had my heart set on this particular project. I'm optimistic about Riverfront and I feel it will stimulate other development in the area. You have to look at what Detroit can be in twenty or thirty years. I've worked with many of you before and I trust you will understand my feelings for Detroit and my commitment to it."

Cockrel stood to respond. Although his greeting to Fisher had been friendly, he began by saying: "We've all heard of you, all read about you, what you've done for Detroit." Next he used humor, cracking that he hoped he would be here in the year 2000. Then Cockrel stated: "I have taken a position of opposition to aspects of financing the plan. There would be a general-fund depletion while we are experiencing dire economic times and are on the verge of collapse. Yet, we are still seeing the executive branch come to us with the tax-abatement plan. I'm concerned that the city's general fund will not be sufficient to extend a certain quality of life to its citizens, that its ability to do so will be negatively affected by the tax abatement. I feel the city is at a point fiscally where it can't afford it. Does it have to be an all-or-nothing-at-all proposition? I'm prepared to open the door to see if there is room for compromise. I want to know why Riverfront Associates has to operate on the assumption that they have to have a twelve-year 100 percent tax abatement. There are those who say they don't want to see that happen in Detroit."

Fisher replied: "I understand your concerns. But it depends on whether you look at the short term or the long term. What I'm looking at is ten or twelve years in the short-term history of the city. It is important to attract industry so you're building a tax base for the future. You have to decide which is best — that or leave the city fallow and not develop it."

Fisher asked Miles Jaffe to explain the importance of the abatement. In effect, Jaffe said that because the FHA was insuring the mortgage, they had to be assured that the developers could attract enough tenants so that the rental income would be sufficient to pay off the mortgage. The abatement would give the developers an edge with the FHA; without it, they wouldn't get the federal funds they had to have to build Riverfront.

There was some more discussion around the room, desultory questions and answers about Riverfront, but the face-off between Fisher and Cockrel, which the press had predicted would be "a knock-down brawl," was done. The headline in the next day's *Detroit News* heralded the media's disappointment: "Cockrel, Fisher 'row' fizzles."

Ken Cockrel voted against the tax break, the only council member to do so. But perhaps as Young said, Cockrel was not truly convinced that Riverfront was bad for Detroit. On July 18, Fisher was going through the mail in his office when he opened a package from Cockrel. The cover letter said: "Dear Max: I enjoyed our repartee during the council session of June 4 so much, I've decided to give you the T-shirt off my back.

No formal Detroit wardrobe is complete without this basic black thread. As you move toward groundbreaking on the river, I wish you good fortune with the development."

Enclosed was a T-shirt stenciled with the refrain, "Tax Max and his pal, Al!"

A week later, Fisher replied: "Dear Ken: Sorry that I took the shirt off your back, but I think I'll keep it as a memento, especially if we can have groundbreaking soon. I enjoy our discussions and am looking forward to seeing you soon."

The formal opposition to Riverfront was over.

June 15, 1982, was the official groundbreaking for the project. Fisher, Taubman and Young donned hard hats for photographers and turned over the first shovels of Riverfront dirt. Cockrel did not attend, but almost everyone who had a hand in the development did. A brightly striped tent half the size of a football field could not hold all the bankers, lawyers, and city, state and federal officials. They heard a speech by Young, who called Taubman "the reluctant dragon," and said Riverfront was what his administration was about. They heard a speech by Taubman, who made it clear that he and Fisher were "going to make [Riverfront] work." They heard a speech by Fisher, who stuffed a prepared text into his jacket as he approached the podium and then spoke earnestly about his "dream," a dream that he did not elaborate on.

Following the ceremony, as Fisher was being driven to the Renaissance Center, where he and Taubman were hosting a prime rib luncheon in the River Room for the tentful of people, he confessed to a guest that he had been afraid of boring his audience. The men in the car were quiet amid the tinted glass, leather and air-conditioning. Fisher was lost in his thoughts. His guest in the backseat remembered an elaboration he had heard of Fisher's "dream" from someone close enough to have shared Fisher's private thoughts when he sat late at night staring into the marble fireplace in his garden room.

"Riverfront and RenCen," he said, "were to be Max and Henry's bookends. It went all the way back to the riots and their vision of a new Detroit. You could look at Detroit from

Windsor and see Henry's RenCen and Coleman's Joe Louis Arena and Max and Al's two apartment towers and understand the dynamics of Detroit at a glance. Max made a public promise after the riots, after he sold the Fisher Building, to put money back into Detroit. He wasn't going to be forced off that pledge."

Fisher broke the silence in the car, picking up the phone cradled next to him in the front seat and calling his office to ask if there were any messages. He hung up and turned to his guest in the back. "You think it went all right?" he asked. "I didn't talk too long?"

The car glided to a stop outside the Renaissance Center; Fisher stepped out and disappeared inside the RenCen, into a roomful of congratulations.

He had not talked too long. He had waited for the better part of decade to see his vision rise along the river. By the spring of 1984, the first tower opened to renters; that fall, the second tower opened, and after two years their occupancy remained above 95 percent. In the summer of 1990, ground was broken for a third tower. The project, however, steadily loses money. Between 1978 and 1991, Fisher and Taubman lost more than $30 million. But Riverfront was built. Fisher was discharging his responsibilities, closing circles, paying off his personal obligation to Detroit.

And he still had a decade to go before the year 2000.

Chapter 19

BEGINNINGS AND ENDINGS

D URING THE CARTER administration, Fisher retained his unofficial position as the "dean of American Jewry." However, since he was a Republican, he lost his access to the Oval Office and was unable to function as an intermediary between Washington and Jerusalem. Although gratified by his efforts at Detroit Renaissance and with Riverfront Associates, Fisher discovered that for him life outside the inner circles of national government was painful.

The extent to which he missed his diplomatic work was underscored on March 26, 1979, a cool spring Monday afternoon, when Max and Marjorie Fisher were among the 1,500 guests at the White House who watched as President Sadat of Egypt and Prime Minister Begin of Israel signed the Arabic, Hebrew and English versions of the first peace treaty between Israel and an Arab country — the Camp David accords.

That evening, the guests attended a dinner to celebrate the signing. One hundred thirty tables were arrayed beneath an enormous yellow-striped tent on the South Lawn; Columbia River salmon in aspic, roast beef, spring vegetables, a hazelnut and chocolate mousse, and three wines were served. Marjorie and Max were seated on the outer rim of the dining area, as were all Republicans. Marjorie could not see Carter, Begin and Sadat from behind the worsted wool-and-silk wall of guests. But Max was tall enough to spot them over the crowd — senators, representatives from the House, former and current State Department officials, and prominent members of the American Jewish and Arab communities — converging on the center of the tent to congratulate the leaders.

Political scientist Steven Spiegel has written that it was

the work of the Nixon and Ford administrations that "created the conditions for and initiated a new Arab-Israeli peace process, beginning with a limited settlement." Fisher agreed with this assertion and was proud of the small part he played in helping to facilitate the disengagements after the Yom Kippur War. But throughout the Camp David process, and now, in this grand hour of triumph, he was forced to sit on the sidelines. The 1980 election was approaching and Fisher — perhaps never more than on that chilly spring evening on the White House lawn — was burning to involve himself again.

While the Fishers watched the crowd, Prime Minister Begin, standing with Carter and Sadat, turned and saw Max above the throng of well wishers. Begin waved for Max to join him. Slowly, the Fishers wended their way toward the prime minister. Begin greeted the Fishers, then introduced Max to Carter, saying, "Mr. President, I want you to meet the most important member of your country's Jewish community."

As Fisher and Carter shook hands, the president replied: "Yes, I've heard of him."

Begin then introduced the Fishers to Sadat, who was standing with his wife, Jehan. Max shook hands and congratulated the Egyptian leader. Marjorie recalls feeling struck by Sadat's presence, his grace. She wanted to offer more than a perfunctory greeting to a man whom she had come to admire for his courage in pursuit of peace. She uttered the first thing that popped into her head: "All humanity is one entity."

President Sadat smiled. Jehan Sadat asked: "Would you please repeat what you said, dear?"

Marjorie repeated it and Jehan Sadat thanked her.

The exchange has a tragic footnote. Four years after that evening, the Fishers were in New York City to attend a sixtieth birthday party for Henry Kissinger at the Pierre Hotel. By then, President Sadat was dead — assassinated by Islamic fundamentalists in Nasr City on October 6, 1981. As the Fishers began walking from their hotel to Kissinger's party, it started to rain. Egypt's ambassador to the United States, Ashraf A. Ghorbal, offered them a ride. Marjorie hurried into the backseat of the car. With a sudden shock of recognition, Marjorie realized that the woman sitting next to her was Jehan Sadat. With a sad smile crossing her face, Jehan Sadat said: "All humanity is one entity."

*   *   *

Almost exactly one year after the Camp David accords were signed, Fisher was in the midst of a presidential campaign. On March 6, it was announced in Washington, D.C., that Fisher and other prominent Republicans were establishing a national draft committee for former President Gerald Ford. Behind Fisher's decision was that Ford was his closest ally in the ensemble of 1980 presidential hopefuls, and that the present front-runner and winner of the New Hampshire primary, former Governor Ronald Reagan, was aligned with the right wing of the GOP, a conclave in which Fisher was not comfortable.

Ford himself hinted that he would again try for the presidency. Like Fisher, he was not at home with the party's right wing. During an interview at his office in Rancho Mirage, California, Ford, referring to Reagan's conservatism, said that "there is the growing sentiment [in Republican circles around the country] that Governor Reagan cannot win the election." Reagan campaign manager, William J. Casey, suspected that Ford was publicly disparaging Reagan's chances because he was still angry with Reagan for challenging him for the 1976 nomination. Ford had been an incumbent; Reagan should have waited his turn. His loss to Carter was close and Ford felt that the Reagan challenge had proved to be a pivotal difference.

In the late winter of 1980, though, Ford was reluctant to declare his candidacy since, as political observer Elizabeth Drew wrote, he "was leading what many would consider the good life — Palm Springs, Vail, well-paid speeches, an ample income, respectful treatment as a former president . . . all [of which] might be spoiled if he actually ran." But the announcement of the draft committee and Fisher's involvement in it caused a stir. Insiders doubted that the Ford committee would have been formed unless the former president had privately consented to run.

Whatever happened on the political front, Fisher, as chairman of the Detroit Renaissance, had his civic duty to consider. He (with the help of his friend, prominent Republican and Detroit industrialist, Robert Evans) had been lobbying for two years to bring the 1980 Republican National Convention to financially strapped Detroit, while almost no one running the GOP wished to come. Party leaders were eager to avoid Detroit without offending Fisher. They claimed the city was unsafe. This perception was sharpened in January 1980, when Detroit's police officers threatened a walkout if a pay hike the city clearly could not afford was not granted. In response, Fisher convened several Sunday-morning meetings in his garden room, and union leaders reached a compromise with Detroit Mayor Coleman Young that would keep them working.

Fisher argued that not only would the business be good for Detroit, but the city's negative image had been distorted by the press, and the media's presence during the convention would prove it. Republican leaders were not convinced. In the end, Detroit was selected as the site of the convention because of Fisher's friendships. Former President Ford recalls hearing the story that Detroit and Dallas finished in a dead heat as host for the 1980 RNC. The balloting was secret, but it was rumored afterward that GOP National Chairman William E. Brock, a close friend of Fisher, cast the deciding vote that brought all those Republicans in their red-and-yellow golf caps to Detroit. After the convention ended without incident and everyone agreed that Detroit had been a wonderful host, Brock joked to Fisher that he had spent more than a few "sleepless nights" over his vote, a vote cast chiefly on Fisher's word that Republicans would be welcomed in the predominantly African-American, blue-collar city.

Ford's potential candidacy did not materialize. On April 3, he wrote Fisher to thank him for his $1,000 contribution to the Draft Ford Committee and stated that his "decision not to be a candidate was a terribly difficult one but, all things considered, I believe it was in the best interest of the Republican

Party and the nation. I hope you and others understand. I will
be at the GOP convention and will play whatever constructive role will help the cause of defeating President Carter." At
the bottom of the letter, Ford penned in a postscript: "You
always come through. J."

Ford told Fisher that if Reagan were nominated he would
campaign for him, but the Reagan organization was skeptical,
believing that Ford's resentment about 1976 would keep him
off the campaign trail. And they were disturbed about it.
Casey biographer, Joseph Persico, cites a memo that Casey
sent Reagan in the spring of 1980: "Of all the Republicans,"
wrote Casey, "Jerry Ford is the one who can hurt us or help us
most." Casey was troubled by Reagan's image as a dedicated
right-winger — a Barry Goldwater with an arsenal of down-to-
earth folksiness and TV-charm. Ford was the quintessential
moderate, and Casey wanted him aboard.

Reagan was cognizant of his image. He thought that it
was unfair — a holdover from his stance against campus activists when he was governor of California. "I don't think I had
any other choice but to take a strong stand [against the radi-
cals]," says Reagan. "I think those people were being guided
by the Communists. The Communists' whole purpose was to
keep the trouble going. One of their weapons against me was
that whole thing of my being a right-wing maniac. This was
the word they spread. It was pretty shameless."

The label stuck, and Casey knew that a more moderate
Reagan would be more attractive to voters. Casey contacted
Fisher through Theodore Cummings, who was a friend of both
Reagan and Fisher. Reagan did not know Fisher well, but, by
1980, he says Fisher's stature was such that Republican presi-
dents and Republican presidential candidates "inherited him."

"Max," says Reagan, "has always been willing to lend his
support. It's very much a part of him, and it's valuable to
those of us who may find ourselves temporarily servants of
the people." Reagan was eager to access Fisher's contacts and
skills, which the former president says, "would have been
impossible for me to master."

In late April, Fisher went to Ted Cummings's home in

Beverly Hills, California. Casey asked him to come upstairs, where Fisher spoke with the candidate and his campaign manager.

"You're going to need Jerry Ford to win this thing," Fisher told them.

Displaying a flair for understatement, Reagan replied: "I don't think he's too friendly."

Fisher said: "Call him up and talk to him."

Reagan smiled, saying: "If you think I should, I'll do it."

Casey was eager for Fisher to sign on with Reagan. He knew that if Reagan had Fisher with him, then Ford would probably join as well. Casey told Fisher that Ford had been mentioned as a possible choice for the vice presidency. Fisher replied that he didn't know if Ford would be interested. Casey told him to talk about it with the former president. Then Casey said that some of the Reagan campaign people opposed the idea of a fund-raiser in Detroit because the candidate had not garnered enough support among corporations. The campaign people were afraid that a bad showing would embarrass Reagan and highlight his lack of corporate backing.

"Max," Casey asked, "how do you think we'll do in Detroit?"

"I'll take care of it," Fisher said.

On May 14, Fisher and Robert Evans held a cocktail party and a dinner that netted $330,000 for the Reagan campaign. Also of primary importance was the effect of these fund-raisers on the press's perception of Reagan.

On Friday, May 16, Bill Peterson of *The Washington Post* wrote: "Ronald Reagan is finally picking up the support of one group that has long eluded him — the corporate boardroom crowd." Peterson recounted Reagan's successful speech at a Detroit Economic Club luncheon, where he sat between Thomas Murphy, chairman of General Motors, and William Agee, chairman of Bendix Corp. Then Peterson said: "The $1,000 fund-raising dinner was even more impressive. The guest list included top executive officers from General Motors, Owens-Illinois, Burroughs Corp., Marathon Oil, K-Mart, Ford Motors, and a host of other companies. Henry

Ford II didn't make it, but he sold $10,000 in tickets."

Following his swing through Michigan, Reagan got busy mending fences. As Fisher had advised him, Reagan phoned Ford. In June, he visited him in Rancho Mirage. Immediately after the meeting, Ford called Fisher at the Regency Hotel in New York City. Ford said that the visit had gone well; there had been some more talk of Ford taking the vice-presidential spot and creating a dream ticket. Ford told Fisher that he declined the offer, adding that as much as he would like to campaign for Reagan, he was going to be tied up with speaking engagements to raise $600,000 for the completion of the Ford Library on the main campus of the University of Michigan at Ann Arbor. Fisher got in touch with Casey and explained about the Ford Library and the need for a further gesture from the Reagan people.

"What kind of gesture?" Casey inquired.

Fisher said: "Maybe if help with the library was offered."

The details were quickly arranged. Fisher and Casey assumed the fund-raising chores, so that Ford was free to campaign for Reagan. Fisher, who had already raised over $500,000 for the library, made another pledge to get things rolling. Casey himself gave $5,000. By July 14, the opening night of the Republican Convention, the money was raised.

Gerald Ford delivered. In his speech to the 10,000 delegates who were assembled at Joe Louis Arena on the banks of the Detroit River, the former president said: "Elder statesmen are supposed to sit quietly and smile wisely from the sidelines. I've never been much for sitting. I've never spent much time on the sidelines. . . . So when this convention fields a team for Governor Reagan, count me in."

Reagan and Casey thanked Fisher profusely for bringing Ford aboard. And Reagan loved Ford's speech. His phrase, "count me in," intrigued him. Perhaps Ford was interested in being his running mate. Reagan authorized Casey to meet with a Ford team, led by former Secretary of State Henry Kissinger, to investigate the feasibility of fielding such a ticket.

As newspaper reporters, network correspondents and not a few GOP insiders were tracking down the former president for a comment, Ford and his wife — with a mob of Secret Service agents at their heels — exited the arena's backstage entrance, where Fisher was waiting for them in his burgundy Lincoln. The Fords rode with Fisher to his house in Franklin. That Monday evening, July 14, was Jerry Ford's sixty-seventh birthday; Fisher would turn seventy-two on Tuesday, and so they sat on the red chintz-covered chairs in Fisher's garden room, eating coconut cake and chatting about the convention with Betty Ford and Marjorie Fisher, former Ambassador Leonard K. Firestone and his wife, Nickie, and the Fishers' daughter, Mary, who had worked as an advance person in the Ford White House, helping to arrange the innumerable details associated with the president's travels.

The serious political talk came the next morning when Fisher and Ford met in Fisher's upstairs library. Negotiations were proceeding between the Ford and Reagan camp to draw up the dream ticket. Fisher and Ford discussed the possibility for several hours, determining that there were three main reasons why such a ticket was not feasible: spheres of responsibility could not be adequately defined; their staffs would never be able to co-exist peacefully and productively; and the situation would be too competitive for their wives, neither of whom would fully be acknowledged as first lady.

Ford concluded: "Even though it can't be done, we still have to listen to the Reagan proposal out of sense of deference."

Fisher agreed that Ford should listen politely but try to guard against too much talk of a Reagan-Ford ticket, which could hurt the ultimate ticket in November. Private negotiations between the camps lagged on for thirty-six hours, with the attendant speculations in the press, but, in reality, the matter was closed. The official conclusion occurred late Wednesday night when Ford met alone with Reagan. Ford departed the hotel suite smiling and Reagan told his staff: "His answer was no. He didn't think it was right for him or me. I'm going to call George [H.] Bush."

Ford campaigned wholeheartedly for Reagan; Fisher mined his network for funds and worked the Jewish community. Given Reagan's far-right image, Fisher encountered resistance to him. One member of the community asked Fisher: "Do you think Reagan can find Israel on a map?" Fisher replied that he could do far more than that. Before the election, Fisher spoke to Reagan about Israel on three separate occasions and he came away agreeing with what Richard Nixon later privately told him: that of all the presidents since 1948, Ronald Reagan had the strongest emotional commitment to the Jewish State.

Two years after leaving the presidency, Reagan explains the roots of his personal tie to Israel: "Though there are religious differences between Christianity and Judaism," he says, "we worship the same God: the Holy Land is the Holy Land to a great many of us. And then, after the trials and tribulations of the Jews during the Second World War, the idea of them having a homeland there again with all the traditions that go with it, is something that every American should be able to appreciate. All of us in America go back in our ancestry to some other part of the world. There is no nation like us. Except Israel. Both nations are melting pots. All of us in the United States have a feeling for our heritage as well as the fact that we are Americans. And so it is with the Jews and Israel — everyone coming from somewhere else to live in freedom."

During the 1980 campaign, Fisher — as he had done with Nixon — helped Reagan explain his thinking on Israel and Soviet Jewry to the organized American Jewish community. On September 3, Reagan addressed a B'nai B'rith forum in Washington, D.C. Fisher had worked on the speech with Reagan adviser Richard V. Allen. The speech contained specific attacks on the Carter administration's relationship to Israel and the Soviet Union. Within the opening thirty seconds, the candidate said: "In defending Israel's right to exist, we defend the very values upon which our nation is built. The long agony of Jews in the Soviet Union is never far from our minds and hearts. All these suffering people ask is that their families get the chance to work where they choose, in freedom and peace. They will not be forgotten by a Reagan administration."

Additionally, Fisher touted Reagan's position in Israel,

speaking to Prime Minister Menachem Begin and other leaders, and telling *The Jerusalem Post* that Reagan was "much more moderate than he is perceived and his commitment to Israel is firmly based on his assessment of Israel's importance to the United States as a reliable ally in a vital strategic area. An America led by Reagan would be a [more] convincing America in the international arena — and thus an America that Israel could safely rely on."

Yet once Reagan soundly defeated Carter in the 1980 election, Fisher did not enjoy the same easy access to the Oval Office that he had during previous Republican administrations. His personal relationship with Reagan, while congenial, did not include the kind of closeness that he had shared with Nixon and Ford. As *Washington Post* reporter Lou Cannon points out in *President Reagan: The Role of a Lifetime*, as a latecomer to politics and an outsider in Washington, "Reagan lacked the network of alliances and friendships normally forged by politicians as they scramble up the career ladder." As president, however, Reagan did depend on what Cannon calls "offstage influences." Among the most influential of these was Richard Nixon.

Seven years had passed since Nixon had resigned the presidency, and by now he had some cause for contentment. He had published his memoirs and was writing on foreign affairs. He was not free from the taint of Watergate and scholars would quarrel over the value of his accomplishments. But at last his geopolitical achievements, from the partial strategic arms limitation treaty with the Soviet Union to the path he cleared to the People's Republic of China — what Henry Kissinger calls Nixon's "seminal contributions" — were beginning to be acknowledged.

Democrats and Republicans alike sought Nixon's advice — but out of the public eye. Michael Oksenberg, a member of the National Security Council under Carter, was sent to brief Nixon after relations with China were normalized. Nixon became a consultant to President Reagan and others in his administration on issues ranging from the defense budget to the squabbles among the staff in the West Wing of the White

House. One of the recommendations Nixon made to Reagan was that he talk to Fisher.

In a private memo to the White House, Nixon wrote: "I have a suggestion to make on Mideast policy, generally and particularly with regard to relations with Israel. As you know better than I, you are overwhelmed with people inside and outside the government who profess to speak for the Jewish community. Many of them are simply in business for themselves or for their particular constituencies. By far, the best man we worked with and one who was invaluable when Kissinger was working out the disengagement plans on the Egyptian and Syrian fronts was Max Fisher. He knows [the] Israeli government leaders intimately and could always carry the message to Garcia, even if it was unpleasant when we asked him to do so. He also is greatly respected among the various Jewish organizations because of his enormous contributions on the fund-raising front. But most important, he is one of those rare individuals supporting Israel's position who can always be counted upon for total, loyal support for whatever decision is made by the administration. Equally important, he can keep his mouth shut. I would strongly urge that you personally have him down for lunch or a talk, get his advice, and use him for special assignments. I can attest from personal experience that he will never let you down."

In general, though, Reagan opted to leave the finer points of foreign policy to his advisers. Thus, Fisher did not meet with him as he had met with Nixon and Ford. Instead, Fisher found that his access to policy-makers ran through the stylishly appointed, oak-paneled office of Reagan's secretary of state, General Alexander Haig.

Fisher had become friendly with Haig during the Nixon administration, when the general was serving as Kissinger's deputy on the National Security Council and later as Nixon's chief of staff. Haig trusted Fisher, respecting his facility for getting along with the divergent personalities at the White House and in the State Department. Haig says that Fisher's achievements owed much to the fact that "Max was viewed as a patriot and, to his everlasting glory, he's a persistent sonovabitch. There are no ends to which he won't go to communicate his concerns. He traveled enough to Israel so that if you watched him you knew that he had a good feel for the pulse of [Israeli leaders], their demeanor and attitude."

Haig was eager to use Fisher's contacts with the leaders in Israel, believing that "it is always helpful to have an extra channel that influences more formal dialogue." And as the administration got under way, Fisher wasted little time cementing his relationship with the secretary of state. On March 2, he was in Haig's office giving him a reading on the situation in Israel. Although the Labor Party's Shimon Peres was rising in the polls, Fisher said, Begin would win re-election. Fisher was leaving for Israel in two weeks and he promised to meet with Haig when he returned. He also told the secretary of state that he was in the process of bringing leaders of the American Jewish community together with the White House to discuss the controversy over the impending sale of Airborne Warning and Command Systems to Saudi Arabia.

AWACS, flying radar systems that are used to pinpoint incoming aircraft or missiles and to direct the launching of defensive or offensive missiles, became a conundrum for Haig as he was taking office. Since 1948, every administration has considered selling arms to Arab nations and weathered the corresponding political flak. Yet perhaps no administration had to wrestle with this problem as quickly as the Reagan White House.

Says Haig: "The Carter administration had made a commitment to the Saudi government. And we were faced with this horrible dilemma of a foreign commitment we had to honor. And so I started, during the transition, making this clear to my Israeli counterpart, [Foreign Minister] Yitzhak Shamir. And basically the Israeli government was prepared to accept the sale."

Much of the American Jewish community, and the Congress, were not prepared to accept it, and the administration came under fire. According to Haig, the conflict over the sale was unnecessary.

"Of course," says Haig, "the Jewish community, unaware of my dialogue with Shamir, was pushing against the sale. But the problem was that [Secretary of Defense Caspar W.] Weinberger made a public statement that not only were we selling the Saudis AWACS, we were going to sell them [advanced sidewinder air-to-air missiles and extra fuel tanks designed to increase the AWACS range approximately 900 miles]. And then Shamir is blown out of the saddle by Begin. And that's when the rail really started. The whole controversy was a direct result of the lack of discipline in the Reagan administration and Weinberger's Arabist proclivities."

It also cheapened what Haig believes are the two most important commodities in foreign policy, "reliability and consistency." He says that if the Reagan administration hoped to draw the Saudis into the American camp at the expense of the U.S.-Israeli relationship, then they were stumbling over faulty logic. "You cannot impress new friends by screwing old friends," Haig states. "Because they say to themselves: 'Today it's an old friend getting screwed; tomorrow it'll be me.'"

Fisher was thrust into the controversy within the organized American Jewish community, which was lobbying to kill the sale. Haig feels that "some people accept the conventional wisdom that the American Jewish community wields unprecedented influence on U.S. policy-making. Based on my experience, I don't find it to be true. There is no dominant thinking in the American Jewish community. There's the left and the right. Max's influence came from his Republicanism and that we had a Republican president who had confidence in him. Max didn't get anything, in practical terms, by being the Republican Party's guru on Israel. He took a lot of heat, with all the infighting, which is a product of the Jewish community being a philosophical potpourri. But the stereotype of Jewish money and Jewish control is appalling. I've seen it in practice and they're not as influential as portrayed — by both sides. Everybody likes to think they are influencing things — especially when organizations have been put together to accomplish missions along those lines. But that influence is just not there."

Yet many in the Reagan administration, exquisitely sensitive to public opinion and hoping to get the AWACS sale through Congress with a minimum of warring in the press, agreed to meet with a delegation of thirty-two Jewish Republican leaders on the afternoon of March 11. The agenda, though, was not to include the sale, but rather Reagan's initiatives for prodding the lagging economy.

On the morning prior to the White House encounter, Fisher chaired a closed-door meeting with Jewish leaders at the Hay-Adams Hotel. Senator Rudolph E. Boschwitz of Minnesota, a Jewish Republican and chairman of the Senate Foreign Relations Subcommittee on the Middle East, was at the Hays-Adams along with Thomas A. Dine, the new executive director of the American Israel Public Affairs Committee (AIPAC), the official pro-Israel lobbying organization in Congress. Boschwitz informed the group that eleven of the seventeen members of the Foreign Relations Committee supported a resolution blocking the sale — all eight Democrats and three Republicans. Boschwitz then stated that he was vehemently opposed to the sale. He urged the delegation to argue against it with Reagan, claiming that if they did not the administration would exploit the silence of the Jewish community during its congressional lobbying efforts.

Fisher was incensed. Nothing angered him more than what he deemed reckless judgment, and Boschwitz's suggestion ran counter to everything he regarded as sacrosanct when dealing with oppositional points of view. What, he asked the delegation, was to be gained by attacking the administration? Making it appear as though the American Jewish community were forcing Congress to choose between Reagan and Begin? Deals were never closed in the spirit of confrontation. Better to work behind closed doors. Besides, the Israeli government had made a deal with the White House not to push for a confrontation. Furthermore, Fisher said, there were strategic considerations. Any lasting Middle East peace, said Fisher, will involve the cooperation of the Saudis. The bottom line is not the AWACS, but who will have influence — and how much — with the Arabs? The United States or the Soviet Union, which is not friendly toward Israel? If the White House wins this debate, then Saudi Arabia will be in the administration's debt, which is good for America and good for Israel.

Fisher was sharply rebuffed by the majority of the group. Although no one said it, many thought that he was again acting as the administration's court Jew. Tom Dine circulated AIPAC's six-page memorandum protesting the sale. A vote was taken, which favored the drafting of a statement opposing the deal. Fisher was chosen to read it to the president. Then the delegation left for the White House.

In the Cabinet Room, Reagan was flanked by Fisher and Ted Cummings. Seated across the table were Vice President George Bush, with the Jewish delegation filling the rest of the chairs at the table and along the walls. After the reporters were ushered out, Reagan spoke about his domestic economic program. He did not mention Israel.

Fisher responded with the prepared statement. According to the text, he was supposed to say, "We are deeply disturbed by, and opposed to, the proposed sale of equipment to enhance the offensive capability of the Saudi Arabian F-15s without a change in Saudi opposition toward the Camp David peace process." Instead, he substituted, "We are a little bit disturbed by," and dropped "opposed to."

Those in the delegation who supported the statement were angry, but Fisher held his ground: he would not embarrass the president in public; all of Fisher's experience with government officials taught him this was not an effective way to play the game. Reagan, affable as always, replied by assuring the group that the United States would make certain that the balance of arms, in qualitative terms, would remain in Israel's favor and reaffirmed his campaign commitments toward Israel.

Immediately after the session, Fisher spoke at a White House news conference. His tone was conciliatory, but he was obviously annoyed at Republican Jewish leaders who had criticized him because he thought it was in everyone's best interest not to clash publicly with the White House. Israeli leaders, he said, would have to make up their own minds about the sale, and perhaps they already had, since it appeared they were ready to live with a deal whereby Israel would receive an additional $600 million in military loans.

Less than a week later, Fisher was in Israel bluntly telling *The Jerusalem Post*: "I don't think the White House meeting was useful." When he returned to Detroit, he phoned Haig, informing the secretary of state that further discussions were needed on the AWACS — maybe at a small meeting, a forum that would not be used as a staging area to attack the administration. Haig told him to set it up.

Yet by the time this group gathered on June 25, the situation had radically shifted.

Reagan had been shot on March 31. The next day, during a National Security Council meeting chaired by Vice President Bush, Defense Secretary Weinberger pressed for — and won — NSC-approval to sell the additional equipment to Saudi Arabia. Haig was reportedly skeptical about giving the Saudis such sophisticated equipment, but his role within the administration was being undermined by Weinberger, Reagan's domestic advisers and the secretary of state's embarrassing "I'm-in control-here" statement after Reagan was wounded.

On June 7, 1981, the relationship between Washington and Jerusalem underwent further strain. While the debate over AWACS raged, the Israeli government's immediate focus was not on Saudi Arabia, but on Iraq. With physical assistance from France and Italy, Iraqi leader Saddam Hussein had been able to construct a nuclear reactor in his country and was developing nuclear weapons. According to Amos Perlmutter, biographer of Israeli Prime Minister Menachem Begin, in the eyes of Begin, a survivor of the Holocaust, "Hussein was Hitler, and the nuclear reactor at Osirak was a technologically advanced version of the Final Solution."

On June 7, the Israeli Air Force destroyed the reactor. The Reagan administration openly deplored Israel's actions. In an unprecedented move, they suspended shipments of F-16 aircraft to the Israelis and approved a U.N. Security Council condemnation of Israel. The American Jewish community was vexed by the condemnation, a feeling that intensified when the press revealed that President Reagan telephoned his ambassador to the United Nations, Jeane J. Kirkpatrick, at her vacation home in St. Remy, France, to congratulate her on her deft handling of the resolution.

Thus, on June 25, when a small delegation of Republican Jews, headed by Fisher, met with White House counselor Edwin Meese III to convey their opposition to the administration's proposed sale of the AWACS, the Saudi sale was no longer the predominant topic of concern. Fisher said that the community was disturbed by the administration's treatment of Israel — in general. Meese answered that the administration still supported the Israelis, in spite of the recent strain. Meese listened to them, and then departed. Nothing, Fisher thought, had been accomplished.

In July, two weeks after his seventy-third birthday, Fisher went to Washington and spoke privately with Secretary of State Haig for an hour. The secretary applauded the Israeli raid on Iraq and said that the administration was being short-sighted: Hussein should not have nuclear weapons. (Nearly a decade later, in January 1991, with the Persian Gulf War under way, Fisher recalled Begin's decision and his conversation with Haig, and commented that time had proven both of them right.) However, Haig told Fisher, the administration resented Begin's pre-emptive actions, not only in Iraq but now with his attack on the PLO in Lebanon. Haig suggested that discussions with Begin should get started to resolve these issues. Fisher said that he would speak to Begin. Haig and Fisher also discussed the problems, from Haig's vantage point, of formulating foreign policy in the Reagan White House, with Meese and National Security Adviser Richard Allen coordinating policy for the president, and Weinberger under-cutting Haig at every opportunity. Fisher said that the Israelis were aware of this and were not trying to make things more difficult for the secretary.

Sadat was assassinated in October, and senators, who were drawing near to a vote on the AWACS, were worried that defeating the sale would promote instability in the region. The sale was passed by the Senate at the end of October, and the Reagan administration, attempting to mend fences with the American Jewish community, scheduled a meeting with their leaders on November 19. Two hours before the meeting, Fisher met with Haig. The secretary told him that Meese and Weinberger were again intruding on foreign policy. Later, in his notes of the meeting, Fisher wrote: "Haig is a good man. He is going to need some help."

At the White House, President Reagan told American Jewish leaders that the proposed level of U.S.-and-Israeli strategic cooperation would be substantive, not "cosmetic." The leaders voiced their distress over the anti-Semitic rhetoric that emerged around the AWACS debate. The meeting, however, did little to mitigate the bitterness that lingered between Washington and Jerusalem.

While entangled in the controversy, Fisher briefly turned his attention to business. On January 7, 1982, U.S. Steel purchased Marathon Oil, paying $125 per share. Fisher, with 665,115 shares of Marathon stock, realized over $83 million. Then, before the year was out, Fisher's interest in the Irvine Ranch came to a highly profitable conclusion. Al Taubman and Donald Bren, co-chairman of Irvine Co., were at odds over which one of them was running Irvine. Bren offered to buy out the partnership for $518 million. With California real estate in a slump and land-use regulations hindering further development, Fisher prevailed upon Taubman to sell, and Bren purchased Irvine Co. Taubman walked away with $140 million; Fisher with $100 million.

Less profitable, but more enjoyable for Fisher, the ex-football lineman, was his investment with Taubman in the Michigan Panthers of the United States Football League. The USFL had a short run; the owners lost millions, but Fisher was consoled by the fact that the Panthers won a league championship.

One afternoon, not long after the Irvine sale, Taubman phoned Fisher. The gist of the conversation, Fisher says, was that Taubman wanted to buy Sotheby's Holdings, the parent of the then-financially ailing London-based art auction house. The British government had been dragging its heels on a

$100-million takeover bid from two New York businessmen, Marshall Cogan and Stephen Swid. When Cogan and Swid heard that Taubman was interested in buying Sotheby's, they contacted Fisher and asked him why Taubman was competing with them. Fisher replied: "Al's got a $140 million burning a hole in his pocket and he's looking around to invest it."

Six months later, Taubman, Fisher, Henry Ford II, Milton Petrie and Leslie H. Wexner, owner of the Limited clothing stores, acquired Sotheby's for $139 million. (In 1990, *Fortune* magazine, in reference to the group's profits, would dub the five men, "the $400 million friendship.") It was rumored that Henry Ford II helped push the deal through by putting in a good word with Queen Elizabeth II.

Fisher had scant time to savor his success. Secretary of State Haig was increasingly disgusted with his eroding power in the administration and was reportedly angered at the White House's condemnation of Israel for attacking the PLO in Beirut. So, in late June 1982, Haig resigned. With the nomination of George Shultz as his successor, Fisher was cast into the middle of a shrill debate within the organized Jewish community, a segment of which contended that Shultz was as obdurate an Arabist, and therefore as anti-Israel, as Defense Secretary Weinberger.

* * *

In November of 1990, at the 59th annual meeting of the Council of Jewish Federations, George Shultz told the following tale. It seems that he was on a business trip in London, when the White House, with its fabled proficiency for locating anyone in the world, called a phone booth he happened to be ambling past. Shultz picked up the phone and President Reagan was on the line proposing that he take the job of secretary of state. Shultz accepted, and as soon as he hung up, the phone rang again. He answered it.

"Hello, George," said Fisher. "I hear you're going to be the new secretary of state. How can I help you?"

The apocryphal story was indicative of the working relationship that developed between Fisher and the new secretary of state. "Whenever Max wanted to talk with me," says Shultz, "he could call and talk. He had easy access to me and I relied on Max for advice on all kinds of things, including our work with Israel and the peace process."

The objections that some members of the organized American Jewish community expressed about Shultz's nomination centered on his employer: since 1974, Shultz had been executive president of the California-based Bechtel Group, a private multibillion dollar engineering and construction firm with strong ties to oil-rich Arab states. (Before becoming secretary of defense, Weinberger had served as Bechtel's general counsel.) Journalist Laton McCartney, author of *Friends in High Places: The Bechtel Story*, asserts that Bechtel ran "deep with country-club-style anti-Semitism," a charge that Shultz denies.

"Bechtel was unjustly accused," says Shultz. "The spill over about [the company] being internally anti-Semitic was totally wrong. One of our chief officers was Jewish, but we didn't think of it that way — we just thought of him as a terrific guy. People didn't even know that one of [Stephen D. Bechtel Jr.'s] sons-in-law was Jewish."

It was not the rumored anti-Semitism that rankled some in the Jewish community, but Bechtel's business with Libya and Saudi Arabia, and its adherence to the Arab boycott — the same financial bludgeon that Arab nations wielded against the Ford Motor Company when Henry II decided to do business with Israel in the 1970s.

"As far as the Arab boycott goes," Shultz says, "Bechtel did a lot of business with various Arab countries and didn't do any business with Israel, although it had tried on one or two occasions — I happen to know. But it didn't. Bechtel was rather careful legally about what it did. And in the end, the record proves it."

Fisher was appalled by the charges that Shultz was either anti-Semitic or hostile toward Israel. He had known Shultz since 1969, when Nixon appointed him secretary of labor. They established, Fisher says, an immediate rapport. It is not hard to see why. Both men were courtly and soft-spoken, but direct, with a good eye for the bottom line, and a conciliatory style that masked the steel core of natural, and tough, negotiators.

In conversation with Shultz, Fisher learned how the then-secretary of labor viewed the strategic importance of Israel to the United States and how he had developed an appreciation for Israeli patriotism.

In the mid-1960s, Shultz was the dean of the University of Chicago's graduate school of business, and he became friendly with a student from Israel, Yosef Levy.

"Joe was a terrific young man," says Shultz. "He had charm and he was savvy. My wife and I had a custom of having a party at the end of each quarter for the students on the dean's list — a fairly select group — and Joe was always there. So we came to know and admire him. When the [Six-Day War] broke out [on June 5, 1967], before we even realized Joe had [returned to his army unit in Israel], we heard that he had been killed on the Golan Heights. My wife and I were stunned.

"We also learned something about Israel from him. The ultimate compliment a school like the University of Chicago can pay a graduate student is to invite him to be on the faculty. And we would have invited Joe. But it was very clear that his idea was to come and study and then go back to Israel. He had no interest in staying in the United States. It was such a contrast to students from so many other countries who spend half their time figuring out how to stay here. So it taught us something about Israel. And when he went back to fight — he didn't wait for somebody to call. As soon as he heard [about the war], he left. When I went to Israel in 1969, as secretary of labor, I visited his parents [to offer my condolences]."

On June 28, Fisher was in Jerusalem for meetings at the Jewish Agency when he fired off a congratulatory cable to Shultz, stating: "I resent the implications that you might be biased in your judgment because of your present business association [with the Bechtel Group]. I have always known you to be a fair, honorable man with a real sense of integrity. Be assured of my cooperation."

Next, Fisher cabled Ed Meese at the White House, asking

him to "please convey to the president my congratulations for his appointment of George Shultz as secretary of state. I have known George for many years and find him to be a man of great integrity and ability with a sense of fairness. I am prepared to publicly support him. If you want to use this statement of support you may do so. If there is anything else I can do, please contact me."

Finally, Fisher cabled the chairman of the Senate's Foreign Relations Committee, Senator Charles H. Percy, a Republican from Illinois, telling him, in effect, what he had told Meese. However worded, though, Fisher's meaning was clear: If the organized Jewish community protests the appointment, or works against the confirmation, Fisher was willing to do whatever was possible to see that Shultz became secretary of state.

After flying back to the United States, Fisher went to see Haig at his home. As with Nixon's loss in 1960, Fisher knew how painful the reality of fair-weather political friends could be, and so he supported Haig on his decision and commiserated with him over his predicament in the administration.

Meantime, Shultz was easily confirmed as secretary of state, and he began consulting frequently with Fisher. Although Shultz says that "it's better for the government to use official diplomatic channels," for communicating its positions, and remains "an advocate for using the ambassador," he found talking with Fisher helpful.

Says Shultz: "I felt that Max was the person who knew the straight story and whose opinion carried real [weight in Israel and in the American Jewish community]. So I instinctively turned to him. You could speak confidentially to him and trust him. He was always on the level. He didn't try to manipulate. He told you what he believed and what he was going to do. Whenever he went to Israel he would check in with me, and when he got back he would check in again. He could give you a sense of people's thinking."

Fisher could also help mediate between the organized American Jewish community and the administration, which was crucial to Shultz, since President Reagan was preparing to set forth his plan for Middle East peace, and the administration was going to need the support of the Jewish community.

"Before President Reagan made his speech we had a lot of discussions with people about what to do," explains Shultz, who, like Fisher, was a dedicated consensus builder. "The Israelis were in Beirut. We had just gotten the PLO out and the situation in Lebanon seemed to have settled down a bit. We felt that Lebanon was one issue, but the West Bank and Gaza were deeper problems, and we wanted to address them. I had extensive confrontations with the Senate Foreign Relations Committee and the House. I consulted with Max and a group of leaders from the American Jewish community. We put out a position, saying, 'Here's what we are going to propose. What do you think? What are your ideas?' They were being consulted throughout the process. I think there was a pretty good reception to [our peace plan] in the United States and Europe, and in the American Jewish community. And one of the reasons was that we had listened to people, so if somebody tried to upset our decisions, they wouldn't be able to."

Shultz reached out to the American Jewish community because he feels they are an integral part of U.S. foreign policy toward Israel. "One of the unique things about America is that everybody here is, in a sense, from somewhere else," says Shultz. "So, if you're secretary of state, you realize that there are all of these constituencies out there. For example, the biggest Polish city outside of Warsaw is Chicago. And so if you're going to do something about Poland, you'd better see what the people in Chicago think. And if you're not thinking about Poland, then they are going to remind you to think about Poland. It's characteristic of our foreign policy that we care more about what's happening in various countries than most other countries do about what's going on someplace else. And the reason is that we have this variety of constituencies. The American Jewish community is a strong, well-organized group and I think it performs a useful role in this unique aspect of American foreign policy. And we shouldn't apologize for listening to them or any other [ethnic or religious] community."

On August 5, Fisher and a group of Jewish leaders met

with Shultz, Vice President Bush and Defense Secretary Weinberger. Fisher's notes on the meeting reveal that the three administration officials agreed that Lebanon should be a free state and the PLO eliminated. But they also expressed the same opinion — that Israel's continued bombing and shelling of Beirut was too harsh and that the top priority after the conflict ended was autonomy for the Palestinians.

The group's reactions were mixed. Like the majority of American Jewry, Fisher and the other leaders did not oppose Palestinian autonomy because they questioned the moral right of Palestinians to have a state, or an entity, of their own. Their objections were founded on their fear for Israel's safety once this homeland was created. If the administration could design a plan that allotted Israel defensible borders and extracted a dependable commitment to peace from Palestinian leadership, then possibly the situation could be resolved. Ideas of how to accomplish these goals were fired back and forth. Discussions were heated, but compared to the tensions over the AWACS sale, Fisher judged the meeting to be a success.

On September 1, 1982, President Reagan unfurled his blueprint for Middle East peace. The Reagan Plan recommended that Jordanian-Palestinian-Israeli negotiations begin, with a seat reserved at the bargaining table for the PLO. It also called for a Palestinian entity on the West Bank in association with Jordan.

Israeli Prime Minister Begin violently rejected the plan, grousing in private that Israel had just defeated the PLO and now Reagan was resurrecting them. In all likelihood, Begin, with his legalistic bent, objected to the plan on what he perceived as more legitimate and meaningful grounds.

Ever since the 1967 Six-Day War, Israel had been amenable to swapping land for peace, and had done so with Egypt. Yet land is Israel's sole bargaining chip with Arab nations, and therefore to tolerate the wording of a proposal that challenges their sovereignty over any territory under their control robs them of these chips — the lone currency and hope they have for peace. What appeared to be hairsplitting by Begin was a bid to preserve the long-term prospect for peace. For a prime minister to do otherwise would be irresponsible. And this conviction was not limited to the legalistic Begin. Seven years later, it kindled Israeli Prime Minister Yitzhak Shamir's fiery resistance to President George Bush's characterization of East Jerusalem as "occupied territory."

The Reagan administration went about the business of marketing its proposal. On September 12, Shultz spoke before 300 people at a United Jewish Appeal big-gifts dinner in New York City. Fisher, wrapped up in preliminary discussions on the Sotheby purchase, could not attend. But Shultz asked Fisher to review a draft of his speech and the secretary of state incorporated some of Fisher's suggestions into the text. Standing before the audience, in the midst of his defense of the Reagan Plan, Shultz departed from his written speech and said: "I'm not sure my good friend, Max Fisher, would agree with everything I have to say, but — "

The audience laughed. Then applause broke out around the room.

Whatever the validity of the administration's initiatives, events worked to undermine peace. Four days after Shultz's speech, Lebanese Phalangists massacred Palestinians in the Sabra and Shatila refugee camps in Lebanon. The massacre brought protests over Israel's invasion of Lebanon to a head. Consequently, Israel's Kahan Commission ruled that Israeli General Ariel Sharon was indirectly responsible for the killing by allowing the Phalangists into the camps.

On October 28, Fisher met alone with Shultz in Washington, and tried to assist the secretary in inducing the Begin government to accept, at least in part, the Reagan Plan. Fisher advised Shultz to be patient and low-key; overtly criticizing Begin would harden his stance, as would cutting Israel out of the process to resolve the conflict in Lebanon. Begin should be invited to the United States for a visit, Fisher said, and then pressed to meet with King Hussein of Jordan. This would stimulate movement on that aspect of the plan and perhaps force a showdown on West-Bank rule. Meanwhile, the Palestinians should be pressured to recognize Israel's right to exist.

Finally, Fisher said, Begin's wife, Aliza was dying. The prime minister had always described her as more than a helpmate, but as the one person in the world to whom he could talk. President Reagan, said Fisher, should send Begin a letter expressing his concern for Aliza's failing health.

His efforts notwithstanding, Fisher was pessimistic about peace. Of all the secretary of states with whom Fisher dealt, he was, in outlook and demeanor, most similar to George Shultz, and because of their similarities Fisher was also the most candid with him. In their telephone conversations over the next few months, Fisher expressed his doubts about the Israelis and Palestinians reaching common ground.

Feeling that he had unintentionally disheartened the secretary of state, he wrote to Shultz: "I didn't mean to be quite as negative because I believe there is an opportunity for peace and the initiatives that you are taking are ones that I wholeheartedly support. As a result of your meeting [with American Jewish leaders, they have] a very warm personal feeling about you. They may have not agreed with some of the administration's ideas, but on a personal level you have their confidence, which is vital. George, please don't get discouraged. I still see the light at the end of the tunnel and if there is anything I can do to make that light brighter, please don't hesitate to call upon me."

One of the things that Fisher could do was to help Egyptian President Hosni Mubarak settle a dispute with Begin over the town of Taba, south of Eilat, in the Sinai peninsula. A stipulation of the peace treaty between Israel and Egypt was that Israel would return the entire Sinai. However, an Israeli company had built a resort hotel in Taba, and Begin did not want to give it to Egypt. In February, Fisher was contacted by Egyptian Ambassador Ghorbal. The ambassador requested that Fisher go to Egypt and speak with Mubarak. Later that month, Fisher flew to Aswan. He was greeted with as much pomp and circumstance as a head of state, with a red carpet rolled out to the door of his jet. Fisher spoke with a number of Mubarak's Cabinet ministers, and then he met with the Egyptian president.

Mubarak said: "I need to talk to Mr. Begin about Taba."

After a half-century of deal making, Fisher's response was understandable. "Why don't you call him on the phone?" he asked.

Despite Egypt's formal treaty with Israel, Mubarak had his relationship with other Arab states to consider, and so he replied: "I cannot do that."

Fisher nodded. "All right," he said. "What can I do?"

"You have influence in Israel," Mubarak said. "Speak to Mr. Begin. Tell him that he agreed to return 100 percent of the Sinai, and Taba is part of that agreement. Taba has become such a symbol to Egyptians, you would think it was their ancient capital."

Mubarak suggested that the dispute be brought before an international arbitration board. That sounded reasonable, said Fisher, but he asked Mubarak why he didn't try to improve the relationship between Egypt and Israel, adding that it would be better for all concerned if the Egyptian diplomatic connection to Israel was more cordial.

"Yes," Mubarak said. "It would. I will talk to my ministers."

Fisher said: "I'll speak to Mr. Begin."

Fisher flew to Israel and spoke to the prime minister. Begin, who was reputed to be far fonder of talking than listening, heard Fisher out. Fisher suggested that arbitration was the answer. Begin said that he would take Fisher's recommendation under advisement.

Back in the United States, Fisher updated Shultz and Ambassador Ghorbal on his meetings. He told Ghorbal to inform Mubarak that the Israelis would most likely opt for arbitration. Ultimately, several years later, after then-Prime Minister Shimon Peres agreed to international arbitration, Taba was awarded to Egypt. Fisher, indulging in some wishful thinking, would comment that much of the friction over territory in the Middle East would be more peacefully resolved if it were treated as business — like companies hondling over prices.

Meanwhile, Middle East peace was nowhere in sight. In November 1982, Begin's wife, Aliza, died. Her death, coupled with the worsening situation in Lebanon and the Israelis' clamorous opposition to the war's mounting casualties, took their toll on Begin, who sank into a depression from which he never completely recovered. Upon resigning in September 1983, Begin retreated to his Jerusalem apartment at 1 Zemach Street and became, in the words of Pulitzer-Prize-winning journalist, Thomas L. Friedman, "one of the most remarkable cases in political history: a man totally engaged in his country's politics . . . [and] his nation's greatest orator, who overnight became a man of silence."

*   *   *

After twelve years as chairman of the Board of Governors of the Jewish Agency, Fisher's tenure was ending. Having voted for Willkie in 1940 because he did not think any president, even FDR, should serve more than two four-year terms, Fisher believed that it was bad for the Agency to have the post of chairman so identified with one person. Yet knowing this did not make stepping down any easier. The reconstituted Jewish Agency was largely his creation and he had trouble letting go.

On June 22, 1983, Fisher was honored at a dinner in the hall of the Jerusalem Great Synagogue. The next evening at the closing session of the Jewish Agency Assembly, he officially stepped down as BOG chairman, telling the audience that "as much as I may have given, I have received much more in return. I can't help but think of my parents — how proud they would have been to know that their son would some day be privileged to stand in the hall of the Knesset, in Jerusalem, in the presence of the leadership of Israel and of world Jewry, to talk about Jewish unity."

Later, his wistfulness was touched with a hint of anger when he told an interviewer, "This isn't the end of my career. This is *during* my career." That his prediction proved to be accurate did not lessen his sadness at relinquishing the chairmanship.

In recognition of Fisher's achievement at the Agency, he was unanimously elected founding chairman of the Board of Governors.

THE DAY'S NOT ENDED

O N JUNE 25, 1984, Max Fisher was bar mitzvahed at the Western Wall in Jerusalem. The bar mitzvah is a ceremony in which a thirteen-year-old boy is commanded to accept his share of Jewish responsibility and becomes a man. Fisher, growing up in the Christian community of Salem, was sixty-three years late.

But there he was, at eight-thirty on a Monday morning, the sunlight hot and bright on the *Kotel*, the sacred Wall, the only standing vestige of the ancient Temple. Thirty-five of Fisher's family and friends gathered. At the Wall, Fisher ran his hands over the stones and leaned forward to kiss them. Even in the simmering heat, the stones were cool. A journalist later reported that Fisher was crying when he put on his *tallit*, the fringed prayer shawl, and his *tefillin*, small boxes mounted on leather straps — one for the arm and one for the head — with biblical verses written on parchment and enclosed in each box. Fisher was summoned to the Torah and recited the transliterated Hebrew prayers from an index card. Then, looking up, he said: "This is the most fortunate day of my life."

Following the service, Marjorie hosted a brunch at the King David Hotel. For years, Marjorie had accompanied Max on his travels, and Max was aware of her sacrifice. In his final speech as chairman of the Board of Governors, he told the audience that his profound involvement with the Jewish Agency had "deepened my love and appreciation for my wife, Marjorie, who encouraged me, despite the strain on her."

By early November 1984, the strain of those years on Marjorie finally overwhelmed her. Although Marjorie says that she had been drinking alcohol excessively since the late 1950s, her consumption followed a regular — and for her, manageable — pattern. Each evening, at five o'clock, she began drinking vodka, and she drank until it was time for dinner at seven. But in November 1984, while Marjorie was in Palm Beach, she detected a change in her habit: she was now drinking from after dinner until she fell asleep. One sip made her drunk, proving that she no longer had any tolerance for alcohol.

"I would wake up in the morning," says Marjorie, "and I had trouble remembering what had happened the night before. During the day I would forget things. I realized that my drinking was controlling my life. I was frightened, and one evening, I said to Max: 'I'm in trouble.'"

On the evening Marjorie told Max about her fears, two of their daughters, Mary Fisher and Julie Cummings, were at the house. During a discussion about available treatment, Mary convinced her mother to sign into the Betty Ford Center in Rancho Mirage, and phoned to make the arrangements. On November 21, 1984, Marjorie checked in.

She lived in a dormitory with twenty women. Every morning began with a meditation walk, then breakfast at seven, followed by lectures, group-therapy sessions, individual meetings with a counselor, films, recreation, and study and quiet times before dinner. At night, Marjorie says, she did homework — "readings and written assignments that help you understand yourself and the disease of the alcoholism."

The third week of Marjorie's treatment was family week, and Max, four of their children, two sons-in-law, a daughter-in-law, and a grandson arrived to attend sessions that taught them more about themselves and the difficulties created by alcohol. During these sessions, Max heard about the price, in detail, that his children had paid for his commitments to causes. Initially, as would be expected from someone so reticent, he was terribly uncomfortable with the process, his chair swiveled to the outside of the group. Marjorie Aronow recalled how her parents had never been around while she was growing up. Julie Cummings repeated what she had been saying for years: "I gave my father to the world." Phillip Fisher was crying, and told Max how his immersion in business, philanthropy and politics had robbed him of a father, and he resented it.

Max put his arm around Phillip and turned toward the group. His voice thick, he said: "I had no idea."

Mary Fisher recalls: "My father was in shock. We had always been scared to tell him how lonely we felt because he wasn't there. We were amazed that he stayed around the center for five days. It was the longest time we ever had his undivided attention. It wasn't just getting him to understand how we felt, but our whole family changed. We became more aware of each other, and what my mother had done, in Dad's absence, to keep us together."

Adds Julie Cummings: "I give Dad a lot of credit for going through it. He was just filled with emotion. After those sessions, he became a different person."

So did Marjorie Fisher. Following one month of treatment at the Betty Ford Center, she promised herself that she would never drink again.

* * *

Despite the feuding over the AWACS sale and the Reagan Plan, the relationship between the administration and the American Jewish community was, for the most part, harmonious. Primarily, this was because President Reagan, always emotionally attached to Israel, also considered the Israelis a vital asset in the conflict between the United States and Soviet Union. (Reagan was the first president to bestow formal approval on increased strategic cooperation between the two allies.) In addition, according to Hedrick Smith, author of *The Power Game*, Secretary of State Shultz became "disillusioned with the Arabs after seeing Lebanon — under Syrian pressure — wriggle out of the Lebanon-Israel agreement that Shultz had mediated in May 1983. Since then, Shultz had worked to increase aid to Israel, and he had come to bank on the Israeli relationship — so much so that . . . he wanted to insulate American-Israeli relations from political ups and downs."

Fisher was disappointed that the congenial relations between the administration and the Israeli government did not win electoral support for the president from the Jewish community. Although Reagan effortlessly won re-election, defeating Walter Mondale by 17 million votes, he attracted just 35 percent of Jewish voters — a 4 percent drop from 1980.

In light of these results, Fisher, along with a coterie of Jewish Republicans, established the National Jewish Coalition. Headquartered in Washington, D.C., the NJC's stated goals are to sensitize Republican decision makers to the concerns of Jews and to encourage Jewish participation in Republican politics. However, it is not a lobbying group or a PAC. In a sense, the coalition was simply the institutionalization of the work that Fisher had started in 1960. Fisher reasoned that even if most Jews didn't cast their ballots for a Republican presidential candidate, then at least the NJC would formally tie American Jewry to the GOP and, of greater importance, to Republican administrations.

* * *

During the second Reagan administration, peace in the Middle East remained close enough to fuel the dream and far enough away to frustrate the dreamers. In 1984, when the Labor Party's Shimon Peres became prime minister of Israel's coalition government, a compromise seemed plausible. While the Likud Party — Peres's partner in the coalition — opposed resolving the Palestinian problem by relinquishing any part of the West Bank or transferring control to local Palestinians, Peres was more malleable. He felt that to cling to the entire West Bank would either force Israel to absorb 2 million Arabs or to institute deportations. For Peres, neither choice was a viable option.

The coalition government did not diminish Fisher's status as a quiet diplomat. Shimon Peres explains that this is because Fisher "occupies a position, not a post," and, more important, because he is politically adept.

Peres states: "I compare Max to a ship that has both engines and sails. When Max has the wind with him, he uses his sails. When he needs to propel himself further, he uses his engines. Max is a very good sailor."

Within the Israeli government, says Peres, Fisher was welcomed by the left and right wing. Fisher had long cultivated this flexibility — the key being that when it came to the inner machinations of Israel, he stayed staunchly apolitical.

"I'm not an Israeli citizen," says Fisher, "so I don't have to take a position on politics or anything else. The only thing I feel comfortable doing is offering advice based on the facts I might have. And I offer my services to both Labor and Likud. Besides, if it looks as though I've favored Likud, I'll lose credibility with Labor. If I tell the Labor Party what they want to hear, then I'll lose credibility with the Likud. So the best thing for me to do is make myself available."

Although Fisher declined to take a public stand on how Israel should handle the Palestinians and the prospect of bartering land for peace, his opinion about what course would be best to follow was closer to the attitude favored by Labor's Peres than to the one of Likud leader Yitzhak Shamir. (Peres would be prime minister for two years and then switch jobs with Shamir, who was serving as foreign minister.) As far back as 1974, Fisher had privately warned members of the Israeli Cabinet that building settlements on the West Bank would have grave political consequences in Israel and the United States. If they didn't offer some kind of a deal, then terms would be forced on them by geopolitical circumstances. Over the long haul, Fisher repeatedly told Israel's leaders, the Israelis would find it difficult to hang on to all of the territory captured during the Six-Day War.

As soon as Peres was in office, he sought to use Fisher's "credibility and clout." He wanted Fisher to assure the Reagan administration that he was committed to seeking peace.

In a February meeting at Foggy Bottom, Fisher spoke to Secretary Shultz, who, while delighted with Peres's resolve, was guarded about his chances. Fisher also asked Shultz if he would continue to pursue emigration for Ethiopian and Soviet Jews. Shultz said that he would raise the topics with the Ethiopian government and the Russians. The secretary added that under no circumstances would the United States put Israel in the middle when it came to discussing the regional conflict with the Kremlin, and he asked Fisher to relay this promise to Peres. In addition, said Shultz, Fisher should tell Peres that when it comes to arms sales, Israel would be a priority and their security will in no way be hampered.

During the spring and fall of 1985, Peres, in secret discussions with King Hussein of Jordan, attempted to arrange an accommodation that would give Jordan and Israel administrative powers over the West Bank and Gaza Strip, with the final status of these areas to be determined in joint negotiations among the Israelis, Jordanians and local Palestinians. Meantime, no new Jewish settlements would be built on the West Bank, and Israel would return 500,000 acres of land to Jordan.

Tragically, as has so often happened in the Middle East, violence scuttled the peace initiative. On October 1, 1985, Israeli F-16 jets attacked PLO headquarters in Tunis, killing nearly two dozen of Yasser Arafat's staff. Less than a week later, four Palestinian terrorists hijacked an Italian cruise ship, the *Achille Lauro*, and in the process murdered an ailing sixty-four-year-old American, Leon Klinghoffer, throwing his body overboard.

Fisher, in a talk with Shultz, said that he still hoped a private deal could be struck between Israel and King Hussein. Shultz favored the quiet approach — unpublicized face-to-face meetings between heads of state — referring to it as applying the "Fisher Principle." But just over a year later, on December 8, 1987, with the Likud's Shamir now piloting the government and Peres ensconced at the foreign ministry, the *intifada* broke out in the Gaza Strip. The Israeli army mobilized to quell the rioting Palestinians, and peace vanished amid clouds of tear gas and daily hailstorms of stones.

As the *intifada* swept through the territories, a potentially divisive issue arose between Israel and American Jewry. The issue was rooted in how the Israeli government would continue to interpret its Law of Return. The law gives every Jew the right to immigrate to Israel and be granted automatic citizenship. Determining exactly who qualifies as a Jew is another matter. According to Jewish law, *halakhah*, a Jew is someone born to a Jewish mother or converted in accordance with *halakhic* rituals.

In order to secure a majority during what Prime Minister Yitzhak Shamir describes as his "intricate and difficult coalition negotiations," he courted representatives from four ultra-Orthodox religious parties. As a condition of joining Shamir's coalition, the leaders of these parties demanded that only strictly Orthodox conversions be recognized by the Israeli government. Anyone who converted without complying to the letter of the law would not be considered Jewish and therefore have no right to immigrate to Israel under the Law of Return.

Initially, Shamir appeared to acquiesce to their demands. The reaction in the American Jewish community, observed *The New York Times*, was filled with "heat and outrage." American Jews, 90 percent of whom are non-Orthodox, are the strongest and most generous supporters of Israel in the world. They are also exceedingly broad-minded about conversions performed by rabbis from other streams of religious life, namely Conservative and Reform. It seemed unimaginably painful that Israel would classify the rapidly expanding percentage of American converts to Judaism as Gentiles.

Fisher and a host of Jewish leaders flew to Israel to discuss the "who-is-a-Jew" debate with the prime minister. For Shamir, Fisher "represents the synthesis between the policies and aspirations of the United States and the goals and ideals of the Jewish people." He says that since assuming the prime ministership, he has valued Fisher's ability "to explain the outlook and philosophy of the Republican Party to the Israeli leadership, and by the same token, to convey to his Republican colleagues the sentiments and attitudes that exist in Israel."

In sum, then, Shamir respects Fisher for his political wisdom. This was fortunate because while several American leaders argued against the anti-democratic posture of letting the Orthodox demarcate the boundaries of Jewishness, Fisher's advice to Shamir was based in the realpolitik. He told the prime minister that to alienate Jews in the United States would be unwise. The White House and Congress, said Fisher, when determining the breadth of their support for the Israelis, are mightily aware of how their Jewish constituents feel about Israel. Hence, to divide American Jewry would consequently divide support for Israel in Washington.

"Of course," says Shamir, "the viewpoint of a friend like Max Fisher was given very serious attention."

The prime minister claims that he assured the leadership that "there was no intention whatsoever of delegitimizing any Jew." In the end, Shamir installed his government without transfiguring the law and, for all practical purposes, the question of who is a Jew was returned to the lofty — and Fisher believed more appropriate — realm of theological speculation.

* * *

In 1988, Fisher reached his eightieth birthday. Accolades rolled in from around the world. Letters arrived from family and friends, from presidents and prime ministers, senators and congressmen, governors, secretaries of state and foreign ministers, and Marjorie bound each one in a leather scrapbook. Having spent his political life out of the spotlight, Fisher felt gratified by the appreciative notes — signs that the discreet niche he had carved for himself was so widely recognized and respected by Washington insiders. Ronald Reagan's last chief of staff, Howard H. Baker, wrote: "In the lobby just outside the White House mess, hangs a large portrait of you presenting an award to the president earlier this year. I think that as we celebrate your eightieth birthday . . . it's especially appropriate that the photograph occupy such a prominent spot in the busiest intersection of the West Wing."

Besides the letters, several parties were given in Fisher's honor. Al Taubman hosted a stag luncheon at the Detroit Club, and fifty of Fisher's chums flew in from such distant spots as

Alaska and England. There was a dinner cruise down the Detroit River — for family and some longtime friends — aboard the yacht *Brownie's III*. Since 1988 was an election year and Fisher was now laboring in his seventh presidential campaign, it was only fitting that one of the celebrations should have a pragmatic political edge. In the early fall, President Reagan came to the Westin Hotel in Detroit and spoke to over 1,200 Republicans at a $1,000-a-plate dinner in Fisher's honor. (Numerous guests paid $5,000 to have their pictures snapped with Fisher and the president.) Over $2 million was raised at the dinner, the proceeds going to the Michigan GOP.

Reagan was munificent in his remarks about Fisher, enumerating his efforts on behalf of the Republican Party and the United States, telling the audience that, "to put it simply, Max is a legend." To demonstrate how much of a legend, Reagan recounted the following story.

At the 1980 Republican nominating convention in Detroit, when Reagan was selected to run for the presidency, hundreds of people converged on the platform to congratulate him. A dear friend, said Reagan, was watching the celebration on TV in a hotel lounge in California. He was enjoying it immensely. Suddenly, a man — in all probability a Detroiter — who was seated nearby, asked him: "Hey, mister, who're all those people up on the podium with Max Fisher?"

"I didn't mind [when my friend told me what happened]," said the president, "since Max is one of the few men who's been around longer than I have."

Reagan would honor Fisher again right before he left office by awarding him the Presidential Citizens Medal (along with such Americans as James S. Brady, William F. Buckley Jr., Malcolm S. Forbes, Max M. Kampelman, Colin L. Powell and Edward Teller). The medal, the second highest honor a private citizen can receive, is given at the discretion of the president. As Reagan commented at the White House ceremony, Fisher was awarded the medal for his "generous acts of philanthropy, dedicated civic service and [for his leadership] of the Jewish community."

Yet perhaps the greatest tribute that Fisher received in his eightieth year was an invitation to come to New Orleans in August and address the Republican National Convention. He had spent so many decades backstage, the prospect of standing before the national political footlights — even at this late date — was intimidating. He meticulously prepared his speech and flew to New Orleans a day early to rehearse it onstage. On the morning of August 15, Fisher waited in the wings while Maureen Reagan introduced him — with the typical bombast of political conventions — as a "great Republican and great American." Dressed in his trademark dark navy suit, a light blue shirt and slate-gray patterned tie, Fisher strode briskly out to face the delegates and television cameras. Resting his hands on the podium and leaning toward the audience, Fisher began by trumpeting the qualifications of George Bush for the presidency. Then, as in campaigns past, he set his sights on American Jewry.

"We Jews," said Fisher, "are a people of the book, a people who treasure the written word. What, then, are we to think of a party whose platform ignores our basic communal needs and historical fears? Don't take my word for it. Look at the Democratic platform yourself. And as you turn the pages, ask yourself, where is the Democratic platform condemning anti-Semitism? Where is the Democratic platform plank condemning the U.N. resolution on Zionism as racism? Where is the Democratic platform supporting the cries of Soviet Jewry? And where is the Democratic platform rejecting an independent Palestinian state?

"My friends, the Democratic platform of past years contained much of the language you long to hear, but we cannot find it in that platform today. This spring seven state Democratic conventions voted to recommend that the Democratic platform support an independent Palestinian state. Thank God, this motion was never put to vote. But next year, what?

"My friends, the Republican Party will not support an independent Palestinian state because it is wrong. Wrong not only for Israel, but also for America. . . . And I say to you, my fellow American Jews, come join with me, and with this great political party which shares your values, and which has labored steadily to earn your trust and respect. The Republican Party's interests are your interests, its goals are your goals."

Fisher's criticism of the Democrat's agenda was not only based on his objection to a Palestinian state. After all, he wanted Israel and the Palestinians to live in peace. Obviously, this peace would include some sort of compromise. Yet throughout the 1988 campaign, Fisher sensed something more frightening in the Democratic camp than support for the Palestinians: he felt that the party had been commandeered by its vociferously anti-Semitic left wing.

On October 1, Fisher released a statement to the press charging that the campaign of the Democratic candidate for the presidency, Governor Michael S. Dukakis of Massachusetts, was infected with "the poison of anti-Semitism." Fisher was referring to three members of the Democratic National Committee — Ruth Ann Skaff of the Arab American Institute in Texas for recognizing the Palestinian Liberation Organization; Los Angeles City Councilman Robert Farrell for likening the Israelis to the Nazis in their treatment of Arabs on the West Bank; and the Reverend Willie Barrow, executive director of the Chicago-based Operation PUSH, who was a vocal fan of the black separatist, Louis Farrakhan. Among a flurry of anti-Semitic jabs, Farrakhan had referred to Judaism as a "gutter religion," and told students at Michigan State University that Jews "suck the blood out of the black community, and [then] . . . feel we have no right now to say something about it."

Fisher thought it ironic that the first person to answer his charges was the Reverend Jesse Jackson, who was campaigning for Dukakis in Ann Arbor, Michigan. In the 1984 campaign, Jackson had referred to New York City as "Hymietown." He was also a defender of Farrakhan. (Maybe Jackson felt that he owed the Nation of Islam leader, since in 1984 Farrakhan threatened Milton Coleman, the journalist who reported Jackson's characterization of New York, with death.) Acting as though he were above criticism on the subject of anti-Semitism, Jackson told the *Detroit Free Press* that

Fisher's accusations were "unfounded [and] unfair," and that people should "focus on the guts of the Dukakis campaign," adding that the governor's "commitment to human rights is beyond reproach."

In short order, Skaff denied Fisher's charges; Farrell said he would sign any letter condemning anti-Semitism, though admitted that his earlier comments were excessive; and Barrow said that he was merely lauding Farrakhan's aggressive posture on economic development in black communities.

Fisher was tired of leftists hiding their anti-Semitism behind their anti-Zionist rhetoric. He had been listening to it since the late 1960s. Nor did he have any tolerance for the older, more commonplace right-wing anti-Semitism. Fisher was working at Bush headquarters in Washington, D.C., when revelations surfaced that members of the Bush campaign had links to Nazi and other anti-Semitic organizations. Fisher contacted Bush campaign chairman Jim Baker and demanded that the men be fired.

In an interview with the *Detroit Free Press*, Fisher said: "When it was called to [my] attention that Nazi supporters and others were involved in the Republican campaign, we got rid of them immediately. I just happen to think that should apply to [both] Republicans and [Democrats]."

On Election Day, Bush surpassed Dukakis by 8 percent of the popular vote. The governor recovered quite a bit of lost ground against the vice president in the week before the election. But a *New York Times*/CBS News Poll indicated that the voters had "made up their minds earlier and, by a large margin, for Mr. Bush."

The vice president won 35 percent of the Jewish vote, which historically was above average. However, given the Democrats' support for the Palestinians and the flagrant anti-Semitism by some celebrated members of its left wing, Fisher was surprised that Bush did not receive more backing from Jews at the polls. The NJC, only four years old, had not made any substantial headway against the voting habits of Jews. However, once Bush took office in January 1989, there was another surprise in store for Fisher — this one more pleasant than his dismay over Jewish voting patterns. For it was in the wake of the inauguration that Fisher was able to gauge just how far his role had evolved in the two decades since Nixon defeated Humphrey in 1968.

* * *

George Klein, who in 1991 was a national co-chairman of the NJC, was brought to the United States from Austria as a child by his parents, who were fleeing the Nazis. His father, Stephen, an observant Jew, founded the New York-based Barton's candy company. By 1973, George was executive vice president of the family business and had worked with Fisher on Nixon's re-election campaign.

According to Klein, it was after 1968 that some small segments of the organized Jewish community became increasingly aware of "the importance of building a relationship with the White House." However, says Klein, "these type of links take time. A relationship with someone who becomes president is personal and must develop over a period of years. Legislators are continuously campaigning; they always need your help. A president only needs you once or twice in eight years."

Fisher, notes Klein, understood this process. His achievements were already universally acknowledged by the organized elements of American Jewry. But it became clear after the Ford administration that his rank as *the* Jewish Republican was recognized by those in the GOP who hoped — or managed — to become president.

Says Klein: "Max's relationship to George Bush is a good example of this recognition. Although he and Bush are friendly, Max was not the Jewish Republican closest to Bush when he became president. Still, when it was time for the Jewish community and the administration to talk, Max was the one who was called. And when he comes to a discussion at the White House, the president gives him an honored place — the chair to his right — and asks him to open the meeting. Max is a full-fledged political tradition, and Republican presidents have picked up on it."

George Bush cannot recall when he first encountered Fisher, but says that he has known him for two decades. Fisher speculates that he met the future president in the 1970s, while Bush, already an ex-congressman from Texas and ex-ambassador to the United Nations, was Republican National Chairman. Bush describes his relationship with Fisher as "affectionate and respectful," feelings that Fisher reciprocates. Unlike his relationships with Nixon, Ford and Reagan, though, Fisher's relationship with Bush was not grounded in common experiences. Sixteen years his senior, Fisher belonged to a different political generation: the seminal influence on Fisher's early manhood was the Depression; for Bush, it was the Second World War. Nor could their backgrounds have been more different. Bush was the scion of aristocratic New Englanders, a graduate of Yale. His father, Prescott, a prosperous investment banker, was elected to the U.S. Senate from Connecticut in 1952. It was a far cry from Fisher's beginnings as a Jewish immigrant's son.

In the 1950s, Bush did make a respectable mark in the oil business. He may have heard of Fisher and Aurora, except by the time Bush became successful, Fisher was in the process of selling the company. The two men did share a similar style. Bush, as a *Time* magazine cover story declared on August 21, 1989, was "Mr. Consensus," who kept his political cards close to his vest in an effort to prevent "coalitions from forming in opposition." This was Fisher's standard operating procedure for running organizations.

Certainly, Bush was not blind to the assistance that Fisher could provide. As George Klein and others have observed, well before 1988 Fisher had fashioned his own permanent position. Still, this is not sufficient to account for the expansive role that Bush authorized him to play — a role that, to some degree, depends on the trust of, and access to, the president.

Of course, Bush recognizes Fisher's standing among organized American Jewry. The president says that Fisher "understands the special circumstances that Israel faces in protecting its national security, and he represents the strong feelings and support of America's Jewish population. He is a unique spokesman for U.S. policy in Israel, and for Israel's policy in the United States." But, for the president, Fisher's standing is a partial requirement for his job. In fact, Bush concedes that it is only his "very personal relationship" with Fisher that "allows him to utilize Max as a personal emissary."

So it stands to reason that something about Fisher appealed to the president beyond the politically expedient — some aspect of Fisher that created a bond between them. Perhaps it was the respect that many sons of privilege have for self-made men who achieve wealth and status and yet retain their willingness to pitch in and work hard. As a young man, Bush had passed up his father's investment banking business, refusing to take full advantage of his privilege, and chased oil in Texas. This, at least, was an aspect of Fisher that then-Vice President Bush highlighted during a dinner at the Madison Hotel in Washington on February 28, 1986.

The dinner was given by Leonard and Suzanne Garment for Max and Marjorie. Henry Kissinger spoke, as did George Shultz and several of the Fishers' family and friends. In his introduction of Max, Vice President Bush said: "We know of his love for Israel. The joy of [Soviet refusnik Natan] Scharansky finally going home. The agony of the [Israeli] athletes [murdered at the 1972 Olympics] in Munich. All of these things. I think of Max. What it meant to him. And his being a kind of constant conscience to us in government. Now and in the past.

"But there's another dimension of Max," said Bush, "that hasn't been mentioned tonight. And that's pure gut American politics. A motel in northern Michigan with the ceilings so low you could hardly stand up. They don't even give away free soap there. And here's Max Fisher. Could have bought the thing twenty times over. Shaking hands with the precinct delegates and rolling up his sleeves and participating in that grass-roots course of American politics that really makes this country tick. And when you get going too high, he'll bring you down to earth. When you've had the hell kicked out of you, he'll lift you up. And we all feel that way about him. He's our friend."

Bush's perception of Fisher as a friend was important, because by July 1989, as Bush faced what Fred Barnes of *The New Republic* labeled "the first crisis of his presidency," all was far from well between Washington and Jerusalem, and Fisher would find himself caught in the cross fire.

* * *

On the night of July 28, Israeli commandos raided the southern Lebanese village of Jibchit, abducting Sheik Abdul Karim Obeid, a leader of the Shiite fundamentalist Hizballah — the Party of God. Closely allied with Iran, Hizballah was holding most of the Western hostages. The Israeli government planned to swap Obeid for three Israeli soldiers who had been taken prisoner years before in Lebanon. At a press conference hours after the abduction, Bush lashed out at Israel, saying: "I don't think kidnapping and violence help the cause of peace."

Two days later, a group representing Hizballah threatened to kill a captured leader of a U.N. observer team — U.S. Marine Lieutenant Colonel William Higgins — if Obeid was not released. Israeli Defense Minister Yitzhak Rabin proposed to exchange Obeid and 150 Lebanese Shiitie prisoners for the three Israeli POWs and all the Western hostages. Secretary of State Baker approved of Rabin's counteroffer. But while Israel prepared to announce its terms, Hizballah released a video-tape of Higgins, hanging by the neck, bound, blindfolded and dead. Hizballah then stated that American hostage Joseph Cicippio would be next if Obeid and an unspecified number of Palestinians and Lebanese guerrillas were not freed.

Ultimately, the evidence suggested that Higgins had been murdered prior to Obeid's abduction. For the moment, though, the White House was concerned about Cicippio and feared that the United States could be drawn into a military confrontation in Lebanon because of Israel's foray. Angered by this possible scenario, the administration cabled the Israeli government, questioning its motivation, timing and strategy in kidnapping Obeid — all of it in language that one Israeli official portrayed to *The Jerusalem Post* as "almost insulting." Israeli leaders, particularly Prime Minister Shamir, were so offended by the cable that they did not reply.

Fisher watched helplessly as the strain between the two allies increased. The White House issued a statement urging "all parties who hold hostages in the Middle East" to release them. Again, Israeli leaders were offended, since the statement appeared to equate Israel's abduction of Obeid with the kidnappings carried out by Lebanese extremists. Fisher was flabbergasted when Minority Leader Robert Dole asserted on the Senate floor that Israel had acted without regard for the lives of American hostages, adding that "a little more responsibility on the part of the Israelis would be refreshing."

Cicippio was granted a reprieve by his captors. Meantime, Shamir claimed publicly that there was "no deterioration whatsoever" in relations between Israel and the United States, and that the rumors of a crisis between Jerusalem and Washington were "wrong." Fisher disagreed, and after the president's spokesman, Marlin Fitzwater, told the press that "many people" in the White House concurred with Dole's statement, Fisher decided it was time to schedule a talk with the president.

On August 8, five Jewish leaders met with Bush: Seymour Reich, chairman of the Presidents Conference; Malcolm Hoenlein, the Conference executive director; Ed Levy, president of AIPAC; George Klein and Richard Fox from the National Jewish Coalition, and Fisher (whose official title was now honorary chairman of the NJC). With Bush was his chief of staff, John H. Sununu, Vice President Dan Quayle, National Security Adviser Brent Scowcroft and several other aides. Nailing down the talk with Bush was a coup, since the White House, worried about appearing to side with Israel's U.S. supporters, had not even listed the meeting on the president's daily schedule.

Bush opened by saying that he was anxious to hear from the group. He did want to let them know that he was terribly troubled by the hostage situation. He said that, personally, he felt a tremendous responsibility for the Americans being held in Lebanon. And, quite simply, because Israel had abducted Obeid, their lives were now in more danger than ever before.

An observer at the meeting, who prefers not to be identified, later said that when Bush finished there was an uncomfortable silence — people shifting in their seats. The president had drawn a line. Although he had said that he was more than willing to listen to another perspective, he wanted the group to know that his main priority here was not geopolitics, but the safety of the hostages.

Bush waited for a response. According to Seymour Reich, in meetings with government officials "Max never tried to make himself the focal point and always deferred to the head of the Presidents Conference. He wanted the administration to know that this was coming from the community, not from him." But now, instead of answering Bush, Reich said: "Mr. President, I think we'd all like to hear from Max."

Fisher began by stating that this delegation considered itself a friend of the president. But the community was upset about Dole's comments and Fitzwater's support. Both men had created a distortion in the minds of the American public and energized feelings against Israel that were contrary to the best interests of the United States. He cited a *Washington Post* poll that showed a majority of Americans considered Dole's statements to border on the intemperate. The administration should remember that America's long-term strategic interests were with Israel. The rift between Washington and Jerusalem was unnecessary and the tensions counterproductive.

Bush replied that he was aware of the tensions, though the U.S. relationship with Israel transcended any momentary distress. He then discussed the lack of communication between the United States and the Israelis, saying that it would be helpful to know what they were up to in Lebanon, especially if American lives were on the line. He guaranteed that he would not abide any irreparable breaches between the two governments while he was president — he would do what was necessary to shore up the relationship. He said he was not going to shift U.S. policy because the views of a particular government in Israel did not coincide with the way the administration looked at things. Bush was referring to the Likud Party and not just to their activities in Lebanon, but their policy of continuing to build settlements on the West Bank. For several minutes, the president spoke knowledgeably about the political strife in Israel between Likud and Labor.

Then members of the delegation answered the president, touching on the anger that had been engendered in the Jewish community by the comparison of the Obeid abduction to the Hizballah kidnappings. They also said that though this may be the age of *glasnost*, the Soviet Union had not radically altered its tactics in the Middle East; the Kremlin still supported terrorism and sold weapons to Israel's enemies.

Bush listened, then intimated that what he truly wanted was for the delegation to pass along the message to Shamir that the breakdown in communication between the United States and Israel was deeply distressing to the White House and should not continue. Fisher appreciated that, in approach and personality, Bush and Shamir were not the perfect couple. Bush was highly verbal, relying on personal contacts that he nurtured in long conversations over the phone. Shamir was quiet, a listener, and more formal; he would not call when a note would do.

Bush again reassured the group that the U.S. relationship with Israel would remain on solid ground. As the meeting broke up, Fisher lingered, talking with the president. He reiterated the spot that Shamir was in — how strongly the Israeli public felt about the return of their prisoners. He doubted that the prime minister had intended to back Bush into a political corner or to endanger the hostages. He would speak to Shamir, but he wouldn't push him. Bush thanked Fisher and they shook hands.

"Those are handsome cufflinks," Fisher said to the president. They were gold and engraved with the presidential seal.

Bush smiled, removed the cufflinks from his shirt and handed them to Fisher.

"They're yours, Max," the president said.

The meeting was officially over.

The next day, Shamir telephoned Bush. Their conversation was cordial. They discussed, in general terms, the hostage situation and how Israel expected to address it. But, *The New York Times* reported, Bush later mentioned to some associates that he did not get specific answers to his questions. Shamir followed up his phone call with a letter that did provide some explanation for Israel's abduction of Obeid, but again he did not directly answer the president.

Due to differing objectives and styles, the relationship between Bush and Shamir would not be easygoing. Their personal uneasiness, however, would create a greater opportunity for Fisher to work the diplomatic back-channel.

Bush, though, is reluctant to admit the existence of an unofficial channel. He says that what Fisher does is "not a matter of back-channeling, because there is no substitute for our diplomacy abroad. But it is important to have private citizens to help explain our position in Israel. And Max Fisher can provide personal and direct explanations for our policies in his discussions with Jewish leaders. He has been helpful in our discussions with Prime Minister Shamir for some time."

Shamir, like Bush, is hesitant to characterize Fisher's work as operating in a back-channel. The prime minister states that "there is the closest contact between the governments of the United States and Israel through their respective ambassadors and embassy personnel, and by means of fairly frequent meetings between ministers from both countries. There is also close contact with members of Congress, the media and the public. Accordingly, almost all the needs are served through the regular diplomatic channels. However, because of the open, democratic nature of the two societies, there are occasions when the personal intervention of a man of the stature of Max Fisher is helpful on both sides of the ocean. This has been the role of Max Fisher throughout the years, and his contribution has been invaluable."

By February 1990, when Fisher went to Israel for eight days to attend meetings at the Jewish Agency, the hostage crisis had receded. But a perpetual dispute between the United

States and Israel was about to boil over. The dispute centered on Israel's ongoing settlement of the West Bank. The Bush administration was trying to arrange talks between the Israelis and Palestinians. Invariably, such arrangements threw the matter of land into bold relief. But now, with the Soviet Union's more flexible posture toward emigration, hundreds of thousands of Soviet Jews were streaming into Israel. This highlighted the question of where the Israeli government intended to settle them. Thus, during Fisher's visit, the settlement issue topped the agenda. He met privately three times with Prime Minister Shamir, twice with Deputy Prime Minister Peres, and held two long conversations with Defense Minister Rabin.

As Fisher later told Bush, the Israeli leaders promised him that there was "no government policy to settle [the Russian Jews] in the West Bank or Gaza and no new incentives for them to go there. . . . Prime Minister Shamir assured me that no American money and no new Israeli government money would be spent on absorbing them in the territories." Shimon Peres pointed out to Fisher that "no new settlements could be built without the approval of the Labor Party Cabinet ministers and that they would not agree to any such decision."

Fisher also told the president that while there were some small existing incentives for settlement in the territories, they "were unlikely to have a significant impact on where the Soviet Jews actually settle. In my judgment, however, the cancellation of these incentives is more than is politically feasible for the PM in today's environment."

One of Fisher's talks with Shamir focused on the peace process. Shamir said that he was committed to dealing with the Palestinians, but was "being distracted by the turmoil in his own party." He had been working closely with Rabin, in private consultations. The prime minister felt that he had 65 percent of the Likud behind him. He preferred to consolidate his political base before taking any large steps. After listening to the prime minister, Fisher says that he told him, "in very clear terms," that it "would be difficult for the United States to keep everybody in place behind his initiative if he did not take a positive decision now."

Several weeks later, Fisher gave Bush his assessment of Shamir's willingness to pursue peace. "This is a fateful and very difficult decision for Israel to make," said Fisher. "For the first time in the history of the state, Israel will be legitimizing the Palestinians as its negotiating partner. I sense that the country is swinging behind the idea of making this decision, but we should expect significant political fallout. I am confident that there will be positive movement soon. When the PM moves forward, however, he will need your public support."

When Fisher returned from his February trip to Israel, he organized his observations in writing for the president. Before he could communicate with Bush, though, the situation underwent a radical transformation.

At a press conference in early March, the president stated that he did "not believe there should be new settlements in the West Bank or in East Jerusalem." Casting doubts on Israeli sovereignty over Jerusalem, was, in the words of *The New York Times*, "a departure from usual Washington practice." East Jerusalem, along with the Gaza Strip and the West Bank, had been wrested from Jordan after King Hussein ordered the shelling of West Jerusalem in the 1967 Six-Day War. Officially, the United States has never recognized the Israeli annexation of this land, so technically the U.S government sees East Jerusalem as occupied territory. However, U.S. administrations have protested Israeli expansion into the West Bank territories while tolerating it in the neighborhoods of East Jerusalem.

Bush's pronouncement caused a furor in Israel, especially at the present moment, because the government, split between Likud and Labor, was deliberating over whether to participate in American-sponsored negotiations with the Palestinians. Organized American Jewry was also taken aback by Bush's statement. And since Fisher was going to speak to the president anyway about his February visit, he added an addendum to his written report. While in Israel, Fisher had spent a considerable amount of time in Jerusalem with Mayor Teddy Kollek, touring the housing sites where some Soviet Jews would be settled. The sites in the eastern part of the city, Fisher assured Bush, were on "uninhabited, government-owned land." Kollek was concerned about any infringement of the rights of Jerusalem's Arab residents.

It was a mistake, Fisher suggested to Bush, for the administration to link Jerusalem to the issue of settlements.

"I know that your position, and that of the Republican Party, is whatever the outcome of negotiations, Jerusalem should remain unified. If that is the case, it cannot be treated in the same way as settlements in the West Bank. Jerusalem requires a political compromise, but it is not subject to territorial compromise. This is the consensus issue in the American Jewish community and Israel."

According to Fisher, the most profound impact of the president's linkage was on the ever-fragile potential for peace.

"I do not think it is politically wise," said Fisher, "to adopt a position that Jews should not settle in Jerusalem. At a very delicate stage in the peace process, it can only produce a strong negative response in Israel and the American Jewish community. They remember what happened to Jewish holy sites before 1967 despite international guarantees given in 1948."

Then, tactfully, Fisher closed his remarks with a reference to Bush's statement: "In view of what has happened, it will take considerable patience and work to keep the peace process on track."

In a brief handwritten note dated March 8, Bush thanked Fisher for his comments, calling them "most helpful." Unfortunately, less than a week later, Fisher's prediction about the dubious political wisdom of challenging Israel's sovereignty over Jerusalem proved accurate. For Fisher, the turn of events was a prime illustration of how rapidly events could spiral downward in the Middle East when the Israelis perceived — justifiably or not — that they had been abandoned by their most powerful ally, the United States.

On March 13, the disagreement between Labor and Likud

over peace talks with the Palestinians came to a head. Wary of a U.S. administration that appeared to deem Jerusalem up for grabs, Shamir rejected the terms suggested by the United States for entering into a dialogue with the Palestinians. Consequently, the government collapsed. Tensions escalated. On May 20, a deranged Israeli murdered seven Arab laborers. Rioting ensued between Palestinians and Israeli security forces. Seven died; five hundred were injured, and the violence spilled from the territories to towns inside Israel. On May 30, an attack on an Israeli beach by terrorists in speedboats was repulsed. PLO chairman Yasser Arafat denied that his organization was involved.

What ensued, Fisher thought, was depressingly predictable. With their security under attack, Israelis swung to the political right. By June 8, Prime Minister Shamir assembled a government — the most hawkish in Israel's history — which was committed, in principle, to developing Jewish settlements in the occupied territories. This was, Fisher knew, precisely what the Bush administration had hoped to avoid. Two weeks later, the president suspended talks with the PLO because Arafat would not condemn the recent terrorist attack. It was too little, too late. Israel was already politically isolated. And another opportunity was lost.

Fisher continued working to facilitate a productive dialogue between Bush and Shamir. But on August 2, when Iraqi tanks rumbled into Kuwait and Bush ordered U.S. forces to Saudi Arabia, it was obvious to Fisher that the Middle East cards would be shuffled again.

As Desert Shield gave way to Desert Storm, Fisher traveled to Jerusalem for meetings. He watched from the balcony of his room at the King David Hotel as Iraqi Scuds sparked in the night skies above Israel. He spoke with Shamir and admired the prime minister's political courage for not retaliating against Saddam Hussein and thereby preserving the U.S.-Arab coalition. What Fisher found most amazing was that throughout the Gulf War, Soviet Jews kept landing in Tel Aviv; even the threat of gas attacks did not deter them; they were given gas masks as they stepped off the planes.

From August 2, 1990, until February 27, 1991, when Bush halted the allied offensive against Iraq, 137,313 Russian Jews poured into Israel. Fisher had had a hand in opening the gates. It was among the few of his contributions that was known outside the top levels of government — a contribution that led Board of Governors chairman Mendel Kaplan to announce to the Jewish Agency that "in one decisive step, Max Fisher has changed the course of Jewish history."

★ ★ ★

In 1979, the Soviet Union permitted 51,320 of its Jews to emigrate. Sixty percent of them came to the United States, while the rest went to Israel. Vastly outnumbered by their Arab enemies, Israel was not only proud to rescue these Jews from the oppressive conditions in the Soviet Union, they also needed immigrants, particularly ones like the Russians, who were, as a rule, educated and equipped with a multitude of skills. But as global competition between the United States and the Soviet Union fermented, the Kremlin choked off Jewish emigration. Additionally, those who applied for exit visas often lost their jobs; many were harassed by the KGB. Between 1980 and 1987, only 46,206 were permitted to leave, nearly all of them bolting to America. Then, with the ascendancy of Mikhail Gorbachev, the situation changed.

During the spring of 1988, Soviet Jews were leaving Russia at the rate of approximately 1,000 a month. By fall, the number had doubled. The Israeli government was angry since the emigrants were, for the most part, only able to exit the Soviet Union because they held visas to Israel. Then, once the emigrants reached Vienna or traveled on to one of the European holding centers — for example, Ladispoli, in Rome — they applied for entry to the United States. As a result, the centers were jammed with people waiting to enter America. And Gorbachev was promising that more Jews could emigrate.

In 1988, Carmi Schwartz was the executive vice president of the Council of Jewish Federations. He saw the growing problem and phoned Fisher. What were they going to do about the Jews in Rome? At first, Fisher turned to Secretary of State Shultz for assistance.

Says Schwartz: "Shultz was an enormous help. He cared like hell; he brought up Soviet Jewry at every encounter with the Russians. It was always on his agenda: one, because he felt deeply about it; he went to Moscow during Passover, had a seder in the embassy and invited a group of refusniks to join him. And two, I felt Soviet Jewry was important to Shultz because of his relationship with Max. He had a special friendship with Max. And it was ever-present."

That summer, the director of the CJF's Washington action office, Mark Talisman, called Schwartz, warning him that the Soviet Jews, already caught in a logjam, were about to become even more backed up.

Recalls Talisman: "In July 1988, Attorney General Edwin Meese sent a letter to National Security Adviser Colin Powell. Essentially, the letter said that the 1980 Refugee Act needed to be followed in regard to all refugees — including Soviet Jews. Now, Jews who were virtually prisoners in the Soviet Union would be in the position of having to prove on a case-by-case basis that they were being persecuted. This happened as the numbers started to soar, and the whole system got boxed up."

Schwartz instructed Talisman to contact Fisher.

"Max attended meeting upon meeting to try and get this straightened out," says Talisman. "The crisis was a serious one. By October 1988, we were beginning to organize, but it was an election year; many people in Congress were on the road campaigning. We weren't able to get anyone to focus on the situation until January 1989, when the Bush administration came in. [Deputy Secretary of State Lawrence S.] Eagleburger understood the idiocy of it. Thousands of Soviet Jews were stuck in Rome; it was costing organized American Jewry $8 per person — over $300,000 a day; it was a waste. And the human wreckage was really tragic. Refusniks who had suffered horribly were being ordered by the U.S. government to report in detail how they had a well-founded fear of persecution. Had Kafka been alive, he'd only have to be a stenographer."

The Bush administration wanted to help. But annual immigration slots are limited and there were budgetary constraints. Under the Refugee Act, the United States funds immigrants at $935 per head a year. The American Jewish community was covering the rest of the cost. During 1989, the Soviet Union issued exit visas to 71,196 Jews — up from 18,965 the previous year. At the holding centers, the situation was becoming intolerable — grim reminders of the displaced persons camps that rose in the aftermath of the Holocaust. Meanwhile, the U.S. administration was pressing Jewish organizations to assist them in fixing acceptable immigration numbers.

Fisher felt that putting that question to a broad spectrum of Jewish organizations was a disaster-waiting-to-happen, because where the Soviet Jews should reside — in the United States or Israel — was the subject of an explosive debate between American Jews and Israelis.

Martin S. Kraar, who succeeded Carmi Schwartz as the executive vice president of the CJF in the fall of 1989, explains the American view: "The position that the majority of us took was that the Soviet Jews were entitled to decide where they wanted to live. We may have preferred that they go to Israel, but we were not going to rescue them from an oppressive society, bring them into a free one, and then make their first personal decision for them. Nor once they entered the United States were we going to allow them to become destitute. Our mandate is to help Jews and so our services were made available to them."

Juxtaposed to this stance is the one espoused by Mendel Kaplan, a South African who now spends six months a year in Israel and serves as the chairman of the Jewish Agency Board of Governors.

"We, in Israel," says Kaplan "do not believe in Soviet Jews going to America — in moving them from one diaspora to another. To us, the freedom of choice that American Jews spoke about was a negation of Jewish leadership. I believe that

Jews should have a right to move anywhere they want. But they should not use public Jewish funds to do it. The Soviet Jews were being referred to as refugees, which means that the person is politically persecuted and has nowhere else to go. But every Jew in the world does have a place — Israel. The word 'refugee' is offensive to us because Israel is their home."

Inevitably, this conflict ignited a firestorm among the leading philanthropic institutions of Jewish life.

"We ended up with over 35,000 people stacked up in Rome," says Martin Kraar. "The Jewish Agency was yelling at the federations, and the federations, upset about the cost of maintaining Rome, were yelling at the Jewish Agency because they weren't in Rome trying to convince people to come to Israel."

With conditions swiftly deteriorating, Fisher embarked on a course that was unprecedented for him and ran contrary to his reputation as the foremost consensus builder in the organized Jewish world. Before presenting the dilemma to the established organizations for open debate, Fisher invited Mark Talisman, Mandell (Bill) L. Berman, president of the Council of Jewish Federations, and Shoshana Cardin, head of the National Conference on Soviet Jewry, to form a quartet with him. Dubbing it the "No Name Committee," Fisher took this intimate representative body to talk with the administration about clearing the Soviet Jews through the bureaucracy.

The motivation for Fisher's decision was a blend of pragmatism and personal considerations. On a practical level, Fisher believed that the tug-of-war over where the Russian emigrants belonged would prevent organized Jewry from actually seeing them through to safety. Because of the guilt over the Holocaust — the pledge that it would never happen again — rescuing Soviet Jewry was among the most impassioned concerns of Jewish organizations. During the Nixon administration, Fisher had seen these emotions gather the community behind the Jackson-Vanik legislation — in his view, a disastrous error in judgment. As Fisher had vainly tried to point out to organized American Jewry in the 1970s, the

Kremlin was bound to react by cutting off emigration. This was the eventual outcome, and Fisher promised himself to avoid mishaps arising from the raw emotionalism of the circumstances.

Personally, Fisher did not want this opportunity to skate past him. Over the last several years, he had felt the passing of time as never before. In September 1987, Henry Ford II had died. Fisher had lost an irreplaceable presence in his life. Every morning, as he sat in his office in the Fisher Building, he would glance up from his desk to look at the framed picture of his friend that he kept nearby. The photograph was taken by Ford's wife, Kathy, in Henry's final months, and for Fisher it emphasized how the years had sped past. At the age of eighty, Fisher knew, second chances were scarce. The Soviet Union was undergoing an avalanche of change; anti-Semitism was on the rise; Gorbachev was staring at domestic challenges that defied the imagination; his grip on the reins of power was by no means steady; and the doors could shut on Russian Jewry as suddenly as they had opened. Fisher wanted this settled — now.

Bill Berman remembers that one morning Fisher phoned and said that he needed him in Washington. That was Berman's introduction to the No Name Committee.

"At our first meeting with Deputy Secretary of State Eagleburger, he came in, saw Max sitting in an easy chair, smiled and said: 'I know where the power is here.' Everyone laughed. It was obvious how friendly they were. That meeting was very cordial. We explained that we hoped to get the State Department in synch with Congress. The need was obvious: we had close to 40,000 Soviet Jews stuck in the pipeline, and they wanted to enter the United States — not Israel."

For Shoshana Cardin, the contribution of the No Name Committee was twofold.

"The administration offered us approximately 25,000 slots," says Cardin. "We told them that we needed 40,000 so we could reunify families, and that the Jewish community could afford to pay for that number and keep the immigrants from becoming wards of the state. Financially, we did not want to overburden the federations. Many of the Soviet Jews who were coming here neither had anchor families or resources. Then we asked the U.S. government to press the Kremlin to let Soviet Jews apply for exit visas to either America or Israel. Max was convinced that first of all, Israel needed the immigrants, while the American Jewish community did not; two, that the Soviet Jews would be lost if they came here, whereas in Israel they would be returned to the Jewish people. The whole thing could have taken years to work out. It was a stroke of genius in that Max was able to do this in a relatively short time."

The U.S. government agreed to accept 40,000 Russian Jews — nearly all that were clogging the pipeline. This meant that if you were a Jew in the Soviet Union and chose to emigrate, then another year would pass before you would even be considered for entrance into the United States. A dual-track system was then instituted by the Kremlin; Russian Jews now had a choice between applying for a visa to the United States or Israel.

Stanley Horowitz, who, as head of the United Jewish Appeal, would assist with the fund-raising efforts on behalf of Soviet Jews, identifies the net results of these changes: "The true impact of what Max did was now the Jews in Russia had to decide where they wanted to go when they were in the Soviet Union. They could no longer take an Israeli visa, go to Vienna, be recognized as refugees and then come to the United States. With only 40,000 openings a year, America was now unavailable as a home for the majority of Soviet Jewish emigrants. So the Russian Jews chose to fly to Tel Aviv."

The last details for Fisher to help set in motion were the new and immense fund-raising requirements. In February 1990, a special General Assembly of the Council of Jewish Federations convened in Miami Beach. Members of the CJF consented to undertake a fund-raising campaign, Operation Exodus, for the express purpose of settling the Soviet immigrants in Israel — an atypical move for the CJF, which customarily confines its work to filling domestic needs. The goal of Operation Exodus was $420 million, and American Jewish communities pledged to provide their allocated sum from the proceeds of this special campaign or, if necessary, from money that they would borrow to cover their commitment.

In March, even before the official kickoff of the campaign, Fisher attended a United Jewish Appeal breakfast in New York City with, among others, Edgar Bronfman and Leslie Wexner. Before the orange juice was served, Fisher was called to the phone. Former Ambassador Walter Annenberg, a close friend from the Nixon and Ford administrations, was on the line.

"Max," said Annenberg, "I feel keenly about this. I'd like to be helpful. What are you looking for?"

Never one to be shy in pursuit of a good cause, Fisher replied: "How about five million a year for three years?"

"Fine," Annenberg said.

After hanging up, it occurred to Fisher that the size of Annenberg's commitment might stimulate the generosity of the big givers at the breakfast. Fisher called the ambassador back and asked if he could announce his pledge in public. Of course, Annenberg said.

"Walter's pledge," says Fisher, "was a real spark. I made the announcement, and by the time coffee was poured $58 million was pledged to Operation Exodus."

During 1990, Soviet Jewish immigration to Israel reached 181,759. Through the first six months of 1991, nearly 87,000 more arrived. PLO leader Yasser Arafat was shocked. In an interview, he complained that the inrush of Soviet Jews was more ominous for the Arabs than the creation of Israel.

With luck, Fisher thought, Arafat would be right. By December 1992, estimates claimed, over 1 million Soviet Jews will have come to Israel. Even with the drastic absorption dilemma generated by the inflow, Fisher was confident that over the long run the increased population would bring stability to the region; he concurred with what his friend, Simcha Dinitz, chairman of the Executive of the Jewish Agency, told *The Jerusalem Post*: "The immigrants will bring peace."

* * *

Playing so large a part in steering Soviet Jewry to Israel should have been enough for Fisher — the culmination of a lifetime of building bridges between Washington and Jerusalem. Prime Minister Yitzhak Shamir had told him that it was "a miracle." Maybe it was, Fisher thought, and he was pleased with his contribution, but it wasn't sufficient to satisfy him. His gnawing sense of having left things undone was never far below the surface.

History, Fisher knew, could not be trusted. History had recorded almost nothing of his role, and what it did record was often incorrect. Recently, he had read an essay by the distinguished Israeli political commentator, Moshe Zak. Zak wrote that Fisher had been enlisted by Nixon to persuade Golda Meir to accept the Rogers Plan, and alluded to Fisher again as one of the Republican Jews recruited by Ford to pressure Yitzhak Rabin during the 1975 Reassessment. Nothing could be further from the truth. But perhaps Fisher had wanted it that way — to leave no tracks, to live out of the limelight and savor his own brand of freedom.

Still, there were moments when he enjoyed a respite from his feelings of dissatisfaction — for instance, over the Memorial Day weekend of 1991 — as he sat in his glass-walled garden room in Detroit and another drama, to which he had lent his hand, unfolded.

Beginning on Friday, May 24, the Israeli government began an emergency airlift of 14,500 Ethiopian Jews — almost the entire Jewish population of that country. More than two dozen planes were in the air simultaneously, and each craft had two or three people to a seat. Less than forty-four hours later, the Ethiopians were safely in Israel.

For years, at countless meetings, Fisher had asked the White House and State Department to back Israel's attempts to ingather the Ethiopians, and argued their case whenever he could. In 1984, when a famine forced nearly 8,000 Ethiopian Jews to flee into the Sudan, Fisher raised the issue again with the administration. He found several sympathetic listeners, particularly then-Vice President George Bush. Assigned by President Reagan to oversee the logistics of the situation, Bush was relentless in his efforts to free the Ethiopian Jews caught in the Sudan, becoming the driving force behind a covert operation that ferried 7,000 of them to Israel. Neighboring Arab countries soon pressured the Ethiopian and Sudanese governments to halt further emigration. By March 1985, eight hundred Ethiopian Jews were still trapped in the Sudan. Vice President Bush stepped in again, sending U.S. C-130 Hercules transports to fly the 800 to Israel.

"George Bush's repeated efforts on behalf of the Ethiopian Jews were remarkable," says Fisher. "Had he not been personally involved, I doubt they would have survived."

The plight of the Ethiopian Jews wore on until the spring of 1991, when President Menguistu Haile Mariam of Ethiopia came under siege by rebels. Fisher was on the phone to Washington during this period, trying to find a way out for the Ethiopian Jews. He contacted the White House. Bush, now the president, needed little prodding. For a third time, he took the situation in hand, appointing former Senator Rudy Boschwitz as his special envoy to Ethiopia. Boschwitz urged Menguistu to let the Jews go. In May, Menguistu fled the country. Bush threw his personal weight behind the rescue mission. He sent a letter to the acting head of the Ethiopian government, Lieutenant General Tesfaye Gebre-Kidan, promising him that the United States would assist in bringing the civil war to an end if the Jews were immediately allowed to depart for Israel. Gebre-Kidan consented. Meanwhile, Bush prevailed upon the State Department to convince the rebels to delay capturing the capital until the Jews were gone.

Now, sitting in his Detroit garden room, Fisher was reading about the airlift in *The Times*. When the newsprint was piled at his feet, he phoned the president, praising him for his help in seeing the Ethiopian Jews to safety. Yes, Fisher said, he had talked with the prime minister in Israel. Israelis were dancing at Ben-Gurion Airport, while the Ethiopians knelt down to kiss the tarmac. Fisher and Bush moved on to more personal matters: the president's illness — the atrial fibrillation, an erratically fast heartbeat, that had recently been diagnosed. Fisher assured him that he had no need to worry; he had been suffering from the same thing for almost twenty years. All you had to do was take your medication and keep busy. The president laughed, and they said goodbye.

Fisher slouched in his chair, stretching out his legs and closing his eyes. The early summer sunlight lit the glass wall behind him. A longtime associate, much involved in organized world Jewry, was sitting on the couch across from Fisher. He commented that it had been quite a noteworthy day; the Ethiopians being airlifted to freedom was an accomplishment on the order of saving the Soviet Jews.

Suddenly, Fisher straightened in his chair and opened his eyes; they narrowed, taking on his familiar look of concentration, and strangely, defiance.

"The day's not ended," Fisher said.

ACKNOWLEDGEMENTS

This book could not have been written without the help of dozens of people. First, of course, is Max M. Fisher, who provided me with the opportunity to sift through his archives and shared hundreds of hours of his memories and observations with me. His wife, Marjorie, was no less generous with her time; she fielded my questions day or night, and I will always respect her forthrightness when it came to discussing the more challenging moments of her life.

Many others (some of whom sadly passed away before this book was completed), contributed their time to *Quiet Diplomat*, and I will forever be in their debt. I hope this list is complete, but if not, I offer my deepest apologies: Nathan Appleman, Marjorie Fisher Aronow, David Aronow, Bernadine Aubert, Yehuda Avner, Mandell L. Berman, Philip Bernstein, Harold Berry, Louis Berry, Floyd Bornstein, Matt Brooks, John Bugas, Joyce Switow Burkoff, Stanley T. Burkoff, George H. Bush, Shoshana Cardin, Hannah Chinitz, Walker L. Cisler, Howard Cohen, Fred E. Cope, Julie Fisher Cummings, Peter Cummings, Simcha Dinitz, Zvi Dinstein, Robert J. Dixon, Melvin Dubinsky, Leon Dulzin, Daniel J. Elazar, Sol Eisenberg, Arthur G. Elliott Jr., Ephraim Evon, Hortense Falk, Ron Firth, Mary Fisher, Phillip W. Fisher, Marlin Fitzwater, Steven Flax, Edsel Ford II, Gerald R. Ford, Henry Ford II, Norris Friedlander, Leonard Garment, Suzanne Garment, Bertram Gold, Irving L. Goldman, Uri Gordon, William Haber, Alexander M. Haig Jr., Gottlieb Hammer, Betty M. Hansen, Dwight Havens, Yehuda Hellman, Shari Hillman, Malcolm Hoenlein, Jerold C. Hoffberger, Charles Hoffman, Jason Honigman, Stanley B. Horowitz, Charles Horvath, Dennis N. Horwitz, Clay Howell, Joseph L. Hudson, Calvin Hughes,

Eliezer Jaffe, Miles Jaffe, Jacob Javits, Mendel Kaplan, Irving Kessler, Henry A. Kissinger, George Klein, Martin S. Kraar, Teddy Kollek, David Lissy, Bill Kovach, David J. Mahoney, Morton L. Mandel, Aron M. Mathieu, Robert E. McCabe, Paul W. McCracken, Kathryn McIntosh, Sharon Ross Medsker, Ruth Miles, Israel Miller, William G. Milliken, Seymour Milstein, John N. Mitchell, Richard G. Morse, Robert A. Mosbacher Sr., Joseph Nederlander, Richard M. Nixon, Kathy O'Connor, Shlomo Osherov, Shimon Peres, Joseph E. Persico, Martin R. Pollner, Yitzhak Rabin, Ronald W. Reagan, Seymour Reich, Charles Roessler, George W. Romney, Anne Fisher Rose, Lew Rose, Harry Rosen, Gail Fisher Rossen, Herschel Schacter, Avraham Schenker, Maurice S. Schiller, Shirley Krell Schlafer, Alan E. Schwartz, Carmi Schwartz, Yitzhak Shamir, Jane Fisher Sherman, Larry Sherman, George P. Shultz, Joseph J. Sisco, William G. Slaughter Jr., Maurice H. Stans, Al Stark, Jacob Stein, Mark Talisman, Dorothy Fisher Tessler, Frank Tessler, Melvin I. Urofsky, Richard VanDusen, Richard Van Tiem, A. Alfred Taubman, Remer Tyson, Howard Weisband, Henry Penn Wenger, Joseph J. Wright, Henry K. Yaggi Jr., Coleman A. Young, Chaim Zohar.

I would also like to thank Irving Bernstein, Zelig Chinitz and Arthur Klebanoff for their wise comments on the manuscript; Jerome Eckstein, for being my teacher then and now; Peter Iselin, Judith Sokoloff, Elizabeth Coccio and M.S. Solow for their editorial assistance; Sam Bloch, for turning a manuscript into a book; Gus Cardinali, who guided me through Detroit and provided history lessons at every corner; Elizabeth Stephens for helping me comb the Fisher Archives and always knowing where to look; Beth Brinser, my research assistant, who saved me countless months of digging; and my wife, Annis, whose loving encouragement and sage advice sustained me from the first page of this book to the last.

NOTES

Introduction
EISENHOWER AND THE REVELATIONS OF SINAI

SOURCES

Books, newspapers, journals, documents:

Ambrose, *Eisenhower: The President*; Ambrose, *Nixon: The Education of a Politician 1913-1962*; Bartlett, *Bartlett's Familiar Quotations, Fifteenth Edition*; Blitzer, *Between Washington & Jerusalem: A Reporter's Notebook*; Bundon, *Ike: His Life and Times*; Delury, ed., *The 1975 World Almanac*; El Azhary, *Political Cohesion of American Jews in American Politics: A Reappraisal of Their Role in Presidential Elections*; Karp, *To Give Life: The UJA and the Shaping of the American Jewish Community*; Sachar, *A History of Israel From the Rise of Zionism to Our Time*; Spiegel, *The Other Arab-Israeli Conflict: Making America's Middle East Policy, from Truman to Reagan.*

The New York Times.
American Jewish Archives.

Fisher Archives.

Oral History:
Max M. Fisher

Interviews:
Max M. Fisher, Malcolm Hoenlein, Richard M. Nixon.

NOTES

Fisher goes to Eisenhower: Max M. Fisher interview.

Art of the possible: Max M. Fisher interview. The remark "Politics is the art of the possible" has been attributed to Bismarck, who also said — in a speech on March 15, 1884 — "Politics is not a science . . . but an art." Bartlett, *Bartlett's Familiar Quotations, Fifteenth Edition*, p. 53.

Operate in background: Max M. Fisher interview.

"Dean of American Jewry": Malcolm Hoenlein interview.

UJA study: Karp, *To Give Life: The UJA and the Shaping of the American Jewish Community*, p. 142.

The farm in Pennsylvania; Eisenhower in frail health: Ambrose, *Eisenhower: The President*, pp. 628-629. **Glass-enclosed sun porch:** Ambrose, *Eisenhower: The President*, pp. 628-629.

Fisher saw Eisenhower as a strong president: Max M. Fisher interview. Historians have been re-examining the accepted hands-off vision of Eisenhower's presidency. On *The New York Times'* op-ed page, July 26, 1989, Professor Fred I. Greenstein of Princeton University, wrote: "But today, students of the presidency acknowledge that, in his own way, Ike was an activist president and a shrewd, informed leader. . . . The new assessment of Eisenhower's leadership began in the early 1980s as scholars digested a mass of hitherto-classified documents from his White House."

Eisenhower reminisces about 1945: *Max M. Fisher Addresses 1964-1968*, p. 76; Max M. Fisher interview; Max M. Fisher OH. The OH designation for oral history refers to a collection of taped and written interviews conducted by David Zurawik for the Fisher Archives.

Discussing GOP, politics, history: Max M. Fisher interview; Max M. Fisher OH.

Nasser nationalized Suez Canal: Sachar, *A History of Israel From the Rise of Zionism to Our Time*, p. 486. **Nasser, a national hero:** Sachar, *A History of Israel From the Rise of Zionism to Our Time*, p. 486. **France, England and Israel scheme:** Spiegel, *The Other Arab-Israeli Conflict: Making America's Middle East Policy, from Truman to Reagan*, pp. 73-74.

Israelis attack enrages Eisenhower: Spiegel, *The Other Arab-Israeli Conflict: Making America's Middle East Policy, from Truman to Reagan*, pp. 74-75. **Ominous message to Ben-Gurion:** Sachar, *A History of Israel From the Rise of Zionism to Our Time*, p. 503.

Israel ignores message: Sachar, *A History of Israel From the Rise of Zionism to Our Time*, p. 503. **U.S. supports U.N. charter:** Sachar, *A History of Israel From the Rise of Zionism to Our Time*, **p. 503. U.S. threatens to cut Israeli financial aid:** Spiegel, *The Other Arab-Israeli Conflict: Making America's Middle East Policy, from Truman to Reagan;* pp. 76-77, Blitzer, *Between Washington & Jerusalem: A Reporter's Notebook*, p. 12.

Israel withdraws: Spiegel, *The Other Arab-Israeli Conflict: Making America's Middle East Policy, from Truman to Reagan*, p. 77.

Very bad timing politically: Richard M. Nixon interview.

Stevenson captures Jewish vote: El Azhary, *Political Cohesion of American Jews in American Politics: A Reappraisal of Their Role in Presidential Elections*, p. 23.

Eisenhower ignores American Jewish concerns in making Suez Canal crisis decisions: *American Jewish Archives*, Volume XL, April 1988, p. 84; Bundon, *Ike: His Life and Times*, p. 55.

After Suez, British world power ebbed: Richard M. Nixon interview.

U.S. had to act alone: Richard M. Nixon interview.

Eisenhower, no second thoughts: Ambrose, *Nixon: The Education of a Politician 1913-1962*, p. 420.

"Never should have pressured Israel to evacuate": Max M. Fisher interview; Max M. Fisher OH.

Expressed regrets to others: Max M. Fisher, Richard M. Nixon interviews.

Thought it was a mistake: Richard M. Nixon interview.

"If I had had a Jewish adviser": Max M. Fisher interview; Max M. Fisher OH.

An epiphany: Max M. Fisher interview; Max M. Fisher OH.

Thanked Eisenhower: Max M. Fisher interview; Max M. Fisher OH.

UJA awards ceremony: *Max M. Fisher Addresses, 1964-1968*, p. 73, Fisher Archives. **Speaks of Koening, Alexander, Eisenhower:** *Max M. Fisher Addresses, 1964-1968*, p. 75, Fisher Archives. **Yom Kippur visit:** *Max M. Fisher Addresses, 1964-1968*, p. 76.

"A sunnier day will be coming soon": *Max M. Fisher Addresses, 1964-1968*, Fisher Archives.

Eisenhower illness: Ambrose, *Eisenhower: The President*, p. 669.

"Someone like Max can change the president's mind": Richard M. Nixon interview.

Chapter 1

WHAT NORMAN ROCKWELL NEVER DREAMED

SOURCES

Books, journals, newspapers:

Applebaum, *The Fishers: A Family Portrait*; Behrman, ed., *Strive and Succeed: Two novels by Horatio Alger*; Gerber, ed., *Anti-Semitism in America*; Howe, *The World of our Fathers*; Kallen, *"Of Them Which Say They Are Jews" and Other Essays on the Jewish Struggle for Survival*; Levinger, *A History of the Jews in the United States*; Sims, *The Klan. The Quaker*, 1923-1926

Midstream, Monthly Detroit.

The Salem (Ohio) *News.*

Fisher Archives.

Interviews:

Fred E. Cope, Robert J. Dixon, Ron Firth, Marjorie Switow Fisher, Max M. Fisher, Charles M. Roessler, Anne Fisher Rose, Gail Fisher Rossen, Henry Yaggi Jr.

NOTES

Two million Jews emigrate to U.S.: Levinger, *A History of the Jews in the United States*, p. 265. **Malka Brody's birthday:** Malka's (Mollie's) birth year was 1887, although it is not formally recorded. Her birthday was celebrated by the family on Valentine's Day, a tradition started by Marjorie in the 1950s.

July 15, 1908: Applebaum, *The Fishers: A Family Portrait*, p. 15

Salem history: Robert J. Dixon, Ron Firth interviews. **William Fisher adapted:** Anne Fisher Rose interview.

Always enough food for the guests: Anne Fisher Rose interview.

Max and his fifteen-minute piano practices: Gail Fisher Rossen interview.

"Sonny boy": Gail Fisher Rossen interview.

"Yiddishe Mameh": Max M. Fisher interview.

"Haunt Jewish sons": Howe, *The World of Our Fathers*, p. 174.

"Jewish mother": *Midstream*, February 1967.

The Jewish National Fund box: Max M. Fisher interview.

Demanding, determined women: *Midstream*, February 1967.

Driven to be a success: Max M. Fisher interview.

Philosophy of wealth: Behrman, S.N., editor, *Strive and Succeed, two novels by Horatio Alger*, pp. iii, iv.

Lee Chamberlain: Max M. Fisher interview.

Chamberlain description: Charles M. Roessler interview.

"Dedicated to Scouting and the boys": Charles M. Roessler interview.

"Came back as one of the boys": Max M. Fisher interview.

"Football practice and your dad's booze": Charles B. Coffee to Max M. Fisher, January 24, 1981, Fisher Archives.

"Max was always trying to improve": Fred E. Cope interview.

"Pugnacious as hell": Max M. Fisher interview.

Jewish identity: Kallen, *"Of Them Which Say They Are Jews" and Other Essays on the Jewish Struggle for Survival.* p. 36

Ohio and the Ku Klux Klan: Sims, *The Klan*, pp. 60-61.

"All show and no blow": Henry K. Yaggi Jr. interview.

Hometown recollections: Max M. Fisher, Anne Fisher Rose interviews.

"'Dirty Jew'": Anne Fisher Rose interview.

"'Had his moments with being Jewish'": *Monthly Detroit*, July 1980.

"Rabbi" equals "Joe" or "Butch": Henry K. Yaggi Jr. interview.

"He was called 'Rabbi' and stuff like that": Fred E. Cope interview.

"'Steppin' Fetchit": Fred E. Cope interview.

"Selection of the center": *The Salem* (Ohio) *News*, December 1, 1925.

American anti-Semitism: Gerber, ed., "The 'Mythical Jew' and 'Jew next door,'" in Nineteenth Century America, *Anti-Semitism in American History.*

"Exemption": Rose, *Strangers in Their Midst*, p. 139.

"Biculturalism": Rose, *Strangers in Their Midst*, p. 139.

"Growing up in Salem": Fisher remarks to Salem Alumni Association, June 10, 1972, Fisher Archives.

"Making the desert bloom again": Fisher remarks to Salem Alumni Association, June 10, 1972, Fisher Archives.

"I never left": Fisher remarks to Salem Alumni Association, June 10, 1972, Fisher Archives.

Amazed they invited him to return: Max M. Fisher interview.

Chapter 2
THE ROAD NOT TAKEN
SOURCES

Newspapers:
The Ohio Lantern.

Fisher Archives.

Oral History:
Max M. Fisher.
Council of Jewish Federations Oral History Project.

Interviews:
Peter Cummings, Max M. Fisher, Aron M. Mathieu.

NOTES

10,000 students at Ohio State University: Max M. Fisher interview.

"Wide, wide doors" of OSU: *Max M. Fisher Addresses 1969-1972*, p. 139, Fisher Archives.

"You are Jewish": Max M. Fisher interview; Max M. Fisher CJF OH.

"More Jewish": Max M. Fisher interview; Max M. Fisher CJF OH.

"Going to be a big success": Max M. Fisher interview; Max M. Fisher CJF OH.

Dealing with uncertainties: Max M. Fisher; Max M. Fisher CJF OH.

Introduced to formalized Judaism: Max M. Fisher CJF OH.

Involved in Hillel: Max M. Fisher CJF OH.

"Very shy": Confidential interview.

President of fraternity: Aron M. Mathieu interview.

Filling up on chili: Max M. Fisher interview; Max M. Fisher OH.

"This Jew boy's not very smart": Max M. Fisher interview; Max M. Fisher CJF OH.

"No problem relating to Christians": Max M. Fisher interview; Max M. Fisher CJF OH.

Self scrutiny: Max M. Fisher interview; Max M. Fisher CJF OH.

"Call to the Work of the World": *The Ohio Lantern*, June 10, 1930. The entire text of Hudson's speech is printed in this student newspaper.

Award in Cleveland instead: Max M. Fisher, Peter Cummings interviews.

Chapter 3
IN PURSUIT OF HORATIO ALGER
SOURCES
Books, journals, newspapers:
Applebaum, *The Fishers: A Family Portrait;* Conot, *An American Odyssey;* Ferry, *The Buildings of Detroit;* Hurt, *Texas Rich;* Lacey, *Ford: The Men and the Machine;* Owen, *Trek of the Oil Finders: A History of Exploration for Petroleum;* Spence, *Portrait in Oil: How the Ohio Oil Company Grew to Become Marathon;* Yaffe, *The American Jews;* Yergin, *The Prize: The Epic Quest for Oil, Money & Power.*

Forbes.

Detroit Free Press, The Detroit News, The Mellus Newspapers.

Fisher Archives.

Interviews:
Nathan Appleman, Irving Bernstein, Harold Berry, Floyd Bornstein, Joyce Switow Burkoff, Stanley T. Burkoff, Julie Fisher Cummings, Marjorie Switow Fisher, Max M. Fisher, Norris Friedlander, Irving L. "Bucky" Goldman, Dennis N. Horwitz, Kathryn McIntosh, Maurice S. Schiller, Shirley Krell Schlafer, Jane Fisher Sherman, Larry Sherman, William E. Slaughter Jr., A. Alfred Taubman, Henry Penn Wenger.

NOTES
Max arrives in Detroit: Applebaum, *The Fishers: A Family Portrait,* pp. 37-38.
Richman Brothers' career ended: Max M. Fisher interview.
$15-a-week salesman: Applebaum, *The Fishers: A Family Portrait,* pp. 40-41.
Saw automobile as a basic factor in American lives: Max M. Fisher remarks to Salem Alumni Association, June 10, 1972, Fisher Archives.
Detroit ravaged by Depression: Conot, *American Odyssey,* pp. 260, 275. **Detroit's starved children:** Conot, *American Odyssey,* p. 283.
Couldn't give away oil: *Detroit Free Press,* October 28, 1979.
Strolling West Grand Boulevard: Max M. Fisher interview. **Fisher Building shadow:** Ferry, *The Buildings of Detroit,* p. 334. **Built in 1928, Detroit's "New Center":** Lacey, *Ford: The Men and the Machine,* p. 567. **Gothic in design:** Lacey, *Ford: The Men and the Machine,* p. 567.
Detroit hostile to Jews: Conot, *American Odyssey,* pp. 326-327. **Father Coughlin's anti-Semitic invectives:** Conot, *American Odyssey,* pp. 281-282, 368.
No money for vaudeville shows: *Detroit Free Press,* October 28, 1979.
Schiller joins Keystone: Maurice S. Schiller interview.
Hunting geese to make a deal: Maurice S. Schiller interview.
Keystone operations inefficient and in the red: Applebaum, *The Fishers: A Family Portrait,* pp. 41-42.
Oil discovered in eastern Michigan: Owen, *The Trek of the Oil Finders: A History of Exploration for Petroleum,* pp. 610-615. **Keystone small venture in crude refining:** Applebaum, *The Fishers: A Family Portrait,* pp. 42-43.
Two hundred barrels: *Detroit Free Press,* October 28, 1979.
Voted for FDR: *Detroit Free Press,* October 28, 1979.
Cuban vacation and suit: Max M. Fisher interview; *Detroit Free Press,* October 28, 1979.
Keystone plant burned to ground: Max M. Fisher interview.

Max wanted to rebuild refinery, William blamed refinery for fire: Max M. Fisher interview.

Henry Wenger a Swiss immigrant, Max's mentor in business: Henry Penn Wenger, William Slaughter, Max M. Fisher interviews.

"Must have hoodwinked them": *Forbes*, September 14, 1981.

Fisher's figures "made sense": William Slaughter interview.

Fisher among first Jews in oil business: Henry Penn Wenger interview.

Convinced his father to allow use of Keystone land for refinery: Applebaum, *The Fishers: A Family Portrait*, p. 45; Max M. Fisher, William Slaughter interviews.

Fisher meets, courts and marries Sylvia Krell: Max M. Fisher, Jane Fisher Sherman, Shirley Krell Schlafer interview.

"You have to do something different": *Forbes*, September 14, 1981.

Sylvia pregnant: Max M. Fisher interview.

Fisher and The Ohio Oil Company deal made with a handshake: *Forbes*, September 14, 1981; Applebaum, *The Fishers: A Family Portrait*, pp. 46-47; Max M. Fisher interview.

Jane born, Sylvia moves to Tucson to preserve health: Max M. Fisher, Jane Fisher Sherman interviews.

Max working day and night: Bucky Goldman interview.

Max loved the adventure of the oil business: Maurice S. Schiller, Max M. Fisher interviews.

Description of Dallas: Hurt, *Texas Rich*, p. 85.

Pray, then Fisher and Schiller carrying $150,000 in cash: Max M. Fisher, Maurice S. Schiller interviews.

Description of Donnell: See Spence, *Portrait in Oil*.

The Ohio kept its bargain even in World War II's darkest days: Max M. Fisher interview; *Forbes*, September 14, 1981.

Aurora emerged World War II prospering, "Aurora type": Max M. Fisher, William Slaughter interviews; The Mellus Newspapers, February 15, 1951; Fisher Archives.

"Calories don't count if they come from your plate": Jane Fisher Sherman, Julie Fisher Cummings interviews.

Max fighting migraine headaches: Nathan Appleman, Jane Fisher Sherman, Marjorie Switow Fisher, Max M. Fisher interviews.

Sylvia Fisher dies: Jane Fisher Sherman, Max M. Fisher, Sylvia Krell Schlafer interviews.

Mollie and William Fisher move to Florida: Applebaum, *The Fishers: A Family Portrait* pp. 73-80, Norris Friedlander interview. **Marjorie newly divorced, not looking for dates:** Marjorie Switow Fisher, Joyce Switow Burkoff interviews.

"How's my hair?": Joyce Switow Burkoff interview.

Max widowed, rejected most dates: Max M. Fisher interview.

"Hello, Scarlett": Max M. Fisher, Marjorie Switow Fisher interviews.

"Hi, Rhett": Max M. Fisher, Marjorie Switow Fisher interviews.

Max pursued Marjorie: Max M. Fisher, Marjorie Switow Fisher interviews.

"He was such a gentlemen": Marjorie Switow Fisher interview.

"Your fish is black": Joyce Switow Burkoff, Stanley T. Burkoff interviews.

Max fixes *kreplach* **for Marjorie's family:** Joyce Switow Burkoff, Stanley T. Burkoff interviews.

Max calls Marjorie from Cuba to propose: Max M. Fisher, Marjorie Switow Fisher, Bucky Goldman interviews.

Max and Marjorie married in New York City: Marjorie Switow Fisher, Nathan Appleman interviews.

First visit to Israel, 1954: Max M. Fisher interview. This story was recounted often by Fisher in his speeches. See, for example, *Max M. Fisher Addresses 1964-1968*, pp. 196-197, Fisher Archives.

Shut down immigration: Max M. Fisher interview; *Max M. Fisher Addresses 1964-1968*, pp. 196-197, Fisher Archives.

"Never close the gates": Max M. Fisher interview; *Max M. Fisher Addresses 1964-1968*, pp. 196-197, Fisher Archives.

Calling in cards: Yaffe, *The American Jew*, pp. 173-174.

Fisher-New Center Company: Harold Berry, Floyd Bornstein, Dennis N. Horwitz interviews; *The Detroit News*, December 27, 1962. The breakdown of FNC was as follows: Fisher owned 25 percent of FNC; Henry E. Wenger and William E. Slaughter Jr. had 15 percent; Louis Berry, his son Harold, and his daughter, Mrs. Selma Berry Snider, owned 30 percent; George Seyburn owned 25 percent, and David Miro, Berry's attorney, owned 5 percent.

Fisher Building a Detroit symbol: *The Detroit News*, December 27, 1962.

Saved expense of new nameplate: Lacey, *Ford: The Men and the Machine*, p. 567.

Chapter 4
BUILDING BRIDGES
SOURCES
Books, journals, newspapers, manuscripts:

Applebaum, *The Fishers: A Family Portrait*; Biale, *Power and Powerlessness in Jewish History*; Ford with Chase, *The Times of My Life*; Eisenhower, *Pat Nixon: The Untold Story*; Karp, *Haven and Home: A History of the Jews in America, To Give Life: The UJA and the Shaping of the American Jewish Community*; Tuchman, *Practicing History*; Woocher, *Sacred Survival: The Civil Religion of American Jews*.

Harper's, People.

Detroit Free Press, Detroit Jewish News, The Jewish Standard, Jewish Telegraphic Agency.

Feingold, "The UJA in American Jewish Consciousness." An unpublished manuscript.

Fisher Archives.

Interviews:

Irving Bernstein, Philip Bernstein, Joyce Switow Burkoff, Zelig S. Chinitz, Julie Fisher Cummings, Marjorie Switow Fisher, Mary Fisher, Max M. Fisher, Phillip W. Fisher, Gottlieb Hammer, Richard M. Nixon, Jane Fisher Sherman, Larry Sherman, Elizabeth A. Stephens.

NOTES
Fisher elected UJA Chairman: Karp, *To Give Life: The UJA and the Shaping of the American Jewish Community*, p. 138.

'American Jewish leader': *Max M. Fisher Addresses 1964-1968*, p. 21.

UJA leadership passed Eastern European Jews: Karp, *Haven and Home: A History of the Jews in America*, p. 332. " **'Homeless, tempest-tost'":** *Max M. Fisher Addresses 1964-1968*, p. 57.

"Fisher, the Eastern European prince": Irving Bernstein interview. **"A different kind of Jew":** Irving Bernstein interview.

Old Money versus New Money: Irving Bernstein interview; Karp, *Haven and Home: A History of the Jews in America*, p. 332.

German Jews anti-Zionist: Karp, *To Give Life: The UJA and the Shaping of the American Jewish Community*, p. 332.

Reluctant yet to fund Israel: Biale, *Power and Powerlessness in Jewish History*, p. 177.

Question of dual allegiance: *People*, August 7, 1989.

Zionism invoked loyalty questions: Tuchman, *Practicing History*, p. 215.

Jews "peculiarly fitted for the attainment of American ideals": Karp, *Haven and Home: A History of the Jews in America*, pp. 249-250.

Fisher saw U.S.-Israeli policies complementary: Max M. Fisher interview.

"Where's the dual allegiance?": Max M. Fisher interview.

Cooperation for a coalition: Max M. Fisher, Zelig S. Chinitz interviews. **"A single step":** *Max M. Fisher Addresses 1964-1968*, pp. 17-21, Fisher Archives; Max M. Fisher interview.

UJA coordinates campaigns: Feingold, "The UJA in American Jewish Consciousness," Unpublished manuscript.

UJA organizational role: Feingold, "The UJA in American Jewish Consciousness," Unpublished manuscript. **Volunteers and professionals amalgam:** Max M. Fisher, Irving Bernstein, Zelig S. Chinitz interviews.

Business, charity, not run alike: Max M. Fisher interview.

Set policy, then direct it: Max M. Fisher OH.

Didn't interfere: Irving Bernstein interview.

Corporate, philanthropic interests: Applebaum, *The Fishers: A Family Portrait*, pp. 98-100; *Detroit Free Press*, June 28, 1963.

"Compartmentalize things": Max M. Fisher interview.

"I never made it": Max M. Fisher interview.

Constant telephone contact: Richard M. Nixon, Max M. Fisher, Marjorie Switow Fisher, Irving Bernstein, Zelig S. Chinitz, Gottlieb Hammer, Jane Fisher Sherman, Larry Sherman, Elizabeth A. Stephens interviews.

Appreciate him asking your opinion: Richard M. Nixon, Max M. Fisher, Marjorie Switow Fisher, Irving Bernstein, Zelig S. Chinitz, Gottlieb Hammer, Jane Fisher Sherman, Larry Sherman, Elizabeth A. Stephens interviews.

Knew where you stood with Max: Confidential interview.

"Softened the atmosphere": Confidential interview.

"Gentleness and welcome": Irving Bernstein interview.

Class replaces religion: *Harper's*, March 1955.

Rich know the poor in Salem: Confidential interview.

Common purpose: Max M. Fisher interview.

Social occasions: Irving Bernstein interview.

Marjorie provided a "gracious social atmosphere": Irving Bernstein interview. **Social planning to Marjorie:** Marjorie Switow Fisher, Max M. Fisher interviews. **"Proud to have them":** Marjorie Switow Fisher interview.

Life of a politician's wife: *Detroit Free Press*, March 16, 1965; Marjorie Switow Fisher interview.

"I had no idea": Marjorie Switow Fisher interview.

Perfectionist: Marjorie Switow Fisher interview.

"I'm fourth": Marjorie Switow Fisher interview.

"Bowl of charities": *Detroit Free Press*, September 24, 1967. **Hiding vitamin pills:** *Detroit Free Press*, September 24, 1967.

Exacted a price: Marjorie Switow Fisher, Max M. Fisher, Joyce Switow Burkoff, Phillip W. Fisher, Julie Fisher Cummings, Mary Fisher interviews.

UJA and federations friction, money, power: Feingold, "The UJA in American Jewish Consciousness," pp. 32-33, unpublished manuscript.

Tension in purposes: Feingold, "The UJA in American Jewish Consciousness," pp. 32-33, unpublished manuscript.

Opposed incorporation: Feingold, "The UJA in American Jewish Consciousness," pp. 32-33, unpublished manuscript; Max M. Fisher interview.

American Jews identified with Israel: Woocher, *Sacred Survival: The Civil Religion of American Jews*, p. 58.

"A Chosen Generation": Woocher, *Sacred Survival: The Civil Religion of American Jews*, p. 58.

Fisher cornered both sides: Max M. Fisher interview.

"Responsibility to all the Jewish people": Max M. Fisher interview.

"More that unites than divides": Max M. Fisher interview.

Israel basis for dramatic giving: Max M. Fisher, Irving Bernstein, Zelig S. Chinitz interviews. **Giving doubled at wars:** 1988 report to the United Jewish Appeal's National Allocations Committee, Fisher Archives.

UJA, Federations, "symbiotic": Karp, *To Give Life: The UJA and the Shaping of American Jewish Community*, pp. 142-143. **Big cities, big givers:** Max M. Fisher, Zelig S. Chinitz, Irving Bernstein, Philip Bernstein interviews.

"Salesmen for the UJA": Max M. Fisher, Zelig S. Chinitz, Irving Bernstein, Philip Bernstein interviews.

"Formal and cool": *The Jewish Standard*, March 20, 1981.

Max the representative of Jewish community unified entity: Karp, *Haven and Home: A History of the Jews in America*, p. 333.

"Grass Roots Man": *Detroit Jewish News*, December 18, 1964.

UJA and CJF leader: Applebaum, *The Fishers: A Family Portrait*, pp. 98-100.

Long range allocations agreements: Feingold, "The UJA in American Jewish Consciousness," p. 33, unpublished manuscript.

"Unique leader of American Jewish community": Jewish Telegraphic Agency, March 19, 1981. **"Achieving Jewish unity":** Jewish Telegraphic Agency, March 19, 1981.

"Builder of bridges": Jewish Telegraphic Agency, March 19, 1981.

Chapter 5
FISHER AND NIXON: LONELY MEN OF FAITH
SOURCES

Books, journals, newspapers:
Ambrose, *Nixon: The Education of a Politician 1913-1962*; Brodie, *Richard M. Nixon: The Shaping of His Character*; Goldwater, *Goldwater*; Hammer, *Good Faith and Credit*; Lurie, *The Running of Richard Nixon*; Nixon, *In The Arena, Six Crises, RN: The Memoirs of Richard Nixon*; Safire, *Before the Fall*; Wills, *Nixon Agonistes*; Witcover, *The Resurrection of Richard Nixon*.
The Detroit Magazine.
Detroit Free Press, Detroit Jewish News, The Wall Street Journal.

Fisher Archives.

Oral History:
Max M. Fisher, Jason Honigman, Joseph L. Hudson, Richard M. Nixon.

Interviews:
Irving Bernstein, Stanley T. Burkoff, Zelig S. Chinitz, Marjorie Switow Fisher, Max M. Fisher, Leonard Garment, David H. Lissy, David J. Mahoney, Seymour

Milstein, Richard G. Morse, Joseph Nederlander, Richard M. Nixon, George W. Romney, Jane Fisher Sherman, Jacob Stein, Elizabeth A. Stephens, Joseph J. Wright.

NOTES

Fisher and Nixon meet, 1959: Max M. Fisher, Richard M. Nixon interviews; Max M. Fisher, Richard M. Nixon OH. **Talk to VP Nixon UJA problem:** Max M. Fisher interview; Max M. Fisher OH. **UJA tax-exempt status challenged:** Feingold, "United Jewish Appeal in American Consciousness, pp. 34-35, unpublished manuscript.

Nixon sympathetic to UJA problem: Max M. Fisher interview. **Investigation repulsed:** Feingold, "United Jewish Appeal in American Consciousness," p. 35, unpublished manuscript. **Funds restructured:** Hammer, *Good Faith and Credit*, pp. 129-135. **Regular Fisher-Nixon meetings:** Max M. Fisher, Richard M. Nixon interviews; Max M. Fisher, Richard M. Nixon OH.

"We could discuss issues": Richard M. Nixon OH.

"Shared same philosophy": Max M. Fisher interview; Max M. Fisher OH.

Immersed selves in work: Max M. Fisher, Richard M. Nixon interviews. **"Hardest-working man":** Ambrose, *Nixon: The Education of a Politician 1913-1962*, p. 75. **Respected others' hard work:** Ambrose, *Nixon: The Education of a Politician 1913-1963*, p. 122. **"Nothing could be more pitiful":** Wills, *Nixon Agonistes*, p. 28. **Contempt for the idle rich:** Wills, *Nixon Agonistes*, p. 28.

Incapable of relaxing: A number of people interviewed discussed Fisher's inability to relax. Consistently, it was heard from his wife and children, and various colleagues: for example, Zelig S. Chinitz, Philip Bernstein, David H. Lissy and Joseph L. Hudson.

Max spent Caribbean cruise on telephone: Jason Honigman OH.

1958, Nixon decided to run: Nixon, *Six Crises*, pp. 356-358.

Motive for support less obvious: Max M. Fisher interview; Max M. Fisher OH.

Less government best for economic growth: Max M. Fisher interview; Max M. Fisher OH.

Voted for Wendell Willkie: Max M. Fisher, Jane Fisher Sherman interviews.

Jewish vote taken for granted by Democrats: Max M. Fisher interview.

1960 mark of Fisher's entrance into national political fund-raising: Max M. Fisher interview.

Determined to campaign in every state: Ambrose, *Nixon: The Education of a Politician 1913-1962*, pp. 603-604.

Able to fund only one telethon: Max M. Fisher interview; Nixon, *Six Crisis*, pp. 440-441.

Difficulties raising money for telethon: David J. Mahoney interview.

Max raised $250,000 immediately: David J. Mahoney interview.

If not for Fisher, no telethon: David J. Mahoney interview.

Nixon loses closest race in presidential history: Ambrose, *The Education of a Politician 1913-1962*, p. 606. **A shift of one-tenth of one percent:** Ambrose, *The Education of a Politician 1913-1962*, p. 607.

Fisher's admiration for Nixon increased: Max M. Fisher interview. **Texas, Chicago voting fraud rumors:** Ambrose, *The Education of a Politician 1913-1962*, p. 606. **Daley's deathbed confession:** Max M. Fisher, Leonard Garment interviews.

Supporters encouraged Nixon to contest election: Ambrose, *The Education of a Politician 1913-1962*, p. 606; Nixon, *Six Crisis*, p. 489. **No recount:** Max M. Fisher interview. **L.A. Law:** Max M. Fisher interview; Nixon, *Six Crisis*, pp. 489-490. **Pat in D.C, Nixon in L.A. eating TV dinners:** Nixon, *RN: The Memoirs of Richard Nixon*, pp. 231-232. **"Were often the first to desert":** Nixon, *RN: The Memoirs of Richard Nixon*, pp. 231-232.

Fisher did not desert: Richard M. Nixon to Max M. Fisher, December 9, 1960, Fisher Archives.

"Renewed determination": Richard M. Nixon to Max M. Fisher, January 3, 1961, Fisher Archives.

Nixon still running: Max M. Fisher interview.

Steady contact, Nixon values Fisher: Max M. Fisher, Richard M. Nixon interviews. **"Unbounded admiration" for Fisher:** Richard M. Nixon to Peter Golden, June 22, 1989.

"Great personal loyalty": Richard M. Nixon OH.

1961, Republican Party leader: Ambrose, *Nixon: The Education of a Politician 1913-1962*, p. 629, Nixon, *RN: The Memoirs of Richard Nixon*, p. 231. **Times-Mirror syndicate political columns:** Nixon, *RN: The Memoirs of Richard Nixon*, p. 232. **May 1961 speaking tour:** Nixon, *RN: The Memoirs of Richard Nixon*, p. 236.

A rested Nixon: Ambrose, *Nixon: The Education of a Politician 1913-1962*, p. 634. **How to win the "Negro vote":** *Detroit Free Press*, May 10, 1961. **Nixon would lead GOP to middle ground:** *The Detroit Free Press*, May 10, 1961.

Fisher congratulates Nixon on speech: Max M. Fisher to Richard M. Nixon, May 11, 1961, Fisher Archives.

Pressure to seek California governorship: Nixon, *RN: The Memoirs of Richard Nixon*, pp. 236-237.

Pluses in California governorship election: Max M. Fisher to Richard M. Nixon, July 28, 1961, Fisher Archives.

"Keen sense of timing": *The Wall Street Journal*, February 8, 1978. **Ambivalent about California race:** Nixon, *RN: The Memoirs of Richard Nixon*, p. 239. **Will seek your advice again:** Richard M. Nixon to Max M. Fisher, August 15, 1961, Fisher Archives.

Merits of California race, GOP leadership: Nixon, *Six Crisis*, pp. 356, 455.

Benefit of your advice: Max M. Fisher interview; Richard M. Nixon to Max M. Fisher, September 1, 1961, Fisher Archives.

Nixon announces candidacy for California governorship: Nixon, *RN: The Memoirs of Richard Nixon*, pp. 240-241. **Using position as "stepping-stone" to presidency:** Ambrose, *Nixon The Education of a Politician 1913-1962*, p. 648. **Voters believed charge:** Ambrose, *Nixon: The Education of a Politician 1913-1962*, p. 650. **Nixon thanks Fisher for support in 1960 election:** Richard M. Nixon to Max M. Fisher, November 8, 1961, Fisher Archives.

Autographed copy of *Six Crisis***:** Richard M. Nixon to Max M. Fisher, Fisher Archives. The autographed copy of *Six Crisis* is also in the Fisher Archives. **Sent advance copies to prominent Republicans:** Ambrose, *Nixon: The Education of a Politician 1913-1962*, p. 639. **"Ability to fill the highest office":** Max M. Fisher to Richard M. Nixon, April 10, 1962, Fisher Archives.

Fisher "helpful" to Nixon 1962 campaign: Max M. Fisher interview. **$1.42 million for 1962 campaign:** Ambrose, *Nixon: The Education of a Politician 1913-1962*, p. 670. **Contributors unwilling to fund gubernatorial campaign:** Ambrose, *Nixon: The Education of a Politician 1913-1962*, p. 655. **Tight budget:** Ambrose, *Nixon: The Education of a Politician 1913-1962*, p. 656.

Premonition of loss: Richard M. Nixon to Max M. Fisher, July 18, 1962, Fisher Archives. **"Our new home in Beverly Hills":** Richard M. Nixon to Max M. Fisher, July 18, 1962, Fisher Archives.

Watched returns at the Beverly Hills Hotel: Lurie, *The Running of Richard Nixon*, p. 267. **Fisher called Nixon:** Max M. Fisher, George W. Romney interviews; Max M. Fisher, Richard M. Nixon OH.

"Not going to quite make it": Max M. Fisher, George W. Romney interviews; Max M. Fisher, Richard M. Nixon OH.

"Looked terrible and felt worse": Nixon, *RN: The Memoirs of Richard Nixon*, p. 245. **"My last press conference":** Ambrose, *Nixon: The Education of a Politician 1913-1962*, p. 672.

Nixon, "sore loser": Ambrose, *Nixon: The Education of a Politician 1913-1962*, p. 672. **Nixon walking out of history:** Ambrose, *Nixon: The Education of a Politician 1913-1962*, p. 673.

Disappointed with loss: Max M. Fisher interview. **Knew Nixon not done with politics:** Max M. Fisher interview.

"Not the end of political activity for you": Max M. Fisher to Richard M. Nixon, December 4, 1962, Fisher Archives.

Sent Fisher California oranges: Richard M. Nixon to Max M. Fisher, February 28, 1963, Fisher Archives.

Relocates to New York City, done with politics: Nixon, *RN: The Memoirs of Richard Nixon*, p. 247. **Nixon joins Wall Street law firm:** Safire, *Before the Fall*, p. 21. **"General utility musician":** Leonard Garment interview. **Told Fisher of Daley's dying regret:** Leonard Garment interview.

Took it upon self to orient Nixon to NYC: Leonard Garment interview.

Wall Street not Nixon's arena: Leonard Garment interview.

Nixon in "wilderness": Safire, *Before the Fall*, p. 45.

"The Baruch of the heartland": Richard M. Nixon OH.

Jewish had "to be twice as good": Max M. Fisher interview.

Goldwater GOP candidate for 1964: Goldwater, *Goldwater*, p. 27; Nixon, *RN: The Memoirs of Richard Nixon*, p. 262.

Fisher, Nixon, Romney meet to discuss Goldwater: Max M. Fisher OH.

Romney critical of Goldwater's "extremism": Nixon, *RN: The Memoirs of Richard Nixon*, pp. 260-262. **Nixon attempts to persuade Romney to run:** Max M. Fisher OH.

Muddled story: Max M. Fisher OH.

Nixon thought Romney was going to run: Witcover, *The Resurrection of Richard Nixon*, p. 93.

Nixon sends apologies for mix-up: Max M. Fisher OH.

Nixon-Fisher similarities: Leonard Garment interview.

Myth of Nixon's disregard for common man: Ambrose, *Nixon: The Education of a Politician 1913-1962*, p. 587.

Kennedy and people thinking he was "real friend of the working man": Ambrose, *Nixon: The Education of a Politician 1913-1962*, p. 587.

Alex a stone dresser from Europe yet employed in barber shop: Names and places have been altered to protect the privacy of "Alex" and his family.

Nixon's difficult childhood: Nixon, *RN: The Memoirs of Richard Nixon*, pp. 9-12.

Fisher agrees to assist, asks for more information: Max M. Fisher to Richard M. Nixon, August 11, 1964, Fisher Archives.

Nixon himself supplies information: Richard M. Nixon to Max M. Fisher, August 31, 1964, Fisher Archives.

Fisher instructs attorney to find Alex a job at gas station: Max M. Fisher interview; handwritten note dated September 3, 1964, on the letter from Richard M. Nixon to Max M. Fisher, August 31, 1964, Fisher Archives.

"Can't take without giving something back": *The Detroit Magazine*, September 24, 1967.

Gift giving and fund-raising a vocation: *The Detroit Magazine*, September 24, 1967.

Recognized Max's private philanthropy: Stanley T. Burkoff interview.

Frequented same barber as Max: Stanley T. Burkoff interview.

"Put barber's and manicurist's children through school": Stanley T. Burkoff interview.

Financially aided friends and strangers: Elizabeth A. Stephens, Joseph Nederlander, confidential interviews. **Asked for help, blank check in the mail same day:** Confidential interview.

Financial backer and mentor: Joseph J. Wright, Richard G. Morse interviews.

Fisher calls law school trustee: Joseph J. Wright interview.

"The determination never to despair": Nixon, *RN: The Memoirs of Richard M. Nixon*, pp. 12-13.

"Fear of loss of control": Brodie, *Richard M. Nixon: The Shaping of His Character*, p. 445. **"You stay calm":** Max M. Fisher interview.

Nixon astounded: Richard M. Nixon OH. **Fisher knew Nixon background only through the press:** Max M. Fisher to Richard M. Nixon, May 30, 1978, Fisher Archives.

Nixon unaware of Fisher's Horatio Alger success: Richard M. Nixon to Max M. Fisher, January 29, 1982, Fisher Archives.

Aversion to personal confrontation: Nixon, *RN: The Memoirs of Richard Nixon*, p. 6.

"I get along": Max M. Fisher interview.

"An introvert in an extrovert's profession": Nixon, *In the Arena*, p. 222.

Max so secretive: Marjorie Switow Fisher interview.

Fisher didn't tell everything: Jacob Stein interview.

Begin knocks on suite door: Seymour Milstein interview.

Turned down public career: Max M. Fisher interview.

"Last press conference": Ambrose, *Nixon: The Education of a Politician 1912-1962*, p. 670.

Chapter 6

FISHER AND ROMNEY

AND

THE LEGACY OF THE SIX-DAY WAR

SOURCES

Books, journals, newspapers:

Candee, ed., *Current Biography 1958*; Collier, Horowitz, *The Fords: An American Epic*; Delury, ed., *The 1975 World Almanac*; Elazar, Cohen, *The Jewish Polity: Jewish Organizations from Biblical Times to the Present*; Harris, *Romney's Way: A Man and an Idea*; Kahn, *The Passionate People*; Javits, *Javits: The Autobiography of a Public Man*; Mollenhoff, *George Romney: Mormon in Politics*; Moritz, ed., *Current Biography 1963*; Nixon, *RN: The Memoirs of Richard Nixon*; Schiff, *A History of the Israeli Army*; Stans, *The Terrors of Justice*; White, *The Making of the President-1968*; Wills, *Nixon Agonistes*; Urofsky, *We Are One!*.

Commentary, Detroit, Forbes, Monthly Detroit.

Detroit Free Press, The Detroit News, The Jerusalem Post, The New York Times, The Wall Street Journal.

Fisher Archives.

Oral History:

Max M. Fisher, Henry Ford II, William Haber, Jason Honigman, George W. Romney, Remer Tyson, Richard VanDusen.

Interviews:
Nathan Appleman, Harold Berry, Zelig S. Chinitz, Arthur G. Elliott Jr., Max M. Fisher, Yitzhak Rabin.

NOTES

"Hollywood's Central Casting": White, *The Making of the President-1968*, p. 37.

Romney's corporate career: Candee, ed., *Current Biography 1958*, pp. 366-367.

Rambler, American Motors profiting, Michigan in trouble: Mollenhoff, *George Romney: Mormon in Politics*, p. 162. **State General Fund depleted:** Mollenhoff, *George Romney: Mormon in Politics*, p. 164. **Soapy Williams goes to Washington:** Moritz, ed., *Current Biography 1963*, pp. 467-468. **Williams advocate of personal, corporate income tax:** Moritz, ed., *Current Biography 1963*, p. 468.

Citizens for Michigan: Mollenhoff, *George Romney: Mormon in Politics*, p. 164. **Romney "Con-Con" delegate:** White, *The Making of the President*, p. 37.

Nixon urged Romney into politics: Harris, *Romney's Way: A Man and an Idea*, p. 218. **Robert McNamara urged Romney also:** Wills, *Nixon Agonistes*, p. 194. **Mormon faith:** Mollenhoff, *George Romney: Mormon in Politics*, p. 171. **Fasted and prayed for twenty-four hours before deciding to seek GOP gubernatorial nomination:** *George Romney: Mormon in Politics*, p. 171. **Romney campaign staff selected:** Max M. Fisher interview; Max M. Fisher OH; *Monthly Detroit*, July 1980. **Honigman asked to be campaign fund-raiser:** Max M. Fisher interview; Max M. Fisher, Jason Honigman OH; *Monthly Detroit*, July 1980.

Hated asking for money: Jason Honigman OH.

Fisher not apprehensive asking for money: Jason Honigman OH.

Promised to ask Fisher to join staff: Jason Honigman OH.

Golfing in snow, waiting for football games on television: Jason Honigman OH.

Thought Romney "top notch": Max M. Fisher interview.

Met Romney on way to a board meeting: George W. Romney OH.

"I was selling him": George W. Romney OH.

"We just hit it off": Max M. Fisher interview.

Management skills, moderate attitudes appealed to Fisher: Max M. Fisher interview. **Romney's position on race:** White, *The Making of the President-1968*, p. 36. **Dismissed a Michigan GOP leader with John Birch Society affiliation:** Mollenhoff, *George Romney: Mormon in Politics*, p. 180. **Sought black community input:** Mollenhoff, *George Romney: Mormon in Politics*, p. 177.

Time for change: Max M. Fisher to Jake L. Hamon, May 30, 1962, Fisher Archives.

Fisher had to be accepted by Romney advisers: Max M. Fisher interview; George W. Romney, Richard VanDusen OH; *Monthly Detroit*, July 1980. **Met in Romney's formal living room:** Max M. Fisher interview; George W. Romney, Richard VanDusen OH; *Monthly Detroit*, July 1980. **Impressed by Fisher's questioning:** Max M. Fisher interview; George W. Romney, Richard VanDusen OH; *Monthly Detroit*, July 1980. **Didn't know they were being tested by Fisher:** Max M. Fisher OH.

Decided Romney could win: Max M. Fisher OH. **Fisher dispelled doubts:** *Monthly Detroit*, July 1980. **I want your money before I ask others for theirs:** Max M. Fisher interview; Max M. Fisher, Richard VanDusen OH; *Monthly Detroit*, July 1980.

They complied: Max M. Fisher interview; Max M. Fisher, Richard VanDusen OH; *Monthly Detroit*, July 1980. **Fisher gave $20,000:** Max M. Fisher interview. **Fisher accepted:** Richard VanDusen OH.

Max responsible for how money spent: Richard VanDusen OH.

Fisher's appointment announced: George W. Romney press statement, March 28, 1962, Fisher Archives.

Max a real coup for organization: Richard VanDusen OH.

Romney wanted to be detached from fund-raising: George W. Romney OH. **Max got it done properly:** George W. Romney OH. **"Max Fisher and a telephone":** Remer Tyson, OH. **Political and charity fund-raising similar:** Max M. Fisher interview.

"Give without feeling fleeced": Max M. Fisher interview.

Idea of producing compact: *The Detroit News*, March 29, 1970. **Big Three not eager to give to Romney:** *The Detroit News*, March 29, 1970. **Romney an ingrate:** Elton F. MacDonald to Max M. Fisher, June 12, 1962, Fisher Archives

"I wooed them": Max M. Fisher interview. **Max got just about everybody:** *The Detroit News*, March 29, 1970.

Gave them same pitch: Max M. Fisher interview. **Told them face-to-face Romney better for industry:** Max M. Fisher interview.

Not as simple as "economic sensibilities": Henry Ford II OH. **You do it because Max asked:** Henry Ford II OH.

GM executive Bunkie Knudsen anted up: Collier, Horowitz, *The Fords: An American Epic*, pp. 303, 338. **Knudsen suitably forthcoming:** Max M. Fisher interview. **Gave check for $5,000:** Max M. Fisher to Semon E. Knudsen, August 28, 1962, Fisher Archives. **Fund-raisers at country clubs:** Arthur G. Elliott Jr. interview; Richard VanDusen OH.

Never saw anything like it: Richard VanDusen OH.

Power fund-raising: Richard VanDusen OH.

Max worked the room: Arthur G. Elliott Jr. interview.

Solicited funds from business, social, Jewish acquaintances: Max M. Fisher list of pledge balances due for 1962 Romney gubernatorial campaign, May 28, 1962, Fisher Archives. **Had friends solicit contributions:** Max M. Fisher interview. **Levy an example:** Max M. Fisher list of pledge balances due for 1962 Romney gubernatorial campaign, May 28, 1962, Fisher Archives. **"A committee of one":** Max M. Fisher to Edward C. Levy, May 21, 1962, Fisher Archives. **Sent a pack of pledge cards:** Max M. Fisher to Edward C. Levy, May 21, 1962, Fisher Archives. **Asked Nathan Appleman:** Nathan Appleman interview. **Asked Leonard Friedman:** Max M. Fisher to Leonard Friedman, May 30, 1962, Fisher Archives; Max M. Fisher interview. **Connected by Jewish causes:** Max M. Fisher to Leonard Friedman, September 12, 1963, Fisher Archives. **Need money to "combat great reserves of the unions":** Max M. Fisher to Leonard Friedman, May 30, 1962, Fisher Archives. **Contacted Jake L. Hamon:** Max M. Fisher interview. **Hamon gave generously:** Max M. Fisher to Jake L. Hamon, May 30, 1962, Fisher Archives. **"A Texan in Michigan":** Jake L. Hamon to Max M. Fisher, May 15, 1962, Fisher Archives.

Discretion appreciated: Max M. Fisher to Jake L. Hamon, May 30, 1962, Fisher Archives.

Romney jobs loss: Mollenhoff, *George Romney: Mormon in Politics*, p. 187. **Kennedy-Johnson campaign for Democratic nominee:** Mollenhoff, *George Romney: Mormon in Politics*, p. 187. **"Coattails leadership":** Mollenhoff, *George Romney: Mormon in Politics*, p. 187.

At task until November: Max M. Fisher interview. **Spent over $450,000:** Harris, *Romney's Way: A Man and an Idea*, p. 236. **Raised nearly one million dollars:** Arthur G. Elliott Jr., Max M. Fisher interviews.

"Never ran out of money": Arthur G. Elliott Jr., Max M. Fisher interviews.

Romney wins election by narrow margin: Mollenhoff, *George Romney: Mormon in Politics*, p. 188. **Moderate Republican split into Democratic-black, labor vote:** Mollenhoff, *George Romney: Mormon in Politics*, p. 189.

As feared, Goldwater lost heavily: *The 1975 World Almanac*, p. 735. **GOP split into factions:** Goldwater, *Goldwater*, p. 174.

Can't reject hard-core Goldwater voters: Richard M. Nixon to Max M. Fisher, December 28, 1964, Fisher Archives.

"Presidential timber": *Detroit*, September 24, 1967. **Romney had long coat-tails:** Mollenhoff, *George Romney: Mormon in Politics*, p. 251.

Romney could win in 1968: *Detroit Free Press*, December 11, 1966. **"Holier-than-thou" appearance:** *Detroit Free Press*, December 11, 1966. **Commitment to ideals:** Max M. Fisher interview. **"Super Boy Scout":** *Detroit Free Press*, December 11, 1966.

Money, money, money: Stans, *The Terrors of Justice*, p. 23. **Romney had access to steady cash flow:** *Detroit Free Press*, December 11, 1966.

Romney at UJA fund-raiser: *The New York Times*, December 9, 1966.

Salutes generosity, responsibility: *The New York Times*, December 9, 1966.

Fisher access to national, international Jewish community: *The New York Times*, December 9, 1966.

Arab threats to Israel: Schiff, *A History of the Israeli Army*, p. 124.

"American Jews are here!": *Max M. Fisher Addresses 1964-1968*, p. 182.

First meeting with Yitzhak Rabin: Max M. Fisher interview.

"I always trusted him": Yitzhak Rabin interview.

Estimates "beyond belief": Max M. Fisher OH.

"There's going to be war": Max M. Fisher, Harold Berry interviews.

Fund-raising's finest hours: Zelig S. Chinitz interview. **Money poured in:** *The Jerusalem Post*, August 10, 1967; Max M. Fisher interview. **Gave all they could:** Urofsky, *We Are One!*, p. 356.

"Every last possible dollar": *Max M. Fisher Addresses 1964-1968*, pp. 181-188.

Raised over $430 million in 1967: Urofsky, *We Are One!*, p. 356.

Israel the "religion" of American Jews: *Commentary*, March 1989.

"From the Heights of June": *The Jerusalem Post*, October 30, 1967; *Max M. Fisher Addresses 1964-1968*, pp. 197-198.

American Jewish polity: For a more detailed discussion of this term and its relationship to Jewish political activity see Elazar and Cohen, *The Jewish Polity: Jewish Organizations from Biblical Times to the Present*, p. 5. **"Max became a devout Zionist":** Kahn, *The Passionate People*, pp. 230-231. **"The kind of people the nicer type of Jew can be":** Kahn, *The Passionate People*, pp. 230-231.

Never had a Max Fisher here: Kahn, *The Passionate People*, p. 231.

Get Max Fisher: William Haber OH.

"Max is *the* symbol": William Haber OH. **"The symbolism of Max Fisher":** William Haber OH.

Owed success to smiling fortune: *Detroit*, September 24, 1967.

"I didn't know any better": *Forbes*, September 14, 1981.

"I never felt I had it made": Max M. Fisher interview.

New York convenient meeting place: *The New York Times*, December 29, 1966.

Fisher "quite unshakable": *Detroit*, September 24, 1967.

Romney "a great symbol": *Detroit*, September 24, 1967.

Fisher has no plans for himself: *Detroit*, September 24, 1967.

"Benevolent presence": Kahn, *The Passionate People*, p. 231. **"A rare gift of empathy":** *Detroit*, September 24, 1967.

Fund-raiser and adviser: George Romney OH.

Fisher and Javits friends since 1950s: Javits, *Javits: The Autobiography of a Public Man*, p. 282. **Unique as Jewish Republicans:** Max M. Fisher interview. **Concerned about GOP direction, frequent telephone calls:** Max M. Fisher interview. **Early**

Sunday morning calls: Marian Javits to Max M. Fisher, July 15, 1988, Fisher Archives.

Invited to lunch with Romney: Javits, *Javits: The Autobiography of a Public Man*, p. 354, Max M. Fisher interview. **Romney-Javits ticket proposed:** Javits, *Javits: The Autobiography of a Public Man*, p. 354; Max M. Fisher interview.

Romney announces ticket: Javits, *Javits: The Autobiography of a Public Man*, p. 354.

Press knocking on Javits' door: Javits, *Javits: The Autobiography of a Public Man*, p. 354.

Can't elect Nixon: *Detroit Free Press*, December 11, 1966.

Fisher knew Nixon still viable: Max M. Fisher interview; Max M. Fisher OH.

"Vindicated with a vengeance": Nixon, *RN: The Memoirs of Richard Nixon*, p. 277.

"A prerequisite for my own comeback": Nixon, *RN: The Memoirs of Richard Nixon*, p. 277. **Max financed Nixon's 1966 travels:** Richard M. Nixon OH.

Maintained contact with all contenders: Max M. Fisher OH.

Max moves "where the power is": *Monthly Detroit*, July 1980.

"Can't please everybody": *Monthly Detroit*, July 1980; Max M. Fisher interview.

Chapter 7

In the Heat of the Summer

SOURCES

Books, journals, newspapers, and documents:
Ambrose, *Nixon: The Triumph of a Politician 1962-1972*; Conot, *American Odyssey*; Fine, *Violence in the Model City*; Green, *The Cynics' Lexicon*; Hertzberg, *The Jews in America*; Shachtman, *Decade of Shocks*; White, *The Making of the President-1968*.

The Detroit News, *The Times-Picayune*, *The Newark Sunday News*, *The New York Times*.

Fortune.

MMF Addresses 1964-1968, *MMF Addresses 1969-1972*.

Fisher Archives.

Oral History:
Marjorie Switow Fisher, Joseph L. Hudson, John M. Mitchell, George W. Romney.

Interviews:
Gus Cardinali, Marjorie Switow Fisher, Max M. Fisher, Steven Flax, Richard M. Nixon, Richard Van Tiem, A. Alfred Taubman.

NOTES

"To win the nomination": Ambrose, *Nixon: The Triumph of a Politician 1962-1972*, p. 102. **Let Romney lead:** Ambrose, *Nixon: The Triumph of a Politician 1962-1972*, p. 105. **Staging dramatic come from behind victory:** Ambrose, *Nixon: The Triumph of a Politician 1962-1972*, p. 105. **Mitchell wary of Nixon's strategy:** John N. Mitchell OH; Ambrose, *Nixon: The Triumph of a Politician 1962-1972* , p. 133.

"Max Fisher's support meant a hell of a lot in '68": John N. Mitchell OH. **"Didn't dream [campaign] would cost as much":** Richard M. Nixon interview. **"Just because I'm for George doesn't mean I'm against you":** Max M. Fisher interview.

Detroit's turn, July 23, 1967: Conot, *American Odyssey*, pp. 523-525.

Fisher wanted to see riot for himself: Max M. Fisher, Richard Van Tiem interviews.

"Decade of shocks": Shachtman, *Decade of Shocks*.

Indescribable sadness: Max M. Fisher interview.

Couldn't fix Detroit: Max M. Fisher interview.

"Then I called the governor": Max M. Fisher interview.

Detroit "bombed": Conot, *American Odyssey*, pp. 535-536. **Romney requests federal troops:** Conot, *American Odyssey*, pp. 536-537. **Johnson hesitates to help a Republican governor:** Conot, *American Odyssey*, pp. 536-537. **Paratroopers arrive eighteen hours after request made.** Fine, *Violence in the Model City*, p. 214.

"Politicians quibbled while the city burned": Gus Cardinali interview.

$42.5 million in damages: Fine, *Violence in the Model City*, p. 297-299. **"First urban coalition in the United States":** Conot, *American Odyssey*, p. 541.

"Max still had a fervent vision of something better": Joseph L. Hudson OH.

Enraged by Johnson's stalling: Max M. Fisher interview.

"As business helps in meeting social problems it truly helps itself": *Max M. Fisher Addresses 1969-1972*, p. 63, Fisher Archives. **"Jews advancing social justice":** Hertzberg, *The Jews in America*, pp. 379-380.

"It isn't the way they are working today": *Max M. Fisher Addresses 1969-1972*, p. 59, Fisher Archives.

Fisher advises against a Romney 1964 presidential race: Max M. Fisher interview.

"'They are gunning for you.'": Max M. Fisher OH.

"Max is no media innocent": Steven Flax interview.

Taubman and the media: *Fortune*, April 9, 1990. **"Par with inside traders":** A. Alfred Taubman interview. **"Fisher lamented":** *The Detroit News*, March 8, 1981.

Nothing to fear from media: Max M. Fisher, A. Alfred Taubman interviews.

"Max is basically a listener": A. Alfred Taubman interview.

"Max has good judgment": George W. Romney OH.

Romney knocked off campaign course. George W. Romney OH. **Gallup Poll:** *The New York Times*, August 22, 1967. **"Ten top people":** *The Detroit News*, August 21, 1967.

Already had $2 million in contribution commitments: Fisher, OH; copies of the checks, Fisher Archives.

"An 'E' for effort": Max M. Fisher to George W. Romney, March 7, 1963, and Gordon transcript, Fisher Archives.

"Lou liked George": Max M. Fisher OH.

No off-camera Romney aides: White, *The Making of the President-1968*, p. 59. **"No television performance":** Green, *The Cynic's Lexicon*, p. 147.

Position inconsistent accusation: White, *The Making of the President-1968*, p. 59.

"Greatest brainwashing over Vietnam": White, *The Making of the President-1968*, p. 60

"Statement blew out of the water": Max M. Fisher OH.

Romney declares candidacy: *The New York Times*, February 28, 1968. **Gains in New Hampshire:** *The Times-Picayune*, January 30, 1968.

"Prominent business people": Max M. Fisher to Nelson A. Rockefeller, January 29, Fisher Archives. **Who's who in Michigan:** Rockefeller Luncheon final guest list, Fisher Archives.

Small black-tie dinner: February 23-24, 1968 Rockefeller itinerary, Fisher Archives. **Luncheon began at noon:** February 23-24, 1968 Rockefeller itinerary, Fisher Archives. **Rockefeller submarined nomination:** George W. Romney OH.

"**I'm not a candidate**": *The New York Times*, February 25, 1968.

Reporters rudely cross-examining Rockefeller: Marjorie Switow Fisher interview.

Across the country: *The Newark News*, February 25, 1968.

By then, Rockefeller in New York: Max M. Fisher, Marjorie Switow Fisher interviews.

Another major Romney fund-raising affair: *The New York Times*, February 25, 1968.

The Fishers relaxed: Marjorie Switow Fisher interview.

"**Is Mr. Fisher there?**": Marjorie Switow Fisher interview; Marjorie Switow Fisher OH. "**I'll tell my husband**": Marjorie Switow Fisher interview; Marjorie Switow Fisher OH.

Caught two fish: Marjorie Switow Fisher interview; Marjorie Switow Fisher OH.

Rockefeller used me to woo Fisher: George W. Romney OH.

Max was loyal: George W. Romney OH.

Saw it differently: Max M. Fisher interview; Max M. Fisher OH.

Chapter 8
THE FINAL CURTAIN
SOURCES

Books, journals, newspapers:

Ambrose, *Nixon: The Triumph of a Politician 1962-1972*; Delury, ed., *The 1975 World Almanac*; El Azhary, *Political Cohesion of American Jews in American Politics: A Reappraisal of Their Role in Presidential Elections*; Levitan, *Jews in American Life*; Murphy, *Fortas: The Rise and Ruin of a Supreme Court Justice*; Persico, *The Imperial Rockefeller*; Safire, *Before the Fall*; Stans, *The Terrors of Justice*; Urofsky, *We Are One!*; White, *The Making of the President-1968*.

The National Jewish Monthly.

The Birmingham (Michigan) *Observer & Eccentric, The California Jewish Record, The Detroit News, The Grand Rapids* (Michigan) *Press, The Jerusalem Post;* The Jewish Telegraphic Agency Daily News Bulletin, *The National Observer, The New York Times.*

Fisher Archives.

Oral History:

Irving Bernstein, Sol Eisenberg, Marjorie Switow Fisher, Max M. Fisher, Yehuda Hellman, John N. Mitchell, Richard M. Nixon, George W. Romney, Herschel Schacter, Maurice H. Stans.

Interviews:

Marjorie Switow Fisher, Max M. Fisher, Richard M. Nixon, Martin R. Pollner, George W. Romney, Elizabeth A. Stephens.

NOTES

Refunded surplus money: Max M. Fisher interview; Max M. Fisher OH. "**This money should be returned**": March 4, 1968 letters to contributors, Fisher Archives.

Thanks for the 14 cents: *The Detroit News*, August 21, 1967. **Responsibility for how it's spent:** *The Detroit News*, August 21, 1967.

Surprised with refunds: Illustrated by John B. Martin to Max M. Fisher, March 11, 1968, Fisher Archives.

Rockefeller romances Fisher: Max M. Fisher interview.

Rockefeller confers with GOP: Persico, *The Imperial Rockefeller*, p. 67. **Not a candidate for presidency:** Max M. Fisher interview; Max M. Fisher OH; *The New York Times*, March 22, 1968.

Rockefeller indecisive: Max M. Fisher OH.

Johnson not running: *The New York Times*, April 1, 1968. **Democratic candidacy open:** White, *The Making of the President-1968*, pp. 347-348.

Nixon at Romney's house with Fisher: *The Birmingham* (Michigan) *Observer & Eccentric*, April 25, 1968. **The urban crisis and the vice presidency:** George W. Romney interview. **Romney withholds Michigan's support of Nixon:** Max M. Fisher OH.

Kept options open: George W. Romney interview.

Owed Romney neutrality: Max M. Fisher interview; Max M. Fisher OH.

Nixon noncommittal: *The Birmingham* (Michigan) *Observer & Eccentric*, April 25, 1968. In the author's interviews, Max M. Fisher and George W. Romney confirm Nixon's reply.

Wanted Fisher on board: John N. Mitchell OH.

Romney's pact: Max M. Fisher, John N. Mitchell, George W. Romney OH; *The Birmingham* (Michigan) *Observer & Eccentric*, April 25, 1968.

Mitchells visit Detroit: Max M. Fisher OH.

"We're all in politics": Marjorie Switow Fisher interview; Marjorie Switow Fisher OH.

Kidnapped Max: Marjorie Switow Fisher interview.

Max and Sol Eisenberg: Sol Eisenberg OH. **"Nixon's Court Jew":** Israel Miller interview. **Talk to his "psychiatrist":** Elizabeth A. Stephens interview.

Need your help: Marjorie Switow Fisher interview.

Happy Birthday: Marjorie Switow Fisher interview.

Kept his word to Romney: Max M. Fisher interview. **Agnew nominated:** Ambrose, *Nixon: The Triumph of a Politician 1962-1972*, pp. 174-175.

"A single purpose": Max M. Fisher to Richard M. Nixon, August 12, 1968, Fisher Archives.

"Issues that interest me": Max M. Fisher, Richard M. Nixon interviews.

Tapping familiar sources: Contributors' list, November 6, 1968, Fisher Archives. **Raising both money and votes:** Max M. Fisher interview; Max M. Fisher OH.

Jewish voting power: Safire, *Before the Fall*, pp. 564-565.

Nixon, a friend of the Jews: *The National Observer*, October 28, 1968. **"Talk to them":** Max M. Fisher interview; Max M. Fisher OH.

"Jewish desk": Martin R. Pollner interview.

Expensive proposition: Confidential interview OH.

Fisher introduces Nixon at B'nai B'rith convention: Max M. Fisher interview; Max M. Fisher OH. **"Tipped in Israel's favor":** Safire, *Before the Fall*, p. 565.

Give Israel military superiority: Richard M. Nixon, "The Cradle of Civilization Must Not Be its Grave," September 8, 1968, Fisher Archives. **Published speech:** *The National Jewish Monthly*, October 1968. **Speech mailed to Jewish leaders:** Max M. Fisher to Martin R. Pollner, September 23, 1968, list of recipients, Fisher Archives.

Nixon pleased with reception: Richard M. Nixon to Max M. Fisher, October 5, 1968, Fisher Archives. **Fisher as Nixon's special adviser:** Nixon-Agnew press release, September 26, 1968, Fisher Archives. **Appointment important to Jews:** *The Jerusalem Post*, September 27, 1968.

Humphrey trailing by 15 points: White, *The Making of the President-1968*, pp. 355-356. **"Shorten the war":** Boller, *Presidential Campaigns*, p. 325.

Nixon lead cut to 5 points: White, *The Making of the President-1968*, pp. 356-357. **Campaign money cupboards bare:** *The Grand Rapids* (Michigan) *Press*, October 11, 1968.

Little money left: *The Grand Rapids* (Michigan) *Press*, October 11, 1968.

Fisher funnels funds into GOP: *The Grand Rapids* (Michigan) *Press*, October 11, 1968.

Humphrey asks Fisher to raise money for him: Max M. Fisher interview; Max M. Fisher OH.

Humphrey asks again: Max M. Fisher OH.

Thought Max would split funds: John N. Mitchell OH.

Haunted by lack of funds: White, *The Making of the President-1968*, p. 257.

Funds make the difference: Confidential interview OH.

Max was magnificent: Maurice H. Stans OH.

Flattered Max asked for their help: Herschel Schacter OH.

Max makes commitment himself: Richard M. Nixon OH.

Ability as "luck": Max M. Fisher interview; Max M. Fisher OH.

Fears for Israel's survival: Hertzberg, *The Jews in America*, pp. 369-370. **Nixon unequivocal stance pro-Israel:** *The California Jewish Record*, October 11, 1968.

Anti-Semitism of black militants: *Commentary*, February 1948.

Anti-Semitic motif: Hertzberg, *The Jews in America*, p. 371. **Jews targets of urban rioting:** *The National Observer*, October 28, 1968.

Running for sheriff: Boller, *Presidential Campaigns*, p. 330. **"Unexpected dividend":** *California Jewish Record*, October 11, 1968.

One Jewish vote for Nixon: *The National Observer*, October 11, 1968.

Jewish Democrats for Nixon: *The National Observer*, October 11, 1968.

Shift in Jewish vote: *The National Observer*, October 11, 1968.

Jews prominent in Nixon campaign: *The National Observer*, October 11, 1968.

Johnson nominates Fortas: Ambrose, *Nixon: The Triumph of a Politician 1962-1972*, pp. 159-160.

Sides with Republican Senators: *The New York Times*, June 22, 1968.

Fisher advises against siding with Senate filibuster: Max M. Fisher interview. No Jew occupied a Cabinet post until 1906, when President Theodore Roosevelt appointed Oscar S. Straus to serve in the newly created Department of Commerce and Labor. Straus also held what was considered the Jewish diplomatic assignment of American representative to Turkey under presidents Cleveland, McKinley and Taft. High diplomatic posts, throughout United States history, have been deemed by presidents to be more acceptable for Jews than positions in the Cabinets. President Monroe appointed the first one, Mordechai Manuel Noah, as consul to Tunis. See Levitan, *Jews in American Life*, pp. 156-157. **Nixon changes policy:** Murphy, *Fortas: The Rise and Ruin of a Supreme Court Justice*, pp. 473-475.

Integrate Jewish community into day-to-day policies: Max M. Fisher interview; Max M. Fisher OH.

Leader of your community: Herschel Schacter OH.

Fisher trusted Nixon: Irving Bernstein OH.

Politicking wouldn't happen again: Max M. Fisher OH.

George Ball in Humphrey's campaign: Nixon-Agnew press release, October 18, 1968, Fisher Archives.

"Concerned Citizens for Nixon": Nixon-Agnew press release, October 18, 1968, Fisher Archives.

The Presidents Conference: Urofsky, *We Are One!*, pp. 300-301.

Nixon invited to confer with "authentic leaders of American Jewish commu-

nity": Herschel Schacter to Max M. Fisher, September 12, 1968, Fisher Archives.

A historic meeting: Yehuda Hellman OH.

Might be cruel to Nixon: Max M. Fisher OH.

Nixon at Presidents' Conference: Jewish Telegraphic Agency Daily News Bulletin, October 22, 1968, Max M. Fisher interview; Max M. Fisher OH.

Triumphant meeting: Jewish Telegraphic Agency Daily News Bulletin, October 22, 1968.

Election influenced by Vietnam: Ambrose, *Nixon: The Triumph of a Politician 1962-1972*, pp. 211-212.

Election Day: Marjorie Switow Fisher interview; *The Detroit News*, November 7, 1968.

Nixon wins by 1 percent: Max M. Fisher, Marjorie Switow interviews; Ambrose, *Nixon: The Triumph of a Politician 1962-1972*, pp. 219, 221; Delury, ed., *The 1975 World Almanac*, p. 735.

Fisher to Nixon headquarters: Max M. Fisher interview.

"Century Club": Stans, *The Terrors of Justice*, p. 141.

$60,000 of own money: Max M. Fisher interview. **Amount raised:** Stans, *The Terrors of Justice*, p. 140. **Jewish vote:** El Azhary, *Political Cohesion of American Jewish Politics: A Reappraisal of Their Role in Presidential Elections*, p. 27.

Fisher's national identity as Jewish Republican leader: Richard M. Nixon interview.

Baruch: Levitan, *Jews in American Life*, pp. 227-229.

Fisher and the community consciousness: Yehuda Hellman OH.

Fisher politicized Jewish America: Yehuda Hellman OH.

Chapter 9
LEARNING HIS PART: 1969-1970
THE NIXON WHITE HOUSE, PART I
SOURCES

Books, newspapers:

Chinitz, *A Common Agenda: The Reconstitution of the Jewish Agency*; Collier, Horowitz, *The Fords: An American Epic*; Fine, *Violence in the Model City*; Hoffman, *The Smoke Screen: Israel, Philanthropy and American Jews*; Kissinger, *The White House Years*; Meir, *My Life*; Nixon, *RN: The Memoirs of Richard Nixon*; Rabin, *The Rabin Memoirs*; Spiegel, *The Other Arab-Israeli Conflict: Making America's Middle East Policy, from Truman to Reagan*.

Detroit Free Press, Detroit News, The Kansas City Times, The New York Times.

The Nixon Presidential Materials Project.

Fisher Archives.

Oral History:

John Bugas, Henry Ford II, Max M. Fisher, John N. Mitchell, Joseph J. Sisco.

Interviews:

Philip Bernstein, Daniel J. Elazar, Marjorie Switow Fisher, Max M. Fisher, Leonard Garment, Bill Kovach, Paul W. McCracken, Israel Miller, Richard M. Nixon, Jacob Stein.

NOTES

Knew Fisher would not accept ambassadorship: Richard M. Nixon interview. **"He didn't need status":** Richard M. Nixon interview.

Wanted a position for Romney, given HUD: Max M. Fisher, Richard M. Nixon interviews.

"Keeping his eye on the ball": Max M. Fisher interview.

Topics of interest: Max M. Fisher, Richard M. Nixon interviews.

Direct foreign policy from White House: Nixon, *RN: The Memoirs of Richard Nixon*, p. 343; Kissinger, *White House Years*, p. 11. **"A strong administrator":** Nixon, *RN: The Memoirs of Richard Nixon*, p. 339.

Kissinger National Security Adviser: Nixon, *RN: The Memoirs of Richard Nixon*, p. 341.

"Necessary to use private communications": Richard M. Nixon interview.

Fisher named American Jewish community liaison: Max M. Fisher interview.

Informed on matters of Jewish community: John R. Brown memo to H.R. Haldeman, April 11, 1969, The Nixon Presidential Materials Project.

Fisher at Eshkol's funeral: *Detroit Free Press*, February 27, 1969. **Potential for aiding Israel dim:** Max M. Fisher interview.

Fisher office at HUD: *Detroit Free Press*, April 27, 1969. **"New measure of reliance on voluntary efforts":** *Detroit Free Press*, April 27, 1969.

Uniting leaders from black and white communities: Max M. Fisher interview.

"Serious postriot confrontation": Fine, *Violence in the Model City*, p. 418. **Republic of New Africa meeting at New Bethel Church:** Fine, *Violence in the Model City*, p. 418. **Detroit patrolman killed:** Fine, *Violence in the Model City*, pp. 418-419.

Police arrest 142: Fine, *Violence in the Model City*, p. 418.

Crockett and Calahan clash: Fine, *Violence in the Model City*, p. 419.

Detroit police publicly critical of Crockett: Fine, *Violence in the Model City*, p. 421.

Crockett defends ruling: Fine, *Violence in the Model City*, pp. 421-422.

Black community supports Crockett: Fine, *Violence in the Model City*, p. 422.

New Detroit, Inc., already investigating police-community relations: *The Detroit News*, April 3, 1969.

Threatens to "raise hell": *The Detroit News*, April 3, 1969.

Fisher mollifies Harrington: Max M. Fisher OH; *The Detroit News*, April 3, 1969.

Calmly examine the facts: *The Detroit News*, April 3, 1969.

Crockett an "honest man": Max M. Fisher OH; *The Detroit News*, April 3, 1969.

Big guys on "niggers' side": Fine, *Violence in the Model City*, p. 422.

Kept own anger in check: Max M. Fisher interview. **Unite to solve same dilemma:** Max M. Fisher interview.

New Detroit, Inc. adopts report vindicating Crockett: *The Detroit News*, May 3, 1969.

Demanding NDI-commissioned report of police: *The Detroit News*, November 21, 1969.

NDI asked to pay for unreleased study: *The Detroit News*, November 21, 1969. **Not going to pay:** *The Detroit News*, November 21, 1969.

Police implemented suggested changes: Fine, *Violence in the Model City*, p. 424.

Romney and Fisher create National Center for Voluntary Action in 1969: President Richard Nixon's Daily Diary, April 15, 1969, The Nixon Presidential Materials Project. **Brief Nixon on NCVA:** President Richard Nixon's Daily Diary, April 19, 1969, The Nixon Presidential Materials Project.

Fisher elected CJF president: Max M. Fisher interview. **General Assembly picketed by college students:** Max M. Fisher, Philip Bernstein interviews. **Planned to disrupt plenary session:** Philip Bernstein interview.

Fisher invited them in: Philip Bernstein interview. **"You will be involved":** Philip Bernstein interview.

JDL threaten to disrupt Assembly: Max M. Fisher, Philip Bernstein interviews. **"Acted as if they weren't there":** Philip Bernstein interview.

Role between Washington and Jerusalem unclear: Max M. Fisher interview. **Nixon had spot for him:** Richard M. Nixon interview.

Fisher similar to Colonel House: Richard M. Nixon interview.

House a close friend of Wilson: Richard M. Nixon interview.

Woodrow Wilson an "ideal" for presidency: Nixon, *Leaders*, p. 337.

"Excellent credentials" with Israelis and Nixon: Richard M. Nixon interview.

Building up a responsible person: Richard M. Nixon interview.

Support for Israel in U.S.: Richard M. Nixon interview.

Max's loyalty not divided: Richard M. Nixon interview.

Egyptian's War of Attrition, 1969: Meir, *My Life*, p. 298. **Israel needed resupply of U.S. military aircraft:** Spiegel, *The Other Arab-Israeli Conflict: Making America's Middle East Policy, from Truman to Reagan*, p. 185.

U.S. reluctant to furnish aircraft: Spiegel, *The Other Arab-Israeli Conflict: Making America's Middle East Policy, from Truman to Reagan*, p. 161. **Deal made in 1968, U.S. slow to deliver:** Spiegel, *The Other Arab-Israeli Conflict: Making America's Middle East Policy, from Truman to Reagan*, p. 163. **Nixon slow to fill order:** Spiegel, *The Other Arab-Israeli Conflict: Making America's Middle East Policy, from Truman to Reagan*, p. 170. **Nixon distanced White House from Middle East policy:** Spiegel, *The Other Arab-Israeli Conflict: Making America's Middle East Policy, from Truman to Reagan* pp. 170-172. **Kept Kissinger away from Middle East:** *The Other Arab-Israeli Conflict: Making America's Middle East Policy, from Truman to Reagan* p. 176.

U.N. Resolution 242, November 22, 1967: *The Other Arab-Israeli Conflict: Making America's Middle East Policy, from Truman to Reagan*, p. 156. **"Affirmed positions by each side":** Spiegel, *The Other Arab-Israeli Conflict: Making America's Middle East Policy, from Truman to Reagan*, p. 156.

Rogers wanted pre-1967 borders: Spiegel, *The Other Arab-Israeli Conflict: Making America's Middle East Policy, from Truman to Reagan*, p. 186. **Meir not accepting of Arab's "verbal reliability":** Spiegel, *The Other Arab-Israeli Conflict: Making America's Middle East Policy, from Truman to Reagan*, p. 183.

Meir calls Fisher for assistance: Max M. Fisher interview.

"Two oak trees": Max M. Fisher OH.

Needed to speak with Nixon: Max M. Fisher OH.

Calls Garment: Max M. Fisher interview.

Meir credits Fisher for Nixon link: Max M. Fisher interview.

Max was discreet: Richard M. Nixon interview.

Reporters as "quasi-government officials": Bill Kovach interview.

Mollie Fisher dies: *Detroit Free Press*, August 9, 1969.

Max her "sonny boy": Max M. Fisher interview. **Max's tears as he prayed:** Marjorie Switow Fisher interview.

Qaddafi takes over Libya: Spiegel, *The Other Arab-Israeli Conflict: Making America's Middle East Policy, from Truman to Reagan*, p. 167. **Targets Marathon Oil because of Fisher:** Max M. Fisher, Joseph J. Sisco OH.

Still an oil man: Max M. Fisher interview. **Qaddafi threatened to nationalize Marathon:** Joseph J. Sisco, Max M. Fisher OH.

Talked with John Bugas: John Bugas OH.

Resigned from Marathon board: John Bugas OH.

Accepted resignation: John Bugas OH.

Meir and Nixon meet: Spiegel, *The Other Arab-Israeli Conflict: Making America's Middle East Policy, from Truman to Reagan*, p. 179. **White House dinner:** Max M. Fisher interview. **Meir confident of U.S. relationship:** Meir, *My Life*, p. 330.

"Reservoir of good will": Max M. Fisher memorandum to Richard M. Nixon, October 9, 1969, Fisher Archives.

Optimism short-lived: Spiegel, *The Other Arab-Israeli Conflict: Making America's Middle East Policy, from Truman to Reagan*, p. 186.

Meir shaken by Rogers Plan: Meir, *My Life*, p. 331. **Meir sending Fisher personal emissaries:** Golda Meir to Max M. Fisher, December 29, 1969, Fisher Archives.

Evidence of bountiful Soviet arms to Egypt: Max M. Fisher interview.

American Jewish community outraged by Rogers Plan: Max M. Fisher interview.

Called Sisco, a man he respected: Max M. Fisher interview. **"Fast and close friends":** Joseph J. Sisco OH.

"A consummate diplomat": Joseph J. Sisco OH.

Administration not pressuring Israel to accept plan: Max M. Fisher interview. **Sisco endorsed further economic and military aid to Israel:** Max M. Fisher interview.

Fisher called a "court Jew": Israel Miller, Jacob Stein, Irving Bernstein interviews.

"Court Jew": Biale, *Power and Powerlessness in Jewish History*, pp. 98-99.

Community unrealistic: Max M. Fisher interview. **Rogers Plan unrealistic:** Nixon, *RN: The Memoirs of Richard Nixon*, p. 479.

American Jewish community leaders meet with Rogers: *The Kansas City Times*, January 13, 1970.

Rogers didn't belong in foreign affairs: Max M. Fisher interview.

Credibility weakened: Max M. Fisher interview.

Jewish community concerned about Nixon administration: Max M. Fisher to Richard M. Nixon, January 12, 1970, Fisher Archives.

Predicts protest over Pompidou's visit: Max M. Fisher to Richard M. Nixon, January 12, 1970, Fisher Archives.

How to keep Jewish community cool: Max M. Fisher to Richard M. Nixon, January 12, 1970, Fisher Archives.

"Max took risks supporting me": Richard M. Nixon interview. **Reaffirm support for Israel:** Max M. Fisher interview.

Rogers Plan disapproval: *The New York Times*, January 26, 1970.

"Israel is one of its friends": *The New York Times*, January 26, 1970.

President "shares our concerns": *The New York Times*, January 26, 1970.

Johnson administration jets not delivered: Max M. Fisher interview.

Knew Kissinger mostly from newspaper accounts: Max M. Fisher interview.

Fisher asks Kissinger aid in delivering promised jets to Israel: Max M. Fisher interview.

"Go see John Mitchell": Max M. Fisher interview.

"Nixon valued his political judgment": Kissinger, *White House Years*, p. 369; Nixon, *RN: The Memoirs of Richard Nixon*, pp. 433-434.

"Political science not taught at universities": Kissinger, *White House Years*, p. 33.

Mitchell's death: Max M. Fisher interview; *The New York Times*, November 10, 1988.

Mitchell never wanted to be in Washington: Max M. Fisher interview.

Crying at sight of Soviet Jews in U.S.: Max M. Fisher interview.

Spoke with Mitchell about jets: Max M. Fisher interview.

Induced others to make decisions: John N. Mitchell OH.

Handling things "outside of the State Department and the NSC": John N. Mitchell OH.

Believed Israel would get Phantoms: Max M. Fisher interview. **Sympathy for Israel, especially from John Mitchell:** Rabin, *The Rabin Memoirs*, p. 165.

Protest predictions accurate: Max M. Fisher to Richard M. Nixon, January 12, 1970, Fisher Archives. **Pompidou harassed in Chicago:** Spiegel, *The Other Arab-Israeli Conflict: Making America's Middle East Policy, from Truman to Reagan*, p. 186. **Madame Pompidou upset:** Nixon, *RN: The Memoirs of Richard Nixon*, p. 480. **Nixon goes to Pompidou dinner:** Safire, *Before the Fall*, p. 566; Spiegel, *The Other Arab-Israeli Conflict: Making America's Middle East Policy, from Truman to Reagan*, p. 186. **Garment called Fisher:** Safire, *Before the Fall*, p. 566; Leonard Garment, Max M. Fisher interviews. **Nixon in a pique:** Safire, *Before the Fall*, p. 567.

Announces postponement of Phantom delivery: Spiegel, *The Other Arab-Israeli Conflict: Making America's Middle East Policy, from Truman to Reagan*, p. 186. **Attempt to "slow down the arms race":** Nixon, *RN: The Memoirs of Richard Nixon*, p. 480.

Rabin in secret meeting with Nixon: Rabin, *The Rabin Memoirs*, p. 169. **Will supply Israel with arms needs "by way of Kissinger":** Rabin, *The Rabin Memoirs*, p. 171.

"How Israel got her Phantoms": John N. Mitchell OH.

Dayan presented Fisher with 1200 B.C. beer jug: Max M. Fisher interview.

Fisher knew Israel getting jets: Max M. Fisher interview. **Speculation on NCVA resignation:** *The Detroit News*, March 17, 1970.

"Timing turned out to be bad": White House Memorandum, Murray Chotiner to Peter Flanigan, May 5, 1970, The Nixon Presidential Materials Project.

Wanted Henry Ford II to replace him: Max M. Fisher interview. **Ford "an LBJ man down the line":** Collier, Horowitz, *The Fords: An American Epic*, p. 354. **Fisher free to tackle economy:** Max M. Fisher interview.

"Discussed the whole field": Richard M. Nixon interview.

Economic discussions with McCracken: Max M. Fisher interview.

"He had access": Paul W. McCracken interview.

Nixon and Fisher discuss the economy: Max M. Fisher, Richard M. Nixon interviews.

Suggests Nixon involve business leaders in economic decisions: Max M. Fisher to Richard M. Nixon, June 13, 1970, Fisher Archives.

Decided to try a forum for industry leaders and government: Paul W. McCracken interview.

Nixon creates National Commission of Productivity: Richard M. Nixon to Max M. Fisher, June 18, 1970, Fisher Archives.

Thinking "so close": Richard M. Nixon to Max M. Fisher, June 18, 1970, Fisher Archives.

"Max brought in five or six CEOs": Paul W. McCracken interview.

Max elected UIA chairman: Max M. Fisher interview.

"The gilded funnel": Hoffman, *The Smoke Screen: Israel, Philanthropy and American Jews*, p. 134. **"The least known":** Hoffman, *The Smoke Screen: Israel, Philanthropy and American Jews*, p. 134. **"Most clout":** Hoffman, *The Smoke Screen: Israel, Philanthropy and American Jews*, p. 135. **UIA funnel to Jewish Agency:** Hoffman, *The Smoke Screen: Israel, Philanthropy and American Jews*, p. 135.

Jewish Agency Israeli government branch: Daniel Elazar interview. **"'Second line' for party placements":** Chinitz, *A Common Agenda: The Reconstitution of the Jewish Agency*, p. 11.

Chapter 10
The Strongest Single Link
Reconstituting the Jewish Agency for Israel

SOURCES

Books, documents, newspapers:
Chinitz, *A Common Agenda: The Reconstitution of the Jewish Agency for Israel*; Jaffe, *Givers and Spenders*; Halperin, *The Political World of American Zionism*; Hoffman, *The Smoke Screen: Israel, Philanthropy and American Jews*; Rose, *Chaim Weizmann*; Sachar, *A History of Israel From the Rise of Zionism to Our Time.*
The Jewish Agency for Israel: A Brief Description.
Jewish Telegraphic Agency Daily News Bulletin, *National Jewish Post*, Jewish Agency *Youth Aliya Newsletter.*

Fisher Archives.

Oral History:
Melvin Dubinsky, Max M. Fisher, Jerold C. Hoffberger, Moshe Rivlin, Harry Rosen.

Interviews:
Leon Dulzin, Daniel J. Elazar, Max M. Fisher, Uri Gordon, Charles Hoffman, Eliezer D. Jaffe, Mendel Kaplan, Morton L. Mandel, Jane Fisher Sherman.

NOTES

1897 first Zionist Congress: Rose, *Chaim Weizmann*, p. 45. **Practical Zionism:** Halperin, *The Political World of American Zionism*, pp. 6-7. **Homeland sustained by world Jewry:** Hoffman, *The Smoke Screen: Israel, Philanthropy and American Jews*, p. 39.

Herzl died 1904: Sachar, *A History of Israel From the Rise of Zionism to Our Time*, p. 63. **Balfour declaration:** Sachar, *A History of Israel From the Rise of Zionism to Our Time*, p. 109. **A Jewish Agency:** Chinitz, *A Common Agenda: The Reconstitution of the Jewish Agency for Israel*, p. 1.

To build a homeland: Chinitz, *A Common Agenda: The Reconstitution of the Jewish Agency for Israel*, pp. 4-6.

Need for a Jewish state: United Israel Appeal pamphlet, *The Jewish Agency for Israel: A Brief Description.*

Jewish Agency political ties: Hoffman, *The Smoke Screen: Israel, Philanthropy and American Jews*, p. 42. **To ingather "exiles":** United Israel Appeal pamphlet, *The Jewish Agency for Israel: A Brief Description.* **Diaspora life unhealthy:** Jewish Telegraphic Agency Daily News Bulletin, April 24, 1991.

Seeking a purpose: Chinitz, *A Common Agenda: The Reconstitution of the Jewish Agency for Israel*, p. 10.

Looked up to Pincus: Max M. Fisher interview.

Resent non-Zionists: Hoffman, *The Smoke Screen: Israel, Philanthropy and American Jews*, p. 126.

Some say in money spent: Melvin Dubinsky OH.

"Wellsprings of support" for Israel: Chinitz, *A Common Agenda: The Reconstitution of the Jewish Agency for Israel*, p. 15.

A secular Jew: Max M. Fisher interview.

Responsible for Israel's existence: Max M. Fisher interview.

Philanthropists, Zionist politics: Max M. Fisher interview.

Businessmen not interested in philosophy: Max M. Fisher interview.

"Strongest single link": Max M. Fisher interview.

No right to be involved: Hoffman, *The Smoke Screen: Israel, Philanthropy and American Jews*, p. 134.

He will be a Zionist: *National Jewish Post*, October 2, 1970. **Arabs deemed me a Zionist:** *National Jewish Post*, October 2, 1970.

Function same as ideology: Harry Rosen OH. **Reconstitution impossible without Fisher:** Moshe Rivlin OH.

Powerful yet "a mobilizer of people": Moshe Rivlin OH.

Allow all to speak: Max M. Fisher OH.

Some objection to this style: Morton L. Mandel interview.

"Max is a consensus builder": Morton L. Mandel interview.

Jewish Agency, WZO restructured with some diaspora control: Max M. Fisher interview; Chinitz, *A Common Agenda: The Reconstitution of the Jewish Agency for Israel*, p. 23.

"Carry the welfare of Israel in his heart": *Max M. Fisher Addresses 1969-1972*, pp. 158-163, Fisher Archives.

"Sloppy, wasteful philanthropy": Jaffe, *Givers and Spenders*, p. 7.

"He made a lousy deal": Eliezer D. Jaffe interview.

"Change had to be evolutionary": Hoffman, *Smoke Screen: Israel, Philanthropy and American Jews*, p. 135.

Hoffberger "a more assertive approach": Hoffman, *Smoke Screen: Israel, Philanthropy and American Jews*, pp. 176-177.

"Balanced all the factions": Jerold C. Hoffberger OH.

Agency jobs perks of patronage system: Max M. Fisher interview.

Liked Begin: Max M. Fisher interview.

Dispensing jobs to political cronies: Max M. Fisher interview.

Next treasurer: Max M. Fisher interview.

Agency jobs prerogative of political party: Max M. Fisher interview.

"Not anymore": Max M. Fisher interview.

"New Zionists": Max M. Fisher interview.

"Functional, not ideological": Max M. Fisher interview. **Caesarea Conference held to understand each other:** Max M. Fisher interview; Chinitz, *A Common Agenda: The Reconstitution of the Jewish Agency for Israel*, pp. 67-92.

All Jews belong in Israel: Gordon, *My Zionism*, Jewish Agency-Youth Aliya newsletter, Fisher Archives.

Education Fisher's project: Hoffman, *Smoke Screen: Israel, Philanthropy and American Jews*, p. 164.

"I never had a Jewish education": Leon Dulzin interview.

Two Jewish diaspora funds: Hoffman, *Smoke Screen: Israel, Philanthropy and American Jews*, p. 165.

Jewish Agency links diaspora to Israel: Daniel Elazar interview.

Chapter 11
PERSONAL BUSINESS

SOURCES

Books, journals:

Aricha, *Hour of the Clown*; Collier, Horowitz, *The Fords An American Epic*; Hayes, *Henry A Life of Henry Ford II*; Kiska, *Detroit's Powers & Personalities*; Lacey, *Ford: The Men and the Machine*; Rose, *Chaim Weizmann*.

Monthly Detroit .

Fisher Archives.

Oral History:
Henry Ford II, Teddy Kollek.

Interviews:
Marjorie Fisher Aronow, Irving Bernstein, Joyce Switow Burkoff, Stanley T. Burkoff, Julie Fisher Cummings, Marjorie Switow Fisher, Mary Fisher, Max M. Fisher, Phillip W. Fisher, Edsel B. Ford II, Norris Friedlander, Sharon Ross Medsker, Alan E. Schwartz, Elizabeth A. Stephens.

NOTES

Max constantly away from home, Marjorie accompanied him: Marjorie Switow Fisher interview.

Playing gin rummy with Princess of Morocco using Israel and Morocco as "stakes": Marjorie Switow Fisher interview.

Meir not amused with Marjorie's winnings: Max M. Fisher, Marjorie Switow Fisher interviews.

Plot to kill Max "Fischer": Aricha, *Hour of the Clown*, p. 9.

FBI guarding children, shotguns on kitchen table: Julie Fisher Cummings interview.

No intention of being scared off: Max M. Fisher interview.

Tried to shake FBI guard: Stanley T. Burkoff interview.

"These people are not as important as we are": Mary Fisher interview.

Telephone "favorite instrument": *Monthly Detroit* , July 1980.

Couldn't spank the children: Marjorie Fisher Aronow interview.

"I miss the children": Marjorie Switow Fisher interview.

Compensated by bringing children along on business, philanthropy trips: Max M. Fisher interview. **Accompanied father to Israel:** Phillip W. Fisher, Max M. Fisher interviews.

1969 rebellion against father: Phillip W. Fisher interview.

Vietnam greatest source of conflict: Max M. Fisher, Phillip W. Fisher interviews.

Supported Nixon's decision: Max M. Fisher to Richard M. Nixon, May 2, 1970, Fisher Archives.

"What's Nixon doing?": Phillip W. Fisher interview.

Didn't want to be unyielding with own son: Max M. Fisher interview.

"You make up your mind": Phillip W. Fisher interview.

Opportunity to be reacquainted: Max M. Fisher, Phillip W. Fisher interviews.

Itinerary: Max M. Fisher, Phillip W. Fisher interviews.

"Your father has died": Phillip W. Fisher interview. **"He froze":** Phillip W. Fisher interview.

In control: Phillip W. Fisher interview.

Didn't want him to be alone, met with Meir, etc., and returned to Detroit to plan funeral: Phillip W. Fisher interview.

Stroked his father's hair: Sharon Ross Medsker interview.

Father declined invitation to White House, gave him Nixon-signed place card: Max M. Fisher interview.

William proud of Max: Norris Friedlander interview.

"His word was his bond": Irwin Groner eulogy, January 27, 1971, Fisher Archives.

Found the place card Nixon had signed: Max M. Fisher interview.

Taubman and Ford II close friends: Max M. Fisher interview.

"Granddad killed my father": Lacey, *Ford: The Men and the Machine*, p. 434.

Gave Chaim Weizmann a Lincoln limousine: Rose, *Chaim Weizmann*, pp. 457-458.

Schwartz Detroit's "legal patriarch": Kiska, *Detroit's Powers & Personalities*, pp. 190-191.

Time for Jewish members at Detroit Club: Alan E. Schwartz interview.

"How do we deal with this?": Alan E. Schwartz interview.

"Just let it sit": Alan E. Schwartz interview.

Accepted a year later: Alan E. Schwartz interview.

Ford and Fisher "trusted each other": Alan E. Schwartz interview.

"Angel on my father's shoulder": Edsel Ford II interview.

Valued Fisher's listening ability: Edsel Ford II interview.

"Max has been a mentor for me": Edsel Ford II interview.

"Does things from the heart": Max M. Fisher interview.

"I could count on Max": Henry Ford II OH.

Encouraged Kathleen DuRoss romance: Marjorie Switow Fisher interview.

Ford ignores Arab boycott, opens assembly plant in Israel: Hayes, *Henry A Life of Henry Ford II*, p. 114; Max M. Fisher interview.

"Nobody's gonna tell me": Lacey, *Ford: The Men and the Machine*, p. 568.

Holds Fisher in high esteem: Teddy Kollek OH.

"You're full of shit": Collier, Horowitz, *The Fords An American Epic*, pp. 361.

Wanted to see the Suez Canal: Hayes, *Henry A Life of Henry Ford II*, p. 124.

Helicopter crash in the Sinai: Hayes, *Henry A Life of Henry Ford II*, p. 124.

"He's looking for oil": Irving Bernstein interview.

Scattered shells could signal oil: Max M. Fisher interview.

"I want the religious guy": Irving Bernstein interview.

Allowed to switch helicopters: Irving Bernstein interview.

Invested in Israel because he wanted to not necessarily economic sense: Hayes, *Henry A Life of Henry Ford II*, p. 127.

Need to do what was right: Max M. Fisher interview.

Palm Beach vacation: Max M. Fisher interview.

Insisted on sunny winter vacation: Marjorie Switow Fisher interview.

Woke with a start: Max M. Fisher interview.

"His skin turned gray": Marjorie Switow Fisher interview. **Suffered arrhythmia, should reduce stress:** Max M. Fisher, Marjorie Switow Fisher interviews.

Round of health problems: Max M. Fisher interview.

Stretched too thin: Max M. Fisher interview.

Dating someone nine years her senior: Julie Fisher Cummings interview.

Frightened by drinking: Max M. Fisher, Marjorie Switow Fisher interviews.

"Beside himself with Marjorie's drinking": Confidential interview.

Didn't blame Max: Marjorie Switow Fisher interview.

Blamed self: Max M. Fisher interview.

"All it will take is will power": Max M. Fisher notes, January 1, 1973, Fisher Archives.

Gauged own self: Max M. Fisher, Marjorie Switow Fisher interviews.

Involvement cost more than imagined: Max M. Fisher, Marjorie Switow Fisher interviews.

Chapter 12
PLAYING HIS ROLE: 1971-1974
THE NIXON WHITE HOUSE:
PART II

SOURCES

Books, journals, newspapers:
Ambrose, *Nixon: The Triumph of a Politician 1962-1972*; Associated Press (The), *The World in 1972*; Bernstein, *To Dwell In Unity*; Delury, ed., *The 1975 World Almanac and Book of Facts*; Destler, *Presidents, Bureaucrats and Foreign Policy, the Politics of Organizational Reform*; Meir, *My Life*; Nixon, *In the Arena, RN: The Memoirs of Richard Nixon*; Ognibene, *The Life and Politics of Henry M. Jackson*; Quandt, *Decade of Decisions: American Foreign Policy Toward the Arab-Israeli Conflict 1967-1976*; Sachar, *A History of Israel From the Rise of Zionism to Our Time*; Safire, *Before the Fall*; Spiegel, *The Other Arab-Israeli Conflict: Making America's Middle East Policy, from Truman to Reagan*; Stans, *The Terrors of Justice*; Thorton, *The Nixon-Kissinger Years*; Urofsky, *We Are One!*.

Judaism, National Journal
Jewish Telegraphic Agency Daily News Bulletin, *The Detroit News*, *The Evening Star*, *The New York Times*, *The Philadelphia Inquirer*, *The Washington Post*.

Fisher Archives.

Oral History:
Melvin Dubinsky, Leonard Garment, Israel Miller, Herschel Schacter, Maurice H. Stans.

Interviews:
Simcha Dinitz, Marjorie Switow Fisher, Max M. Fisher, Leonard Garment, Alexander M. Haig Jr., Henry A. Kissinger, Richard M. Nixon, Jacob Stein.

NOTES
"Stop shooting, start talking": Spiegel, *The Other Arab-Israeli Conflict: Making America's Middle East Policy, from Truman to Reagan*, p. 193. **Unofficial ceasefire violated within days by Egypt:** Spiegel, *The Other Arab-Israeli Conflict: Making America's Middle East Policy, from Truman to Reagan*, p. 194; Thorton, *The Nixon-Kissinger Years*, p. 48. **Nasser dead:** Thorton, *The Nixon-Kissinger Years*, p. 58. **Sadat reluctant to sign treaty:** Spiegel, *The Other Arab-Israeli Conflict: Making America's Middle East Policy, from Truman to Reagan*, p. 215.

Syria backs PLO in Jordan: Thorton, *The Nixon-Kissinger Years*, p. 55. **Jordanian crisis:** Spiegel, *The Other Arab-Israeli Conflict: Making America's Middle East Policy, from Truman to Reagan*, p. 201.

"Fulfill Israel's needs for military weapons": Ognibene, *The Life and Politics of Henry M. Jackson*, p. 183.

"Monkey wrench" into détente: Urofsky, *We Are One!*, p. 419.

Second only to Israel: Urofsky, *We Are One!*, p, 420.

"Leningrad 11": *The New York Times*, June 22, 1970. **Two sentenced to death:** *The New York Times*, December 25, 1970.

Seven days to appeal: *The New York Times*, December 25, 1970.

Rogers asked to intercede: *The New York Times*, December 30, 1970.

Nixon says "trust me"; sentence commuted: Max M. Fisher interview.

Couldn't publicly pressure Soviets into releasing Jewry: Max M. Fisher interview. **Jewish Defense League bombs Soviet Embassy:** *The Detroit News*, January 12, 1971.

Nixon denounces violence: *The Detroit News*, January 12, 1971. **Telegram to Nixon renouncing act:** *The Detroit News*, January 12, 1971.

Dividing time between Jewish Agency and GOP: Max M. Fisher interview. **Understands the Soviet Jews' situation:** Max M. Fisher interview. For example, in a June 21, 1971, *Jerusalem Post* news article, Fisher said that President Nixon "understands the problem very well and takes a very positive stand on it, much more so than he is usually given credit for."

CRP established: *National Journal*, September 11, 1971. **Fisher eager to garner Jewish vote for Nixon:** Max M. Fisher interview.

In constant telephone contact with political pulse: Max M. Fisher interview.

Campaign advice to John Mitchell: Max M. Fisher to John N. Mitchell, August 16, 1971, Fisher Archives.

"Broad-based vote-getting effort": *The New York Times*, July 7, 1972. **Goldberg coordinating events:** Lawrence Goldberg memorandum for Committee To Re-elect the President, July 5, 1972, Fisher Archives.

Money and votes: Maurice H. Stans OH.

Henry Ford II gave $100,000: Max M. Fisher interview.

"Jewish money": Safire, *Before the Fall*, p. 572.

Fisher contacts across the country: Max M. Fisher interview.

Kosher luncheon: *The Evening Star*, March 7, 1972.

Canvassed thirty states: *The Washington Post*, October 10, 1972. **Speech in Philadelphia:** *The Philadelphia Inquirer*, June 11, 1972.

"How much for Luxembourg?": Maurice H. Stans OH.

Hurricane Agnes: Associated Press (The), *The World in 1972*, p. 113.

CJF restores losses suffered by Jewish community: Bernstein, *To Dwell In Unity*, p. 195.

Aiming for Jewish Democrats' votes: Max M. Fisher interview.

Jewish Democrat voting trend began in 1928: *Judaism*, Summer 1988, p. 277.

Roosevelt cemented trend: *Judaism*, Summer 1988, p. 277.

Citing Nixon's economic, military aid to Israel: *The Philadelphia Inquirer*, June 11, 1972.

McGovern Democratic presidential nominee: Associated Press (The), *The World in 1972*, p. 101.

McGovern unreliable for Israel: *Judaism*, Summer 1988, p. 277.

Fisher converts Jewish Democrats: *The New York Times*, July 7, 1972.

"Send signs": Max M. Fisher interview. **Schacter deliver RNC convention opening prayer:** Max M. Fisher interview.

Not a Republican: Herschel Schacter OH.

"Best dinner": Max M. Fisher interview.

"$8 million": Max M. Fisher to John N. Mitchell, December 5, 1972, Fisher Archives. **"Sitting this election out":** Max M. Fisher to Leonard Garment, October 9, 1972, Fisher Archives.

Personal satisfaction: Max M. Fisher interview.

Taxi cab ride: Max M. Fisher interview.

Nixon-American Jewish leaders meet: Max M. Fisher notes, September 26, 1972, Fisher Archives.

Projecting Jewish vote: Max M. Fisher notes, September 26, 1972, Fisher Archives.

"I know you've worked": Max M. Fisher notes, September 26, 1972, Fisher Archives.

Make Jewish community comfortable at White House: Max M. Fisher notes, September 26, 1972, Fisher Archives.

Can't embarrass Soviets: Max M. Fisher notes, September 26, 1972, Fisher Archives.

No question for Israel: Max M. Fisher notes, September 26, 1972, Fisher Archives.

Discussed issues with thirty-one Jewish leaders: Synopsis of Meeting with President Nixon at Waldorf-Astoria Hotel, New York City, September 26, 1972, Fisher Archives.

"A quota is a sign": Safire, *Before the Fall*, p. 571. **"I ask you to trust me":** Synopsis of Meeting with President Nixon at Waldorf-Astoria Hotel, New York City, September 26, 1972, Fisher Archives.

Nixon government "consoling but ineffective": Jewish Telegraphic Agency Daily News Bulletin, September 29, 1972.

"Shock" at administration's views: Jewish Telegraphic Agency Daily News Bulletin, September 29, 1972.

Fisher calls Pincus: Max M. Fisher interview. **"Bless President Nixon":** Jewish Telegraphic Agency Daily News Bulletin, October 3, 1972.

Fisher returns to campaign trail: Max M. Fisher interview.

Nixon cuts deal with Jackson: Ambrose, *Nixon: The Triumph of a Politician 1962-1972*, pp. 615-616. **Nuclear arms pact:** Ambrose, *Nixon: The Triumph of a Politician 1962-1972*, pp. 615-616. **"Bum deal":** Ambrose, *Nixon: The Triumph of a Politician 1962-1972*, p. 615.

Delayed signing treaty in May: Ambrose, *Nixon: The Triumph of a Politician 1962-1972*, p. 615. **Trade linked to Vietnam:** Ambrose, *Nixon: The Triumph of a Politician 1962-1972*, p. 616.

Nixon releases Republican senators: Ambrose, *Nixon: The Triumph of a Politician 1962-1972*, p. 616.

Jackson amendment before Senate: Ambrose, *Nixon: The Triumph of a Politician 1962-1972*, p. 617. **4,500 Jews in October:** Ambrose, *Nixon: The Triumph of a Politician 1962-1972*, p. 617.

Nixon rewards Soviets: Ambrose, *Nixon: The Triumph of a Politician 1962-1972*, p. 617.

Nixon defeats McGovern by widest margin: Delury, ed., *The 1975 World Almanac and Book of Facts*, p. 735. **Jewish vote reached 40 percent for Nixon:** "Jewish Voter Division: Final Report" prepared by Lawrence Y. Goldberg of the Nixon re-election committee, Fisher Archives; Max M. Fisher interview. **"Issues rather than tradition":** Max M. Fisher to John N. Mitchell, December 5, 1972, Fisher Archives. **"Jewish constituency welcome at the White House":** Max M. Fisher to John N. Mitchell, December 5, 1972, Fisher Archives.

"Fisher mafia": Richard M. Nixon interview.

Vietnam peace accords signed: Nixon, *RN: The Memoirs of Richard Nixon*, p. 757. **Middle East truce sinking:** For example, Thorton, *The Nixon-Kissinger*, pp. 228-229. **Ismael, then Meir, visits Washington:** Spiegel, *The Other Arab-Israeli Conflict: Making America's Middle East Policy, from Truman to Reagan*, p. 237. **Meir promised more weapons as trade for peace:** Spiegel, *The Other Arab-Israeli Conflict: Making America's Middle East Policy, from Truman to Reagan*, p. 238.

Meir dinner, "Jewish leadership, thrilled to be invited": Max M. Fisher to Richard M. Nixon, March 8, 1973, Fisher Archives. **Offered Fisher ambassadorship, or administrative spot again:** Max M. Fisher interview. **Fisher declined:** Max M. Fisher interview. **Working with Ehrlichman on energy matters:** Max M. Fisher interview.

"Offered Max any job he wants": Max M. Fisher, Richard M. Nixon interviews.

"He's lazy": Max M. Fisher interview.

"Smallest check": *The Jerusalem Post*, April 8, 1973; Max M. Fisher interview.

"Rallying point for both sides": Nixon, *RN: The Memoirs of Richard Nixon*, p. 875.

Fisher invites Jackson to Palm Beach: Max M. Fisher interview. **"How many Jews?"**: Max M. Fisher interview.

"A hundred thousand": Max M. Fisher interview.

"Jackson-Vanik was a mistake": Richard M. Nixon interview.

"It showed Max at his best": Richard M. Nixon interview.

April 19 meeting with American Jewish leaders: Max M. Fisher notes, April 19, 1973, Fisher Archives.

"The Kremlin won't listen": Max M. Fisher interview.

Vaguely-worded press release: Urofsky, *We Are One!*, pp. 421-422.

Dissident Soviet Jews' letter: Urofsky, *We Are One!*, pp. 421-422.

"With all your problems:" Max M. Fisher to Richard M. Nixon, April 19, 1973, Fisher Archives.

Nixon thanked Fisher for support: Max M. Fisher interview. **"Do not hesitate to call"**: Max M. Fisher to Richard M. Nixon, May 14, 1973, Fisher Archives.

Couldn't see president out of office: Max M. Fisher interview.

SALT II talks: Nixon, *RN: The Memoirs of Richard Nixon*, p. 877. **Nixon admitted to "plumbers"**: *The New York Times*, May 23, 1973.

"Deeply grateful for your words of encouragement": Richard M. Nixon to Max M. Fisher, June 4, 1973, Fisher Archives.

Fisher worried: Max M. Fisher interview.

Fisher at Brezhnev White House dinner: Jacob Stein, Max M. Fisher interviews.

Received criticism for dining with Brezhnev: Jacob Stein interview.

Signal to Brezhnev: Max M. Fisher interview.

Specifically introduced to Brezhnev: Max M. Fisher, Jacob Stein interviews.

"The road will be wider": Jacob Stein interview.

Dobrynin brought into conversation: Jacob Stein, Max M. Fisher interviews.

Nixon and Brezhnev sign pact, fly to San Clemente: Nixon, *RN: The Memoirs of Richard Nixon*, p. 881.

Fisher asks Stein to do something about anti-Soviet protest planned in San Clemente: Jacob Stein interview.

Able to relocate protest march: Jacob Stein interview.

Fishers and Steins invited to Russian Embassy: Max M. Fisher, Jacob Stein interviews.

Wives preferred not to attend: Max M. Fisher, Jacob Stein interviews.

Dobrynin preferred wives attend: Max M. Fisher, Jacob Stein interviews.

"Say things the administration can't say": Max M. Fisher, Jacob Stein interviews.

Kept meetings with Kissinger quiet: Jacob Stein interview.

Encouraged American Jewish community to apply pressure: Max M. Fisher interview.

Brezhnev understood democracy: Max M. Fisher interview.

Social front maintained: Jacob Stein interview. **"Exchanging polite nonsense"**: Jacob Stein interview.

Gave Dobrynin an earful about Soviet treatment of Jews: Jacob Stein interview.

"Levels of immigration are going up": Max M. Fisher, Jacob Stein interviews.

Put the Jews on a plane, send them to the U.S.: Max M. Fisher, Jacob Stein interviews.

"Could you do that?": Max M. Fisher, Jacob Stein interviews.

Lunch served, discussion softens: Max M. Fisher interview. **Situation could be eased "without confrontation":** Max M. Fisher to Leonard Garment, August 11, 1973, Fisher Archives.

"Frank and friendly visit": Max M. Fisher to Leonard Garment, August 11, 1973, Fisher Archives.

Nixon threatened with a subpoena: Nixon, *RN: The Memoirs of Richard Nixon*, p. 901.

"Be assured of my cooperation and support": Max M. Fisher to Richard Nixon, August 3, 1974, Fisher Archives.

"Always valued your friendship": Richard M. Nixon to Max M. Fisher, August 14, 1973, Fisher Archives.

Nixon predicted war to Kissinger: Kissinger, *Years of Upheaval*, p. 211; Spiegel, *The Other Arab-Israeli Conflict: Making America's Middle East Policy, from Truman to Reagan*, p. 237. **"Last major foreign-policy decision":** Nixon, *In the Arena*, p. 335.

October 6, 1973, Egypt and Syria attack Israel: Sachar, *A History of Israel From the Rise of Zionism to Our Time*, p. 755.

Major Jewish organizations meet in New York, confident of Israeli victory: Jacob Stein interview. **Scheduled fund-raiser for Shoreham Hotel, October 9:** Jacob Stein interview.

Unprecedented Israeli losses: Spiegel, *The Other Arab-Israeli Conflict: Making America's Middle East Policy, from Truman to Reagan*, p. 250. **Soviets resupplying Arab clients:** Sachar, *A History of Israel From the Rise of Zionism to Our Time*, pp. 755-768.

Sought U.S. military aid to Israel: Max M. Fisher interview; Spiegel, *The Other Arab-Israeli Conflict: Making America's Middle East Policy from Truman to Reagan*, pp. 250-251. **"At all hours of the day and the night":** Meir, *My Life*, p. 362. **"Contacts in the U.S. government were so intimate":** Simcha Dinitz interview.

Dinitz tells Fisher of Israel's desperation: Simcha Dinitz, Max M. Fisher interviews. **"Max was a one-man campaign":** Leonard Garment OH.

Letter urging president to resupply Israel: Jacob Stein interview.

Nixon and Fisher meet, October 9: Max M. Fisher interview. **Tapes subject of debate, Agnew under investigation:** Nixon, *RN: The Memoirs of Richard Nixon*, pp. 923-926. **Nixon reads letter:** Max M. Fisher interview.

"I'm asking you now": Max M. Fisher interview.

Nixon assured Fisher of Israeli resupply: Max M. Fisher interview.

Israel calling saying they were in trouble, 'thought that Max had been had by the president": Jacob Stein interview. **Fisher "called Kissinger":** Jacob Stein interview.

"Logistical" problems: Max M. Fisher, Jacob Stein interviews.

Kissinger blamed for delay, he blamed the Defense Department: Quandt, *Decade of Decisions: American Foreign Policy Toward the Arab-Israeli Conflict 1967-1976*, p. 175.

Kissinger used Defense Department as diplomatic device: Thorton, *The Nixon-Kissinger Years*, pp. 241-242.

"There has to be a limit to ingratitude": Henry A. Kissinger interview.

"Bureaucratic" delay: Richard M. Nixon interview.

"Just send them all": Richard M. Nixon interview.

"Nixon deserves the credit for it": Alexander M. Haig Jr. interview.

22,000 tons of equipment delivered: Sachar, *A History of Israel From the Rise of Zionism to Our Time*, p. 770.

Airlift "made our victory possible": Meir, *My Life*, p. 362.

Jacobson and Truman: Sachar, *A History of Israel From The Rise of Zionism to Our Time*, pp. 302-303. **U.S. recognizes Israel:** Sachar, *A History of Israel From The Rise of Zionism to Our Time*, p. 312.

Not committed to statehood: Sachar, *A History of Israel From the Rise of Zionism to Our Time*, p. 291.

Airlift as "strategic considerations": Richard M. Nixon interview.

"Foreign affairs primacy to the president": Destler, *Presidents, Bureaucrats and Foreign Policy, the Politics of Organizational Reform*, pp. 85-86.

"Max gave prestige to the Presidents Conference": Israel Miller OH.

"Harsh words between Scoop and us": Jacob Stein interview.

"Legislation was a mistake": Jacob Stein interview.

MFN denied Soviet Union: Nixon, *RN: The Memoirs of Richard Nixon*, p. 876. **Emigration dwindled:** Jacob Stein interview. **Fisher frustrated:** Max M. Fisher interview.

"No intention of resigning": Max M. Fisher interview. On page 981 of *RN: The Memoirs of Richard Nixon*, the former president recalls that he specifically said: "And I want you to know that I have no intention whatever of ever walking away from the job the people elected me to do for the people of the United States." **Didn't "expect to be impeached":** Max M. Fisher interview.

"Those Jew boys": *The Detroit News*, May 15, 1974. **"Do the same thing once in a while":** *The Detroit News*, May 15, 1974. **"Hate to have my business meetings recorded":** Max M. Fisher interview. **Nixon as anti-Semitic ludicrous:** Max M. Fisher interview.

Fisher called to testify: Max M. Fisher interview; notes on memorandum, Fisher Archives. **Mitchell and Stans indicted:** Stans, *The Terrors of Justice*, p. 302. **Mitchell and Stans acquitted in Vesco case:** Stans, *The Terrors of Justice*, p. 343. **"Innocents in the line of fire":** Stans, *The Terrors of Justice*, p. 79. **Stans fined $5,000:** Stans, *The Terrors of Justice*, pp. 370-374. **Mitchell indicted again:** Stans, *The Terrors of Justice*, p. 329.

"Max was compassionate": Maurice H. Stans OH.

"Pay his price": Max M. Fisher interview.

Not names to be associated with: Max M. Fisher interview. Haldeman and Mitchell convicted: Associated Press (The), *The World in 1974*, pp. 227-232.

"What was his price?": Max M. Fisher interview.

Acknowledged $250,000 contribution: Max M. Fisher interview.

Fisher testifies before grand jury: Max M. Fisher interview.

Furious at questions of his integrity: Max M. Fisher interview.

Chapter 13

OLD FRIENDS

SOURCES

Books, newspapers, documents:

Biale, *Power and Powerlessness in Jewish History*; Ford, *A Time to Heal*; Nixon, *In the Arena, RN: The Memoirs of Richard Nixon*; Smith, *The Power Game*.

Detroit Free Press, The Jerusalem Post, The Birmingham (Michigan) *Observer & Eccentric*.

Fisher Archives.

Gerald R. Ford Library:

Oral History:
    Max M. Fisher, Gerald R. Ford, Richard M. Nixon.

Interviews:
    Marjorie Switow Fisher, Max M. Fisher, Gerald R. Ford, Leonard Garment, Maurice S. Schiller.

NOTES

Fisher in audience as Ford sworn in: Max M. Fisher OH.

Ford was the right man, right place: *The Birmingham* (Michigan) *Observer & Eccentric*, August 26, 1974.**"Jews into American political elite":** Biale, *Power and Powerlessness in Jewish History*, p. 181.

"Access is primary": Smith, *The Power Game*. **"Max had access":** Gerald. R. Ford interview.

John Connally, first VP choice: Nixon, *RN: The Memoirs of Richard Nixon*, p. 905. **Fisher's integrity and fund-raising services invaluable to GOP:** Richard M. Nixon, Max M. Fisher OH; Gerald R. Ford, Max M. Fisher interviews. **Officials are not "movable objects":** Max M. Fisher, confidential interviews.

"Max was trusted": Leonard Garment interview. **From Nixon to Bush, they call him:** Leonard Garment interview.

Ford knew Fisher from 1960s: Gerald R. Ford interview; Gerald R. Ford OH.

Max's reputation helps raise money: Gerald R. Ford OH.

Something special about Ford: Max M. Fisher interview.

1964, Fisher suggests Ford seek vice presidency: Marjorie Switow Fisher interview.

Wanted to be Speaker of the House: Marjorie Switow Fisher interview.

Ford asks Fisher for aid in Griffin's U.S. Senate race: Gerald R. Ford to Max M. Fisher, February 14, 1966, Fisher Archives. **"Legislating for a Better America":** Program guide, The Economic Club of Detroit's Ladies' Night Dinner, November 17, 1969, Fisher Archives. **Rabbi Abba Hillel Silver Award:** Gerald R. Ford to Max M. Fisher, February 28, 1973. **"Warmest personal regards":** Gerald R. Ford to Max M. Fisher, November 9, 1973.

"A close friend": Ford, *A Time to Heal*, p. 247. **"My old friend":** Ford, *A Time to Heal*, p. 286.

Betting on Michigan, Ohio State football games: Max M. Fisher OH.

Not by nature suspicious: Ford, *A Time to Heal*, p. 6.

Grand Rapids highly conservative: Ford, *A Time to Heal*, p. 46.

A few Jewish students: Gerald R. Ford interview.

"And Max is a good example": Gerald R. Ford interview.

Max generated trust and respect: Ford, *A Time to Heal*, pp. 188-189.

"Max would always tell me what he thought": Gerald R. Ford interview.

Could tell Ford the way it was: Max M. Fisher OH.

"Assured of my continued friendship": Max M. Fisher to Richard M. Nixon, August 26, 1974, Fisher Archives.

"How grateful we are to you": Max M. Fisher interview.

Friendship is "deeply cherished": Richard M. Nixon to Max M. Fisher, December 20, 1974, Fisher Archives.

"When you lose, you hear from your friends": Nixon, *In the Arena*, p. 32.

Nixon called: *Detroit Free Press Sunday Magazine*, January 11, 1976.

"Mr. President": The President's Daily Diary, August 26, 1974, Gerald R. Ford Library; Ford, *A Time to Heal*, p. 349.

Deal directly with the president: Max M. Fisher notes on meeting with Gerald R. Ford, August 26, 1974, Fisher Archives. **Help with energy and Israel:** Max M. Fisher notes on meeting with Gerald R. Ford, August 26, 1974, Fisher Archives.

Early meeting is "crucial": Max M. Fisher notes on meeting with Gerald R. Ford, August 26, 1974, Fisher Archives.

"President Ford's longtime support": *The Jerusalem Post*, September 2, 1974. **Greetings for Rabin and Meir:** *The Jerusalem Post*, September 13, 1974.

Conference on inflation: L. William Seidman to William G. Milliken, September 23, 1974, Executive MC3-1, Gerald R. Ford Library; Gerald R. Ford to Max M. Fisher, October 23, 1974, Executive MC3-1, Gerald R. Ford Library. **Advising Secretary of Interior:** The President's Daily Diary, October 29, 1974, Gerald R. Ford Library. **Seven-year energy program:** Memorandum of Information for the file, October 28, 1974, Executive PR 7-1, Gerald R. Ford Library. **Fisher's suggestions in use:** Memorandum of Information for the file, October 28, 1974, Executive PR 7-1, Gerald R. Ford Library. **Fisher energy program:** Max M. Fisher interview.

"Cost me a fortune": Max M. Fisher, Gerald R. Ford interviews; Gerald R. Ford OH.

Finer points of access: Max M. Fisher notes on meeting with Gerald R. Ford, November 23, 1975, Fisher Archives. **Arrange Ford meeting with American Jewish leaders:** Max M. Fisher notes on meeting with Gerald R. Ford, November 23, 1975, Fisher Archives.

Recommends Garment for UN job: collects bet from Ford: Max M. Fisher interview: Max M. Fisher notes on meeting with Gerald R. Ford, November 23, 1975.

Fisher meets with Ford, Cheney, McCracken: The President's Daily Diary, December 8, 1974, Gerald R. Ford Library. **McCracken convinced inflation defeated:** Memorandum of Information for the File, December 24, 1974, Executive BE 5, Gerald R. Ford Library. **Fisher economic suggestions:** Max M. Fisher notes on meeting with President Gerald R. Ford, Paul W. McCracken, and Richard B. Cheney, December 8, 1974, Fisher Archives.

Ford meets Jewish American leaders: Memorandum of Information for the File, December 20, 1974, Executive RM 3-2, Gerald R. Ford Library.

Israel can count on U.S.: Memorandum of Information for the File, December 20, 1974, Executive RM 3-2, Gerald R. Ford Library.

Negotiations a quid pro quo: Max M. Fisher notes on meeting with Gerald R. Ford and Jewish American leaders, December 20, 1974, Fisher Archives.

"Never be another Munich": Max M. Fisher notes on meeting with Gerald R. Ford and Jewish American leaders, December 20, 1974, Fisher Archives.

"You impressed the group": Max M. Fisher to Gerald R. Ford, December 20, 1974 Fisher Archives; Executive RM 3-2, Gerald R. Ford Library.

"Old friend, Max Fisher": Ford, *A Time to Heal*, p. 286.

Chapter 14
THE REASSESSMENT
SOURCES
Books, journals, newspapers:
Aronson, *Conflict and Bargaining in the Middle East: An Israeli Perspective*; Associated Press (The), *The World in 1975*; Blitzer, *Between Washington & Jerusalem: A Reporter's Notebook*; Ford, *A Time to Heal*; Golan, *The Secret Conversations*

of Henry Kissinger; Karnow, *Vietnam: A History;* Kissinger, *White House Years, Years of Upheaval;* Rabin, *Pinkas Sherut [Ledger of Service] Volume Two, The Rabin Memoirs;* Sachar, *A History of Israel: Volume II;* Quandt, *Decade of Decisions: American Foreign Policy Toward the Arab-Israeli Conflict 1967-1976.*
Newsweek.
The Jerusalem Post, Jewish Chronicle News Service, Haaretz, The New York Times.

Fisher Archives.

Gerald R. Ford Library.

Oral History:
Max M. Fisher, Joseph J. Sisco.
Council of Jewish Federations Oral History Project.

Interviews:
Irving Bernstein, Marjorie Switow Fisher, Max M. Fisher, Gerald R. Ford, Betty M. Hansen, Henry A. Kissinger, Shlomo Osherov, Yitzhak Rabin.

NOTES

Meir a political casualty of war: Sachar, *History of Israel: Volume II*, p. 5.
Everything for nothing: Rabin, *The Rabin Memoirs*, pp. 245-247.
Public pledge of nonbelligerency: Golan, *The Secret Conversations of Henry Kissinger*, pp. 222-223. **Israel cede oil fields and passes:** Golan, *The Secret Conversations of Henry Kissinger*, p. 230. **Israel flexible:** Golan, *The Secret Conversations of Henry Kissinger*, p. 230.
Secretary shuttling ten days in March: Golan, *The Secret Conversations of Henry Kissinger*, p. 232. **Discrepancies not solved:** Rabin, *The Rabin Memoirs*, p. 255. **Egypt wouldn't state nonbelligerency:** Quandt, *Decade of Decisions: American Foreign Policy Toward the Arab-Israeli Conflict 1967-1976*, p. 265. **"New Egyptian proposals to Rabin":** Golan, *The Secret Conversations of Henry Kissinger*, p. 235. **Peace but not at any price:** Golan, *The Secret Conversations of Henry Kissinger*, p. 236.
March 21 Ford letter: Quandt, *Decade of Decisions: American Foreign Policy Toward the Arab-Israeli Conflict 1967-1976*, p. 265. **Begin to reassess U.S.-Israeli relations:** Rabin, *The Rabin Memoirs*, p. 256.
Israeli stance hardens: Aronson, *Conflict and Bargaining in the Middle East: An Israeli Perspective*, p. 248.
Sadat won't promise nonbelligerency: Quandt, *Decade of Decisions: American Foreign Policy Toward the Arab-Israeli Conflict 1967-1976*, p. 266.
Deceived operationally: Henry A. Kissinger interview.
"Why lose cards?": Yitzhak Rabin interview. **Not the final step:** Yitzhak Rabin interview.
Farewell statement to Israel: *The New York Times*, March 24, 1975. **"Humiliating" the United States:** *Jewish Chronicle News Service*, May 29, 1975. **Most "acrimonious" period:** Blitzer, *Between Washington & Jerusalem: A Reporter's Notebook*, p. 209.
Support for Israel could be curbed: Ford, *A Time to Heal*, p. 247. **Israel losing big picture:** Gerald R. Ford interview.
U.S. chokehold on arms: *Newsweek*, April 14, 1975. **Diplomatic relations slowed:** *Newsweek*, April 14, 1975.
Career Arabists used in reassessment process: *Newsweek*, April 14, 1975. **Kissinger encourages other countries to pressure Israel:** *Newsweek*, April 14, 1975.
American Jewish leaders rally to Israel's defense: *Newsweek*, April 14, 1975. **Tactics work, only 7 percent pro-Arab:** *Newsweek*, April 14, 1975.

Kissinger effected by outcry: Henry A. Kissinger interview. **"Really felt the pressure":** Henry A. Kissinger interview.

Ford more disappointed: Henry A. Kissinger interview. **Dinitz in action before Kissinger back in U.S.:** Henry A. Kissinger interview.

American Jewish community "terribly misinformed": Gerald R. Ford interview.

Max is "very smart, very wise": Gerald R. Ford interview.

Reassessment jolted community: Ford, *A Time to Heal*, p. 247.

Max ushered into Oval Office: The President's Daily Diary, March 27, 1975, Gerald R. Ford Library. **Ford not alone:** The President's Daily Diary, March 27, 1975, Gerald R. Ford Library. **"Mad as hell":** Ford, *A Time to Heal*, p. 247.

Met for 40 minutes: The President's Daily Diary, March 27, 1975, Gerald R. Ford Library. **Foreign policy losing credibility:** Ford, *A Time to Heal*, p. 244. **Moderate Arab assassinated:** Associated Press (The), *The World in 1975*, pp. 43-44. **Fall of Saigon:** Karnow, *Vietnam: A History*, pp. 684-685.

Trusted Ford and Kissinger: Max M. Fisher interview.

"Shuttle diplomacy": Kissinger, *Years of Upheaval*, p. 799. **Max is a "problem solver":** Joseph J. Sisco OH.

He listened: Max M. Fisher interview.

Ford, Kissinger disappointed, hurt: Max M. Fisher notes, Oval Office meeting with Ford and Kissinger, March 29, 1975, Fisher Archives.

Settled down the president: Max M. Fisher notes, Oval Office meeting with Ford and Kissinger, March 29, 1975, Fisher Archives.

Fisher talks to Israeli government: Max M. Fisher, Gerald R. Ford interviews."**Kissinger picking on Rabin":** *The Jerusalem Post*, April 8, 1975.

"Never called a press conference": Gerald R. Ford interview.

"Outside consultants pressuring Israel": Spiegel, *The Other Arab-Israeli Conflict Making America's Middle East Policy from Truman to Reagan* p. 312.

Max never tried to fool: Gerald R. Ford interview.

Kissinger trusted Fisher: Henry A. Kissinger interview.

Max conveyed administration's thinking: Henry A. Kissinger interview.

Difficult to convey message: Outline and notes of Max M. Fisher's Oval Office conversation with President Gerald R. Ford and Secretary of State Henry A. Kissinger, March 27, 1975 Fisher Archives; Max M. Fisher interview.

Controversy mushrooming: Max M. Fisher OH.

Notes of meeting, exhausting: Max M. Fisher interview.

"Situation not encouraging": *Haaretz*, March 31, 1975. Translated by Zelig S. Chinitz.

Story fed by American Jewish community: Confidential interview.

Agency business as usual: Max M. Fisher, Zelig S. Chinitz, Shlomo Osherov interviews.

Both had faith in me: Max M. Fisher interview.

Fisher meets with Israeli leaders, Israel did not mislead Kissinger: Max M. Fisher interview; Max M. Fisher OH. An outline of Fisher's agenda from April 3-5, 1975 is contained in Fisher's notes for his meeting with President Gerald R. Ford and Henry A. Kissinger, April 9, 1975, Fisher Archives.

Fisher, Rabin "speak in four eyes": Max M. Fisher, Yitzhak Rabin interviews; Rabin, *The Rabin Memoirs*, pp. 152-153.

Rabin saw American Jewish role differently: Rabin, *The Rabin Memoirs*, pp. 228-229.

Not an Israeli Army private: Max M. Fisher interview.

"Not being much of friend by lying": Max M. Fisher interview.

Rabin saw Fisher as a "cold Jew": Irving Bernstein interview. **Max's reserve, Rabin's lack of trust:** Irving Bernstein interview.

Madison Hotel owned by Marshal Coyne: Rabin, *The Rabin Memoirs*, p. 220. **Fisher's life story:** Irving Bernstein interview.

Rabin trusts Fisher's commitment: Yitzhak Rabin interview.

Max Jewish, but loyal American: Yitzhak Rabin interview.

Middle East interests besides Israel: Max M. Fisher OH.

Rabin no Golda Meir: Max M. Fisher interview.

Rabin a "brilliant strategist": Max M. Fisher interview.

Talked "point by point": Yitzhak Rabin interview.

Israelis want peace, but cautious of Sadat: Max M. Fisher, Yitzhak Rabin interviews. For further insight into Rabin's perceptions of Sadat, see Rabin, *The Rabin Memoirs*, pp. 249-250; Max M. Fisher notes on meeting with Ford and Kissinger, April 9, 1975 Fisher Archives; Max M. Fisher CJF OH.

Rabin, Fisher, talk for five hours: Max M. Fisher interview.

"The process will resume": Yitzhak Rabin interview.

"Max moves its hinges": Rabin, *Pinkas Sherut Volume Two* [*Ledger of Service*], p. 352. Paragraph translated by Zelig S. Chinitz.

Chapter 15
BEHIND THE WHITE HOUSE DOOR
SOURCES
Books, newspapers, journals:

Javits, *Javits: The Autobiography of a Public Man*; McGinniss, *The Selling of the President*; Meir, *My Life*; Rabin, *The Rabin Memoirs*; Spiegel, *The Other Arab-Israeli Conflict: Making America's Middle East Policy, from Truman to Reagan.*

Chicago Daily News, Detroit Free Press, Detroit Jewish News, The Detroit News, Haaretz, The Jerusalem Post, The London Jewish Times, The New York Post, The New York Times, The Washington Post.

Newsweek, Regardie's.

Fisher Archives.

The Gerald R. Ford Library.

Oral History:

Max M. Fisher, Leonard Garment.
Council of Jewish Federations Oral History Project.

Interviews:

Max M. Fisher, Gerald R. Ford, Leonard Garment, Henry A. Kissinger.

NOTES

Fisher "to coax Israelis": *The New York Post*, April 5, 1975. **Israel 'misled him':** *Haaretz*, April 7, 1975, Zelig S. Chinitz translation, Fisher Archives.

"Absolutely false": *The Detroit News*, April 10, 1975.

Kissinger meets with Morgenthau, Wiesel, and Kampelman: *The Jerusalem Post*, April 4, 1975. **Kissinger "very sad":** *The Jerusalem Post*, April 4, 1975. **Kissinger "too did not sleep at night":** *The Detroit News*, April 4, 1975.

Fisher en route to Washington: Max M. Fisher Daily Schedule, April 8-9, 1975, Fisher Archives. **Kissinger reluctant to start new peace talks:** *The New York Times*,

April 8, 1975. **Fisher not in "Israel on a special mission":** *The New York Times*, April 8, 1975.

Meeting with Rumsfeld: Max M. Fisher notes, meeting with Donald Rumsfeld and Henry A. Kissinger, April 8, 1975, Fisher Archives. **Kissinger still "emotional":** Max M. Fisher notes, meeting with Donald Rumsfeld and Henry A. Kissinger, April 8, 1975, Fisher Archives.

Dinner meeting with Javits: Max M. Fisher Daily Schedule, April 8-9, 1975, Fisher Archives.

Fisher "had a greater influence regarding Israel": Javits, *Javits: The Autobiography of a Public Man* , p. 282. **Fisher's "intercessions" for United States and Israel:** Javits, *Javits: The Autobiography of a Public Man*, p. 282.

Javits and Fisher discuss peace talks crisis: Max M. Fisher interview. **Javits to help resolve differences:** *The Jerusalem Post*, April 8, 1975.

Rift had to be healed before Ford's speech: Max M. Fisher OH.

Garment at United Nations: Leonard Garment interview. **"Taken me through the toughest times":** Leonard Garment to Max M. Fisher, July 15, 1988, Fisher Archives.

Garment's personal tragedy: *Regardie's*, October 1987, p. 89. **Garment relied on Fisher's advice:** Leonard Garment interview; Max M. Fisher to Leonard Garment, April 20, 1987, Fisher Archives. **Garment recognized usefulness to leaders:** Leonard Garment interview.

"Wanted the benefit of his wisdom": Leonard Garment interview.

Garment and Fisher prepare paper to be presented to Ford and Kissinger: Max M. Fisher, Leonard Garment interviews.

Free-associative thinking: Leonard Garment interview.

"A master of the arcane Washington art": *Regardie's*, October 1987.

Formality of presentation significant: Max M. Fisher, Leonard Garment interviews.

Read a paper: Leonard Garment interview.

"Study a person's character": Max M. Fisher interview.

"Ford had genuine respect for Max": Leonard Garment interview.

"One of the most important meetings in the history of American-Israeli relations": Leonard Garment OH.

Finished paper at 3 a.m.: Max M. Fisher, Leonard Garment OH.

Ford meeting with advisers: President Gerald Ford's Daily Diary, April 9, 1975, Gerald R. Ford Library. **Went to White House:** Max M. Fisher, Leonard Garment OH; Max M. Fisher interview.

"No comment": Max M. Fisher OH.

Fisher, Kissinger and Ford in Oval Office: President Gerald Ford's Daily Diary, April 9, 1975, Gerald R. Ford Library; Max M. Fisher interview; in addition, photographs in the Fisher Archives, showing Fisher in a variety of meetings with Ford and Kissinger, indicate this seating arrangement was typical.

Read statement to Kissinger and Ford: The entire text of the document that Fisher read to Ford and Kissinger, dated April 9, 1975, is in the Fisher Archives and the Gerald R. Ford Library; Max M. Fisher interview. **United States is Israel's "only real friend":** Meir, *My Life*, p. 372.

Israel would never retreat to 1967 borders: Rabin, *The Rabin Memoirs*, p. 263.

"Max, I want to thank you": Max M. Fisher notes on Ford and Kissinger meeting, April 9, 1975, Fisher Archives; Max M. Fisher, Gerald R. Ford, Henry A. Kissinger interviews; Max M. Fisher CJF OH.

Fords asks for copy of statement: Max M. Fisher on Ford and Kissinger meeting, April 9, 1975, Fisher Archives; Max M. Fisher, Gerald R. Ford, Leonard Garment, Henry A. Kissinger interviews; Max M. Fisher CJF OH; Max M. Fisher OH.

"**Personal and private visit**": *Detroit Free Press*, April 10, 1975.

Fisher seated with Ford family: *The Washington Post*, April 11, 1975.

America and Middle East: *The New York Times*, April 11, 1975, contains full text of President Gerald R. Ford's speech.

Formal reading of thoughts "turned out to be correct": Leonard Garment to David Zurawik, October 11, 1982, Fisher Archives.

"**Jewish portfolio**": Spiegel, *The Other Arab-Israeli Conflict: Making America's Middle East Policy, from Truman to Reagan*, p. 235.

Fisher had Ford's private telephone number: Max M. Fisher interview.

Chatting with Ford, talking politics: President Gerald Ford's Daily Diary, April 11, 1975, Gerald R. Ford Library; Max M. Fisher notes on meeting with Donald Rumsfeld, Ronald Nessen and Max Friedersdorf, Fisher Archives.

Kissinger calls Fisher in Detroit: Max M. Fisher Daily Schedule, April 8-9, 1975, Fisher Archives; Max M. Fisher interview; Max M. Fisher CJF OH.

Kissinger and Fisher attentive friends: Correspondence between Henry A. Kissinger and Max M. Fisher found in Fisher Archives.

Kissinger waives lecture fee for Fisher: *The New York Post*, November 5, 1982.

"**To me you are the greatest**": Max M. Fisher to Henry A. Kissinger, March 27, 1983, Fisher Archives.

"**A lodestar of the American Jewish community**": Henry A. Kissinger to Max M. Fisher, July 15, 1988, Fisher Archives.

"**Thank you for helping me turn the president around**": Max M. Fisher interview.

Purpose of call clear: Max M. Fisher interview.

Israeli sympathizers vocal in reassessment opposition: *The London Jewish Times*, May 29, 1975; *Newsweek*, April 14, 1975.

"**It's not true**": Max M. Fisher interview.

Fisher optimistic about re-establishing Israel, Egypt talks: Max M. Fisher notes, April 30, 1975, Fisher Archives.

Fisher and 1976 presidential elections: Max M. Fisher notes, April 30, 1975, Fisher Archives. **Story of April 9 meeting:** *The London Jewish Times*, May 9, 1975.

"**It never happened**": Henry A. Kissinger interview.

"**American Jews Against Ford**": *Time*, May 12, 1975; AJAF brochure, Fisher Archives.

Senators advocate strong Israeli military assistance: *The New York Times*, May 23, 1975.

Israelis "overplaying their hand": Ford, *A Time to Heal*, pp. 287-288.

Fisher seeks to defuse power struggle: Max M. Fisher notes, May 27, 1975, Fisher Archives. **Develop fresh ideas:** Ford, *A Time to Heal*, p. 287. **Fisher relays new Israeli formulations:** Max M. Fisher notes, May 27, 1975, Fisher Archives.

Fisher sees opportunity to resolve dispute: Max M. Fisher notes, May 26, 1975, Fisher Archives.

Seeks "to maintain a climate of trust": Max M. Fisher notes, May 26, 1975, Fisher Archives.

Israel "must take the initiative": Max M. Fisher notes, May 26, 1975, Fisher Archives.

Israel must "keep the negotiations alive": Max M. Fisher notes, May 26, 1975, Fisher Archives.

"**What's holding them back?**": Max M. Fisher notes, May 26, 1975, Fisher Archives.

Think Kissinger "will take advantage of them": Max M. Fisher notes, May 26, 1975, Fisher Archives.

Demonstrate flexibility: Max M. Fisher notes, May 26, 1975, Fisher Archives.

Looking for flexibility from Sadat: Max M. Fisher notes, May 26, 1975, Fisher Archives.

"A commitment from Sadat not to use force to settle their differences": Max M. Fisher notes, May 26, 1975, Fisher Archives.

"A lot of face-saving": Max M. Fisher notes, May 26, 1975, Fisher Archives.

Sees room for negotiation: Max M. Fisher notes, May 26, 1975, Fisher Archives.

Sadat and Ford discuss Sinai buffer zone: Ford, *A Time to Heal*, p. 290.

Ford and Rabin discuss Sinai buffer zone: Ford, *A Time to Heal*, p. 292.

"Have to leave the passes": Max M. Fisher notes, June 13, 1975, Fisher Archives. **Refusal "based on political necessities":** Max M. Fisher notes, June 13, 1975, Fisher Archives.

Fisher to speak with Rabin and Allon: Max M. Fisher notes, June 13, 1975, Fisher Archives.

Fisher review Israel's options for Rabin and Allon: Max M. Fisher notes, July 1, 1975, Fisher Archives.

"One more shot at negotiations": Max M. Fisher notes, July 1, 1975, Fisher Archives.

Rabin and Kissinger meet secretly: Spiegel, *The Other Arab-Israeli Conflict: Making America's Middle East Policy, from Truman to Reagan*, pp. 298-299.

Fisher brings Kissinger and American Jewish leaders together to discuss the negotiations: Max M. Fisher notes, August 18, 1975, Fisher Archives.

Israel would have U.S. full backing: Max M. Fisher notes, August 18, 1975, Fisher Archives.

Congress must approve of U.S. presence in Sinai: Max M. Fisher notes, August 18, 1975, Fisher Archives.

Leaders "reassured": Max M. Fisher notes, August 18, 1975, Fisher Archives.

Sinai II agreement reached: Spiegel, *The Other Arab-Israeli Conflict: Making America's Middle East Policy, from Truman to Reagan*, p. 301.

U.S. pledges massive military and economic aid to Israel: *The Other Arab-Israeli Conflict: Making America's Middle East Policy, from Truman to Reagan*, p. 301.

Discussed "matter of Mideast settlement very thoroughly": Max M. Fisher notes, August 27, 1975, Fisher Archives.

Campaign finances discouraging: Max M. Fisher notes, August 27, 1975, Fisher Archives.

Economic policies could adversely affect Republican campaign: Max M. Fisher notes, August 27, 1975, Fisher Archives.

"Thoroughly satisfactory": Max M. Fisher notes, August 27, 1975, Fisher Archives. **Nixon pardon a burden to election victory:** Max M. Fisher interview.

Sinai II signed: Spiegel, *The Other Arab-Israeli Conflict: Making America's Middle East Policy, from Truman to Reagan*, p. 302.

Fisher praises Sinai II: *Chicago Daily News*, September 2, 1975.

American Jewish leaders swayed by Ford and Kissinger to support Sinai II: *Detroit Jewish News*, September 12, 1975.

Congress approves agreement: Spiegel, *The Other Arab-Israeli Conflict: Making American's Middle East Policy, from Truman to Reagan*, p. 305. **Assad of Syria critical of Sinai II:** Spiegel, *The Other Arab-Israeli Conflict: Making America's Middle East Policy, from Truman to Reagan*, p. 303.

Chapter 16

Lessons Learned

SOURCES

Books, journals, newspapers:
Ford, *A Time to Heal*; Golan, *The Secret Conversations of Henry Kissinger*; Spiegel, *The Other Arab-Israeli Conflict: Making America's Middle East Policy, from Truman to Reagan*; Rabin, *The Rabin Memoirs*; Raviv, Melman, *Every Spy a Prince: The Complete History of Israel's Intelligence Community*; Wallach, Wallach, *Arafat: In the Eyes of the Beholder*.

Forbes, New York.

The Boston Globe, Davar, Detroit Free Press, The Detroit News, The Jerusalem Post, Jewish Telegraphic Agency Daily News Bulletin; (New York) *Daily News, The New York Times, The Wall Street Journal.*

Fisher Archives.

Gerald R. Ford Library.

Interviews:
Max M. Fisher, Gerald R. Ford, Dennis N. Horwitz, Seymour Milstein, Robert A. Mosbacher Sr.

NOTES

Difficult to win election: Ford, *A Time to Heal*, p. 344.

Fisher "rare public appearance" for GOP fund-raiser: *Detroit Free Press*, September 21, 1975. **Aiming for $500,000:** *Detroit Free Press*, September 21, 1975.

Ford speaks at $50-ticket fund-raiser: *The New York Times*, October 11, 1975. **New election laws restricted individual, PAC giving:** Max M. Fisher interview.

Fisher urges Ford to straighten campaign: Max M. Fisher notes, October 15, 1975, Fisher Archives. **Mosbacher takes reins:** Max M. Fisher interview. **"Wouldn't have done as well without Max":** Robert A. Mosbacher Sr. interview.

President Ford Committee underway: Executive S06 PL PL2, Gerald R. Ford Library.

Ford reduces transitional aid to Israel: Spiegel, *The Other Arab-Israeli Conflict: Making America's Middle East Policy from Truman to Reagan*, pp. 306-308.

Reports on visit with Rabin: Max M. Fisher notes, December 13, 1975, Fisher Archives.

Compromise on aid to Israel: Max M. Fisher notes, December 13, 1975, Fisher Archives.

Ford's political standing in Jewish community: Max M. Fisher notes, December 13, 1975, Fisher Archives.

Ford winning in early primaries: Ford, *A Time to Heal*, pp. 367-368. **Expected Reagan to quit:** Ford, *A Time to Heal*, pp. 374, 388.

Flack about selling jets to Egypt: Spiegel, *The Other Arab-Israeli Conflict: Making America's Middle East Policy from Truman to Reagan*, p. 307. **Calls sale "cynical and dangerous":** *The Jerusalem Post*, March 10, 1976. **Congress could defeat sale:** *The Jerusalem Post*, March 10, 1976.

Avert political fallout: Max M. Fisher notes, March 10, 1975, Fisher Archives.

New Arab relationship at Israel's expense: Max M. Fisher notes, March 10, 1975, Fisher Archives.

Keep Sadat in U.S. pocket: Max M. Fisher notes, March 10, 1975, Fisher Archives.

Political ramifications: Max M. Fisher notes, March 10, 1975, Fisher Archives.

Limited to calendar year: Max M. Fisher notes, March 10, 1975, Fisher Archives.

Suggests meeting with American Jewish leaders: Max M. Fisher notes, March 10, 1975, Fisher Archives.

Ford set on sale: Max M. Fisher notes, March 10, 1975, Fisher Archives.

Sale fails, Israel loses: Max M. Fisher notes, March 10, 1975, Fisher Archives.

Transitional quarter aid questioned: Max M. Fisher notes, March 10, 1975, Fisher Archives.

Passman "foxy old guy": Max M. Fisher notes, March 10, 1975, Fisher Archives.

Need political credit for Ford campaign: Max M. Fisher notes, March 10, 1975, Fisher Archives.

"Arms supply precedent" concerns: Jewish Telegraphic Agency Daily News Bulletin, March 13, 1975.

Move Sadat from Soviet influence: Spiegel, *The Other Arab-Israeli Conflict: Making America's Middle East Policy from Reagan to Truman*, p. 307; Max M. Fisher, Gerald R. Ford interviews.

Not worth the fuss: Max M. Fisher notes, March 17, 1975, Fisher Archives.

Symbolic aid to Egypt: Max M. Fisher notes, March 17, 1975, Fisher Archives.

Ford in command of situation: Max M. Fisher notes, March 17, 1975, Fisher Archives.

Ford suffers primary defeat: Ford, *A Time to Heal*, p. 375.

Scranton criticizes East Jerusalem settlement: Spiegel, *The Other Arab-Israeli Conflict: Making America's Middle East Policy from Truman to Reagan*, pp. 306-307.

"A warm attitude to the Jewish community": *Davar*, April 7, 1976. **Words were misinterpreted:** Max M. Fisher notes, undated except for March-April 1976, Fisher Archives.

Fisher grilled by press: Max M. Fisher interview.

Reacts to criticism: *The Jerusalem Post*, April 2, 1976; see also *Davar*, April 7, 1976, translation by Zelig S. Chinitz, Fisher Archives.

People forget the $4 billion: *The Jerusalem Post*, April 2, 1976.

Palestinians root of conflict: *The Jerusalem Post*, April 2, 1976.

Ethnic slurs about Kissinger: Rabin, *The Rabin Memoirs*, p. 271.

Kissinger accused of blocking arms to Israel during Yom Kippur War: Golan, *The Secret Conversations of Henry Kissinger*, p. 50. **Arms could ruin future U.S.-Arab, Moscow relations:** Golan, *The Secret Conversations of Henry Kissinger*, p. 46.

Kissinger first secretary of state Jews meet: *The Jerusalem Post*, April 2, 1976.

"Nixon and Kissinger delivered the goods, in time": *The Jerusalem Post*, April 2, 1976.

Compare Nixon and Ford to Kennedy-Johnson: *The Jerusalem Post*, April 2, 1976. **Interview published across the U.S.:** See, for example, the (New York) *Daily News*, April 3, 1976; *Detroit Free Press*, April 3, 1976. **Others disagreed with Fisher's assessment:** *The Boston Globe*, April 12, 1976.

Campaign laws restrict ethnic outreach: Max M. Fisher interview.

Fisher and Ford discuss Ford's standing in Jewish community: Max M. Fisher interview.

Ford says U.S. guarantees Israel's freedom: *The New York Times*, May 14, 1976.

Reagan fund-raising telethon: Ford, *A Time to Heal*, pp. 375-376. **Reagan raises $1.5 million and attacks Ford's foreign policy:** Ford, *A Time to Heal*, p. 376. **Reagan wins five primaries:** Ford, *A Time to Heal*, p. 381. **Ford wins three, including Mich-**

igan, yet Reagan ahead 528 to 479: Ford, *A Time to Heal*, pp. 384-386. **Ford regains lead 992 to 886:** Ford, *A Time to Heal*, p. 389.

Fisher brings American Jewish leaders to Ford's White House: Max M. Fisher notes, June 24, 1976, Fisher Archives.

Ford "extraordinary": Max M. Fisher notes, June 24, 1976, Fisher Archives. **Israel receives $275 million:** *The New York Times*, June 26, 1976.

Kissinger and Fisher meet: Max M. Fisher notes, July 2, 1976, Fisher Archives. **Entebbe hijacking:** Raviv, Melman, *Every Spy a Prince: The Complete History of Israel's Intelligence Community*, pp. 216-217.

Ford tells Fisher to tell Rabin not to retaliate against PLO: Max M. Fisher notes, July 2, 1976, Fisher Archives. **PLFP Arafat rival:** Wallach, Wallach, *Arafat: In the Eyes of the Beholder*, pp. 438-440. **If Israel backed down, wouldn't help their cause:** Max M. Fisher notes, July 2, 1976, Fisher Archives. **Ford, Fisher, Kissinger meet:** Max M. Fisher notes, July 2, 1976, Fisher Archives. **Campaign needs organization:** Max M. Fisher notes, July 2, 1976, Fisher Archives. **Baker chosen to head campaign organization:** Ford, *A Time to Heal*, p. 410. **Nonsectarian citizens for Ford:** Max M. Fisher notes, July 2, 1976, Fisher Archives.

Raid on Entebbe: Max M. Fisher interview. **Carter-Mondale ticket:** Max M. Fisher interview.

Fisher a Michigan delegate: Gerald R. Ford to Max M. Fisher, July 13, 1976, Fisher Archives. **Fisher ensured a rabbi gave one benediction at GOP convention:** Max M. Fisher interview.

Fisher predicts Ford on first ballot: *The Jerusalem Post*, August 17, 1976. **Ford wins nomination, first ballot:** Ford, *A Time to Heal*, p. 399.

Polls give Carter gaping lead over Ford: Ford, *A Time to Heal*, p. 409. **Ford trails Carter by as much as 9.5 million votes:** Ford, *A Time to Heal*, p. 409. **"Convert 130,000 Carter supporters a day":** Ford, *A Time to Heal*, p. 409.

Public financing of campaign: *The New York Times*, April 28, 1976. **Ford campaign staff discuss strategy to win American Jewish vote:** *The Jerusalem Post*, September 21, 1976. **Ford hosts luncheon for select American Jewish leaders:** E, PT, Briefing Paper David H. Lissy to Gerald R. Ford, September 20, 1976, Gerald R. Ford Library. **Ford reiterates commitment to Israel:** E, PT, Briefing Paper, David H. Lissy to Gerald R. Ford, September 20, 1976, Gerald R. Ford Library.

Speech would "turn the tide": *The Jerusalem Post*, September 21, 1976.

"Importance of direct communication to the American Jewish community": Robert A. Cohn to Max M. Fisher, October 18, 1976, Fisher Archives.

Jews had to believe candidate aware of their needs: Max M. Fisher interview. **Reagan wouldn't campaign for Ford:** Ford, *A Time to Heal*, p. 424.

"No Soviet domination in Eastern Europe": Ford, *A Time to Heal*, p. 422. **Carter quick to capitalize on error:** Ford, *A Time to Heal*, p. 423.

Ford kept campaigning: Ford, *A Time to Heal*, pp. 431-432.

Waiting for election results: Max M. Fisher interview. **Victory party arranged:** Max M. Fisher interview. **Carter winning Deep South:** Ford, *A Time to Heal*, p. 433. **Fisher aided Ford with Jewish vote:** Max M. Fisher interview. **Carter wins New York:** Ford, *A Time to Heal*, p. 433-434. **Pennsylvania and Texas to Carter:** Ford, *A Time to Heal*, p. 434. **"It's over":** Max M. Fisher interview.

"The most disappointing moment in my life": Max M. Fisher interview. **CBS places Jewish vote for Ford at 32 percent:** *New York*, December 6, 1976. **Ford received 40 percent of Jewish vote:** Max M. Fisher interview. **No longer unkosher to vote Republican:** *New York*, December 6, 1976.

Eli Black and United Brands: *The Wall Street Journal*, February 14, 1975. **Merged company with J. Morrell and other food producers:** *The Wall Street Journal*, May 13, 1975.

Combine business with social conscious: *The Wall Street Journal*, February 14, 1975. **"The most socially conscious American company in the hemisphere":** *The Wall Street Journal*, February 14, 1975.

Banana taxes, natural disasters cause dramatic losses: *The Wall Street Journal*, February 14, 1975. **High cattle-feed costs:** *The Wall Street Journal*, February 14, 1975. **$43 million lost in 1974:** *The Wall Street Journal*, May 13, 1975.

Black jumps to his death: *The New York Times*, February 4, 1975. **Corporate life stress:** *The New York Times*, February 14, 1975.

Bribes to South American and European officials discovered: *The Wall Street Journal*, May 13, 1975.

Fisher asked to be acting chairman: *The Wall Street Journal*, February 8, 1978. **Business community surprised:** *Forbes*, June 1, 1976. **United Brands stock plummeting, legal troubles soaring:** *The New York Times*, May 14, 1975; Max M. Fisher interview.

"Wanted to know if I could still run a big corporation": Max M. Fisher interview. **Increased stock in company:** Dennis N. Horwitz interview. **Controlled over 5 percent of stock:** *The Wall Street Journal*, February 8, 1978.

Wallace W. Booth chosen president, CEO: *The Wall Street Journal*, May 13, 1975. **Senior VP at Rockwell International:** *The Wall Street Journal*, May 13, 1975.

Fisher's presence increases stock value by 13 percent: *The New York Times*, May 14, 1975. **Fisher United Brands' chairman:** *The New York Times*, August 1, 1975. **Fisher subpoenaed by SEC:** *The Detroit News*, August 14, 1975. **Investigating foreign payments:** Max M. Fisher interview. **SEC suit settled:** *The Wall Street Journal*, January 28, 1976.

"Unusual" settlement: *The Wall Street Journal*, January 28, 1976. **SEC granted permanent access to United Brands' books:** *The Wall Street Journal*, January 28, 1976.

Fisher and Milsteins dig into running company: *The Wall Street Journal*, August 1, 1975.

Reminded Fisher of running Aurora: Max M. Fisher interview. **Milstein ate hot dog part:** Paul Milstein to Max M. Fisher, July 15, 1988, Fisher Archives.

Involved with corporate hierarchy: Max M. Fisher interview. **Fisher's style criticized by some employees:** *The Wall Street Journal*, February 8, 1978.

Didn't call to ask about golf game: *The Wall Street Journal*, February 8, 1978.

Suggests "go back to work": Seymour Milstein interview. **"I am working":** Seymour Milstein interview

"Company's not being managed": Seymour Milstein interview

Big time commitment necessary: Seymour Milstein interview.

Needed somebody in charge of operations, next bribe, someone goes to jail: Seymour Milstein interview; *The Wall Street Journal*, January 31, 1977.

"Max persuaded me": Seymour Milstein interview.

Other directors agreed with Fisher: Seymour Milstein interview.

"Talk to Wally Booth": Seymour Milstein interview.

"Not happy with how you run things": Seymour Milstein interview.

"Friendly difference of opinion": *The Wall Street Journal*, January 31, 1977.

Voted to move from Boston to New York: Seymour Milstein interview.

Executives complained about move: *The Wall Street Journal*, February 8, 1978.

Not sorry to lose complaining executives: Max M. Fisher interview.

Fisher resigns post: *The Detroit News*, May 18, 1978. **Stock worth up 540 percent:** *The Wall Street Journal*, May 14, 1975, Dennis N. Horwitz interview.

Fisher honorary chairman: *The Detroit News*, May 18, 1978.

Chapter 17
RENAISSANCE MAN

SOURCES

Books, newspapers:
Chafets, *Devil's Night*; Collier, Horowitz, *The Fords: An American Epic*; Darden, Hill, Thomas, Thomas, *Detroit: Race and Uneven Development*; Kiska, *Detroit's Powers & Personalities*; Lacey, *Ford: The Men and the Machine*.

The Detroit News; *The Milwaukee Journal*; *The New York Post*; *The New York Times Sunday Magazine*; *The* (Albany, N.Y.) *Times Union*.

Fisher Archives.

Oral History:
Marjorie Switow Fisher, Dwight Havens.

Interviews:
Max M. Fisher, Robert E. McCabe, Coleman A. Young.

NOTES

"What can we do for Detroit?": Marjorie Switow Fisher interview; Marjorie Switow Fisher OH.

Trying to rescue Detroit: Dwight Havens OH.

"Got some good news": Dwight Havens OH. **Ford willing if other significant Detroit leaders would help:** Dwight Havens OH.

Resigned from NDI in January 1970: *The Detroit News*, January 12, 1970. **Forum for expressing ideas, frustrations:** *The Detroit News*, August 18, 1968. **Concrete solutions, not ideas:** Max M. Fisher OH.

Couldn't pin Henry Ford II: Dwight Havens OH.

Ford agrees to co-chair efforts: Dwight Havens OH.

Visited Roche in the early morning: Dwight Havens OH.

Right to the point: Dwight Havens, Max M. Fisher OH.

Detroit Renaissance founded: Darden, Hill, Thomas, Thomas: *Detroit: Race and Uneven Development*, p. 46.

"Max was beautiful": Dwight Havens OH.

"What can we do for Detroit?" speech: *Max M. Fisher Addresses 1969-1972*, p. 142, Fisher Archives.

Roll-call of Detroit Renaissance directors: *Max M. Fisher Addresses 1969-1972*, pp. 143-145, Fisher Archives.

Year 2000: Max M. Fisher interview.

Detroit's Devil's Night: Robert E. McCabe, Max M. Fisher interviews; Chafets, *Devil's Night*.

"Champagne Bob": Robert E. McCabe interview; Kiska, *Detroit's Powers & Personalities*, p. 190.

Accustomed to discussing urban redevelopment: Robert E. McCabe interview.

"We'd like you to come out and run it": Robert E. McCabe interview.

Lured McCabe to Detroit for simple advice-giving, persuaded him to stay: Robert E. McCabe interview.

Detroit no longer producing 80 percent of U.S. passenger cars: Collier, Horowitz, *The Fords: An American Epic*, p. 419.

"A rudderless city": *The Milwaukee Journal*, May 31, 1977.

Decentralization of industry: Coleman A. Young interview.

Expressways destroyed Detroit's tax base: Coleman A. Young interview.

"It was a double-con": Coleman A. Young interview.

Racism as Detroit's base problem: Chayfets, *The New York Times Sunday Magazine*, July 29, 1990.

Fisher sees less histrionic explanations: Max M. Fisher interview.

New York City suffering violence as much as Detroit: *New York Post*, September 7, 1990; *The* (Albany, N.Y.) *Times Union*, September 9, 1990; *New York Post*, September 10, 1990.

Revise notions of cities and look to the future: *The Milwaukee Journal*, May 31, 1977.

Riverfront development studied: Darden, Hill, Thomas, Thomas, *Detroit: Race and Uneven Development*, p. 46.

Irony of suburban trio pushing city revitalization: Robert E. McCabe interview.

Irony not lost: Max M. Fisher interview; Lacey, *Ford: The Men and the Machine*, p. 572.

Good intentions not marketable: Lacey, *Ford: The Men and the Machine*, pp. 573-574.

Fisher and Ford by the pool: Max M. Fisher, Marjorie Switow Fisher interviews.

Henry Ford II takes on rebuilding Detroit: Lacey, *Ford: The Men and the Machine*, p. 575. **"RenCen":** Darden, Hill, Thomas, Thomas, *Detroit: Race and Uneven Development*, p. 47. **"Urban village":** Darden, Hill, Thomas, Thomas, *Detroit: Race and Uneven Development*, p. 49.

"The Man Who Gave Ford the Better Idea": *The Milwaukee Journal*, May 31, 1977; Darden, Hill, Thomas, Thomas, *Detroit: Race and Uneven Development*, p. 49.

"RenCen" criticism: Darden, Hill, Thomas, Thomas, *Detroit: Race and Uneven Development*, pp. 50-51.

A financial disaster, few tenants, ferocious landlord: Darden, Hill, Thomas, Thomas, *Detroit: Race and Uneven Development*, pp. 51-53.

Defaulted on second mortgage: Darden, Hill, Thomas, Thomas, *Detroit: Race and Uneven Development*, pp. 51-54.

"Max and Hank the Deuce recognized" the economic risks: Coleman A. Young interview.

Pedestrian traffic on increase: Robert E. McCabe interview.

Not for the money but for the year 2000: Max M. Fisher interview.

Chapter 18

DOWN BY THE RIVER

SOURCES

Books, journals, newspapers:
Darden, Hill, Thomas, Thomas, *Detroit: Race and Uneven Development*.
Fortune, *M Inc.*.
Detroit Free Press, *The Detroit News*, *The New York Times*.

Fisher Archives.

Oral History:
Louis Berry, Max M. Fisher, Miles Jaffe, A. Alfred Taubman.

Interviews:
Marjorie Switow Fisher, Max M. Fisher, Phillip W. Fisher, Dennis N. Horwitz,

Calvin Hughes, Robert E. McCabe, Kathryn McIntosh, Elizabeth A. Stephens, Coleman A. Young.

NOTES

Selling the Fisher Building: *The Detroit News*, January 4, 1974. **Fisher reluctant:** Louis Berry OH.

Blue about the Smith or Jones Building: Kathryn McIntosh interview.

"Probably not": Kathryn McIntosh interview.

Sale netted $11.1 million: Max M. Fisher interview; Max M. Fisher worksheet sale of Fisher-New Center Stock, December 28, 1973, Fisher Archives. **Pledge not to change building's name:** *The Detroit News*, January 4, 1974.

Not quitting the city: *The Detroit News*, January 4, 1974. **"Learn to liquidate":** Max M. Fisher notes, January 1, 1973, Fisher Archives.

Nothing financially pressing: Max M. Fisher interview.

Fisher loathed debts: Phillip W. Fisher interview.

Learned about chits: Phillip W. Fisher interview.

Social responsibility to pay something back: *Max M. Fisher Addresses 1969-1972*, pp. 203-206.

"Strong binding factor between" black civil rights struggle and Jewish community: Coleman A. Young interview.

"Owed a lot": Max M. Fisher interview.

More than he was able to imagine: Max M. Fisher OH.

"Application of power to realize an urban development project": Darden, Hill, Thomas, Thomas, *Detroit: Race and Uneven Development*, p. 58.

Penn Central sells Fisher's dream site for $10 million: A. Alfred Taubman OH.

Willing to wait to get his way: Max M. Fisher OH.

Not without Max: A. Alfred Taubman OH.

Max influenced Al and Henry: Coleman A. Young interview.

Max responsible for the Detroit Renaissance mission: Coleman A. Young interview.

Detroit use of CETA funds vetoed: *Detroit Free Press*, July 30, 1976. **"Punitive and vindictive":** *Detroit Free Press*, July 30, 1976. **Coleman calls Fisher for help:** Max M. Fisher OH. **Ford reverses ruling for Detroit:** *Detroit Free Press*, July 30, 1976.

Ensured city and state had stake: Max M. Fisher OH.

"Max Fisher bill": *Detroit Free Press*, December 18, 1976.

Milliken signs "Max Fisher bill": *Detroit Free Press*, January 14, 1977. **"Early rider aboard the Carter train":** *Fortune*, April 21, 1980. **"Detroit will still have a friend in the White House":** Coleman A. Young interview.

"Nationwide reputation for corruption and incompetence": *Detroit Free Press*, September 5, 1977. **Binford cleaned up office:** *Detroit Free Press*, September 5, 1977.

Binford against Fisher's Riverfront: *Detroit Free Press*, September 5, 1977.

Young activates his Washington "Detroit-made mini-machine": *Fortune*, April 21, 1980.

Binford had a new job: Confidential interview.

Fisher, Taubman and eight minor partners: Dennis N. Horwitz interview; Riverfront News Release, June 15, 1982, Fisher Archives.

Irvine Ranch deal: *M Inc.*, September 1990.

Dealing with private individuals easier than public agencies: A. Alfred Taubman OH.

One roadblock after another: Max M. Fisher OH.

Riverfront plans finalized: Darden, Hill, Thomas, Thomas, *Detroit: Race and Uneven Development*, p. 58.

Compromise with Conservation Clubs: *The Detroit News*, September 13, 1980.

No comment about dislocated rats: Max M. Fisher OH.

Safire criticizes Detroit: *The New York Times*, April 30, 1981.

Fisher rebuttal to criticism: *The New York Times*, July 11, 1981. **Fisher's reply a message to Washington:** Max M. Fisher OH.

Riverfront an animated puzzle: Miles Jaffe OH.

Jackson Pollock puzzle: Miles Jaffe OH.

Still willing to take a risk: Miles Jaffe OH.

"If this can be done without breaking me, I want it built": Miles Jaffe OH.

Able to sell bonds privately to Chemical Bank: Miles Jaffe OH.

"Men who are for real": Miles Jaffe OH.

Power of Fisher's political and financial contacts: Darden, Hill, Thomas, Thomas, *Detroit: Race and Uneven Development*, pp. 58-59.

Riverfront financed with private and public funds: Riverfront Financing Statement, June 15, 1982, Fisher Archives.

Tax abatement proposal: *Detroit Free Press*, April 2, 1979.

"Rich folks gotta have apartments, too": *Detroit Free Press*, April 2, 1979.

"Has to make rents affordable": *Detroit Free Press*, April 2, 1979.

"See what kind of man he is": *Detroit Free Press*, April 2, 1979.

Fisher and Cockrel at opposite ends in 1979: *Detroit Free Press*, April 23, 1984; *Detroit Free Press*, April 27, 1979.

Cockrel's "progressive, socialist agenda": *Detroit Free Press*, April 27, 1979.

Attacked tax-breaks for "millionaires": *Detroit Free Press*, October 7, 1979.

Young, "a neo-colonialist puppet": *Detroit Free Press*, October 7, 1979.

"At the time the niggers first resisted slavery": *Detroit Free Press*, October 7, 1979.

Detroit Alliance for a Rational Economy: *Detroit Free Press*, October 7, 1979.

"Tax Max and his pal Al" petition: Riverfront Petition, Fisher Archives.

"Growth of the black power concept is healthy": *The Detroit News Sunday Magazine*, February 23, 1969.

"If they think I'm going to make so much money": Max M. Fisher OH.

"They just want to throw darts at you": Max M. Fisher OH.

Young, Fisher "keep their eyes on the ball": Miles Jaffe OH.

Issue is the investment: Max M. Fisher, Coleman A. Young interviews.

"You get the job done": Max M. Fisher interview.

"No room for pie-in-the-sky": Coleman A. Young interview.

"We all know the council is going to roll over": *Detroit Free Press*, June 5, 1981.

Cockrel's rhetoric "to prove how radical he was": Coleman A. Young interview.

"Max is one of the most admired white people in the city's black community": Robert E. McCabe interview.

Cockrel chose the wrong target: Coleman A. Young interview.

Max "is not swayed by differences": Coleman A. Young interview.

Fisher and Cockrel showdown: Calvin Hughes interview; Max M. Fisher OH; The Detroit City Council Notes, June 4, 1981; *The Detroit News*, June 5, 1981.

Riverfront facing "a real time constraint": *The Detroit News*, June 5, 1981.

"Cooperation and understanding of the City Council is needed": Detroit City Council Notes, June 4, 1981; *The Detroit News*, June 5, 1981.

"What you've done for Detroit": The Detroit City Council Notes, June 4, 1981; *The Detroit News*, June 5, 1981.

"Or leave the city fallow and not develop it": Detroit City Council Notes, June 4, 1981; *The Detroit News*, June 5, 1981.

Jaffe explains abatement's importance: Detroit City Council Notes, June 4, 1981.

"Cockrel, Fisher 'row' fizzles": *The Detroit News*, June 4, 1981.

"I've decided to give you the T-shirt off my back": Kenneth V. Cockrel to Max M. Fisher, July 17, 1981, Fisher Archives.

"Tax Max and His Pal Al!" T-shirt: Max M. Fisher interview.

Filed T-shirt in Riverfront file: Elizabeth A. Stephens interview.

"Sorry that I took the shirt off your back": Max M. Fisher to Kenneth V. Cockrel, July 24, 1981, Fisher Archives.

Official RenCen groundbreaking ceremony: Max M. Fisher interview.

Max's and Henry's "bookends": Confidential OH.

"You think it went all right": Max M. Fisher OH.

Riverfront deficit twice the Fisher Building sale profit: Max M. Fisher, Dennis N. Horwitz, Elizabeth A. Stephens interviews.

I am indebted to David Zurawik for his detailed notes on the ground-breaking ceremony for Riverfront, and the draft of his account of Fisher's car ride from the ceremony to the luncheon at the Renaissance Center.

Chapter 19
BEGINNINGS AND ENDINGS

SOURCES

Books, journals, newspapers:

Cannon, *President Reagan: The Role of a Lifetime*; Drew, *Portrait of an Election*; Friedman, *From Beirut to Jerusalem*; Ford, *A Time to Heal*; McCartney, *Friends in High Places: The Bechtel Story*; Perlmutter, *The Life and Times of Menachem Begin*; Persico, *Casey*; Sadat, *A Woman of Egypt*; Spiegel, *The Other Arab-Israeli Conflict: Making America's Middle East Policy, from Truman to Reagan*.

Fortune, Newsweek.

The Detroit News, (Southern California) *Herald Examiner, The Jerusalem Post, The New York Times, The* (Albany, N.Y.) *Times Union, The Washington Post.*

Fisher Archives.

Oral History:

Gerald R. Ford.

Interviews:

Marjorie Fisher Aronow, Zelig S. Chinitz, Julie Fisher Cummings, Marjorie Switow Fisher, Mary Fisher, Max M. Fisher, Philip W. Fisher, Alexander M. Haig Jr, Dennis N. Horwitz, Richard M. Nixon, Ronald R. Reagan, George P. Shultz.

NOTES

Life outside national circles: Max M. Fisher interview.

Camp David accords: Max M. Fisher interview; *The New York Times*, March 27, 1979.

Dinner menu: Max M. Fisher interview; *The New York Times*, March 27, 1979.

Republicans at outer rim: Marjorie Switow Fisher interview. **Max tall enough to see:** Marjorie Switow Fisher interview.

Nixon and Ford set stage: Spiegel, *The Other Arab-Israeli Conflict: Making*

America's Middle East Policy, from Truman to Reagan, p. 314. **Played a part:** Max M. Fisher interview.

"Most important member of Jewish community": Marjorie Switow Fisher interview.

"I've heard of him": Marjorie Switow Fisher interview. **"All humanity is one entity":** Marjorie Switow Fisher interview.

"Please repeat": Marjorie Switow Fisher interview.

Jehan Sadat thanked her: Marjorie Switow Fisher interview.

Sadat assassinated: Sadat, Jehan, *A Woman of Egypt*, pp. 13-14. **A sad smile, "all humanity is one entity":** Marjorie Switow Fisher interview.

Draft Ford Committee announced: *The Detroit News*, March 7, 1980. **Fisher uncomfortable with right-wing GOP:** Max M. Fisher interview.

"Reagan cannot win": (Southern California) *Herald Examiner*. **Casey suspected Ford still angry:** Persico, *Casey*, p. 186. **Reagan pivotal in 1976 campaign:** Ford, *A Time to Heal*, p. 437.

Leading the "good life": Drew, *Portrait of an Election*, p. 17. **Insiders believed Ford consented:** Max M. Fisher interview.

Max still active in Detroit's business: Max M. Fisher interview.

Lobbying for GOP convention in Detroit: Max M. Fisher interview.

Brock's deciding vote: Max M. Fisher interview.

"You always come through": Gerald R. Ford to Max M. Fisher, April 3, 1980, Fisher Archives.

Reagan organization skeptical: Persico, *Casey*, p. 186. **Ford can help or hurt the most:** Persico, *Casey*; p. 186. **Casey wanted Ford:** Persico, *Casey*, p. 186.

Right-wing maniac label: Ronald W. Reagan interview.

Casey contacted Fisher: Max M. Fisher interview.

"Inherited" Max: Ronald W. Reagan interview.

Reagan eager to use Fisher: Ronald W. Reagan interview. **Reagan and Casey meet with Fisher:** Max M. Fisher interview.

Need Jerry Ford to win: Max M. Fisher interview.

"Not too friendly: Max M. Fisher interview.

"Call him up": Max M. Fisher interview.

"You think I should": Max M. Fisher interview.

Casey needed both Ford and Fisher: Max M. Fisher interview.

How will we do in Detroit?: Max M. Fisher interview.

"I'll take care of it": Max M. Fisher interview.

Detroit Reagan fund-raiser: *The Washington Post*, May 16, 1980. **"Corporate boardroom crowd" for Reagan:** *The Washington Post*, May 16, 1980.

Reagan visits Ford: Persico, *Casey*, p. 187.

Need for further gesture: Max M. Fisher interview.

"What kind of gesture?": Max M. Fisher interview.

Help with Ford Library funds: Max M. Fisher interview.

Casey and Fisher free up Ford: Max M. Fisher interview. **Casey gave $5,000:** Persico, *Casey*, p. 186. **Money raised by July 14:** Max M. Fisher interview.

"Count me in": Persico, *Casey*, p. 187.

Reagan and Casey thanked Fisher: Max M. Fisher interview. **Reagan proposes Ford as VP:** Persico, *Casey*, p. 187.

Ford and Fisher celebrate birthdays: Mary Fisher interview.

Ford and Fisher discuss offer: Max M. Fisher interview.

Listen out of deference: Max M. Fisher interview.

Guard against talk: Max M. Fisher interview.

Matter closed: Max M. Fisher interview.

"His answer was no": Casey, *Persico*, p. 188.

Reagan able to find Israel on a map: Max M. Fisher interview.

Reagan's strong emotional commitment to Israel: Max M. Fisher, Richard M. Nixon interviews.

"To live in freedom": Ronald W. Reagan interview.

Fisher input into Reagan's B'nai B'rith speech: Max M. Fisher interview. **Soviet Jews remembered by a Reagan administration:** Max M. Fisher notes, September 3, 1980, Fisher Archives; *The New York Times*, September 4, 1980.

Reagan a reliable Israeli ally: *The Jerusalem Post*, July 3, 1980.

"Reagan lacked the network": Cannon, *President Reagan: The Role of a Lifetime*, p. 65. **"Offstage influences":** Cannon, *President Reagan: The Role of a Lifetime*, p. 65. **Nixon influential upon Reagan:** Cannon, *President Reagan: The Role of a Lifetime*, p. 73

Nixon's "seminal contributions": *Newsweek*, May 19, 1986.

Nixon became a political consultant: *Newsweek*, May 19, 1986.

Trust Max implicitly: Richard M. Nixon memorandum, Fisher Archives, circa 1981. This memorandum is part of a larger memorandum, but it exists in the Fisher Archives as only a single page. It is clear from the content that it was sent at the beginning of the Reagan administration — since Nixon writes that he will later make some specific suggestions regarding the Middle East. I assume that the Middle East would have been among the first topics that Nixon wrote about to Reagan. On page 76 of Lou Cannon's *Role of a Lifetime*, he dates the first memorandum Nixon sent Reagan, November 17, 1980. The section regarding Fisher could not have been far behind.

Max seen as a "patriot": Alexander M. Haig Jr. interview.

"Helpful to have an extra channel": Alexander M. Haig Jr. interview. **Haig and Fisher meet:** Max M. Fisher notes, March 2, 1981, Fisher Archives.

Selling arms to Arabs conundrum: Spiegel, *The Other Arab-Israeli Conflict: Making America's Middle East Policy, from Truman to Reagan*, pp. 407-408.

Israel prepared to accept sale: Alexander M. Haig Jr. interview.

"Weinberger's Arabist proclivities": Alexander M. Haig Jr. interview.

"Reliability and consistency": Alexander M. Haig Jr. interview.

Myth of Jewish influence: Alexander M. Haig Jr. interview.

Boschwitz against sale-American Jewish leaders prepare statement: Max M. Fisher interview.

Administration's "Court Jew": Confidential interview; *The Jerusalem Post*, March 13, 1980.

Fisher amends statement's text: *The Jerusalem Post*, March 13, 1980.

Public embarrassment of president not way to play game: Max M. Fisher interview. **Reagan reaffirms support of Israel:** *The Jerusalem Post*, March 13, 1981.

Fisher's tone conciliatory: *The Jerusalem Post*, March 13, 1981.

"White House meeting not useful": *The Jerusalem Post*, March 17, 1981.

"I'm-in-control-here": Spiegel, *The Other Arab-Israeli Conflict: Making America's Middle East Policy, from Truman to Reagan*, p. 408.

"Hussein was Hitler": Perlmutter, *The Life and Times of Menachem Begin*, p. 362.

U.S. approves U.N. condemnation of Israel's actions: Spiegel, *The Other Arab-Israeli Conflict: Making America's Middle East Policy, from Truman to Reagan*, p. 409. **American Jewish community incensed:** Max M. Fisher interview. **Meet with Meese to voice concern:** Max M. Fisher interview.

Haig only one in Reagan administration to support Israeli destruction of Iraqi nuclear plant, vindicated in 1991: Max M. Fisher interview. On July 10, 1991 in an interview on Israeli radio, Begin, breaking his self-imposed silence, commented that the Persian Gulf War vindicated his decision to bomb Iraq. Begin said: "When the

Scuds landed here [during the Gulf War] many people understood, even those who criticized us at the time for an act of provocation, that they were wrong and we were right." *The* (Albany, N.Y.) *Times Union*, July 12, 1991.

Haig undercut in Reagan administration: Max M. Fisher notes, November 1981, Fisher Archives.

Bitterness between Washington and Jerusalem: Max M. Fisher notes, November 1981, Fisher Archives.

$83 million profit: Dennis N. Horwitz interview. **Sold Irvine Ranch shares for $100 million profit:** Max M. Fisher interview.

Panthers won league, lost money: Max M. Fisher interview.

British government dragging heals: *The New York Times*, July 29, 1983. **"Burning a hole in his pocket":** Max M. Fisher interview.

"The $400 million friendship": *Fortune*, April 9, 1990.

A word with the Queen: *Fortune*, April 9, 1990.

Reagan, then Fisher track him down to a telephone booth in London: George P. Shultz interview.

"How can I help you?": George P. Shultz interview.

Max "had easy access to me": George P. Shultz interview.

Bechtel "deep with country-club-style anti-Semitism": McCartney, *Friends in High Places: The Bechtel Story*, p. 183.

Refutes accusation of Bechtel's anti-Semitism: George P. Shultz interview.

Arab boycott: George P. Shultz interview.

Fisher and Shultz first met in 1969: Max M. Fisher interview.

Shultz respect for Israel: Max M. Fisher interview.

Favored student killed in Six-Day War: George P. Shultz interview.

"Taught us something about Israel": George P. Shultz interview. The former secretary of state adds: "In the summer of 1988, [during the *intifada*], Joe's ninety-year-old father was stabbed to death in Jerusalem by a Palestinian. I sent roses to his widow."

"I resent the implications": Max M. Fisher cable to George P. Shultz, June 29, 1982, Fisher Archives.

"Prepared to publicly support him": Max M. Fisher cable to Edwin Meese III, June 29, 1982, Fisher Archives.

Cabled support to Senate Foreign Relations Committee: Max M. Fisher cable to Charles H. Percy, June 29, 1982, Fisher Archives.

Commiserated with Haig: Alexander M. Haig Jr. to Max M. Fisher, July 15, 1988, Fisher Archives.

Shultz consulted with Fisher: George P. Shultz interview.

"Could speak confidentially and trust" Fisher: George P. Shultz interview.

Max as mediator between American Jewish community and Reagan administration: George P. Shultz interview.

Should consider all the constituencies: George P. Shultz interview.

Lebanon a free state, eliminate PLO: Max M. Fisher notes, August 5, 1982, Fisher Archives.

Begin rejects Reagan Plan: Max M. Fisher interview.

Meeting a success: Max M. Fisher notes, August 5, 1982, Fisher Archives.

Shultz speech to UJA: Zelig S. Chinitz interview.

Laughter and applause: Zelig S. Chinitz interview.

Refugee camp massacre: Friedman, *From Beirut to Jerusalem*, p. 161. **Sharon responsible:** Perlmutter, *The Life and Times of Menachem Begin*, pp. 387-388.

Begin's wife dying, Fisher advises Reagan to send a letter: Max M. Fisher notes, October 28, 1982, Fisher Archives.

Reluctant to surrender Taba resort: Max M. Fisher interview.

Mubarak wants to speak with Begin: Max M. Fisher interview.
"Call him on the phone": Max M. Fisher interview.
"I cannot do that": Max M. Fisher interview.
"What can I do": Max M. Fisher interview. **Taba part of the Sinai agreement:** Max M. Fisher interview.
Suggest connection be more cordial: Max M. Fisher interview.
Mubarak agreed: Max M. Fisher interview.
"I'll speak to Mr. Begin": Max M. Fisher interview.
Begin heard Fisher out: Max M. Fisher interview.
Taba to Egypt via arbitration: Max M. Fisher interview. **Treat territories as business commodities:** Max M. Fisher interview.
Begin "a man of silence": Friedman, *From Beirut to Jerusalem*, p. 178.
Jewish Agency tenure ending: Max M. Fisher interview. **Difficult to let go:** Max M. Fisher interview.
"This is during my career": Max M. Fisher OH.
Founding Chairman of the Board of Governors: Max M. Fisher interview.

Epilogue
THE DAY'S NOT ENDED

Sources
Books, documents, newspapers, manuscripts:
Blitzer, *Between Washington & Jerusalem: A Reporter's Notebook*; Johnson, ed., *Information Please Almanac 1991*; Reagan with Novak, *My Turn: The Memoirs of Nancy Reagan*; Regan, *For the Record: From Wall Street to the White House*; Smith, *The Power Game: How Washington Works*; Wallach, Wallach, *Arafat: In the Eyes of the Beholder*.

Weekly Compilation of Presidential Documents, Soviet Jewry Research Bureau.

The New Republic, Time.

Detroit Free Press, The Jerusalem Post, The New York Times, The (Albany, N.Y.) *Times Union, The Village Voice.*

Stanley B. Horowitz memoirs (unpublished).

Fisher Archives.

Interviews:
Marjorie Fisher Aronow, Mandell L. Berman, Matt Brooks, Shoshana Cardin, Zelig S. Chinitz, Julie Fisher Cummings, Marjorie Switow Fisher, Mary Fisher, Max M. Fisher, Phillip W. Fisher, Shari Hillman, Malcolm Hoenlein, Charles Horvath, Mendel Kaplan, George Klein, Martin S. Kraar, Shimon Peres, Ronald W. Reagan, Seymour Reich, Carmi Schwartz, Elizabeth A. Stephens, Mark Talisman.

NOTES
Gathering of family, friends: Zelig S. Chinitz interview. **Kissed the cool stones:** Max M. Fisher interview. **"Most fortunate day":** Zelig S. Chinitz interview. **Strain on Marjorie telling:** Marjorie Switow Fisher interview. **"I'm in trouble":** Marjorie Switow Fisher interview; *Detroit Free Press*, November 3, 1985.
Checked into the Betty Ford Center: Mary Fisher interview; *Detroit Free Press*, November 3, 1985.
Learning to understand alcoholism: Marjorie Switow Fisher interview; *Detroit Free Press*, November 3, 1985.

Family week: *Detroit Free Press*, November 3, 1985. **Max heard about the price:** Julie Fisher Cummings interview. **Turned chair outward:** Julie Fisher Cummings interview. **Parents never around:** Marjorie Fisher Aronow interview. **"Gave my father to the world":** Julie Fisher Cummings interview. **Crying at session:** Phillip W. Fisher interview.

"I had no idea": Phillip W. Fisher interview.

"My father was in shock": Mary Fisher interview.

"He became a different person": Julie Fisher Cummings interview.

Never drink again: Marjorie Switow Fisher interview.

Strategic cooperation between Israel and U.S. formalized: Blitzer, *Between Washington & Jerusalem: A Reporter's Notebook*, p. 240. **Shultz banked on Israeli-U.S. relationship:** Smith, *The Power Game: How Washington Works*, p. 224.

Disappointed in Jewish electoral support: Max M. Fisher interview. **Reagan re-elected:** Johnson, ed., *Information Please Almanac 1991*, p. 637. **Thirty-five percent of Jewish voters and four percent drop from 1980:** Max M. Fisher interview.

National Jewish Coalition established: Shari Hillman interview. **Formal ties to Republican administration:** Max M. Fisher, Matt Brooks interviews.

Peres and Palestinian issue; secret talks with Hussein: Wallach, Wallach, *Arafat: In the Eyes of the Beholder*, p. 313.

"A position, not a post": Shimon Peres interview.

"A very good sailor": Shimon Peres interview.

Fisher welcomed by left, right wings: Shimon Peres interview.

Maintains apolitical stance, retains credibility: Max M. Fisher interview.

Fisher advice on West Bank settlements: Max M. Fisher interview.

Peres sought out Fisher: Max M. Fisher interview.

Shultz delighted with Peres's resolve: Max M. Fisher interview. **Israel a priority:** Max M. Fisher notes, February 11, 1985, Fisher Archives.

Israelis attack PLO headquarters: Wallach, Wallach, *Arafat: In the Eyes of the Beholder*, p. 313. *Achille Lauro* **hijacked:** Wallach, Wallach, *Arafat: In the Eyes of the Beholder*, p. 323.

Private deals: Max M. Fisher interview. **"Fisher Principle":** George P. Shultz to Max M. Fisher, October 14, 1987, Fisher Archives.

Questions over Law of Return: Zelig S. Chinitz interview.

"Difficult coalition negotiations": Yitzhak Shamir to Peter Golden, January 2, 1991, Fisher Archives. **Included ultra-Orthodox:** *The New York Times*, November 13, 1988. **Demanded strict adherence to Orthodox conversions:** Zelig S. Chinitz interview.

American Jewish community's reaction: *The New York Times*, December 3, 1988, November 13, 1988. **American Jewish converts as Gentiles:** *The New York Times*, December 3, 1988.

Fisher "synthesis": Yitzhak Shamir to Peter Golden, January 2, 1991, Fisher Archives. **Values Fisher's ability to interpret signals:** Yitzhak Shamir to Peter Golden, January 2, 1991, Fisher Archives.

Advised Shamir against alienating American Jews: Max M. Fisher interview.

Fisher "given very serious attention": Yitzhak Shamir to Peter Golden, January 2, 1991, Fisher Archives.

"No intention whatsoever of delegitimizing any Jew": Yitzhak Shamir to Peter Golden, January 2, 1991, Fisher Archives.

Eightieth birthday: Max M. Fisher, Marjorie Switow Fisher interviews.

Fisher portrait "in the busiest intersection of the West Wing": Howard H. Baker to Max M. Fisher, June 28, 1988, Fisher Archives.

Birthday luncheon and dinner cruise: Marjorie Switow Fisher, Elizabeth A.

Stephens interviews; *Detroit Free Press*, April 17, 1988. **GOP fund-raiser honoring Fisher:** *Detroit Free Press*, October 7, 1988.

"Max is a legend": Videotape of Michigan Republican Party fund-raiser: Max M. Fisher Tribute, November 8, 1988, Fisher Archives.

"On the podium with Max Fisher": Videotape of Michigan Republican Party fund-raiser: Max M. Fisher Tribute, November 8, 1988, Fisher Archives.

"Been around longer than I have": Videotape of Michigan Republican Party fund-raiser: Max M. Fisher Tribute, November 8, 1988, Fisher Archives.

Presidential Citizens Medal: Charles Horvath interview; *Weekly Compilation of Presidential Documents*, Volume 25, Number 3, pp. 69-98. Published by Office of the Federal Register, National Archives and Records Administration, Washington, D.C.

Democratic Platform ignores Jewish concerns: Max M. Fisher notes, August 15, 1988, Fisher Archives.

Democratic support for Palestinian state: Max M. Fisher notes, August 15, 1988, Fisher Archives.

Republican Party's interests same as American Jews: Max M. Fisher notes, August 15, 1988, Fisher Archives.

Democrats ruled by anti-Semitic faction: Max M. Fisher interview.

"Poison of anti-Semitism": *Detroit Free Press*, October 2, 1988. **Farrakhan's anti-Semitic remarks:** *Detroit Free Press*, October 2, 1988; *The New York Times*, March 29, 1990; *The New York Post*, June 3, 1991.

Jackson responds: Max M. Fisher interview; *Detroit Free Press*, October 2, 1988. **Reporter threatened by Farrakhan:** *The Village Voice*, August 15, 1989. **Jackson calls accusations "unfair":** *Detroit Free Press*, October 2, 1988.

Three explain anti-Semitic remarks: *Detroit Free Press*, October 2, 1988.

Hiding behind anti-Zionism: Max M. Fisher interview. **Fisher demands Republicans fire anti-Semitic campaigners:** *Detroit Free Press*, October 2, 1988.

Got rid of Nazi supporters: *Detroit Free Press*, October 2, 1988.

Voters decided early for Bush: *The New York Times*, November 10, 1988.

Bush received 35 percent of Jewish vote: Max M. Fisher interview. **Thought more Jews would have responded to Democrats' anti-Semitism:** Max M. Fisher interview.

George Klein background: George Klein interview.

White House relationship important: George Klein interview.

Fisher "*the* Jewish Republican": George Klein interview.

"A full-fledged political tradition": George Klein interview.

Bush-Fisher relationship for two decades: George Bush according to Marlin Fitzwater to Peter Golden, April 5, 1991, Fisher Archives. **Fisher remembers first meeting:** Max M. Fisher interview. **"Affectionate and respectful":** George Bush according to Marlin Fitzwater to Peter Golden, April 5, 1991, Fisher Archives. **Bush borne of aristocratic New England:** Johnson, ed., *Information Please Almanac 1991*, p. 663.

Bush success in oil business: Johnson, ed., *Information Please Almanac 1991*, p. 663. **"Mr. Consensus":** *Time*, August 21, 1989.

Bush values "very personal relationship" with Fisher: George Bush according to Marlin Fitzwater to Peter Golden, April 5, 1991, Fisher Archives.

Madison Hotel dinner: Max M. Fisher interview.

Kissinger, Shultz among speakers: Audiotape, Madison Hotel dinner, February 28, 1986, Fisher Archives. **Fisher a "constant conscience to us in government":** Audiotape, Madison Hotel dinner, February 28, 1986, Fisher Archives.

"Pure gut American politics": Audiotape, Madison Hotel dinner, February 28, 1986, Fisher Archives.

"First crisis of his presidency": *The New Republic*, August 28, 1989.

Israelis abduct Sheik Obeid: *Time*, August 14, 1989.

Bush critical of Israel: *The New Republic*, August 28, 1989.

Hizballah threatens to kill Higgins, Israelis counteroffer: *Time*, August 14, 1989. Higgins executed: *Time*, August 14, 1989. Cicippio to be killed next if Hizballah demands not met, U.S. feared military intervention: *Time*, August 14, 1989. U.S. cable to Shamir: *The Jerusalem Post*, August 26, 1989. U.S. calls for release of all hostages: *The New York Times*, August 17, 1989. Dole critical of Israeli action: *Time*, August 14, 1989. Fisher flabbergasted: Max M. Fisher interview.

"No deterioration": *The Jerusalem Post*, August 26, 1989. Time to talk with the president: *The New York Times*, August 17, 1989; Max M. Fisher interview.

Five American Jewish leaders confer with Bush and others: *The Jerusalem Post*, August 9, 1989. Meeting not on president's daily schedule: *The Jerusalem Post*, August 9, 1989.

Israeli action further endangered American hostages' lives: Confidential interview.

Primary concern for hostages' safety: Confidential interview.

"From the community, not from him": Seymour Reich interview. "Like to hear from Max": Seymour Reich interview.

Rift counterproductive: Max M. Fisher interview.

Bush reveals thinking about U.S.-Israeli relationship: Confidential interview.

Kremlin still supports terrorism: Confidential interview.

Bush asks delegation to pass message to Shamir: Confidential interview. Bush and Shamir not perfect couple: Max M. Fisher interview. Won't pressure Shamir: Confidential interview.

Fisher lingers with Bush: Malcolm Hoenlein interview.

"Handsome cufflinks": Malcolm Hoenlein interview.

Bush handed Fisher cufflinks: Malcolm Hoenlein interview.

"They're yours": Malcolm Hoenlein interview.

Bush "reaffirmed" ties: *The Jerusalem Post*, August 9, 1989.

Shamir phoned Bush: *The New York Times*, August 17, 1989.

"Fisher can provide personal and direct explanations": George Bush according to Marlin Fitzwater to Peter Golden, April 5, 1991, Fisher Archives.

"Personal intervention of a man of the stature of Max Fisher is helpful": Yitzhak Shamir to Peter Golden, January 2, 1991, Fisher Archives.

No new money for settlement of Russian Jews in territories: Max M. Fisher to George H. Bush, March 5, 1991, Fisher Archives.

Existing incentives small but important politically: Max M. Fisher to George H. Bush, March 5, 1991, Fisher Archives.

Shamir committed to Palestinian deal: Max M. Fisher to George H. Bush, March 5, 1991, Fisher Archives.

Advised Shamir: Max M. Fisher to George H. Bush, March 5, 1991, Fisher Archives.

Palestinians as negotiating partner: Max M. Fisher to George H. Bush, March 5, 1991, Fisher Archives.

Bush calls for no new settlements in East Jerusalem: *The New York Times*, March 9, 1991. Tolerated East Jerusalem settlements: *The New York Times*, March 9, 1991.

Israel and American Jewry stunned by criticism: *The New York Times*, March 9, 1991. Addendum to report: Max M. Fisher interview.

Settlements on "uninhabited, government-owned land": Max M. Fisher to George H. Bush, March 5, 1990, Fisher Archives.

"Political" not "territorial compromise": Max M. Fisher to George H. Bush, March 5, 1990, Fisher Archives.

Bush position evokes "strong negative response": Max M. Fisher to George H. Bush, March 5, 1990, Fisher Archives. **Peace process needs "considerable patience and work":** Max M. Fisher to George H. Bush, March 5, 1990, Fisher Archives.

"Most helpful": George H. Bush to Max M. Fisher, March 8, 1990, Fisher Archives.

Shamir government collapses: Johnson, ed., *Information Please Almanac 1991*, p. 979. **Arab laborers murdered:** Johnson, ed., *Information Please Almanac 1991*, p. 981.

Hawkish Israeli government: Johnson, ed., *Information Please Almanac 1991*, p. 982. **PLO talks suspended:** Johnson, ed., *Information Please Almanac 1991*, p. 982.

Watched Soviet Jews and Iraqi Scuds arrive in Israel simultaneously: Max M. Fisher interview.

137,313 Soviet Jews into Israel: Soviet Jewry Research Bureau, July 1991. **"Fisher has changed the course of Jewish history":** Stanley B. Horowitz, *Memoirs*, (unpublished), 1991.

51,320 Russian Jews emigrated, 1979: Soviet Jewry Research Bureau, July 1990. **46,206 next 8 years:** Soviet Jewry Research Bureau, July 1990.

Mass exodus of Soviet Jews: Soviet Jewry Research Bureau, July 1990. **Jammed into Ladispoli:** Carmi Schwartz interview.

Soviet Jewry important to Shultz because of Max: Carmi Schwartz interview.

Meese letter endangers Soviet Jews' emigration: Mark Talisman interview.

Told Talisman to call Fisher: Carmi Schwartz interview.

Refusniks had to prove persecution: Mark Talisman interview.

$935 per refugee: Martin S. Kraar interview. **71,196 Soviet Jews released in 1989:** Soviet Jewry Research Bureau, July 1990. **Soviet Jewry relocation debate:** Martin S. Kraar interview.

"Israel is their home": Mendel Kaplan interview.

"Stacked up in Rome": Martin S. Kraar interview.

"No Name Committee": Max M. Fisher interview.

Berman called for No Name Committee: Mandell L. Berman interview.

Eagleburger fond of Fisher: Mandell L. Berman interview.

"A stroke of genius": Shoshana Cardin interview.

Visas to U.S. or Israel: Martin S. Kraar, Shoshana Cardin interviews.

Had to decide destination in Soviet Union: Stanley B. Horowitz interview.

Funding Operation Exodus: Yitzhak Shamir to Peter Golden, January 2, 1991, Fisher Archives.

United Jewish Appeal breakfast: *The Jerusalem Post*, March 20, 1990.

Walter Annenberg calls: Max M. Fisher interview.

"I'd like to be helpful": Max M. Fisher interview.

Five million a year: Max M. Fisher interview.

"Fine": Max M. Fisher interview.

Donation made public: Max M. Fisher interview.

$58 million pledged: Max M. Fisher interview.

181,759 Soviet Jews to Israel: Soviet Jewry Research Bureau, 1990-1991. **87,000 in 1991's first half:** Soviet Jewry Research Bureau, 1990-1991.

Arafat complaining: *The* (Albany, N.Y.) *Times Union*, April 27, 1990.

Over 1 million by December 1992: Max M. Fisher interview.

"Immigrants will bring peace": *The Jerusalem Post*, July 14, 1990; Max M. Fisher interview.

"A miracle": Yitzhak Shamir to Peter Golden, January 2, 1991, Fisher Archives. **Things undone:** Max M. Fisher interview.

Zak column: *The Jerusalem Post*, October 5, 1991.

14,500 Ethiopian Jews evacuated within thirty-six hours: *The New York Times*, May 26, 1991.

Ethiopian Jews used as hostages for Israeli weapons: *The New York Times*, May 25 and 26, 1991. **Calling everybody in Washington:** Max M. Fisher, Zelig S. Chinitz interviews.

Intervention to assist Jews: *The New York Times*, May 25 and 26, 1991; Max M. Fisher interview.

Fisher phones Bush: Max M. Fisher interview.

A successful day: Zelig S. Chinitz interview.

Look of defiance: Zelig S. Chinitz interview.

"The day's not ended": Zelig S. Chinitz interview.

SELECTED BIBLIOGRAPHY

Alger, Horatio. *Strive and Succeed*, two novels by Horatio Alger. (Behrman, S.N., editor.) New York: Holt, Rhinehart and Winston, 1967.

Alterman, Eric. "The Spin Doctor." *Regardie's*, October 1987.

Ambrose, Stephen E. *Eisenhower: The President.* New York: Simon and Schuster, 1984.

——————. *Nixon: The Education of a Politician 1913-1962* . New York: Simon and Schuster, 1987.

——————. *Nixon: The Triumph of a Politician 1962-1972.* New York: Simon and Schuster, 1989.

Amos, Colin; Becker, Peter; Crowley, Lyle; Dana, Will; Domanick, Joe; Dunkel, Tom; Enfield, Susan; Finke, Nikki; Fisher, Susan; Gardner, Amanda; Gimmelson, Debbie; Huang, Nellie; Hubbel, Stephen; Kaplan, Michael; Kessler, Brad; Louis, Errol T.; Meyer, Thomas J.; McHugh, Pratt, Mary; Clare; Ralston, Jeannie; Reed, Lisa; Shaver, Katie; Sherman, Jean; Stewart, Jill; Sullivan Jr., Robert E.; Tomasky, Michael; Thomas, Bill; Waldman, Tom; Willensky, Diana; Wilkinson, Francis. "Power Brokers." *M Inc.*, September 1990.

Applebaum, Phillip. *The Fishers: A Family Portrait.* Detroit: Harlo Press, 1982.

Aricha, Amos. *Hour of the Clown.* New York: New American Library, 1981.

Arion, Asher. *Politics in Israel.* Chatham, New Jersey: Chatham House Publishers, Inc., 1985.

Aronoff, Myron J. *Israeli Vision and Divisions: Cultural Change and Political Conflict.* New Brunswick, New Jersey: Transaction Publishers, 1989.

Aronson, Schlomo. *Conflict and Bargaining in the Middle East: An Israeli Perspective.* Baltimore: Johns Hopkins University Press, 1978.

Asher, Jerry with Hammel, Eric. *Duel for the Golan.* New York: William Morrow and Company, 1987.

Associated Press (The). *The World in 1972.* New York: Western Publishing Company, Inc., 1973.

——————. *The World in 1973.* New York: Western Publishing Company, Inc., 1974.

——————. *The World in 1974.* New York: American Can Company, Printing Division, 1975.

——————. *The World in 1975.* United States: The Associated Press, 1976.

Bakal, Carl. *Charity U.S.A.: An Investigation into the Hidden World of the Multibillion Dollar Charity Industry.* New York: Times Books, 1979.

Baldwin, James. "The Harlem Ghetto." *Commentary*, February 1948.

Baltzell, E. Digby. "The Protestant Establishment." *Harper's*, March 1955.

Bartlett, John. *Bartlett's Familiar Quotations*, Fifteenth Edition. Boston: Little, Brown and Company, 1980.

Bernstein, Philip. *To Dwell in Unity: The Jewish Federation Movement in America Since 1960.* Philadelphia: The Jewish Publication Society of America, 1983.

Biale, David. *Power and Powerlessness in Jewish History*. New York: Schocken Books, 1986.

Birmingham, Stephen. *Our Crowd*. New York: Harper & Row Publishers, 1967.

_____. *The Rest of Us: The Rise of America's Eastern European Jews*. London: MacDonald, 1984.

Blau, Zena Smith. "In Defense of the Jewish Mother." *Midstream*, February 1967.

Blitzer, Wolf. *Between Washington & Jerusalem : A Reporter's Notebook*: New York: Oxford University Press, 1985.

Blum, Jerome. *Lord and Peasant in Russia*. Princeton, New Jersey: Princeton University Press, 1961.

Boller, Jr., Paul F. *Presidential Anecdotes*. New York: Penguin Books, 1982.

_____. *Presidential Campaigns*. New York: Oxford University Press, 1985.

Boy Scouts of America and Harcout, William. *The Official Boy Scout Handbook*. Irving, Texas: Boy Scouts of America, 1988

Brodie, Fawn M. *Richard M. Nixon: The Shaping of his Character*. Cambridge: Harvard University Press, 1983.

Brown, Terry, P. and Gallese, Liz, Roman. "Quiet Operator." *The Wall Street Journal*, February 8, 1978.

Brzezinski, Zbigniew. *Power and Principle: Memoirs of the National Security Adviser*. New York: Farrar Straus Giroux, 1985.

Bundon, Piers. *Ike: His Life and Times*. New York: Harper and Row Publishers, 1986.

Caldwell, Dan, Editor. *Henry Kissinger: His Personality and Policies*. Durham, North Carolina: Duke University Press, 1983.

Candee, Marjorie, ed. Current Biography 1958. New York: H.W. Wilson Company, 1953.

Cannon, Lou. *President Reagan: The Role of a Lifetime*. New York: Simon and Schuster, 1991.

Cardone, Barbara. *Used but Useful. A review of the Used Oil Management Program in New York State*. Albany, New York: Legislative Commission on Toxic Substances and Hazardous Wastes, October 1986.

Carter, Jimmy. *Keeping Faith: Memoirs of a President*. New York: Bantam Books, 1982.

_____. *The Blood of Abraham*. London: Sidgwick & Jackson, 1985.

Chafets, Ze'ev. *Heroes and Hustlers, Hard Hats and Holy Men: Inside the New Israel*. New York: William Morrow and Company, Inc., 1986.

_____. *Members of the Tribe: On the Road in Jewish America*. New York: Bantam Books, 1988.

_____. "The Tragedy of Detroit." *The New York Times Sunday Magazine*, July 29, 1990.

_____. *Devil's Night: And Other True Tales of Detroit*. New York: Random House, 1990.

Chesin, M.D., Eli S. *President Nixon's Psychiatric Profile*. New York: Peter H. Wyden, 1973.

Cheyfitz, Kirk. "The Power Broker." *Monthly Detroit*, July 1980.

Chinitz, Zelig S. *A Common Agenda: The Reconstitution of the Jewish Agency for Israel*. Jerusalem: Jerusalem Center for Public Affairs, 1985.

Cleveland Directory Company. *Cleveland City Directory*. Cleveland, Ohio, 1925-1931.

Collier, Peter and Horowitz, David. *The Fords: An American Epic*. New York: Summit Books, 1987.

Conot, Robert. *American Odyssey*. Detroit: Wayne State University Press, 1986.

Cope, Alexis, Mendenhall, Thomas, Hooper, Osman Castle. *History of the Ohio*

State University (three volumes). The Ohio State University Press. Columbus, Ohio, 1920, 1922, 1926.

Couch, Ernie and Jill. *Ohio Trivia*. Nashville, Tennessee: Rutledge Hill Press, 1988.

Darden, Joe T.; Child Hill, Richard; Thomas, June and Thomas, Richard. *Detroit: Race and Uneven Development*. Philadelphia: Temple University Press, 1987.

Dayan, Moshe. *Story of My Life*. London: Sphere Books Limited, 1976.

Delury, George E., Executive Editor. *The World Almanac & Book of Facts 1975*. New York: Newspaper Enterprise Association, Inc., 1974.

Destler, I.M. *Presidents, Bureaucrats and Foreign Policy: The Politics of Organizational Reform*. Princeton, New Jersey: Princeton University Press, 1972.

Dinnerstein, Leonard and Palsson, Mary Dale, editors. *Jews in the South*. Baton Rouge, Louisiana: Louisiana State University Press, 1973.

Drew, Elizabeth. *Portrait of an Election: 1980*. New York: Simon and Schuster, 1981.

Eban, Abba. *An Autobiography*. New York: Random House, 1977.

Ehrlichman, John. *Witness to Power - The Nixon Years*. New York: Pocket Books, 1982.

Eisenhower, Julie Nixon. *Pat Nixon: The Untold Story*. New York: Simon and Schuster, 1986.

El Azhary, M.S. *Political Cohesion of American Jews in American Politics: A Reappraisal of Their Role in Presidential Elections*. Washington, D.C.: University Press of America, 1980.

el-Sadat, Anwar. *In Search of Identity: An Autobiography*. New York: Harper & Row, Publishers, 1977.

Elazar, Daniel J. and Cohen, Stuart A. *The Jewish Polity: Jewish Political Organizations from Biblical Times to the Present*. Bloomington: Indiana University Press, 1985.

Encyclopedia Judaica. Volume 4 Jerusalem: Keter, Publishing House Ltd., 1971.

——————. Volume 16 Jerusalem: The Jerusalem Encyclopedia Judaica/The Macmillan Company, 1971.

Enos, John Lawrence. *Petroleum Progress and Profits: A History of Process Innovation*. Cambridge, Massachusetts: MIT Press, 1962.

Ewen, Lynda Ann. *Corporate Power and Urban Crisis in Detroit*. Princeton, New Jersey: Princeton University Press, 1978.

Fein, Leonard. *Where are We? The Inner Life of America's Jews*. New York: Harper & Row, Publishers, 1988.

Feingold, Henry. "The UJA in American Jewish Consciousness." New York: United Jewish Appeal, 1983 (unpublished).

Ferry, W. Hawkins. *The Buildings of Detroit*. Detroit: Wayne State University Press, 1968.

Fine, Sidney. *Violence in the Model City*. Ann Arbor: The University of Michigan Press, 1989.

Finke, Nikki. "Power Brokers." *M Inc.*, September 1990.

Flax, Steven. "When do you build character?" *Forbes*, September 14, 1981.

Ford, Betty, with Chase, Chris. *The Times of My Life*. New York: Ballantine Books, 1978.

Ford, Gerald R. *A Time to Heal*. New York: Harper & Row, Publishers and The Reader's Digest Association, Inc., 1979.

Fox, Moshe. "Backing the 'Good Guys': American Governmental Policy, 'Jewish Influence' and the Sinai Campaign of 1956." *The American Jewish Archives*, April 1988.

Friedman, Thomas L. *From Beirut to Jerusalem*. New York: Farrar Straus Giroux, 1989.

Gardner, Ralph, D. *Horatio Alger*. Mendota, Illinois: The Wayside Press, 1964.

George, Alexander L. and Juliette L. *Woodrow Wilson and Colonel House: A Personality Study*. New York: Dover Publications, Inc., 1964.

Gerber, David A., ed. *Anti-Semitism in American History*. Urbana and Chicago: University of Illinois Press, 1987

Golan, Matti. Translation by Friedman, Ina. *Shimon Peres*. New York: St. Martin's Press, 1982.

——————. Translation by Stern, Ruth Geyra, and Stern, Sol. *The Secret Conversations of Henry Kissinger*. New York: Quadrangle/The New York Times Book Co., 1976.

Goldin, Milton. *Why They Give: American Jews and Their Philanthropies*. New York: Macmillan Publishing Co., Inc., 1976.

Goldwater, Barry M. *Goldwater*. New York: Doubleday, 1988.

Grant, James. *Bernard Baruch: The Adventures of a Wall Street Legend*. New York: Simon and Schuster, 1983.

Grayzel, Solomon. *A History of the Jews*. Philadelphia: The Jewish Publication Society of America, 1969.

Green, Jonathan, editor. *The Cynic's Lexicon*. New York: St. Martin's Press, 1984.

Green, Mark J. *The Other Government: The Unseen Power of Washington Lawyers*. New York: Grossman Publishers, a division of The Viking Press, 1975.

Grose, Peter. *Israel in the Mind of America*. New York: Schocken Books, 1984.

Gross, Ken. "Picks and Pans." *People*, August 7, 1989.

Guzzardi, Jr., Walter. "A Determined Detroit Struggles to Find a New Economic Life." *Fortune*, April 21, 1980.

Halberstam, David. *The Powers that Be*. New York: Laurel, 1979.

Halperin, Samuel. *The Political World of American Zionism*. Silver Spring, Maryland: Information Dynamics, Inc., 1985.

Halpern, Ben. *A Clash of Heroes: Brandeis, Weizmann, and American Zionism*. New York: Oxford University Press, 1987.

Hammer, Gottlieb. *Good Faith and Credit*. New York: Cornwall Books, 1985.

Harris, T. George. *Romney's Way: A Man and An Idea*. Englewood Cliffs, New Jersey: Prentice-Hall, Inc., 1968.

Hayes, Walter. *Henry: A Life of Henry Ford II*. New York: Grove Weidenfeld, 1990.

Hersh, Seymour M. *The Price of Power*. New York: Summit Books, 1983.

Hertzberg, Arthur. *The Jews in America*. New York: Simon and Schuster, 1989.

Hoffman, Charles. *The Smoke Screen: Israel, Philanthropy and American Jews*. Silver Spring, Maryland: Eshel Books, 1989.

Howe, Irving. *The World of our Fathers*. New York: Simon and Schuster, 1976.

Howett, Thomas R., Mary B. *The Salem Story: 1806-1956: Sesqui Centennial Souvenir Hand Book*. Salem, Ohio: The Budget Press, 1956.

Hoyt, Edwin P. *Horatio's Boys*. Radnor, Pennsylvania: Chilton Book Company, 1974.

Hughes, Jonathan. *The Vital Few: The Entrepreneur & American Economic Progress*. New York: Oxford University Press, 1986.

Hughes, Emmet, John. *The Ordeal of Power: A Political Memoir of the Eisenhower Years*. New York: Atheneum, 1963.

Hurt III, Harry. *Texas Rich: The Hunt Dynasty from the Early Oil Days through the Silver Crash*. New York: W.W. Norton & Company, 1982.

Jaffe, Eliezer D. *Givers and Spenders The Politics of Charity in Israel*. Jerusalem: Ariel Publishing House, 1985.

Javits, *Jacob K. Javits: The Autobiography of a Public Man*. Boston: Houghton Mifflin Company, 1981.

Jaworski, Leon. *The Right and the Power*. New York: Pocket Books, 1977.

Johnson, Paul. *Modern Times*. New York: Harper & Row, Publishers, 1983.

Kahn, Roger. *The Passionate People.* New York: William Morrow & Company, Inc., 1968.

Johnson, Otto, editor. *Information Please Almanac 1991.* Boston: Houghton Mifflin Company, 1991.

Kallen, Horace, M. *Of Them Which Say They are Jews and Other Essays on the Jewish Struggle for Survival.* New York: Bloch Publishing Company, 1954.

Karnow, Stanley. *Vietnam: A History.* New York: The Viking Press, 1983.

Karp, Abraham J. *Haven and Home: A History of the Jews in America.* New York: Schocken Books, 1985.

——————. *To Give Life: The UJA and the Shaping of the American Jewish Community.* New York: Schocken Books, 1980.

Kiska, Tim. *Detroit's Powers & Personalities.* Rochester Hills, Michigan: Momentum Books, Ltd., 1989.

Kissinger, Henry A. *American Foreign Policy: A Global View.* Singapore: Institute of Southeast Asian Studies, 1982.

——————. *American Foreign Policy, Third Edition.* New York: W.W. Norton & Company, Inc., 1977.

——————. *A World Restored: Metternich, Castlereagh and the Problems of Peace, 1812-1822.* Boston: Houghton Mifflin Company, 1957.

——————. *Observations: Selected Speeches and Essays 1982-1984.* Boston: Little, Brown and Company, 1985.

——————. *White House Years.* Boston: Little, Brown and Company, 1979.

——————. *Years of Upheaval.* Boston: Little, Brown and Company, 1982.

Kolko, Gabriel. *Main Currents in Modern American History.* New York: Pantheon Books, 1976.

Kurtzman, Dan. *Ben-Gurion: Prophet of Fire.* New York: Simon and Schuster, 1983.

Lacey, Robert. *Ford: The Men and the Machine.* New York: Ballantine Books, 1986.

Lavine, Harold. *Smoke-Filled Rooms.* Englewood Cliffs, New Jersey: Prentice-Hall, Inc., 1970.

Learsi, Rufus. *Fulfillment: The Epic Story of Zionism.* New York: Herzl Press, 1972.

Levinger, Lee, J. *A History of the Jews in the United States.* New York: Union of American Hebrew Congregations, 1949.

Levitan, Tina. *Jews in American Life.* New York: Hebrew Publishing Company, 1969.

Little, Jeffrey B. and Rhodes, Lucien. *Understanding Wall Street 2nd Edition.* Blue Ridge Summit, Pennsylvania: Liberty House, 1987.

Lookstein, Haskel. *Were We Our Brothers Keepers? The Public Response of American Jews to the Holocaust, 1938-1944.* New York: Vintage Books. 1988.

Lurie, Leonard. *The Running of Richard Nixon.* New York: Coward, McCann & Geoghegan, Inc., 1972.

McCartney, Laton. *Friends in High Places: The Bechtel Story The Most Secret Corporation and How It Engineered the World.* New York: Simon and Schuster, 1988.

McElvaine, Robert S. *The Great Depression.* United States: Times Books, a division of Random House, Inc. New York, 1984.

McGinniss, Joe. *The Selling of the President, 1968.* New York: Penguin books, 1988.

Meir, Golda. *My Life.* London: Futura, 1975.

Michaels, James W., editor. "The Forbes Four Hundred." *Forbes,* September 13, 1982.

——————. "The Forbes Four Hundred." *Forbes,* October 24, 1989.

——————. "The Forbes Four Hundred." *Forbes,* October 22, 1990.

Mohs, Mayo. "Troubled Land of Zion." *Time,* May 18, 1981.

Murphy, Bruce Allen. *Fortas: The Rise and Ruin of a Supreme Court Justice.* New York: William Morrow and Company, Inc., 1988.

Mollenhoff, Clark R. *George Romney: Mormon in Politics*. New York: Meredith Press, 1968.

Moritz, Charles, ed.. Current Biography 1963. New York: H.W. Wilson Company, 1968.

Nixon, Richard M. *A New Road for America: Major Policy Statements, From March 1970 to October 1971*. Garden City, New York: A Readers Digest Press Book, Doubleday & Company, Inc., 1972.

_____. *In the Arena*. New York: Simon and Schuster, 1990.

_____. *Leaders*. New York: Warner Books, 1982.

_____. *Setting the Course: Major Policy Statements by President Richard Nixon*. New York: A Readers Digest Press Book, Funk & Wagnalls, 1970.

_____. *Six Crises*, New York: Warner Books, 1979.

_____. *RN: The Memoirs of Richard Nixon*. New York: A Touchstone Book, Simon and Schuster, 1970.

Noonan, Peggy. *What I Saw at the Revolution: A Political Life in the Reagan Era*. New York: Random House, 1990.

O'Brien, Conor Cruise. *The Siege: The Saga of Israel and Zionism*. New York: Simon and Schuster, 1986.

Ognibene, Peter J. *Scoop: The Life and Politics of Henry M. Jackson*. Briarcliff Manor, New York: Stein and Day, Publishers, 1975.

Owen, Edgar Wesley. *The Trek of the Oil Finders: A History of Exploration for Petroleum*. Tulsa, Oklahoma: American Association of Petroleum Geologists, 1975.

Persico, Joseph E. *Casey*. New York: Viking, 1990.

_____. *The Imperial Rockefeller*. New York: Simon and Schuster, 1982.

Perlmutter, Amos. *The Life and Times of Menachem Begin*. Garden City, New York: Doubleday & Company, Inc. 1987.

Perlmutter, Nathan and Perlmutter, Ruth. *The Real Anti-Semitism in America*. New York: Arbor House, 1982.

Podhoretz, Norman. *Commentary*, March 1989.

Printer's Ink. February 10, 1956.

Quandt, William B. *Decade of Decisions: American Foreign Policy Toward the Arab-Israeli Conflict, 1967-1976*. Berkeley and Los Angeles, California and London: University of California Press and University of California Press, Ltd., 1977.

Rabin, Yitzhak, *Pinkas Sherut* Volume Two, [*Ledger of Service.*] Tel Aviv: Maariv Publications, 1979.

_____. *The Rabin Memoirs*. Boston: Little, Brown and Company, 1979.

Rabinowitz, Ezekiel. *Justice Louis D. Brandeis: The Zionist Chapter of His Life*. New York: Philosophical Library, 1968.

Raviv, Dan and Melman, Yossi. *Every Spy a Prince: The Complete History of Israel's Intelligence Community*. Boston: Houghton Mifflin Company. 1990.

Reagan, Nancy. *My Turn*. New York: Random House, 1989.

Reagan, Ronald. *An American Life*. New York: Simon and Schuster, 1990.

Regan, Donald T. *For the Record*. New York: St. Martin's Press, 1989.

Rockaway, Robert A. *The Jews of Detroit: From the Beginning 1762-1914*. Detroit: Wayne State University Press, 1986.

Rose, Peter I. *Strangers in Their Midst*. Merrick, New York: Richwood Publishing Company, 1977.

Rose, Norman. *Chaim Weizmann*. New York: Elisabeth Sifton Books/ Viking, 1986.

Rubin, Jeffrey Z., editor. *Dynamics of Third Party Intervention: Kissinger in the Middle East*. New York: Praeger Publishers, 1983.

Rubin, Ronald I., *New York* "Help for the Republicans: The Jewish Vote" December 6, 1976.

Sachar, Howard M. *A History of Israel From the Rise of Zionism to Our Time.* New York: Alfred A. Knopf, 1986.

_____. *A History of Israel: Volume II.* New York: Oxford University Press, 1987.

_____. *Diaspora. An Inquiry into the Contemporary Jewish World.* New York: Harper and Row, Publishers, 1985.

Sadat, Jehan. *A Woman of Egypt.* New York: Pocket Books, 1987.

Safire, William. *Before the Fall.* New York: Doubleday & Company, 1975.

Schiff, Ze'ev. *A History of the Israeli Army.* New York: MacMillan Publishing Company, 1985.

_____ and Ya'ari, Ehud. Edited and Translated by Friedman, Ina. *Intifada.* New York: Simon and Schuster, 1990.

Schulzinger, Avrum. "Max Fisher: The Millionaire Who's Riding A Revolution." *Detroit News Sunday Magazine,* February 23, 1969.

Select Committee on Presidential Campaign Activities. *Hearings Before the Select Committee on Presidential Campaign Activities of the United States Senate of the United States*

Senate Ninety-Third Congress First Session Watergate and Related Activities Phase I: Watergate Investigation, Books 1 and 2. Washington: U.S. Government Printing Office, 1973.

Shachtman, Tom. *Decade of Shocks.* New York: Poiseden Press, 1983.

Shaffer, Dale, E. *Historical Firsts in Salem.* Salem, Ohio, 1987.

_____. *Reflections of Salem's Past.* Salem, Ohio, 1984.

_____. *Some Remembrances of Salem's Past.* Salem, Ohio, 1983.

_____. *Yesterday in Salem: A Collection of Nostalgic Articles.* Salem, Ohio. 1986.

Sims, Patsy. *The Klan.* New York: Stein and Day, 1978.

Sittig, Marshall. "Catalytic Cracking Techniques in Review." *Petroleum Refiner,* October 1952.

Smith, Hedrick. *The Power Game: How Washington Works.* New York: Random House, 1988.

Smith, Patricia B. "Detroit's Gentle, Massive Max Fisher." *Detroit Magazine,* September 24, 1967.

Solomon, Herbert, L. "The Republican Party and the Jews." *Judaism.* Summer 1988.

Spence, Hartzell. *Portrait in Oil: How the Ohio Oil Company Grew to Become Marathon.* New York: McGraw-Hill Book Company, Inc., 1962.

Spiegel, Steven L. *The Other Arab-Israel Conflict: Making America's Middle East Policy, from Truman to Reagan.* Chicago: The University of Chicago Press, 1985.

Stans, Maurice H. *The Terrors of Justice.* New York: Everest House, 1978.

Thornton, Richard C. *The Nixon-Kissinger Years.* New York: Paragon House, 1989.

Tillem, Ivan L., editor. *The 1986 Jewish Almanac.* New York: Pacific Press, 1985.

_____. *The 1987-88 Jewish Almanac.* New York: Pacific Press, 1987.

Tuchman, Barbara W. *Practicing History.* New York: Ballantine Books, 1982.

Tumin, Melvin M. "Conservative Trends in American Jewish Life." *Judaism,* Spring 1964.

Urofsky, Melvin I. *We Are One!* Garden City, New York: Anchor Press/Doubleday, 1978.

Vonada, Damaine. *Ohio: Matters of Fact.* Wilmington, Ohio: Orange Frazer Press, 1987.

Wallach, Janet and John. *Arafat: In the Eyes of the Beholder.* New York: Lyle Stuart, 1990.

White, Theodore. *The Making of the President-1968*. New York: Atheneum Publishers, 1969.

——————. *The Making of the President-1972*. New York: Atheneum Publishers, 1973.

Wiesel, Elie. *The Jews of Silence*. New York: Signet Books, 1967.

Wigoder, Geoffrey, editor-in-chief. *The Encyclopedia of Judaism*. New York: Macmillan Publishing Company, 1989.

Wills, Gary. *Nixon Agonistes*. New York: New American Library, 1971.

Witcover, Jules. *The Resurrection of Richard Nixon*. New York: G.P. Putnam's Sons, 1970.

Woocher, Jonathan S. *Sacred Survival: The Civil Religion of American Jews*. Bloomington & Indianapolis: Indiana University Press, 1986.

Yaffe, James. *The American Jews*. New York: Random House, 1968.

Yergin, Daniel. *The Prize: The Epic Quest for Oil, Money & Power*. New York: Simon and Schuster, 1991.

INDEX

Sucher, William C., 53
Suez Canal, v, viii, 193, 195, 247, 248, 255, 287, 352
Suez Crisis, v-ix, 85
Summit II, 281
Sununu, John, 460
Surdam, Robert, 379, 381, 384
Swainson, John B., 115, 123
Swid, Stephen, 434
Switow, Harry, 58
Switow, Florence, 58, 59

Talisman, Mark, 469, 471
Taubman, Alfred A., 65-67, 68, 104, 122, 145, 147-149, 151, 243, 244, 249, 382, 383, 387, 388, 391, 397, 399, 401, 402, 405, 406, 408, 411, 412, 414, 415, 433-434, 451
Temple Beth El, 219
terHorst, Jerald F., 209
Thatcher, Margaret, viii
Thieu, President, 177-178
Thorton, Richard C., 290
Torczyner, Jacques, 220
Tristar Development, Inc., 392, 393
Truman, Harry S., 244, 293, 321
Tuchman, Barbara W., 74
Tucker, Charles M., Jr., 117
Tyson, Remer, 119

United Brands Co., 370-377
United Farm Workers Union, 371
United Foundation of Detroit, 64, 65, 70, 116, 381
United Fruit Company, 42, 370, 371
United Israel Appeal (UIA), 173, 213-214, 218, 263, 276, 310
United Jewish Appeal (UJA), i, iii, vi, ix, 62-63, 70, 72-73, 75, 84, 85, 125, 127, 128, 130, 131, 134, 161, 167, 171, 173, 174, 194, 212, 213, 218 219, 220, 241, 246, 263, 264, 287, 310, 323, 324, 346, 440
UJA-CJF cooperation, 80-84
U.N. Resolution 242, 194
United States Football League, 433

U.S. Steel, 433
Urofsky, Melvin I., 256

VanDusen, Richard, 115, 116, 118-119, 121
Vanik, Charles A., 274
Van Tiem, Richard, 141
Vaughan, Sarah, 378
Versailles Treaty, 191
Vesco, Robert, 297
Vietnam War, 127, 142, 150-151, 154, 157, 167, 169, 177, 194, 239, 273, 275, 283, 312, 317, 352, 354
von Bismarck, Otto, ii

Wallace, George C., 157, 171
Wallace, Mike, 148
Warburg, Edward, 72, 73
Warburg, Felix, 73, 84
War of Attrition, 193, 205, 221
War of Independence (Israel), v
Warren, Earl, Chief Justice, 172
Washington, Dinah, 378
Watergate, 142, 156, 206, 280, 281, 286-287, 296-299, 301, 312, 425
Wayne State University, 407
Weinberger, Caspar, 428, 431, 432, 433, 434, 435, 439
Weizmann, Chaim, 214, 216, 225, 293
Weizman, Ezer, 248
Wenger, Henry E., 38-41, 42, 46, 67, 250
Wenger, Henry Penn (Penny), 39-40, 67
West Bank, 356, 357, 361, 362, 366, 438, 440, 448, 463
Westmoreland, William, Gen., 151
Wexler, William A., Dr., 204, 257, 263, 271
Wexner, Leslie, 434, 474
Whalen, Kenneth, 382
Whinery, Laura Mae, 13
Whitaker, John, 100
White Panthers, 407
White, Theodore, 117
Whitney, Cornelius, 281
Whitney, Marylou, 281